Anxiety and The Prospect of Hope

Readings in the Twentieth Century and Beyond

Editors:
David O. Sutton
Eric Wallman
Mark Williams
Areej Zufari

D0841328

CENGAGE
Learning™

Australia • Brazil • Japan • Korea • Mexico • Singapore • Spain • United Kingdom • United States

CENGAGE
Learning™

**Anxiety and
The Prospect of Hope:
Readings in the Twentieth
Century and Beyond**

CLASSICS OF WESTERN THOUGHT SERIES: THE MODERN
WORLD, VOLUME III, 4TH EDITION
Edgar F. Knoebel, Editor
© 1988 Cengage Learning. All rights reserved.

ON SARTRE, 1ST EDITION
KAMBER
© 2000 Cengage Learning. All rights reserved.

Executive Editors:

Maureen Staudt
Michael Stranz

CLASSICS OF WESTERN THOUGHT SERIES: THE ANCIENT
WORLD, VOLUME I, 4TH EDITION
Source 3 Authors
© 1988 Cengage Learning. All rights reserved.

Senior Project Development
Manager:

Linda deStefano

Marketing Specialist:

Courtney Sheldon

Senior Production/
Manufacturing Manager:

Donna M. Brown

PreMedia Manager:

Joel Brennecke

Sr. Rights Acquisition
Account Manager:

Todd Osborne

Cover Image:
Getty Images*

*Unless otherwise noted, all cover
images used by Custom Solutions,
a part of Cengage Learning, have
been supplied courtesy of Getty
Images with the exception of the
Earthviewcover image, which has
been supplied by the National
Aeronautics and Space
Administration (NASA).

ALL RIGHTS RESERVED. No part of this work covered by the copyright herein
may be reproduced, transmitted, stored or used in any form or by any means
graphic, electronic, or mechanical, including but not limited to photocopying,
recording, scanning, digitizing, taping, Web distribution, information networks,
or information storage and retrieval systems, except as permitted under
Section 107 or 108 of the 1976 United States Copyright Act, without the prior
written permission of the publisher.

For product information and technology assistance, contact us at
Cengage Learning Customer & Sales Support, 1-800-354-9706

For permission to use material from this text or product,
submit all requests online at **cengage.com/permissions**
Further permissions questions can be emailed to
permissionrequest@cengage.com

This book contains select works from existing Cengage Learning resources and
was produced by Cengage Learning Custom Solutions for collegiate use. As such,
those adopting and/or contributing to this work are responsible for editorial
content accuracy, continuity and completeness.

Compilation © 2010. Cengage Learning.

ISBN-13: 978-1-111-63174-1

ISBN-10: 1-111-63174-3

Cengage Learning
5191 Natorp Boulevard
Mason, Ohio 45040
USA

Cengage Learning is a leading provider of customized learning solutions with
office locations around the globe, including Singapore, the United Kingdom,
Australia, Mexico, Brazil, and Japan. Locate your local office at:
international.cengage.com/region.

Cengage Learning products are represented in Canada by Nelson Education, Ltd.
For your lifelong learning solutions, visit **www.cengage.com/custom.**
Visit our corporate website at **www.cengage.com.**

Printed in the United States
of America

Contents

1

T. S. Eliot

Lovesong of J. Alfred Prufrock

T. S. Eliot (1888–1965) was born in St. Louis, Missouri, and moved to England, where he became a British citizen in 1927. Educated at Harvard University, the University of Paris (Sorbonne), and Merton College, Oxford, he worked initially at the International Department of Lloyd's Bank. He then joined the publishing house of Faber and Faber, which eventually published his poems. One of the most dominant forces in modern poetry, Eliot is best known for Prufrock and Other Observations *(1917),* The Waste Land *(1922), and* Four Quartets *(1943). He also wrote several major plays including* Murder in the Cathedral *(1936) and* The Cocktail Party *(1950) and major works of literary criticism including* The Sacred Wood *(1920) and* Essays, Ancient and Modern *(1936). In 1948 he was awarded the Nobel Prize for Literature.*

S'io credessi che mia risposta fosse
A persona che mai tornasse al mondo,
Questa fiamma staria senza piu scosse.
Ma perciocche giammai di questo fondo
Non torno vivo alcun, s'i'odo il vero,
Senza tema d'infamia ti rispondo.

Let us go then, you and I,
When the evening is spread out against the sky
Like a patient etherized upon a table;
Let us go, through certain half-deserted streets,
The muttering retreats
Of restless nights in one-night cheap hotels
And sawdust restaurants with oyster-shells:
Streets that follow like a tedious argument
Of insidious intent
To lead you to an overwhelming question . . .
Oh, do not ask, "What is it?"
Let us go and make our visit.

In the room the women come and go
Talking of Michelangelo.

The yellow fog that rubs its back upon the window-panes,
The yellow smoke that rubs its muzzle on the window-panes
Licked its tongue into the corners of the evening,
Lingered upon the pools that stand in drains,
Let fall upon its back the soot that falls from chimneys,
Slipped by the terrace, made a sudden leap,
And seeing that it was a soft October night,
Curled once about the house, and fell asleep.

And indeed there will be time
For the yellow smoke that slides along the street,
Rubbing its back upon the window-panes;
There will be time, there will be time
To prepare a face to meet the faces that you meet;
There will be time to murder and create,
And time for all the works and days of hands
That lift and drop a question on your plate;
Time for you and time for me,
And time yet for a hundred indecisions,
And for a hundred visions and revisions,
Before the taking of a toast and tea.

In the room the women come and go
Talking of Michelangelo.

And indeed there will be time
To wonder, "Do I dare?" and, "Do I dare?"
Time to turn back and descend the stair,
With a bald spot in the middle of my hair—
(They will say: "How his hair is growing thin!")
My morning coat, my collar mounting firmly to the chin,
My necktie rich and modest, but asserted by a simple pin—
(They will say: "But how his arms and legs are thin!")
Do I dare
Disturb the universe?
In a minute there is time
For decisions and revisions which a minute will reverse.
For I have known them all already, known them all—
Have known the evenings, mornings, afternoons,
I have measured out my life with coffee spoons;
I know the voices dying with a dying fall
Beneath the music from a farther room.
⠀⠀⠀So how should I presume?
And I have known the eyes already, known them all—
The eyes that fix you in a formulated phrase, And when I am
⠀⠀⠀formulated, sprawling on a pin, When I am pinned and
⠀⠀⠀wriggling on the wall, Then how should I begin
To spit out all the butt-ends of my days and ways?
And how should I presume?

And I have known the arms already, known them all—
Arms that are braceleted and white and bare
(But in the lamplight, downed with light brown hair!)
Is it perfume from a dress
That makes me so digress?
Arms that lie along a table, or wrap about a shawl.
⠀⠀⠀And should I then presume?
⠀⠀⠀And how should I begin?

***

Shall I say, I have gone at dusk through narrow streets
And watched the smoke that rises from the pipes
Of lonely men in shirt-sleeves, leaning out of windows? . . .

I should have been a pair of ragged claws
Scuttling across the floors of silent seas.

***

And the afternoon, the evening, sleeps so peacefully!
Smoothed by long fingers,
Asleep . . . tired . . . or it malingers,
Stretched on the floor, here beside you and me.
Should I, after tea and cakes and ices,
Have the strength to force the moment to its crisis?
But though I have wept and fasted, wept and prayed,
Though I have seen my head (grown slightly bald) brought in
    upon a platter,
I am no prophet—and here's no great matter;
I have seen the moment of my greatness flicker,
And I have seen the eternal Footman hold my coat, and snicker,
And in short, I was afraid.
And would it have been worth it, after all,
After the cups, the marmalade, the tea,
Among the porcelain, among some talk of you and me,
Would it have been worth while,
To have bitten off the matter with a smile,
To have squeezed the universe into a ball
To roll it toward some overwhelming question,
To say: "I am Lazarus, come from the dead,
Come back to tell you all, I shall tell you all"—
If one, settling a pillow by her head,
    Should say: "That is not what I meant at all.
    That is not it, at all."

And would it have been worth it, after all,
Would it have been worth while,

After the sunsets and the dooryards and the sprinkled streets,
After the novels, after the teacups, after the skirts that trail along
    the floor—
And this, and so much more?—
It is impossible to say just what I mean!
But as if a magic lantern threw the nerves in patterns on a screen:
Would it have been worth while
If one, settling a pillow or throwing off a shawl,
And turning toward the window, should say:
    "That is not it at all,
    That is not what I meant, at all."

★★★

No! I am not Prince Hamlet, nor was meant to be;
Am an attendant lord, one that will do
To swell a progress, start a scene or two,
Advise the prince; no doubt, an easy tool,
Deferential, glad to be of use,
Politic, cautious, and meticulous;
Full of high sentence, but a bit obtuse;
At times, indeed, almost ridiculous—
Almost, at times, the Fool.

I grow old . . . I grow old . . .
I shall wear the bottoms of my trousers rolled.
Shall I part my hair behind? Do I dare to eat a peach?
I shall wear white flannel trousers, and walk upon the beach.
I have heard the mermaids singing, each to each.

I do not think that they will sing to me.

I have seen them riding seaward on the waves
Combing the white hair of the waves blown back
When the wind blows the water white and black.

We have lingered in the chambers of the sea
By sea-girls wreathed with seaweed red and brown
Till human voices wake us, and we drown.

UNDERSTANDING MEANING

1. What kind of person is J. Alfred Prufrock, and what kind of world does he live in?
2. What is the relationship between Dante's *Inferno,* which Eliot quotes in the beginning of the poem, and Prufrock's "overwhelming question"?

EVALUATING ELEMENTS

1. What different levels of diction do you find used throughout the poem?
2. What images does Eliot use to show upper-class society?

APPRECIATING LANGUAGE

1. How does Eliot use repetition for emphasis?
2. What specific questions does Prufrock continue to ask at the party and when he is alone?

WRITING SUGGESTIONS

1. Analyze patterns of interior monologues within the poem. Then describe how they reveal important information about Prufrock's view of society and his place in it.
2. Research the many allusions in Eliot's poem. Then discuss the importance of those allusions to the meaning of the poem.

2

Hugo Ball

Dada Manifesto

Dada is a new tendency in art. One can tell this from the fact that until now nobody knew anything about it, and tomorrow everyone in Zurich will be talking about it. Dada comes from the dictionary. It is terribly simple. In French it means "hobby horse". In German it means "good-bye", "Get off my back", "Be seeing you sometime". In Romanian: "Yes, indeed, you are right, that's it. But of course, yes, definitely, right". And so forth.

An International word. Just a word, and the word a movement. Very easy to understand. Quite terribly simple. To make of it an artistic tendency must mean that one is anticipating complications. Dada psychology, dada Germany cum indigestion and fog paroxysm, dada literature, dada bourgeoisie, and yourselves, honoured poets, who are always writing with words but never writing the word itself, who are always writing around the actual point. Dada world war without end, dada revolution without beginning, dada, you friends and also-poets, esteemed sirs, manufacturers, and evangelists. Dada Tzara, dada Huelsenbeck, dada m'dada, dada m'dada dada mhm, dada dera dada, dada Hue, dada Tza.

How does one achieve eternal bliss? By saying dada. How does one become famous? By saying dada. With a noble gesture and delicate propriety. Till one goes crazy. Till one loses consciousness. How can one get rid of everything that smacks of journalism, worms, everything nice and right, blinkered, moralistic, europeanised, enervated? By saying dada. Dada is the world soul, dada is the pawnshop. Dada is the world's best lily-milk soap. Dada Mr Rubiner, dada Mr Korrodi. Dada Mr Anastasius Lilienstein. In plain language: the hospitality of the Swiss is something to be profoundly appreciated. And in questions of aesthetics the key is quality.

I shall be reading poems that are meant to dispense with conventional language, no less, and to have done with it. Dada Johann Fuchsgang Goethe. Dada Stendhal. Dada Dalai Lama, Buddha, Bible, and Nietzsche. Dada m'dada. Dada mhm dada da. It's a question of connections, and of loosening them up a bit to start with. I don't want words that other people have invented. All the words are other people's inventions. I want my own stuff, my own rhythm, and vowels and consonants too, matching the rhythm and all my own. If this pulsation is seven yards long, I want words for it that are seven yards long. Mr Schulz's words are only two and a half centimetres long.

It will serve to show how articulated language comes into being. I let the vowels fool around. I let the vowels quite simply occur, as a cat meows . . . Words emerge, shoulders of words, legs, arms, hands of words. Au, oi, uh. One shouldn't let too many words out. A line of poetry is a chance to get rid of all the filth that clings to this accursed language, as if put there by stockbrokers' hands, hands worn smooth by coins. I want the word where it ends and begins. Dada is the heart of words.

Each thing has its word, but the word has become a thing by itself. Why shouldn't I find it? Why can't a tree be called Pluplusch, and Pluplubasch when it has been raining? The word, the word, the word outside your domain, your stuffiness, this laughable impotence, your stupendous smugness, outside all the parrotry of your self-evident limitedness. The word, gentlemen, is a public concern of the first importance.

3

James Joyce

Araby

James Joyce (1882–1941) was born in Dublin, Ireland, and was given a strict Jesuit education at schools such as Belvedere College in Dublin. During his last year at Belvedere, Joyce began to reject his Catholic faith, choosing instead to study modern languages at University College, Dublin. Joyce's literary hero was playwright Henrik Ibsen, whose plays embodied a theme that intrigued Joyce: the cost of individual rebellion in the face of community conformity. In order to read and write about Ibsen's plays, Joyce taught himself Norwegian. In 1902, Joyce left home, religion, and country to spend the rest of his life as an exile in Europe. He lived briefly in Paris, Trieste, and Zurich, teaching school and writing stories about the various forms of intellectual paralysis he perceived in his homeland. Joyce published these stories, Dubliners, in 1914 and in 1916, produced a semi-autobiographical account of his own development as a writer, A Portrait of the Artist as a Young Man. In 1920, Joyce moved back to Paris, where he found support and sympathy for the literary innovations in his masterpiece, Ulysses (1922). Complex and uncompromising in its language, the book created such a public controversy that it was banned in the United States until a high court cleared the way for its publication in 1933. His writing ignored and often misunderstood, Joyce spent the remaining years of his life working on his final experimental epic, Finnegans Wake (1939). "Araby," reprinted from Dubliners, tells of a young boy's disappointment.

"Araby" by James Joyce from DUBLINERS by James Joyce, copyright 1916 by B. W. Heubsch. Definitive text copyright © 1967 by the Estate of James Joyce. Used by permission of Viking Penguin, a division of Penguin Group (USA) Inc.

North Richmond Street, being blind, was a quiet street except at the hour when the Christian Brothers' School set the boys free. An uninhabited house of two storeys stood at the blind end, detached from its neighbours in a square ground. The other houses of the street, conscious of decent lives within them, gazed at one another with brown imperturbable faces.

The former tenant of our house, a priest, had died in the back drawing-room. Air, musty from having been long enclosed, hung in all the rooms, and the waste room behind the kitchen was littered with old useless papers. Among these I found a few paper-covered books, the pages of which were curled and damp: *The Abbot,* by Walter Scott, *The Devout Communicant* and *The Memoirs of Vidocq.* I liked the last best because its leaves were yellow. The wild garden behind the house contained a central apple-tree and a few straggling bushes, under one of which I found the late tenant's rusty bicycle-pump. He had been a very charitable priest; in his will he had left all his money to institutions and the furniture of his house to his sister.

When the short days of winter came dusk fell before we had well eaten our dinners. When we met in the street the houses had grown sombre. The space of sky above us was the colour of ever-changing violet and towards it the lamps of the street lifted their feeble lanterns. The cold air stung us and we played till our bodies glowed. Our shouts echoed in the silent street. The career of our play brought us through the dark muddy lanes behind the houses where we ran the gauntlet of the rough tribes from the cottages, to the back doors of the dark dripping gardens where odours arose from the ashpits, to the dark odorous stables where a coachman smoothed and combed the horse or shook music from the buckled harness. When we returned to the street light from the kitchen windows had filled the areas. If my uncle was seen turning the corner we hid in the shadow until we had seen him safely housed. Or if Mangan's sister came out on the doorstep to call her brother in to his tea we watched her from our shadow peer up and down the street. We waited to see whether she would remain or go in and, if she remained, we left our shadow and walked up to Mangan's steps resignedly. She was waiting for us, her figure defined by the light from the half-opened door. Her brother always teased her before he obeyed and I stood by the railings looking at her. Her dress swung as she moved her body and the soft rope of her hair tossed from side to side.

Every morning I lay on the floor in the front parlour watching her door. The blind was pulled down to within an inch of the sash so that I could not be seen. When she came out on the doorstep my heart leaped. I ran to the hall, seized my books and followed her. I kept her brown figure always in my eye, and, when we came near the point at which our ways diverged, I quickened my pace and passed her. This happened morning after morning. I had never spoken to her, except for a few casual words, and yet her name was like a summons to all my foolish blood.

Her image accompanied me even in places the most hostile to romance. On Saturday evenings when my aunt went marketing I had to go to carry some of the parcels. We walked through the flaring streets, jostled by drunken men and bargaining women, amid the curses of labourers, the shrill litanies of shop-boys who stood on guard by the barrels of pigs' cheeks, the nasal chanting of street-singers, who sang a *come-all-you* about O'Donovan Rossa, or a ballad about the troubles in our native land. These noises converged in a single sensation of life for me: I imagined that I bore my chalice safely through a throng of foes. Her name sprang to my lips at moments in strange prayers and praises which I myself did not understand. My eyes were often full of tears (I could not tell why) and at times a flood from my heart seemed to pour itself out into my bosom. I thought little of the future. I did not know whether I would ever speak to her or not or, if I spoke to her, how I could tell her of my confused adoration. But my body was like a harp and her words and gestures were like fingers running upon the wires.

One evening I went into the back drawing-room in which the priest had died. It was a dark rainy evening and there was no sound in the house. Through one of the broken panes I heard the rain impinge upon the earth, the fine incessant needles of water playing in the sodden beds. Some distant lamp or lighted window gleamed below me. I was thankful that I could see so little. All my senses seemed to desire to veil themselves and, feeling that I was about to slip from them, I pressed the palms of my hands together until they trembled, murmuring: *"O love! O love!"* many times.

At last she spoke to me. When she addressed the first words to me I was so confused that I did not know what to answer. She asked me was I going to *Araby.* I forgot whether I answered yes or no. It would be a splendid bazaar, she said she would love to go.

"And why can't you?" I asked.

While she spoke she turned a silver bracelet round and round her wrist. She could not go, she said, because there would be a retreat that week in her convent. Her brother and two other boys were fighting for their caps and I was alone at the railings. She held one of the spikes, bowing her head towards me. The light from the lamp opposite our door caught the white curve of her neck, lit up her hair that rested there and, falling, lit up the hand upon the railing. It fell over one side of her dress and caught the white border of a petticoat, just visible as she stood at ease.

"It's well for you," she said.

"If I go," I said, "I will bring you something."

What innumerable follies laid waste my waking and sleeping thoughts after that evening! I wished to annihilate the tedious intervening days. I chafed against the work of school. At night in my bedroom and by day in the classroom her image came between me and the page I strove to read. The syllables of the word *Araby* were called to me through the silence in which my soul luxuriated and cast an Eastern enchantment over me. I asked for leave to go to the bazaar on Saturday night. My aunt was surprised and hoped it was not some Freemason affair. I answered few questions in class. I watched my master's face pass from amiability to sternness; he hoped I was not beginning to idle. I could not call my wandering thoughts together. I had hardly any patience with the serious work of life which, now that it stood between me and my desire, seemed to me child's play, ugly monotonous child's play.

On Saturday morning I reminded my uncle that I wished to go to the bazaar in the evening. He was fussing at the hallstand, looking for the hat-brush, and answered curtly:

"Yes, boy, I know."

As he was in the hall I could not go into the front parlour and lie at the window. I left the house in bad humour and walked slowly towards the school. The air was pitilessly raw and already my heart misgave me.

When I came home to dinner my uncle had not yet been home. Still it was early. I sat staring at the clock for some time and, when its ticking began to irritate me, I left the room. I mounted the staircase and gained the upper part of the house. The high cold empty gloomy rooms liberated me and I went from room to room singing. From the front window I saw my companions playing below in the street. Their cries reached me weakened and indistinct and, leaning my forehead against the cool glass, I looked over at the dark house where she lived. I may have stood there for an hour, seeing nothing but the brown-clad figure cast by my imagination, touched discreetly by the lamplight at the curved neck, at the hand upon the railing and at the border below the dress.

When I came downstairs again I found Mrs. Mercer sitting at the fire. She was an old garrulous woman, a pawnbroker's widow, who collected used stamps for some pious purpose. I had to endure the gossip of the tea-table. The meal was prolonged beyond an hour and still my uncle did not come. Mrs. Mercer stood up to go: she was sorry she couldn't wait any longer, but it was after eight o'clock and she did not like to be out late, as the night air was bad for her. When she had gone I began to walk up and down the room, clenching my fists. My aunt said:

"I'm afraid you may put off your bazaar for this night of Our Lord."

At nine o'clock I heard my uncle's latchkey in the halldoor. I heard him talking to himself and heard the hallstand rocking when it had received the weight of his overcoat. I could interpret these signs. When he was midway through his dinner I asked him to give me the money to go to the bazaar. He had forgotten.

"The people are in bed and after their first sleep now," he said. I did not smile. My aunt said to him energetically:

"Can't you give him the money and let him go? You've kept him late enough as it is."

My uncle said he was very sorry he had forgotten. He said he believed in the old saying: "All work and no play makes Jack a dull boy." He asked me where I was going and, when I had told him a second time he asked me did I know *The Arab's Farewell to his Steed*. When I left the kitchen he was about to recite the opening lines of the piece to my aunt.

I held a florin tightly in my hand as I strode down Buckingham Street towards the station. The sight of the streets thronged with buyers and glaring with gas recalled to me the purpose of my journey. I took my seat in a third-class carriage of a deserted train. After an intolerable delay the train moved out of the station slowly. It crept onward among ruinous houses and over the twinkling river. At Westland Row Station a crowd of people pressed to the carriage doors; but the porters moved them back, saying that it was a special train for the bazaar. I remained alone in the bare carriage. In a few minutes the train drew up beside an improvised wooden platform. I passed out on to the road and saw by the lighted dial of a clock that it was ten minutes to ten. In front of me was a large building which displayed the magical name.

I could not find any sixpenny entrance and, fearing that the bazaar would be closed, I passed in quickly through a turnstile, handing a shilling to a weary-looking man. I found myself in a big hall girdled at half its height by a gallery. Nearly all the stalls were closed and the greater part of the hall was in darkness. I recognised a silence like that which pervades a church after a service. I walked into the centre of the bazaar timidly. A few people were gathered about the stalls which were still open. Before a curtain, over which the words *Café Chantant* were written in coloured lamps, two men were counting money on a salver. I listened to the fall of the coins.

Remembering with difficulty why I had come I went over to one of the stalls and examined porcelain vases and flowered tea-sets. At the door of the stall a young lady was talking and laughing with two

young gentlemen. I remarked their English accents and listened vaguely
to their conversation.

"Oh, I never said such a thing!"

"Oh, but you did!"

"Oh, but I didn't!"

"Didn't she say that?"

"Yes. I heard her."

"Oh, there's a . . . fib!"

Observing me the young lady came over and asked me did I wish
to buy anything. The tone of her voice was not encouraging; she
seemed to have spoken to me out of a sense of duty. I looked humbly
at the great jars that stood like eastern guards at either side of the dark
entrance to the stall and murmured:

"No, thank you."

The young lady changed the position of one of the vases and went
back to the two young men. They began to talk of the same subject.
Once or twice the young lady glanced at me over her shoulder.

I lingered before her stall, though I knew my stay was useless, to
make my interest in her wares seem the more real. Then I turned away
slowly and walked down the middle of the bazaar. I allowed the two
pennies to fall against the sixpence in my pocket. I heard a voice call
from one end of the gallery that the light was out. The upper part of
the hall was now completely dark.

Gazing up into the darkness I saw myself as a creature driven and
derided by vanity; and my eyes burned with anguish and anger.

4

Wallace Stevens

Anecdote of the Jar

Wallace Stevens (1879–1955) was born in Reading, Pennsylvania, and educated at Harvard University. On graduation, he worked at several law firms and eventually for an insurance company, the Hartford Accidental and Indemnity Company. He spent the rest of his life with the company but managed to write poetry in his spare time. His "poetry of ideas" is most evident in poems such as "Peter Quince at the Clavier" and "Sunday Morning" (1915). His most notable collections are Harmonium (1923), The Auroras of Autumn (1950), and Collected Poems (1954).

I placed a jar in Tennessee,
And round it was, upon a hill.
It made the slovenly wilderness
Surround that hill.

The wilderness rose up to it,
And sprawled around, no longer wild.
The jar was round upon the ground
And tall and of a port in air.

"Anecdote of the Jar" from THE COLLECTED POEMS OF WALLACE STEVENS by Wallace Stevens, copyright 1954 by Wallace Stevens and renewed 1982 by Holly Stevens. Used by permission of Alfred A. Knopf, a division of Random House, Inc.

It took dominion everywhere.
The jar was gray and bare.
It did not give of bird or bush,
Like nothing else in Tennessee.

UNDERSTANDING MEANING

1. What is reflected in the jar?
2. What is the relationship between the jar and nature?

EVALUATING ELEMENTS

1. What images in the poem stand out?
2. How does each stanza present the jar?

APPRECIATING LANGUAGE

1. Why does the poet describe the wilderness as "slovenly" in line 3?
2. What does the poet mean by the use of the verb "give" in line 11?

WRITING SUGGESTIONS

1. Analyze the progression of images and perceptions of the jar in each stanza, and explore the relationship between seeing and being in the poem.
2. Research cubist art and relate what you learn to Stevens's poem.

5

Tristan Tzara

The Dada Manifesto

The magic of a word - DADA - which for journalists has opened the door to an unforeseen world, has for us not the slightest importance.

To launch a manifesto you have to want: A.B. & C., and fulminate against 1, 2, & 3, work yourself up and sharpen your wings to conquer and circulate lower and upper case As, Bs & Cs, sign, shout, swear, organise prose into a form that is absolutely and irrefutably obvious, prove its ne plus ultra and maintain that novelty resembles life in the same way as the latest apparition of a harlot proves the essence of God. His existence had already been proved by the accordion, the landscape and soft words. * To impose one's A.B.C. is only natural - and therefore regrettable. Everyone does it in the form of a crystalbluff-madonna, or a monetary system, or pharmaceutical preparations, a naked leg being the invitation to an ardent and sterile Spring. The love of novelty is a pleasant sort of cross, it's evidence of a naive don't-give-a-damn attitude, a passing, positive, sign without rhyme or reason. But this need is out of date, too. By giving art the impetus of supreme simplicity - novelty - we are being human and true in relation to innocent pleasures; impulsive and vibrant in order to crucify boredom. At the lighted crossroads, alert, attentive, lying in wait for years, in the forest. * I am writing a manifesto and there's nothing I want, and yet I'm saying certain things, and in principle I am against manifestos, as I am against principles (quantifying measures of the moral value of every phrase - too easy; approximation was invested by the impressionists). *

I'm writing this manifesto to show that you can perform contrary actions at the same time, in one single, fresh breath; I am against action; as for continual contradiction, and affirmation too, I am neither for nor against them, and I won't explain myself because I hate common sense.

DADA - this is a word that throws up ideas so that they can be shot down; every bourgeois is a little playwright, who invents different subjects and who, instead of situating suitable characters on the level of his own intelligence, like chrysalises on chairs, tries to find causes or objects (according to whichever psychoanalytic method he practices) to give weight to his plot, a talking and self-defining story. *

Every spectator is a plotter, if he tries to explain a word (to know!) From his padded refuge of serpentine complications, he allows his instincts to be manipulated. Whence the sorrows of conjugal life.

To be plain: The amusement of redbellies in the mills of empty skulls.

image of a hand pointing to the right DADA DOES NOT MEAN ANYTHING

If we consider it futile, and if we don't waste our time over a word that doesn't mean anything... The first thought that comes to these minds is of a bacteriological order: at least to discover its etymological, historical or psychological meaning. We read in the papers that the negroes of the Kroo race call the tail of a sacred cow: DADA. A cube, and a mother, in a certain region of Italy, are called: DADA. The word for a hobby horse, a children's nurse, a double affirmative in Russian and Romanian, is also: DADA. Some learned journalists see it as an art for babies, other Jesuscallingthelittlechildrenuntohim saints see it as a return to an unemotional and noisy primitivism - noise and monotonous. A sensitivity cannot be built on the basis of a word; every sort of construction converges into a boring sort of perfection, a stagnant idea of a golden swamp, a relative human product. A work of art shouldn't be beauty per se, because it is dead; neither gay nor sad, neither light nor dark; it is to rejoice or maltreat individualities to serve them up the cakes of sainted haloes or the sweat of a meandering chase through the atmosphere. A work of art is never beautiful, by decree, objectively, for everyone. Criticism is, therefore, useless; it only exists subjectively, for every individual, and without the slightest general characteristic. Do people imagine they have found the psychic basis common to all humanity? The attempt of Jesus, and the Bible, conceal, under their ample, benevolent wings: shit, animals and days. How can anyone hope to order the chaos that constitutes that infinite, formless variation: man? The principle: "Love thy neighbour" is hypocrisy. "Know thyself" is utopian, but more acceptable because it includes malice. No pity. After the carnage we are left with the hope of a purified humanity. I always speak about myself because I don't want to convince, and I have no right to drag others in my wake, I'm not compelling anyone to follow me, because everyone makes his art in his own way, if he knows anything about the joy that rises like an arrow up to the astral strata, or that which descends into the mines stewn with the flowers of corpses and fertile spasms. Stalactites: look everywhere for them, in creches magnified by pain, eyes as white as angels' hares. Thus DADA was born* , out of a need for independence, out of mistrust for the community. People who join us keep their freedom. We don't accept any theories. We've had enough of the cubist and futurist academies: laboratories of formal ideas. Do we make art in order to earn money and keep the dear bourgeoisie happy? Rhymes have the smack of money, and inflexion slides along the line of the stomach in profile. Every group of artists has ended up at this bank, straddling various comets. Leaving the door open to the possibility of wallowing in comfort and food.

Here we are dropping our anchor in fertile ground.

Here we really know what we are talking about, because we have experienced the trembling and the awakening. Drunk with energy, we are revenants thrusting the trident into heedless flesh. We are streams of curses in the tropical abundance of vertiginous *a line image of a squiggle consisting of overlapping curves and zigzags* vegetation, resin and rain is our sweat, we bleed and burn with thirst, our blood is strength.

Cubism was born out of a simple manner of looking at objects: Cezanne painted a cup twenty centimetres lower than his eyes, the cubists look at it from above, others complicate it appearance by cutting a vertical section through it and soberly placing it to one side (I'm not forgetting the creators, nor the seminal reasons of unformed matter that they rendered definitive). ★ The futurist sees the same cup in movement, a succession of objects side by side, mischievously embellished by a few guide-lines. This doesn't stop the canvas being either a good or a bad painting destined to form an investment for intellectual capital. The new painter creates a world whose elements are also its means, a sober, definitive, irrefutable work. The new artist protests: he no longer paints (symbolic and illusionistic reproduction) but creates directly in stone, wood, iron, tin, rocks, or locomotive structures capable of being spun in all directions by the limpid wind of the momentary sensation. ★ Every pictorial or plastic work is unnecessary , even if it is a monster which terrifies servile minds, and not a sickly-sweet object to adorn the refectories of animals in human garb, those illustrations of the sad fable of humanity. - A painting is the art of making two lines, which have been geometrically observed to be parallel, meet on a canvas, before our eyes, in the reality of a world that has been transposed according to new conditions and possibilities. This world is neither specified nor defined in the work, it belongs, in its innumerable variations, to the spectator. For its creator it has neither case nor theory. Order = disorder; ego = non-ego; affirmation - negation: the supreme radiations of an absolute art. Absolute in the purity of its cosmic and regulated chaos, eternal in that globule that is a second which has no duration, no breath, no light and no control. ★ I appreciate an old work for its novelty. It is only contrast that links us to the past. ★ Writers who like to moralise and discuss or ameliorate psychological bases have, apart from a secret wish to win, a ridiculous knowledge of life, which they may have classified, parcelled out, canalised; they are determined to see its categories dance when they beat time. Their readers laugh derisively, but carry on: what's the use?

There is one kind of literature which never reaches the voracious masses. The work of creative writers, written out of the author's real necessity, and for his own benefit. The awareness of a supreme egoism, wherein laws become significant. ★ Every page should explode, either because of its profound gravity, or its vortex, vertigo, newness, eternity, or because of its staggering absurdity, the enthusiasm of its principles, or its typography. On the one hand there is a world tottering in its flight, linked to the resounding tinkle of the infernal gamut; on the other hand, there are: the new men. Uncouth, galloping, riding astride on hiccups. And there is a mutilated world and literary medicasters in desperate need of amelioration.

I assure you: there is no beginning, and we are not afraid; we aren't sentimental. We are like a raging wind that rips up the clothes of clouds and prayers, we are preparing the great spectacle of disaster, conflagration and decomposition. Preparing to put an end to mourning, and to replace tears by sirens spreading from one continent to another. Clarions of intense joy, bereft of that poisonous sadness. ★ DADA is the mark of abstraction; publicity and business are also poetic elements.

I destroy the drawers of the brain, and those of social organisation: to sow demoralisation everywhere, and throw heaven's hand into hell, hell's eyes into heaven, to reinstate the fertile wheel of a universal circus in the Powers of reality, and the fantasy of every individual.

A philosophical questions: from which angle to start looking at life, god, ideas, or anything else. Everything we look at is false. I don't think the relative result is any more important than the choice of patisserie or cherries for dessert. The way people have of looking hurriedly at things from the opposite point of view, so as to impose their opinions indirectly, is called dialectic, in other words, heads I win and tails you lose, dressed up to look scholarly.

If I shout:

Ideal, Ideal, Ideal

Knowledge, Knowledge, Knowledge

Boomboom, Boomboom, Boomboom

I have recorded fairly accurately Progress, Law, Morals, and all the other magnificent qualities that various very intelligent people have discussed in so many books in order, finally, to say that even so everyone has danced according to his own personal boomboom, and that he's right about his boomboom: the satisfaction of unhealthy curiosity; private bell-ringing for inexplicable needs; bath; pecuniary difficulties; a stomach with repercussions on to life; the authority of the mystical baton formulated as the grand finale of a phantom orchestra with mute bows, lubricated by philtres with a basis of animal ammonia. With the blue monocle of an angel they have dug out its interior for twenty sous worth of unanimous gratitude. ★ If all of them are right, and if all pills are only Pink, let's try for once not to be right. ★ People think they can explain rationally, by means of thought, what they write. But it's very relative. Thought is a fine thing for philosophy, but it's relative. Psychoanalysis is a dangerous disease, it deadens man's anti-real inclinations and systematises the bourgeoisie. There is no ultimate Truth. Dialectics is an amusing machine that leads us (in banal fashion) to the opinions which we would have held in any case. Do people really think that, by the meticulous subtlety of logic, they have demonstrated the truth and established the accuracy of their opinions? Even if logic were confined by the senses it would still be an organic disease. To this element, philosophers like to add: The power of observation. But this magnificent quality of the mind is precisely the proof of its impotence. People observe, they look at things from one or several points of view, they choose them from amongst the millions that exist. Experience too is the result of chance and of individual abilities. ★ Science revolts me when it becomes a speculative system and loses its utilitarian character - which is so useless - but is at least individual. I hate slimy objectivity, and harmony, the science that considers that everything is always in order. Carry on, children, humanity ... Science says that we are nature's servants: everything is in order, make both love and war. Carry on, children, humanity, nice kind bourgeois and virgin journalists... ★ I am against systems; the most acceptable system is that of have none on no principle. ★ To complete oneself, to perfect oneself in one's own pettiness to the point of filling the little vase of oneself with oneself, even the courage to fight for and against thought, all this can suddenly infernally propel us into the mystery of daily bread and the lilies of the economic field.

DADAIST SPONTANEITY

What I call the I-don't-give-a-damn attitude of life is when everyone minds his own business, at the same time as he knows how to respect other individualities, and even how to stand up for himself, the two-step becoming a national anthem, a junk shop, the wireless (the wireless telephone) transmitting Bach fugues, illuminated advertisements for placards for brothels, the organ broadcasting carnations for God, all this at the same time, and in real terms, replacing photography and unilateral catechism.

Active simplicity.
The incapacity to distinguish between degrees of light: licking the twilight and floating in the huge mouth filled with honey and excrement. Measured against the scale of Eternity, every action is vain - (if we allow thought to have an adventure whose result would be infinitely grotesque - an important factor in the awareness of human incapacity). But if life is a bad joke, with neither goal nor initial accouchement, and because we believe we ought, like clean chrysanthemums, to make the best of a bad bargain, we have declared that the only basis of understanding is: art. It hasn't the importance that we, old hands at the spiritual, have been lavishing on it for centuries. Art does nobody any harm, and those who are capable of taking an interest in it will not only receive caresses, but also a marvellous chance to people the country of their conversation. Art is a private thing, the artist makes it for himself; a comprehensible work is the product of a journalist, and because at this moment I enjoy mixing this monster in oil paints: a paper tube imitating the metal that you press and automatically squeeze out hatred, cowardice and villainy. The artist, or the poet, rejoices in the venom of this mass condensed into one shopwalker of this trade, he is glad to be insulted, it proves his immutability. The author or the artist praised by the papers observes that his work has been understood: a miserable lining to a collaborating with the heat of an animal incubating the baser instincts. Flabby, insipid flesh multiplying itself with the aid of typographical microbes.

We have done violence to the snivelling tendencies in our natures. Every infiltration of this sort is macerated diarrhoea. To encourage this sort of art is to digest it. What we need are strong straightforward, precise works which will be forever misunderstood. Logic is a complication. Logic is always false. It draws the superficial threads of concepts and words towards illusory conclusions and centres. Its chains kill, an enormous myriapod that asphyxiates independence. If it were married to logic, art would be living in incest, engulfing, swallowing its own tail, which still belongs to its body, fornicating in itself, and temperament would become a nightmare tarred and feathered with protestantism, a monument, a mass of heavy, greyish intestines.

But suppleness, enthusiasm and even the joy of injustice, that little truth that we practise as innocents and that makes us beautiful: we are cunning, and our fingers are malleable and glide like the

line image of loops with a few "x"s along their length

branches of that insidious and almost liquid plant; this injustice is the indication of our soul, say the cynics. This is also a point of view; but all flowers aren't saints, luckily, and what is divine in us is the awakening of anti-human action. What we are talking about here is a paper flower for the buttonhole of gentlemen who frequent the ball of masked life, the kitchen of grace, our white, lithe or fleshy girl cousins. They make a profit out of what we have selected. The contradiction and unity of opposing poles at the same time may be true. IF we are absolutely determined to utter this platitude, the appendix of alibidinous, evil-smelling morality. Morals have an atrophying effect, like every other pestilential product of the intelligence. Being governed by morals and logic has made it impossible for us to be anything other than impassive towards policemen - the cause of slavery - putrid rats with whom the bourgeois are fed up to the teeth, and who have infected the only corridors of clear and clean glass that remained open to artists.

Every man must shout: there is great destructive, negative work to be done. To sweep, to clean. The cleanliness of the individual materialises after we've gone through folly, the aggressive, complete folly of a world left in the hands of bandits who have demolished and destroyed the centuries. With neither aim nor plan, without organisation: uncontrollable folly, decomposition. Those who are strong in word or in strength will survive, because they are quick to defend themselves; the agility of their limbs and feelings flames on their faceted flanks.

Morals have given rise to charity and pity, two dumplings that have grown like elephants, planets, which people call good. There is nothing good about them. Goodness is lucid, clear and resolute, and ruthless towards compromise and politics. Morality infuses chocolate into every man's veins. This task is not ordained by a supernatural force, but by a trust of ideas-merchants and academic monopolists. Sentimentality: seeing a group of bored and quarrelling men, they invented the calendar and wisdom as a remedy. By sticking labels on to things, the battle of the philosophers we let loose (money-grubbing, mean and meticulous weights and measures) and one understood once again that pity is a feeling, like diarrhoea in relation to disgust, that undermines health, the filthy carrion job of jeopardising the sun. I proclaim the opposition of all the cosmic faculties to that blennorrhoea of a putrid sun that issues from the factories of philosophical thought, the fight to the death, with all the resources of

DADAIST DISGUST

Every product of disgust that is capable of becoming a negation of the family is dada; DADA; acquaintance with all the means hitherto rejected by the sexual prudishness of easy compromise and good manners: DADA; abolition of logic, dance of those who are incapable of creation: DADA; every hierarchy and social equation established for values by our valets: DADA; every object, all objects, feelings and obscurities, every apparition and the precise shock of parallel lines, are means for the battle of: DADA; the abolition of memory: DADA; the abolition of archaeology: DADA the abolition of prophets: DADA; the abolition of the future: DADA; the absolute and indiscutable belief in every god that is an immediate product of spontaneity: DADA; the elegant and unprejudiced leap from on harmony to another sphere; the trajectory of a word, a cry, thrown into the air like an acoustic disc; to respect all individualities in their folly of the moment, whether serious, fearful, timid, ardent, vigorous, decided or enthusiastic; to strip one's church of every useless and unwieldy accessory; to spew out like a luminous cascade any offensive or loving thought, or to cherish it - with the lively satisfaction that it's all precisely the same thing - with the same intensity in the bush, which is free of insects for the blue-blooded, and gilded with the bodies of archangels, with one's soul. Liberty: DADA DADA DADA; – the roar of contorted pains, the interweaving of contraries and all contradictions, freaks and irrelevancies: LIFE.

6

T.S. Eliot

The Waste Land

Nam Sibyllam quidem Cumis ego ipse oculis meis
vidi in ampulla pendere, et cum illi pueri dicerent:
Σίβυλλα τί θέλεις; respondenbat illa: ἀποθανεῖν θέλο.

I. THE BURIAL OF THE DEAD

APRIL is the cruellest month, breeding
Lilacs out of the dead land, mixing
Memory and desire, stirring
Dull roots with spring rain.
Winter kept us warm, covering
Earth in forgetful snow, feeding
A little life with dried tubers.
Summer surprised us, coming over the Starnbergersee
With a shower of rain; we stopped in the colonnade,
And went on in sunlight, into the Hofgarten,
And drank coffee, and talked for an hour.
Bin gar keine Russin, stamm' aus Litauen, echt deutsch.
And when we were children, staying at the archduke's,
My cousin's, he took me out on a sled,
And I was frightened. He said, Marie,

Marie, hold on tight. And down we went.
In the mountains, there you feel free.
I read, much of the night, and go south in the winter.

What are the roots that clutch, what branches grow
Out of this stony rubbish? Son of man,
You cannot say, or guess, for you know only
A heap of broken images, where the sun beats,
And the dead tree gives no shelter, the cricket no relief,
And the dry stone no sound of water. Only
There is shadow under this red rock,
(Come in under the shadow of this red rock),
And I will show you something different from either
Your shadow at morning striding behind you
Or your shadow at evening rising to meet you;
I will show you fear in a handful of dust.
Frisch weht der Wind
Der Heimat zu.
Mein Irisch Kind,
Wo weilest du?
'You gave me hyacinths first a year ago;
'They called me the hyacinth girl.'
—Yet when we came back, late, from the Hyacinth garden,
Your arms full, and your hair wet, I could not
Speak, and my eyes failed, I was neither
Living nor dead, and I knew nothing,
Looking into the heart of light, the silence.
Od' und leer das Meer.

Madame Sosostris, famous clairvoyante,
Had a bad cold, nevertheless
Is known to be the wisest woman in Europe,
With a wicked pack of cards. Here, said she,
Is your card, the drowned Phoenician Sailor,
(Those are pearls that were his eyes. Look!)
Here is Belladonna, the Lady of the Rocks,

The lady of situations.
Here is the man with three staves, and here the Wheel,
And here is the one-eyed merchant, and this card,
Which is blank, is something he carries on his back,
Which I am forbidden to see. I do not find
The Hanged Man. Fear death by water.
I see crowds of people, walking round in a ring.
Thank you. If you see dear Mrs. Equitone,
Tell her I bring the horoscope myself:
One must be so careful these days.

Unreal City,
Under the brown fog of a winter dawn,
A crowd flowed over London Bridge, so many,
I had not thought death had undone so many.
Sighs, short and infrequent, were exhaled,
And each man fixed his eyes before his feet.
Flowed up the hill and down King William Street,
To where Saint Mary Woolnoth kept the hours
With a dead sound on the final stroke of nine.
There I saw one I knew, and stopped him, crying 'Stetson!
'You who were with me in the ships at Mylae!
'That corpse you planted last year in your garden,
'Has it begun to sprout? Will it bloom this year?
'Or has the sudden frost disturbed its bed?
'Oh keep the Dog far hence, that's friend to men,
'Or with his nails he'll dig it up again!
'You! hypocrite lecteur!—mon semblable,—mon frère!'

II. A GAME OF CHESS

THE Chair she sat in, like a burnished throne,
Glowed on the marble, where the glass
Held up by standards wrought with fruited vines
From which a golden Cupidon peeped out
(Another hid his eyes behind his wing)
Doubled the flames of sevenbranched candelabra

Reflecting light upon the table as
The glitter of her jewels rose to meet it,
From satin cases poured in rich profusion;
In vials of ivory and coloured glass
Unstoppered, lurked her strange synthetic perfumes,
Unguent, powdered, or liquid—troubled, confused
And drowned the sense in odours; stirred by the air
That freshened from the window, these ascended
In fattening the prolonged candle-flames,
Flung their smoke into the laquearia,
Stirring the pattern on the coffered ceiling.
Huge sea-wood fed with copper
Burned green and orange, framed by the coloured stone,
In which sad light a carvèd dolphin swam.
Above the antique mantel was displayed
As though a window gave upon the sylvan scene
The change of Philomel, by the barbarous king
So rudely forced; yet there the nightingale
Filled all the desert with inviolable voice
And still she cried, and still the world pursues,
'Jug Jug' to dirty ears.
And other withered stumps of time
Were told upon the walls; staring forms
Leaned out, leaning, hushing the room enclosed.
Footsteps shuffled on the stair.
Under the firelight, under the brush, her hair
Spread out in fiery points
Glowed into words, then would be savagely still.

'My nerves are bad to-night. Yes, bad. Stay with me.
'Speak to me. Why do you never speak? Speak.
'What are you thinking of? What thinking? What?
'I never know what you are thinking. Think.'

I think we are in rats' alley
Where the dead men lost their bones.

'What is that noise?'
                The wind under the door.
'What is that noise now? What is the wind doing?'
                Nothing again nothing.
                         'Do
'You know nothing? Do you see nothing? Do you remember
'Nothing?'
    I remember
Those are pearls that were his eyes.
'Are you alive, or not? Is there nothing in your head?'
                But
O O O O that Shakespeherian Rag—
It's so elegant
So intelligent
'What shall I do now? What shall I do?'
'I shall rush out as I am, and walk the street
'With my hair down, so. What shall we do to-morrow?
'What shall we ever do?'
                The hot water at ten.
And if it rains, a closed car at four.
And we shall play a game of chess,
Pressing lidless eyes and waiting for a knock upon the door.

When Lil's husband got demobbed, I said—
I didn't mince my words, I said to her myself,
HURRY UP PLEASE IT'S TIME
Now Albert's coming back, make yourself a bit smart.
He'll want to know what you done with that money he gave you
To get yourself some teeth. He did, I was there.
You have them all out, Lil, and get a nice set,
He said, I swear, I can't bear to look at you.
And no more can't I, I said, and think of poor Albert,
He's been in the army four years, he wants a good time,
And if you don't give it him, there's others will, I said.
Oh is there, she said. Something o' that, I said.

Then I'll know who to thank, she said, and give me a straight
  look.
HURRY UP PLEASE IT'S TIME
If you don't like it you can get on with it, I said.
Others can pick and choose if you can't.
But if Albert makes off, it won't be for lack of telling.
You ought to be ashamed, I said, to look so antique.
(And her only thirty-one.)
I can't help it, she said, pulling a long face,
It's them pills I took, to bring it off, she said.
(She's had five already, and nearly died of young George.)
The chemist said it would be alright, but I've never been the
  same.
You *are* a proper fool, I said.
Well, if Albert won't leave you alone, there it is, I said,
What you get married for if you don't want children?
HURRY UP PLEASE IT'S TIME
Well, that Sunday Albert was home, they had a hot gammon,
And they asked me in to dinner, to get the beauty of it hot—
HURRY UP PLEASE IT'S TIME
HURRY UP PLEASE IT'S TIME
Goonight Bill. Goonight Lou. Goonight May. Goonight.
Ta ta. Goonight. Goonight.
Good night, ladies, good night, sweet ladies, good night, good
  night.

III. THE FIRE SERMON

THE river's tent is broken: the last fingers of leaf
Clutch and sink into the wet bank. The wind
Crosses the brown land, unheard. The nymphs are departed.
Sweet Thames, run softly, till I end my song.
The river bears no empty bottles, sandwich papers,
Silk handkerchiefs, cardboard boxes, cigarette ends
Or other testimony of summer nights. The nymphs are departed.
And their friends, the loitering heirs of city directors;

Departed, have left no addresses.
By the waters of Leman I sat down and wept...
Sweet Thames, run softly till I end my song,
Sweet Thames, run softly, for I speak not loud or long.
But at my back in a cold blast I hear
The rattle of the bones, and chuckle spread from ear to ear.

A rat crept softly through the vegetation
Dragging its slimy belly on the bank
While I was fishing in the dull canal
On a winter evening round behind the gashouse
Musing upon the king my brother's wreck
And on the king my father's death before him.
White bodies naked on the low damp ground
And bones cast in a little low dry garret,
Rattled by the rat's foot only, year to year.
But at my back from time to time I hear
The sound of horns and motors, which shall bring
Sweeney to Mrs. Porter in the spring.
O the moon shone bright on Mrs. Porter
And on her daughter
They wash their feet in soda water
Et, O ces voix d'enfants, chantant dans la coupole!

Twit twit twit
Jug jug jug jug jug jug
So rudely forc'd.
Tereu

Unreal City
Under the brown fog of a winter noon
Mr. Eugenides, the Smyrna merchant
Unshaven, with a pocket full of currants
C.i.f. London: documents at sight,
Asked me in demotic French
To luncheon at the Cannon Street Hotel

Followed by a weekend at the Metropole.

At the violet hour, when the eyes and back
Turn upward from the desk, when the human engine waits
Like a taxi throbbing waiting,
I Tiresias, though blind, throbbing between two lives,
Old man with wrinkled female breasts, can see
At the violet hour, the evening hour that strives
Homeward, and brings the sailor home from sea,
The typist home at teatime, clears her breakfast, lights
Her stove, and lays out food in tins.
Out of the window perilously spread
Her drying combinations touched by the sun's last rays,
On the divan are piled (at night her bed)
Stockings, slippers, camisoles, and stays.
I Tiresias, old man with wrinkled dugs
Perceived the scene, and foretold the rest—
I too awaited the expected guest.
He, the young man carbuncular, arrives,
A small house agent's clerk, with one bold stare,
One of the low on whom assurance sits
As a silk hat on a Bradford millionaire.
The time is now propitious, as he guesses,
The meal is ended, she is bored and tired,
Endeavours to engage her in caresses
Which still are unreproved, if undesired.
Flushed and decided, he assaults at once;
Exploring hands encounter no defence;
His vanity requires no response,
And makes a welcome of indifference.
(And I Tiresias have foresuffered all
Enacted on this same divan or bed;
I who have sat by Thebes below the wall
And walked among the lowest of the dead.)
Bestows on final patronising kiss,
And gropes his way, finding the stairs unlit...

She turns and looks a moment in the glass,
Hardly aware of her departed lover;
Her brain allows one half-formed thought to pass:
'Well now that's done: and I'm glad it's over.'
When lovely woman stoops to folly and
Paces about her room again, alone,
She smoothes her hair with automatic hand,
And puts a record on the gramophone.

'This music crept by me upon the waters'
And along the Strand, up Queen Victoria Street.
O City city, I can sometimes hear
Beside a public bar in Lower Thames Street,
The pleasant whining of a mandoline
And a clatter and a chatter from within
Where fishmen lounge at noon: where the walls
Of Magnus Martyr hold
Inexplicable splendour of Ionian white and gold.

The river sweats
Oil and tar
The barges drift
With the turning tide
Red sails
Wide
To leeward, swing on the heavy spar.
The barges wash
Drifting logs
Down Greenwich reach
Past the Isle of Dogs.
        Weialala leia
        Wallala leialala

Elizabeth and Leicester
Beating oars
The stern was formed

A gilded shell
Red and gold
The brisk swell
Rippled both shores
Southwest wind
Carried down stream
The peal of bells
White towers
    Weialala leia
    Wallala leialala

'Trams and dusty trees.
Highbury bore me. Richmond and Kew
Undid me. By Richmond I raised my knees
Supine on the floor of a narrow canoe.'
'My feet are at Moorgate, and my heart
Under my feet. After the event
He wept. He promised "a new start".
I made no comment. What should I resent?'
'On Margate Sands.
I can connect
Nothing with nothing.
The broken fingernails of dirty hands.
My people humble people who expect
Nothing.'
    la la

To Carthage then I came

Burning burning burning burning
O Lord Thou pluckest me out
O Lord Thou pluckest

burning

IV. DEATH BY WATER

PHLEBAS the Phoenician, a fortnight dead,
Forgot the cry of gulls, and the deep seas swell
And the profit and loss.
        A current under sea
Picked his bones in whispers. As he rose and fell
He passed the stages of his age and youth
Entering the whirlpool.
        Gentile or Jew
O you who turn the wheel and look to windward,
Consider Phlebas, who was once handsome and tall as you.

V. WHAT THE THUNDER SAID

AFTER the torchlight red on sweaty faces
After the frosty silence in the gardens
After the agony in stony places
The shouting and the crying
Prison and place and reverberation
Of thunder of spring over distant mountains
He who was living is now dead
We who were living are now dying
With a little patience

Here is no water but only rock
Rock and no water and the sandy road
The road winding above among the mountains
Which are mountains of rock without water
If there were water we should stop and drink
Amongst the rock one cannot stop or think
Sweat is dry and feet are in the sand
If there were only water amongst the rock
Dead mountain mouth of carious teeth that cannot spit
Here one can neither stand nor lie nor sit
There is not even silence in the mountains

But dry sterile thunder without rain
There is not even solitude in the mountains
But red sullen faces sneer and snarl
From doors of mudcracked houses
                    If there were water

        And no rock
        If there were rock
        And also water
        And water
        A spring
        A pool among the rock
        If there were the sound of water only
        Not the cicada
        And dry grass singing
        But sound of water over a rock
        Where the hermit-thrush sings in the pine trees
        Drip drop drip drop drop drop drop
        But there is no water

Who is the third who walks always beside you?
When I count, there are only you and I together
But when I look ahead up the white road
There is always another one walking beside you
Gliding wrapt in a brown mantle, hooded
I do not know whether a man or a woman
—But who is that on the other side of you?

What is that sound high in the air
Murmur of maternal lamentation
Who are those hooded hordes swarming
Over endless plains, stumbling in cracked earth
Ringed by the flat horizon only
What is the city over the mountains
Cracks and reforms and bursts in the violet air
Falling towers

Jerusalem Athens Alexandria
Vienna London
Unreal

A woman drew her long black hair out tight
And fiddled whisper music on those strings
And bats with baby faces in the violet light
Whistled, and beat their wings
And crawled head downward down a blackened wall
And upside down in air were towers
Tolling reminiscent bells, that kept the hours
And voices singing out of empty cisterns and exhausted wells.

In this decayed hole among the mountains
In the faint moonlight, the grass is singing
Over the tumbled graves, about the chapel
There is the empty chapel, only the wind's home.
It has no windows, and the door swings,
Dry bones can harm no one.
Only a cock stood on the rooftree
Co co rico co co rico
In a flash of lightning. Then a damp gust
Bringing rain

Ganga was sunken, and the limp leaves
Waited for rain, while the black clouds
Gathered far distant, over Himavant.
The jungle crouched, humped in silence.
Then spoke the thunder
D a
Datta: what have we given?
My friend, blood shaking my heart
The awful daring of a moment's surrender
Which an age of prudence can never retract
By this, and this only, we have existed
Which is not to be found in our obituaries

Or in memories draped by the beneficent spider
Or under seals broken by the lean solicitor
In our empty rooms
D A
Dayadhvam: I have heard the key
Turn in the door once and turn once only
We think of the key, each in his prison
Thinking of the key, each confirms a prison
Only at nightfall, aetherial rumours
Revive for a moment a broken Coriolanus
D A
Damyata: The boat responded
Gaily, to the hand expert with sail and oar
The sea was calm, your heart would have responded
Gaily, when invited, beating obedient
To controlling hands

        I sat upon the shore
Fishing, with the arid plain behind me
Shall I at least set my lands in order?

London Bridge is falling down falling down falling down

Poi s'ascose nel foco che gli affina
Quando fiam ceu chelidon—O swallow swallow
Le Prince d'Aquitaine à la tour abolie
These fragments I have shored against my ruins
Why then Ile fit you. Hieronymo's mad againe.
Datta. Dayadhvam. Damyata.

   Shantih shantih shantih

7

e. e. cummings

Buffalo Bill's

Buffalo Bill's
defunct
            who used to
            ride a watersmooth-silver
                                    stallion
and break onetwothreefourfive pigeonsjustlikethat
                                            Jesus
he was a handsome man
                        and what i want to know is
how do you like your blueeyed boy
Mister Death

"Buffalo Bill's". Copyright 1923, 1951, © 1991 by the Trustees for the E. E. Cummings Trust. Copyright © 1976 by George James Firmage, from COMPLETE POEMS: 1904–1962 by E. E. Cummings, edited by George J. Firmage. Used by permission of Liveright Publishing Corporation.

8

William Carlos Williams

Red Wheelbarrow

William Carlos Williams (1883–1963) was born in Rutherford, New Jersey, and educated at the University of Pennsylvania, where he earned an M.D. In 1910 he opened a pediatrics practice in Rutherford, New Jersey, where, except for a trip to Europe, he lived and practiced medicine for the rest of his life. Although his early poetry is associated with Imagism, he later declared himself an "objectivist," asserting that "there are no ideas but in things." His major long poem, Paterson (1946–1958), recounts the history of local people and predicaments.

so much depends
upon

a red wheel
barrow

glazed with rain
water

beside the white
chickens

"Red Wheelbarrow" by William Carlos Williams, from COLLECTED POEMS: 1909–1939, VOLUME I, copyright © 1938 by New Directions Publishing Corp. Reprinted by permission of New Directions Publishing Corp.

UNDERSTANDING MEANING

1. What is described in the poem?
2. What depends on the red wheelbarrow?

EVALUATING ELEMENTS

1. How does the poet rely on images, rather than verbs, to indicate what has happened?
2. How does the first stanza provide a way of interpreting the other three stanzas?

APPRECIATING LANGUAGE

1. What does the poet imply about relationships between things and people in the first stanza?
2. What statement does the poem make about beauty?

WRITING SUGGESTIONS

1. Analyze the images in terms of color, shape, and texture and how elements of one impact elements of the others.
2. Research theories of "seeing" in the visual arts, and apply what you learn to Williams's poem.

9

André Breton

Manifesto of Surrealism

So strong is the belief in life, in what is most fragile in life – *real* life, I mean – that in the end this belief is lost. Man, that inveterate dreamer, daily more discontent with his destiny, has trouble assessing the objects he has been led to use, objects that his nonchalance has brought his way, or that he has earned through his own efforts, almost always through his own efforts, for he has agreed to work, at least he has not refused to try his luck (or what he calls his luck!). At this point he feels extremely modest: he knows what women he has had, what silly affairs he has been involved in; he is unimpressed by his wealth or his poverty, in this respect he is still a newborn babe and, as for the approval of his conscience, I confess that he does very nicely without it. If he still retains a certain lucidity, all he can do is turn back toward his childhood which, however his guides and mentors may have botched it, still strikes him as somehow charming. There, the absence of any known restrictions allows him the perspective of several lives lived at once; this illusion becomes firmly rooted within him; now he is only interested in the fleeting, the extreme facility of everything. Children set off each day without a worry in the world. Everything is near at hand, the worst material conditions are fine. The woods are white or black, one will never sleep.

But it is true that we would not dare venture so far, it is not merely a question of distance. Threat is piled upon threat, one yields, abandons a portion of the terrain to be conquered. This imagination which knows no bounds is henceforth allowed to be exercised only in strict accordance with the laws of an arbitrary utility; it is incapable of assuming this inferior role for very long and, in the vicinity of the twentieth year, generally prefers to abandon man to his lusterless fate.

Though he may later try to pull himself together on occasion, having felt that he is losing by slow degrees all reason for living, incapable as he has become of being able to rise to some exceptional situation such as love, he will hardly succeed. This is because he henceforth belongs body and soul to an imperative practical necessity which demands his constant attention. None of his gestures will be expansive, none of his ideas generous or far-reaching. In his mind's eye, events real or imagined will be seen only as they relate to a welter of similar events, events in which he has not participated, *abortive* events. What am I saying: he will judge them in relationship to one of these events whose consequences are more reassuring than the others. On no account will he view them as his salvation.

Beloved imagination, what I most like in you is your unsparing quality.

There remains madness, "the madness that one locks up," as it has aptly been described. That madness or another.... We all know, in fact, that the insane owe their incarceration to a tiny number of legally reprehensible acts and that, were it not for these acts their freedom (or what we see as their freedom) would not be threatened. I am willing to admit that they are, to some degree, victims of their imagination, in that it induces them not to pay attention to certain rules – outside of which the species feels threatened – which we are all supposed to know and respect. But their profound indifference to the way in which we judge them, and even to the various punishments meted out to them, allows us to suppose that they derive a great deal of comfort and consolation from their imagination, that they enjoy their madness sufficiently to endure the thought that its validity does not extend beyond themselves. And, indeed, hallucinations, illusions, etc., are not a source of trifling pleasure. The best controlled sensuality partakes of it, and I know that there are many evenings when I would gladly that pretty hand which, during the last pages of Taine's *L'Intelligence,* indulges in some curious misdeeds. I could spend my whole life prying loose the secrets of the insane. These people are honest to a fault, and their naiveté has no peer but my own. Christopher Columbus should have set out to discover America with a boatload of madmen. And note how this madness has taken shape, and endured.

It is not the fear of madness which will oblige us to leave the flag of imagination furled.

The case against the realistic attitude demands to be examined, following the case against the materialistic attitude. The latter, more poetic in fact than the former, admittedly implies on the part of man a kind of monstrous pride which, admittedly, is monstrous, but not a new and more complete decay. It should above all be viewed as a welcome reaction against certain ridiculous tendencies of spiritualism. Finally, it is not incompatible with a certain nobility of thought.

By contrast, the realistic attitude, inspired by positivism, from Saint Thomas Aquinas to Anatole France, clearly seems to me to be hostile to any intellectual or moral advancement. I loathe it, for it is made up of mediocrity, hate, and dull conceit. It is this attitude which today gives birth to these ridiculous books, these insulting plays. It constantly feeds on and derives strength from the newspapers and stultifies both science and art by assiduously flattering the lowest of tastes; clarity bordering on stupidity, a dog's life. The activity of the best minds feels the effects of it; the law of the lowest common denominator finally prevails upon them as it does upon the others. An amusing result of this state of affairs, in literature for example, is the generous supply of novels. Each person adds his personal little "observation" to the whole. As a cleansing antidote to all this, M. Paul Valéry recently suggested that an anthology be compiled in which the largest possible number of opening passages from novels be offered; the resulting insanity, he predicted, would be a source of considerable edification. The most famous authors would be included. Such a though reflects great credit on Paul Valéry who, some time ago, speaking of novels, assured me that, so far as he was concerned, he would continue to refrain from writing: "The Marquise went out at five." But has he kept his word?

If the purely informative style, of which the sentence just quoted is a prime example, is virtually the rule rather than the exception in the novel form, it is because, in all fairness, the author's ambition is severely circumscribed. The circumstantial, needlessly specific nature of each of their notations leads me to believe that they are perpetrating a joke at my expense. I am spared not even one of the character's slightest vacillations: will he be fairhaired? what will his name be? will we first meet him during the summer? So many questions resolved once and for all, as chance directs; the only discretionary power left me is to close the book, which I am careful to do somewhere in the vicinity of the first page. And the descriptions! There is nothing to which their vacuity can be compared; they are nothing but so many superimposed images taken from some stock catalogue, which the author utilizes more and more whenever he chooses; he seizes the opportunity to slip me his postcards, he tries to make me agree with him about the clichés:

> The small room into which the young man was shown was covered with yellow wallpaper: there were geraniums in the windows, which were covered with muslin curtains; the setting sun cast a harsh light over the entire setting…. There was nothing special about the room. The furniture, of yellow wood, was all very old. A sofa with a tall back turned down, an oval table opposite the sofa, a dressing table and a mirror set against the pierglass, some chairs along the walls, two or three etchings of no value portraying some German girls with birds in their hands — such were the furnishings. (Dostoevski, Crime and Punishment)

I am in no mood to admit that the mind is interested in occupying itself with such matters, even fleetingly. It may be argued that this school-boy description has its place, and that at this juncture of the book the author has his reasons for burdening me. Nevertheless he is wasting his time, for I refuse to go into his room. Others' laziness or fatigue does not interest me. I have too unstable a notion of the continuity of life to equate or compare my moments of depression or weakness with my best moments. When one ceases to feel, I am of the opinion one should keep quiet. And I would like it understood that I am not accusing or condemning lack of originality as such. I am only saying that I do not take particular note of the empty moments of my life, that it may be unworthy for any man to crystallize those which seem to him to be so. I shall, with your permission, ignore the description of that room, and many more like it.

Not so fast, there; I'm getting into the area of psychology, a subject about which I shall be careful not to joke.

The author attacks a character and, this being settled upon, parades his hero to and fro across the world. No matter what happens, this hero, whose actions and reactions are admirably predictable, is compelled not to thwart or upset—even though he looks as though he is—the calculations of which he is the object. The currents of life can appear to lift him up, roll him over, cast him down, he will still belong to this *readymade* human type. A simple game of chess which doesn't interest me in the least—man, whoever he may be, being for me a mediocre opponent. What I cannot bear are those wretched discussions relative to such and such a move, since winning or losing is not in question. And if the game is not worth the candle, if objective reason does a frightful job—as indeed it does—of serving him who calls upon it, is it not fitting and proper to avoid all contact with these categories? "Diversity is so vast that every different tone of voice, every step, cough, every wipe of the nose, every sneeze...."★ (Pascal.) If in a cluster of grapes there are no two alike, why do you want me to describe this grape by the other, by all the others, why do you want me to make a palatable grape? Our brains are dulled by the incurable mania of wanting to make the unknown known, classifiable. The desire for analysis wins out over the sentiments.★★ (Barrès, *Proust.*) The result is statements of undue length whose persuasive power is attributable solely to their strangeness and which impress the reader only by the abstract quality of their vocabulary, which moreover is ill-defined. If the general ideas that philosophy has thus far come up with as topics of discussion revealed by their very nature their definitive incursion into a broader or more general area. I would be the first to greet the news with joy. But up till now it has been nothing but idle repartee; the flashes of wit and other niceties vie in concealing from us the true thought in search of itself, instead of concentrating on obtaining successes. It seems to me that every act is its own justification, at least for the person who has been capable of committing it, that it is endowed with a radiant power which the slightest gloss is certain to diminish. Because of this gloss, it even in a sense ceases to happen. It gains nothing to be thus distinguished. Stendhal's heroes are subject to the comments and appraisals—appraisals which are more or less successful—made by that author, which add not one whit to their glory. Where we really find them again is at the point at which Stendahl has lost them.

We are still living under the reign of logic: this, of course, is what I have been driving at. But in this day and age logical methods are applicable only to solving problems of secondary interest. The absolute rationalism that is still in vogue allows us to consider only facts relating directly to our experience. Logical ends, on the contrary, escape us. It is pointless to add that experience itself has found itself increasingly circumscribed. It paces back and forth in a cage from which it is more and more difficult to make it emerge. It too leans for support on what is most immediately expedient, and it is protected by the sentinels of common sense. Under the pretense of civilization and progress, we have managed to banish from the mind everything that may rightly or wrongly be termed superstition, or fancy; forbidden is any kind of search for truth which is not in conformance with accepted practices. It was, apparently, by pure chance that a part of our mental world which we pretended not to be concerned with any longer—and, in my opinion by far the most important part—has been brought back to light. For this we must give thanks to the discoveries of Sigmund Freud. On the basis of these discoveries a current of opinion is finally forming by means of which the human explorer will be able to carry his investigation much further, authorized as he will henceforth be not to confine himself solely to the most summary realities. The imagination is perhaps on the point of reasserting itself, of reclaiming its rights. If the depths of our mind contain within it strange forces capable of augmenting those on the surface, or of waging a victorious battle against them, there is every reason to seize them—first to seize them, then, if need be, to submit them to the control of our reason. The analysts themselves have everything to gain by it. But it is worth noting that no means has been designated a priori for carrying out this undertaking, that until further notice it can be construed to be the province of poets as well as scholars, and that its success is not dependent upon the more or less capricious paths that will be followed.

Freud very rightly brought his critical faculties to bear upon the dream. It is, in fact, inadmissible that this considerable portion of psychic activity (since, at least from man's birth until his death, thought offers no solution of continuity, the sum of the moments of the dream, from the point of view of time, and taking into consideration only the time of pure dreaming, that is the dreams of sleep, is not inferior to the sum of the moments of reality, or, to be more precisely limiting, the moments of waking) has still today been so grossly neglected. I have always been amazed at the way an ordinary observer lends so much more credence and attaches so much more importance to waking events than to those occurring in dreams. It is because man, when he ceases to sleep, is above all the plaything of his memory, and in its normal state memory takes pleasure in weakly retracing for him the circumstances of the dream, in stripping it of any real importance, and in dismissing the only *determinant* from the point where he thinks he has left it a few hours before: this firm hope, this concern. He is under the impression of continuing something that is worthwhile. Thus the dream finds itself reduced to a mere parenthesis, as is the night. And, like the night, dreams generally contribute little to furthering our understanding. This curious state of affairs seems to me to call for certain reflections:

1) Within the limits where they operate (or are thought to operate) dreams give every evidence of being continuous and show signs of organization. Memory alone arrogates to itself the right to excerpt from dreams, to ignore the transitions, and to depict for us rather a series of dreams than the *dream itself.* By the same token, at any given moment we have only a distinct notion of realities, the coordination of which is a question of will.* (Account must be taken of the *depth* of the dream. For the most part I retain only what I can glean from its most superficial layers. What I most enjoy contemplating about a dream is everything that sinks back below the surface in a waking state, everything I have forgotten about my activities in the course of the preceding day, dark foliage, stupid branches. In "reality," likewise, I prefer to *fall.*) What is worth noting is that nothing allows us to presuppose a greater dissipation of the elements of which the dream is constituted. I am sorry to have to speak about it according to a formula which in principle excludes the dream. When will we have sleeping logicians, sleeping philosophers? I would like to sleep, in order to surrender myself to the dreamers, the way I surrender myself to those who read me with eyes wide open; in order to stop imposing, in this realm, the conscious rhythm of my

thought. Perhaps my dream last night follows that of the night before, and will be continued the next night, with an exemplary strictness. *It's quite possible,* as the saying goes. And since it has not been proved in the slightest that, in doing so, the "reality" with which I am kept busy continues to exist in the state of dream, that it does not sink back down into the immemorial, why should I not grant to dreams what I occasionally refuse reality, that is, this value of certainty in itself which, in its own time, is not open to my repudiation? Why should I not expect from the sign of the dream more than I expect from a degree of consciousness which is daily more acute? Can't the dream also be used in solving the fundamental questions of life? Are these questions the same in one case as in the other and, in the dream, do these questions already exist? Is the dream any less restrictive or punitive than the rest? I am growing old and, more than that reality to which I believe I subject myself, it is perhaps the dream, the difference with which I treat the dream, which makes me grow old.

2) Let me come back again to the waking state. I have no choice but to consider it a phenomenon of interference. Not only does the mind display, in this state, a strange tendency to lose its bearings (as evidenced by the slips and mistakes the secrets of which are just beginning to be revealed to us), but, what is more, it does not appear that, when the mind is functioning normally, it really responds to anything but the suggestions which come to it from the depths of that dark night to which I commend it. However conditioned it may be, its balance is relative. It scarcely dares express itself and, if it does, it confines itself to verifying that such and such an idea, or such and such a woman, has made an impression on it. What impression it would be hard pressed to say, by which it reveals the degree of its subjectivity, and nothing more. This idea, this woman, disturb it, they tend to make it less severe. What they do is isolate the mind for a second from its solvent and spirit it to heaven, as the beautiful precipitate it can be, that it is. When all else fails, it then calls upon chance, a divinity even more obscure than the others to whom it ascribes all its aberrations. Who can say to me that the angle by which that idea which affects it is offered, that what it likes in the eye of that woman is not precisely what links it to its dream, binds it to those fundamental facts which, through its own fault, it has

lost? And if things were different, what might it be capable of? I would like to provide it with the key to this corridor.

3) The mind of the man who dreams is fully satisfied by what happens to him. The agonizing question of possibility is no longer pertinent. Kill, fly faster, love to your heart's content. And if you should die, are you not certain of reawaking among the dead? Let yourself be carried along, events will not tolerate your interference. You are nameless. The ease of everything is priceless.

What reason, I ask, a reason so much vaster than the other, makes dreams seem so natural and allows me to welcome unreservedly a welter of episodes so strange that they could confound me now as I write? And yet I can believe my eyes, my ears; this great day has arrived, this beast has spoken.

If man's awaking is harder, if it breaks the spell too abruptly, it is because he has been led to make for himself too impoverished a notion of atonement.

4) From the moment when it is subjected to a methodical examination, when, by means yet to be determined, we succeed in recording the contents of dreams in their entirety (and that presupposes a discipline of memory spanning generations; but let us nonetheless begin by noting the most salient facts), when its graph will expand with unparalleled volume and regularity, we may hope that the mysteries which really are not will give way to the great Mystery. I believe in the future resolution of these two states, dream and reality, which are seemingly so contradictory, into a kind of absolute reality, a *surreality*, if one may so speak. It is in quest of this surreality that I am going, certain not to find it but too unmindful of my death not to calculate to some slight degree the joys of its possession.

A story is told according to which Saint-Pol-Roux, in times gone by, used to have a notice posted on the door of his manor house in Camaret, every evening before he went to sleep, which read: THE POET IS WORKING.

A great deal more could be said, but in passing I merely wanted to touch upon a subject which in itself would require a very long and much more detailed discussion; I shall come back to it. At this juncture, my intention was merely to mark a point by noting the *hate of the marvelous* which rages in certain men, this absurdity beneath which they try to bury it. Let us not mince words: the marvelous is always beautiful, anything marvelous is beautiful, in fact only the marvelous is beautiful.

In the realm of literature, only the marvelous is capable of fecundating works which belong to an inferior category such as the novel, and generally speaking, anything that involves storytelling. Lewis' *The Monk* is an admirable proof of this. It is infused throughout with the presence of the marvelous. Long before the author has freed his main characters from all temporal constraints, one feels them ready to act with an unprecedented pride. This passion for eternity with which they are constantly stirred lends an unforgettable intensity to their torments, and to mine. I mean that this book, from beginning to end, and in the purest way imaginable, exercises an exalting effect only upon that part of the mind which aspires to leave the earth and that, stripped of an insignificant part of its plot, which belongs to the period in which it was written, it constitutes a paragon of precision and innocent grandeur.* (What is admirable about the fantastic is that there is no longer anything fantastic: there is only the real.) It seems to me none better has been done, and that the character of Mathilda in particular is the most moving creation that one can credit to this *figurative* fashion in literature. She is less a character than a continual temptation. And if a character is not a temptation, what is he? An extreme temptation, she. In *The Monk* the "nothing is impossible for him who dares try" gives it its full, convincing measure. Ghosts play a logical role in the book, since the critical mind does not seize them in order to dispute them. Ambrosio's punishment is likewise treated in a legitimate manner, since it is finally accepted by the critical faculty as a natural denouement.

It may seem arbitrary on my part, when discussing the marvelous, to choose this model, from which both the Nordic literatures and Oriental literatures have borrowed time and time again, not to mention the religious literatures of every country. This is because most of the examples which these literatures could have furnished me with are tainted by puerility, for the simple reason that they are addressed to children. At an early age children are weaned on the marvelous, and later on they fail to retain a sufficient virginity of mind to thoroughly enjoy fairy tales. No matter how charming they may be, a grown man would think he were reverting to childhood by nourishing himself on fairy tales, and I am the first to admit that all such tales are not suitable for him. The fabric of adorable improbabilities must be made a trifle more subtle the older we grow, and we are still at the age of waiting for this kind of spider.... But the faculties do not change radically. Fear, the attraction of the unusual, chance, the taste for things extravagant are all devices which we can always call upon without fear of deception. There are fairy tales to be written for adults, fairy tales still almost blue.

The marvelous is not the same in every period of history: it partakes in some obscure way of a sort of general revelation only the fragments of which come down to us: they are the romantic *ruins,* the modern *mannequin,* or any other symbol capable of affecting the human sensibility for a period of time. In these areas which make us smile, there is still portrayed the incurable human restlessness, and this is why I take them into consideration and why I judge them inseparable from certain productions of genius which are, more than the others, painfully afflicted by them. They are Villon's gibbets, Racine's Greeks, Baudelaire's couches. They coincide with an eclipse of the taste I am made to endure, I whose notion of taste is the image of a big spot. Amid the bad taste of my time I strive to go further than anyone else. It would have been I, had I lived in 1820, I "the bleeding nun," I who would not have spared this cunning and banal "let us conceal" whereof the parodical Cuisin speaks, it would have been I, I who would have reveled in the enormous metaphors, as he says, all phases of the "silver disk." For today I think of a *castle,* half of which is not necessarily in ruins; this castle belongs to me, I picture it in a rustic setting, not far from Paris. The outbuildings are too numerous to mention, and, as for the interior, it has been frightfully restored, in such manner as to leave nothing to be desired from the viewpoint of comfort. Automobiles are parked before the door, concealed by the shade of trees. A few of my friends are living here as permanent guests: there is Louis Aragon leaving; he only has time enough to say hello; Philippe Soupault gets up with the stars, and Paul Eluard, our great Eluard, has not yet come home. There are Robert Desnos and Roger Vitrac out on the grounds poring over an ancient edict on duelling; Georges Auric, Jean Paulhan; Max Morise, who rows so well, and Benjamin Péret, busy with his equations with birds; and Joseph Delteil; and Jean Carrive; and Georges Limbour, and Georges Limbours (there is a whole hedge of Georges Limbours); and Marcel Noll; there is T. Fraenkel waving to us from his captive balloon, Georges Malkine, Antonin Artaud, Francis Gérard, Pierre Naville, J.-A. Boiffard, and after them Jacques Baron and his brother, handsome and cordial, and so many others besides, and gorgeous women, I might add. Nothing is too good for these young men, their wishes are, as to wealth, so many commands. Francis Picabia comes to pay us a call, and last week, in the hall of mirrors, we received a certain Marcel Duchamp whom we had not hitherto known. Picasso goes hunting in the neighborhood. The spirit of *demoralization* has elected domicile in the castle, and it is with it we have to deal every time it is a question of contact with our fellowmen, but the doors are always open, and one does not begin by "thanking" everyone, you know. Moreover, the solitude is vast, we don't often run into one another. And anyway, isn't what matters that we be the masters of ourselves, the masters of women, and of love too?

I shall be proved guilty of poetic dishonesty: everyone will go parading about saying that I live on the rue Fontaine and that he will have none of the water that flows therefrom. To be sure! But is he certain that this castle into which I cordially invite him is an image? What if this castle really existed! My guests are there to prove it does; their whim is the luminous road that leads to it. We really live by our fantasies when we *give free reign to them*. And how could what one might do bother the other, there, safely sheltered from the sentimental pursuit and at the trysting place of opportunities?

Man proposes and disposes. He and he alone can determine whether he is completely master of himself, that is, whether he maintains the body of his desires, daily more formidable, in a state of anarchy. Poetry teaches him to. It bears within itself the perfect compensation for the miseries we endure. It can also be an organizer, if ever, as the result of a less intimate disappointment, we contemplate taking it seriously. The time is coming when it decrees the end of money and by itself will break the bread of heaven for the earth! There will still be gatherings on the public squares, and *movements* you never dared hope participate in. Farewell to absurd choices, the dreams of dark abyss, rivalries, the prolonged patience, the flight of the seasons, the artificial order of ideas, the ramp of danger, time for everything! May you only take the trouble to *practice* poetry. Is it not incumbent upon us, who are already living off it, to try and impose what we hold to be our case for further inquiry?

It matters not whether there is a certain disproportion between this defense and the illustration that will follow it. It was a question of going back to the sources of poetic imagination and, what is more, of remaining there. Not that I pretend to have done so. It requires a great deal of fortitude to try to set up one's abode in these distant regions where everything seems at first to be so awkward and difficult, all the more so if one wants to try to take someone there. Besides, one is never sure of really being there. If one is going to all that trouble, one might as well stop off somewhere else. Be that as it may, the fact is that the way to these regions is clearly marked, and that to attain the true goal is now merely a matter of the travelers' ability to endure.

We are all more or less aware of the road traveled. I was careful to relate, in the course of a study of the case of Robert Desnos entitled ENTRÉE DES MÉDIUMS,★ (See *Les Pas perdus,* published by N.R.F.) that I had been led to" concentrate my attention on the more or less partial sentences which, when one is quite alone and on the verge of falling asleep, become perceptible for the mind without its being possible to discover what provoked them." I had then just attempted the poetic adventure with the minimum of risks, that is, my aspirations were the same as they are today but I trusted in the slowness of formulation to keep me from useless contacts, contacts of which I completely disapproved. This attitude involved a modesty of thought certain vestiges of which I still retain. At the end of my life, I shall doubtless manage to speak with great effort the way people speak, to apologize for my voice and my few remaining gestures. The virtue of the spoken word (and the written word all the more so) seemed to me to derive from the faculty of foreshortening in a striking manner the exposition (since there was exposition) of a small number of facts, poetic or other, of which I made myself the substance. I had come to the conclusion that Rimbaud had not proceeded any differently. I was composing, with a concern for variety that deserved better, the final poems of *Mont de piété,* that is, I managed to extract from the blank lines of this book an incredible advantage. These lines were the closed eye to the operations of thought that I believed I was obliged to keep hidden from the reader. It was not deceit on my part, but my love of shocking the reader. I had the illusion of a possible complicity, which I had more and more difficulty giving up. I had begun to cherish words excessively for the space they allow around them, for their tangencies with countless other words which I did not utter. The poem BLACK FOREST derives precisely from this state of mind. It took me six months to write it, and you may take my word for it that I did not rest a single day. But this stemmed from the opinion I had of myself in those days, which was high, please don't judge me too harshly. I enjoy these stupid confessions. At that point cubist pseudo-poetry was trying to get a foothold, but it had emerged defenseless from Picasso's brain, and I was thought to be as dull as dishwater (and still am). I had a sneaking suspicion, moreover, that from the viewpoint of poetry I was off on the wrong road, but I hedged my bet as best I could, defying lyricism with salvos of definitions and formulas (the Dada phenomena were waiting in the wings, ready to come on stage) and pretending to search for an application of poetry to advertising (I went so far as to claim that the world would end, not with a good book but with a beautiful advertisement for heaven or for hell).

In those days, a man at least as boring as I, Pierre Reverdy, was writing:

The image is a pure creation of the mind.

It cannot be born from a comparison but from a juxtaposition of two more or less distant realities.

The more the relationship between the two juxtaposed realities is distant and true, the stronger the image will be—the greater its emotional power and poetic reality... *
(Nord-Sud, March 1918)

These words, however sibylline for the uninitiated, were extremely revealing, and I pondered them for a long time. But the image eluded me. Reverdy's aesthetic, a completely a posteriori aesthetic, led me to mistake the effects for the causes. It was in the midst of all this that I renounced irrevocably my point of view.

One evening, therefore, before I fell asleep, I perceived, so clearly articulated that it was impossible to change a word, but nonetheless removed from the sound of any voice, a rather strange phrase which came to me without any apparent relationship to the events in which, my consciousness agrees, I was then involved, a phrase which seemed to me insistent, a phrase, if I may be so bold, *which was knocking at the window*. I took cursory note of it and prepared to move on when its organic character caught my attention. Actually, this phrase astonished me: unfortunately I cannot remember it exactly, but it was something like: "There is a man cut in two by the window," but there could be no question of ambiguity, accompanied as it was by the faint visual image* (Were I a painter, this visual depiction would doubtless have become more important for me than the other. It was most certainly my previous predispositions which decided the matter. Since that day, I have had occasion to concentrate my attention voluntarily on similar apparitions, and I know they are fully as clear as auditory phenomena. With a pencil and white sheet of paper to hand, I could easily trace their outlines. Here again it is not a matter of drawing, but *simply of tracing*. I could thus depict a tree, a wave, a musical instrument, all manner of things of which I am presently incapable of providing even the roughest sketch. I would plunge into it, convinced that I would find my way again, in a maze of lines which at first glance would seem to be going nowhere. And, upon opening my eyes, I would get the very strong impression of something "never seen." The proof of what I am saying has been provided many times by Robert Desnos: to be convinced, one has only to leaf through the pages of issue number 36 of *Feuilles libres* which contains several of his drawings (*Romeo and Juliet*, *A Man Died This Morning*, etc.) which were taken by this magazine as the drawings of a madman and published as such.) of a man walking cut half way up by a window perpendicular to the axis of his body. Beyond the slightest shadow of a doubt, what I saw was the simple reconstruction in space of a man leaning out a window. But this window having shifted with the man, I realized that I was dealing with an image of a fairly rare sort, and all I could think of was to incorporate it into my material for poetic construction. No sooner had I granted it this capacity than it was in fact succeeded by a whole series of phrases, with only brief pauses between them, which surprised me only slightly less and left me with the impression of their being so gratuitous that the control I had then exercised upon myself seemed to me illusory and all I could think of was putting an end to the interminable quarrel raging within me.* (Knut Hamsum ascribes this sort of revelation to which I had been subjected as deriving from *hunger,* and he may not be wrong. (The fact is I did not eat every day during that period of my life). Most certainly the manifestations that he describes in these terms are clearly the same:

"The following day I awoke at an early hour. It was still dark. My eyes had been open for a long time when I heard the clock in the apartment above strike five. I wanted to go back to sleep, but I couldn't; I was wide awake and a thousand thoughts were crowding through my mind.

"Suddenly a few good fragments came to mind, quite suitable to be used in a rough draft, or serialized; all of a sudden I found, quite by chance, beautiful phrases, phrases such as I had never written. I repeated them to myself slowly, word by word; they were excellent. And there were still more coming. I got up and picked up a pencil and some paper that were on a table behind my bed. It was as though some vein had burst within me, one word followed another, found its proper place, adapted itself to the situation, scene piled upon scene, the action unfolded, one retort after another welled up in my mind, I was enjoying myself immensely. Thoughts came to me so rapidly and continued to flow so abundantly that I lost a whole host of delicate details, because my pencil could not keep up with them, and yet I went as fast as I could, my hand in constant motion, I did not lose a minute. The sentences continued to well up within me, I was pregnant with my subject."

Apollinaire asserted that Chirico's first paintings were done under the influence of cenesthesic disorders (migraines, colics, etc.).)

Completely occupied as I still was with Freud at that time, and familiar as I was with his methods of examination which I had some slight occasion to use on some patients during the war, I resolved to obtain from myself what we were trying to obtain from them, namely, a monologue spoken as rapidly as possible without any intervention on the part of the critical faculties, a monologue consequently unencumbered by the slightest inhibition and which was, as closely as possible, akin to *spoken thought*. It had seemed to me, and still does—the way in which the phrase about the man cut in two had come to me is an indication of it—that the speed of thought is no greater than the speed of speech, and that thought does not necessarily defy language, nor even the fast-moving pen. It was in this frame of mind that Philippe Soupault—to whom I had confided these initial conclusions – and I decided to blacken some paper, with a praiseworthy disdain for what might result from a literary point of view. The ease of execution did the rest. By the end of the first day we were able to read to ourselves some fifty or so pages obtained in this manner, and begin to compare our results. All in all, Soupault's pages and mine proved to be remarkably similar: the same overconstruction, shortcomings of a similar nature, but also, on both our parts, the illusion of an extraordinary verve, a great deal of emotion, a considerable choice of images of a quality such that we would not have been capable of preparing a single one in longhand, a very special picturesque quality and, here and there, a strong comical effect. The only difference between our two texts seemed to me to derive essentially from our respective tempers. Soupault's being less static than mine, and, if he does not mind my offering this one slight criticism, from the fact that he had made the error of putting a few words by way of titles at the top of certain pages, I suppose in a spirit of mystification. On the other hand, I must give credit where credit is due and say that he constantly and vigorously opposed any effort to retouch or correct, however slightly, any passage of this kind which seemed to me unfortunate. In this he was, to be sure, absolutely right.* (I believe more and more in the infallibility of my thought with respect to myself, and this is too fair. Nonetheless, with this *thought-writing*, where one is at the mercy of the first outside distraction, "ebullutions" can occur. It would be inexcusable for us to pretend otherwise. By definition, thought is strong, and incapable of catching itself in error. The blame for these obvious weaknesses must be placed on suggestions that come to it from without.) It is, in fact, difficult to appreciate fairly the various elements present: one may even go so far as to say that it is impossible to appreciate them at a first reading. To you who write, these elements are, on the surface, *as strange to you as they are to anyone else,* and naturally you are wary of them. Poetically speaking, what strikes you about them above all is their *extreme degree of immediate absurdity,* the quality of this absurdity, upon closer scrutiny, being to give way to everything admissible, everything legitimate in the world: the disclosure of a certain number of properties and of facts no less objective, in the final analysis, than the others.

In homage to Guillaume Apollinaire, who had just died and who, on several occasions, seemed to us to have followed a discipline of this kind, without however having sacrificed to it any mediocre literary means, Soupault and I baptized the new mode of pure expression which we had at our disposal and which we wished to pass on to our friends, by the name of SURREALISM. I believe that there is no point today in dwelling any further on this word and that the meaning we gave it initially has generally prevailed over its Apollinarian sense. To be even fairer, we could probably have taken over the word SUPERNATURALISM employed by Gérard de Nerval in his dedication to the *Filles de feu.*★ (And also by Thomas Carlyle in *Sartor Resartus* ([Book III] Chapter VIII, "Natural Supernaturalism"), 1833-34.) It appears, in fact, that Nerval possessed to a tee the spirit with which we claim a kinship, Apollinaire having possessed, on the contrary, naught but *the letter,* still imperfect, of Surrealism, having shown himself powerless to give a valid theoretical idea of it. Here are two passages by Nerval which seem to me to be extremely significant in this respect:

I am going to explain to you, my dear Dumas, the phenomenon of which you have spoken a short while ago. There are, as you know, certain storytellers who cannot invent without identifying with the characters their imagination has dreamt up. You may recall how convincingly our old friend Nodier used to tell how it had been his misfortune during the Revolution to be guillotined; one became so completely convinced of what he was saying that one began to wonder how he had managed to have his head glued back on.

...And since you have been indiscreet enough to quote one of the sonnets composed in this SUPERNATURALISTIC dream-state, as the Germans would call it, you will have to hear them all. You will find them at the end of the volume. They are hardly any more obscure than Hegel's metaphysics or Swedenborg's MEMORABILIA, and would lose their charm if they were explained, if such were possible; at least admit the worth of the expression....** (See also *L'Idéoréalisme* by Saint-Pol-Roux.)

Those who might dispute our right to employ the term SURREALISM in the very special sense that we understand it are being extremely dishonest, for there can be no doubt that this word had no currency before we came along. Therefore, I am defining it once and for all:

SURREALISM, *n.* Psychic automatism in its pure state, by which one proposes to express—verbally, by means of the written word, or in any other manner—the actual functioning of thought. Dictated by the thought, in the absence of any control exercised by reason, exempt from any aesthetic or moral concern.

ENCYCLOPEDIA. *Philosophy.* Surrealism is based on the belief in the superior reality of certain forms of previously neglected associations, in the omnipotence of dream, in the disinterested play of thought. It tends to ruin once and for all all other psychic mechanisms and to substitute itself for them in solving all the principal problems of life. The following have performed acts of ABSOLUTE SURREALISM: Messrs. Aragon, Baron, Boiffard, Breton, Carrive, Crevel, Delteil, Desnos, Eluard, Gérard, Limbour, Malkine, Morise, Naville, Noll, Péret, Picon, Soupault, Vitrac.

They seem to be, up to the present time, the only ones, and there would be no ambiguity about it were it not for the case of Isidore Ducasse, about whom I lack information. And, of course, if one is to judge them only superficially by their results, a good number of poets could pass for Surrealists, beginning with Dante and, in his finer moments, Shakespeare. *In the course of the various attempts I have made to reduce what is, by breach of trust, called genius, I have found nothing which in the final analysis can be attributed to any other method than that.*

Young's *Nights* are Surrealist from one end to the other; unfortunately it is a priest who is speaking, a bad priest no doubt, but a priest nonetheless.

Swift is Surrealist in malice,

Sade is Surrealist in sadism.

Chateaubriand is Surrealist in exoticism.

Constant is Surrealist in politics.

Hugo is Surrealist when he isn't stupid.

Desbordes-Valmore is Surrealist in love.

Bertrand is Surrealist in the past.

Rabbe is Surrealist in death.

Poe is Surrealist in adventure.

Baudelaire is Surrealist in morality.

Rimbaud is Surrealist in the way he lived, and elsewhere.

Mallarmé is Surrealist when he is confiding.

Jarry is Surrealist in absinthe.

Nouveau is Surrealist in the kiss.

Saint-Pol-Roux is Surrealist in his use of symbols.

Fargue is Surrealist in the atmosphere.

Vaché is Surrealist in me.

Reverdy is Surrealist at home.

Saint-Jean-Perse is Surrealist at a distance.

Roussel is Surrealist as a storyteller.

Etc.

I would like to stress the point: they are not always Surrealists, in that I discern in each of them a certain number of preconceived ideas to which—very naively!—they hold. They hold to them because they had not *heard the Surrealist voice*, the one that continues to preach on the eve of death and above the storms, because they did not want to serve simply to orchestrate the marvelous score. They were instruments too full of pride, and this is why they have not always produced a harmonious sound.* (I could say the same of a number of philosophers and painters, including, among the latter, Uccello, from painters of the past, and, in the modern era, Seurat, Gustave Moreau, Matisse (in "La Musique," for example), Derain, Picasso, (by far the most pure), Braque, Duchamp, Picabia, Chirico (so admirable for so long), Klee, Man Ray, Max Ernst, and, one so close to us, André Masson.)

But we, who have made no effort whatsoever to filter, who in our works have made ourselves into simple receptacles of so many echoes, modest *recording instruments* who are not mesmerized by the drawings we are making, perhaps we serve an even nobler cause. Thus do we render with integrity the "talent" which has been lent to us. You might as well speak of the talent of this platinum ruler, this mirror, this door, and of the sky, if you like.

We do not have any talent; ask Philippe Soupault:

"Anatomical products of manufacture and low-income dwellings will destroy the tallest cities."

Ask Roger Vitrac:

"No sooner had I called forth the marble-admiral than he turned on his heel like a horse which rears at the sight of the North star and showed me, in the plane of his two-pointed cocked hat, a region where I was to spend my life."

Ask Paul Eluard:

"This is an oft-told tale that I tell, a famous poem that I reread: I am leaning against a wall, with my verdant ears and my lips burned to a crisp."

Ask Max Morise:

"The bear of the caves and his friend the bittern, the vol-au-vent and his valet the wind, the Lord Chancellor with his Lady, the scarecrow for sparrows and his accomplice the sparrow, the test tube and his daughter the needle, this carnivore and

his brother the carnival, the sweeper and his monocle, the Mississippi and its little dog, the coral and its jug of milk, the Miracle and its Good Lord, might just as well go and disappear from the surface of the sea."

Ask Joseph Delteil:

"Alas! I believe in the virtue of birds. And a feather is all it takes to make me die laughing."

Ask Louis Aragon:

"During a short break in the party, as the players were gathering around a bowl of flaming punch, I asked a tree if it still had its red ribbon."

And ask me, who was unable to keep myself from writing the serpentine, distracting lines of this preface.

Ask Robert Desnos, he who, more than any of us, has perhaps got closest to the Surrealist truth, he who, in his still unpublished works★ (NOUVELLES HÉBRIDES, DÉSORDRE FORMEL, DEUIL POUR DEUIL.) and in the course of the numerous experiments he has been a party to, has fully justified the hope I placed in Surrealism and leads me to believe that a great deal more will still come of it. Desnos *speaks Surrealist* at will. His extraordinary agility in orally following his thought is worth as much to us as any number of splendid speeches which are lost, Desnos having better things to do than record them. He reads himself like an open book, and does nothing to retain the pages, which fly away in the windy wake of his life.

SECRETS OF THE MAGICAL SURREALIST ART

Written Surrealist composition

or

first and last draft

After you have settled yourself in a place as favorable as possible to the concentration of your mind upon itself, have writing materials brought to you. Put yourself in as passive, or receptive, a state of mind as you can. Forget about your genius, your talents, and the talents of everyone else. Keep reminding yourself that literature is one of the saddest roads that leads to everything. Write quickly, without any preconceived subject, fast enough so that you will not remember what you're writing and be tempted to reread what you have written. The first sentence will come spontaneously, so compelling is the truth that with every passing second there is a sentence unknown to our consciousness which is only crying out to be heard. It is somewhat of a problem to form an opinion about the next sentence; it doubtless partakes both of our conscious activity and of the other, if one agrees that the fact of having written the first entails a minimum of perception. This should be of no importance to you, however; to a large extent, this is what is most interesting and intriguing about the Surrealist game. The fact still remains that punctuation no doubt resists the absolute continuity of the flow with which we are concerned, although it may seem as necessary as the arrangement of knots in a vibrating cord. Go on as long as you like. Put your trust in the inexhaustible nature of the murmur. If silence threatens to settle in if you should ever happen to make a mistake—a mistake, perhaps due to carelessness—break off without hesitation with an overly clear line. Following a word the origin of which seems suspicious to you, place any letter whatsoever, the letter "l" for example, always the letter "l," and bring the arbitrary back by making this letter the first of the following word.

How not to be bored any longer when with others

This is very difficult. Don't be at home for anyone, and occasionally, when no one has forced his way in, interrupting you in the midst of your Surrealist activity, and you, crossing your arms, say: "It doesn't matter, there are doubtless better things to do or not do. Interest in life is indefensible Simplicity, what is going on inside me, is still tiresome to me!" or an other revolting banality.

To make speeches

Just prior to the elections, in the first country which deems it worthwhile to proceed in this kind of public expression of opinion, have yourself put on the ballot. Each of us has within himself the potential of an orator: multicolored loin cloths, glass trinkets of words. Through Surrealism he will take despair unawares in its poverty. One night, on a stage, he will, by himself, carve up the eternal heaven, that *Peau de l'ours*. He will promise so much that any promises he keeps will be a source of wonder and dismay. In answer to the claims of an entire people he will give a partial and ludicrous vote. He will make the bitterest enemies partake of a secret desire which will blow up the countries. And in this he will succeed simply by allowing himself to be moved by the immense word which dissolves into pity and revolves in hate. Incapable of failure, he will play on the velvet of all failures. He will be truly elected, and women will love him with an all-consuming passion.

To write false novels

Whoever you may be, if the spirit moves you burn a few laurel leaves and, without wishing to tend this meager fire, you will begin to write a novel. Surrealism will allow you to: all you have to do is set the needle marked "fair" at "action," and the rest will follow naturally. Here are some characters rather different in appearance; their names in your handwriting are a question of capital letters, and they will conduct themselves with the same ease with respect to active verbs as does the impersonal pronoun "it" with respect to words such as "is raining," "is," "must," etc. They will command them, so to speak, and wherever observation, reflection, and the faculty of generalization prove to be of no help to you, you may rest assured that they will credit you with a thousand intentions you never had. Thus endowed with a tiny number of physical and moral characteristics, these beings who in truth owe you so little will thereafter deviate not one iota from a certain line of conduct about which you need not concern yourself any further. Out of this will result a plot more or less clever in appearance, justifying point by point this moving or comforting denouement about which you couldn't care less. Your false novel will simulate to a marvelous degree a real novel; you will be rich, and everyone will agree that "you've really got a lot of guts," since it's also in this region that this something is located.

Of course, by an analogous method, and provided you ignore what you are reviewing, you can successfully devote yourself to false literary criticism.

How to catch the eye of a woman you pass in the street

....

....

....

....

....

Against death

Surrealism will usher you into death, which is a secret society. It will glove your hand, burying therein the profound M with which the word Memory begins. Do not forget to make proper arrangements for your last will and testament: speaking personally, I ask that I be taken to the cemetery in a moving van. May my friends destroy every last copy of the printing of the *Speech concerning the Modicum of Reality.*

❀ ❀

Language has been given to man so that he may make Surrealist use of it. To the extent that he is required to make himself understood, he manages more or less to express himself, and by so doing to fulfill certain functions culled from among the most vulgar. Speaking, reading a letter, present no real problem for him, provided that, in so doing, he does not set himself a goal above the mean, that is, provided he confines himself to carrying on a conversation (for the pleasure of conversing) with someone. He is not worried about the words that are going to come, nor about the sentence which will follow after the sentence he is just completing. To a very simple question, he will be capable of making a lightning-like reply. In the absence of minor tics acquired through contact with others, he can without any ado offer an opinion on a limited number of subjects; for that he does not need to "count up to ten" before speaking or to formulate anything whatever ahead of time. Who has been able to convince him that this faculty of the first draft will only do him a disservice when he makes up his mind to establish more delicate relationships? There is no subject about which he should refuse to talk, to write about prolifically. All that results from listening to oneself, from reading what one has written, is the suspension of the occult, that admirable help. I am in no hurry to understand myself (basta! I shall always understand myself). If such and such a sentence of mine turns out to be somewhat disappointing, at least momentarily, I place my trust in the following sentence to redeem its sins; I carefully refrain from starting it over again or polishing it. The only thing that might prove fatal to me would be the slightest loss of impetus. Words, groups of words *which follow one another,* manifest among themselves the greatest solidarity. It is not up to me to favor one group over the other. It is up to a miraculous equivalent to intervene—and intervene it does.

Not only does this unrestricted language, which I am trying to render forever valid, which seems to me to adapt itself to all of life's circumstances, not only does this language not deprive me of any of my means, on the contrary it lends me an extraordinary lucidity, and it does so in an area where I least expected it. I shall even go so far as to maintain that it instructs me and, indeed, I have had occasion to use *surreally* words whose meaning I have forgotten. I was subsequently able to verify that the way in which I had used them corresponded perfectly with their definition. This would leave one to believe that we do not "learn," that all we ever do is "relearn." There are felicitous turns of speech that I have thus familiarized myself with. And I am not talking about the *poetic consciousness of objects* which I have been able to acquire only after a spiritual contact with them repeated a thousand times over.

The forms of Surrealist language adapt themselves best to dialogue. Here, two thoughts confront each other; while one is being delivered, the other is busy with it; but how is it busy with it? To assume that it incorporates it within itself would be tantamount to admitting that there is a time during which it is possible for it to live completely off that other thought, which is highly unlikely. And, in fact, the attention it pays is completely exterior; it has only time enough to approve or reject—generally reject—with all the consideration of which man is capable. This mode of language, moreover, does not allow the heart of the matter to be plumbed. My attention, prey to an entreaty which it cannot in all decency reject, treats the opposing thought as an enemy; in ordinary conversation, it "takes it up" almost always on the words, the figures of speech, it employs; it puts me in a position to turn it to good advantage in my reply by distorting them. This is true to such a degree that in certain pathological states of mind, where the sensorial disorders occupy the patient's complete attention, he limits himself, while continuing to answer the questions, to seizing the last word spoken in his presence or the last portion of the Surrealist sentence some trace of which he finds in his mind.

Q. "How old are you?" A. "You." *(Echolalia.)*

Q. "What is your name?" A. "Forty-five houses." *(Ganser syndrome, or beside-the-point replies.)*

There is no conversation in which some trace of this disorder does not occur. The effort to be social which dictates it and the considerable practice we have at it are the only things which enable us to conceal it temporarily. It is also the great weakness of the book that it is in constant conflict with its best, by which I mean the most demanding, readers. In the very short dialogue that I concocted above between the doctor and the madman, it was in fact the madman who got the better of the exchange. Because, through his replies, he obtrudes upon the attention of the doctor examining him—and because he is not the person asking the questions. Does this mean that his thought at this point is stronger? Perhaps. He is free not to care any longer about his age or name.

Poetic Surrealism, which is the subject of this study, has focused its efforts up to this point on reestablishing dialogue in its absolute truth, by freeing both interlocutors from any obligations and politeness. Each of them simply pursues his soliloquy without trying to derive any special dialectical pleasure from it and without trying to impose anything whatsoever upon his neighbor. The remarks exchanged are not, as is generally the case, meant to develop some thesis, however unimportant it may be; they are as disaffected as possible. As for the reply that they elicit, it is, in principle, totally indifferent to the personal pride of the person speaking. The words, the images are only so many springboards for the mind of the listener. In *Les Champs magnétiques,* the first purely Surrealist work, this is the way in which the pages grouped together under the title *Barrières* must be conceived of—pages wherein Soupault and I show ourselves to be impartial interlocutors.

Surrealism does not allow those who devote themselves to it to forsake it whenever they like. There is every reason to believe that it acts on the mind very much as drugs do; like drugs, it creates a certain state of need and can push man to frightful revolts. It also is, if you like, an artificial paradise, and the taste one has for it derives from Baudelaire's criticism for the same reason as the others. Thus the analysis of the mysterious effects and special pleasures it can produce—in many respects Surrealism occurs as a *new vice* which does not necessarily seem to be restricted to the happy few; like hashish, it has the ability to satisfy all manner of tastes—such an analysis has to be included in the present study.

1. It is true of Surrealist images as it is of opium images that man does not evoke them; rather they "come to him spontaneously, despotically. He cannot chase them away; for the will is powerless now and no longer controls the faculties."* (Baudelaire.) It remains to be seen whether images have ever been "evoked." If one accepts, as I do, Reverdy's definition it does not seem possible to bring together, voluntarily, what he calls "two distant realities." The juxtaposition is made or not made, and that is the long and the short of it. Personally, I absolutely refuse to believe that, in Reverdy's work, images such as

In the brook, there is a song that flows

or:

Day unfolded like a white tablecloth

or:

The world goes back into a sack

reveal the slightest degree of premeditation. In my opinion, it is erroneous to claim that "the mind has grasped the relationship" of two realities in the presence of each other. First of all, it has seized nothing consciously. It is, as it were, from the fortuitous juxtaposition of the two terms that a particular light has sprung, *the light of the image,* to which we are infinitely sensitive. The value of the image depends upon the beauty of the spark obtained; it is, consequently, a function of the difference of potential between the two conductors. When the difference exists only slightly, as in a comparison,★ (Compare the image in the work of Jules Renard.) the spark is lacking. Now, it is not within man's power, so far as I can tell, to effect the juxtaposition of two realities so far apart. The principle of the association of ideas, such as we conceive of it, militates against it. Or else we would have to revert to an elliptical art, which Reverdy deplores as much as I. We are therefore obliged to admit that the two terms of the image are not deduced one from the other by the mind for the specific purpose of producing the spark, that they are the simultaneous products of the activity I call Surrealist, reason's role being limited to taking note of, and appreciating, the luminous phenomenon.

And just as the length of the spark increases to the extent that it occurs in rarefied gases, the Surrealist atmosphere created by automatic writing, which I have wanted to put within the reach of everyone, is especially conducive to the production of the most beautiful images. One can even go so far as to say that in this dizzying race the images appear like the only guideposts of the mind. By slow degrees the mind becomes convinced of the supreme reality of these images. At first limiting itself to submitting to them, it soon realizes that they flatter its reason, and increase its knowledge accordingly. The mind becomes aware of the limitless expanses wherein its desires are made manifest, where the pros and cons are constantly consumed, where its obscurity does not betray it. It goes forward, borne by these images which enrapture it, which scarcely leave it any time to blow upon the fire in its fingers. This is the most beautiful night of all, the *lightning-filled night:* day, compared to it, is night.

The countless kinds of Surrealist images would require a classification which I do not intend to make today. To group them according to their particular affinities would lead me far afield; what I basically want to mention is their common virtue. For me, their greatest virtue, I must confess, is the one that is arbitrary to the highest degree, the one that takes the longest time to translate into practical language, either because it contains an immense amount of seeming contradiction or because one of its terms is strangely concealed; or because, presenting itself as something sensational, it seems to end weakly (because it suddenly closes the angle of its compass), or because it derives from itself a ridiculous *formal* justification, or because it is of a hallucinatory kind, or because it very naturally gives to the abstract the mask of the concrete, or the opposite, or because it implies the negation of some elementary physical property, or because it provokes laughter. Here, in order, are a few examples of it:

The ruby of champagne. (LAUTRÉAMONT)

Beautiful as the law of arrested development of the breast in adults, whose propensity to growth is not in proportion to the quantity of molecules that their organism assimilates. (LAUTRÉAMONT)

A church stood dazzling as a bell. (PHILIPPE SOUPAULT)

In Rrose Sélavy's sleep there is a dwarf issued from a well who comes to eat her bread at night. (ROBERT DESNOS)

On the bridge the dew with the head of a tabby cat lulls itself to sleep. (ANDRÉ BRETON)

A little to the left, in my firmament foretold, I see—but it's doubtless but a mist of blood and murder—the gleaming glass of liberty's disturbances. (LOUIS ARAGON)

In the forest aflame

The lions were fresh. (ROBERT VITRAC)

*The color of a woman's stockings is not necessarily in the likeness of her eyes, which
led a philosopher who it is pointless to mention, to say: "Cephalopods have more
reasons to hate progress than do quadrupeds." (MAX MORISE)*

1st. Whether we like it or not, there is enough there to satisfy several demands of the mind. All these images seem to attest to the fact that the mind is ripe for something more than the benign joys it allows itself in general. This is the only way it has of turning to its own advantage the ideal quantity of events with which it is entrusted.* (Let us no forget that, according to Novalis' formula, "there are series of events which run parallel to real events. Men and circumstances generally modify the ideal train of circumstances, so that is seems imperfect; and their consequences are also equally imperfect. Thus it was with the Reformation; instead of Protestantism, we got Lutheranism.") These images show it the extent of its ordinary dissipation and the drawbacks that it offers for it. In the final analysis, it's not such a bad thing for these images to upset the mind, for to upset the mind is to put it in the wrong. The sentences I quote make ample provision for this. But the mind which relishes them draws therefrom the conviction that it is on the *right track;* on its own, the mind is incapable of finding itself guilty of cavil; it has nothing to fear, since, moreover, it attempts to embrace everything.

2nd. The mind which plunges into Surrealism relives with glowing excitement the best part of its childhood. For such a mind, it is similar to the certainty with which a person who is drowning reviews once more, in the space of less than a second, all the insurmountable moments of his life. Some may say to me that the parallel is not very encouraging. But I have no intention of encouraging those who tell me that. From childhood memories, and from a few others, there emanates a sentiment of being unintegrated, and then later of *having gone astray,* which I hold to be the most fertile that exists. It is perhaps childhood that comes closest to one's "real life"; childhood beyond which man has at his disposal, aside from his laissez-passer, only a few complimentary tickets; childhood where everything nevertheless conspires to bring about the effective, risk-free possession of oneself. Thanks to Surrealism, it seems that opportunity knocks a second time. It is as though we were still running toward our salvation, or our perdition. In the shadow we again see a precious terror. Thank God, it's still only Purgatory. With a shudder, we cross what the occultists call *dangerous territory.* In my wake I raise up monsters that are lying in wait; they are not yet too ill-disposed toward me, and I am not lost, since I fear them. Here are "the elephants with the heads of women and the flying lions" which used to make Soupault and me tremble in our boots to meet, here is the "soluble fish" which still frightens me slightly. POISSON SOLUBLE, am I not the soluble fish, I was born under the sign of Pisces, and man is soluble in his thought! The flora and fauna of Surrealism are inadmissible.

3rd. I do not believe in the establishment of a conventional Surrealist pattern any time in the near future. The characteristics common to all the texts of this kind, including those I have just cited and many others which alone could offer us a logical analysis and a careful grammatical analysis, do not preclude a certain evolution of Surrealist prose in time. Coming on the heels of a large number of essays I have written in this vein over the past five years, most of which I am indulgent enough to think are extremely disordered, the short anecdotes which comprise the balance of this volume offer me a glaring proof of what I am saying. I do not judge them to be any more worthless, because of that, in portraying for the reader the benefits which the Surrealist contribution is liable to make to his consciousness.

Surrealist methods would, moreover, demand to be heard. Everything is valid when it comes to obtaining the desired suddenness from certain associations. The pieces of paper that Picasso and Braque insert into their work have the same value as the introduction of a platitude into a literary analysis of the most rigorous sort. It is even permissible to entitle POEM what we get from the most random assemblage possible (observe, if you will, the syntax) of headlines and scraps of headlines cut out of the newspapers:

POEM

A burst of laughter

# of sapphire in the island of Ceylon

The most beautiful straws

HAVE A FADED COLOR

UNDER THE LOCKS

on an isolated farm

FROM DAY TO DAY

the pleasant

grows worse

coffee

preaches for its saint

THE DAILY ARTISAN OF YOUR BEAUTY

MADAM,

of silk stockings

is not

A leap into space

A STAG

Love above all

Everything could be worked out so well

PARIS IS A BIG VILLAGE

Watch out for

the fire that covers

THE PRAYER

of fair weather

Know that

The ultraviolet rays

have finished their task

short and sweet

THE FIRST WHITE PAPER

OF CHANCE

Red will be

The wandering singer

WHERE IS HE?

in memory

in his house

AT THE SUITORS' BALL

I do

as I dance

What people did, what they're going to do

And we could offer many many more examples. The theater, philosophy, science, criticism would all succeed in finding their bearings there. I hasten to add that future Surrealist techniques do not interest me.

Far more serious, in my opinion* (Whatever reservations I may be allowed to make concerning responsibility in general and the medico-legal considerations which determine an individual's degree of responsibility—complete responsibility, irresponsibility, limited responsibility (sic)—however difficult it may be for me to accept the principle of any kind of responsibility, I would like to know how the first punishable offenses, the Surrealist character of which will be clearly apparent, will be *judged*. Will the accused be acquitted, or will he merely be given the benefit of the doubt because of extenuating circumstances? It's a shame that the violation of the laws governing the Press is today scarcely repressed, for if it were not we would soon see a trial of this sort: the accused has published a book which is an outrage to public decency. Several of his "most respected and honorable" fellow citizens have lodged a complaint against him, and he is also charged with slander and libel. There are also all sorts of other charges against him, such as insulting and defaming the army, inciting to murder, rape, etc. The accused, moreover, wastes no time in agreeing with the accusers in "stigmatizing" most of the ideas expressed. His only defense is claiming that he does not consider himself to be the author of his book, said book being no more and no less than a Surrealist concoction which precludes any question of merit or lack of merit on the part of the person who signs it; further, that all he has done is copy a document without offering any opinion thereon, and that he is at least as foreign to the accused text as is the presiding judge himself.

What is true for the publication of a book will also hold true for a whole host of other acts as soon as Surrealist methods begin to enjoy widespread favor. When that happens, a new morality must be substituted for the prevailing morality, the source of all our trials and tribulations.)—I have intimated it often enough—are the applications of Surrealism to action. To be sure, I do not believe in the prophetic nature of the Surrealist word. "It is the oracle, the things I say."* (Rimbaud.) Yes, *as much as I like,* but what of the oracle itself?** (Still, STILL.... We must absolutely get to the bottom of this. Today, June 8, 1924, about one o'clock, the voice whispered to me: "Béthune, Béthune." What did it mean? I have never been to Béthune, and have only the vaguest notion as to where it is located on the map of France. Béthune evokes nothing for me, not even a scene from *The Three Musketeers.* I should have left for Béthune, where perhaps there was something awaiting me; that would have been to simple, really. Someone told me they had read in a book by Chesterton about a detective who, in order to find someone he is looking for in a certain city, simply scoured from roof to cellar the houses which, from the outside, seemed somehow abnormal to him, were it only in some slight detail. This system is as good as any other.

Similarly, in 1919, Soupault went into any number of impossible buildings to ask the concierge whether Philippe Soupault did in fact live there. He would not have been surprised, I suspect, by an affirmative reply. He would have gone and knocked on his door.) Men's piety does not fool me. The Surrealist voice that shook Cumae, Dodona, and Delphi is nothing more than the voice which dictates my less irascible speeches to me. My *time* must not be its time, why should this voice help me resolve the childish problem of my destiny? I pretend, unfortunately, to act in a world where, in order to take into account its suggestions, I would be obliged to resort to two kinds of interpreters, one to translate its judgements for me, the other, impossible to find, to transmit to my fellow men whatever sense I could make out of them. This world, in which I endure what I endure (don't go see), this modern world, I mean, what the devil do you want me to do with it? Perhaps the Surrealist voice will be stilled, I have given up trying to keep track of those who have disappeared. I shall no longer enter into, however briefly, the marvelous detailed description of my years and my days. I shall be like Nijinski who was taken last year to the Russian ballet and did not realize what spectacle it was he was seeing. I shall be alone, very alone within myself, indifferent to all the world's ballets. What I have done, what I have left undone, I give it to you.

And ever since I have had a great desire to show forbearance to scientific musing, however unbecoming, in the final analysis, from every point of view. Radios? Fine. Syphilis? If you like. Photography? I don't see any reason why not. The cinema? Three cheers for darkened rooms. War? Gave us a good laugh. The telephone? Hello. Youth? Charming white hair. Try to make me say thank you: "Thank you." Thank you. If the common man has a high opinion of things which properly speaking belong to the realm of the laboratory, it is because such research has resulted in the manufacture of a machine or the discovery of some serum which the man in the street views as affecting him directly. He is quite sure that they have been trying to improve his lot. I am not quite sure to what extent scholars are motivated by humanitarian aims, but it does not seem to me that this factor constitutes a very marked degree of goodness. I am, of course, referring to true scholars and not to the vulgarizers and popularizers of all sorts who take out patents. In this realm as in any other, I believe in the pure Surrealist joy of the man who, forewarned that all others before him have failed, refuses to admit defeat, sets off from whatever point he chooses, along any other path save a reasonable one, and arrives wherever he can. Such and such an image, by which he deems it opportune to indicate his progress and which may result, perhaps, in his receiving public acclaim, is to me, I must confess, a matter of complete indifference. Nor is the material with which he must perforce encumber himself; his glass tubes or my metallic feathers... As for his method, I am willing to give it as much credit as I do mine. I have seen the inventor of the cutaneous plantar reflex at work; he manipulated his subjects without respite, it was much more than an "examination" he was employing; *it was obvious that he was following no set plan.* Here and there he formulated a remark, distantly, without nonetheless setting down his needle, while his hammer was never still. He left to others the futile task of curing patients. He was wholly consumed by and devoted to that sacred fever.

Surrealism, such as I conceive of it, asserts our complete *nonconformism* clearly enough so that there can be no question of translating it, at the trial of the real world, as evidence for the defense. It could, on the contrary, only serve to justify the complete state of distraction which we hope to achieve here below. Kant's absentmindedness regarding women, Pasteur's absentmindedness about "grapes," Curie's absentmindedness with respect to vehicles, are in this regard profoundly symptomatic. This world is only very relatively in tune with thought, and incidents of this kind are only the most obvious episodes of a war in which I am proud to be participating. "Ce monde n'est que très relativement à la mesure de la pensée et les incidents de ce genre ne sont que les épisodes jusqu'ici les plus marquants d'une guerre d'indépendence à laquelle je me fais gloire de participer." Surrealism is the "invisible ray" which will one day enable us to win out over our opponents. "You are no longer trembling, carcass." This summer the roses are blue; the wood is of glass. The earth, draped in its verdant cloak, makes as little impression upon me as a ghost. It is living and ceasing to live which are imaginary solutions. Existence is elsewhere.

10

Bertrand Russell

Why I am not a Christian

As your Chairman has told you, the subject about which I am going to speak to you tonight is "Why I Am Not a Christian." Perhaps it would be as well, first of all, to try to make out what one means by the word *Christian*. It is used these days in a very loose sense by a great many people. Some people mean no more by it than a person who attempts to live a good life. In that sense I suppose there would be Christians in all sects and creeds; but I do not think that that is the proper sense of the word, if only because it would imply that all the people who are not Christians—all the Buddhists, Confucians, Mohammedans, and so on—are not trying to live a good life. I do not mean by a Christian any person who tries to live decently according to his lights. I think that you must have a certain amount of definite belief before you have a right to call yourself a Christian. The word does not have quite such a full-blooded meaning now as it had in the times of St Augustine and St. Thomas Aquinas. In those days, if a man said that he was a Christian it was known what he meant. You accepted a whole collection of creeds which were set out with great precision, and every single syllable of those creeds you believed with the whole strength of your convictions.

"Why I Am Not A Christian" by Bertrand Russell from "Why I Am Not A Christian" by Bertrand Russell (Simon & Schuster). Copyright © The Bertrand Russell Peace Foundation Ltd. Used by permission.

WHAT IS A CHRISTIAN?

Nowadays it is not quite that. We have to be a little more vague in our meaning of Christianity. I think, however, that there are two different items which are quite essential to anybody calling himself a Christian. The first is one of a dogmatic nature—namely, that you must believe in God and immortality. If you do not believe in those two things, I do not think that you can properly call yourself a Christian. Then, further than that, as the name implies, you must have some kind of belief about Christ. The Mohammedans, for instance, also believe in God and in immortality, and yet they would not call themselves Christians. I think you must have at the very lowest the belief that Christ was, if not divine, at least the best and wisest of men. If you are not going to believe that much about Christ, I do not think you have any right to call yourself a Christian. Of course, there is another sense, which you find in *Whitaker's Almanack* and in geography books where the population of the world is said to be divided into Christians, Mohammedans, Buddhists, fetish worshipers, and so on; and in that sense we are all Christians. The geography books count us all in, but that is purely geographical sense, which I suppose we can ignore. Therefore I take it that when I tell you why I am not a Christian I have to tell you two different things: first, why I do not believe in God and in immortality, and, secondly, why I do not think that Christ was the best and wisest of men, although I grant him a very high degree of moral goodness.

But for the successful efforts of unbelievers in the past, I could not take so elastic a definition of Christianity as that. As I said before, in olden days it had a much more full-blooded sense. For instance, it included the belief in hell. Belief in eternal hell-fire was an essential item of Christian belief until pretty recent times. In this country, as you know, it ceased to be an essential item because of a decision of the Privy Council, and from that decision the Archbishop of Canterbury and the Archbishop of York dissented, but in this country our religion is settled by Act of Parliament, and therefore the Privy Council was able to override their Graces and hell was no longer necessary to a Christian. Consequently I shall not insist that a Christian must believe in hell.

THE EXISTENCE OF GOD

To come to this question of the existence of God: it is a large and serious question, and if I were to attempt to deal with it in any adequate manner I should have to keep you here until Kingdom Come, so that you will have to excuse me if I deal with it in a somewhat summary fashion. You know, of course, that the Catholic Church has laid it down as a dogma that the existence of God can be proved by the unaided reason. That is a somewhat curious dogma, but it is one of their dogmas. They had to introduce it because at one time the freethinkers adopted the habit of saying that there were such and such arguments which mere reason might urge against the existence of God, but of course they knew as a matter of faith that a God did exist. The arguments and the reasons were set out at great length, and the Catholic Church felt that they must stop it. Therefore they laid it down that the existence of God can be proved by the unaided reason and they had to set up what they considered were arguments to prove it. There are, of course, a number of them, but I shall take only a few.

The First-Cause Argument

Perhaps the simplest and easiest to understand is the argument of the First Cause. (It is maintained that everything we see in this world has a cause, and as you go back in the chain of causes further and further you must come to a First Cause, and to that

First Cause you give the name of God.) That argument, I suppose, does not carry very much weight nowadays, because, in the first place, cause is not quite what it used to be. The philosophers and the men of science have got going on cause, and it has not anything like the vitality it used to have; but, apart from that, you can see that the argument that there must be a First Cause is one that cannot have any validity. I may say that when I was a young man and was debating the questions very seriously in my mind, I for a long time accepted the argument of the First Cause, until one day, at the age of eighteen, I read John Stuart Mill's Autobiography, and I there found this sentence: "My father taught me that the question 'Who made me?' cannot be answered, since it immediately suggests the further question 'Who made God?'" That very simple sentence showed me, as I still think, the fallacy in the argument of the First Cause. If everything must have a cause, then God must have a cause. If there can be anything without a cause, it may just as well be the world as God, so that there cannot be any validity in that argument. It is exactly of the same nature as the Hindu's view, that the world rested upon an elephant and the elephant rested upon a tortoise; and when they said, "How about the tortoise?" the Indian said, "Suppose we change the subject." The argument is really no better than that. There is no reason why the world could not have come into being without a cause; nor, on the other hand, is there any reason why it should not have always existed. There is no reason to suppose that the world had a beginning at all. The idea that things must have a beginning is really due to the poverty of our imagination. Therefore, perhaps, I need not waste any more time upon the argument about the First Cause.

The Natural-Law Argument

Then there is a very common argument from natural law. That was a favorite argument all through the eighteenth century, especially under the influence of Sir Isaac Newton and his cosmogony. People observed the planets going around the sun according to the law of gravitation and they thought that God had given a behest to these planets to move in that particular fashion, and that was why they did so. That was, of course, a convenient and simple explanation that saved them the trouble of looking any further for explanations of the law of gravitation. Nowadays we explain the law of gravitation in a somewhat complicated fashion that Einstein has introduced. I do not propose to give you a lecture on the law of gravitation, as interpreted by Einstein, because that again would take some time; at any rate, you no longer have the sort of natural law that you had in the Newtonian system, where, for some reason that nobody could understand, nature behaved in a uniform fashion. We now find that a great many things we thought were natural laws are really human conventions. You know that even in the remotest depths of stellar space there are still three feet to a yard. That is, no doubt, a very remarkable fact, but you would hardly call it a law of nature. And a great many things that have been regarded as laws of nature are of that kind. On the other hand, where you can get down to any knowledge of what atoms actually do, you will find they are much less subject to law than people thought, and that the laws at which you arrive are statistical averages of just the sort that would emerge from chance. There is, as we all know, a law that if you throw dice you will get double sixes only about once in thirty-six times, and we do not regard that as evidence that the fall of the dice is regulated by design; on the contrary, if the double sixes came every time we should think that there was design. The laws of nature are of that sort as regards a great many of them. They are statistical averages such as would emerge from the laws of chance; and that makes this whole business of natural law much less impressive than it formerly was. Quite apart from that, which represents the momentary state of science that may change tomorrow, the whole idea that natural laws imply a lawgiver is due to a confusion between natural and human laws. Human laws are behests commanding you to behave a certain way, in which way you may choose to behave, or you may choose not to behave; but natural laws are a description of how things do in fact behave, and being a mere description of what they in fact do, you cannot argue that there must be somebody who told them to do that, because even supposing that there were, you are then faced with the question, "Why did God issue just those natural laws and no others?" If you say that he did it simply from his own good pleasure, and without any reason, you then find that there is something which is not subject to law and so your train of natural law is interrupted. If you say, as more orthodox theologians do, that in all the laws which God issues he had a reason for giving those laws rather than others—the reason, of course, being to create the best universe, although you would never think it to look at it—if there were a reason for the laws which God gave, then God himself was subject to law, and therefore you do not get any advantage by introducing God as an intermediary. You have really a law outside and anterior to the divine edicts, and God does not serve your purpose, because he is not the ultimate lawgiver. In short, this whole argument about natural law no longer has anything like the strength that it used to have. I am traveling on in time in my review of the arguments. The arguments that are used for the existence of God change their character as time goes on. They were at first hard intellectual arguments embodying certain quite definite fallacies. As we come to modern times they become less respectable intellectually and more and more affected by a kind of moralizing vagueness.

The Argument from Design

The next step in this process brings us to the argument from design. You all know the argument from design: Everything in the world is made just so that we can manage to live in the world, and if the world was ever so little different, we could not manage to live in it. That is the argument from design. It sometimes takes a rather curious form; for instance, it is argued that rabbits have white tails in order to be easy to shoot. I do not know how rabbits would view that application. It is an easy argument to parody. You all know Voltaire's remark, that obviously the nose was designed to be such as to fit spectacles. That sort of parody has turned out to be not nearly so wide off the mark as it might have seemed in the eighteenth century, because since the time of Darwin we understand much better why living creatures are adapted to their environment. It is not that their environment was made to be suitable to them but they grew to be suitable to it, and that is the basis of adaptation. There is no evidence of design about it.

When you come to look into this argument from design, it is a most astonishing thing that people can believe that this world, with all the things that are in it, with all its defects, should be the best that omnipotence and omniscience have been able to produce in millions of years. I really cannot believe it. Do you think that, if you were granted omnipotence and omniscience and millions of years in which to perfect your world, you could produce nothing better than the Ku Klux Klan or the Fascists? Moreover, if you accept the ordinary laws of science, you have to suppose that human life and life in general on this planet will die out in due course: it is a stage in the decay of the solar system; at a certain stage of decay you get the sort of conditions of temperature and so forth which are suitable to protoplasm, and there is life for a short time in the life of the whole solar system. You see in the moon the sort of thing to which the earth is tending—something dead, cold, and lifeless.

I am told that that sort of view is depressing, and people will sometimes tell you that if they believed that they would not be able to go on living. Do not believe it; it is all nonsense. Nobody really worries much about what is going to happen millions of years hence. Even if they think they are worrying too much about that, they are really deceiving themselves. They are worried about something much more mundane, or it may merely be a bad digestion; but nobody is really seriously rendered unhappy by the thought of something that is going to happen to this world millions and millions of years hence. Therefore, although it is of course a gloomy view to suppose that life will die out—at least I suppose we may say so, although sometimes when I contemplate the things that people do with their lives I think it is almost a consolation—it is not such as to render life miserable. It merely makes you turn your attention to other things.

. . . Of course I know that the sort of intellectual arguments that I have been talking to you about are not what really moves people. What really moves people to believe in God is not any intellectual argument at all. Most people believe in God because they have been taught from early infancy to do it, and that is the main reason.

Then I think that the next most powerful reason is the wish for safety, a sort of feeling that there is a big brother who will took after you. That plays a very profound part in influencing people's desire for a belief in God.

THE CHARACTER OF CHRIST

I now want to say a few words upon a topic which I often think is not quite sufficiently dealt with by Rationalists, and that is the question whether Christ was the best and the wisest of men. It is generally taken for granted that we should all agree that that was so. I do not myself. I think that there are a good many points upon which

I agree with Christ a great deal more than the professing Christians do. I do not know that I could go with Him all the way, but I could go with Him much further than most professing Christians can. You will remember that He said, "Resist not evil: but whosoever shall smite thee on thy right cheek, turn to him the other also." That is not a new precept or a new principle. It was used by Lao-tse and Buddha some 500 or 600 years before Christ, but it is not a principle which as a matter of fact Christians accept. I have no doubt that the present Prime Minister [Stanley Baldwin], for instance, is a most sincere Christian, but I should not advise any of you to go and smite him on one cheek. I think you might find that he thought this text was intended in a figurative sense.

Then there is another point which I consider excellent. You will remember that Christ said "Judge not lest ye be judged." That principle I do not think you would find was popular in the law courts of Christian countries. I have known in my time quite a number of judges who were very earnest Christians, and none of them felt that they were acting contrary to Christian principles in what they did. Then Christ says "Give to him that asketh of thee, and from him that would borrow of thee turn not thou away." That is a very good principle. Your Chairman has reminded you that we are not here to talk politics, but I cannot help observing that the last general election was fought on the question of how desirable it was to turn away from him that would borrow of thee, so that one must assume that the Liberals and Conservatives of this country are composed of people who do not agree with the teaching of Christ, because they certainly did very emphatically turn away on that occasion.

Then there is one other maxim of Christ which I think has a great deal in it, but I do not find that it is very popular among some of our Christian friends. He says, "If thou wilt be perfect, go and sell that which thou hast, and give to the poor." That is a very excellent maxim, but, as I say, it is not much practiced. All these, I think, are good maxims, although they are a little difficult to live up to. I do not profess to live up to them myself, but then, after all, it, is not quite the same thing as for a Christian.

Defects in Christ's Teaching

Having granted the excellence of these maxims, I come to certain points in which I do not believe that one can grant either the superlative wisdom or the superlative goodness of Christ as depicted in the Gospels; and here I may say that one is not concerned with the historical question. Historically it is quite doubtful whether Christ ever existed at all, and if He did we do not know anything about Him, so that I am not concerned with the historical question, which is a very difficult one, I am concerned with Christ as He appears in the Gospels, taking the Gospel narrative as it stands, and there one does find some things that do not seem to be very wise. For one thing, He certainly thought that His second coming would occur in clouds of glory before the death of all the people who were living at that time. There are a great many texts that prove that. He says, for instance, "Ye shall not have gone over the cities of Israel till the Son of Man become." Then He says, "There are some standing here which shall not taste death till the Son of Man comes into His Kingdom"; and there are a lot of places where it is quite clear that He believed that His second coming would happen during the lifetime of many then living. That was the belief of His earlier followers, and it was the basis of a good deal of His moral teaching. When He said, "Take no thought for the morrow," and things of that sort, it was very largely because He thought that the second coming was going to be very soon, and that all ordinary mundane affairs did not count. I have, as a matter of fact, known some Christians who did believe that the second coming was imminent. I knew a parson who frightened his congregation terribly by telling them that the second coming was very imminent indeed, but they were much consoled when they found that he was planting trees in his garden. The early Christians did really believe it, and they did abstain from such things as planting trees in their gardens, because they did accept from Christ the belief that the second coming was imminent. In that respect, clearly He was not so wise as some other people have been, and He was certainly not superlatively wise.

The Moral Problem

Then you come to moral questions. There is one very serious defect to my mind in Christ's moral character, and that is that He believed in hell. I do not myself feel that any person who is really profoundly humane can believe in everlasting punishment. Christ certainly, as depicted in the Gospels did believe in everlasting punishment, and one does find repeatedly a vindictive fury against those people who would not listen to His preaching—an attitude which is not uncommon with preachers, but which does somewhat detract from superlative excellence. You do not, for instance find that attitude in Socrates. You find him quite bland and urbane toward the people who would not listen to him; and it is, to my mind, far more worthy of a sage to take that line than to take the line of indignation. You probably all remember the sort of things that

Socrates was saying when he was dying, and the sort of things that he generally did say to people who did not agree with him.

You will find that in the Gospels Christ said, "Ye serpents, ye generation of vipers, how can ye escape the damnation of hell." That was said to people who did not like His preaching. It is not really to my mind quite the best tone, and there are a great many of these things about hell. There is, of course, the familiar text about the sin against the Holy Ghost: "Whosoever speaketh against the Holy Ghost it shall not be forgiven him neither in this World nor in the world to come." That text has caused an unspeakable amount of misery in the world, for all sorts of people have imagined that they have committed the sin against the Holy Ghost, and thought that it would not be forgiven them either in this world or in the world to come. I really do not think that a person with a proper degree of kindliness in his nature would have put fears and terrors of that sort into the world.

Then Christ says, "The Son of Man shall send forth His angels, and they shall gather out of His kingdom all things that offend, and them which do iniquity, and shall cast them into a furnace of fire; there shall be wailing and gnashing of teeth"; and He goes on about the wailing and gnashing of teeth; and He goes on about the wailing and gnashing of teeth. It comes in one verse after another, and it is quite manifest to the reader that there is a certain pleasure in contemplating wailing and gnashing of teeth, or else it would not occur so often. Then you all, of course, remember about the sheep and the goats; how at the second coming He is going to divide the sheep from the goats, and He is going to say to the goats, "Depart from me, ye cursed, into everlasting fire." He continues, "And these shall go away into everlasting fire." Then He says again, "If thy hand offend thee, cut it off; it is better for thee to enter into life maimed, than having two hands to go into hell, into the fire that never shall be quenched; where the worm dieth not and the fire is not quenched." He repeats that again and again also. I must say that I think all this doctrine, that hell-fire is a punishment for sin, is a doctrine of cruelty. It is a doctrine that put cruelty into the world and gave the world generations of cruel torture; and the Christ of the Gospels, if you could take Him as His chroniclers represent Him, would certainly have to be considered partly responsible for that.

There are other things of less importance. There is the instance of the Gadarene swine, where it certainly was not very kind to the pigs to put the devils into them and make them rush down the hill to the sea. You must remember that He was omnipotent, and He could have made the devils simply go away; but He chose to send them into the pigs. Then there is the curious story of the fig tree, which always rather puzzled me. You remember what happened about the fig tree. "He was hungry; and seeing a fig tree afar off having leaves, He came if happily He might find anything thereon; and when He came to it He found nothing but leaves, for the time of figs was not yet. And Jesus answered and said unto it: 'No man eat fruit of thee hereafter for ever . . .' and Peter . . . saith unto Him: 'Master, behold the fig tree which thou cursedst is withered away.'" This is a very curious story, because it was not the right time of year for figs, and you really could not blame the tree. I cannot myself feel that either in the matter of wisdom or in the matter of virtue Christ stands quite as high as some other people known to history. I think I should put Buddha and Socrates above Him in those respects.

THE EMOTIONAL FACTOR

As I said before, I do not think that the real reason why people accept religion has anything to do with argumentation. They accept religion on emotional grounds. One is often told that it is a very wrong thing to attack religion, because religion makes men virtuous. So I am told; I have not noticed it. You know, of course, the parody of that argument in Samuel Butler's book, *Erewhon Revisited*. You will remember that in *Erewhon* there is a certain Higgs who arrives in a remote country, and after spending some time there he escapes from that country in a balloon. Twenty years later he comes back to that country and finds a new religion in which he is worshipped under the name of the "Sun Child," and it is said that he ascended into heaven. He finds that the Feast of the Ascension is about to be celebrated, and he hears Professors Hanky and Panky say to each other that they never set eyes on the man Higgs, and they hope they never will; but they are the high priests of the religion of the Sun Child. He is very indignant, and he comes up to them, and he says, "I am going to expose all this humbug and tell the people of Erewhon that it was only I, the man Higgs, and I went up in a balloon." He was told, "You must not do that, because all the morals of this country are bound round this myth, and if they once know that you did not ascend into heaven they will all become wicked"; and so he is persuaded of that and he goes quietly away.

That is the idea—that we should all be wicked if we did not hold to the Christian religion. It seems to me that the people who have held to it have been for the most part extremely wicked. You find this curious fact, that the more intense has been the religion of any period and the more profound has been the dogmatic belief, the greater has been the cruelty and the worse has been the state of affairs. In the so-called ages of faith, when men really did believe the Christ religion in all its completeness, there was the Inquisition, with its tortures; there were millions of unfortunate women burned as witches; and there was every kind of cruelty practiced upon all sorts of people in the name of religion.

You find as you look around the world that every single bit of progress in humane feeling, every improvement in the criminal law, every step toward the diminution of war, every step toward better treatment of the colored races, or every mitigation of slavery, every moral progress that there has been in the world, has been consistently opposed by the organized churches of the world. I say quite deliberately that the Christian religion, as organized in its churches, has been and still is the principal enemy of moral progress in the world.

HOW THE CHURCHES HAVE RETARDED PROGRESS

You may think that I am going too far when I say that that is still so. I do not think that I am. Take one fact. You will bear with me if I mention it. It is not a pleasant fact, but the churches compel one to mention facts that are not pleasant. Supposing that in this world that we live in today an inexperienced girl is married to a syphilitic man, in that case the Catholic Church says, "That is an indissoluble sacrament. You must endure celibacy or stay together. And if you stay together, you must not use birth control to prevent the birth of syphilitic children." Nobody whose natural sympathies have not been warped by dogma, or whose moral nature was not absolutely dead to all sense of suffering, could maintain that it is right and proper that that state of things should continue.

That is only an example. There are a great many ways in which, at the present moment, the church, by its insistence upon what it chooses to call morality, inflicts upon all sorts of people undeserved and unnecessary suffering. And of course, as we know, it is in its major part an opponent still of progress and of improvement in all the ways that diminish suffering in the world, because it has chosen to label as morality a certain narrow set of rules of conduct which have nothing to do with human happiness, and when you say that this or that ought to be done because it would make for human happiness they think that has nothing to do with the matter at all. "What has human happiness to do with morals? The object of morals is not to make people happy."

FEAR, THE FOUNDATION OF RELIGION

Religion is based, I think, primarily and mainly upon fear. It is partly the terror of the unknown and partly, as I have said, the wish to feel that you have a kind of elder brother who will stand by you in all your troubles and disputes. Fear is the basis of the whole thing—fear of the mysterious, fear of defeat, fear of death. Fear is the parent of cruelty, and therefore it is no wonder if cruelty and religion have gone hand in hand. It is because fear is at the basis of those two things. In this world we can now begin a little to understand things, and a little to master them by help of science, which has forced its way step by step against the Christian religion, against the churches, and against the opposition of all the old precepts. Science can help us to get over this craven fear in which mankind has lived for so many generations. Science can teach us, and I think our own hearts can teach us, no longer to look around for imaginary supports, no longer to invent allies in the sky, but rather to look to our own efforts here below to make this world a fit place to live in, instead of the sort of place that the churches in all these centuries have made it.

WHAT WE MUST DO

We want to stand upon our own feet and look fair and square at the world—its good facts, its bad facts, its beauties, and its ugliness; see the world as it is and be not afraid of it. Conquer the world by intelligence and not merely by being slavishly subdued by the terror that comes from it. The whole conception of God is a conception derived for the ancient Oriental despotisms. It is a conception quite unworthy of free men. When you hear people in church debasing themselves and saying that they are miserable sinners, and all the rest of it, it seems contemptible and not worthy of self-respecting human beings. We ought to stand up and look the world frankly in the face. We ought to make the best we can of the world and if it is not so good as we wish, after all it will still be better than what these others have made of it in all these ages. A good world needs knowledge, kindliness, and courage; it does not need a regretful hankering after the past or a fettering of the free intelligence by the words uttered long ago by ignorant men. It needs a fearless outlook and a free intelligence. It needs hope for the future not looking back all the time toward a past that is dead, which we trust will be far surpassed by the future that our intelligence can create.

11

Zora Neale Hurston

How It Feels to be Colored Me

I am colored but I offer nothing in the way of extenuating circumstances except the fact that I am the only Negro in the United States whose grandfather on the mother's side was not an Indian chief.

I remember the very day that I became colored. Up to my thirteenth year I lived in the little Negro town of Eatonville, Florida. It is exclusively a colored town. The only white people I knew passed through the town going to or coming from Orlando. The native whites rode dusty horses, the Northern tourists chugged down the sandy village road in automobiles. The town knew the Southerners and never stopped cane chewing when they passed. But the Northerners were something else again. They were peered at cautiously from behind curtains by the timid. The more venturesome would come out on the porch to watch them go past and got just as much pleasure out of the tourists as the tourists got out of the village.

The front porch might seem a daring place for the rest of the town, but it was a gallery seat to me. My favorite place was atop the gate-post. Proscenium box for a born first-nighter. Not only did I enjoy the show, but I didn't mind the actors knowing that I liked it. I usually spoke to them in passing. I'd wave at them and when they returned my salute, I would say something like this: "Howdy-do-well-I-thank-you-where-you-goin'?" Usually the automobile or the horse paused at this, and after a queer exchange of compliments, I would probably "go a piece of the way" with them, as we say in farthest Florida. If one of my family happened to come to the front in time to see me, of course negotiations would be rudely broken off. But even so, it is clear that I was the first "welcome-to-our-state" Floridian, and I hope the Miami Chamber of Commerce will please take notice.

During this period, white people differed from colored to me only in that they rode through town and never lived there. They liked to hear me "speak pieces" and sing and wanted to see me dance the parse-me-la, and gave me generously of their small silver for doing these things, which seemed strange to me for I wanted to do them so much that I needed bribing to stop. Only they didn't know it. The colored people gave no dimes. They deplored any joyful tendencies in me, but I was their Zora nevertheless. I belonged to them, to the nearby hotels, to the county—everybody's Zora.

But changes came in the family when I was thirteen, and I was sent to school in Jacksonville. I left Eatonville, the town of the oleanders, as Zora. When I disembarked from the river-boat at Jacksonville, she was no more. It seemed that I had suffered a sea change. I was not Zora of Orange County any more, I was now a little colored girl. I found it out in certain ways. In my heart as well as in the mirror, I became a fast brown—warranted not to rub nor run.

But I am not tragically colored. There is no great sorrow dammed up in my soul, nor lurking behind my eyes. I do not mind at all. I do not belong to the sobbing school of Negrohood who hold that nature somehow has given them a lowdown dirty deal and whose feelings are all hurt about it. Even in the helter-skelter skirmish that is my life, I have seen that the world is to the strong regardless of a little pigmentation more or less. No, I do not weep at the world—I am too busy sharpening my oyster knife.

Someone is always at my elbow reminding me that I am the granddaughter of slaves. It fails to register depression with me. Slavery is sixty years in the past. The operation was successful and the patient is doing well, thank you. The terrible struggle that made me an American out of a potential slave said "On the line!" The Reconstruction said "Get set!"; and the generation before said "Go!" I am off to a flying start and I must not halt in the stretch to look behind and weep. Slavery is the price I paid for civilization, and the choice was not with me. It is a bully adventure and worth all that I have paid through my ancestors for it. No one on earth ever had a greater chance for glory. The world to be won and nothing to be lost. It is thrilling to think—to know that for any act of mine, I shall get twice as much praise or twice as much blame. It is quite exciting to hold the center of the national stage, with the spectators not knowing whether to laugh or to weep.

The position of my white neighbor is much more difficult. No brown specter pulls up a chair beside me when I sit down to eat. No dark ghost thrusts its leg against mine in bed. The game of keeping what one has is never so exciting as the game of getting.

I do not always feel colored. Even now I often achieve the unconscious Zora of Eatonville before the Hegira*. I feel most colored when I am thrown against a sharp white background.

For instance at Barnard.† "Beside the waters of the Hudson" I feel my race. Among the thousand white persons, I am a dark rock surged upon, overswept by a creamy sea. I am surged upon and overswept, but through it all, I remain myself. When covered by the waters, I am; and the ebb but reveals me again.

Sometimes it is the other way around. A white person is set down in our midst, but the contrast is just as sharp for me. For instance, when I sit in the drafty basement that is The New World Cabaret with a white person, my color comes. We enter chatting about any little nothing that we have in common and are seated by the jazz waiters. In the abrupt way that jazz orchestras have, this one plunges into a number. It loses no time in circumlocutions, but gets right down to business. It constricts the thorax and splits the heart with its tempo and narcotic harmonies. This orchestra grows rambunctious, rears on its hind legs and attacks the tonal veil with primitive fury, rending it, clawing it until it breaks through the jungle beyond. I follow those heathen—follow them exultingly. I dance wildly inside myself; I yell within, I whoop; I shake my assegai‡ above my head, I hurl it true to the mark yeeeooww! I am in the jungle and living in the jungle way. My face is painted red

---

* Exodus or pilgrimage: Hurston refers here to the migration of millions of African Americans from the South to the North in the early 20th century. (All notes from Norton Field Guide to Writing with Readingsunless otherwise cited)

† Barnard: Barnard College in New York City, where Hurston received her BA in 1927.

‡ Assegai: a weapon for throwing or hurling, usually a light spear or javelin made of wood and pointed withiron. (Wikipedia)

and yellow and my body is painted blue. My pulse is throbbing like a war drum. I want to slaughter something—give pain, give death to what, I do not know. But the piece ends. The men of the orchestra wipe their lips and rest their fingers. I creep back slowly to the veneer we call civilization with the last tone and find the white friend sitting motionless in his seat, smoking calmly.

"Good music they have here," he remarks, drumming the table with his fingertips.

Music! The great blobs of purple and red emotion have not touched him. He has only heard what I felt. He is far away and I see him but dimly across the ocean and the continent that have fallen between us. He is so pale with his whiteness then and I am so colored.

At certain times I have no race, I am me. When I set my hat at a certain angle and saunter down Seventh Avenue, Harlem City, feeling as snooty as the lions in front of the Forty-Second Street Library, for instance. So far as my feelings are concerned, Peggy Hopkins Joyce* on the Boule Mich with her gorgeous raiment, stately carriage, knees knocking together in a most aristocratic manner, has nothing on me. The cosmic Zora emerges. I belong to no race nor time. I am the eternal feminine with its string of beads.

I have no separate feeling about being an American citizen and colored. It merely astonishes me. How can any deny themselves the pleasure of my company! It's beyond me.

But in the main, I feel like a brown bag of miscellany propped against a wall. Against a wall in company with other bags, white, red and yellow. Pour out the contents, and there is discovered a jumble of small things priceless and worthless. A first-water diamond†, an empty spool, bits of broken glass, lengths of string, a key to a door long since crumbled away, a rusty knife blade, old shoes saved for a road that never was and never will be, a nail bent under the weight of things too heavy for any nail, a dried flower or two, still a little fragrant. In your hand is the brown bag. On the ground before you is the jumble it held—so much like the jumble in the bags, could they be emptied,

---

* American actress and celebrity (1893-1957). Boule Mich: Boulevard St. Michel, a street on the left bank of Paris.
† A diamond of the highest quality (Answers.com)

that all might be dumped in a single heap and the bags refilled without altering the content of any greatly. A bit of colored glass more or less would not matter. Perhaps that is how the Great Stuffer of Bags filled them in the first place—who knows?

12

Various Authors

Modern Poetry

Modern literature cannot be understood apart from the intellectual crisis of Western culture. These times have seen the alienation of human beings from their environment and from themselves, as well as the fragmentation of the concepts of self and society, with accompanying uncertainty, anxiety, and despair. In addition, many young poets of the early twentieth century were sent into the cauldron of the First World War. The intensity of their experiences compelled them to convey to others the infernal scenes they were forced to witness.

Modern poets, in trying to cope with a hostile world and their own alienation from it, have written with relentless, analytic frankness, often tinged with mockery of humanity's tragic plight. They have discarded traditional techniques and have experimented freely, while insisting on the need for a rigorous poetic discipline. Many have used a new vocabulary that aims at both precision and allusiveness; this dual character has often made their poems difficult, requiring the reader's most careful and informed attention. The following selection of poets and poems offers a considerable range of modern subjects and styles.

Robert Lee Frost (1874-1963), the renowned American poet and educator, wrote "After Apple-Picking" (1914), an excellent example of his art. The poem appears to be a realistic account of a rural New England scene. It is written in the ordinary rhythms of speech, but its surface simplicity is deceiving. The poem skillfully suggests, through the metaphor of apple harvesting, one individual's weariness with life and his growing sense of wonder about his mortality.

The poem titled "In Flanders Fields" became the most famous and memorable English poem to come out of the First World War. It was written by John McCrae *(1872-1918), a Canadian physician who felt, a few weeks into the war, that his services were needed in the Allied war effort. Urged on by his patriotism, he sailed to Europe and was assigned as a medical officer to a Canadian artillery unit. In 1915 this unit was operating in Flanders (western Belgium), where it suffered heavy losses to a powerful German sweep toward Paris. The soldiers' sacrifices seemed to McCrae to serve an important and noble purpose: had the Germans taken Paris, the Allies could have lost the war. The poem holds to this heroic note and calls upon others to join the war effort—in order to keep faith with the dead soldiers.*

As the murderous trench warfare ground on at the western front, the tone of war poetry changed decisively. This is displayed in the work of **Siegfried Sassoon** *(1886-1967), a decorated English infantry officer. His poem "A Working Party," was written in 1916, while Sassoon was in France, fighting against the Germans. As the struggle dragged on, devouring young men like an insatiable monster, Sassoon concluded that the war had become one of aggression and conquest, prolonged by those who held power in England. Following the publication of his anti-war views, he was sent to a hospital in Scotland to recover from "shell shock." While there he wrote more poems about different aspects of the war. One of them, titled "Glory of Women," was a biting comment on the role of women on the home front.*

Wilfred Owen *(1893-1918) picked up the theme of bitterness toward the unending slaughter. As the cynical poem "Dulce et Decorum Est" (1917) so vividly describes, death and suffering were ever present—be it through bullets, poison gas, or bursting artillery shells. In june 1917, Owen (like Sassoon) was sent to a hospital in Scotland because of shell shock. While back home, he saw many young men whom war had reduced to a pitiable state^as portrayed in his poem "Disabled" (1917). The brutality of war had robbed these men of a meaningful future and of everything that makes life worthwhile and enjoyable. (Owen himself was ordered back to frontline duty in 1918 and was killed on November 4, exactly one week before the Armistice took effect.)*

Yvan Goll *(1891-1950) was born in Alsace and grew up in Lorraine, the two provinces situated between France and Germany, and claimed by both over many centuries. It is not surprising, then, that Goll grew up bi-culturally, writing with equal skill in both languages. Seeing the nations of Europe tearing savagely into each other during the First World War caused the poet pain, despair, and compassion for all those whose lives had been damaged.*

Goll expressed his anguish in a number of poems, among them eleven that bear the title "Recitative" (1916). The poem numbered "VIH" tells about the cruelty and misery of war, the staggering number of casualties, and the never-ending succession of battles. For even in the worst days of the war there were on each side enough politicians and generals who, claiming to see light at the end of the tunnel, persuaded the nation to send their sons into yet another battle—to their deaths.

The shock and depression from the war persisted even after its end in 1918. **William Butler Yeats** *(1865-1939), the Irish poet and nationalist, expresses in his poem "The Second Coming" (1921) a grim view of the future in harsh, broken rhythms and astringent, symbolic language. Turning from the sentimental, Christian hope for an age of peace, Yeats sees beyond the chaos of his times the coming of an iron age of anarchy and brutality.*

Among the literary figures in America after the war, **Louis Untermeyer** *(1885-1977) claims a prominent place. Much of his long and productive life was given to writing poetry, biographies, children's books, and the publishing of anthologies. The topics of Untermeyer's poems—generally insightful and friendly, on occasion humorous—range across the entire spectrum of human experience. The poem "The Flaming Circle" (1923) reflects a particular strand of thought among some modern philosophers, namely, that humans remain strangers to each other. Even intimate union between them is but temporary, followed by separation and aloneness.*

Wystan Hugh (W.H.) Auden *(1907-1973) proved to be one of the most prolific writers of his century. Among his many literary creations are poems, plays, texts for operas and films, as well as travel reports. Auden was the son of a well-to-do English physician who provided him with an excellent education. While in his teens, Auden began to write poetry, and soon it became clear to him that writing, and above all the writing of poems, was to be his life's work.*

Much of Auden's inspiration came from his travels—which carried him to Germany, Iceland, Spain, China, and the United States. He remained in America from 1939 to 1948 and became a citizen in 1946. The 1920s and 1930s were plagued with political problems, social and economic dislocations, and bitter ideological controversies. Auden found these a rich source of themes which he expressed in his poems, and he also participated actively in several movements for social reform.

The poem "The Unknown Citizen" was written in 1939, with its title suggested by the Tomb of the Unknown Soldier. It is a caricature of the sheeplike organization man—who, like millions of others, has become submerged in modern bureaucratic mass society. The hero of this poem is the "well-adjusted," conforming person—devoid of critical thinking or independent action. Auden is saying here that a person of this type, though well intentioned and well cared for by the state, fails as a **creative** *human being.*

ROBERT FROST

*After Apple-Picking**

My long two-pointed ladder's sticking through a tree
Toward heaven still,
And there's a barrel that I didn't fill
Beside it, and there may be two or three
Apples I didn't pick upon some bough.
But I am done with apple-picking now.
Essence of winter sleep is on the night,
The scent of apples: I am drowsing off.
I cannot rub the strangeness from my sight
I got from looking through a pane of glass
I skimmed this morning from the drinking trough
And held against the world of hoary grass.
It melted, and I let it fall and break.
But I was well
Upon my way to sleep before it fell,
And I could tell
What form my dreaming was about to take.
Magnified apples appear and disappear,
Stem end and blossom end,
And every fleck of russet showing clear.
My instep arch not only keeps the ache,
It keeps the pressure of a ladder-round.
I feel the ladder sway as the boughs bend.
And I keep hearing from the cellar bin
The rumbling sound
Of load on load of apples coming in.
For I have had too much
Of apple-picking: I am overtired
Of the great harvest I myself desired.
There were ten thousand thousand fruit to touch,
Cherish in hand, lift down, and not let fall.

---

* Modern Poetry "After Apple-Picking." Copyright 1930, 1939, © 1969 by Holt, Rinehart and Winston, Inc. Copyright © 1958 by Robert Frost. Copyright © 1967 by Lesley Frost Ballantine. Reprinted from *The Poetry of Robert Frost,* ed. Edward Connery Lathem, by permission of Henry Holt and Company, Inc.

For all
That struck the earth,
No matter if not bruised or spiked with stubble,
Went surely to the cider-apple heap
As of no worth.
One can see what will trouble
This sleep of mine, whatever sleep it is.
Were he not gone,
The woodchuck could say whether it's like his
Long sleep, as I describe its coming on,
Or just some human sleep.

JOHN MCCRAE

In Flanders Fields*

In Flanders fields the poppies blow
Between the crosses, row on row,
    That mark our place; and in the sky
    The larks, still bravely singing, fly
Scarce heard amid the guns below.

We are the Dead. Short days ago
We lived, felt dawn, saw sunset glow,
    Loved and were loved, and now we lie
    In Flanders fields.

---

* MODERN POETRY John McCrae, "In Flanders Fields," from *The Penguin Book of First World War Poetry,* ed. Jon Silkin. New York: Viking Penguin, Inc., 1981. Copyright © Jon Silkin, 1979, 1981. Page 85.

Take up our quarrel with the foe:
To you from failing hands we throw
   The torch; be yours to hold it high.
If ye break faith with us who die
We shall not sleep, though poppies grow
   In Flanders fields.

SIEGFRIED SASSOON

A Working Party*

Three hours ago he blundered up the trench,
Sliding and poising, groping with his boots;
Sometimes he tripped and lurched against the walls
With hands that pawed the sodden bags of chalk.
He couldn't see the man who walked in front;
Only he heard the drum and rattle of feet
Stepping along barred trench boards, often splashing
Wretchedly where the sludge was ankle-deep.

Voices would grunt 'Keep to your right—make way!'
When squeezing past some men from the front-line:
White faces peered, puffing a point of red;
Candles and braziers glinted through the chinks
And curtain-flaps of dug-outs; then the gloom
Swallowed his sense of sight; he stooped and swore
Because a sagging wire had caught his neck.

A flare went up; the shining whiteness spread
And flickered upward, showing nimble rats
And mounds of glimmering sand-bags, bleached with rain;
Then the slow silver moment died in dark.
The wind came posting by with chilly gusts
And buffeting at corners, piping thin.
And dreary through the crannies; rifle-shots
Would split and crack and sing along the night,

* Modern Poetry "A Working Party" from *The Collected Poems of Siegfried Sassoon* by Siegfried Sassoon. Copyright 1918, 1920 by E. P. Dutton & Co.; 1936, 1946, 1947, 1948 by Siegfried Sassoon. Reprinted by permission of Viking Penguin, Inc.

And shells came calmly through the drizzling air
To burst with hollow bang below the hill.

Three hours ago he stumbled up the trench;
Now he will never walk that road again:
He must be carried back, a jolting lump
Beyond all need of tenderness and care.
He was a young man with a meagre wife
And two small children in a Midland town;
He showed their photographs to all his mates,
And they considered him a decent chap
Who did his work and hadn't much to say,
And always laughed at other people's jokes
Because he hadn't any of his own.

That night when he was busy at his job
Of piling bags along the parapet,*
He thought how slow time went, stamping his feet
And blowing on his fingers, pinched with cold.
He thought of getting back by half-past twelve,
And tot† of rum to send him warm to sleep
In draughty dug-out frowsty‡ with the fumes
Of coke,§ and full of snoring weary men.

He pushed another bag along the top,
Craning his body outward; then a flare
Gave one white glimpse of No Man's Land and wire;
And as he dropped his head the instant split
His startled life with lead, and all went out.

---

*Earthen embankment shielding the top of the trench.
†Small drink.
‡ Stuffy, musty.
§ A solid fuel made from coal.

*Glory of Women**
You love us when we're heroes, home on leave,
Or wounded in a mentionable place.
You worship decorations; you believe
That chivalry redeems the war's disgrace.
You make us shells. You listen with delight,
By tales of dirt and danger fondly thrilled.
You crown our distant ardors while we fight,
And mourn our laurelled memories when we're killed.

You can't believe that British troops 'retire'
When hell's last horror breaks them, and they run,
Trampling the terrible corpses—blind with blood.
O German mother dreaming by the fire,
While you are knitting socks to send your son
His face is trodden deeper in the mud.

WILFRED OWEN

Duke et Decorum Est†
Bent double, like old beggars under sacks,
Knock-kneed, coughing like hags, we cursed through sludge,
Till on the haunting flares we turned our backs
And towards our distant rest began to trudge.
Men marched asleep. Many had lost their boots
But limped on, blood-shod. All went lame; all blind;
Drunk with fatigue; deaf even to the hoots
Of gas shells dropping softly behind.

Gas! Gas! Quick, boys!—An ecstasy of fumbling,
Fitting the clumsy helmets just in time;
But someone still was yelling out and stumbling,
And flound'ring like a man in fire or lime . . .

* Modern Poetry "Glory of Women," from *The Collected Poems of Siegfried Sassoon* by Siegfried Sassoon. Copyright 1918, 1920 by E. P. Dutton & Co.; 1936, 1946, 1947, 1948 by Siegfried Sassoon. Reprinted by permission of Viking Penguin, Inc.
† Modern Poetry Wilfred Owen, "Dulce et Decorum Est," from *The Penguin Book of First World War Poetry,* ed. Jon Silkin. New York: Viking Penguin, Inc., 1981. Copyright ©JonSilkin, 1979, 1981. Pp. 182-83.

Dim, through the misty panes* and thick green light,
As under a green sea, I saw him drowning.

In all my dreams, before my helpless sight,
He plunges at me, guttering, choking, drowning.

If in some smothering dreams you too could pace
Behind the wagon that we flung him in,
And watch the white eyes writhing in his face,
His hanging face, like a devil's sick of sin;
If you could hear, at every jolt, the blood
Come gargling from the froth-corrupted lungs,

Obscene as cancer, bitter as the cud
Of vile, incurable sores on innocent tongues,—
My friend, you would not tell with such high zest
To children ardent for some desperate glory,
The old Lie: Dulce et decorum est
Pro patria mori.†

Disabled‡

He sat in a wheeled chair, waiting for dark,
And shivered in his ghastly suit of grey,
Legless, sewn short at elbow. Through the park
Voices of boys rang saddening like a hymn,
Voices of play and pleasure after day,
Till gathering sleep had mothered them from him.

★   ★   ★

---

* Goggles fitted in the gas mask.
† "Dulce. . . mori." Latin, by the Roman poet Horace (65-8 B.c.): "It is sweet and fitting to die for one's country."
‡ Modern Poetry Wilfred Owen, "Disabled," from *The Penguin Book of First World War Poetry,* ed. Jon Silkin. New York: Viking Penguin, Inc., 1981. Copyright ©Jon Silkin, 1979, 1981. Pp. 184-85.

About this time Town used to swing so gay
When glow-lamps budded in the light blue trees,
And girls glanced lovelier as the air grew dim,
—In the old times, before he threw away his knees.
Now he will never feel again how slim
Girls' waists are, or how warm their subtle hands.
All of them touch him like some queer disease.

★   ★   ★

There was an artist silly for his face,
For it was younger than his youth, last year.
Now, he is old; his back will never brace;
He's lost his color very far from here,
Poured it down shell-holes till the veins ran dry,
And half his lifetime lapsed in the hot race
And leap of purple spurted from his thigh.

★   ★   ★

One time he liked a bloodsmear down his leg,
After the matches, carried shoulder-high.
It was after football, when he'd drunk a peg,
He thought he'd better join.—He wonders why.
Someone had said he'd look a god in kilts,
That's why; and maybe, too, to please his Meg,
Aye, that was it, to please the giddy jilts
He asked to join. He didn't have to beg;
Smiling they wrote his lie: aged nineteen years.
Germans he scarcely thought of; all their guilt,
And Austria's,* did not move him. And no fears
Of Fear came yet. He thought of jewelled hilts
For daggers in plaid socks; of smart salutes;
And care of arms; and leave; and pay arrears;
Esprit de corps;† and hints for young recruits.
And soon, he was drafted out with drums and cheers.

★   ★   ★

Some cheered him home, but not as crowds cheer Goal.
Only a solemn man who brought him fruits

---

* Austria and Germany were allies in the First World War.
† French, the spirit of comradeship and related ideals shared by a group.

Thanked him; and then inquired about his soul.

★ ★ ★

Now, he will spend a few sick years in institutes,
And do what things the rules consider wise,
And take whatever pity they may dole.
Tonight he noticed how the women's eyes
Passed from him to the strong men that were whole.
How cold and late it is! Why don't they come
And put him into bed? Why don't they come?

YVAN GOLL

Recitative (VIII)*
Like a grey wall around Europe
The long battle ran.
The never-ending battle, the bogged-down battle, the softening-
up battle,
The battle that was never the final battle.
Oh, the monotony of trench-warfare! Oh, trench-grave! Oh, sleep
of starvation!
The bridges built of corpses!
The roads surfaced with corpses!
The walls cemented with corpses!
For months on end the horizon stared mysteriously and glassily
like a dead man's eye.
For years on end the distance rang like the same old passing-bell.
The days were as alike as a pair of graves.
Oh, you heroes!
Crawling out on wet nights, mewling in the bitter cold, you from
your all-electric cities!
The sentry swapped ten nights' sleep for one cigarette; whole
regiments gambled away eternity for ten yards of wasteland.
Full-blooded curses spat into the starlit mire. Damp cellars littered
with tinny booty captured from the enemy.
Oh, you Greek dancers, dwarfed in lousy caverns! Popping up like
Indians in fancy-dress when the drums sounded the attack:

* Modern Poetry Yvan Goll, "Recitative (VIII)," trans, from the German and reprinted by permission of Patrick Bridgwater. From *The Penguin Book of First World War Poetry*, ed, Jon Silkin. Copyright ©Jon Silkin, 1979, 1981. (New York: Viking Penguin, Inc., 1981) Page 242.

Before sticking your bayonet into his groin, did not one of you see
the Christ-like look of his opponent, did not one of you notice
that the man over there had a kingly heart full of love?
Did not one of you still believe in his own and mankind's
conscience?
You brothers, fellow-men! Oh, you heroes!

WILLIAM BUTLER YEATS

The Second Coming*†

Turning and turning in the widening gyre‡
The falcon cannot hear the falconer;§
Things fall apart; the center cannot hold;
Mere anarchy is loosed upon the world,
The blood-dimmed tide is loosed, and everywhere
The ceremony of innocence is drowned;
The best lack all conviction, while the worst
Are full of passionate intensity.
Surely some revelation is at hand;
Surely the Second Coming is at hand.
The Second Coming! Hardly are those words out
When a vast image out of Spiritus Mundi¶
Troubles my sight: somewhere in sands of the desert
A shape with lion body and the head of a man,
A gaze blank and pitiless as the sun,
Is moving its slow thighs, while all about it
Reel shadows of the indignant desert birds.
The darkness drops again; but now I know
That twenty centuries of stony sleep
Were vexed to nightmare by a rocking cradle,
And what rough beast, its hour come round at last,
Slouches towards Bethlehem to be born?

---

* Modern Poetry William Butler Yeats, "The Second Coming." Reprinted with permission of Macmillan Publishing Company from *Collected Poems* by William Butler Yeats. Copyright 1924 by Macmillan Publishing Company, renewed 1952 by Bertha Geòrgie Yeats. Pp. 346-47.
† The biblical prophecy of the Second Coming of Jesus is used as the poem's underlying theme.
‡ Circular, or spiral, motion.
§ Christ.
¶ Latin: World Spirit.

LOUIS UNTERMEYER

The Flaming Circle*

Though for fifteen years you have chaffed† me across the table,
Slept in my arms and fingered my plunging heart,
I scarcely know you; we have not known each other.
For all the fierce and casual contacts, something keeps us apart.

Are you struggling, perhaps, in a world that I see only dimly,
Except as it sweeps toward the star on which I stand alone?
Are we swung like two planets, compelled in our separate orbits,
Yet held in a flaming circle far greater than our own?

Last night we were single, a radiant core of completion,
Surrounded by flames that embraced us but left no burns,
Today we are only ourselves; we have plans and pretensions;
We move in dividing streets with our small and different
concerns.

Merging and rending, we wait for the miracle. Meanwhile
The fire runs deeper, consuming these selves in its growth.
Can this be the mystical marriage—this clash and communion;
This pain of possession that frees and encircles us both?

W. H. AUDEN

The Unknown Citizen‡

To JS/07/M/378
This Marble Monument is Erected by the State

He was found by the Bureau of Statistics to be
One against whom there was no official complaint,
And all the reports on his conduct agree

---

* Modern Poetry "The Flaming Circle" from *Roast Leviathan* by Louis Untermeyer. (New York: Harcourt, Brace and Co., 1923). Copyright 1923 by Harcourt Brace Jovano-vich, Inc. ; renewed 1951 by Louis Untermeyer. Reprinted by permission of the publisher. Pp. 25-26.
† Good-natured teasing.
‡ Modern Poetry "The Unknown Citizen." Copyright 1940 and renewed 1968 by W. H. Auden. Reprinted from *W. H. Auden: Collected Poems,* ed. Edward Mendelson, by permission of Random House, Inc. Pp. 85—86.

That, in the modern sense of an old-fashioned word, he was a
  saint,
For in everything he did he served the Greater Community.
Except for the War till the day he retired
He worked in a factory and never got fired,
But satisfied his employers, Fudge Motors Inc.
Yet he wasn't a scab or odd in his views,
For his Union reports that he paid his dues,
(Our report on his Union shows it was sound)
And our Social Psychology workers found
That he was popular with his mates and liked a drink.
The Press are convinced that he bought a paper every day
And that his reactions to advertisements were normal in every
  way.
Policies taken out in his name prove that he was fully insured,
And his Health-card shows he was once in hospital but left it
  cured.
Both Producers Research and High-Grade Living declare
He was fully sensible to the advantages of the Installment Plan
And had everything necessary to the Modern Man,
A gramophone, a radio, a car and a frigidaire.
Our researchers into Public Opinion are content
That he held the proper opinions for the time of year;
When there was peace, he was for peace; when there
                              was war, he went.
He was married and added five children to the population,
Which our Eugenist* says was the right number for a parent of
                              his generation,
And our teachers report that he never interfered with their
  education.
Was he free? Was he happy? The question is absurd:
Had anything been wrong, we should certainly have heard.

---

* An official charged with supervising the improvement of the genetic qualities of the
population.

13

Adolf Hitler

My Struggle

THE *First World War and the Bolshevik Revolution were severe blows to the European liberal order. The destruction of the traditional social system and its values and the spiritual uprooting of the European masses gave rise to a widespread popular reaction against liberalism, democracy, and the complex urban-industrial revolution that had nurtured them. Adolf Hitler (1889-1945) became the demonic prophet and leader of this counterrevolution.*

As a young man, Hitler led an aimless existence in prewar Austria and Germany. After the war, in which he served with great personal satisfaction, he devoted his life to political affairs, joining the National Socialist (**Nazi**) *German Workers' Party and soon becoming its leader* (**Führer**). *In 1923 he led an unsuccessful revolt against the government, for which he served a short term in prison; but he went on to transform the Nazi party into the mass movement that would, within a decade, dominate Germany. In doing so, he played on the frustrations of a people in defeat and economic depression and, for the most part, in distress over the dislocations brought on by industrialization and urbanization. The party he headed won allegiance through mass propaganda and terror, and in 1933 he became dictator of the nation. As head of state he instituted a nationalist, collectivist, and militarist regime based on romantic notions of people* (**Volk**) *and race, and led the Germans into a series of annexations and invasions that developed into the Second World War.*

Hitler had expounded his program in an exciting but confused book called **Mein Kampf** *(My Struggle), which was written during his prison term and published*

MY STRUGGLE Adolf Hitler, *Mein Kampf,* trans. Ralph Manheim (Boston: Houghton Mifflin, 1943), 51, 64-65, 107, 118-19, 177-81, 214-15, 231, 286, 288, 290, 294, 305-306, 314-16, 318-20, 324-27, 382-85, 391, 393-94, 402-405, 623, 642-43, 645-46, 652-54, 661, 682.

sometime between 1925 and 1927. Supposedly the story of his early life and the development of his ideas and the Nazi movement, the book is a mixture of half truths, big lies, scurrilous attacks, and idealistic emotional appeals intended to arouse in the reader resentment and hatred toward others. He denounces Marxism, Jews, bourgeois liberals, and democracy as the sources of Germany's ills; and he calls for a "regenerated" German nation, attached to its sacred soil, purified in its racial make-up, and devotedly following its leaders to world supremacy. The "bible" of Nazi Germany, the book remains a classic exhibition of violent hatred and irrationality.

The following selection from **Mein Kampf**—*in which sections have been rearranged for the sake of clarity—illustrates Hitler's views on what he believed to be a Marxist-Jewish conspiracy against the German people; the natural inequality of races and the superiority of the Aryan race; the* **Volk** *as the natural human unit and the primacy of the German* **Volk**; *the nature and purposes of propaganda in the creation of a successful mass movement dedicated to the achievement of Nazi objectives; and the need for Germany to conquer more soil for its people. Though largely discredited at present, some of Hitler's ideas still have appeal among those disenchanted with the course of Western civilization and those who feel uncomfortable in a pluralistic society.*

MARXISM

I began to make myself familiar with the founders of [Marxism] in order to study the foundations of the movement. If I reached my goal more quickly than at first I had perhaps ventured to believe, it was thanks to my newly acquired, though at that time not very profound, knowledge of the Jewish question. This alone enabled me to draw a practical comparison between the reality and the theoretical flim-flam of the founding fathers of Social Democracy, since it taught me to understand the language of the Jewish people, who speak in order to conceal or at least to veil their thoughts; their real aim is not therefore to be found in the lines themselves, but slumbers well concealed between them.

For me this was the time of the greatest spiritual upheaval I have ever had to go through.

I had ceased to be a weak-kneed cosmopolitan and become an anti-Semite.* . . .

The Jewish doctrine of Marxism rejects the aristocratic principle of Nature and replaces the eternal privilege of power and strength by the mass of numbers and their dead weight. Thus it denies the value of personality in man, contests the significance of nationality and race, and thereby withdraws from humanity the premise of its existence and its culture. As a foundation of the universe, this doctrine would bring about the end of any order intellectually conceivable to man. And as, in this greatest of all recognizable organisms, the result of an application of such a law could only be chaos, on earth it could only be destruction for the inhabitants of this planet.

If, with the help of his Marxist creed, the Jew is victorious over the other peoples of the world, his crown will be the funeral wreath of humanity and this planet will, as it did thousands of years ago, move through the ether devoid of men.

Eternal Nature inexorably avenges the infringement of her commands.

Hence today I believe that I am acting in accordance with the will of the Almighty Creator: *by defending myself against the Jew, I am fighting for the work of the Lord.* . . .

Only a knowledge of the Jews provides the key with which to comprehend the inner, and consequently real, aims of Social Democracy.

The erroneous conceptions of the aim and meaning of this party fall from our eyes like veils, once we come to know this people, and from the fog and mist of social phrases rises the leering grimace of Marxism. . . .

Marxist doctrine is a brief spiritual extract of the philosophy of life that is generally current today. And for this reason alone any struggle of our so-called bourgeois world against it is impossible, absurd in fact, since this bourgeois world is also essentially infected by these poisons, and worships a view of life which in general is distinguished from the Marxists only by degrees and personalities. The bourgeois world is Marxist, but believes in the possibility of the rule of certain groups of

---

* One who hates Jews and Jewish things.

men (bourgeoisie), while Marxism itself systematically plans to hand the world over to the Jews. . . .

... A Germany saved from these mortal enemies of her existence and her future would possess forces which the whole world could no longer have stifled. *On the day when Marxism is smashed in Germany, her fetters will in truth be broken forever.* For never in our history have we been defeated by the strength of our foes, but always by our own vices and by the enemies in our own camp. . . .

JEWS

The Jew of all times has lived in the states of other peoples, and there formed his own state, which, to be sure, habitually sailed under the disguise of 'religious community' as long as outward circumstances made a complete revelation of his nature seem inadvisable. But as soon as he felt strong enough to do without the protective cloak, he always dropped the veil and suddenly became what so many of the others previously did not want to believe and see: the Jew.

The Jew's life as a parasite in the body of other nations and states explains a characteristic which once caused Schopenhauer*. . . to call him the 'great master in lying.' Existence impels the Jew to lie, and to lie perpetually, just as it compels the inhabitants of the northern countries to wear warm clothing.

His life within other peoples can only endure for any length of time if he succeeds in arousing the opinion that he is not a people but a 'religious community,' though of a special sort.

And this is the first great lie. . . .

The Jew has always been a people with definite racial characteristics and never a religion; only in order to get ahead he early sought for a means which could distract unpleasant attention from his person. And what would have been more expedient and at the same time more innocent than the 'embezzled' concept of a religious community? For here, too, everything is borrowed or rather stolen. Due to his own original special nature, the Jew cannot possess a religious institution,

---

* Arthur Schopenhauer (1788-1860), a German philosopher and chief expounder of pessimism.

if for no other reason because he lacks idealism in any form, and hence belief in a hereafter is absolutely foreign to him. And a religion in the Aryan* sense cannot be imagined which lacks the conviction of survival after death in some form. . . .

The Jew also becomes liberal and begins to rave about the necessary progress of mankind.

Slowly he makes himself the spokesman of a new era.

Also, of course, he destroys more and more thoroughly the foundations of any economy that will really benefit the people. By way of stock shares he pushes his way into the circuit of national production which he turns into a purchasable or rather tradable object, thus robbing the enterprises of the foundations of a personal ownership. Between employer and employee there arises that inner estrangement which later leads to political class division.

Finally, the Jewish influence on economic affairs grows with terrifying speed through the stock exchange. He becomes the owner, or at least the controller, of the national labor force.

To strengthen his political position he tries to tear down the racial and civil barriers which for a time continue to restrain him at every step. To this end he fights with all the tenacity innate in him for religious tolerance. . . .

He always represents himself personally as having an infinite thirst for knowledge, praises all progress, mostly, to be sure, the progress that leads to the ruin of others; for he judges all knowledge and all development only according to its possibilities for advancing his nation, and where this is lacking, he is the inexorable mortal enemy of all light, a hater of all true culture. He uses all the knowledge he acquires in the schools of other peoples, exclusively for the benefit of his race. . . .

His ultimate goal ... is the victory of 'democracy,' or, as he understands it: the rule of parliamentarianism. It is most compatible with his requirements; for it excludes the personality—and puts in its

---

* Indo-European, as differentiated from Jewish. (The Indo-European peoples, as a large *language* group, were believed to have originated in north-central Europe and to have dispersed westward, southward, and eastward beginning around 3000 B.C. Some race theorists, followed by Hitler, insisted that the Indo-Europeans constituted a distinctive and superior *racial* group, which they called "Aryans.")

place the majority characterized by stupidity, incompetence, and last but not least, cowardice. . . .

. . . While on the one hand he organizes capitalist methods of human exploitation to their ultimate consequence, [the Jew] approaches the very victims of his spirit and his activity and in a short time becomes the leader of their struggle against himself. 'Against himself' is only figuratively speaking; for the great master of lies understands as always how to make himself appear to be the pure one and to heap the blame on others. Since he has the gall to lead the masses, it never even enters their heads that this might be the most infamous betrayal of all times.

And yet it was.

Scarcely has the [proletariat] grown out of the general economic shift than the Jew, clearly and distinctly, realizes that it can open the way for his own further advancement. First, he used the bourgeoisie as a battering-ram against the feudal world, then the worker against the bourgeois world, if formerly he knew how to swindle his way to civil rights in the shadow of the bourgeoisie, now he hopes to find the road to his own domination in the worker's struggle for existence.

From now on the worker has no other task but to fight for the future of the Jewish people. Unconsciously he is harnessed to the service of the power which he thinks he is combating. He is seemingly allowed to attack capital, and this is the easiest way of making him fight for it. In this the Jew keeps up an outcry against international capital and in truth he means the national economy which must be demolished in order that the international stock exchange can triumph over its dead body. . . .

Thus there arises a pure movement entirely of manual workers under Jewish leadership, apparently aiming to improve the situation of the worker, but in truth planning the enslavement and with it the destruction of all non-Jewish peoples.

The general pacifistic paralysis of the national instinct of self-preservation ... in the circles of the so-called intelligentsia* is transmitted to the broad masses and above all to the bourgeoisie by the activity

---

* The educated class, the intellectuals.

of the big papers which today are always Jewish. Added to these two weapons of disintegration comes a third and by far the most terrible, the organization of brute force. As a shock and storm troop, Marxism is intended to finish off what the preparatory softening up with the first two weapons has made ripe for collapse. . . .

Here [the Jew] stops at nothing, and in his vileness he becomes so gigantic that no one need be surprised if among our people the personification of the devil as the symbol of all evil assumes the living shape of the Jew.

The ignorance of the broad masses about the inner nature of the Jew, the lack of instinct and narrow-mindedness of our upper classes, make the people an easy victim for this Jewish campaign of lies. . . .

With satanic joy in his face, the black-haired Jewish youth lurks in wait for the unsuspecting girl whom he defiles with his blood, thus stealing her from her people. With every means he tries to destroy the racial foundations of the people he has set out to subjugate. Just as he himself systematically ruins women and girls, he does not shrink back from pulling down the blood barriers for others, even on a large scale. It was and it is Jews who bring the Negroes into the Rhineland,* always with the same secret thought and clear aim of ruining the hated white race by the necessarily resulting bastardization, throwing it down from its cultural and political height, and himself rising to be its master.

For a racially pure people which is conscious of its blood can never be enslaved by the Jew. In this world he will forever be master over bastards and bastards alone.

And so he tries systematically to lower the racial level by a continuous poisoning of individuals.

And in politics he begins to replace the idea of democracy by the dictatorship of the proletariat.

In the organized mass of Marxism he has found the weapon which lets him dispense with democracy and in its stead allows him to subjugate and govern the peoples with a dictatorial and brutal fist.

---

* A reference to the French occupation of the Rhineland after the First World War; some of the French troops were blacks from French colonial Africa.

He works systematically for revolutionization in a twofold sense: economic and political.

Around peoples who offer too violent a resistance to attack from within he weaves a net of enemies, thanks to his international influence, incites them to war, and finally, if necessary, plants the flag of revolution on the very battlefields.

In economics he undermines the states until the social enterprises which have become unprofitable are taken from the state and subjected to his financial control.

In the political field he refuses the state the means for its self-preservation, destroys the foundations of all national self-maintenance and defense, destroys faith in the leadership, scoffs at its history and past, and drags everything that is truly great into the gutter.

Culturally he contaminates art, literature, the theater, makes a mockery of natural feeling, overthrows all concepts of beauty and sublimity, of the noble and the good, and instead drags men down into the sphere of his own base nature.

Religion is ridiculed, ethics and morality represented as outmoded, until the last props of a nation in its struggle for existence in this world have fallen.

Now begins the great last revolution. In gaining political power the Jew casts off the few cloaks that he still wears. The democratic people's Jew becomes the blood-Jew and tyrant over peoples. In a few years he tries to exterminate the national intelligentsia and by robbing the peoples of their natural intellectual leadership makes them ripe for the slave's lot of permanent subjugation.

The most frightful example of this kind is offered by Russia, where he killed or starved about thirty million people with positively fanatical savagery, in part amid inhuman tortures, in order to give a gang of Jewish journalists and stock exchange bandits domination over a great people.

The end is not only the end of freedom of the peoples oppressed by the Jew, but also the end of this parasite upon the nations. After the death of his victim, the vampire sooner or later dies too. . . .

The Jewish train of thought in all this is clear. The Bolshevization of Germany*—that is, the extermination of the national folkish . . . intelligentsia to make possible the sweating of the German working class under the yoke of Jewish world finance—is conceived only as a preliminary to the further extension of this Jewish tendency of world conquest. As often in history, Germany is the great pivot in the mighty struggle. If our people and our state become the victim of these bloodthirsty and avaricious Jewish tyrants of nations, the whole earth will sink into the snares of this octopus; if Germany frees herself from this embrace, this greatest of dangers to nations may be regarded as broken for the whole world. . . .

. . . The striving of the Jewish people for world domination .. . is just as natural as the urge of the Anglo-Saxon to seize domination of the earth. And just as the Anglo-Saxon pursues this course in his own way and carries on the fight with his own weapons, likewise the Jew. He goes his way, the way of sneaking in among the nations and boring from within, and he fights with his weapons, with lies and slander, poison and corruption, intensifying the struggle to the point of bloodily exterminating his hated foes. *In Russian Bolshevism† we must see the attempt undertaken by the Jews in the twentieth century to achieve world domination.* . . .

RACE AND THE FOLKISH PHILOSOPHY

For me and all true National Socialists there is but one doctrine: people and fatherland.

What we must fight for is to safeguard the existence and reproduction of our race and our people, the sustenance of our children and the purity of our blood, the freedom and independence of the fatherland, so that our people may mature for the fulfillment of the mission allotted it by the creator of the universe.

Every thought and every idea, every doctrine and all knowledge, must serve this purpose. And everything must be examined from this point of view and used or rejected according to its utility. Then no theory will stiffen into a dead doctrine, since it is life alone that all things must serve. . . .

---

* The turning of Germany into a Communist state on the Russian Bolshevik model.
† Soviet communism.

No more than Nature desires the mating of weaker with stronger individuals, even less does she desire the blending of a higher with a lower race, since, if she did, her whole work of higher breeding, over perhaps hundreds of thousands of years, might be ruined with one blow.

Historical experience offers countless proofs of this. It shows with terrifying clarity that in every mingling of Aryan blood with that of lower peoples the result was the end of the cultured people. North America, whose population consists in by far the largest part of Germanic elements who mixed but little with the lower colored peoples, shows a different humanity and culture from Central and South America, where the predominantly Latin immigrants often mixed with the aborigines on a large scale. By this one example, we can clearly and distinctly recognize the effect of racial mixture. The Germanic inhabitant of the American continent, who has remained racially pure and unmixed, rose to be master of the continent; he will remain the master as long as he does not fall a victim to defilement of the blood.

The result of all racial crossing is therefore in brief always the following:

(a) Lowering of the level of the higher race;
(b) Physical and intellectual regression and hence the beginning of a slowly but surely progressing sickness.

To bring about such a development is, then, nothing else but to sin against the will of the eternal creator. . . .

Everything we admire on this earth today—science and art, technology and inventions—is only the creative product of a few peoples and originally perhaps of *one* race. On them depends the existence of this whole culture. If they perish, the beauty of this earth will sink into the grave with them. . . .

It is idle to argue which race or races were the original representative of human culture and hence the real founders of all that we sum up under the word 'humanity.' It is simpler to raise this question with regard to the present, and here an easy, clear answer results. All the human culture, all the results of art, science, and technology that we see before us today, are almost exclusively the creative product of the Aryan. This very fact admits of the not unfounded inference that he alone was the founder of all higher humanity, therefore representing the prototype of all that we understand by the word 'man.' He is the Prometheus* of mankind from whose bright forehead the divine spark of genius has sprung at all times, forever kindling anew that fire of knowledge which illumined the night of silent mysteries and thus caused man to climb the path to mastery over the other beings of this earth. Exclude him—and perhaps after a few thousand years darkness will again descend on the earth, human culture will pass, and the world turn to a desert.

If we were to divide mankind into three groups, the founders of culture, the bearers of culture, the destroyers of culture, only the Aryan could be considered as the representative of the first group. From him originate the foundations and walls of all human creation, and only the outward form and color are determined by the changing traits of character of the various peoples. He provides the mightiest building stones and plans for all human progress and only the execution corresponds to the nature of the varying men and races. . . .

. . . Just as in the life of the outstanding individual, genius or extraordinary ability strives for practical realization only when spurred on by special occasions, likewise in the life of nations the creative forces and capacities which are present can often be exploited only when definite preconditions invite.

We see this most distinctly in connection with the race which has been and is the bearer of human cultural development—the Aryans. As soon as Fate leads them toward special conditions, their latent abilities begin to develop in a more and more rapid sequence and to mold themselves into tangible forms. The cultures which they found in such cases are nearly always decisively determined by the existing soil, the given climate, and—the subjected people. This last item, to be sure, is almost the most decisive. The more primitive the technical foundations for a cultural activity, the more necessary is the presence of human helpers who, organizationally assembled and employed, must replace the force of the machine. Without this possibility of using lower human beings, the Aryan would never have been able to

---

* In Greek mythology, an ancient god who stole fire from heaven and gave it to humankind.

take his first steps toward his future culture; just as without the help of various suitable beasts which he knew how to tame, he would not have arrived at a technology which is now gradually permitting him to do without these beasts. . . .

The folkish* philosophy finds the importance of mankind in its basic racial elements. In the state it sees on principle only a means to an end and construes its end as the preservation of the racial existence of man.

Thus, it by no means believes in an equality of the races, but along with their difference it recognizes their higher or lesser value and feels itself obligated, through this knowledge, to promote the victory of the better and stronger, and demand the subordination of the inferior and weaker in accordance with the eternal will that dominates this universe. Thus, in principle, it serves the basic aristocratic idea of Nature and believes in the validity of this law down to the last individual. It sees not only the different value of the races, but also the different value of individuals. From the mass it extracts the importance of the individual personality, and thus, in contrast to disorganizing Marxism, it has an organizing effect. It believes in the necessity of an idealization of humanity, in which alone it sees the premise for the existence of humanity. But it cannot grant the right to existence even to an ethical idea if this idea represents a danger for the racial life of the bearers of a higher ethics; for in a bastardized and niggerized world all the concepts of the humanly beautiful and sublime, as well as all ideas of an idealized future of our humanity, would be lost forever. . . .

And so the folkish philosophy of life corresponds to the innermost will of Nature, since it restores that free play of forces which must lead to a continuous mutual higher breeding, until at last the best of humanity, having achieved possession of this earth, will have a free path for activity in domains which will lie partly above it and partly outside it.

We all sense that in the distant future humanity must be faced by problems which only a highest race, become master people and

---

* Originating from the people (*Volk*) and benefiting them.

supported by the means and possibilities of an entire globe, will be equipped to overcome. . . .

It is self-evident that so general a statement of the meaningful content of a folkish philosophy can be interpreted in thousands of ways. And actually we find hardly a one of our newer political formations which does not base itself in one way or another on this world view. And, by its very existence in the face of the many others, it shows the difference of its conceptions. And so the Marxist world view, led by a unified top organization, is opposed by a hodge-podge of views which even as ideas are not very impressive in face of the solid, hostile front. Victories are not gained by such feeble weapons! Not until the international world view—politically led by organized Marxism—is confronted by a folkish world view, organized and led with equal unity, will success, supposing the fighting energy to be equal on both sides, fall to the side of eternal truth.

A philosophy can only be organizationally comprehended on the basis of a definite formulation of that philosophy, and what dogmas represent for religious faith, party principles are for a political party in the making.

Hence an instrument must be created for the folkish world view which enables it to fight, just as the Marxist party organization creates a free path for internationalism.

This is the goal pursued by the National Socialist German Workers' Party. . . .

THE STATE

All these views have their deepest root in the knowledge that the forces which create culture and values are based essentially on racial elements and that the state must, therefore, in the light of reason, regard its highest task as the preservation and intensification of the race, this fundamental condition of all human cultural development. . . .

It is, therefore, the first obligation of a new movement, standing on the ground of a folkish world view, to make sure that its conception of the nature and purpose of the state attains a uniform and clear character.

Thus the basic realization is: *that the state represents no end, but a means. It is, to be sure, the premise for the formation of a higher human culture, but not its cause, which lies exclusively in the existence of a race capable of culture.* Hundreds of exemplary states might exist on earth, but if the Aryan culture-bearer died out, there would be no culture corresponding to the spiritual level of the highest peoples of today. We can go even farther and say that the fact of human state formation would not in the least exclude the possibility of the destruction of the human race, provided that superior intellectual ability and elasticity would be lost due to the absence of their racial bearers. . . .

This glorious creative ability was given only to the Aryan, whether he bears it dormant within himself or gives it to awakening life, depending whether favorable circumstances permit this or an inhospitable Nature prevents it.

From this the following realization results:

The state is a means to an end. Its end lies in the preservation and advancement of a community of physically and psychically homogeneous creatures. This preservation itself comprises first of all existence as a race and thereby permits the free development of all the forces dormant in this race. Of them a part will always primarily serve the preservation of physical life, and only the remaining part the promotion of a further spiritual development. Actually the one always creates the precondition for the other.

States which do not serve this purpose are misbegotten, monstrosities in fact. The fact of their existence changes this no more than the success of a gang of bandits can justify robbery. . . .

Thus, the highest purpose of a folkish state is concern for the preservation of those original racial elements which bestow culture and create the beauty and dignity of a higher mankind. We, as Aryans, can conceive of the state only as the living organism of a nationality which not only assures the preservation of this nationality, but by the development of its spiritual and ideal abilities leads it to the highest freedom.

But what they try to palm off on us as a state today is usually nothing but a monstrosity born of deepest human error, with untold misery as a consequence. . . .

Anyone who does not want the earth to move toward [racial mixing] must convert himself to the conception that it is the function above all of the Germanic states first and foremost to call a fundamental halt to any further bastardization.

The generation of our present notorious weaklings will obviously cry out against this, and moan and complain about assaults on the holiest human rights. *No, there is only one holiest human right, and this right is at the same time the holiest obligation, to wit: to see to it that the blood is preserved pure and, by preserving the best humanity, to create the possibility of a nobler development of these beings.*

A folkish state must therefore begin by raising marriage from the level of a continuous defilement of the race, and give it the consecration of an institution which is called upon to produce images of the Lord and not monstrosities halfway between man and ape.

The protest against this on so-called *humane* grounds is particularly ill-suited to an era which on the one hand gives every depraved degenerate the possibility of propagating, but which burdens the products themselves, as well as their contemporaries, with untold suffering, while on the other hand every drug store and our very street peddlers offer the means for the prevention of births for sale even to the healthiest parents. In this present-day state of law and order in the eyes of its representatives, this brave, bourgeois-national society, the prevention of the procreative faculty in sufferers from syphilis, tuberculosis, hereditary diseases, cripples, and cretins is a crime, while the actual suppression of the procreative faculty in millions of the very best people is not regarded as anything bad and does not offend against the morals of this hypocritical society, but is rather a benefit to its short-sighted mental laziness. For otherwise these people would at least be forced to rack their brains about providing a basis for the sustenance and preservation of those beings who, as healthy bearers of our nationality, should one day serve the same function with regard to the coming generation.

How boundlessly unideal and ignoble is this whole system! People no longer bother to breed the best for posterity, but let things slide along as best they can. If our churches also sin against the image of the Lord, whose importance they still so highly emphasize, it is entirely because of the line of their present activity which speaks always of the spirit and lets its bearer, the man, degenerate into a depraved proletarian. Afterwards, of course, they make foolish faces and are full of amazement at the small effect of the Christian faith in their own country, at the terrible 'godlessness,' at this physically botched and hence spiritually degenerate rabble, and try with the Church's Blessing, to make up for it by success with the Hottentots and Zulu Kaffirs.* While our European peoples, thank the Lord, fall into a condition of physical and moral leprosy, the pious missionary wanders off to Central Africa and sets up Negro

---

* African tribes (representing all such "primitive" peoples), whom Hitler loathed.

missions until there, too, our 'higher culture' turns healthy, though primitive and inferior, human beings into a rotten brood of bastards.

It would be more in keeping with the intention of the noblest man in this world if our two Christian churches, instead of annoying Negroes with missions which they neither desire nor understand, would kindly, but in all seriousness, teach our European humanity that where parents are not healthy it is a deed pleasing to God to take pity on a poor little healthy orphan child and give him father and mother, than themselves to give birth to a sick child who will only bring unhappiness and suffering on himself and the rest of the world.

The folkish state must make up for what everyone else today has neglected in this field. *It must set race in the center of all life. It must take care to keep it pure. It must declare the child to be the most precious treasure of the people. It must see to it that only the healthy beget children; that there is only one disgrace: despite one's own sickness and deficiencies, to bring children into the world, and one highest honor: to renounce doing so. And conversely it must be considered reprehensible: to withhold healthy children from the nation. Here the state must act as the guardian of a millennial future in the face of which the wishes and the selfishness of the individual must appear as nothing and submit. It must put the most modern medical means in the service of this knowledge. It must declare unfit for propagation all who are in any way visibly sick or who have inherited a disease and can therefore pass it on, and put this into actual practice. Conversely, it must take care that the fertility of the healthy woman is not limited by the financial irresponsibility of a state regime which turns the blessing of children into a curse for the parents. It must put an end to that lazy, nay criminal, indifference with which the social premises for a fecund* family are treated today, and must instead feel itself to be the highest guardian of this most precious blessing of a people. Its concern belongs more to the child than to the adult. . . .*

In the folkish state, finally, the folkish philosophy of life must succeed in bringing about that nobler age in which men no longer are concerned with breeding dogs, horses, and cats, but in elevating man himself, an age in which the one knowingly and silently renounces, the other joyfully sacrifices and gives.

---

* Fertile, capable of procreating many children.

That this is possible may not be denied in a world where hundreds and hundreds of thousands of people voluntarily submit to celibacy,* obligated and bound by nothing except the injunction of the Church.

Should the same renunciation not be possible if this injunction is replaced by the admonition finally to put an end to the constant and continuous original sin of racial poisoning, and to give the Almighty Creator beings such as He Himself created?. . .

PROPAGANDA

The broad masses of the people can be moved only by the power of speech. And all great movements are popular movements, volcanic eruptions of human passions and emotional sentiments, stirred either by the cruel Goddess of Distress or by the firebrand of the word hurled among the masses; they are not the lemonade-like outpourings of literary aesthetes and drawing-room heroes.

Only a storm of hot passion can turn the destinies of peoples, and he alone can arouse passion who bears it within himself.

It alone gives its chosen one the words which like hammer blows can open the gates to the heart of a people.

But the man whom passion fails and whose lips are sealed—he has not been chosen by Heaven to proclaim its will. . . .

In general the art of all truly great national leaders at all times consists among other things primarily in not dividing the attention of a people, but in concentrating it upon a single foe. The more unified the application of a people's will to fight, the greater will be the magnetic attraction of a movement and the mightier will be the impetus of the thrust. It belongs to the genius of a great leader to make even adversaries far removed from one another seem to belong to a single category, because in weak and uncertain characters the knowledge of having different enemies can only too readily lead to the beginning of doubt in their own right.

Once the wavering mass sees itself in a struggle against too many enemies, objectivity will put in an appearance, throwing open the

---

* Unmarried state.

question whether all others are really wrong and only their own people or their own movement are in the right.

And this brings about the first paralysis of their own power. Hence a multiplicity of different adversaries must always be combined so that in the eyes of the masses of one's own supporters the struggle is directed against only one enemy. This strengthens their faith in their own right and enhances their bitterness against those who attack it. . . .

The function of propaganda does not lie in the scientific training of the individual, but in calling the masses' attention to certain facts, processes, necessities, and so forth, whose significance is thus for the first time placed within their field of vision.

The whole art consists in doing this so skillfully that everyone will be convinced that the fact is real, the process necessary, the necessity correct, and so forth. But since propaganda is not and cannot be the necessity in itself, since its function, like the poster, consists in attracting the attention of the crowd, and not in educating those who are already educated or who are striving after education and knowledge, its effect for the most part must be aimed at the emotions and only to a very limited degree at the so-called intellect.

All propaganda must be popular and its intellectual level must be adjusted to the most limited intelligence among those it is addressed to. Consequently, the greater the mass it is intended to reach, the lower its purely intellectual level will have to be. But if, as in propaganda for sticking out a war, the aim is to influence a whole people, we must avoid excessive intellectual demands on our public, and too much caution cannot be exerted in this direction.

The more modest its intellectual ballast, the more exclusively it takes into consideration the emotions of the masses, the more effective it will be. And this is the best proof of the soundness or unsoundness of a propaganda campaign, and not success in pleasing a few scholars or young aesthetes.

The art of propaganda lies in understanding the emotional ideas of the great masses and finding, through a psychologically correct form, the way to the attention and thence to the heart of the broad masses. The fact that our bright boys do not understand this merely shows how mentally lazy and conceited they are.

Once we understand how necessary it is for propaganda to be adjusted to the broad mass, the following rule results:

It is a mistake to make propaganda many-sided, like scientific instruction, for instance.

The receptivity of the great masses is very limited, their intelligence is small, but their power of forgetting is enormous. In consequence of these facts, all effective propaganda must be limited to a very few points and must harp on these in slogans until the last member of the public understands what you want him to understand by your slogan. As soon as you sacrifice this slogan and try to be many-sided, the effect will piddle away, for the crowd can neither digest nor retain the material offered. In this way the result is weakened and in the end entirely cancelled out.

Thus we see that propaganda must follow a simple line and correspondingly the basic tactics must be psychologically sound. . . .

. . . The magnitude of a lie always contains a certain factor of credibility, since the great masses of the people in the very bottom of their hearts tend to be corrupted rather than consciously and purposely evil, and that, therefore, in view of the primitive simplicity of their minds, they more easily fall a victim to a big lie than to a little one, since they themselves lie in little things, but would be ashamed of lies that were too big. . . .

FOREIGN POLICY AND WAR

When the nations on this planet fight for existence—when the question of destiny, 'to be or not to be,' cries out for a solution—then all considerations of humanitarianism or aesthetics crumble into nothingness; for all these concepts do not float about in the ether, they arise from man's imagination and are bound up with man. When he departs from this world, these concepts are again dissolved into nothingness, for Nature does not know them. . . .

But all such concepts become secondary when a nation is fighting for its existence; in fact, they become totally irrelevant to the forms of the struggle as soon as a situation arises where they might paralyze a struggling nation's power of self-preservation. And that has always been their only visible result.

As for humanitarianism, Moltke* said years ago that in war it lies in the brevity of the operation, and that means that the most aggressive fighting technique is the most humane.

But when people try to approach these questions with drivel about aesthetics, and so forth, really only one answer is possible: where the destiny and existence of a people are at stake, all obligation toward beauty ceases. The most unbeautiful thing there can be in human life is and remains the yoke of slavery. . . .

The foreign policy of the folkish state must safeguard the existence on this planet of the race embodied in the state, by creating a healthy, viable natural relation between the nation's population and growth on the one hand and the quantity and quality of its soil on the other hand.

As a healthy relation we may regard only that condition which assures the sustenance of a people on its own soil. Every other condition, even if it endures for hundreds, nay, thousands of years, is nevertheless unhealthy and will sooner or later lead to the injury if not annihilation of the people in question.

Only an adequately large space on this earth assures a nation of freedom of existence.

Moreover, the necessary size of the territory to be settled cannot be judged exclusively on the basis of present requirements, not even in fact on the basis of the yield of the soil compared to the population. For . . . *in addition to its importance as a direct source of a people's food, another significance, that is, a military and political one, must be attributed to the area of a state.* If a nation's sustenance as such is assured by the amount of its soil, the safeguarding of the existing soil itself must also be borne in mind. This lies in the general power-political strength of the state, which in turn to no small extent is determined by geo-military considerations.

Hence, the German nation can defend its future only as a world power. . . .

If the National Socialist movement really wants to be consecrated by history with a great mission for our nation, it must be permeated by knowledge and filled with pain at our true situation in this world; boldly and conscious of its goal, it must take up

---

* Helmuth von Moltke (1800-1891), a German general, remembered for his contributions to the unification of Germany (1864-71).

the struggle against the aimlessness and incompetence which have hitherto guided our German nation in the line of foreign affairs. Then, without consideration of 'traditions' and prejudices, it must find the courage to gather our people and their strength for an advance along the road that will lead this people from its present restricted living space to new land and soil, and hence also free it from the danger of vanishing from the earth or of serving others as a slave nation.

The National Socialist Movement must strive to eliminate the disproportion between our population and our area—viewing this latter as a source of food as well as a basis for power politics—between our historical past and the hopelessness of our present impotence. . . .

And I must sharply attack those folkish pen-pushers who claim to regard such an acquisition of soil as a 'breach of sacred human rights' and attack it as such in their scribblings. One never knows who stands behind these fellows. But one thing is for certain, that the confusion they can create is desirable and convenient to our national enemies. By such an attitude they help to weaken and destroy from within our people's will for the only correct way of defending their vital needs. For no people on this earth possesses so much as a square yard of territory on the strength of a higher will or superior right. Just as Germany's frontiers are fortuitous frontiers, momentary frontiers in the current political struggle of any period, so are the boundaries of other nations' living space. And just as the shape of our earth's surface can seem immutable as granite only to the thoughtless soft-head, but in reality only represents at each period an apparent pause in a continuous development, created by the mighty forces of Nature in a process of continuous growth, only to be transformed or destroyed tomorrow by greater forces, likewise the boundaries of living spaces in the life of nations.

State boundaries are made by man and changed by man. . . .

But we National Socialists must go further. *The right to possess soil can become a duty if without extension of its soil a great nation seems doomed to destruction.* And most especially when not some little nigger* nation or other is involved, but the Germanic mother of life, which has given the present-day world its cultural picture. *Germany will either be a world power or there will be no Germany.* And for world power she needs that magnitude

---

* Hitler's term of contempt for any small, non-Aryan country.

which will give her the position she needs in the present period, and life to her citizens.

14

e. e. cummings

anyone lived in a pretty how town

E. E. Cummings (1894–1962) was born in Cambridge, Massachusetts, and educated at Harvard University. During World War I, he drove an ambulance in Europe and was held captive in a French prison camp, which became the subject of his novel, **The Enormous Room** *(1922). After the war, he associated with the Imagist poets in New York and the expatriate writers in Paris. His eccentric use of punctuation and grammar established his reputation as one of America's best-known and well-liked poets. Although he challenged many writing conventions, his poems respect traditional poetic forms.*

anyone lived in a pretty how town
(with up so floating many bells down)
spring summer autumn winter
he sang his didn't he danced his did.

Women and men (both little and small)
cared for anyone not at all
they sowed their isn't they reaped their same
sun moon stars rain

"anyone lived in a pretty how town". Copyright 1940, © 1968, 1991 by the Trustees for the E. E. Cummings Trust, from COMPLETE POEMS: 1904–1962 by E. E. Cummings, edited by George J. Firmage. Used by permission of Liveright Publishing Corporation.

children guessed (but only a few
and down they forgot as up they grew
autumn winter spring summer)
that noone loved him more by more

when by now and tree by leaf
she laughed his joy she cried his grief
bird by snow and stir by still
anyone's any was all to her

someones married their everyones
laughed their cryings and did their dance
(sleep wake hope and then) they
said their nevers they slept their dream

stars rain sun moon
(and only the snow can begin to explain
how children are apt to forget to remember
with up so floating many bells down)

one day anyone died i guess
(and noone stooped to kiss his face)
busy folk buried them side by side
little by little and was by was

all by all and deep by deep
and more by more they dream their sleep
noone and anyone earth by april
wish by spirit and if by yes.

Women and men (both dong and ding)
summer autumn winter spring
reaped their sowing and went their came
sun moon stars rain

UNDERSTANDING MEANING

1. What is the theme of the poem?
2. How does the syntax of the poem make possible the rhyme and meter set out in the poem?

EVALUATING ELEMENTS

1. How does the use of quatrains in the poem counter the unusual syntax?
2. Who is "anyone," and how does the lack of naming support your answer?

APPRECIATING LANGUAGE

1. How do the jumbled sentences challenge your sense of order?
2. What does Cummings mean when he writes, "reaped their sowing and went their came," and how is that typical of other lines in the poem?

WRITING SUGGESTIONS

1. Analyze each stanza for literal meaning.
2. Research a definition of literary modernism. Then explain how this poem does or does not fit the definition.

15

Asimov

Nightfall

If the stars should appear one night in
a thousand years, how would men believe and adore,
and preserve for many generations
the remembrance of the city of God?
—Emerson

Aton 77, director of Saro University, thrust out a belligerent lower lip and glared at the young newspaperman in a hot fury.

Theremon 762 took that fury in his stride. In his earlier days, when his now widely syndicated column was only a mad idea in a cub reporter's mind, he had specialized in 'impossible' interviews. It had cost him bruises, black eyes, and broken bones; but it had given him an ample supply of coolness and self-confidence. So he lowered the outthrust hand that had been so pointedly ignored and calmly waited for the aged director to get over the worst. Astronomers were queer ducks, anyway, and if Aton's actions of the last two months meant anything; this same Aton was the queer-duckiest of the lot.

Aton 77 found his voice, and though it trembled with restrained emotion, the careful, somewhat pedantic phraseology, for which the famous astronomer was noted, did not abandon him.

'Sir,' he said, 'you display an infernal gall in coming to me with that impudent proposition of yours.' The husky telephotographer of the Observatory, Beenay 25, thrust a tongue's tip across dry lips and interposed nervously, 'Now, sir, after all—'

The director turned to him and lifted a white eyebrow.

'Do not interfere, Beenay. I will credit you with good intentions in bringing this man here; but I will tolerate no insubordination now.'

Theremon decided it was time to take a part. 'Director Aton, if you'll let me finish what I started saying, I think—'

'I don't believe, young man,' retorted Aton, 'that anything you could say now would count much as compared with your daily columns of these last two months. You have led a vast newspaper campaign against the efforts of myself and my colleagues to organize the world against the menace which it is now too late to avert. You have done your best with your highly personal attacks to make the staff of this Observatory objects of ridicule.'

The director lifted a copy of the Saro City *Chronicle* from the table and shook it at Theremon furiously. 'Even a person of your well-known impudence should have hesitated before coming to me with a request that he be allowed to cover today's events for his paper. Of all newsmen, you!'

Aton dashed the newspaper to the floor, strode to the window, and clasped his arms behind his back.

'You may leave,' he snapped over his shoulder. He stared moodily out at the skyline where Gamma, the brightest of the planet's six suns, was setting. It had already faded and yellowed into the horizon mists, and Aton knew he would never see it again as a sane man. He whirled. 'No, wait, come here!' He gestured peremptorily. 'I'll give you your story.'

The newsman had made no motion to leave, and now he approached the old man slowly. Aton gestured outward.

'Of the six suns, only Beta is left in the sky. Do you see it?'

The question was rather unnecessary. Beta was almost at zenith, its ruddy light flooding the landscape to an unusual orange as the brilliant rays of setting Gamma died. Beta was at aphelion. It was small; smaller than Theremon had ever seen it before, and for the moment it was undisputed ruler of Lagash's sky.

Lagash's own sun. Alpha, the one about which it revolved, was at the antipodes, as were the two distant companion pairs. The red dwarf Beta—Alpha's immediate companion—was alone, grimly alone.

Aton's upturned face flushed redly in the sunlight. 'In just under four hours,' he said, 'civilization, as we know it, comes to an end. It will do so because, as you see. Beta is the only sun in the sky.' He smiled grimly.

'Print that! There'll be no one to read it.'

'But if it turns out that four hours pass—and another four—and nothing happens?' asked Theremon softly.

'Don't let that worry you. Enough will happen.'

'Granted! And *still*—it nothing happens?'

For a second time, Beenay 25 spoke. 'Sir, I think you ought to listen to him.'

Theremon said, 'Put it to a vote, Director Aton.'

There was a stir among the remaining five members of the Observatory staff, who till now had maintained an attitude of wary neutrality.

'That,' stated Aton flatly, 'is not necessary.' He drew out his pocket watch. 'Since your good friend, Beenay, insists so urgently, I will give you five minutes. Talk away.'

'Good! Now, just what difference would it make if you allowed me to take down an eyewitness account of what's to come? If your prediction comes true, my presence won't hurt; for in that case my column would never be written. On the other hand, if nothing comes of it, you will just have to expect ridicule or worse. It would be wise to leave that ridicule to friendly hands.'

Aton snorted. 'Do you mean yours when you speak of friendly hands?'

'Certainly!' Theremon sat down and crossed his legs.

'My columns may have been a little rough, but I gave you people the benefit of the doubt every time. After all. this is not the century to preach "The end of the world is at hand" to Lagash. You have to understand that people don't believe the *Book of Revelations* anymore, and it annoys them to have scientists turn aboutface and tell us the Cultists are right after all—'

'No such thing, young man,' interrupted Aton. 'While a great deal of our data has been supplied us by the Cult, our results contain none of the Cult's mysticism. Facts are facts, and the Cult's so-called mythology *has* certain facts behind it. We've exposed them and ripped away their mystery. I assure you that the Cult hates us now worse than you do.'

'I don't hate you. I'm just trying to tell you that the public is in an ugly humor. They're angry.'

Aton twisted his mouth in derision. 'Let them be angry.'

'Yes, but what about tomorrow?'

'There'll be no tomorrow!'

'But if there is. Say that there is—just to see what happens. That anger might take shape into something serious. After all, you know, business has taken a nosedive these last two months. Investors don't really believe the world is coming to an end, but just the same they're being cagy with their money until it's all over. Johnny Public doesn't believe you, either, but the new spring furniture might just as well wait a few months—just to make sure.

'You see the point. Just as soon as this is all over, the business interests will be after your hide. They'll say that if crackpots—begging your pardon—can upset the country's prosperity any time they want, simply by making some cockeyed prediction—it's up to the planet to prevent them.

The sparks will fly, sir.'

The director regarded the columnist sternly. 'And just what were you proposing to do to help the situation?'

'Well'—Theremon grinned—'I was proposing to take charge of the publicity. I can handle things so that only the ridiculous side will show.

It would be hard to stand, I admit, because I'd have to make you all out to be a bunch of gibbering idiots, but if I can get people laughing at you, they might forget to be angry. In return for that, all my publisher asks is an exclusive story.'

Beenay nodded and burst out, 'Sir, the rest of us think he's right.

These last two months we've considered everything but the million-to-one chance that there is an error somewhere in our theory or in our calculations. We ought to take care of that, too.'

There was a murmur of agreement from the men grouped about the table, and Aton's expression became that of one who found his mouth full of something bitter and couldn't get rid of it.

'You may stay if you wish, then. You will kindly refrain, however, from hampering us in our duties in any way. You will also remember that I am in charge of all activities here, and in spite of your opinions as expressed in your columns, I will expect full cooperation and full respect—'

His hands were behind his back, and his wrinkled face thrust forward determinedly as he spoke. He might have continued indefinitely but for the intrusion of a new voice.

'Hello, hello, hello!' It came in a high tenor, and the plump cheeks of the newcomer expanded in a pleased smile. 'What's this morgue-like atmosphere about here? No one's losing his nerve, I hope.'

Aton started in consternation and said peevishly, 'Now what the devil are you doing here, Sheerin? I thought you were going to stay behind in the Hideout.'

Sheerin laughed and dropped his stubby figure into a chair. 'Hideout be blowed! The place bored me. I wanted to be here, where things are getting hot. Don't you suppose I have my share of curiosity? I want to see these Stars the Cultists are forever speaking about.' He rubbed his hands and added in a soberer tone. 'It's freezing outside. The wind's enough to hang icicles on your nose. Beta doesn't seem to give any heat at all, at the distance it is.'

The white-haired director ground his teeth in sudden exasperation. 'Why do you go out of your way to do crazy things, Sheerin? What kind of good are you around here?'

'What kind of good am I around there?' Sheerin spread his palms in comical resignation. 'A psychologist isn't worth his salt in the Hideout.

They need men of action and strong, healthy women that can breed children.

Me? I'm a hundred pounds too heavy for a man of action, and I wouldn't be a success at breeding children. So why bother them with an extra mouth to feed? I feel better over here.'

Theremon spoke briskly. 'Just what is the Hideout, sir?'

Sheerin seemed to see the columnist for the first time. He frowned and blew his ample cheeks out. 'And just who in Lagash are you, redhead?'

Aton compressed his lips and then muttered sullenly, 'That's Theremon 762, the newspaper fellow. I suppose you've heard of him.'

The columnist offered his hand. 'And, of course, you're Sheerin 501 of Saro University. I've heard of you.' Then he repeated, 'What is this Hideout, sir?'

'Well,' said Sheerin, 'we have managed to convince a few people of the validity of our prophecy of—er—doom, to be spectacular about it, and those few have taken proper measures. They consist mainly of the immediate members of the families of the Observatory staff, certain of the faculty of Saro University, and a few outsiders. Altogether, they number about three hundred, but three quarters are women and children.'

'I see! They're supposed to hide where the Darkness and the— er—Stars can't get at them, and then hold out when the rest of the world goes poof.'

'If they can. It won't be easy. With all of mankind insane, with the great cities going up in flames—environment will not be conducive to survival. But they have food, water, shelter, and weapons—'

'They've got more,' said Aton. 'They've got all our records, except for what we will collect today. Those records will mean everything to the next cycle, and *that's* what must survive. The rest can go hang.'

Theremon uttered a long, low whistle and sat brooding for several minutes. The men about the table had brought out a multi-chess board and started a six-member game. Moves were made rapidly and in silence. All eyes bent in furious concentration on the board. Theremon watched them intently and then rose and approached Aton, who sat apart in whispered conversation with Sheerin.

'Listen,' he said, let's go somewhere where we won't bother the rest of the fellows. I want to ask some questions.'

The aged astronomer frowned sourly at him, but Sheerin chirped up, 'Certainly. It will do me good to talk. It always does. Aton was telling me about your ideas concerning world reaction to a failure of the prediction—and I agree with you. I read your column pretty regularly, by the way, and as a general thing I like your views.'

'Please, Sheerin,' growled Aton.

'Eh? Oh, all right. We'll go into the next room. It has softer chairs, anyway.'

There were softer chairs in the next room. There were also thick red curtains on the windows and a maroon carpet on the floor. With the bricky light of Beta pouring in, the general effect was one of dried blood.

Theremon shuddered. 'Say, I'd give ten credits for a decent dose of white light for just a second. I wish Gamma or Delta were in the sky.'

'What are your questions?' asked Aton. 'Please remember that our time is limited. In a little over an hour and a quarter we're going upstairs, and after that there will be no time for talk.'

'Well, here it is.' Theremon leaned back and folded his hands on his chest. 'You people seem so all-fired serious about this that I'm beginning to believe you. Would you mind explaining what it's all about?'

Aton exploded, 'Do you mean to sit there and tell me that you've been bombarding us with ridicule without even finding out what we've been trying to say?'

The columnist grinned sheepishly. 'It's not that bad, sir. I've got the general idea. You say there is going to be a world-wide Darkness in a few hours and that all mankind will go violently insane. What I want now is the science behind it.'

'No, you don't. No, you don't,' broke in Sheerin. 'If you ask Aton for that—supposing him to be in the mood to answer at all—he'll trot out pages of figures and volumes of graphs. You won't make head or tail of it.

Now if you were to ask me, I could give you the layman's standpoint.'

'All right; I ask you.'

'Then first I'd like a drink.' He rubbed his hands and looked at Aton.

'Water?' grunted Aton.

'Don't be silly!'

'Don't you be silly. No alcohol today. It would be too easy to get my men drunk. I can't afford to tempt them.'

The psychologist grumbled wordlessly. He turned to Theremon, impaled him with his sharp eyes, and began.

'You realize, of course, that the history of civilization on Lagash displays a cyclic character—but I mean *cyclic!*'

'I know,' replied Theremon cautiously, 'that that is the current archaeological theory. Has it been accepted as a fact?'

'Just about. In this last century it's been generally agreed upon. This cyclic character is—or rather, was—one of the great mysteries. We've located series of civilizations, nine of them definitely, and indications of others as well, all of which have reached heights comparable to our own, and all of which, without exception, were destroyed by fire at the very height of their culture.

'And no one could tell why. All centers of culture were thoroughly gutted by fire, with nothing left behind to give a hint as to the cause.'

Theremon was following closely. 'Wasn't there a Stone Age, too?'

'Probably, but as yet practically nothing is known of it, except that men of that age were little more than rather intelligent apes. We can forget about that.'

'I see. Go on!'

There have been explanations of these recurrent catastrophes, all of a more or less fantastic nature. Some say that there are periodic rains of fire; some that Lagash passes through a sun every so often; some even wilder things. But there is one theory, quite different from all of these, that has been handed down over a period of centuries.'

'I know. You mean this myth of the "Stars" that the Cultists have in their *Book of Revelations.*'

'Exactly,' rejoined Sheerin with satisfaction. 'The Cultists said that every two thousand and fifty years Lagash entered a huge cave, so that

all the suns disappeared, and there came *total darkness all over the world*!
And then, they say, things called Stars appeared, which robbed men of
their souls and left them unreasoning brutes, so that they destroyed the
civilization they themselves had built up. Of course they mix all this
up with a lot of religio-mystic notions, but that's the central idea.'

There was a short pause in which Sheerin drew a long breath.
'And now we come to the Theory of Universal Gravitation.' He
pronounced the phrase so that the capital letters sounded—and at that
point Aton turned from the window, snorted loudly, and stalked out
of the room.

The two stared after him, and Theremon said, 'What's wrong?'

'Nothing in particular,' replied Sheerin. 'Two of the men were
due several hours ago and haven't shown up yet. He's terrifically short-
handed, of course, because all but the really essential men have gone
to the Hideout.'

'You don't think the two deserted, do you?'

'Who? Faro and Yimot? Of course not. Still, if they're not back
within the hour, things would be a little sticky.' He got to his feet
suddenly, and his eyes twinkled. 'Anyway, as long as Aton is gone—'

Tiptoeing to the nearest window, he squatted, and from the low
window box beneath withdrew a bottle of red liquid that gurgled
suggestively when he shook it.

'I *thought* Aton didn't know about this,' he remarked as he trotted
back to the table. 'Here! We've only got one glass so, as the guest, you
can have it. I'll keep the bottle.'

And he filled the tiny cup with judicious care. Theremon rose to
protest, but Sheerin eyed him sternly.

'Respect your elders, young man.'

The newsman seated himself with a look of anguish on his face.
'Go ahead, then, you old villain.'

The psychologist's Adam's apple wobbled as the bottle upended,
and then, with a satisfied grunt and a smack of the lips, he began again.
'But what do you know about gravitation?'

'Nothing, except that it is a very recent development, not too well
established, and that the math is so hard that only twelve men in Lagash
are supposed to understand it.'

'*Tcha!* Nonsense! Baloney! I can give you all the essential math in a sentence. The Law of Universal Gravitation states that there exists a cohesive force among all bodies of the universe, such that the amount of this force between any two given bodies is proportional to the product of their masses divided by the square of the distance between them.'

'Is that all?'

'That's enough! It took four hundred years to develop it.'

'Why that long? It sounded simple enough, the way you said it.'

'Because great laws are not divined by flashes of inspiration, whatever you may think. It usually takes the combined work of a world full of scientists over a period of centuries. After Genovi 4 I discovered that Lagash rotated about the sun Alpha rather than vice versa—and that was four hundred years ago—astronomers have been working. The complex motions of the six suns were recorded and analyzed and unwoven. Theory after theory was advanced and checked and counterchecked and modified and abandoned and revived and converted to something else. It was a devil of a job.'

Theremon nodded thoughtfully and held out his glass for more liquor.

Sheerin grudgingly allowed a few ruby drops to leave the bottle.

'It was twenty years ago,' he continued after remoistening his own throat, 'that it was finally demonstrated that the Law of Universal Gravitation accounted exactly for the orbital motions of the six suns. It was a great triumph.'

Sheerin stood up and walked to the window, still clutching his bottle.

'And now we're getting to the point. In the last decade, the motions of Lagash about Alpha were computed according to gravity, and if *did not account for the orbit observed;* not even when all perturbations due to the other suns were included. Either the law was invalid, or there was another, as yet unknown, factor involved.'

Theremon joined Sheerin at the window and gazed out past the wooded slopes to where the spires of Saro City gleamed bloodily on the horizon. The newsman felt the tension of uncertainty grow within him as he cast a short glance at Beta. It glowered redly at zenith, dwarfed and evil.

'Go ahead, sir,' he said softly.

Sheerin replied, 'Astronomers stumbled about for year, each proposed theory more untenable than the one before—until Aton had the inspiration of calling in the Cult. The head of the Cult, Sor 5, had access to certain data that simplified the problem considerably. Aton set to work on a new track.

'What if there were another nonluminous planetary body such as Lagash?

If there were, you know, it would shine only by reflected light, and if it were composed of bluish rock, as Lagash itself largely is, then, in the redness of the sky, the eternal blaze of the suns would make it invisible—drown it out completely.'

Theremon whistled. 'What a screwy idea!'

'You think *that's* screwy? Listen to this: Suppose this body rotated about Lagash at such a distance and in such an orbit and had such a mass that its attention would exactly account for the deviations of Lagash's orbit from theory—do you know what would happen?'

The columnist shook his head.

'Well, sometimes this body would get in the way of a sun.' And Sheerin emptied what remained in the bottle at a draft.

'And it does, I suppose,' said Theremon flatly.

'Yes! But only one sun lies in its plane of revolution.' He jerked a thumb at the shrunken sun above. 'Beta! And it has been shown that the eclipse will occur only when the arrangement of the suns is such that Beta is alone in its hemisphere and at maximum distance, at which time the moon is invariably at minimum distance. The eclipse that results, with the moon seven times the apparent diameter of Beta, covers all of Lagash and lasts well over half a day, so that no spot on the planet escapes the effects.

That eclipse comes once every two thousand and forty-nine years.'

Theremon's face was drawn into an expressionless mask.

'And that's my story?'

The psychologist nodded. 'That's all of it. First the eclipse—which will start in three quarters of an hour—then universal Darkness and, maybe, these mysterious Stars—then madness, and end of the cycle.'

He brooded. 'We had two months' leeway—we at the Observatory—
and that wasn't enough time to persuade Lagash of the danger. Two
centuries might not have been enough. But our records are at the
Hideout, and today we photograph the eclipse. The next cycle will *start
off* with the truth, and when the *next* eclipse comes, mankind will at last
be ready for it. Come to think of it, that's part of your story too.'

A thin wind ruffled the curtains at the window as Theremon opened
it and leaned out. It played coldly with his hair as he stared at the crimson
sunlight on his hand. Then he turned in sudden rebellion.

'What is there in Darkness to drive *me* mad?'

Sheerin smiled to himself as he spun the empty liquor bottle with
abstracted motions of his hand. 'Have you ever experienced Darkness,
young man?'

The newsman leaned against the wall and considered. 'No. Can't
say I have. But I know what it is. Just—uh—' He made vague motions
with his fingers and then brightened. 'Just no light. Like in caves.'

'Have you ever been in a cave?'

'In a *cave*! Of course not!'

'I thought not. I tried last week—just to see—but I got out in a
hurry. I went in until the mouth of the cave was just visible as a blur of
light, with black everywhere else. I never thought a person my weight
could run that fast.'

Theremon's lip curled. 'Well, if it comes to that, I guess I wouldn't
have run if I had been there.'

The psychologist studied the young man with an annoyed frown.

'My, don't you talk big! I dare you to draw the curtain.'

Theremon looked his surprise and said, 'What for? If we had four
or five suns out there, we might want to cut the light down a bit for
comfort, but now we haven't enough light as it is.'

'That's the point. Just draw the curtain; then come here and sit
down.'

'All right.' Theremon reached for the tasseled string and jerked.
The red curtain slid across the wide window, the brass rings hissing
their way along the crossbar, and a dusk-red shadow clamped down
on the room.

Theremon's footsteps sounded hollowly in the silence as he made his way to the table, and then they stopped halfway. 'I can't see you, sir,' he whispered.

'Feel your way,' ordered Sheerin in a strained voice.

'But I can't see you, sir.' The newsman was breathing harshly. 'I can't see anything.'

'What did you expect?' came the grim reply. 'Come here and sit down!'

The footsteps sounded again, waveringly, approaching slowly. There was the sound of someone fumbling with a chair. Theremon's voice came thinly,

'Here I am. I feel . . . *ulp* . . . all right.'

'You like it, do you?'

'N—no. It's pretty awful. The walls seem to be—' He paused. 'They seem to be closing in on me. I keep wanting to push them away. But I'm not going *mad*! In fact, the feeling isn't as bad as it was.'

'All right. Draw the curtain back again.'

There were cautious footsteps through the dark, the rustle of Theremon's body against the curtain as he felt for the tassel, and then the triumphant *roo-osh* of the curtain slithering back. Red light flooded the room, and with a cry of joy Theremon looked up at the sun.

Sheerin wiped the moisture off his forehead with the back of a hand and said shakily, 'And that was just a dark room.'

'It can be stood,' said Theremon lightly.

'Yes, a dark room can. But were you at the Jonglor Centennial Exposition two years ago?'

'No, it so happens I never got around to it. Six thousand miles was just a bit too much to travel, even for the exposition.'

'Well, I was there. You remember hearing about the "Tunnel of Mystery" that broke all records in the amusement area—for the first month or so, anyway?'

'Yes. Wasn't there some fuss about it?'

'Very little. It was hushed up. You see, that Tunnel of Mystery was just a mile-long tunnel—with no lights. You got into a little open car and jolted along through Darkness for fifteen minutes. It was very popular—while it lasted.'

'Popular?'

'Certainly. There's a fascination in being frightened *when it's part of a game*. A baby is born with three instinctive fears: of loud noises, of falling, and of the absence of light. That's why it's considered so funny to jump at someone and shout "Boo!" That's why it's such fun to ride a roller coaster. And that's why that Tunnel of Mystery started cleaning up. People came out of that Darkness shaking, breathless, half dead with fear, but they kept on paying to get in.'

'Wait a while, I remember now. Some people came out dead, didn't they?

There were rumors of that after it shut down.'

The psychologist snorted. 'Bah! Two or three died. That was nothing!

They paid off the families of the dead ones and argued the Jonglor City

Council into forgetting it. After all, they said, if people with weak hearts want to go through the tunnel, it was at their own risk—and besides, it wouldn't happen again. So they put a doctor in the front office and had every customer go through a physical examination before getting into the car. That actually *boosted* ticket sales.'

'Well, then?'

'But you see, there was something else. People sometimes came out in perfect order, except that they refused to go into buildings—any buildings; including palaces, mansions, apartment houses, tenements, cottages, huts, shacks, lean-tos, and tents.'

Theremon looked shocked. 'You mean they refused to come in out of the open? Where'd they sleep?'

'In the open.'

'They should have *forced* them inside.'

'Oh, they did, they did. Whereupon these people went into violent hysterics and did their best to bat their brains out against the nearest wall. Once you got them inside, you couldn't keep them there without a strait jacket or a heavy dose of tranquilizer.'

'They must have been crazy.'

'Which is exactly what they were. One person out of every ten who went into that tunnel came out that way. They called in the psychologists, and we did the only thing possible. We closed down the exhibit.' He spread his hands.

'What was the matter with these people?' asked Theremon finally.

'Essentially the same thing that was the matter with you when you thought the walls of the room were crushing in on you in the dark. There is a psychological term for mankind's instinctive fear of the absence of light.

We call it "claustrophobia", because the lack of light is always tied up with enclosed places, so that fear of one is fear of the other. You see?'

'And those people of the tunnel?'

'Those people of the tunnel consisted of those unfortunates whose mentality did not quite possess the resiliency to overcome the claustrophobia that overtook them in the Darkness. Fifteen minutes without light is a long time; you only had two or three minutes, and I believe you were fairly upset.

'The people of the tunnel had what is called a "claustrophobic fixation". Their latent fear of Darkness and enclosed places had crystalized and become active, and, as far as we can tell, permanent. That's what fifteen minutes in the dark will do.'

There was a long silence, and Theremon's forehead wrinkled slowly into a frown. 'I don't believe it's that bad.'

'You mean you don't want to believe,' snapped Sheerin. 'You're afraid to believe. Look out the window!'

Theremon did so, and the psychologist continued without pausing.

'Imagine Darkness—everywhere. No light, as far as you can see. The houses, the trees, the fields, the earth, the sky—black! And Stars thrown in, for all I know—whatever *they* are. Can you conceive it?'

'Yes, I can,' declared Theremon truculently.

And Sheerin slammed his fist down upon the table in sudden passion.

'You lie! You can't conceive that. Your brain wasn't built for the conception any more than it was built for the conception of infinity or of eternity. You can only talk about it. A fraction of the reality upsets you, and when the real thing comes, your brain is going to be presented with the phenomenon outside its limits of comprehension. You will go mad, completely and permanently! There is no question of it!'

He added sadly, 'And another couple of millennia of painful struggle comes to nothing. Tomorrow there won't be a city standing unharmed in all Lagash.'

Theremon recovered part of his mental equilibrium. 'That doesn't follow. I still don't see that I can go loony just because there isn't a sun in the sky—but even if I did, and everyone else did, how does that harm the cities? Are we going to blow them down?'

But Sheerin was angry, too. 'If you were in Darkness, what would you want more than anything else; what would it be that every instinct would call for? Light, damn you, *light*!'

'Well?'

'And how would you get light?'

'I don't know,' said Theremon flatly.

'What's the *only* way to get light, short of a sun?'

'How should I know?'

They were standing face to face and nose to nose.

Sheerin said, 'You bum something, mister. Ever see a forest fire? Ever go camping and cook a stew over a wood fire? Heat isn't the only thing burning wood gives off, you know. It gives off light, and people know that. And when it's dark they want light, and they're going to *get* it.'

'So they bum wood?'

'So they burn whatever they can get. They've got to have light. They've got to burn something, and wood isn't handy—so they'll burn whatever is nearest. They'll have their light—and every center of habitation goes up in flames!'

Eyes held each other as though the whole matter were a personal affair of respective will powers, and then Theremon broke away wordlessly. His breathing was harsh and ragged, and he scarcely noted the sudden hubbub that came from the adjoining room behind the closed door.

Sheerin spoke, and it was with an effort that he made it sound matter-of-fact. 'I think I heard Yimot's voice. He and Faro are probably back. Let's go in and see what kept them.'

'Might as well!' muttered Theremon. He drew a long breath and seemed to shake himself. The tension was broken.

The room was in an uproar, with members of the staff clustering about two young men who were removing outer garments even as they parried the miscellany of questions being thrown at them.

Aton hustled through the crowd and faced the newcomers angrily. 'Do you realize that it's less than half an hour before deadline? Where have you two been?'

Faro 24 seated himself and rubbed his hands. His cheeks were red with the outdoor chill. 'Yimot and I have just finished carrying through a little crazy experiment of our own. We've been trying to see if we couldn't construct an arrangement by which we could simulate the appearance of Darkness and Stars so as to get an advance notion as to how it looked.'

There was a confused murmur from the listeners, and a sudden look of interest entered Aton's eyes. 'There wasn't anything said of this before.

How did you go about it?'

'Well,' said Faro, 'the idea came to Yimot and myself long ago, and we've been working it out in our spare time. Yimot knew of a low one-story house down in the city with a domed roof—it had once been used as a museum, I think. Anyway, we bought it—'

'Where did you get the money?' interrupted Aton peremptorily.

'Our bank accounts,' grunted Yimot 70. 'It cost two thousand credits.'

Then, defensively, 'Well, what of it? Tomorrow, two thousand credits will be two thousand pieces of paper. That's all.'

'Sure.' agreed Faro. 'We bought the place and rigged it up with black velvet from top to bottom so as to get as perfect a Darkness as possible.

Then we punched tiny holes in the ceiling and through the roof and covered them with little metal caps, all of which could be shoved aside simultaneously at the close of a switch. At least we didn't do that part

ourselves; we got a carpenter and an electrician and some others—money
didn't count. The point was that we could get the light to shine through
those holes in the roof, so that we could get a starlike effect.'

Not a breath was drawn during the pause that followed. Aton said
stiffly, 'You had no right to make a private—'

Faro seemed abashed. 'I know, sir—but frankly, Yimot and I thought
the experiment was a little dangerous. If the effect really worked,
we half expected to go mad—from what Sheerin says about all this,
we thought that would be rather likely. We wanted to take the risk
ourselves. Of course if we found we could retain sanity, it occurred to
us that we might develop immunity to the real thing, and then expose
the rest of you the same way.

But things didn't work out at all—'

'Why, what happened?'

It was Yimot who answered. 'We shut ourselves in and allowed
our eyes to get accustomed to the dark. It's an extremely creepy feeling
because the total Darkness makes you feel as if the walls and ceiling are
crushing in on you. But we got over that and pulled the switch. The caps
fell away and the roof glittered all over with little dots of light—'

'Well?'

'Well—nothing. That was the whacky part of it. Nothing happened.
It was just a roof with holes in it, and that's just what it looked like.
We tried it over and over again—that's what kept us so late—but there
just isn't any effect at all.'

There followed a shocked silence, and all eyes turned to Sheerin,
who sat motionless, mouth open.

Theremon was the first to speak. 'You know what this does to this
whole theory you've built up, Sheerin, don't you?' He was grinning
with relief.

But Sheerin raised his hand. 'Now wait a while. Just let me think this
through.' And then he snapped his fingers, and when he lifted his head
there was neither surprise nor uncertainty in his eyes. 'Of course—'

He never finished. From somewhere up above there sounded a
sharp clang, and Beenay, starting to his feet, dashed up the stairs with
a 'What the devil!'

The rest followed after.

Things happened quickly. Once up in the dome, Beenay cast one horrified glance at the shattered photographic plates and at the man bending over them; and then hurled himself fiercely at the intruder, getting a death grip on his throat. There was a wild threshing, and as others of the staff joined in, the stranger was swallowed up and smothered under the weight of half a dozen angry men.

Aton came up last, breathing heavily. 'Let him up!'

There was a reluctant unscrambling and the stranger, panting harshly, with his clothes torn and his forehead bruised, was hauled to his feet. He had a short yellow beard curled elaborately in the style affected by the Cultists. Beenay shifted his hold to a collar grip and shook the man savagely. 'All right, rat, what's the idea? These plates—'

'I wasn't after *them*,' retorted the Cultist coldly. 'That was an accident.'

Beenay followed his glowering stare and snarled, 'I see. You were after the cameras themselves. The accident with the plates was a stroke of luck for you, then. If you had touched Snapping Bertha or any of the others, you would have died by slow torture. As it is—' He drew his fist back.

Aton grabbed his sleeve. 'Stop that! Let him go!'

The young technician wavered, and his arm dropped reluctantly. Aton pushed him aside and confronted the Cultist. 'You're Latimer, aren't you?'

The Cultist bowed stiffly and indicated the symbol upon his hip. I am Latimer 25, adjutant of the third class to his serenity, Sor 5.'

'And'—Aton's white eyebrows lifted—'you were with his serenity when he visited me last week, weren't you?'

Latimer bowed a second time.

'Now, then, what do you want?'

'Nothing that you would give me of your own free will.'

'Sor 5 sent you, I suppose—or is this your own idea?'

'I won't answer that question.'

'Will there be any further visitors?'

'I won't answer that, either.'

Aton glanced at his timepiece and scowled. 'Now, man, what is it your master wants of me? I have fulfilled my end of the bargain.'

Latimer smiled faintly, but said nothing.

'I asked him,' continued Aton angrily, 'for data only the Cult could supply, and it was given to me. For that, thank you. In return I promised to prove the essential truth of the creed of the Cult.'

'There was no need to prove that,' came the proud retort. 'It stands proven by the *Book of Revelations*.'

'For the handful that constitute the Cult, yes. Don't pretend to mistake my meaning. I offered to present scientific backing for your beliefs. And I did!'

The Cultist's eyes narrowed bitterly. 'Yes, you did—with a fox's subtlety, for your pretended explanation backed our beliefs, and at the same time removed all necessity for them. You made of the Darkness and of the Stars a natural phenomenon and removed all its real significance. That was blasphemy.'

'If so, the fault isn't mine. The facts exist. What can I do but state them?'

'Your "facts" are a fraud and a delusion.'

Aton stamped angrily. 'How do you know?'

And the answer came with the certainty of absolute faith. 'I know!'

The director purpled and Beenay whispered urgently. Aton waved him silent. 'And what does Sor 5 want us to do? He still thinks. I suppose, that in trying to warn the world to take measures against the menace of madness, we are placing innumerable souls in jeopardy. We aren't succeeding, if that means anything to him.'

'The attempt itself has done harm enough, and your vicious effort to gain information by means of your devilish instruments must be stopped. We obey the will of the Stars, and I only regret that my clumsiness prevented me from wrecking your infernal devices.'

'It wouldn't have done you too much good,' returned Aton. 'All our data, except for the direct evidence we intend collecting right now, is already safely cached and well beyond possibility of harm.' He smiled grimly. 'But that does not affect your present status as an attempted burglar and criminal.'

He turned to the men behind him. 'Someone call the police at Saro City.'

There was a cry of distaste from Sheerin. 'Damn it, Aton, what's wrong with you? There's no time for that. Here'—he hustled his way forward—'let me handle this.'

Aton stared down his nose at the psychologist. 'This is not the time for your monkeyshines, Sheerin. Will you please let me handle this my own way? Right now you are a complete outsider here, and don't forget it.'

Sheerin's mouth twisted eloquently. 'Now why should we go to the impossible trouble of calling the police—with Beta's eclipse a matter of minutes from now—when this young man here is perfectly willing to pledge his word of honor to remain and cause no trouble whatsoever?'

The Cultist answered promptly, 'I will do no such thing. You're free to do what you want, but it's only fair to warn you that just as soon as I get my chance I'm going to finish what I came out here to do. If it's my word of honor you're relying on, you'd better call the police.'

Sheerin smiled in a friendly fashion. 'You're a determined cuss, aren't you? Well, I'll explain something. Do you see that young man at the window? He's a strong, husky fellow, quite handy with his fists, and he's an outsider besides. Once the eclipse starts there will be nothing for him to do except keep an eye on you. Besides him, there will be myself—a little too stout for active fisticuffs, but still able to help.'

'Well, what of it?' demanded Latimer frozenly.

'Listen and I'll tell you,' was the reply. 'Just as soon as the eclipse starts, we're going to take you, Theremon and I, and deposit you in a little closet with one door, to which is attached one giant lock and no windows. You will remain there for the duration.'

'And afterward,' breathed Latimer fiercely, 'there'll be no one to let me out. I know as well as you do what the coming of the Stars means—I know it far better than you. With all your minds gone, you are not likely to free me. Suffocation or slow starvation, is it? About what I might have expected from a group of scientists. But I don't give my word. It's a matter of principle, and I won't discuss it further.'

Aton seemed perturbed. His faded eyes were troubled.

'Really, Sheerin, locking him—'

'Please!' Sheerin motioned him impatiently to silence. 'I don't think for a moment things will go that far. Latimer has just tried a clever little bluff, but I'm not a psychologist just because I like the sound of the word.' He grinned at the Cultist. 'Come now, you don't really think I'm trying anything as crude as slow starvation. My dear Latimer, if I lock you in the closet, you are not going to see the Darkness, and you are not going to see the Stars. It does not take much knowledge of the fundamental creed of the Cult to realize that for you to be hidden from the Stars when they appear means the loss of your immortal soul. Now, I believe you to be an honorable man. I'll accept your word of honor to make no further effort to disrupt proceedings, if you'll offer it.'

A vein throbbed in Latimer's temple, and he seemed to shrink within himself as he said thickly, 'You have it!' And then he added with swift fury. 'But it is my consolation that you will all be damned for your deeds of today.' He turned on his heel and stalked to the high three-legged stool by the door.

Sheerin nodded to the columnist. 'Take a seat next to him, Theremon—just as a formality. Hey, Theremon!'

But the newspaperman didn't move. He had gone pale to the lips. 'Look at that!' The finger he pointed toward the sky shook, and his voice was dry and cracked.

There was one simultaneous gasp as every eye followed the pointing finger and, for one breathless moment, stared frozenly.

Beta was chipped on one side!

The tiny bit of encroaching blackness was perhaps the width of a fingernail, but to the staring watchers it magnified itself into the crack of doom.

Only for a moment they watched, and after that there was a shrieking confusion that was even shorter of duration and which gave way to an orderly scurry of activity—each man at his prescribed job. At the crucial moment there was no time for emotion. The men were merely scientists with work to do. Even Aton had melted away.

Sheerin said prosaically. 'First contact must have been made fifteen minutes ago. A little early, but pretty good considering the uncertainties involved in the calculation.' He looked about him and then tiptoed to

Theremon, who still remained staring out the window, and dragged him away gently.

'Aton is furious,' he whispered, 'so stay away. He missed first contact on account of this fuss with Latimer, and if you get in his way he'll have you thrown out the window.'

Theremon nodded shortly and sat down. Sheerin stared in surprise at him.

'The devil, man,' he exclaimed, 'you're shaking.'

'Eh?' Theremon licked dry lips and then tried to smile. 'I don't feel very well, and that's a fact.'

The psychologist's eyes hardened. 'You're not losing your nerve?'

'No!' cried Theremon in a flash of indignation. 'Give me a chance, will you? I haven't really believed this rigmarole—not way down beneath, anyway—till just this minute. Give me a chance to get used to the idea.

You've been preparing yourself for two months or more.'

'You're right, at that,' replied Sheerin thoughtfully. 'Listen! Have you got a family—parents, wife, children?'

Theremon shook his head. 'You mean the Hideout, I suppose. No, you don't have to worry about that. I have a sister, but she's two thousand miles away. I don't even know her exact address.'

'Well, then, what about yourself? You've got time to get there, and they're one short anyway, since I left. After all, you're not needed here, and you'd make a darned fine addition—'

Theremon looked at the other wearily. 'You think I'm scared stiff, don't you? Well, get this, mister. I'm a newspaperman and I've been assigned to cover a story. I intend covering it.'

There was a faint smile on the psychologist's face. 'I see.

Professional honor, is that it?'

'You might call it that. But, man. I'd give my right arm for another bottle of that sockeroo juice even half the size of the one you bogged. If ever a fellow needed a drink, I do.'

He broke off. Sheerin was nudging him violently. 'Do you hear that? Listen!'

Theremon followed the motion of the other's chin and stared at the Cultist, who, oblivious to all about him, faced the window, a look of wild elation on his face, droning to himself the while in singsong fashion.

'What's he saying?' whispered the columnist.

'He's quoting *Book of Revelations*, fifth chapter,' replied Sheerin.

Then, urgently, 'Keep quiet and listen, I tell you.'

The Cultist's voice had risen in a sudden increase of fervor: ' "And it came to pass that in those days the Sun, Beta, held lone vigil in the sky for ever longer periods as the revolutions passed; until such time as for full half a revolution, it alone, shrunken and cold, shone down upon Lagash.

' "And men did assemble in the public squares and in the highways, there to debate and to marvel at the sight, for a strange depression had seized them. Their minds were troubled and their speech confused, for the souls of men awaited the coming of the Stars.

' "And in the city of Trigon, at high noon, Vendret 2 came forth and said unto the men of Trigon, 'Lo, ye sinners! Though ye scorn the ways of righteousness, yet will the time of reckoning come. Even now the Cave approaches to swallow Lagash; yea, and all it contains.'

' "And even as he spoke the lip of the Cave of Darkness passed the edge of Beta so that to all Lagash it was hidden from sight. Loud were the cries of men as it vanished, and great the fear of soul that fell upon them.

' "It came to pass that the Darkness of the Cave fell upon Lagash, and there was no light on all the surface of Lagash. Men were even as blinded, nor could one man see his neighbor, though he felt his breath upon his face.

' "And in this blackness there appeared the Stars, in countless numbers, and to the strains of music of such beauty that the very leaves of the trees cried out in wonder.

' "And in that moment the souls of men departed from them, and their abandoned bodies became even as beasts; yea, even as brutes of the wild; so that through the blackened streets of the cities of Lagash they prowled with wild cries.

' "From the Stars there then reached down the Heavenly Flame, and where it touched, the cities of Lagash flamed to utter destruction, so that of man and of the works of man nought remained.

'Even then—"'

There was a subtle change in Latimer's tone. His eyes had not shifted, but somehow he had become aware of the absorbed attention of the other two.

Easily, without pausing for breath, the timbre of his voice shifted and the syllables became more liquid.

Theremon, caught by surprise, stared. The words seemed on the border of familiarity. There was an elusive shift in the accent, a tiny change in the vowel stress; nothing more—yet Latimer had become thoroughly unintelligible.

Sheerin smiled slyly. 'He shifted to some old-cycle tongue, probably their traditional second cycle. That was the language in which the *Book of Revelations* was originally written, you know.'

'It doesn't matter; I've heard enough.' Theremon shoved his chair back and brushed his hair back with hands that no longer shook. 'I feel much better now.'

'You do?' Sheerin seemed mildly surprised.

'I'll say I do. I had a bad case of jitters just a while back.

Listening to you and your gravitation and seeing that eclipse start almost finished me. But this'—he jerked a contemptuous thumb at the yellow-bearded Cultist—'*this* is the sort of thing my nurse used to tell me. I've been laughing at that sort of thing all my life. I'm not going to let it scare me *now*.'

He drew a deep breath and said with a hectic gaiety, 'But if I expect to keep on the good side of myself. I'm going to turn my chair away from the window.'

Sheerin said, 'Yes, but you'd better talk lower. Aton just lifted his head out of that box he's got it stuck into and gave you a look that should have killed you.'

Theremon made a mouth. 'I forgot about the old fellow.' With elaborate care he turned the chair from the window, cast one distasteful look over his shoulder, and said, 'It has occurred to me that there must be considerable immunity against this Star madness.'

The psychologist did not answer immediately. Beta was past its zenith now, and the square of bloody sunlight that outlined the window upon the floor had lifted into Sheerin's lap. He stared at its dusky color thoughtfully and then bent and squinted into the sun itself.

The chip in its side had grown to a black encroachment that covered a third of Beta. He shuddered, and when he straightened once more his florid cheeks did not contain quite as much color as they had had previously.

With a smile that was almost apologetic, he reversed his chair also.

'There are probably two million people in Saro City that are all trying to join the Cult at once in one gigantic revival.' Then, ironically. 'The Cult is in for an hour of unexampled prosperity. I trust they'll make the most of it. Now, what was it you said?'

'Just this. How did the Cultists manage to keep the *Book of Revelations* going from cycle to cycle, and how on Lagash did it get written in the first place? There must have been some sort of immunity, for if everyone had gone mad, who would be left to write the book?'

Sheerin stared at his questioner ruefully. 'Well, now, young man, there isn't any eyewitness answer to that, but we've got a few damned good notions as to what happened. You see. there are three kinds of people who might remain relatively unaffected. First, the very few who don't see the Stars at all: the seriously retarded or those who drink themselves into a stupor at the beginning of the eclipse and remain so to the end. We leave them out—because they aren't really witnesses.

'Then there are children below six, to whom the world as a whole is too new and strange for them to be too frightened at Stars and Darkness. They would be just another item in an already surprising world. You see that, don't you?'

The other nodded doubtfully. 'I suppose so.'

'Lastly, there are those whose minds are too coarsely grained to be entirely toppled. The very insensitive would be scarcely affected—oh, such people as some of our older, work-broken peasants. Well, the children would have fugitive memories, and that, combined with the confused, incoherent babblings of the half-mad morons, formed the basis for the *Book of Revelations*.

'Naturally, the book was based, in the first place, on the testimony of those least qualified to serve as historians; that is, children and morons; and was probably edited and re-edited through the cycles.'

'Do you suppose,' broke in Theremon, 'that they carried the book through the cycles the way we're planning on handing on the secret of gravitation?'

Sheerin shrugged. 'Perhaps, but their exact method is unimportant. They do it, somehow. The point I was getting at was that the book can't help but be a mass of distortion, even if it is based on fact. For instance, do you remember the experiment with the holes in the roof that Faro and Yimot tried—the one that didn't work?'

'Yes.'

'You know why it didn't w—' He stopped and rose in alarm, for Aton was approaching, his face a twisted mask of consternation. *'What's happened?'*

Aton drew him aside and Sheerin could feel the fingers on his elbow twitching.

'Not so loud!' Aton's voice was low and tortured. 'I've just gotten word from the Hideout on the private line.'

Sheerin broke in anxiously. 'They are in trouble?'

'Not *they.*' Aton stressed the pronoun significantly. 'They sealed themselves off just a while ago, and they're going to stay buried till day after tomorrow. They're safe. But the *city.* Sheerin—it's a shambles. You have no idea—' He was having difficulty in speaking.

'Well?' snapped Sheerin impatiently. 'What of it? It will get worse.

What are you shaking about?' Then, suspiciously, 'How do you feel?'

Aton's eyes sparked angrily at the insinuation, and then faded to anxiety once more. 'You don't understand. The Cultists are active. They're rousing the people to storm the Observatory—promising them immediate entrance into grace, promising them salvation, promising them anything. What are we to do, Sheerin?'

Sheerin's head bent, and he stared in long abstraction at his toes. He tapped his chin with one knuckle, then looked up and said crisply, 'Do? What is there to do? Nothing at all. Do the men know of this?'

'No, of course not!'

'Good! Keep it that way. How long till totality?'

'Not quite an hour.'

'There's nothing to do but gamble. It will take time to organize any really formidable mob, and it will take more time to get them out here.

We're a good five miles from the city—'

He glared out the window, down the slopes to where the farmed patches gave way to clumps of white houses in the suburbs; down to where the metropolis itself was a blur on the horizon—a mist in the waning blaze of Beta.

He repeated without turning. 'It will take time. Keep on working and pray that totality comes first.'

Beta was cut in half, the line of division pushing a slight concavity into the still-bright portion of the Sun. It was like a gigantic eyelid shutting slantwise over the light of a world.

The faint clatter of the room in which he stood faded into oblivion, and he sensed only the thick silence of the fields outside. The very insects seemed frightened mute. And things were dim.

He jumped at the voice in his ear. Theremon said. 'Is something wrong?'

'Eh? Er—no. Get back to the chair. We're in the way.' They slipped back to their comer, but the psychologist did not speak for a time. He lifted a finger and loosened his collar. He twisted his neck back and forth but found no relief. He looked up suddenly.

'Are you having any difficulty in breathing?'

The newspaperman opened his eyes wide and drew two or three long breaths. 'No. Why?'

'I looked out the window too long, I suppose. The dimness got me.

Difficulty in breathing is one of the first symptoms of a claustrophobic attack. '

Theremon drew another long breath. 'Well, it hasn't got me yet. Say, here's another of the fellows.'

Beenay had interposed his bulk between the light and the pair in the corner, and Sheerin squinted up at him anxiously. 'Hello, Beenay.'

The astronomer shifted his weight to the other foot and smiled feebly.

'You won't mind if I sit down awhile and join in the talk? My cameras are set, and there's nothing to do till totality.' He paused and eyed the

Cultist, who fifteen minutes earlier had drawn a small, skin-bound book from his sleeve and had been poring intently over it ever since.

'That rat hasn't been making trouble, has he?'

Sheerin shook his head. His shoulders were thrown back and he frowned his concentration as he forced himself to breathe regularly. He said, 'Have you had any trouble breathing, Beenay?'

Beenay sniffed the air in his turn. 'It doesn't seem stuffy to me.'

'A touch of claustrophobia,' explained Sheerin apologetically.

'Ohhh! It worked itself differently with me. I get the impression that my eyes are going back on me. Things seem to blur and—well, nothing is clear. And it's cold, too.'

'Oh, it's cold, all right. That's no illusion.' Theremon grimaced. 'My toes feel as if I've been shipping them cross-country in a refrigerating car.'

'What we need,' put in Sheerin, 'is to keep our minds busy with extraneous affairs. I was telling you a while ago, Theremon, why Faro's experiments with the holes in the roof came to nothing.'

'You were just beginning,' replied Theremon. He encircled a knee with both arms and nuzzled his chin against it.

'Well, as I started to say, they were misled by taking the *Book of Revelations* literally. There probably wasn't any sense in attaching any physical significance to the Stars. It might be, you know, that in the presence of total Darkness, the mind finds it absolutely necessary to create light. This illusion of light might be all the Stars there really are.'

'In other words,' interposed Theremon, 'you mean the Stars are the results of the madness and not one of the causes. Then, what good will

Beenay's photographs be?'

'To prove that it is an illusion, maybe; or to prove the opposite; for all I know. Then again—'

But Beenay had drawn his chair closer, and there was an expression of sudden enthusiasm on his face. 'Say, I'm glad you two got onto this subject.' His eyes narrowed and he lifted one finger. 'I've been thinking about these Stars and I've got a really cute notion. Of course it's strictly ocean foam, and I'm not trying to advance it seriously, but I think it's interesting. Do you want to hear it?'

He seemed half reluctant, but Sheerin leaned back and said, 'Go ahead!

I'm listening.'

'Well, then, supposing there were other suns in the universe.' He broke off a little bashfully. 'I mean suns that are so far away that they're too dim to see. It sounds as if I've been reading some of that fantastic fiction, I suppose.'

'Not necessarily. Still, isn't that possibility eliminated by the fact that, according to the Law of Gravitation, they would make themselves evident by their attractive forces?'

'Not if they were far enough off,' rejoined Beenay, 'really far off—maybe as much as four light years, or even more. We'd never be able to detect perturbations then, because they'd be too small. Say that there were a lot of suns that far off; a dozen or two, maybe.'

Theremon whistled melodiously. 'What an idea for a good Sunday supplement article. Two dozen suns in a universe eight light years across.

Wow! That would shrink our world into insignificance. The readers would eat it up.'

'Only an idea,' said Beenay with a grin, 'but you see the point. During an eclipse, these dozen suns would become visible because there'd be no *real* sunlight to drown them out. Since they're so far off, they'd appear small, like so many little marbles. Of course the Cultists talk of millions of

Stars, but that's probably exaggeration. There just isn't any place in the universe you could put a million suns—unless they touch one another.'

Sheerin had listened with gradually increasing interest. 'You've hit something there, Beenay. And exaggeration is just exactly what would happen.

Our minds, as you probably know, can't grasp directly any number higher than five; above that there is only the concept of "many". A dozen would become a million just like that. A damn good idea!'

'And I've got another cute little notion,' Beenay said. 'Have you ever thought what a simple problem gravitation would be if only you had a sufficiently simple system? Supposing you had a universe in which there was a planet with only one sun. The planet would travel in a perfect ellipse and the exact nature of the gravitational force would be so evident it could be accepted as an axiom. Astronomers on such a world would start off with gravity probably before they even invented the telescope. Naked-eye observation would be enough.'

'But would such a system be dynamically stable?' questioned Sheerin doubtfully.

'Sure! They call it the "one-and-one" case. It's been worked out mathematically, but it's the philosophical implications that interest me.'

'It's nice to think about,' admitted Sheerin, 'as a pretty abstraction— like a perfect gas, or absolute zero.'

'Of course,' continued Beenay, 'there's the catch that life would be impossible on such a planet. It wouldn't get enough heat and light, and if it rotated there would be total Darkness half of each day. You couldn't expect life—which is fundamentally dependent upon light—to develop under those conditions. Besides—'

Sheerin's chair went over backward as he sprang to his feet in a rude interruption. 'Aton's brought out the lights.'

Beenay said, 'Huh,' turned to stare, and then grinned halfway around his head in open relief.

There were half a dozen foot-long, inch-thick rods cradled in Aton's arms. He glared over them at the assembled staff members.

'Get back to work, all of you. Sheerin, come here and help me!'

Sheerin trotted to the older man's side and, one by one, in utter silence, the two adjusted the rods in makeshift metal holders suspended from the walls.

With the air of one carrying through the most sacred item of a religious ritual, Sheerin scraped a large, clumsy match into spluttering life and passed it to Aton, who carried the flame to the upper end of one of the rods.

It hesitated there awhile, playing futilely about the tip, until a sudden, crackling flare cast Aton's lined face into yellow highlights. He withdrew the match and a spontaneous cheer rattled the window.

The rod was topped by six inches of wavering flame! Methodically, the other rods were lighted, until six independent fires turned the rear of the room yellow.

The light was dim, dimmer even than the tenuous sunlight. The flames reeled crazily, giving birth to drunken, swaying shadows. The torches smoked devilishly and smelled like a bad day in the kitchen. But they emitted yellow light.

There was something about yellow light, after four hours of somber, dimming Beta. Even Latimer had lifted his eyes from his book and stared in wonder.

Sheerin warmed his hands at the nearest, regardless of the soot that gathered upon them in a fine, gray powder, and muttered ecstatically to himself. 'Beautiful! Beautiful! I never realized before what a wonderful color yellow is.'

But Theremon regarded the torches suspiciously. He wrinkled his nose at the rancid odor and said, 'What are those things?'

'Wood,' said Sheerin shortly.

'Oh, no, they're not. They aren't burning. The top inch is charred and the flame just keeps shooting up out of nothing.'

'That's the beauty of it. This is a really efficient artificial-light mechanism. We made a few hundred of them, but most went to the Hideout, of course. You see'—he turned and wiped his blackened hands upon his handkerchief—'you take the pithy core of coarse water reeds, dry them thoroughly, and soak them in animal grease. Then you set fire to it and the grease burns, little by little. These torches will burn for almost half an hour without stopping. Ingenious, isn't it? It was developed by one of our own young men at Saro University.'

After the momentary sensation, the dome had quieted. Latimer had carried his chair directly beneath a torch and continued reading, lips moving in the monotonous recital of invocations to the Stars. Beenay had drifted away to his cameras once more, and Theremon seized the opportunity to add to his notes on the article he was going to write for the Saro City *Chronicle* the next day—a procedure he had been following for the last two hours in a perfectly methodical, perfectly conscientious and, as he was well aware, perfectly meaningless fashion. But, as the gleam of amusement in Sheerin's eyes indicated, careful note-taking occupied his mind with something other than the fact that the sky was gradually turning a horrible deep purple-red, as if it were one gigantic, freshly peeled beet; and so it fulfilled its purpose.

The air grew, somehow, denser. Dusk, like a palpable entity, entered the room, and the dancing circle of yellow light about the torches etched itself into ever-sharper distinction against the gathering grayness beyond.

There was the odor of smoke and the presence of little chuckling sounds that the torches made as they burned; the soft pad of one of the men circling the table at which he worked, on hesitant tiptoes; the occasional indrawn breath of someone trying to retain composure in a world that was retreating into the shadow.

It was Theremon who first heard the extraneous noise. It was a vague, unorganized *impression* of sound that would have gone unnoticed but for the dead silence that prevailed within the dome.

The newsman sat upright and replaced his notebook. He held his breath and listened; then, with considerable reluctance, threaded his way between the solarscope and one of Beenay's cameras and stood before the window.

The silence ripped to fragments at his startled shout: '*Sheerin!*'

Work stopped! The psychologist was at his side in a moment. Aton joined him. Even Yimot 70, high in his little lean-back seat at the eyepiece of the gigantic solarscope, paused and looked downward.

Outside, Beta was a mere smoldering splinter, taking one last desperate look at Lagash. The eastern horizon, in the direction of the city, was lost in Darkness, and the road from Saro to the Observatory was a dull-red line bordered on both sides by wooded tracts, the trees of which had somehow lost individuality and merged into a continuous shadowy mass.

But it was the highway itself that held attention, for along it there surged another, and infinitely menacing, shadowy mass.

Aton cried in a cracked voice, 'The madmen from the city! They've come!'

'How long to totality?' demanded Sheerin.

'Fifteen minutes, but . . . but they'll be here in five.'

'Never mind, keep the men working. We'll hold them off. This place is built like a fortress. Aton, keep an eye on our young Cultist just for luck. Theremon, come with me.'

Sheerin was out the door, and Theremon was at his heels. The stairs stretched below them in tight, circular sweeps about the central shaft, fading into a dank and dreary grayness.

The first momentum of their rush had carried them fifty feet down, so that the dim, flickering yellow from the open door of the dome had disappeared and both above and below the same dusky shadow crushed in upon them.

Sheerin paused, and his pudgy hand clutched at his chest. His eyes bulged and his voice was a dry cough. 'I can't . . . breathe . . . Go down . . . yourself. Close all doors—'

Theremon took a few downward steps, then turned.

'Wait! Can you hold out a minute?' He was panting himself. The air passed in and out his lungs like so much molasses, and there was a little germ of screeching panic in his mind at the thought of making his way into the mysterious Darkness below by himself.

Theremon, after all, was afraid of the dark!

'Stay here,' he said. I'll be back in a second.' He dashed upward two steps at a time, heart pounding—not altogether from the exertion—tumbled into the dome and snatched a torch from its holder. It was foul-smelling, and the smoke smarted his eyes almost blind, but he clutched that torch as if he wanted to kiss it for joy, and its flame streamed backward as he hurtled down the stairs again.

Sheerin opened his eyes and moaned as Theremon bent over him. Theremon shook him roughly. 'All right, get a hold on yourself. We've got light.'

He held the torch at tiptoe height and, propping the tottering psychologist by an elbow, made his way downward in the middle of the protecting circle of illumination.

The offices on the ground floor still possessed what light there was, and Theremon felt the horror about him relax.

'Here,' he said brusquely, and passed the torch to Sheerin. 'You can hear *them* outside.'

And they could. Little scraps of hoarse, wordless shouts.

But Sheerin was right; the Observatory was built like a fortress.

Erected in the last century, when the neo-Gavottian style of architecture was at its ugly height, it had been designed for stability and durability rather than for beauty.

The windows were protected by the grillwork of inch-thick iron bars sunk deep into the concrete sills. The walls were solid masonry that an earthquake couldn't have touched, and the main door was a huge oaken slab rein—forced with iron. Theremon shot the bolts and they slid shut with a dull clang.

At the other end of the corridor, Sheerin cursed weakly. He pointed to the lock of the back door which had been neatly jimmied into uselessness.

'That must be how Latimer got in,' he said.

'Well, don't stand there,' cried Theremon impatiently. 'Help drag up the furniture—and keep that torch out of my eyes. The smoke's killing me.'

He slammed the heavy table up against the door as he spoke, and in two minutes had built a barricade which made up for what it lacked in beauty and symmetry by the sheer inertia of its massiveness.

Somewhere, dimly, far off, they could hear the battering of naked fists upon the door; and the screams and yells from outside had a sort of half reality.

That mob had set off from Saro City with only two things in mind: the attainment of Cultist salvation by the destruction of the Observatory, and a maddening fear that all but paralyzed them. There was no time to think of ground cars, or of weapons, or of leadership, or even of organization. They made for the Observatory on foot and assaulted it with bare hands.

And now that they were there, the last flash of Beta, the last ruby-red drop of flame, flickered feebly over a humanity that had left only stark, universal fear!

Theremon groaned, 'Let's get back to the dome!'

In the dome, only Yimot, at the solarscope, had kept his place. The rest were clustered about the cameras, and Beenay was giving his instructions in a hoarse, strained voice.

'Get it straight, all of you. I'm snapping Beta just before totality and changing the plate. That will leave one of you to each camera. You all know about . . . about times of exposure—'

There was a breathless murmur of agreement.

Beenay passed a hand over his eyes. 'Are the torches still burning?

Never mind, I see them!' He was leaning hard against the back of a chair.

'Now remember, don't. . . don't try to look for good shots. Don't waste time trying to get t-two stars at a time in the scope field. One is enough. And . . . and if you feel yourself going, *get away from the camera.*'

At the door, Sheerin whispered to Theremon, 'Take me to Aton. I don't see him.'

The newsman did not answer immediately. The vague forms of the astronomers wavered and blurred, and the torches overhead had become only yellow splotches.

'It's dark,' he whimpered.

Sheerin held out his hand. 'Aton.' He stumbled forward. 'Aton!'

Theremon stepped after and seized his arm. 'Wait, I'll take you.'

Somehow he made his way across the room. He closed his eyes against the Darkness and his mind against the chaos within it.

No one heard them or paid attention to them. Sheerin stumbled against the wall. 'Aton!'

The psychologist felt shaking hands touching him, then withdrawing, a voice muttering, 'Is that you, Sheerin?'

'Aton!' He strove to breathe normally. 'Don't worry about the mob. The place will hold them off.'

Latimer, the Cultist, rose to his feet, and his face twisted in desperation. His word was pledged, and to break it would mean placing his soul in mortal peril. Yet that word had been forced from him and had not been given freely. The Stars would come soon! He could not stand by and allow—And yet his word was pledged.

Beenay's face was dimly flushed as it looked upward at Beta's last ray, and Latimer, seeing him bend over his camera, made his decision. His nails cut the flesh of his palms as he tensed himself.

He staggered crazily as he started his rush. There was nothing before him but shadows; the very floor beneath his feet lacked substance. And then someone was upon him and he went down with clutching fingers at his throat.

He doubled his knee and drove it hard into his assailant. 'Let me up or I'll kill you.'

Theremon cried out sharply and muttered through a blinding haze of pain. 'You double-crossing rat!'

The newsman seemed conscious of everything at once. He heard Beenay croak, 'I've got it. At your cameras, men!' and then there was the strange awareness that the last thread of sunlight had thinned out and snapped.

Simultaneously he heard one last choking gasp from Beenay, and a queer little cry from Sheerin, a hysterical giggle that cut off in a rasp—and a sudden silence, a strange, deadly silence from outside.

And Latimer had gone limp in his loosening grasp. Theremon peered into the Cultist's eyes and saw the blankness of them, staring upward, mirroring the feeble yellow of the torches. He saw the bubble of froth upon Latimer's lips and heard the low animal whimper in Latimer's throat.

With the slow fascination of fear, he lifted himself on one arm and turned his eyes toward the blood-curdling blackness of the window.

Through it shone the Stars!

Not Earth's feeble thirty-six hundred Stars visible to the eye; Lagash was in the center of a giant cluster. Thirty thousand mighty suns shone down in a soul-searing splendor that was more frighteningly cold in its awful indifference than the bitter wind that shivered across the cold, horribly bleak world.

Theremon staggered to his feet, his throat, constricting him to breathlessness, all the muscles of his body writhing in an intensity of terror and sheer fear beyond bearing. He was going mad and knew it, and somewhere deep inside a bit of sanity was screaming, struggling to fight off the hopeless flood of black terror. It was very horrible to go mad and know that you were going mad—to know that in a little minute you would be here physically and yet all the real essence would be dead and drowned in the black madness. For this was the Dark—the Dark and the Cold and the Doom.

The bright walls of the universe were shattered and their awful black fragments were falling down to crush and squeeze and obliterate him.

He jostled someone crawling on hands and knees, but stumbled somehow over him. Hands groping at his tortured throat, he limped toward the flame of the torches that filled all his mad vision.

'Light!' he screamed.

Aton, somewhere, was crying, whimpering horribly like a terribly frightened child. 'Stars—all the Stars—we didn't know at all. We didn't know anything. We thought six stars in a universe is something the Stars didn't notice is Darkness forever and ever and ever and the walls are breaking in and we didn't know we couldn't know and anything—'

Someone clawed at the torch, and it fell and snuffed out. In the instant, the awful splendor of the indifferent Stars leaped nearer to them.

On the horizon outside the window, in the direction of Saro City, a crimson glow began growing, strengthening in brightness, that was not the glow of a sun.

The long night had come again.

16

Jean-Paul Sartre

No Exit

CHARACTERS IN THE PLAY:
the VALET, GARCIN, ESTELLE, and INEZ

SCENE: A drawing-room in Second Empire style. A massive bronze ornament stands on the mantelpiece.

GARCIN [*enters, accompanied by the* ROOM-VALET, *and glances around him*]: Hm! So here we are?

VALET: Yes, Mr. Garcin.

GARCIN: And this is what it looks like?

VALET: Yes.

GARCIN: Second Empire furniture, I observe. . . . Well, well, I dare say one gets used to it in time.

VALET: Some do, some don't.

GARCIN: Are all the rooms like this one?

VALET: How could they be? We cater for all sorts: Chinamen and Indians, for instance. What use would they have for a Second Empire chair?

GARCIN: And what use do you suppose I have for one? Do you know who I was? . . .Oh, well, it's no great matter. And, to tell the truth, I had quite a habit of living among furniture that I didn't relish, and in false positions. I'd even come to like it. A false position in a Louis-Philippe dining room—you know the style?—well, that had its points, you know. Bogus in bogus, so to speak.

VALET: And you'll find that living in a Second Empire drawing-room has its points.

GARCIN: Really? . . .Yes, yes, I dare say. . . . [*He takes another look around.*] Still I certainly didn't expect—this! You know what they tell us down there?

VALET: What about?

GARCIN: About [*makes a sweeping gesture*] this—er—residence.

VALET: Really, sir, how could you believe such cock-and-bull stories? Told by people who'd never set foot here. For, of course, if they had—

GARCIN: Quite so. [*Both laugh. Abruptly the laugh dies from* GARCIN'S *face.*] But I say, where are the instruments of torture?

VALET: The what?

GARCIN: The racks and red-hot pincers and all the other paraphernalia?

VALET: Ah, you must have your little joke, sir.

GARCIN: My little joke? Oh, I see. No, I wasn't joking. [*A short silence. He strolls round the room.*] No mirrors, I notice. No windows. Only to be expected. And nothing breakable. [*Bursts out angrily.*] But damn it all, they might have left me my toothbrush!

VALET: That's good! So you haven't yet got over your—what-do-you-call-it?—sense of human dignity? Excuse me smiling.

GARCIN [*thumping ragefully the arm of an armchair*]: I'll ask you to be more polite. I quite realize the position I'm in, but I won't tolerate . . .

VALET: Sorry, sir. No offense meant. But all our guests ask me the same questions. Silly questions, if you'll pardon my saying so. Where's the torture-chamber? That's the first thing they ask, all of them. They don't bother their heads about the bathroom requisites, that I can assure you. But after a bit, when they've got their nerve back, they start in about their toothbrushes and what-not. Good heavens, Mr. Garcin, can't you use your brains? What, I ask you, would be the point of brushing your teeth?

GARCIN [*more calmly*]: Yes, of course you're right. [*He looks around again.*] And why should one want to see oneself in a looking-glass? But that bronze contraption on the mantelpiece, that's another story. I suppose there will be times when I stare my eyes out at it. Stare my eyes out—see what I mean? . . . All right, let's put our cards on the table. I assure you I'm quite conscious of my position. Shall I tell you what it feels like? A man's drowning, choking, sinking by inches, till only his eyes are just above water. And what does he see? A bronze atrocity by—what's the fellow's name?—Barbedienne. A collector's piece. As in a nightmare. That's their idea, isn't it? . . . No, I suppose you're under orders not to answer questions; and I won't insist. But don't forget, my man, I've a good notion of what's coming to me, so don't you boast you've caught me off my guard. I'm facing the situation, facing it. [*He starts pacing the room again.*] So that's that; no toothbrush. And no bed, either. One never sleeps, I take it?

VALET: That's so.

GARCIN: Just as I expected. *Why* should one sleep? A sort of drowsiness steals on you, tickles you behind the ears, and you feel your eyes closing—but why sleep? You lie down on the sofa and—in a flash, sleep flies away. Miles and miles away. So you rub your eyes, get up, and it starts all over again.

VALET: Romantic, that's what you are.

GARCIN: Will you keep quiet, please! . . . I won't make a scene, I shan't be sorry for myself, I'll face the situation, as I said just now. Face it fairly and squarely. I won't have it springing at me from behind, before I've time to size it up. And you call that being "romantic!" . . . So it comes to this; one doesn't need rest. Why bother about sleep if one isn't sleepy? That stands to reason, doesn't it? Wait a minute, there's a snag somewhere; something disagreeable. Why, now, should it be disagreeable? . . . Ah, I see; it's life without a break.

VALET: What are you talking about?

GARCIN: Your eyelids. We move ours up and down. Blinking, we call it. It's like a small black shutter that clicks down and makes a break. Everything goes black; one's eyes are moistened. You can't imagine how restful, refreshing, it is. Four thousand little rests per hour. Four thousand little respites—just think! . . . So that's the idea. I'm to live without eyelids. Don't act the fool, you know what I mean. No eyelids, no sleep; it follows, doesn't it? I shall never sleep again. But then—how shall I endure my own company? Try to understand. You see, I'm fond of teasing, it's a second nature with me—and I'm used to teasing myself. Plaguing myself, if you prefer; I don't tease nicely. But I can't go on doing that without a break. Down there I had my nights. I slept. I always had good nights. By way of compensation, I suppose. And happy little dreams. There was a green field. Just an ordinary field. I used to stroll in it. . . . Is it daytime now?

VALET: Can't you see? The lights are on.

GARCIN: Ah, yes, I've got it. It's *your* daytime. And outside?

VALET: Outside?

GARCIN: Damn it, you know what I mean. Beyond that wall.

VALET: There's a passage.

GARCIN: And at the end of the passage?

VALET: There's more rooms, more passages, and stairs.

GARCIN: And what lies beyond them?

VALET: That's all.

GARCIN: But surely you have a day off sometimes. Where do you go?

VALET: To my uncle's place. He's the head valet here. He has a room on the third floor.

GARCIN: I should have guessed as much. Where's the light-switch?

VALET: There isn't any.

GARCIN: What? Can't one turn off the light?

VALET: Oh, the management can cut off the current if they want to. But I can't remember their having done so on this floor. We have all the electricity we want.

GARCIN: So one has to live with one's eyes open all the time?

VALET: To *live*, did you say?

GARCIN: Don't let's quibble over words. With one's eyes open. Forever. Always broad daylight in my eyes—and in my head. [*Short silence.*] And suppose I took that contraption on the mantelpiece and dropped it on the lamp—wouldn't it go out?

VALET: You can't move it. It's too heavy.

GARCIN [*seizing the bronze ornament and trying to lift it*]: You're right. It's too heavy. [*A short silence follows.*]

VALET: Very well, sir, if you don't need me any more, I'll be off.

GARCIN: What? You're going? [*The VALET goes up to the door.*] Wait. [VALET *looks around.*] That's a bell, isn't it? [VALET *nods.*] And if I ring, you're bound to come?

VALET: Well, yes, that's so—in a way. But you can never be sure about that bell. There's something wrong with the wiring, and it doesn't always work. [GARCIN *goes to the bell-push and presses the button. A bell purrs outside.*]

GARCIN: It's working all right.

VALET [*looking surprised*]: So it is. [*He, too, presses the button.*] But I shouldn't count on it too much if I were you. It's—capricious. Well, I really must go now. [GARCIN *makes a gesture to detain him.*] Yes, sir?

GARCIN: No, never mind. [*He goes to the mantel piece and picks up a paper-knife.*] What's this?

VALET: Can't you see? An ordinary paper-knife.

GARCIN: Are there books here?

VALET: No.

GARCIN: Then what's the use of this? [VALET *shrugs his shoulders.*] Very well. You can go. [VALET *goes out.*]

[GARCIN *is by himself. He goes to the bronze ornament and strokes it reflectively. He sits down; then gets up, goes to the bell-push, and presses the button. The bell remains silent. He tries two or three times, without success. Then he tries to open the door, also without success. He calls the* VALET *several times, but gets no result. He beats the door with his fists, still calling. Suddenly he grows calm and sits down again. At the same moment the door opens and* INEZ *enters, followed by the* VALET]

VALET: Did you call, sir?

GARCIN [*on the point of answering "Yes"—but then his eyes fall on* INEZ]: No.

VALET [*turning to* INEZ]: This is your room, madam. [INEZ *says nothing.*] If there's any information you require—? [INEZ *still keeps silent, and the* VALET *looks slightly huffed.*] Most of our guests have quite a lot to ask me. But I won't insist. Anyhow, as regards the toothbrush, and the electric bell, and that thing on the mantelshelf, this gentleman can tell you anything you want to know as well as I could. We've had a little chat, him and me. [VALET *goes out.*] [GARCIN *refrains from looking at* INEZ, *who is inspecting the room. Abruptly she turns to* GARCIN.]

INEZ: Where's Florence? [GARCIN *does not reply.*] Didn't you hear? I asked you about Florence. Where is she?

GARCIN: I haven't an idea.

INEZ: Ah, that's the way it works, is it? Torture by separation. Well, as far as I'm concerned, you won't get anywhere. Florence was a tiresome little fool, and I shan't miss her in the least.

GARCIN: I beg your pardon. Who do you suppose I am?

INEZ: You? Why, the torturer, of course.

GARCIN [*looks startled, then bursts out laughing*]: Well, that's a good one! Too comic for words. I the torturer! So you came in, had a look at me, and thought I was—er—one of the staff. Of course, it's that silly fellow's fault; he should have introduced us. A torturer indeed! I'm Joseph Garcin, journalist and man of letters by profession. And as we're both in the same boat, so to speak, might I ask you, Mrs.—?

INEZ [*testily*]: Not "Mrs." I'm unmarried.

GARCIN: Right. That's a start, anyway. Well, now that we've broken the ice, do you *really* think I look like a torturer? And, by the way, how does one recognize torturers when one sees them? Evidently you've ideas on the subject.

INEZ: They look frightened.

GARCIN: Frightened! But how ridiculous! Of whom should they be frightened? Of their victims?

INEZ: Laugh away, but I know what I'm talking about. I've often watched my face in the glass.

GARCIN: In the glass? [*He looks around him.*] How beastly of them! They've removed everything in the least resembling a glass. [*Short silence.*] Anyhow, I can assure you I'm not frightened. Not that I take my position lightly; I realize its gravity only too well. But I'm not afraid.

INEZ [*shrugging her shoulders*]: That's your affair. [*Silence.*] Must you be here all the time, or do you take a stroll outside, now and then?

GARCIN: The door's locked.

INEZ: Oh! . . . That's too bad.

GARCIN: I can quite understand that it bores you having me here. And I too—well, quite frankly, I'd rather be alone. I want to think things out, you know; to set my life in order, and one does that better by oneself. But I'm sure we'll manage to pull along together somehow. I'm no talker, I don't move much; in fact I'm a peaceful sort of fellow. Only, if I may venture on a suggestion, we should make a point of being extremely courteous to each other. That will ease the situation for us both.

INEZ: I'm not polite.

GARCIN: Then I must be polite for two.

[*A longish silence. GARCIN is sitting on a sofa, while INEZ paces up and down the room.*]

INEZ [*fixing her eyes on him*]: Your mouth!

GARCIN [*as if waking from a dream*]: I beg your pardon.

INEZ: Can't you keep your mouth still? You keep twisting it about all the time. It's grotesque.

GARCIN: So sorry. I wasn't aware of it.

INEZ: That's just what I reproach you with. [GARCIN'S *mouth twitches.*] There you are! You talk about politeness, and you don't even try to control your face. Remember you're not alone; you've no right to inflict the sight of your fear on me.

GARCIN [*getting up and going towards her*]: How about you? Aren't you afraid?

INEZ: What would be the use? There was some point in being afraid *before*, while one still had hope.

GARCIN [*in a low voice*]: There's no more hope—but it's still "before." We haven't yet begun to suffer.

INEZ: That's so. [*A short silence.*] Well? What's going to happen?

GARCIN: I don't know. I'm waiting.

[*Silence again.* GARCIN *sits down and* INEZ *resumes her pacing up and down the room.* GARCIN'S *mouth twitches; after a glance at* INEZ *he buries his face in his hands. Enter* ESTELLE *with the* VALET. ESTELLE *looks at* GARCIN, *whose face is still hidden by his hands.*]

ESTELLE [*to* GARCIN]: No. Don't look up. I know what you're hiding with your hands. I know you've no face left. [GARCIN *removes his hands.*] What! [*A short pause, then, in a tone of surprise*] But I don't know you!

GARCIN: I'm not the torturer, madam.

ESTELLE: I never thought you were. I—I thought someone was trying to play a rather nasty trick on me. [*To the* VALET] Is anyone else coming?

VALET: No, madam. No one else is coming.

ESTELLE: Oh! Then we're to stay by ourselves, the three of us, this gentleman, this lady and myself. [*She starts laughing.*]

GARCIN [*angrily*]: There's nothing to laugh about.

ESTELLE [*still laughing*]: It's those sofas. They're so hideous. And just look how they've been arranged. It makes me think of New Year's Day—when I used to visit that boring old aunt of mine, Aunt Mary. Her house is full of horror like that. . . . I suppose each of us has a sofa of his own. Is that one mine? [*To the* VALET] But you can't expect me to sit on that one. It would be too horrible for words. I'm in pale blue and it's vivid green.

INEZ: Would you prefer mine?

ESTELLE: That claret-colored one, you mean? That's very sweet of you, but really—no, I don't think it'd be so much better. What's the good of worrying, anyhow? We've got to take what comes to us, and I'll stick to the green one. [*Pauses.*] The only one which might do at a pinch, is that gentleman's. [*Another pause.*]

INEZ: Did you hear, Mr. Garcin?

GARCIN [*with a slight start*]: Oh—the sofa, you mean. So sorry. [*He rises.*] Please take it, madam.

ESTELLE: Thanks. [*She takes off her coat and drops it on the sofa. A short silence.*] Well, as we're to live together, I suppose we'd better introduce ourselves. My name's Rigault. Estelle Rigault. [GARCIN *bows and is going to announce his name, but* INEZ *steps in front of him.*]

INEZ: And I'm Inez Serrano. Very pleased to meet you.

GARCIN [*bowing again*]: Joseph Garcin.

VALET: Do you require me any longer?

ESTELLE: No, you can go. I'll ring when I want you.

[*Exit* VALET, *with polite bows to everyone.*]

INEZ: You're very pretty. I wish we'd had some flowers to welcome you with.

ESTELLE: Flowers? Yes, I loved flowers. Only they'd fade so quickly here, wouldn't they? It's so stuffy. Oh, well, the great thing is to keep as cheerful as we can, don't you agree? Of course, you, too, are—

INEZ: Yes. Last week. What about you?

ESTELLE: I'm—quite recent. Yesterday. As a matter of act, the ceremony's not quite over. [*Her tone is natural enough, but she seems to be seeing what she describes.*] The wind's blowing my sister's veil all over the place. She's trying her best to cry. Come, dear! Make another effort. That's better. Two tears, two little tears are twinkling under the black veil. Oh dear! What a sight Olga looks this morning! She's holding my sister's arm, helping her along. She's not crying, and I don't blame her, tears always mess one's face up, don't they? Olga was my bosom friend, you know.

INEZ: Did you suffer much?

ESTELLE: No. I was only half conscious, mostly.

INEZ: What was it?

ESTELLE: Pneumonia. [*In the same tone as before*] It's over now, they're leaving the cemetery. Good-by. Good-by. Quite a crowd they are. My husband's stayed at home. Prostrated with grief, poor man. [*To* INEZ] How about you?

INEZ: The gas stove.

ESTELLE: And you, Mr. Garcin?

GARCIA: Twelve bullets through my chest. [ESTELLE *makes a horrified gesture.*] Sorry! I fear I'm not good company among the dead.

ESTELLE: Please, please don't use that word. It's so—so crude. In terribly bad taste, really. It doesn't mean much, anyhow. Somehow I feel we've never been so much alive as now. If we've absolutely got to mention this—this state of things, I suggest we call ourselves—wait!—absentees. Have you been—been absent for long?

GARCIN: About a month.

ESTELLE: Where do you come from?

GARCIN: From Rio.

ESTELLE: I'm from Paris. Have you anyone left down there?

GARCIN: Yes, my wife. [*In the same tone as* ESTELLE *has been using*] She's waiting at the entrance of the barracks. She comes there every day. But they won't let her in. Now she's trying to peep between the bars. She doesn't yet know I'm—absent, but she suspects it. Now she's going away. She's wearing her black dress. So much the better, she won't need to change. She isn't crying, but she never did cry, anyhow. It's a bright, sunny day and she's like a black shadow creeping down the empty street. Those big tragic eyes of hers—with that martyred look they always had. Oh, how she got on my nerves!

[*A short silence.* GARCIN *sits on the central sofa and buries his head in his hands.*]

INEZ: Estelle!

ESTELLE: Please, Mr. Garcin!

GARCIN: What is it?

ESTELLE: You're sitting on my sofa.

GARCIN: I beg your pardon. [*He gets up.*]

ESTELLE: You looked so—so far away. Sorry I disturbed you.

GARCIN: I was setting my life in order. [INEZ *starts laughing.*] You may laugh but you'd do better to follow my example.

INEZ: No need. My life's in perfect order. It tidied itself up nicely of its own accord. So I needn't bother about it now.

GARCIN: Really? You imagine it's so simple as that. [*He runs his hand over his forehead.*] Whew! How hot it is here! Do you mind if—? [*He begins taking off his coat.*]

ESTELLE: How dare you! [*More gently*] No, please don't. I loathe men in their shirt-sleeves.

GARCIN [*putting on his coat again*]: All right. [*A short pause.*] Of course, I used to spend my nights in the newspaper office, and it was a regular Black Hole, so we never kept our coats on. Stiflingly hot it could be. [*Short pause. In the same tone as previously*] Stifling, that it *is*. It's night now.

ESTELLE: That's so. Olga's undressing; it must be after midnight. How quickly the time passes, on earth!

INEZ: Yes, after midnight. They've sealed up my room. It's dark, pitch-dark, and empty.

GARCIN: They've strung their coats on the backs of the chairs and rolled up their shirt-sleeves above the elbow. The air stinks of men and cigar-smoke. [*A short silence.*] I used to like living among men in their shirt-sleeves.

ESTELLE [*aggressively*]: Well, in that case our tastes differ. That's all it proves. [*Turning to* INEZ] What about you? Do you like men in their shirt-sleeves?

INEZ: Oh, I don't care much for men any way.

ESTELLE [*looking at the other two with a puzzled air*]: Really I can't imagine why they put us three together. It doesn't make sense.

INEZ [*stifling a laugh*]: What's that you said?

ESTELLE: I'm looking at you two and thinking that we're going to live together. . . . It's so absurd. I expected to meet old friends, or relatives.

INEZ: Yes, a charming old friend—with a hole in the middle of his face.

ESTELLE: Yes, him too. He danced the tango so divinely. Like a professional. . . . But why, why should we of all people be put together?

GARCIN: A pure fluke, I should say. They lodge folks as they can, in the order of their coming. [*To* INEZ] Why are you laughing?

INEZ: Because you amuse me with your "flukes." As if they left anything to chance! But I suppose you've got to reassure yourself somehow.

ESTELLE [*hesitantly*]: I wonder, now. Don't you think we may have met each other at some time in our lives?

INEZ: Never. I shouldn't have forgotten you.

ESTELLE: Or perhaps we have friends in common. I wonder if you know the Dubois-Seymours?

INEZ: Not likely.

ESTELLE: But *everyone* went to their parties.

INEZ: What's their job?

ESTELLE: Oh, they don't do anything. But they have a lovely house in the country, and hosts of people visit them.

INEZ: I didn't. I was a post-office clerk.

ESTELLE [*recoiling a little*]: Ah, yes. . . . Of course, in that case—[*A pause.*] And you, Mr. Garcin?

GARCIN: We've never met. I always lived in Rio.

ESTELLE: Then you must be right. It's mere chance that has brought us together.

INEZ: Mere chance? Then it's by chance this room is furnished as we see it. It's an accident that the sofa on the right is a livid green, and that one on the left's wine-red. Mere chance? Well, just try to shift the sofas and you'll see the difference quick enough. And that statue on the mantelpiece, do you think it's there by accident? And what about the heat here? How about that? [*A short silence.*] I tell you they've thought it all out. Down to the last detail. Nothing was left to chance. This room was all set for us.

ESTELLE: But really! Everything here's so hideous; all in angles, so uncomfortable. I always loathed angles.

INEZ [*shrugging her shoulders*]: And do you think *I* lived in a Second Empire drawing-room?

ESTELLE: So it was all fixed up beforehand?

INEZ: Yes. And they've put us together deliberately.

ESTELLE: Then it's not mere chance that *you* precisely are sitting opposite *me*? But what can be the idea behind it?

INEZ: Ask me another! I only know they're waiting.

ESTELLE: I never could bear the idea of anyone's expecting something from me. It always made me want to do just the opposite.

INEZ: Well, do it. Do it if you can. You don't even know what they expect.

ESTELLE [*stamping her foot*]: It's outrageous! So something's coming to me from you two? [*She eyes each in turn.*] Something nasty, I suppose. There are some faces that tell me everything at once. Yours don't convey anything.

GARCIN [*turning abruptly towards* INEZ]: Look here! Why are we together? You've given us quite enough hints, you may as well come out with it.

INEZ [*in a surprised tone*]: But I know nothing, absolutely nothing about it. I'm as much in the dark as you are.

GARCIN: We've *got* to know. [*Ponders for a while.*]

INEZ: If only each of us had the guts to tell—

GARCIN: Tell what?

INEZ: Estelle!

ESTELLE: Yes?

INEZ: What have you done? I mean, why have they sent you here?

ESTELLE [*quickly*]: That's just it. I haven't a notion, not the foggiest. In fact, I'm wondering if there hasn't been some ghastly mistake. [*To* INEZ] Don't smile. Just think of the number of people who—who become absentees every day. There must be thousands and thousands, and probably they're sorted out by—by understrappers, you know what I mean. Stupid employees who don't know their job. So they're bound to make mistakes sometimes. . . . Do stop smiling. [*To*

GARCIN] Why don't you speak? If they made a mistake in my case, they may have done the same about you. [*To* INEZ] And you, too. Anyhow, isn't it better to think we've got here by mistake?

INEZ: Is that all you have to tell me?

ESTELLE: What else should I tell? I've nothing to hide. I lost my parents when I was a kid, and I had my young brother to bring up. We were terribly poor and when an old friend of my people asked me to marry him I said yes. He was very well off, and quite nice. My brother was a very delicate child and needed all sorts of attention, so really that was the right thing for me to do, don't you agree? My husband was old enough to be my father, but for six years we had a happy married life. Then two years ago I met the man I was fated to love. We knew it the moment we set eyes on each other. He asked me to run away with him, and I refused. Then I got pneumonia and it finished me. That's the whole story. No doubt, by certain standards, I did wrong to sacrifice my youth to a man nearly three times my age. [*To* GARCIN] Do *you* think that could be called a sin?

GARCIN: Certainly not. [*A short silence.*] And now, tell me, do you think it's a crime to stand by one's principles?

ESTELLE: Of course not. Surely no one could blame a man for that!

GARCIN: Wait a bit! I ran a pacifist newspaper. Then war broke out. What was I to do? Everyone was watching me, wondering: "Will he dare?" Well, I dared. I folded my arms and they shot me. Had I done anything wrong?

ESTELLE [*laying her hand on his arm*]: Wrong? On the contrary. You were—

INEZ [*breaks in ironically*]:—a hero! And how about your wife, Mr. Garcin?

GARCIN: That's simple. I'd rescued her from—from the gutter.

ESTELLE [*to* INEZ]: You see! You see!

INEZ: Yes, I see. [*A pause.*] Look here! What's the point of play-acting, trying to throw dust in each other's eyes? We're all tarred with the same brush.

ESTELLE [*indignantly*]: How dare you!

INEZ: Yes, we are criminals—murderers—all three of us. We're in hell, my pets; they never make mistakes, and people aren't damned for nothing.

ESTELLE: Stop! For heaven's sake—

INEZ: In hell! Damned souls—that's us, all three!

ESTELLE: Keep quiet! I forbid you to use such disgusting words.

INEZ: A damned soul—that's you, my little plaster saint. And ditto our friend there, the noble pacifist. We've had our hour of pleasure, haven't we? There have been people who burned their lives out for our sakes—and we chuckled over it. So now we have to pay the reckoning.

GARCIN [*raising his fist*]: Will you keep your mouth shut, damn it!

INEZ [*confronting him fearlessly, but with a look of vast surprise*]: Well, well! [*A pause.*] Ah, I understand now. I know why they've put us three together.

GARCIN: I advise you to—to think twice before you say any more.

INEZ: Wait! You'll see how simple it is. Childishly simple. Obviously there aren't any physical torments—you agree, don't you? And yet we're in hell. And no one else will come here. We'll stay in this room together, the three of us, for ever and ever. . . . In short, there's someone absent here, the official torturer.

GARCIN [*sotto voce*]: I'd noticed that.

INEZ: It's obvious what they're after—an economy of man-power—or devil-power, if you prefer. The same idea as in the cafeteria, where customers serve themselves.

ESTELLE: Whatever do you mean?

INEZ: I mean that each of us will act as torturer of the two others.

[*There is a short silence while they digest this information.*]

GARCIN [*gently*]: No, I shall never be your torturer. I wish neither of you any harm, and I've no concern with you. None at all. So the solution's easy enough; each of us stays put in his or her corner and takes no notice of the others. You here, you here, and I there. Like soldiers at our posts. Also, we mustn't speak. Not one word. That won't be difficult; each of us has plenty of material for self-communings. I think I could stay ten thousand years with only my thoughts for company.

ESTELLE: Have *I* got to keep silent, too?

GARCIN: Yes. And that way we—we'll work out our salvation. Looking into ourselves, never raising our heads. Agreed?

INEZ: Agreed.

ESTELLE [*after some hesitation*]: I agree.

GARCIN: Then—good-by.

[INEZ *sings to herself. Meanwhile* ESTELLE *has been plying her powder-puff and lipstick. She looks round for a mirror, fumbles in her bag, then turns toward* GARCIN.]

ESTELLE: Excuse me, have you a glass? [GARCIN *does not answer.*] Any sort of glass, a pocket-mirror will do. [GARCIN *remains silent.*] Even if you won't speak to me, you might lend me a glass.

[*His head still buried in his hands,* GARCIN *ignores her.*]

INEZ [*eagerly*]: Don't worry. I've a glass in my bag. [*She opens her bag. Angrily*] It's gone! They must have taken it from me at the entrance.

ESTELLE: How tiresome!

[*A short silence.* ESTELLE *shuts her eyes and sways, as if about to faint.* INEZ *runs forward and holds her up.*]

INEZ: What's the matter?

ESTELLE [*opens her eyes and smiles*]: I feel so queer. [*She pats herself.*] Don't you ever get taken that way? When I can't see myself I begin to wonder if I really and truly exist. I pat myself just to make sure, but it doesn't help much.

INEZ: You're lucky. I'm always conscious of myself—in my mind. Painfully conscious.

ESTELLE: Ah yes, in your mind. But everything that goes on
in one's head is so vague, isn't it? It makes one want to sleep.
[*She is silent for a while.*] I've six big mirrors in my bedroom.
There they are. I can see them. But they don't see me. They're
reflecting the carpet, the settee, the window—but how empty
it is, a glass in which I'm absent! When I talked to people I
always made sure there was one near by in which I could see
myself. I watched myself talking. And somehow it kept me
alert, seeing myself as the others saw me. . . . Oh dear! My
lipstick! I'm sure I've put it on all crooked. No, I can't do
without a looking-glass for ever and ever. I simply can't.
INEZ: Suppose I try to be your glass? Come and pay me a visit,
dear. Here's a place for you on my sofa.
ESTELLE: But—[*Points to* GARCIN.]
INEZ: Oh, he doesn't count.
ESTELLE: But we're going to—to hurt each other. You said it
yourself.
INEZ: Do I look as if I wanted to hurt you?
ESTELLE: One never can tell.
INEZ: Much more likely *you'll* hurt *me*. Still, what does it matter?
If I've got to suffer, it may as well be at your hands, your pretty
hands. Sit down. Come closer. Closer. Look into my eyes.
What do you see?
ESTELLE: Oh, I'm there! But so tiny I can't see myself properly.
INEZ: But *I* can. Every inch of you. Now ask me questions. I'll
be as candid as any looking-glass.
[ESTELLE *seems rather embarrassed and turns to* GARCIN, *as if appealing
to him for help.*]
ESTELLE: Please, Mr. Garcin. Sure our chatter isn't boring you?
[GARCIN *makes no reply.*]
INEZ: Don't worry about him. As I said, he doesn't count. We're
by ourselves. . . . Ask away.
ESTELLE: Are my lips all right?
INEZ: Show! No, they're a bit smudgy.
ESTELLE: I thought as much. Luckily [*throws a quick glance at*
GARCIN] no one's seen me. I'll try again.

INEZ: That's better. No. Follow the line of your lips. Wait! I'll
guide your hand. There. That's quite good.

ESTELLE: As good as when I came in?

INEZ: Far better. Crueler. Your mouth looks quite diabolical that
way.

ESTELLE: Good gracious! And you say you like it! How
maddening, not being able to see for myself! You're quite sure,
Miss Serrano, that it's all right now?

INEZ: Won't you call me Inez?

ESTELLE: Are you sure it looks all right?

INEZ: You're lovely, Estelle.

ESTELLE: But how can I rely upon your taste? Is it the same
as *my* taste? Oh, how sickening it all is, enough to drive one
crazy!

INEZ: I *have* your taste, my dear, because I like you so much.
Look at me. No, straight. Now smile. I'm not so ugly, either.
Am I not nicer than your glass?

ESTELLE: Oh, I don't know. You scare me rather. My reflection
in the glass never did that; of course, I knew it so well. Like
something I had tamed. . . . I'm going to smile, and my smile
will sink down into your pupils, and heaven knows what it will
become.

INEZ: And why shouldn't you "tame" *me*? [*The women gaze at each
other,* ESTELLE *with a sort of fearful fascination.*] Listen! I want you
to call me Inez. We must be great friends.

ESTELLE: I don't make friends with women very easily.

INEZ: Not with postal clerks, you mean? Hullo, what's that—that
nasty red spot at the bottom of your cheek? A pimple?

ESTELLE: A pimple? Oh, how simply foul! Where!

INEZ: There. . . .You know the way they catch larks—with a
mirror? I'm your lark-mirror, my dear, and you can't escape
me. . . . There isn't any pimple, not a trace of one. So what
about it? Suppose the mirror started telling lies? Or suppose I
covered my eyes—as he is doing—and refused to look at you,
all that loveliness of yours would be wasted on the desert air.
No, don't be afraid, I can't help looking at you. I shan't turn

my eyes away. And I'll be nice to you, ever so nice. Only you must be nice to me, too.

[*A short silence.*]

ESTELLE: Are you really—attracted by me?

INEZ: Very much indeed.

[*Another short silence.*]

ESTELLE [*indicating GARCIN by a slight movement of her head*]: But I wish he'd notice me, too.

INEZ: Of course! Because he's a Man! [*To GARCIN*] You've won. [*GARCIN says nothing.*] But look at her, damn it! [*Still no reply from GARCIN.*] Don't pretend. You haven't missed a word of what we've said.

GARCIN: Quite so; not a word. I stuck my fingers in my ears, but your voices thudded in my brain. Silly chatter. Now will you leave me in peace, you two? I'm not interested in you.

INEZ: Not in me, perhaps—but how about this child? Aren't you interested in her? Oh, I saw through your game; you got on your high horse just to impress her.

GARCIN: I asked you to leave me in peace. There's someone talking about me in the newspaper office and I want to listen. And, if it'll make you any happier, let me tell you that I've no use for the "child," as you call her.

ESTELLE: Thanks.

GARCIN: Oh, I didn't mean it rudely.

ESTELLE: You cad!

[*They confront each other in silence for some moments.*]

GARCIN: So that's that. [*Pause.*] You know I begged you not to speak.

ESTELLE: It's *her* fault; she started. I didn't ask anything of her and she came and offered me her—her glass.

INEZ: So you say. But all the time you were making up to him, trying every trick to catch his attention.

ESTELLE: Well, why shouldn't I?

GARCIN: You're crazy, both of you. Don't you see where this is leading us? For pity's sake, keep your mouths shut. [*Pause.*] Now let's all sit down again quite quietly; we'll look at the floor and each must try to forget the others are there.

[*A longish silence.* GARCIN *sits down. The women return hesitantly to their places. Suddenly* INEZ *swings round on him.*]

INEZ: To forget about the others? How utterly absurd! I *feel* you there, in every pore. Your silence clamors in my ears. You can nail up your mouth, cut your tongue out—but you can't prevent your *being there*. Can you stop your thoughts? I hear them ticking away like a clock, tick-tock, tick-tock, and I'm certain you hear mine. It's all very well skulking on your sofa, but you're everywhere, and every sound comes to me soiled because you've intercepted it on its way. Why, you've even stolen my face; you know it and I don't ! And what about her, about Estelle? You've stolen her from me, too; if she and I were alone do you suppose she'd treat me as she does? No, take your hands from your face, I won't leave you in peace—that would suit your book too well. You'd go on sitting there, in a sort of trance, like a yogi, and even if I didn't see her I'd feel it in my bones—that she was making every sound, even the rustle of her dress, for your benefit, throwing you smiles you didn't see. . . . Well, I won't stand for that, I prefer to choose my hell; I prefer to look you in the eyes and fight it out face to face.

GARCIN: Have it your own way. I suppose we were bound to come to this; they knew what they were about, and we're easy game. If they'd put me in a room with men—men can keep their mouths shut. But it's no use wanting the impossible. [*He goes to* ESTELLE *and lightly fondles her neck.*] So I attract you, little girl? It seems you were making eyes at me?

ESTELLE: Don't touch me.

GARCIN: Why not? We might, anyhow, be natural. . . . Do you know, I used to be mad about women? And some were fond of me. So we may as well stop posing, we've nothing to lose. Why trouble about politeness, and decorum, and the rest of it? We're between ourselves. And presently we shall be naked as—as newborn babes.

ESTELLE: Oh, let me be!

GARCIN: As newborn babes. Well, I'd warned you, anyhow.
I asked so little of you, nothing but peace and a little silence.
I'd put my fingers in my ears. Gomez was spouting away as
usual, standing in the center of the room, with all the pressmen
listening. In their shirt-sleeves. I tried to hear, but it wasn't
easy. Things on earth move so quickly, you know. Couldn't
you have held your tongues? Now it's over, he's stopped
talking, and what he thinks of me has gone back into his head.
Well, we've got to see it through somehow. . . . Naked as we
were born. So much the better; I want to know whom I have
to deal with.

INEZ: You know already. There's nothing more to learn.

GARCIN: You're wrong. So long as each of us hasn't made a
clean breast of it—why they've damned him or her—we know
nothing. Nothing that counts. You, young lady, you shall
begin. Why? Tell us why. If you are frank, if we bring our
specters into the open, it may save us from disaster. So—out
with it! Why?

ESTELLE: I tell you I haven't a notion. They wouldn't tell me
why.

GARCIN: That's so. They wouldn't tell me, either. But I've a
pretty good idea. . . . Perhaps you're shy of speaking first?
Right. I'll lead off. [*A short silence.*] I'm not a very estimable
person.

INEZ: No need to tell us that. We know you were a deserter.

GARCIN: Let that be. It's only a side-issue. I'm here because
I treated my wife abominably. That's all. For five years.
Naturally, she's suffering still. There she is: the moment I
mention her, I see her. It's Gomez who interests me, and it's she
I see. Where's Gomez got to? For five years. There! They've
given her back my things; she's sitting by the window, with
my coat on her knees. The coat with the twelve bullet-holes.
The blood's like rust; a brown ring round each hole. It's quite
a museum-piece, that coat; scarred with history. And I used to
wear it, fancy! . . . Now, can't you shed a tear, my love! Surely
you'll squeeze one out—at last? No? You can't manage it? . . .

Night after night I came home blind drunk, stinking of wine
and women. She'd sat up for me, of course. But she never
cried, never uttered a word of reproach. Only her eyes spoke.
Big, tragic eyes. I don't regret anything. I must pay the price,
but I shan't whine. . . . It's snowing in the street. Won't you
cry, confound you? That woman was a born martyr, you know;
a victim by vocation.

INEZ [*almost tenderly*]: Why did you hurt her like that?

GARCIN: It was so easy. A word was enough to make her flinch.
Like a sensitive-plant. But never, never a reproach. I'm fond of
teasing. I watched and waited. But no, not a tear, not a protest.
I'd picked her up out of the gutter, you understand. . . . Now
she's stroking the coat. Her eyes are shut and she's feeling with
her fingers for the bullet-holes. What are you after? What
do you expect? I tell you I regret nothing. The truth is, she
admired me too much. Does that mean anything to you?

INEZ: No. Nobody admired *me*.

GARCIN: So much the better. So much the better for you.
I suppose all this strikes you as very vague. Well, here's
something you can get your teeth into. I brought a half-caste
girl to stay in our house. My wife slept upstairs; she must have
heard—everything. She was an early riser and, as I and the girl
stayed in bed late, she served us our morning coffee.

INEZ: You brute!

GARCIN: Yes, a brute, if you like. But a well-beloved brute. [*A
far-away look comes to his eyes.*] No, it's nothing. Only Gomez, and
he's not talking about *me*. . . . What were you saying? Yes, a
brute. Certainly. Else why should I be here? [*To* INEZ] Your
turn.

INEZ: Well, I was what some people down there called "a
damned bitch." Damned already. So it's no surprise, being here.

GARCIN: Is that all you have to say?

INEZ: No. There was that affair with Florence. A dead men's
tale. With three corpses to it. He to start with; then she and
I. So there's no one left. I've nothing to worry about; it was a
clean sweep. Only that room. I see it now and then. Empty,

with the doors locked. . . . No, they've just unlocked them. "To Let." It's to let; there's a notice on the door. That's—too ridiculous.

GARCIN: Three. Three deaths, you said?

INEZ: Three.

GARCIN: One man and two women?

INEZ: Yes.

GARCIN: Well, well. [*A pause.*] Did he kill himself?

INEZ: He? No, he hadn't the guts for that. Still, he'd every reason; we led him a dog's life. As a matter of fact, he was run over by a tram. A silly sort of end. . . . I was living with them; he was my cousin.

GARCIN: Was Florence fair?

INEZ: Fair? [*Glances at* ESTELLE.] You know, I don't regret a thing; still, I'm not so very keen on telling you the story.

GARCIN: That's all right. . . . So you got sick of him?

INEZ: Quite gradually. All sorts of little things got on my nerves. For instance, he made a noise when he was drinking—a sort of gurgle. Trifles like that. He was rather pathetic really. Vulnerable. Why are you smiling?

GARCIN: Because I, anyhow, am *not* vulnerable.

INEZ: Don't be too sure. . . . I crept inside her skin, she saw the world through my eyes. When she left him, I had her on my hands. We shared a bed-sitting-room at the other end of the town.

GARCIN: And then?

INEZ: Then that tram did its job. I used to remind her every day: "Yes, my pet, we killed him between us." [*A pause.*] I'm rather cruel, really.

GARCIN: So am I.

INEZ: No, you're not cruel. It's something else.

GARCIN: What?

INEZ: I'll tell you later. When I say I'm cruel, I mean I can't get on without making people suffer. Like a live coal. A live coal in others' hearts. When I'm alone I flicker out. For six months I flamed away in her heart, till there was nothing but a cinder.

One night she got up and turned on the gas while I was asleep. Then she crept back into bed. So now you know.

GARCIN: Well! Well!

INEZ: Yes? What's in your mind?

GARCIN: Nothing. Only that it's not a pretty story

INEZ: Obviously. But what matter?

GARCIN: As you say, what matter? [*To* ESTELLE] Your turn. What have you done?

ESTELLE: As I told you, I haven't a notion. I rack my brain, but it's no use.

GARCIN: Right. Then we'll give you a hand. That fellow with the smashed face, who was he?

ESTELLE: Who—who do you mean?

INEZ: You know quite well. The man you were so scared of seeing when you came in.

ESTELLE: Oh, him! A friend of mine.

GARCIN: Why were you afraid of him?

ESTELLE: That's my business, Mr. Garcin.

INEZ: Did he shoot himself on your account?

ESTELLE: Of course not. How absurd you are!

GARCIN: Then why should you have been so scared? He blew his brains out, didn't he? That's how his face got smashed.

ESTELLE: Don't! Please don't go on.

GARCIN: Because of you. Because of you.

INEZ: He shot himself because of you.

ESTELLE: Leave me alone! It's—it's not fair, bullying me like that. I want to go! I want to go!

[*She runs to the door and shakes it.*]

GARCIN: Go if you can. Personally, I ask for nothing better. Unfortunately the door's locked.

[ESTELLE *presses the bell-push, but the bell does not ring.* INEZ *and* GARCIN *laugh.* ESTELLE *swings round on them, her back to the door.*]

ESTELLE [*in a muffled voice*]: You're hateful, both of you.

INEZ: Hateful? Yes, that's the word. Now get on with it. That fellow who killed himself on your account—you were his mistress, eh?

GARCIN: Of course she was. And he wanted to have her to himself alone. That's so, isn't it?

INEZ: He danced the tango like a professional, but he was poor as a church mouse—that's right, isn't it?

[*A short silence.*]

GARCIN: Was he poor or not? Give a straight answer.

ESTELLE: Yes, he was poor.

GARCIN: And then you had your reputation to keep up. One day he came and implored you to run away with him, and you laughed in his face.

INEZ: That's it. You laughed at him. And so he killed himself.

ESTELLE: Did you use to look at Florence in that way?

INEZ: Yes.

[*A short pause, then* ESTELLE *bursts out laughing.*]

ESTELLE: You've got it all wrong, you two. [*She stiffens her shoulders, still leaning against the door, and faces them. Her voice grows shrill, truculent.*] He wanted me to have a baby. So there!

GARCIN: And you didn't want one?

ESTELLE: I certainly didn't. But the baby came, worse luck. I went to Switzerland for five months. No one knew anything. It was a girl. Roger was with me when she was born. It pleased him no end, having a daughter. It didn't please *me*!

GARCIN: And then?

ESTELLE: There was a balcony overlooking the lake. I brought a big stone. He could see what I was up to and he kept on shouting: "Estelle, for God's sake, don't!" I hated him then. He saw it all. He was leaning over the balcony and he saw the rings spreading on the water—

GARCIN: Yes? And then?

ESTELLE: That's all. I came back to Paris—and he did as he wished.

GARCIN: You mean he blew his brains out?

ESTELLE: It was absurd of him, really, my husband never suspected anything. [*A pause.*] Oh, how I loathe you! [*She sobs tearlessly.*]

GARCIN: Nothing doing. Tears don't flow in this place.

ESTELLE: I'm a coward. A coward! [*Pause.*] If you knew how I hate you!

INEZ [*taking her in her arms*]: Poor child! [*To* GARCIN] So the hearing's over. But there's no need to look like a hanging judge.

GARCIN: A hanging judge? [*He glances around him.*] I'd give a lot to be able to see myself in a glass. [*Pause.*] How hot it is! [*Unthinkingly, he takes off his coat.*] Oh, sorry! [*He starts putting it on again.*]

ESTELLE: Don't bother. You can stay in your shirt-sleeves. As things are—

GARCIN: Just so. [*He drops his coat on the sofa.*] You mustn't be angry with me, Estelle.

ESTELLE: I'm not angry with you.

INEZ: And what about me? Are you angry with me?

ESTELLE: Yes.

[*A short silence.*]

INEZ: Well, Mr. Garcin, now you have us in the nude all right. Do your understand things any better for that?

GARCIN: I wonder. Yes, perhaps a trifle better. [*Timidly*] And now suppose we start trying to help each other.

INEZ: I don't need help.

GARCIN: Inez, they've laid their snare damned cunningly—like a cobweb. If you make any movement, if you raise your hand to fan yourself, Estelle and I feel a little tug. Alone, none of us can save himself or herself; we're linked together inextricably. So you can take your choice. [*Pause.*] Hullo? What's happening?

INEZ: They've let it. The windows are wide open, a man is sitting on my bed. *My* bed, if you please! They've let it, let it! Step in, step in, make yourself at home, you brute! Ah, there's a woman, too. She's going up to him, putting her hands on his shoulders. . . . Damn it, why don't they turn the lights on? It's getting dark. Now he's going to kiss her. But that's my room, *my* room! Pitch-dark now. I can't see anything, but I hear them whispering, whispering. Is he going to make love to her on *my* bed? What's that she said? That it's noon and the sun is

shining? I must be going blind. [*A pause.*] Blacked out. I can't
see or hear a thing. So I'm done with the earth, it seems. No
more alibis for me! [*She shudders.*] I feel so empty, desiccated—
really dead at last. All of me's here, in this room. [*A pause.*]
What were you saying? Something about helping me, wasn't it?
GARCIN: Yes.
INEZ: Helping me to do what?
GARCIN: To defeat their devilish tricks.
INEZ: And what do you expect me to do in return?
GARCIN: To help *me*. It only needs a little effort, Inez; just a
spark of human feeling.
INEZ: Human feeling. That's beyond my range. I'm rotten to the
core.
GARCIN: And how about me? [*A pause.*] All the same, suppose
we try?
INEZ: It's no use. I'm all dried up. I can't give and I can't receive.
How could I help you? A dead twig, ready for the burning. [*She
falls silent, gazing at* ESTELLE, *who has buried her head in her hands.*]
Florence was fair, a natural blonde.
GARCIN: Do your realize that this young woman's fated to be
your torturer?
INEZ: Perhaps I've guessed it.
GARCIN: It's through her they'll get you. I, of course, I'm
different—aloof. I take no notice of her. Suppose you had a
try—
INEZ: Yes?
GARCIN: It's a trap. They're watching you, to see if you'll fall
into it.
INEZ: I know. And you're another trap. Do you think they
haven't foreknown every word you say? And of course there's
a whole nest of pitfalls that we can't see. Everything here's
a booby-trap. But what do I care? I'm a pitfall, too. For her,
obviously. And perhaps I'll catch her.
GARCIN: You won't catch anything. We're chasing after each
other, round and round in a vicious circle, like the horses on
a roundabout. That's part of their plan, of course. . . . Drop it,

Inez. Open your hands and let go of everything. Or else you'll bring disaster on all three of us.

INEZ: Do I look the sort of person who lets go? I know what's coming to me. I'm going to burn, and it's to last forever. Yes, I *know* everything. But do you think I'll let go? I'll catch her, she'll see you through my eyes, as Florence saw that other man. What's the good of trying to enlist my sympathy? I assure you I know everything, and I can't feel sorry even for myself. A trap! Don't I know it, and that I'm in a trap myself, up to the neck, and there's nothing to be done about it? And if it suits their book, so much the better!

GARCIN [*gripping her shoulders*]: Well, *I*, anyhow, can feel sorry for you, too. Look at me, we're naked, naked right through, and I can see into your heart. That's one link between us. Do you think I'd want to hurt you? I don't regret anything, I'm dried up, too. But for you I can still feel pity.

INEZ [*who has let him keep his hands on her shoulders until now, shakes herself loose*]: Don't. I hate being pawed about. And keep your pity for yourself. Don't forget, Garcin, that there are traps for you, too, in this room. All nicely set for you. You'd do better to watch your own interests. [*A pause.*] But, if you will leave us in peace, this child and me, I'll see I don't do you any harm.

GARCIN [*gazes at her for a moment, then shrugs his shoulders*]: Very well.

ESTELLE [*raising her head*]: Please, Garcin.

GARCIN: What do you want of me?

ESTELLE [*rises and goes up to him*]: You can help *me*, anyhow.

GARCIN: If you want help, apply to her.

[INEZ *has come up and is standing behind* ESTELLE, *but without touching her. During the dialogue that follows she speaks almost in her ear. But* ESTELLE *keeps her eyes on* GARCIN, *who observes her without speaking, and she addresses her answers to him, as if it were he who is questioning her.*]

ESTELLE: I implore you, Garcin—you gave me your promise, didn't you? Help me quick. I don't want to be left alone. Olga's taken him to a cabaret.

INEZ: Taken whom?

ESTELLE: Peter. . . .Oh, now they're dancing together.

INEZ: Who's Peter?

ESTELLE: Such a silly boy. He called me his glancing stream—
just fancy! He was terribly in love with me. . . . She's persuaded
him to come out with her tonight.

INEZ: Do you love him?

ESTELLE: They're sitting down now. She's puffing like a
grampus. What a fool the girl is to insist on dancing! But I dare
say she does it to reduce. . . . No, of course I don't love him.
He's only eighteen, and I'm not a baby-snatcher.

INEZ: Then why bother about them? What difference does it
make?

ESTELLE: He belonged to me.

INEZ: Nothing on earth belongs to you any more.

ESTELLE: I tell you he was mine. All mine.

INEZ: Yes, he *was* yours—once. But now—try to make him hear,
try to touch him. Olga can touch him, talk to him as much
as she likes. That's so, isn't it? She can squeeze his hands, rub
herself against him—

ESTELLE: Yes, look! She's pressing her great fat chest against
him, puffing and blowing his face. But, my poor little lamb,
can't you see how ridiculous she is? Why don't you laugh at
her? Oh, once I'd have only had to glance at them and she'd
have slunk away. Is there really nothing, nothing left of me?

INEZ: Nothing whatever. Nothing of you's left on earth—not
even a shadow. All you own is here. Would you like that
paper-knife? Or that ornament on the mantelpiece? That blue
sofa's yours. And I, my dear, am yours forever.

ESTELLE: You mine! That's good! Well, which of you two
would dare to call me his glancing stream, his crystal girl? You
know too much about me, you know I'm rotten through and
through. . . . Peter, dear, think of me, fix your thoughts on
me, and save me. All the time you're thinking "my glancing
stream, my crystal girl," I'm only half here. I'm only half
wicked, and half of me is down there with you, clean and
bright and crystal-clear as running water. . . . Oh, just look

at her face, all scarlet, like a tomato. No, it's absurd, we've laughed at her together, you and I, often and often. . . . What's that tune?—I always loved it. Yes, the "St. Louis Blues". . . . All right, dance away, dance away. Garcin, I wish you could see her, you'd die of laughing. Only—she'll never know I *see* her. Yes, I see you, Olga, with your hair all anyhow, and you do look like a dope, my dear. Oh, now you're treading on his toes. It's a scream! Hurry up! Quicker! Quicker! He's dragging her along, bundling her round and round—it's too ghastly! He always said I was so light, he loved to dance with me. [*She is dancing as she speaks.*] I tell you, Olga, I can see you. No, she doesn't care, she's dancing through my gaze. What's that? What's that you said? "Our poor dear Estelle"? Oh, don't be such a humbug! You didn't even shed a tear at the funeral. . . . And she has the nerve to talk to him about her poor dear friend Estelle! How dare she discuss me with Peter? Now then, keep time. She never could dance and talk at once. Oh, what's that? No, no. Don't tell him. Please, please don't tell him. You can keep him, do what you like with him, but please don't tell him about—that! [*She has stopped dancing.*] All right. You can have him now. Isn't it *foul*, Garcin? She's told him everything, about Roger, my trip to Switzerland, the baby. "Poor Estelle wasn't exactly—" No, I wasn't exactly—True enough. He's looking grave, shaking his head, but he doesn't seem so much surprised, not what one would expect. Keep him then—I won't haggle with you over his long eyelashes, his pretty girlish face. They're yours for the asking. His glancing stream, his crystal. Well, the crystal's shattered into bits. "Poor Estelle!" Dance, dance, dance. On with it. But do keep time. One, two. One, two. How I'd love to go down to earth for just a moment, and dance with him again. [*She dances again for some moments.*] The music's growing fainter. They've turned down the lights, as they do for a tango. Why are they playing so softly? Louder, please. I can't hear. It's so far away, so far away. I—I can't hear a sound. [*She stops dancing.*] All over. It's the end. The earth has left me. [*To* GARCIN] Don't turn from me—please. Take me in your arms.

[*Behind* ESTELLE'S *back,* INEZ *signs to* GARCIN *to move away.*]

INEZ [*commandingly*]: Now then, Garcin!

[GARCIN *moves back a step, and glancing at* ESTELLE, *points to* INEZ.]

GARCIN: It's to her you should say that.

ESTELLE [*clinging to him*]: Don't turn away. You're a man, aren't you, and surely I'm not such a fright as all that! Everyone says I've lovely hair and, after all, a man killed himself on my account. You have to look at something, and there's nothing here to see except the sofas and that awful ornament and the table. Surely I'm better to look at than a lot of stupid furniture. Listen! I've dropped out of their hearts like a little sparrow fallen from its nest. So gather me up, dear, fold me to your heart—and you'll see how nice I can be.

GARCIN [*freeing himself from her, after a short struggle*]: I tell you it's to that lady you should speak.

ESTELLE: To her? But she doesn't count, she's a woman.

INEZ: Oh, I don't count? Is that what you think? But, my poor little fallen nestling, you've been sheltering in my heart for ages, though you didn't realize it. Don't be afraid; I'll keep looking at you for ever and ever, without a flutter of my eyelids, and you'll live in my gaze like a mote in a sunbeam.

ESTELLE: A sunbeam indeed! Don't talk such rubbish! You've tried that trick already, and you should know it doesn't work.

INEZ: Estelle! My glancing stream! My crystal!

ESTELLE: *Your* crystal? It's grotesque. Do you think you can fool me with that sort of talk? Everyone knows by now what I did to my baby. The crystal's shattered, but I don't care. I'm just a hollow dummy, all that's left of me is the outside—but it's not for you.

INEZ: Come to me, Estelle. You shall be whatever you like: a glancing stream, a muddy stream. And deep down in my eyes you'll see yourself just as you want to be.

ESTELLE: Oh, leave me in peace. You haven't any eyes. Oh, damn it, isn't there anything I can do to get rid of you? I've an idea. [*She spits in* INEZ'S *face.*] There!

INEZ: Garcin, you shall pay for this.

[*A pause.* GARCIN *shrugs his shoulders and goes to* ESTELLE.]

GARCIN: So it's a man you need?

ESTELLE: Not *any* man. You.

GARCIN: No humbug now. Any man would do your business. As I happen to be here, you want me. Right! [*He grips her shoulders.*] Mind, I'm not your sort at all, really; I'm not a young nincompoop and I don't dance the tango.

ESTELLE: I'll take you as you are. And perhaps I shall change you.

GARCIN: I doubt it. I shan't pay much attention; I've other things to think about.

ESTELLE: What things?

GARCIN: They wouldn't interest you.

ESTELLE: I'll sit on your sofa and wait for you to take some notice of me. I promise not to bother you at all.

INEZ [*with a shrill laugh*]: That's right, fawn on him, like the silly bitch you are. Grovel and cringe! And he hasn't even good looks to commend him!

ESTELLE [*to* GARCIN]: Don't listen to her. She has no eyes, no ears. She's—nothing.

GARCIN: I'll give you what I can. It doesn't amount to much. I shan't love you; I know you too well.

ESTELLE: Do you want me, anyhow?

GARCIN: Yes.

ESTELLE: I ask no more.

GARCIN: In that case—[*He bends over her.*]

INEZ: Estelle! Garcin! You must be going crazy. You're not alone. I'm here too.

GARCIN: Of course—but what does it matter?

INEZ: Under my eyes? You couldn't—couldn't do it.

ESTELLE: Why not? I often undressed with my maid looking on.

INEZ [*gripping* GARCIN'S *arm*]: Let her alone. Don't paw her with your dirty man's hands.

GARCIN [*thrusting her away roughly*]: Take care. I'm no gentleman, and I'd have no compunction about striking a woman.

INEZ: But you promised me; you promised. I'm only asking you to keep your word.

GARCIN: Why should I, considering you were the first to break our agreement?

[INEZ *turns her back on him and retreats to the far end of the room.*]

INEZ: Very well, have it your own way. I'm the weaker party, one against two. But don't forget I'm here, and watching. I shan't take my eyes off you, Garcin; when you're kissing her, you'll feel them boring into you. Yes, have it your own way, make love and get it over. We're in hell; my turn will come.

[*During the following scene she watches them without speaking.*]

GARCIN [*coming back to* ESTELLE *and grasping her shoulders*]: Now then. Your lips. Give me your lips.

[*A pause. He bends to kiss her, then abruptly straightens up.*]

ESTELLE [*indignantly*]: Really! [*A pause.*] Didn't I tell you not to pay attention to her?

GARCIN: You've got it wrong. [*Short silence.*] It's Gomez; he's back in the press-room. They've shut the windows; it must be winter down there. Six months since I—Well, I warned you I'd be absent-minded sometimes, didn't I? They're shivering, they've kept their coats on. Funny they should feel the cold like that, when I'm feeling so hot. Ah, this time he's talking about me.

ESTELLE: Is it going to last long? [*Short silence.*] You might at least tell me what he's saying.

GARCIN: Nothing. Nothing worth repeating. He's a swine, that's all. [*He listens attentively.*] A god-damned bloody swine. [*He turns to* ESTELLE.] Let's come back to—to ourselves. Are you going to love me?

ESTELLE [*smiling*]: I wonder now!

GARCIN: Will you trust me?

ESTELLE: What a quaint thing to ask! Considering you'll be
under my eyes all the time, and I don't think I've much to fear
from Inez, so far as you're concerned.

GARCIN: Obviously. [*A pause. He takes his hands off* ESTELLE'S
shoulders.] I was thinking of another kind of trust. [*Listens.*] Talk
away, talk away, you swine. I'm not there to defend myself. [*To*
ESTELLE] Estelle, you *must* give me your trust.

ESTELLE: Oh, what a nuisance you are! I'm giving you my
mouth, my arms, my whole body—and everything could
be so simple. . . . My trust! I haven't any to give, I'm afraid,
and you're making me terribly embarrassed. You must have
something pretty ghastly on your conscience to make such a
fuss about my trusting you.

GARCIN: They shot me.

ESTELLE: I know. Because you refused to fight. Well, why
shouldn't you?

GARCIN: I—I didn't exactly refuse. [*In a far-away voice*] I must
say he talks well, he makes out a good case against me, but
he never says what I should have done instead. Should I have
gone to the general and said: "General, I decline to fight"? A
mug's game; they'd have promptly locked me up. But I wanted
to show my colors, my true colors, do you understand? I wasn't
going to be silenced. [*To* ESTELLE] So I—I took the train. . . .
They caught me at the frontier.

ESTELLE: Where were you trying to go?

GARCIN: To Mexico. I meant to launch a pacifist newspaper
down there. [*A short silence.*] Well, why don't you speak?

ESTELLE: What could I say? You acted quite rightly, as you
didn't want to fight. [GARCIN *makes a fretful gesture.*] But,
darling, how on earth can I guess what you want me to
answer?

INEZ: Can't you guess? Well, *I* can. He wants you to tell him
that he bolted like a lion. For "bolt" he did, and that's what's
biting him.

GARCIN: "Bolted," "went away,"—we won't quarrel over words.

ESTELLE: But you *had* to run away. If you'd stayed they'd have sent you to jail, wouldn't they?

GARCIN: Of course. [*A pause.*] Well, Estelle, am I a coward?

ESTELLE: How can I say? Don't be so unreasonable, darling. I can't put myself in your skin. You must decide that for yourself.

GARCIN [*wearily*]: I can't decide.

ESTELLE: Anyway, you must remember. You must have had reasons for acting as you did.

GARCIN: I had.

ESTELLE: Well?

GARCIN: But were they the real reasons?

ESTELLE: You've a twisted mind, that's your trouble. Plaguing yourself over such trifles!

GARCIN: I'd thought it all out, and I wanted to make a stand. But was that my real motive?

INEZ: Exactly. That's the question. Was that your real motive? No doubt you argued it out with yourself, you weighed the pros and cons, you found good reasons for what you did. But fear and hatred and all the dirty little instincts one keeps dark—they're motives too. So carry on, Mr. Garcin, and try to be honest with yourself—for once.

GARCIN: Do I really need you to tell me that? Day and night I paced my cell, from the window to the door, from the door to the window. I pried into my heart, I sleuthed myself like a detective. By the end of it I felt as if I'd given my whole life to introspection. But always I harked back to the one thing certain—that I had acted as I did, I'd taken that train to the frontier. But why? Why? Finally I thought: My death will settle it. If I face death courageously, I'll prove I am no coward.

INEZ: And how did you face death?

GARCIN: Miserably. Rottenly. [INEZ *laughs.*] Oh, it was only a physical lapse—that might happen to anyone; I'm not ashamed of it. Only everything's been left in suspense forever. [*To* ESTELLE] Come here, Estelle. Look at me. I want to feel someone looking at me while they're talking about me on earth. . . . I like green eyes.

INEZ: Green eyes! Just hark to him! And you, Estelle, do you like cowards?

ESTELLE: If you knew how little I care! Coward or hero, it's all one—provided he kisses well.

GARCIN: There they are, slumped in their chairs, sucking at their cigars. Bored they look. Half-asleep. They're thinking: "Garcin's a coward." But only vaguely, dreamily. One's got to think of something. "That chap Garcin was a coward." That's what they've decided, those dear friends of mine. In six months' time they'll be saying: "Cowardly as that skunk Garcin." You're lucky, you two; no one on earth is giving you another thought. But I—I'm long in dying.

INEZ: What about your wife, Garcin?

GARCIN: Oh, didn't I tell you? She's dead.

INEZ: Dead?

GARCIN: Yes, she died just now. About two months ago.

INEZ: Of grief?

GARCIN: What else should she die of? So all is for the best, you see; the war's over, my wife's dead, and I've carved out my place in history.

[*He gives a choking sob and passes his hand over his face.* ESTELLE *catches his arm.*]

ESTELLE: My poor darling! Look at me. Please look. Touch me. Touch me. [*She takes his hand and puts it on her neck.*] There! Keep your hand there. [GARCIN *makes a fretful movement.*] No, don't move. Why trouble what those men are thinking? They'll die off one by one. Forget them. There's only me, now.

GARCIN: But *they* won't forget *me*, not they! They'll die, but others will come after them to carry on the legend. I've left my fate in their hands.

ESTELLE: You think too much, that's your trouble.

GARCIN: What else is there to do now? I was a man of action once. . . . Oh, if only I could be with them again, for just one day—I'd fling their lie in their teeth. But I'm locked out; they're passing judgment on my life without troubling about

me, and they're right, because I'm dead. Dead and done with.
[*Laughs.*] A back number.
[*A short pause.*]
ESTELLE [*gently*]: Garcin.
GARCIN: Still there? Now listen! I want you to do me a service.
No, don't shrink away. I know it must seem strange to you,
having someone asking you for help; you're not used to that.
But if you'll make the effort, if you'll only *will* it hard enough,
I dare say we can really love each other. Look at it this way.
A thousand of them are proclaiming I'm a coward; but what
do numbers matter? If there's someone, just one person, to say
quite positively I did not run away, that I'm not the sort who
runs away, that I'm brave and decent and the rest of it—well,
that one person's faith would save me. Will you have that faith
in me? Then I shall love you and cherish you for ever. Estelle—
will you?
ESTELLE [*laughing*]: Oh, you dear silly man, do you think I could
love a coward?
GARCIN: But just now you said—
ESTELLE: I was only teasing you. I like men, my dear, who're
real men, with tough skin and strong hands. You haven't a
coward's chin, or a coward's mouth, or a coward's voice, or a
coward's hair. And it's for your mouth, your hair, your voice, I
love you.
GARCIN: Do you mean this? *Really* mean it?
ESTELLE: Shall I swear it?
GARCIN: Then I snap my fingers at them all, those below and
those in here. Estelle, we shall climb out of hell. [INEZ *gives a
shrill laugh. He breaks off and stares at her.*] What's that?
INEZ [*still laughing*]: But she doesn't mean a word of what she says.
How can you be such a simpleton? "Estelle, am I a coward?"
As if she cared a damn either way.
ESTELLE: Inez, how dare you? [*To* GARCIN] Don't listen to
her. If you want me to have faith in you, you must begin by
trusting me.

INEZ: That's right! That's right! Trust away! She wants a man—
that far you can trust her—she wants a man's arm round her
waist, a man's smell, a man's eyes glowing with desire. And
that's all she wants. She'd assure you were God Almighty if she
thought it would give you pleasure.

GARCIN: Estelle, is it true? Answer me. Is it true?

ESTELLE: What do you expect me to say? Don't you realize how
maddening it is to have to answer questions one can't make
head or tail of? [*She stamps her foot.*] You do make things difficult.
. . . Anyhow, I'd love you just the same, even if you were a
coward. Isn't that enough?

[*A short pause.*]

GARCIN [*to the two women*]: You disgust me, both of you.

[*He goes towards the door.*]

ESTELLE: What are you up to?

GARCIN: I'm going.

INEZ [*quickly*]: You won't get far. The door is locked.

GARCIN: I'll *make* them open it. [*He presses the bell-push. The bell does
not ring.*]

ESTELLE: Please! Please!

INEZ [*to ESTELLE*]: Don't worry, my pet. The bell doesn't work.

GARCIN: I tell you they shall open. [*Drums on the door.*] I can't
endure it any longer, I'm through with you both. [ESTELLE
runs to him; he pushes her away.] Go away. You're even fouler than
she. I won't let myself get bogged in your eyes. You're soft
and slimy. Ugh! [*Bangs on the door again.*] Like an octopus. Like a
quagmire.

ESTELLE: I beg you, oh, I beg you not to leave me. I'll promise
not to speak again, I won't trouble you in any way—but don't
go. I daren't be left alone with Inez, now she's shown her
claws.

GARCIN: Look after yourself. I never asked you to come here.

ESTELLE: Oh, how mean you are! Yes, it's quite true you're a
coward.

INEZ [*going up to ESTELLE*]: Well, my little sparrow fallen from
the nest, I hope you're satisfied now. You spat in my face—

playing up to him, of course—and we had a tiff on his account.
But he's going, and a good riddance it will be. We two women
will have the place to ourselves.

ESTELLE: You won't gain anything. If that door opens, I'm going
too.

INEZ: Where?

ESTELLE: I don't care where. As far from you as I can.

[GARCIN *has been drumming on the door while they talk.*]

GARCIN: Open the door! Open, blast you! I'll endure anything,
your red-hot tongs and molten lead, your racks and prongs
and garrotes—all your fiendish gadgets, everything that burns
and flays and tears—I'll put up with any torture you impose.
Anything, anything would be better than this agony of mind,
this creeping pain that gnaws and fumbles and caresses one
and never hurts quite enough. [*He grips the doorknob and rattles it.*]
Now will you open? [*The door flies open with a jerk, and he just avoids
falling.*] Ah! [*A long silence.*]

INEZ: Well, Garcin? You're free to go.

GARCIN [*meditatively*]: Now I wonder why that door opened.

INEZ: What are you waiting for? Hurry up and go.

GARCIN: I shall not go.

INEZ: And you, Estelle? [ESTELLE *does not move.* INEZ *bursts out
laughing.*] So what? Which shall it be? Which of the three of us
will leave? The barrier's down, why are we waiting? . . . But
what a situation! It's a scream! We're inseparables!

[ESTELLE *springs at her from behind.*]

ESTELLE: Inseparables? Garcin, come and lend a hand. Quickly.
We'll push her out and slam the door on her. That'll teach her
a lesson.

INEZ [*struggling with* ESTELLE]: Estelle! I beg you, let me stay. I
won't go, I won't go! Not into the passage.

GARCIN: Let go of her.

ESTELLE: You're crazy. She hates you.

GARCIN: It's because of her I'm staying here.

[ESTELLE *releases* INEZ *and stares dumbfoundedly at* GARCIN.]

INEZ: Because of me? [*Pause.*] All right, shut the door. It's ten times hotter here since it opened. [GARCIN *goes to the door and shuts it.*] Because of me, you said?

GARCIN: Yes. *You*, anyhow, know what it means to be a coward.

INEZ: Yes, I know.

GARCIN: And you know what wickedness is, and shame, and fear. There were days when you peered into yourself, into the secret places of your heart, and what you saw there made you faint with horror. And then, next day, you didn't know what to make of it, you couldn't interpret the horror you had glimpsed the day before. Yes, you know what evil *costs*. And when you say I'm a coward, you know from experience what that means. Is that so?

INEZ: Yes.

GARCIN: So it's you whom I have to convince; you are of my kind. Did you suppose I meant to go? No, I couldn't leave you here, gloating over my defeat, with all those thoughts about me running in your head.

INEZ: Do you really wish to convince me?

GARCIN: That's the one and only thing I wish for now. I can't hear them any longer, you know. Probably that means they're through with me. For good and all. The curtain's down, nothing of me is left on earth—not even the name of coward. So, Inez, we're alone. Only you two remain to give a thought to me. She—she doesn't count. It's you who matter; you who hate me. If you'll have faith in me I'm saved.

INEZ: It won't be easy. Have a look at me. I'm a hard-headed woman.

GARCIN: I'll give you all the time that's needed.

INEZ: Yes, we've lots of time in hand. *All* time.

GARCIN [*putting his hands on her shoulders*]: Listen! Each man has an aim in life, a leading motive; that's so, isn't it? Well, I didn't give a damn for wealth, or for love. I aimed at being a real man. A tough, as they say. I staked everything on the same horse. . . . Can one possibly be a coward when one's deliberately courted danger at every turn? And can judge a life by a single action?

INEZ: Why not? For thirty years you dreamt you were a hero, and condoned a thousand petty lapses—because a hero, of course, can do no wrong. An easy method, obviously. Then a day came when you were up against it, the red light of real danger—and you took the train to Mexico.

GARCIN: I "dreamt," you say. It was no dream. When I chose the hardest path, I made my choice deliberately. A man is what he wills himself to be.

INEZ: Prove it. Prove it was no dream. It's what one does, and nothing else, that shows the stuff one's made of.

GARCIN: I died too soon. I wasn't allowed time to—to do my deeds.

INEZ: One always dies too soon—or too late. And yet one's whole life is complete at that moment, with a line drawn neatly under it, ready for the summing up. You are—your life, and nothing else.

GARCIN: What a poisonous woman you are! With an answer for everything.

INEZ: Now then! Don't lose heart. It shouldn't be so hard, convincing me. Pull yourself together, man, rake up some arguments. [GARCIN *shrugs his shoulders.*] Ah, wasn't I right when I said you were vulnerable? Now you're going to pay the price, and what a price! You're a coward, Garcin, because I wish it! I wish it—do you hear?—I wish it. And yet, just look at me, see how weak I am, a mere breath on the air, a gaze observing you, a formless thought that thinks you. [*He walks towards her, opening his hands.*] Ah, they're open now, those big hands, those coarse, man's hands! But what do you hope to do? You can't throttle thoughts with hands. So you've no choice, you must convince me, and you're at my mercy.

ESTELLE: Garcin!

GARCIN: What?

ESTELLE: Revenge yourself.

GARCIN: How?

ESTELLE: Kiss me, darling—then you'll hear her squeal.

GARCIN: That's true, Inez. I'm at your mercy, but you're at mine as well.

[*He bends over* ESTELLE. INEZ *gives a little cry.*]

INEZ: Oh, you coward, you weakling, running to women to console you!

ESTELLE: That's right, Inez. Squeal away.

INEZ: What a lovely pair you make! If you could see his big paw splayed out on your back, rucking up your skin and creasing the silk. Be careful, though! He's perspiring, his hand will leave a blue stain on your dress.

ESTELLE: Squeal away, Inez, squeal away! . . . Hug me tight, darling; tighter still—that'll finish her off, and a good thing too!

INEZ: Yes, Garcin, she's right. Carry on with it, press her to you till you feel your bodies melting into each other; a lump of warm, throbbing flesh. . . . Love's a grand solace, isn't it, my friend? Deep and dark as sleep. But I'll see you don't sleep.

ESTELLE: Don't listen to her. Press your lips to my mouth. Oh, I'm yours, yours, yours.

INEZ: Well, what are you waiting for? Do as you're told. What a lovely scene: coward Garcin holding baby-killer Estelle in his manly arms! Make your stakes, everyone. Will coward Garcin kiss the lady, or won't he dare? What's the betting? I'm watching you, everybody's watching, I'm a crowd all by myself. Do you hear the crowd? Do you hear them muttering, Garcin? Mumbling and muttering. "Coward! Coward! Coward! Coward!"—that's what they're saying. . . . It's no use trying to escape, I'll never let you go. What do you hope to get from her silly lips? Forgetfulness? But I shan't forget you, not I! "It's I you must convince." So come to me. I'm waiting. Come along, now. . . . Look how obedient he is, like a well-trained dog who comes when his mistress calls. You can't hold him, and you never will.

GARCIN: Will night never come?

INEZ: Never.

GARCIN: You will always see me?

INEZ: Always.

[GARCIN *moves away from* ESTELLE *and takes some steps across the room. He goes to the bronze ornament.*]

GARCIN: This bronze. [*Strokes it thoughtfully.*] Yes, now's the moment; I'm looking at this thing on the mantelpiece, and I understand that I'm in hell. I tell you, everything's been thought out beforehand. They knew I'd stand at the fireplace stroking this thing of bronze, with all those eyes intent on me. Devouring me. [*He swings round abruptly.*] What? Only two of you? I thought there were more; many more. [*Laughs.*] So this is hell. I'd never have believed it. You remember all we were told about the torture-chambers, the fire and brimstone, the "burning marl." Old wives' tales! There's no need for red-hot pokers. Hell is—other people!

ESTELLE: My darling! Please—

GARCIN [*thrusting her away*]: No, let me be. She is between us. I cannot love you when she's watching.

ESTELLE: Right! In that case, I'll stop her watching. [*She picks up the paper-knife from the table, rushes at* INEZ *and stabs her several times.*]

INEZ [*struggling and laughing*]: But, you crazy creature, what do you think you're doing? You know quite well I'm dead.

ESTELLE: Dead?

[*She drops the knife. A pause.* INEZ *picks up the knife and jabs herself with it regretfully.*]

INEZ: Dead! Dead! Dead! Knives, poison, ropes—all useless. It has happened *already*, do you understand? Once and for all. So here we are, forever. [*Laughs.*]

ESTELLE [*with a peal of laughter*]: Forever. My God, how funny! Forever.

GARCIN [*looks at the two women, and joins in the laughter*]: For ever, and ever, and ever.

[*They slump onto their respective sofas. A long silence. Their laughter dies away and they gaze at each other.*]

GARCIN: Well, well, let's get on with it. . . .

17

Randall Jarrell

The Death of the Ball Turret Gunner

From my mother's sleep I fell into the State,
And I hunched in its belly till my wet fur froze.
Six miles from earth, loosed from the dream of life,
I woke to black flak and the nightmare fighters.
When I died they washed me out of the turret with a hose.

18

Igor Stravinsky

Poetics of Music

Music, like the other arts, has experienced a startling degree of change during the twentieth century—both in style and in content. A composer whose varied works exemplify many of the era's significant musical trends and cultural traditions is Igor Stravinsky (1882-1971).

Born near St. Petersburg (now Leningrad), Russia, Stravinsky studied law—at his parents' insistence—at St. Petersburg University. Becoming acquainted with the established composer Nikolay Rimsky-Korsakov, Stravinsky began to study music privately with him and eventually abandoned the legal profession. Thus he regularly discussed his new compositions with Rimsky-Korsakov, and the older man's orchestral mastery and distinctively Russian musical style had an enduring effect on Stravinsky.

After attending a performance of several early symphonic works by Stravinsky, Sergei Diaghilev, founder and director of the Russian Ballet, commissioned him to compose the scores for a number of ballets. Thus began Stravinsky's explosive rise to prominence among modern composers. The Firebird (1910), the first of these ballets, combines elements of the Russian nationalist tradition with all the exotic orientalism and orchestral sensuality typical of the music of Stravinsky's teacher, Rimsky-Korsakov. The second, Petrushka (1911), is a brashly colorful ballet about puppets come to life. While completing The Firebird, Stravinsky had a daydream about a pagan ritual in which a young girl danced herself to death. This image was the genesis of the third ballet for

Reprinted by permission of the publishers from *Poetics of Music in the Form of Six Lessons* by Igor Stravinsky, trans. A. Knodel and I. Dahl. Cambridge, Mass.: Harvard University Press, Copyright © 1942, 1947, 1970, 1975 by the President and Fellows of Harvard College. [Pp. 11-12, 47-53, 56-57, 63-65.]

Diaghilev, The Rite of Spring (1913), subtitled Pictures of Pagan Russia—a score that represents the culmination of sophisticated primitivism in modern music. Its dynamic opening performance in Paris caused one of the wildest riots in the history of music. The profoundly disturbing effects of the ballet stem from unusual rhythms, dissonant combinations of chords, and, especially, from an elemental power that implacably sweeps the music to a shattering conclusion.

Seeing his native Russia changed by the First World War and the Bolshevik Revolution, Stravinsky eventually moved to France, where he abandoned the romantic Russian features of his earlier compositions and adopted an austere "neoclassical" style. Among his outstanding works of this period are the opera-oratorio Oedipus Rex *(1927), the choral* Symphony of Psalms *(1930), and the full-length opera* The Rake's Progress *(1951), which deliberately re-created Mozart's eighteenth-century style. Deprived of his private income in Russia, Stravinsky began a performing career as pianist and conductor.*

The third major phase of the composer's work was as impressively startling in its results as the earlier two. Stravinsky untiringly moved from the world of musical harmonies derived from traditional scales and modes to the new twelve-note scale or "tone-row" devised by Arnold Schoenberg, his Austro-American contemporary. Stravinsky, around 1955, became a twelve-tone composer who based each work on a series of notes stated as a tone-row in the opening measures. This new technique can be observed, for example, in the ballet Agon *(1957), the orchestral* Variations *(1964), and the choral* Requiem Canticles *(1966).*

In the Poetics of Music *(1947), the book from which the following selection is taken, Stravinsky acknowledges his debt to the great musical tradition. The book is actually a translation of six lectures delivered by him in French at Harvard University during 1939 and 1940. The rapid fall of France to the Germans while Stravinsky was away from Europe for these lectures necessitated the composer's stay in the United States for the duration of the war. (Eventually, he was to live more than a quarter of a century in Hollywood, California.) Stravinsky in these lectures criticizes the vulgarization of music—through commercialization, excessive desire for novelty, and propagandistic requirements. He pleads for order and discipline, for the limitations imposed by cultural forms and the living force of tradition. Although usually regarded as an innovator, Stravinsky reveals himself as a creator who has absorbed the lessons of the past—and who affirms his cultural heritage by building upon it.*

In truth, I should be hard pressed to cite for you a single fact in the history of art that might be qualified as revolutionary. Art is by essence constructive. Revolution implies a disruption of equilibrium. To speak of revolution is to speak of a temporary chaos. Now art is the contrary of chaos. It never gives itself up to chaos without immediately finding its living works, its very existence, threatened.

The quality of being revolutionary is generally attributed to artists in our day with a laudatory intent, undoubtedly because we are living in a period when revolution enjoys a kind of prestige among yesterday's elite. Let us understand each other: I am the first to recognize that daring is the motive force of the finest and greatest acts; which is all the more reason for not putting it unthinkingly at the service of disorder and base cravings in a desire to cause sensation at any price. I approve of daring; I set no limits to it. But likewise there are no limits to the mischief wrought by arbitrary acts.

To enjoy to the full the conquests of daring, we must demand that it operate in a pitiless light. We are working in its favor when we denounce the false wares that would usurp its place. Gratuitous excess spoils every substance, every form that it touches. In its blundering it impairs the effectiveness of the most valuable discoveries and at the same time corrupts the taste of its devotees—which explains why their taste often plunges without transition from the wildest complications to the flattest banalities.

A musical complex, however harsh it may be, is legitimate to the extent to which it is genuine. But to recognize genuine values in the midst of the excesses of sham one must be gifted with a sure instinct that our snobs hate all the more intensely for being themselves completely deprived thereof.

Our vanguard elite, sworn perpetually to outdo itself, expects and requires that music should satisfy the taste for absurd cacophony.

★ ★ ★

We are living at a time when the status of man is undergoing profound upheavals.* Modern man is progressively losing his understanding of values and his sense of proportions. This failure to understand essential realities is extremely serious. It leads us infallibly to the violation of the fundamental laws of human equilibrium. In the domain of music, the consequences of this misunderstanding are these: on one hand there is a tendency to turn the mind away from what I shall call the higher mathematics of music in order to degrade music to servile employment, and to vulgarize it by adapting it to the requirements of an elementary utilitarianism—as we shall soon see on examining Soviet music. On the other hand, since the mind itself is ailing, the music of our time, and particularly the music that calls itself and believes itself *pure,* carries within it the symptoms of a pathologic blemish and spreads the germs of a new original sin. The old original sin was chiefly a sin of knowledge; the new original sin, if I may speak in these terms, is first and foremost a sin of non-acknowledgement—a refusal to acknowledge the truth and the laws that proceed therefrom, laws that we have called fundamental. What then is this truth in the domain of music? And what are its repercussions on creative activity?

Let us not forget that it is written: "Spiritus ubi vult spirat"† (St. John, 3:8). What we must retain in this proposition is above all the word WILL. The Spirit is thus endowed with the capacity of willing. The principle of speculative volition is a fact.

Now it is just this fact that is too often disputed. People question the direction that the wind of the Spirit is taking, not the Tightness of the artisan's work. In so doing, whatever may be your feelings about ontology‡ or whatever your own philosophy and beliefs may be, you must admit that you are making an attack on the very freedom of the spirit—whether you begin this large word with a capital or not. If a believer in Christian philosophy, you would then also have to refuse to

---

* The Second World War was in its first year when Stravinsky delivered his lectures; they were later published as the Poetics of Music (1947). The war caused him to remain in the United States.
† Latin: The Spirit [or wind] blows where it wills.
‡ The branch of philosophy that studies the ultimate nature of reality.

accept the idea of the Holy Spirit. If an agnostic or atheist, you would have to do nothing less than refuse to be a *freethinker* . . .

It should be noted that there is never any dispute when the listener takes pleasure in the work he hears. The least informed of music-lovers readily clings to the periphery of a work; it pleases him for reasons that are most often entirely foreign to the essence of music. This pleasure is enough for him and calls for no justification. But if it happens that the music displeases him, our music-lover will ask you for an explanation of his discomfiture. He will demand that we explain something that is in its essence ineffable.

By its fruit we judge the tree.* Judge the tree by its fruit then, and do not meddle with the roots. Function justifies an organ, no matter how strange the organ may appear in the eyes of those who are not accustomed to see it functioning. Snobbish circles are cluttered with persons who, like one of Montesquieu's characters, wonder how one can possibly be a Persian.† They make me think unfailingly of the story of the peasant who, on seeing a dromedary in the zoo for the first time, examines it at length, shakes his head and, turning to leave, says, to the great delight of those present: "It isn't true."

It is through the unhampered play of its functions, then, that a work is revealed and justified. We are free to accept or reject this play, but no one has the right to question the fact of its existence. To judge, dispute, and criticize the principle of speculative volition which is at the origin of all creation is thus manifestly useless. In the pure state, music is free speculation. Artists of all epochs have unceasingly testified to this concept. For myself, I see no reason for not trying to do as they did. Since I myself was created, I cannot help having the desire to create. What sets this desire in motion, and what can I do to make it productive?

The study of the creative process is an extremely delicate one. In truth, it is impossible to observe the inner workings of this process from

---

* Compare the Gospel of Matthew 12:33: ". . . for the tree is known by its fruit."

† In the fictitious *The Persian Letters* (1721) of the French political philosopher Montesquieu (1689-1755), a Persian letter-writer in Paris exchanges his Persian clothes for European ones. Immediately, he ceases to be an exotic celebrity among the Parisians. "However, if someone chanced to inform them that I was a Persian, I soon heard a murmur all around me: 'Ah! Indeed! He is a Persian? How extraordinary! How can anyone be a Persian?' " (Letter XXX)

the outside. It is futile to try and follow its successive phases in someone else's work. It is likewise very difficult to observe one's self. Yet it is only by enlisting the aid of introspection that I may have any chance at all of guiding you in this essentially fluctuating matter.

Most music-lovers believe that what sets the composer's creative imagination in motion is a certain emotive disturbance generally designated by the name *of inspiration.*

I have no thought of denying to inspiration the outstanding role that has devolved upon it in the generative process we are studying; I simply maintain that inspiration is in no way a prescribed condition of the creative act, but rather a manifestation that is chronologically secondary.

Inspiration, art, artist—so many words, hazy at least, that keep us from seeing clearly in a field where everything is balance and calculation through which the breath of the speculative spirit blows. It is afterwards, and only afterwards, that the emotive disturbance which is at the root of inspiration may arise—an emotive disturbance about which people talk so indelicately by conferring upon it a meaning that is shocking to us and that compromises the term itself. Is it not clear that this emotion is merely a reaction on the part of the creator grappling with that unknown entity which is still only the object of his creating and which is to become a work of art? Step by step, link by link, it will be granted him to discover the work. It is this chain of discoveries, as well as each individual discovery, that give rise to the emotion—an almost physiological reflex, like that of the appetite causing a flow of saliva—this emotion which invariably follows closely the phases of the creative process.

All creation presupposes at its origin a sort of appetite that is brought on by the foretaste of discovery. This foretaste of the creative act accompanies the intuitive grasp of an unknown entity already possessed but not yet intelligible, an entity that will not take definite shape except by the action of a constantly vigilant technique.

This appetite that is aroused in me at the mere thought of putting in order musical elements that have attracted my attention is not at all a fortuitous thing like inspiration, but as habitual and periodic, if not as constant, as a natural need.

This premonition of an obligation, this foretaste of a pleasure, this conditioned reflex, as a modern physiologist would say, shows clearly that it is the idea of discovery and hard work that attracts me. The very act of putting my work on paper, of, as we say, kneading the dough, is for me inseparable from the pleasure of creation. So far as I am concerned, I cannot separate the spiritual effort from the psychological and physical effort; they confront me on the same level and do not present a hierarchy.

The word *artist* which, as it is most generally understood today, bestows on its bearer the highest intellectual prestige, the privilege of being accepted as a pure mind—this pretentious term is in my view entirely incompatible with the role of the *homofaber.**

At this point it should be remembered that, whatever field of endeavor has fallen to our lot, if it is true that we are *intellectuals,* we are called upon not to cogitate, but to perform.

The philosopher Jacques Maritain† reminds us that in the mighty structure of medieval civilization, the artist held only the rank of an artisan. "And his individualism was forbidden any sort of anarchic development, because a natural social discipline imposed certain limitative conditions upon him from without." It was the Renaissance that invented the artist, distinguished him from the artisan and began to exalt the former at the expense of the latter.

At the outset the name artist was given only to the Masters of Arts: philosophers, alchemists, magicians; but painters, sculptors, musicians, and poets had the right to be qualified only as artisans.

> Plying divers implements,
> The subtile artizan implants
> Life in marble, copper, bronze,

---

* Literally (in Latin), skillful man; usually translated as man the maker or man the creator.
† A French Catholic philosopher (1882-1973); like Stravinsky, he remained in America because of the fall of France during his American lecture tour.

says the poet Du Bellay.* And Montaigne† enumerates in his *Essays* the "painters, poets and other artizans." And even in the seventeenth century, La Fontaine‡ hails a painter with the name *of artisan* and draws a sharp rebuke from an ill-tempered critic who might have been the ancestor of most of our present-day critics.

The idea of work to be done is for me so closely bound up with the idea of the arranging of materials and of the pleasure that the actual doing of the work affords us that, should the impossible happen and my work suddenly be given to me in a perfectly completed form, I should be embarrassed and nonplussed by it, as by a hoax.

We have a duty towards music, namely, to invent it.

★ ★ ★

The faculty of observation and of making something out of what is observed belongs only to the person who at least possesses, in his particular field of endeavor, an acquired culture and an innate taste. A dealer, an art-lover who is the first to buy the canvases of an unknown painter who will be famous twenty-five years later under the name of Cézanne§—doesn't such a person give us a clear example of this innate taste? What else guides him in his choices? A flair, an instinct from which this taste proceeds, a completely spontaneous faculty anterior to reflection.

As for culture, it is a sort of upbringing which, in the social sphere, confers polish upon education, sustains and rounds out academic instruction. This upbringing is just as important in the sphere of taste and is essential to the creator who must ceaselessly refine his taste or run the risk of losing his perspicacity. Our mind, as well as our body, requires continual exercise. It atrophies if we do not cultivate it.

It is culture that brings out the full value of taste and gives it a chance to prove its worth simply by its application. The artist imposes a culture upon himself and ends by imposing it upon others. That is how tradition becomes established.

---

* Joachim Du Bellay (1522-60), a French satirical poet.
† Michel de Montaigne (1533-92), a French moralist and creator of the personal essay as a literary form.
‡ Jean de La Fontaine (1621-95), a prolific French scholar, poet, and author of satirical fables.
§ Paul Cézanne (1839-1906), a French Post-Impressionist painter who was a pivotal figure in the redirection of painting away from mere imitation of nature.

Tradition is entirely different from habit, even from an excellent habit, since habit is by definition an unconscious acquisition and tends to become mechanical, whereas tradition results from a conscious and deliberate acceptance. A real tradition is not the relic of a past that is irretrievably gone; it is a living force that animates and informs the present. In this sense the paradox which banteringly maintains that everything which is not tradition is plagiarism, is true . . .

Far from implying the repetition of what has been, tradition presupposes the reality of what endures. It appears as an heirloom, a heritage that one receives on condition of making it bear fruit before passing it on to one's descendants.

Brahms was born sixty years after Beethoven.* From the one to the other, and from every aspect, the distance is great; they do not dress the same way, but Brahms follows the tradition of Beethoven without borrowing one of his habiliments. For the borrowing of a method has nothing to do with observing a tradition. "A method is replaced: a tradition is carried forward in order to produce something new." Tradition thus assures the continuity of creation. The example that I have just cited does not constitute an exception but is one proof out of a hundred of a constant law. This sense of tradition which is a natural need must not be confused with the desire which the composer feels to affirm the kinship he finds across the centuries with some master of the past.

★ ★ ★

A mode of composition that does not assign itself limits becomes pure fantasy. The effects it produces may accidentally amuse but are not capable of being repeated. I cannot conceive of a fantasy that is repeated, for it can be repeated only to its detriment.

Let us understand each other in regard to this word fantasy. We are not using the word in the sense in which it is connected with a definite musical form, but in the acceptation which presupposes an abandonment of one's self to the caprices of imagination. And this presupposes that the composer's will is voluntarily paralyzed. For imagination is not only

---

* Johannes Brahms (1833-97) and Ludwig van Beethoven (1770-1827), two of the great composers of romantic orchestral music.

the mother of caprice but the servant and handmaiden of the creative will as well.

The creator's function is to sift the elements he receives from her, for human activity must impose limits upon itself. The more art is controlled, limited, worked over, the more it is free.

As for myself, I experience a sort of terror when, at the moment of setting to work and finding myself before the infinitude of possibilities that present themselves, I have the feeling that everything is permissible to me. If everything is permissible to me, the best and the worst; if nothing offers me any resistance, then any effort is inconceivable, and I cannot use anything as a basis, and consequently every undertaking becomes futile.

Will I then have to lose myself in this abyss of freedom? To what shall I cling in order to escape the dizziness that seizes me before the virtuality of this infinitude? However, I shall not succumb. I shall overcome my terror and shall be reassured by the thought that I have the seven notes of the scale and its chromatic intervals at my disposal, that strong and weak accents are within my reach, and that in all of these I possess solid and concrete elements which offer me a field of experience just as vast as the upsetting and dizzy infinitude that had just frightened me. It is into this field that I shall sink my roots, fully convinced that combinations which have at their disposal twelve sounds in each octave and all possible rhythmic varieties promise me riches that all the activity of human genius will never exhaust.

What delivers me from the anguish into which an unrestricted freedom plunges me is the fact that I am always able to turn immediately to the concrete things that are here in question. I have no use for a theoretic freedom. Let me have something finite, definite— matter that can lend itself to my operation only insofar as it is commensurate with my possibilities. And such matter presents itself to me together with its limitations. I must in turn impose mine upon it. So here we are, whether we like it or not, in the realm of necessity. And yet which of us has ever heard talk of art as other than a realm of freedom? This sort of heresy is uniformly widespread because it is imagined that art is outside the bounds of ordinary activity. Well, in art as in everything else, one can build only upon a resisting foundation: whatever constantly gives way to pressure, constantly renders movement impossible.

My freedom thus consists in my moving about within the narrow frame that I have assigned myself for each one of my undertakings.

I shall go even further: my freedom will be so much the greater and more meaningful the more narrowly I limit my field of action and the more I surround myself with obstacles. Whatever diminishes constraint, diminishes strength. The more constraints one imposes, the more one frees one's self of the chains that shackle the spirit. . . .

19

Langston Hughes

Harlem

Langston Hughes (1902–1967) was born in Joplin, Missouri, but spent most of his early childhood in Cleveland, Ohio. In the 1920s he attended Columbia University, where he came into contact with the writers, artists, and musicians who were creating the Harlem Renaissance. He showed his poetry to Vachel Lindsey, who was so impressed that he helped Hughes find a publisher. From those beginnings, Hughes went on to be known as the poet laureate of Harlem. In the next five decades, he published poetry, fiction, humor, criticism, and history. He is most famous for introducing the rhythms of black jazz into poetry in collections such as The Weary Blues (1926) and Montage of a Dream Deferred (1951).

What happens to a dream deferred?
   Does it dry up
   like a raisin in the sun?
   Or fester like a sore—
   And then run?

"Harlem (Dream Deferred)" by Langston Hughes, from THE COLLECTED POEMS OF LANGSTON HUGHES by Langston Hughes, copyright © 1994 by The Estate of Langston Hughes. Used by permission of Alfred A. Knopf, a division of Random House, Inc.

Does it stink like rotten meat?
Or crust and sugar over—
like a syrupy sweet?

Maybe it just sags
like a heavy load.

Or does it explode?

UNDERSTANDING MEANING

1. What is the sentiment expressed in the poem, and what is its underlying warning?
2. How does the poem address a cultural, as opposed to a strictly personal, dream?

EVALUATING ELEMENTS

1. What similes do you find in the poem, and how do they suggest a collective progression toward resolution?
2. Why does the poet indent every line except the first?

APPRECIATING LANGUAGE

1. What connotations and denotations are implicit in the nouns used to describe what happens?
2. Why is the last line set in italics?

WRITING SUGGESTIONS

1. Analyze the poem in relation to Hughes's other work, and show how it fits into a larger, general theme in his poetry.
2. Research race relations in the United States in the 1940s and 1950s. Then write an essay that explains the cultural and historical situation of the poem.

20

Aldous Huxley
The Doors of Perception
&
Heaven and Hell

Drugs, known in all ages but more widely available since the advent of modern chemistry, have had varied functions in the twentieth century. Some have been used to relieve pain, some to combat depression or mental illness, and some simply to produce pleasurable sensations. In addition, many people contend, certain drugs can be employed to expand the consciousness of the user. An intellectually distinguished advocate of such psycho-chemical exploration was the writer Aldous Huxley (1894-1963).

Throughout his exceptionally productive literary career (see selection 10), Huxley was interested in ttye idea of psychological liberation. In his later years, considering the failure for many of religious worship, Huxley began to view biochemistry as a means of escaping the confinement of the rationalizing, verbalizing ego. Much of his personal experimentation toward this end is carefully and eloquently recorded in The Doors of Perception *(1954) and* Heaven and Hell *(1956), the sources of the following selection.*

In 1953, under the supervision of a psychiatrist who had written extensively on the biochemistry of schizophrenia (a form of mental disturbance), Huxley swallowed four-tenths of a gram of mescalin. (Mescalin is the active ingredient of peyote, the root of a desert cactus plant that is eaten in religious ceremonies by the Indians of Mexico and the American Southwest. It is also chemically related to LSD, widely known as a hallucinogen—an inducer of false perceptions of the external world.) Within a half-hour, as Huxley relates in The Doors of Perception, *he began to experience "visionary"*

From pp. 67-79, 85-89, and 96-101 in *The Doors of Perception* and *Heaven and Hell* by Aldous Huxley. Copyright (g) 1954, 1955, 1956 by Aldous Huxley. Reprinted by permission of Harper & Row, Publishers, Inc.

effects—not in the subjective, internalized sense that he had initially expected, but rather in the outward "realm of objective fact. " Previously a verbalizer who visualized very poorly, he now saw the objects of his everyday world with an intensity of light and color that revealed their "true Being" It was as if he had walked through the "Door in the Wall" of normal consciousness and returned "wiser but less cocksure, happier but less self-satisfied, humbler . . . yet better equipped to understand the relationship of words to things, of systematic reasoning to the unfathomable Mystery."

In Heaven and Hell, *the sequel to* The Doors of Perception, *Huxley describes the features of the visionary world and the methods by which the visions may be gained. He traces the correspondence between the visions made possible by mescalin and those consistently recorded in religious literature, in folklore and legend, and in certain works of art. Through mescalin and similar drugs, Huxley suggests, "the efficiency of the brain as an instrument for focusing the mind on the problems of life" is lowered. The lowering of the efficiency of the "cerebral reducing valve" permits the "intrusions of biologically useless, but aesthetically and sometimes spiritually valuable material."*

As Huxley indicates in his title, however, there is a visionary hell *as well as a visionary paradise. ("The schizophrenic is like a man permanently under the influence of mescalin and therefore unable to shut off the experience of a reality which he is not holy enough to live with, . . . it never permits him to look at the world with merely human eyes.") Since, as Huxley notes, the effect of such drugs is always conditional on the nature of the individual user, it seems doubtful that any "ideal drug" is possible or even desirable.*

Huxley, nevertheless, advocates the search for a new drug, which — unlike alcohol and tobacco — "will relieve and console our suffering species without doing more harm in the long run than it does good in the short." (Huxley's "ideal drug" should not be identified with the "soma" of his fictional Brave New World; *soma anesthetizes the user to reality, rather than aiding him in penetrating to another level of reality.) It is a sad commentary on contemporary society that some individuals mistakenly point to Huxley's disciplined aesthetic and spiritual searching as justification for their own undisciplined and self-destructive addictions.*

THE DOORS OF PERCEPTION

The urge to transcend self-conscious selfhood is, as I have said, a principal appetite of the soul. When, for whatever reason, men and women fail to transcend themselves by means of worship, good works and spiritual exercises, they are apt to resort to religion's chemical surrogates—alcohol and "goof pills" in the modern West, alcohol and opium in the East, hashish in the Mohammedan world, alcohol and marijuana in Central America, alcohol and coca in the Andes, alcohol and the barbiturates in the more up-to-date regions of South America. In *Poisons Sacrés, Ivresses Divines [Holy Poisons, Heavenly Frenzies]* Philippe de Felice has written at length and with a wealth of documentation on the immemorial connection between religion and the taking of drugs. Here, in summary or in direct quotation, are his conclusions. The employment for religious purposes of toxic substances is "extraordinarily widespread. . . . The practices studied in this volume can be observed in every region of the earth, among primitives no less than among those who have reached a high pitch of civilization. We are therefore dealing not with exceptional facts, which might justifiably be overlooked, but with a general and, in the widest sense of the word, a human phenomenon, the kind of phenomenon which cannot be disregarded by anyone who is trying to discover what religion is, and what are the deep needs which it must satisfy."

Ideally, everyone should be able to find self-transcendence in some form of pure or applied religion. In practice it seems very unlikely that this hoped for consummation will ever be realized. There are, and doubtless there always will be, good churchmen and good churchwomen for whom, unfortunately, piety is not enough. The late G. K. Chesterton,* who wrote at least as lyrically of drink as of devotion, may serve as their eloquent spokesman.

The modern churches, with some exceptions among the Protestant denominations, tolerate alcohol; but even the most tolerant have made no attempt to convert the drug to Christianity, or to sacramen-taize its use. The pious drinker is forced to take his religion in one compartment, his religion-surrogate in another. And perhaps this is inevitable. Drinking cannot be sacramentalized except in religions which set no store on decorum. The worship of Dionysos† or the Celtic god of beer was a loud and disorderly affair. The rites of Christianity are incompatible with even religious drunkenness. This does no harm to the distillers, but is

---

* An English essayist, novelist, poet, and convert to Roman Catholicism (1874-1936).
† The ancient Greek god of wine and fertility.

very bad for Christianity. Countless persons desire self-transcendence and would be glad to find it in church. But, alas, "the hungry sheep look up and are not fed."* They take part in rites, they listen to sermons, they repeat prayers; but their thirst remains unassuaged. Disappointed, they turn to the bottle. For a time at least and in a kind of way, it works. Church may still be attended; but it is no more than the Musical Bank of Butler's *Erewhon*.† God may still be acknowledged; but He is God only on the verbal level, only in a strictly Pickwickian sense.‡ The effective object of worship is the bottle and the sole religious experience is that state of uninhibited and belligerent euphoria which follows the ingestion of the third cocktail.

We see, then, that Christianity and alcohol do not and cannot mix. Christianity and mescalin seem to be much more compatible. This has been demonstrated by many tribes of Indians, from Texas to as far north as Wisconsin. Among these tribes are to be found groups affiliated with the Native American Church, a sect whose principal rite is a kind of Early Christian agape, or love feast, where slices of peyote take the place of the sacramental bread and wine. These Native Americans regard the cactus as God's special gift to the Indians, and equate its effects with the workings of the divine Spirit.

Professor J. S. Slotkin, one of the very few white men ever to have participated in the rites of a Peyotist congregation, says of his fellow worshipers that they are "certainly not stupefied or drunk. . . . They never get out of rhythm or fumble their words, as a drunken or stupefied man would do. . . . They are all quiet, courteous and considerate of one another. I have never been in any white man's house of worship where there is either so much religious feeling or decorum." And what, we may ask, are these devout and well-behaved Peyotists experiencing? Not the mild sense of virtue which sustains the average Sunday churchgoer through ninety minutes of boredom. Not even those high feelings, inspired by thoughts of the Creator and the Redeemer, the Judge and

---

* A quotation from John Milton's *Lycidas* (1637).
† A Utopian satire (1872) by the English novelist and essayist Samuel Butler (1835-1902). *Erewhon* is an anagram of *nowhere*. The Musical Bank is Butler's satirical depiction of a commercially corrupted and ineffectual church where people exchange coins for music.
‡ Understood in an unusual or non-traditional way, like the peculiar meanings given to common words by Mr. Pickwick in Charles Dickens' novel *The Pickwick Papers* (1837).

the Comforter, which animate the pious. For these Native Americans, religious experience is something more direct and illuminating, more spontaneous, less the homemade product of the superficial, self-conscious mind. Sometimes (according to the reports collected by Dr. Slotkin) they see visions, which may be of Christ Himself. Sometimes they hear the voice of the Great Spirit. Sometimes they become aware of the presence of God and of those personal shortcomings which must be corrected if they are to do His will. The practical consequences of these chemical openings of doors into the Other World seem to be wholly good. Dr. Slotkin reports that habitual Peyotists are on the whole more industrious, more temperate (many of them abstain altogether from alcohol), more peaceable than non-Peyotists. A tree with such satisfactory fruits cannot be condemned out of hand as evil.

In sacramentalizing the use of peyote, the Indians of the Native American Church have done something which is at once psychologically sound and historically respectable. In the early centuries of Christianity many pagan rites and festivals were baptized, so to say, and made to serve the purposes of the Church. These jollifications were not particularly edifying; but they assuaged a certain psychological hunger and, instead of trying to suppress them, the earlier missionaries had the sense to accept them for what they were, soul-satisfying expressions of fundamental urges, and to incorporate them into the fabric of the new religion. What the Native Americans have done is essentially similar. They have taken a pagan custom (a custom, incidentally, far more elevating and enlightening than most of the rather brutish carousals and mummeries adopted from European paganism) and given it a Christian significance.

Though but recently introduced into the northern United States, peyote-eating and the religion based upon it have become important symbols of the red man's right to spiritual independence. Some Indians have reacted to white supremacy by becoming Americanized, others by retreating into traditional Indianism. But some have tried to make the best of both worlds, indeed of all the worlds—the best of Indianism, the best of Christianity, and the best of those Other Worlds of transcendental experience, where the soul knows itself as unconditioned and of like nature with the divine. Hence the Native American Church. In it two great appetites of the soul—the urge to independence and self-determination and the urge to s elf-transcendence—were fused with, and interpreted in the light of, a third—the urge to worship, to justify the ways of God to man, to explain the universe by means of a coherent theology.

Lo, the poor Indian, whose untutored mind
*Clothes him in front, but leaves him bare behind.**

But actually it is we, the rich and highly educated whites, who have left ourselves bare behind. We cover our anterior nakedness with some philosophy—Christian, Marxian, Freudo-Physicalist—but abaft we remain uncovered, at the mercy of all the winds of circumstance. The poor Indian, on the other hand, has had the wit to protect his rear by supplementing the fig leaf of a theology with the breechclout of transcendental experience.

I am not so foolish as to equate what happens under the influence of mescalin or of any other drug, prepared or in the future pre-parable, with the realization of the end and ultimate purpose of human life: Enlightenment, the Beatific Vision. All I am suggesting is that the mescalin experience is what Catholic theologians call "a gratuitous grace," not necessary to salvation but potentially helpful and to be accepted thankfully, if made available. To be shaken out of the ruts of ordinary perception, to be shown for a few timeless hours the outer and the inner world, not as they appear to an animal obsessed with survival or to a human being obsessed with words and notions, but as they are apprehended, directly and unconditionally, by Mind at Large—this is an experience of inestimable value to everyone and especially to the intellectual. For the intellectual is by definition the man for whom, in Goethe's† phrase, "the word is essentially fruitful." He is the man who feels that "what we perceive by the eye is foreign to us as such and need not impress us deeply." And yet, though himself an intellectual and one

---

* A parody of lines from Alexander Pope's long philosophical poem *An Essay on Man* (1733): Lo! the poor Indian, whose untutor'd mind Sees God in clouds, or hears him in the wind.
† Johann Wolfgang von Goethe (1749-1832), a German poet and dramatist, was, for much of his life, a romantic concerned with the direct relationship of the human being to external nature.

of the supreme masters of language, Goethe did not always agree with his own evaluation of the word. "We talk," he wrote in middle life, "far too much. We should talk less and draw more. I personally should like to renounce speech altogether and, like organic Nature, communicate everything I have to say in sketches. That fig tree, this little snake, the cocoon on my window sill quietly awaiting its future—all these are momentous signatures. A person able to decipher their meaning properly would soon be able to dispense with the written or the spoken word altogether. The more I think of it, there is something futile, mediocre, even (I am tempted to say) foppish about speech. By contrast, how the gravity of Nature and her silence startle you, when you stand face to face with her, undistracted, before a barren ridge or in the desolation of the ancient hills." We can never dispense with language and the other symbol systems; for it is by means of them, and only by their means, that we have raised ourselves above the brutes, to the level of human beings. But we can easily become the victims as well as the beneficiaries of these systems. We must learn how to handle words effectively; but at the same time we must preserve and, if necessary, intensify our ability to look at the world directly and not through that half opaque medium of concepts, which distorts every given fact into the all too familiar likeness of some generic label or explanatory abstraction.

Literary or scientific, liberal or specialist, all our education is predominantly verbal and therefore fails to accomplish what it is supposed to do. Instead of transforming children into fully developed adults, it turns out students of the natural sciences who are completely unaware of Nature as the primary fact of experience, it inflicts upon the world students of the humanities who know nothing of humanity, their own or anyone else's.

Gestalt psychologists, such as Samuel Renshaw, have devised methods for widening the range and increasing the acuity of human perceptions. But do our educators apply them? The answer is, No.

Teachers in every field of psycho-physical skill, from seeing to tennis, from tightrope walking to prayer, have discovered, by trial and error, the conditions of optimum functioning within their special fields. But have any of the great Foundations financed a project for co-ordinating these empirical findings into a general theory and practice of heightened creativeness? Again, so far as I am aware, the answer is, No.

All sorts of cultists and queer fish teach all kinds of techniques for achieving health, contentment, peace of mind; and for many of their hearers many of these techniques are demonstrably effective. But do we see respectable psychologists, philosophers and clergymen boldly descending into those odd and sometimes malodorous wells, at the bottom of which poor Truth is so often condemned to sit? Yet once more the answer is, No.

And now look at the history of mescalin research. Seventy years ago men of first-rate ability described the transcendental experiences which come to those who, in good health, under proper conditions and in the right spirit, take the drug. How many philosophers, how many theologians, how many professional educators have had the curiosity to open this Door in the Wall? The answer, for all practical purposes, is, None.

In a world where education is predominantly verbal, highly educated people find it all but impossible to pay serious attention to anything but words and notions. There is always money for, there are always doctorates in, the learned foolery of research into what, for scholars, is the all-important problem: Who influenced whom to say what when? Even in this age of technology the verbal humanities are honored. The non-verbal humanities, the arts of being directly aware of the given facts of our existence, are almost completely ignored. A catalogue, a bibliography, a definitive edition of a third-rate versifier's *ipsissima verba,** a stupendous index to end all indexes—any genuinely Alexandrian project is sure of approval and financial support. But when it comes to finding out how you and I, our children and grandchildren, may become more perceptive, more intensely aware of inward and outward reality, more open to the Spirit, less apt, by psychological malpractices, to make ourselves physically ill, and more capable of controlling our own autonomic nervous system—when it comes to any form of non-verbal education more fundamental (and more likely to be of some

---

* Latin: the very words.

practical use) than Swedish drill,* no really respectable person in any really respectable university or church will do anything about it. Verbalists are suspicious of the non-verbal; rationalists fear the given, non-rational fact; intellectuals feel that "what we perceive by the eye (or in any other way) is foreign to us as such and need not impress us deeply." Besides, this matter of education in the non-verbal humanities will not fit into any of the established pigeonholes. It is not religion, not neurology, not gymnastics, not morality or civics, not even experimental psychology. This being so the subject is, for academic and ecclesiastical purposes, non-existent and may safely be ignored altogether or left, with a patronizing smile, to those whom the Pharisees† of verbal orthodoxy call cranks, quacks, charlatans and unqualified amateurs.

"I have always found," Blake‡ wrote rather bitterly, "that Angels have the vanity to speak of themselves as the only wise. This they do with a confident insolence sprouting from systematic reasoning."

Systematic reasoning is something we could not, as a species or as individuals, possibly do without. But neither, if we are to remain sane, can we possibly do without direct perception, the more unsystematic the better, of the inner and outer worlds into which we have been born. This given reality is an infinite which passes all understanding and yet admits of being directly and in some sort totally apprehended. It is a transcendence belonging to another order than the human, and yet it may be present to us as a felt immanence, an experienced participation. To be enlightened is to be aware, always, of total reality in its immanent otherness—to be aware of it and yet to remain in a condition to survive as an animal, to think and feel as a human being, to resort whenever expedient to systematic reasoning. Our goal is to discover that we have always been where we ought to be. Unhappily we make the task exceedingly difficult for ourselves. Meanwhile, however, there are gratuitous graces in the form of partial and fleeting realizations. Under a more realistic, a less exclusively verbal system of education than ours,

---

* A system of exercising the body's muscles and joints.
† Self-righteous, hypocritical people.
‡ William Blake (1757-1827), an English visionary poet and artist. The titles of both of the books by Huxley excerpted here were taken from Blake's revolutionary work *The Marriage of Heaven and Hell* (1790): "If the doors of perception were cleansed every thing would appear to man as it is, infinite."

every Angel (in Blake's sense of that word) would be permitted as a sabbatical treat, would be urged and even, if necessary, compelled to take an occasional trip through some chemical Door in the Wall into the world of transcendental experience. If it terrified him, it would be unfortunate but probably salutary. If it brought him a brief but timeless illumination, so much the better. In either case the Angel might lose a little of the confident insolence sprouting from systematic reasoning and the consciousness of having read all the books.

Near the end of his life Aquinas* experienced Infused Contemplation. Thereafter he refused to go back to work on his unfinished book. Compared with *this*, everything he had read and argued about and written—Aristotle and the Sentences, the Questions, the Propositions, the majestic Summas—was no better than chaff or straw. For most intellectuals such a sit-down strike would be inadvisable, even morally wrong. But the Angelic Doctor had done more systematic reasoning than any twelve ordinary Angels, and was already ripe for death. He had earned the right, in those last months of his mortality, to turn away from merely symbolic straw and chaff to the bread of actual and substantial Fact. For Angels of a lower order and with better prospects of longevity, there must be a return to the straw. But the man who comes back through the Door in the Wall will never be quite the same as the man who went out. He will be wiser but less cocksure, happier but less self-satisfied, humbler in acknowledging his ignorance yet better equipped to understand the relationship of words to things, of systematic reasoning to the unfathomable Mystery which it tries, forever vainly, to comprehend.

HEAVEN AND HELL

Some people never consciously discover their antipodes. Others make an occasional landing. Yet others (but they are few) find it easy to go and come as they please. For the naturalist of the mind, the collector of psychological specimens, the primary need is some safe, easy and reliable method of transporting himself and others from the Old World to the

---

* St. Thomas Aquinas (1225-74), the most influential medieval philosopher—known as the "Angelic Doctor"; his *Summa Theologica* sought to reconcile the truths of reason with those of faith.

New, from the continent of familiar cows and horses to the continent of a wallaby and the platypus.

Two such methods exist. Neither of them is perfect; but both are sufficiently reliable, sufficiently easy and sufficiently safe to justify their employment by those who know what they are doing. In the first case the soul is transported to its far-off destination by the aid of a chemical—either mescalin or lysergic acid.* In the second case, the vehicle is psychological in nature, and the passage to the mind's antipodes is accomplished by hypnosis.† The two vehicles carry the consciousness to the same region; but the drug has the longer range and takes its passengers further into the *terra incognita*.‡

How and why does hypnosis produce its observed effects? We do not know. For our present purposes, however, we do not have to know. All that is necessary, in this context, is to record the fact that some hypnotic subjects are transported, in the trance state, to a region in the mind's antipodes, where they find the equivalent of marsupials—strange psychological creatures leading an autonomous existence according to the law of their own being.

About the physiological effects of mescalin we know a little. Probably (for we are not yet certain) it interferes with the enzyme system that regulates cerebral functioning. By doing so it lowers the efficiency of the brain as an instrument for focusing the mind on the problems of life on the surface of our planet. This lowering of what may be called the biological efficiency of the brain seems to permit the entry into consciousness of certain classes of mental events, which are normally excluded, because they possess no survival value. Similar intrusions of biologically useless, but aesthetically and sometimes spiritually valuable material may occur as the result of illness or fatigue; or they may be induced by fasting, or a period of confinement in a place of darkness and complete silence.

---

* An extremely potent hallucinogen (inducer of false perceptions of the external world) chemically similar to mescalin and to adrenalin; used in the synthesis of LSD.

† In an appendix Huxley also mentions the use of carbon dioxide and the stroboscopie lamp as "two other, less effective aids to visionary experience."

‡ Latin: unknown territory.

A person under the influence of mescalin or lysergic acid will stop seeing visions when given a large dose of nicotinic acid. This helps to explain the effectiveness of fasting as an inducer of visionary experience. By reducing the amount of available sugar, fasting lowers the brain's biological efficiency and so makes possible the entry into consciousness of material possessing no survival value. Moreover, by causing a vitamin deficiency, it removes from the blood that known inhibitor of visions, nicotinic acid. Another inhibitor of visionary experience is ordinary, everyday, perceptual experience. Experimental psychologists have found that, if you confine a man to a "restricted environment," where there is no light, no sound, nothing to smell and, if you put him in a tepid bath, only one, almost imperceptible thing to touch, the victim will very soon start "seeing things," "hearing things" and having strange bodily sensations.

Milarepa, in his Himalayan cavern, and the anchorites* of the Thebaic! followed essentially the same procedure and got essentially the same results. A thousand pictures of the Temptations of St. Anthony bear witness to the effectiveness of restricted diet and restricted environment. Asceticism, it is evident, has a double motivation. If men and women torment their bodies, it is not only because they hope in this way to atone for past sins and avoid future punishments; it is also because they long to visit the mind's antipodes and do some visionary sightseeing. Empirically and from the reports of other ascetics, they know that fasting and a restricted environment will transport them where they long to go. Their self-inflicted punishment may be the door to paradise. (It may also—and this is a point which will be discussed in a later paragraph—be a door into the infernal regions.)

From the point of view of an inhabitant of the Old World, marsupials are exceedingly odd. But oddity is not the same as randomness. Kangaroos and wallabies may lack verisimilitude; but their improbability repeats itself and obeys recognizable laws. The same is true of the psychological creatures inhabiting the remoter regions of our minds. The experiences encountered under the influence of mescalin or deep hypnosis are very

---

* Hermits.

strange; but they are strange with a certain regularity, strange according to a pattern.

What are the common features which this pattern imposes upon our visionary experiences? First and most important is the experience of light. Everything seen by those who visit the mind's antipodes is brilliantly illuminated and seems to shine from within. All colors are intensified to a pitch far beyond anything seen in the normal state, and at the same time the mind's capacity for recognizing fine distinctions of tone and hue is notably heightened. . . .

The typical mescalin or lysergic-acid experience begins with perceptions of colored, moving, living geometrical forms. In time, pure geometry becomes concrete, and the visionary perceives, not patterns, but patterned things, such as carpets, carvings, mosaics. These give place to vast and complicated buildings, in the midst of landscapes, which change continuously, passing from richness to more intensely colored richness, from grandeur to deepening grandeur. Heroic figures, of the kind that Blake called "The Seraphim," may make their appearance, alone or in multitudes. Fabulous animals move across the scene. Everything is novel and amazing. Almost never does the visionary see anything that reminds him of his own past. He is not remembering scenes, persons or objects, and he is not inventing them; he is looking on at a new creation.

The raw material for this creation is provided by the visual experiences of ordinary life; but the molding of this material into forms is the work of someone who is most certainly not the self, who originally had the experiences, or who later recalled and reflected upon them. They are (to quote the words used by Dr. J. R. Smythies in a recent paper in the *American Journal of Psychiatry*) "the work of a highly differentiated mental compartment, without any apparent connection, emotional or volitional, with the aims, interests, or feelings of the person concerned."

Here, in quotation or condensed paraphrase, is Weir Mitchell's account of the visionary world to which he was transported by peyote, the cactus which is the natural source of mescalin.

At his entry into that world he saw a host of "star points" and what looked like "fragments of stained glass." Then came "delicate floating films of color." These were displaced by an "abrupt rush of countless points of white light," sweeping across the field of vision. Next there were zigzag lines of very bright colors, which somehow turned into swelling clouds of still more brilliant hues. Buildings now made their appearance, and then landscapes. There was a Gothic tower of elaborate design with worn statues in the doorways or on stone brackets. "As I gazed, every projecting angle, cornice and even the faces of the stones at their joinings were by degrees covered or hung with clusters of what seemed to be huge precious stones, but uncut stones, some being more like masses of transparent fruit. . . . All seemed to possess an interior light." The Gothic tower gave place to a mountain, a cliff of inconceivable height, a colossal bird claw carved in stone and projecting over the abyss, an endless unfurling of colored draperies, and an efflorescence of more precious stones. Finally there was a view of green and purple waves breaking on a beach "with myriads of lights of the same tint as the waves."

Every mescalin experience, every vision arising under hypnosis, is unique; but all recognizably belong to the same species. The landscapes, the architectures, the clustering gems, the brilliant and intricate patterns— these, in their atmosphere of preternatural light, preternatural color and preternatural significance, are the stuff of which the mind's antipodes are made. Why this should be so, we have no idea. It is a brute fact of experience which, whether we like it or not, we have to accept—just as we have to accept the fact of kangaroos.

From these facts of visionary experience let us now pass to the accounts preserved, in all the cultural traditions, of Other Worlds—the worlds inhabited by the gods, by the spirits of the dead, by man in his primal state of innocence.

Reading these accounts, we are immediately struck by the close similarity between induced or spontaneous visionary experience and the heavens and fairylands of folklore and religion. Preternatural light, preternatural intensity of coloring, preternatural significance— these are characteristic of all the Other Worlds and Golden Ages. And in virtually every case this preternaturally significant light shines on, or shines out of, a landscape of such surpassing beauty that words cannot express it.

Thus in the Greco-Roman tradition we find the lovely Garden of the Hesperides, the Elysian Plain, and the fair Island of Leuke, to which Achilles was translated. Memnon went to another luminous island, somewhere in the East. Odysseus and Penelope traveled in the opposite direction and enjoyed their immortality with Circe in Italy. Still further to the west were the Islands of the Blest, first mentioned by Hesiod and so firmly believed in that, as late as the first century b.c., Sertorius planned to send a squadron from Spain to discover them.

Magically lovely islands reappear in the folklore of the Celts and, at the opposite side of the world, in that of the Japanese. And between Avalon in the extreme West and Horaisan in the Far East, there is the land of Uttarakuru, the Other World of the Hindus. "The land," we read in the *Ramayana*,* "is watered by lakes with golden lotuses. There are rivers by thousands, full of leaves of the color of sapphire and lapis lazuli; and the lakes, resplendent like the morning sun, are adorned by golden beds of red lotus. The country all around is covered by jewels and precious stones, with gay beds of blue lotus, golden-petalled. Instead of sand, pearls, gems and gold form the banks of the rivers, which are overhung with trees of fire-bright gold. These trees perpetually bear flowers and fruit, give forth a sweet fragrance and abound with birds."

Uttarakuru, we see, resembles the landscapes of the mescalin experience in being rich with precious stones. And this characteristic is common to virtually all the Other Worlds of religious tradition. Every paradise abounds in gems, or at least in gemlike objects resembling, as Weir Mitchell puts it, "transparent fruit/' Here, for example, is Ezekiel's version of the Garden of Eden. "Thou hast been in Eden, the garden of God. Every precious stone was thy covering, the sardius, topaz and the diamond, the beryl, the onyx and the jasper, the sapphire, the emerald and the carbuncle, and gold. . . . Thou art the anointed cherub that covereth . . . thou hast walked up and down in the midst of the stones of fire." The Buddhist paradises are adorned with similar "stones of fire.". . .

---

* An ancient Indian epic poem (*ca.* 1000 B.C.).

21

C. Wright Mills

The Higher Immorality

As a result of the massive destruction of life and property in Europe during two world wars, the United States by 1950 had become the leader of the Western nations and held an unprecedented position of world power. An incisive analyst and critic of this new power was C. Wright Mills (1916-1962). Born in Waco, Texas, Mills earned degrees in philosophy and sociology from the University of Texas and, in 1941, a doctorate in sociology and anthropology from the University of Wisconsin. Thereafter he taught sociology at the University of Maryland and, from 1945 until his death, at Columbia University.

Evident in the many works by Mills is his belief that there exists in American society a concentration of power wielded by a small elite group. In his book The Power Elite *(1956), he describes this group as an interlocking triumvirate of those who "rule the big corporations . . . , run the machinery of the state, and . . . direct the military establishment." The following selection is a reprinting of the final chapter of* The Power Elite. *In it Mills attacks the "higher immorality" of that dominating triumvirate which has divorced power from knowledge, substituted "personality" for depth of character, and selected for leadership mediocre men who thrive in a condition of "organized irresponsibility."*

From *The Power Elite* by C. Wright Mills. Copyright © 1956 by Oxford University Press, Inc. Reprinted by permission. [Pp. 343-61.]

The higher immorality can neither be narrowed to the political sphere nor understood as primarily a matter of corrupt men in fundamentally sound institutions. Political corruption is one aspect of a more general immorality; the level of moral sensibility that now prevails is not merely a matter of corrupt men. The higher immorality is a systematic feature of the American elite; its general acceptance is an essential feature of the mass society.

Of course, there may be corrupt men in sound institutions, but when institutions are corrupting many of the men who live and work in them are necessarily corrupted. In the corporate era, economic relations become impersonal—and the executive feels less personal responsibility. Within the corporate worlds of business, war-making and politics, the private conscience is attenuated—and the higher immorality is institutionalized. It is not merely a question of a corrupt administration in corporation, army, or state; it is a feature of the corporate rich, as a capitalist stratum, deeply intertwined with the politics of the military state.

From this point of view, the most important question, for instance, about the campaign funds of ambitious young politicians is not whether the politicians are morally insensitive, but whether or not any young man in American politics, who has come so far and so fast, could very well have done so today without possessing or acquiring a somewhat blunted moral sensibility. Many of the problems of "white-collar crime" and of relaxed public morality, of high-priced vice and of fading personal integrity, are problems of *structural* immorality. They are not merely the problem of the small character twisted by the bad milieu. And many people are at least vaguely aware that this is so. As news of higher immoralities breaks, they often say, "Well, another one got caught today," thereby implying that the cases disclosed are not odd events involving occasional characters but symptoms of a widespread condition. There is good probative evidence that they are right. But what is the underlying condition of which all these instances are symptoms?

1

The moral uneasiness of our time results from the fact that older values and codes of uprightness no longer grip the men and women of the corporate era, nor have they been replaced by new values and codes which would lend moral meaning and sanction to the corporate routines they must now follow. It is not that the mass public has explicitly rejected received codes; it is rather that to many of the members these codes have become hollow. No moral terms of acceptance are available, but neither are any moral terms of rejection. As individuals they are morally defenseless; as groups, they are politically indifferent. It is this generalized lack of commitment that is meant when it is said that "the public" is morally confused.

But, of course, not only "the public" is morally confused in this way. "The tragedy of official Washington," James Reston* has commented, "is that it is confounded at every turn by the hangover of old political habits and outworn institutions but is no longer nourished by the ancient faith on which it was founded. It clings to the bad things and casts away the permanent. It professes belief but does not believe. It knows the old words but has forgotten the melody. It is engaged in an ideological war without being able to define its own ideology. It condemns the materialism of an atheistic enemy, but glorifies its own materialism."

In economic and political institutions the corporate rich now wield enormous power, but they have never had to win the moral consent of those over whom they hold this power. Every such naked interest, every new, unsanctioned power of corporation, farm bloc, labor union, and governmental agency that has risen in the past two generations has been clothed with morally loaded slogans. For what is *not* done in the name of the public interest? As these slogans wear out, new ones are industriously made up, also to be banalized in due course. And all the while, recurrent economic and military crises spread fears, hesitations, and anxieties which give new urgency to the busy search for moral justifications and decorous excuses.

"Crisis" is a bankrupted term, because so many men in high places have evoked it in order to cover up their extraordinary policies and deeds; as a matter of fact, it is precisely the absence of crises that is a cardinal feature of the higher immorality. For genuine crises involve situations in which men at large are presented with genuine alternatives, the moral meanings of which are clearly opened to public debate. The higher immorality, the general weakening of older values and the

---

* An American (Scottish-born) newspaper columnist (1909-).

organization of irresponsibility have not involved any public crises; on the contrary, they have been matters of a creeping indifference and a silent hollowing out.

The images that generally prevail of the higher circles are the images of the elite seen as celebrities. In discussing the professional celebrities, I noted that the instituted elites of power do not monopolize the bright focus of national acclaim. They share it nationally with the frivolous or the sultry creatures of the world of celebrity, which thus serves as a dazzling blind of their true power. In the sense that the volume of publicity and acclaim is mainly and continuously upon those professional celebrities, it is not upon the power elite. So the social visibility of that elite is lowered by the status distraction, or rather public vision of them is through the celebrity who amuses and entertains—or disgusts, as the case may be.

The absence of any firm moral order of belief makes men in the mass all the more open to the manipulation and distraction of the world of the celebrities. In due course, such a "turnover" of appeals and codes and values as they are subjected to leads them to distrust and cynicism, to a sort of Machiavellianism-for-the-little-man. Thus they vicariously enjoy the prerogatives of the corporate rich, the nocturnal antics of the celebrity, and the sad-happy life of the very rich.

But with all this, there is still one old American value that has not markedly declined: the value of money and of the things money can buy—these, even in inflated times, seem as solid and enduring as stainless steel. "I've been rich and I've been poor," Sophie Tucker has said, "and believe me, rich is best." As many other values are weakened, the question for Americans becomes not "Is there anything that money, used with intelligence, will not buy?" but, "How many of the things that money will *not* buy are valued and desired more than what money *will* buy?" Money is the one unambiguous criterion of success, and such success is still the sovereign American value.

Whenever the standards of the moneyed life prevail, the man with money, no matter how he got it, will eventually be respected. A million dollars, it is said, covers a multitude of sins. It is not only that men want money; it is that their very standards are pecuniary. In a society in which the money-maker has had no serious rival for repute and honor, the word "practical" comes to mean useful for private gain, and "common sense," the sense to get ahead financially. The pursuit of the moneyed life is the commanding value, in relation to which the influence of other values has declined, so men easily become morally ruthless in the pursuit of easy money and fast estate-building.

A great deal of American corruption—although not all of it—is simply a part of the old effort to get rich and then to become richer. But today the context in which the old drive must operate has changed. When both economic and political institutions were small and scattered—as in the simpler models of classical economics and Jeffersonian democracy—no man had it in his power to bestow or to receive great favors. But when political institutions and economic opportunities are at once concentrated and linked, then public office can be used for private gain.

Governmental agencies contain no more of the higher immorality than do business corporations. Political men can grant financial favors only when there are economic men ready and willing to take them. And economic men can seek political favors only when there are political agents who can bestow such favors. The publicity spotlight, of course, shines brighter upon the transactions of the men in government, for which there is good reason. Expectations being higher, publics are more easily disappointed by public officials. Businessmen are supposed to be out for themselves, and if they successfully skate on legally thin ice, Americans generally honor them for having gotten away with it. But in a civilization so thoroughly business-penetrated as America, the rules of business are carried over into government—especially when so many businessmen have gone into government. How many executives would really fight for a law requiring a careful and public accounting of all executive contracts and "expense accounts"? High income taxes have resulted in a network of collusion between big firm and higher employee. There are many ingenious ways to cheat the spirit of the tax laws, as we have seen, and the standards of consumption of many high-priced men are determined more by complicated expense accounts than by simple take-home pay. Like prohibition, the laws of income taxes and the regulations of wartime exist without the support of firm business convention. It is merely illegal to cheat them, but it is smart to get away with it. Laws without supporting moral conventions invite crime, but much more importantly, they spur the growth of an expedient, amoral attitude.

A society that is in its higher circles and on its middle levels widely believed to be a network of smart rackets does not produce men with an inner moral sense; a society that is merely expedient does not produce men of conscience. A society that narrows the meaning of "success" to the big money and in its terms condemns failure as the chief vice, raising money to the plane of absolute value, will produce the sharp operator and the shady deal. Blessed are the cynical, for only they have what it takes to succeed.

2

In the corporate world, in the political directorate, and increasingly in the ascendant military, the heads of the big hierarchies and power machines are seen not only as men who have succeeded, but as wielders of the patronage of success. They interpret and they apply to individuals the criteria of success. Those immediately below them are usually members of their clique, of their clientele, sound men as they themselves are sound. But the hierarchies are intricately related to one another, and inside each clique are some whose loyalties are to other cliques. There are personal loyalties as well as official ones, personal as well as impersonal criteria for advancement. As we trace the career of the individual member of various higher circles, we are also tracing the history of his loyalties, for the first and overshadowing fact about the higher circles, from the standpoint of what it takes to succeed within them, is that they are based upon self-co-optation.* The second fact about these hierarchies of success is that they do not form one monolithic structure; they are a complex set of variously related and often antagonistic cliques. The third fact we must recognize is that, in any such world, younger men who would succeed attempt to relate themselves to those in charge of their selection as successes.

Accordingly, the American literature of practical aspiration—which carries the great fetish of success—has undergone a significant shift in its advice about "what it takes to succeed." The sober, personal virtues

---

* The tendency, according to Mills, of those already in the "higher circles" of power to select (co-opt) for advancement into those circles only those who reflect their own career values.

of will power and honesty, of high-mindedness and the constitutional inability to say "yes" to The Easy Road of women, tobacco, and wine—this later nineteenth-century image has given way to "the most important single factor, the effective personality," which "commands attention by charm," and "radiates self-confidence." In this "new way of life," one must smile often and be a good listener, talk in terms of the other man's interests and make the other feel important—and one must do all this sincerely. Personal relations, in short, have become part of "public relations," a sacrifice of selfhood on a personality market, to the sole end of individual success in the corporate way of life. Being justified by superior merit and hard work, but being founded on co-optation by a clique, often on quite other grounds, the elite careerist must continually persuade others and himself as well that he is the opposite of what he actually is.

It is the proud claim of the higher circles in America that their members are entirely self-made. That is their self-image and their well-publicized myth. Popular proof of this is based on anecdotes; its scholarly proof is supposed to rest upon statistical rituals whereby it is shown that varying proportions of the men at the top are sons of men of lower rank. We have already seen the proportions of given elite circles composed of the men who have risen. But what is more important than the proportions of the sons of wage workers among these higher circles is the criteria of admission to them, and the question of who applies these criteria. We cannot from upward mobility infer higher merit. Even if the rough figures that now generally hold were reversed, and 90 per cent of the elite were sons of wage workers—but the criteria of co-optation by the elite remained what they now are—we could not from that mobility necessarily infer merit. Only if the criteria of the top positions were meritorious, and only if they were self-applied, as in a purely entrepreneurial manner, could we smuggle merit into such statistics—from any statistics—of mobility. The idea that the self-made man is somehow "good" and that the family-made man is not good makes moral sense only when the career is independent, when one is on one's own as an entrepreneur. It would also make sense in a strict bureaucracy where examinations control advancement. It makes little sense in the system of corporate co-optation.

There is, in psychological fact, no such thing as a self-made man. No man makes himself, least of all the members of the American elite. In a world of corporate hierarchies, men are selected by those above them in the hierarchy in accordance with whatever criteria they use. In connection with the corporations of America, we have seen the current criteria. Men shape themselves to fit them, and are thus made by the criteria, the social premiums that prevail. If there is no such thing as a self-made man, there is such a thing as a self-used man, and there are many such men among the American elite.

Under such conditions of success, there is no virtue in starting out poor and becoming rich. Only where the ways of becoming rich are such as to require virtue or to lead to virtue does personal enrichment imply virtue. In a system of co-optation from above, whether you began rich or poor seems less relevant in revealing what kind of man you are when you have arrived than in revealing the principles of those in charge of selecting the ones who succeed.

All this is sensed by enough people below the higher circles to lead to cynical views of the lack of connection between merit and mobility, between virtue and success. It is a sense of the immorality of accomplishment, and it is revealed in the prevalence of such views as: "it's all just another racket," and "it's not what you know but who you know." Considerable numbers of people now accept the immorality of accomplishment as a going fact.

Some observers are led by their sense of the immorality of accomplishment to the ideology, obliquely set forth by academic social science, of human relations in industry; still others to the solace of mind provided by the newer literature of resignation, of peace of mind, which in some quietened circles replaces the old literature of frenzied aspiration, of how to get ahead. But, regardless of the particular style of reaction, the sense of the immorality of accomplishment often feeds into that level of public sensibility which we have called the higher immorality. The old self-made man's is a tarnished image, and no other image of success has taken its once bright place. Success itself, as the American model of excellence, declines as it becomes one more feature of the higher immorality.

3

Moral distrust of the American elite—as well as the fact of organized irresponsibility—rests upon the higher immorality, but also upon vague feelings about the higher ignorance. Once upon a time in the United States, men of affairs were also men of sensibility: to a considerable extent the elite of power and the elite of culture coincided, and where they did not coincide they often overlapped as circles. Within the compass of a knowledgeable and effective public, knowledge and power were in effective touch; and more than that, this public decided much that was decided.

"Nothing is more revealing," James Reston has written, "than to read the debate in the House of Representatives in the Eighteen Thirties on Greece's fight with Turkey for independence and the Greek-Turkish debate in the Congress in 1947. The first is dignified and eloquent, the argument marching from principle through illustration to conclusion; the second is a dreary garble of debating points, full of irrelevancies and bad history." George Washington in 1783 relaxed with Voltaire's "letters" and Locke's "On Human Understanding"; Eisenhower read cowboy tales and detective stories. For such men as now typically arrive in higher political, economic and military circles, the briefing and the memorandum seem to have pretty well replaced not only the serious book, but the newspaper as well. Given the immorality of accomplishment, this is perhaps as it must be, but what is somewhat disconcerting about it is that they are below the level on which they might feel a little bit ashamed of the uncultivated style of their relaxation and of their mental fare, and that no self-cultivated public is in a position by its reactions to educate them to such uneasiness.

By the middle of the twentieth century, the American elite have become an entirely different breed of men from those who could on any reasonable grounds be considered a cultural elite, or even for that matter cultivated men of sensibility. Knowledge and power are not truly united inside the ruling circles; and when men of knowledge do come to a point of contact with the circles of powerful men, they come not as peers but as hired men. The elite of power, wealth, and celebrity do not have even a passing acquaintance with the elite of culture, knowledge and sensibility; they are not in touch with them—although the ostentatious fringes of the two worlds sometimes overlap in the world of the celebrity.

Most men are encouraged to assume that, in general, the most powerful and the wealthiest are also the most knowledgeable or, as they might say, "the smartest." Such ideas are propped up by many little slogans about those who "teach because they can't *do*" and about "if you're so smart, why aren't you rich?" But all that such wisecracks mean is that those who use them assume that power and wealth are sovereign values for all men and especially for men "who are smart." They assume also that knowledge always pays off in such ways, or surely ought to, and that the test of genuine knowledge is just such pay-offs. The powerful and the wealthy *must* be the men of most knowledge, otherwise how could they be where they are? But to say that those who succeed to power must be "smart," is to say that power *is* knowledge. To say that those who succeed to wealth must be smart, is to say that wealth *is* knowledge.

The prevalence of such assumptions does reveal something that is true: that ordinary men, even today, are prone to explain and to justify power and wealth in terms of knowledge or ability. Such assumptions also reveal something of what has happened to the kind of experience that knowledge has come to be. Knowledge is no longer widely felt as an ideal; it is seen as an instrument. In a society of power and wealth, knowledge is valued as an instrument of power and wealth, and also, of course, as an ornament in conversation.

What knowledge does to a man (in clarifying what he is, and setting him free)—that is the personal ideal of knowledge. What knowledge does to a civilization (in revealing its human meaning, and setting it free)—that is the social ideal of knowledge. But today, the personal *and* the social ideals of knowledge have coincided in what knowledge does *for* the smart guy—it gets him ahead; and for the wise nation—it lends cultural prestige, sanctifying power with authority.

Knowledge seldom lends power to the man of knowledge. But the supposed, and secret, knowledge of some men-on-the-make, and their very free use thereof, has consequence for other men who have not the power of defense. Knowledge, of course, is neither good nor bad, nor is its use good or bad. "Bad men increase in knowledge as fast as good men," John Adams wrote, "and science, arts, taste, sense and letters, are employed for the purpose of injustice as well as for virtue." That was in 1790; today we have good reason to know that it is so.

The problem of knowledge and power is, and always has been, the problem of the relations of men of knowledge with men of power. Suppose we were to select the one hundred most powerful men, from all fields of power, in America today and line them up. And then, suppose we selected the one hundred most knowledgeable men, from all fields of social knowledge, and lined them up. How many men would be in *both* our line-ups? Of course our selection would depend upon what we mean by power and what we mean by knowledge—especially what we mean by knowledge. But, if we mean what the words seem to mean, surely we would find few if any men in America today who were in both groups, and surely we could find many more at the time the nation was founded than we could find today. For, in the eighteenth century, even in this colonial outpost, men of power pursued learning, and men of learning wen often in positions of power. In these respects we have, I believe, suffered grievous decline.

There is little union in the same persons of knowledge and power but persons of power do surround themselves with men of some knowledge, or at least with men who are experienced in shrewd dealings. The man of knowledge has not become a philosopher king; but he has often become a consultant, and moreover a consultant to a man who is neither king-like nor philosophical. It is, of course, true that the chairman of the pulp writers section of the Authors' League helped a leading senator "polish up the speeches he delivered in the 1952 senatorial campaign." But it is not natural in the course of their careers for men of knowledge to meet with those of power. The links between university and government are weak, and when they do occur, the man of knowledge appears as an "expert" which usually means as a hired technician. Like most others in this society, the man of knowledge is himself dependent for his livelihood upon the job, which nowadays is a prime sanction of thought control. Where getting ahead requires the good opinions of more powerful others, their judgments become prime objects of concern. Accordingly, in so far as intellectuals serve power directly—in a job hierarchy—they often do so unfreely.

The democratic man assumes the existence of a public, and in his rhetoric asserts that this public is the very seat of sovereignty. Two things are needed in a democracy: articulate and knowledgeable publics, and political leaders who if not men of reason are at least reasonably responsible to such knowledgeable publics as exist. Only where publics and leaders are responsive and responsible, are human affairs in democratic order, and only when knowledge has public relevance is this order possible. Only when mind has an autonomous basis, independent of power, but powerfully related to it, can mind exert its force in the shaping of human affairs. This is democratically possible only when there exists a free and knowledgeable public, to which men of knowledge may address themselves, and to which men of power are truly responsible. Such a public and such men—either of power or of knowledge—do not now prevail, and accordingly, knowledge does not now have democratic relevance in America.

The characteristic member of the higher circles today is an intellectual mediocrity, sometimes a conscientious one, but still a mediocrity. His intelligence is revealed only by his occasional realization that he is not up to the decisions he sometimes feels called upon to confront. But usually he keeps such feelings private, his public utterances being pious and sentimental, grim and brave, cheerful and empty in their universal generality. He is open only to abbreviated and vulgarized, predigested and slanted ideas. He is a commander of the age of the phone call, the memo, and the briefing.

By the mindlessness and mediocrity of men of affairs, I do not, of course, mean that these men are not sometimes intelligent—although that is by no means automatically the case. It is not, however, primarily a matter of the distribution of "intelligence"—as if intelligence were a homogeneous something of which there may be more or less. It is rather a matter of the type of intelligence, of the quality of mind that is selected and formed. It is a matter of the evaluation of substantive rationality as the chief value in a man's life and character and conduct. That evaluation is what is lacking in the American power elite. In its place there are "weight" and "judgment" which count for much more in their celebrated success than any subtlety of mind or force of intellect.

All around and just below the weighty man of affairs are his technical lieutenants of power who have been assigned the role of knowledge and even of speech: his public relations men, his ghost, his administrative assistants, his secretaries. And do not forget The Committees. With the increased means of decision, there is a crisis of understanding among the political directorate of the United States, and accordingly, there is often a commanding indecision.

The lack of knowledge as an experience among the elite ties in with the malign ascendancy of the expert, not only as fact but as legitimation. When questioned recently about a criticism of defense policies made by the leader of the opposition party, the Secretary of Defense replied, "Do you think he is an expert in the matter?" When pressed further by reporters he asserted that the "military chiefs think it is sound, and I think it is sound," and later, when asked about specific cases, added: "In some cases, all you can do is ask the Lord." With such a large role so arrogantly given to God and to experts, what room is there for political leadership? Much less for public debate or what is after all every bit as much a political and a moral as a military issue. But then, from before Pearl Harbor,* the trend has been the abdication of debate and the collapse of opposition under the easy slogans of bi-partisanship.

Beyond the lack of intellectual cultivation by political personnel and advisory circle, the absence of publicly relevant mind has come to mean that powerful decisions and important policies are not made in such a way as to be justified or attacked; in short, debated in any intellectual form. Moreover, the attempt to so justify them is often not even made. Public relations displace reasoned argument; manipulation and undebated decisions of power replace democratic authority. More and more, since the nineteenth century, as administration has replaced politics, the decisions of importance do not carry even the panoply of reasonable discussion, but are made by God, by experts, and by men like Mr. Wilson.†

---

* That is, even before the attack by Japanese naval air forces against the American naval base at Pearl Harbor, in Hawaii—December 7, 1941—and the subsequent entry of the United States into the Second World War.
† Charles Wilson (1890-1961), Secretary of Defense during President Dwight D. Eisenhower's first administration (1953-57).

More and more the area of the official secret expands, as well as the area of the secret listening in on those who might divulge in public what the public, not being composed of experts with Q clearance,* is not to know. The entire sequence of decisions concerning the production and the use of atomic weaponry has been made without any genuine public debate, and the facts needed to engage in that debate intelligently have been officially hidden, distorted, and ever lied about. As the decisions become more fateful, not only for Americans but literally for mankind, the sources of information are closed up, and the relevant facts needed for decision (even the decision; made!) are, as politically convenient "official secrets," withheld from the heavily laden channels of information.

In those channels, meanwhile, political rhetoric seems to slide lower and lower down the scale of cultivation and sensibility. The height of such mindless communications to masses, or what an thought to be masses, is probably the demagogic assumption that suspicion and accusation, if repeated often enough, somehow equal proof of guilt—just as repeated claims about toothpaste or brands of cigarettes are assumed to equal facts. The greatest kind of propaganda with which America is beset, the greatest at least in terms of volume and loudness, is commercial propaganda for soap and cigarettes and automobiles; it is to such things, or rather to Their Names, that this society most frequently sings its loudest praises. What is important about this is that by implication and omission, by emphasis and sometimes by flat statement, this astounding volume of propaganda for commodities is often untruthful and misleading; and is addressed more often to the belly or to the groin than to the head or to the heart. Public communications from those who make powerful decisions, or who would have us vote them into such decision-making places, more and more take on those qualities of mindlessness and myth which commercial propaganda and advertising have come to exemplify.

In America today, men of affairs are not so much dogmatic as they are mindless. Dogma has usually meant some more or less elaborated

* A government security classification that allowed those possessing it to have access to "secret" information.

justification of ideas and values, and thus has had some features (however inflexible and closed) of mind, of intellect, of reason. Nowadays what we are up against is precisely the absence of mind of any sort as a public force; what we are up against is a disinterest in and a fear of knowledge that might have liberating public relevance. What this makes possible are decisions having no rational justifications which the intellect could confront and engage in debate.

It is not the barbarous irrationality of dour political primitives that is the American danger; it is the respected judgments of Secretaries of State, the earnest platitudes of Presidents, the fearful self-righteousness of sincere young American politicians from sunny California. These men have replaced mind with platitude, and the dogmas by which they are legitimated are so widely accepted that no counter-balance of mind prevails against them. Such men as these are crackpot realists: in the name of realism they have constructed a paranoid reality all their own; in the name of practicality they have projected a Utopian image of capitalism. They have replaced the responsible interpretation of events with the disguise of events by a maze of public relations; respect for public debate with unshrewd notions of psychological warfare; intellectual ability with agility of the sound, mediocre judgment; the capacity to elaborate alternatives and gauge their consequences with the executive stance.

4

Despite—perhaps because of—the ostracism of mind from public affairs, the immorality of accomplishment, and the general prevalence of organized irresponsibility, the men of the higher circles benefit from the total power of the institutional domains over which they rule. For the power of these institutions, actual or potential, is ascribed to them as the ostensible decision-makers. Their position: and their activities, and even their persons, are hallowed by these ascriptions; and, around all the high places of power, there is a penumbra* of prestige in which the political directorate, the corporate rich, the admirals and generals are bathed. The elite of a society, however modest its individual member, embodies the prestige of the society's power. Moreover, few

---

* Surrounding atmosphere.

individuals in positions of such authority can long resist the temptation to base their self-images, at least in part, upon the sounding board of the collectivity which they head. Acting as the representative of his nation, his corporation, his army, in due course, he comes to consider himself and what he says and believes as expressive of the historically accumulated glory of the great institutions with which he comes to identify himself. When he speaks in the name of his country or its cause, its past glory also echoes in his ears.

Status, no longer rooted primarily in local communities, follows the big hierarchies, which are on a national scale. Status follows the big money, even if it has a touch of the gangster about it. Status follows power, even if it be without background. Below, in the mass society, old moral and traditional barriers to status break down and Americans look for standards of excellence among the circles above them, in terms of which to model themselves and judge their self-esteem. Yet nowadays, it seems easier for Americans to recognize such representative men in the past than in the present. Whether this is due to a real historical difference or merely to the political ease and expediency of hindsight is very difficult to tell. At any rate it is a fact that in the political assignments of prestige there is little disparagement of Washington, Jefferson, and Lincoln, but much disagreement about current figures. Representative men seem more easily recognizable after they have died; contemporary political leaders are merely politicians; they may be big or little, but they are not great, and increasingly they are seen in terms of the higher immorality.

Now again status follows power, and older types of exemplary figures have been replaced by the fraternity of the successful—the professional executives who have become the political elite, who are now the *official* representative men. It remains to be seen whether they will become representative men in the images and aspirations of the mass public, or whether they will endure any longer than the displaced liberals of the 'thirties. Their images are controversial, deeply involved in the immorality of accomplishment and the higher immorality in general. Increasingly, literate Americans feel that there is something synthetic about them. Their style and the conditions under which they become "big" lend themselves too readily to the suspicion of the build-up; the shadows of the ghost writer and the make-up man loom too large; the slickness of the fabrication is too apparent.

We should, of course, bear in mind that men of the higher circles may or may not seek to impose themselves as representative upon the underlying population, and that relevant public sectors of the population may or may not accept their images. An elite may try to impose its claims upon the mass public, but this public may not cash them in. On the contrary, it may be indifferent or even debunk their values, caricature their image, laugh at their claim to be representative men.

In his discussion of models of national character, Walter Bagehot* does not go into such possibilities; but it is clear that for our contemporaries we must consider them, since precisely this reaction has led to a sometimes frenzied and always expensive practice of what is known as "public relations." Those who have both power and status are perhaps best off when they do not actively have to seek acclaim. The truly proud old families will not seek it; the professional celebrities are specialists in seeking it actively. Increasingly, the political, economic, and military elite—as we have seen—compete with the celebrities and seek to borrow their status. Perhaps those who have unprecedented power without the aura of status, will always seek it, even if uneasily, among those who have publicity without power.

For the mass public, there is the status distraction of the celebrity, as well as the economic distraction of war prosperity; for the liberal intellectual, who does look to the political arena, there is the political distraction of the sovereign localities and of the middle levels of power, which sustain the illusion that America is still a self-balancing society. If the mass media focus on the professional celebrities, the liberal intellectuals, especially the academic social scientists among them, focus upon the noisy middle levels. Professional celebrities and middle-level politicians are the most visible figures of the system; in fact, together they tend to monopolize the communicated or public scene that is visible to the members of the mass society, and thus to obscure and to distract attention from the power elite.

---

* A British philosopher and political theorist (1826-77).

The higher circles in America today contain, on the one hand, the laughing, erotic, dazzling glamour of the professional celebrity, and, on the other, the prestige aura of power, of authority, of might and wealth. These two pinnacles are not unrelated. The power elite is not so noticeable as the celebrities, and often does not want to be; the "power" of the professional celebrity is the power of distraction. America as a national public is indeed possessed of a strange set of idols. The professionals, in the main, are either glossy little animals or frivolous clowns; the men of power, in the main, rarely seem to be models of representative men.

Such moral uneasiness as prevails among the American elite themselves is accordingly quite understandable. Its existence is amply confirmed by the more serious among those who have come to feel that they represent America abroad. There, the double-faced character of the American celebrity is reflected both by the types of Americans who travel to play or to work, and in the images many literate and articulate Europeans hold of "Americans." Public honor in America tends now to be either frivolous or grim; either altogether trivial or portentous of a greatly tightened-up system of prestige.

The American elite is not composed of representative men whose conduct and character constitute models for American imitation and aspiration. There is no set of men with whom members of the mass public can rightfully and gladly identify. In this fundamental sense, America is indeed without leaders. Yet such is the nature of the mass public's morally cynical and politically unspecified distrust that it is readily drained off without real political effect. That this is so, after the men and events of the last thirty years, is further proof of the extreme difficulty of finding and of using in America today the political means of sanity for morally sane objectives.

America—a conservative country without any conservative ideology—appears now before the world a naked and arbitrary power, as, in the name of realism, its men of decision enforce their often crackpot definitions upon world reality. The second-rate mind is in command of the ponderously spoken platitude. In the liberal rhetoric, vagueness, and in the conservative mood, irrationality, are raised to principle. Public relations and the official secret, the trivializing campaign and the terrible fact clumsily accomplished, are replacing the reasoned debate of political ideas in the privately incorporated economy, the military ascendancy, and the political vacuum of modern America.

The men of the higher circles are not representative men; their high position is not a result of moral virtue; their fabulous success is not firmly connected with meritorious ability. Those who sit in the seats of the high and the mighty are selected and formed by the means of power, the sources of wealth, the mechanics of celebrity, which prevail in their society. They are not men selected and formed by a civil service that is linked with the world of knowledge and sensibility. They are not men shaped by nationally responsible parties that debate openly and clearly the issues this nation now so unintelligent^ confronts. They are not men held in responsible check by a plurality of voluntary associations which connect debating publics with the pinnacles of decision. Commanders of power unequaled in human history, they have succeeded within the American system of organized irresponsibility.

22

Lewis Mumford

The City in History

Among the alarming trends in the social organization of the United States i.
the continuing deterioration within the core of its large cities. Many q today's
centers function poorly, are inhabited by large numbers of the unem ployed and
dispossessed, and are, for many residents, physically and psychologically hazardous.
The most eloquent and prolific critic of the failures it planning and administering
American cities has been Lewis Mumfort (1895-1990).

Born and raised in the New York City area, Mumford studied at variou.
colleges in the region but never received a degree. Instead, he became a self-taught
student of the city itself, using its superb libraries, museums, and theaters as the
basis for his personal curriculum. In later years his youthful wanderings through
the city would be reflected in his essays on architecture for The New Yorker
magazine. Because of his outstanding popular and scholarly contributions to
urban theory, Mumford, though having earned no academic degree, was appointed
to professorships at such distinguished universities as Dartmouth, Stanford,
Pennsylvania, and M.I.T.

The first lengthy work by Mumford, The Story of Utopia (1922), foreshadowed
the direction of most of his subsequent writings on urban living. By the 1930s he
was advocating the girdling of cities with parklike "green belts" and the constructing
of new cities built to the pedestrian's scale, with an "organic" relationship among
the various urban functions. After the Second World War, he worried about
the destruction of American cities through massive "urban renewal" encroaching
highway systems, and nuclear war.

From *The City in History*, © 1961, by Lewis Mumford. Reprinted from chapters 16 and 17 by permission of Harcourt Brace Jovanovich, Inc.

The City in History *(1961), from which the following selection is taken, is a book in which Mumford summarizes much of his prior theorizing, thereby creating a most searching general inquiry into the human prospect. He begins with a detailed historical essay on the nature, origin, and development of cities, from the earliest villages to the contemporary metropolis, then proceeds to document what he considers to be unnecessary evils of modern urban life. Mumford observes, for example, that the exodus from central city to suburbs has resulted in a class-segregated "low-grade uniform environment." In his view, this "purposeless expansion" of the new metropolis—useful only to the land speculator—has resulted in a dehumanizing, mechanically oriented mass society dominated by technology. Mumford contends, however, that there is still hope for the urban situation. He believes that an "organic" solution—a solution geared to people, not machines—is still possible.*

SUBURBIA—AND BEYOND

The Historic Suburb

All through history, those who owned or rented land outside the city's walls valued having a place in the country, even if they did not actively perform agricultural labor: a cabin, a cottage, a vine-shaded shelter, built for temporary retreat if not for permanent occupancy. Early city dwellers did not wait for rapid transportation to take advantage of this rural surcease. As long as the city remained relatively compact and self-contained, it was possible to keep a balance between rural and urban occupations, yes, and between rural and urban pleasures: eating, drinking, dancing, athletic sports, love-making, every manner of relaxation had a special aura of festivity in a verdant, sunlit landscape. One of the chief penalties for continued urban growth was that it put this pleasurable setting at such a distance and confined it more and more to the ruling classes. . . .

The early appearance of the suburb points to another, even more important, fact: the life-maintaining agencies, gardening and farming, recreation and games, health sanatoria and retreats belong to the surrounding countryside, even when the functions they fostered spring from the town's needs or deficiencies. By the eighteenth century, it is true, the romantic movement had produced a new rationale for the suburban exodus, and the increasingly smoky and overcrowded town provided a new incentive. But it would be an error to regard suburbanism as a mere derivative of this ideology, for it had older, deeper roots. What needs to be accounted for is not the cult of nature that became popular in the eighteenth century, affecting everything from medicine to education, from architecture to cookery, but rather the obstinacy with which people had often clung for centuries to a crowded, depleted, denatured, and constricted environment, whose chief solace for misery was the company of equally miserable people. ...

The ultimate outcome of the suburb's alienation from the city became visible only in the twentieth century, with the extension of the democratic ideal through the instrumentalities of manifolding and mass production. In the mass movement into suburban areas a new kind of community was produced, which caricatured both the historic city and the archetypal suburban refuge: a multitude of uniform, unidentifiable houses, lined up inflexibly, at uniform distances, on uniform roads, in a treeless communal waste, inhabited by people of the same class, the same income, the same age group, witnessing the same television performances, eating the same tasteless prefabricated foods, from the same freezers, conforming in every outward and inward respect to a common mold, manufactured in the central metropolis. Thus the ultimate effect of the suburban escape in our time is, ironically, a low-grade uniform environment from which escape is impossible. What has happened to the suburban exodus in the United States now threatens, through the same mechanical instrumentalities, to take place, at an equally accelerating rate, everywhere else—unless the most vigorous countermeasures are taken.

★ ★ ★

The Suburban Way of Life

★ ★ ★

By the very nature of the retreat, the suburb could be identified by a number of related social characteristics. And first, it was a segregated community, set apart from the city, not merely by space but by class stratification: a sort of green ghetto dedicated to the elite. That smug Victorian phrase, "We keep ourselves to ourselves," expresses the spirit of the suburb, in contrast to the city; for the city, by its nature, is a multi-form non-segregated environment. Little groups may indeed form social islands within a city, as the various tribes tended to do in the early cities of Islam, or again as people from a Greek or a Polish village might form temporary nests together in the same block in Chicago or New York. But the metropolis was a mixture of people who came from different places, practiced different occupations, encountered other personalities, meeting and mingling, co-operating and clashing, the rich with the poor, the proud with the humble.

Except where the suburb enclosed an original small town core, it tended to remain a one-class community, with just a sufficient fringe of tradesmen and servants to keep it going—the latter often condemned to use the central metropolis as their dormitory. Segregation, in practice, means compulsory association, or at least cohabitation; for if there are any choices, they lie outside the immediate community. Hence the great residual freedom of the suburbanite is that of locomotion. For esthetic and intellectual stimulus, the suburb remains dependent upon the big city: the theater, the opera, the orchestra, the art gallery, the university, the museum are no longer part of the daily environment. The problem of reestablishing connections, on a regional rather than a metropolitan basis, is one of the main problems of city planning in our time.

Not merely did the suburb keep the busier, dirtier, more productive enterprises at a distance, it likewise pushed away the creative activities of the city. Here life ceased to be a drama, full of unexpected challenges and tensions and dilemmas: it became a bland ritual of competitive spending. "Half your trouble," Rudyard Kipling wrote to William James in 1896, "is the curse of America—sheer, hopeless, well-ordered boredom; and that is going some day to be the curse of the world." Kipling put his finger, at that early date, upon the weakness of the suburban way of life.

Thus the genuine biological benefits of the suburb were undermined by its psychological and social defects: above all, the irreality of its retreat. In the town poor men demonstrated: beggars held out their hands in the street: disease spread quickly from poor quarters to the residences of the comfortable, via the delivery boy, the washerwoman, the seamstress, or other necessary menials: the eye, if not carefully averted, would, on a five-minute walk in any direction, behold a slum, or at least a slum child, ragged and grimy.

Even in the heyday of Coketown,* sensitive and intelligent souls could not remain long in such an environment without banding together to do something about it: they would exhort and agitate, hold meetings and form parades, draw up petitions and besiege legislators, extract money from the rich and dispense aid to the poor, founding soup kitchens and model tenements, passing housing legislation and acquiring land for parks, establishing hospitals and health centers, libraries and universities, in which the whole community played a part and benefitted.

In the suburb one might live and die without marring the image of an innocent world, except when some shadow of its evil fell over a column in the newspaper. Thus the suburb served as an asylum for the preservation of illusion. Here domesticity could flourish, forgetful of the exploitation on which so much of it was based. Here individuality could prosper, oblivious of the pervasive regimentation beyond. This was not merely a child-centered environment: it was based on a childish view of the world, in which reality was sacrificed to the pleasure principle.

As an attempt to recover what was missing in the city, the suburban exodus could be amply justified, for it was concerned with primary human needs. But there was another side: the temptation to retreat from unpleasant realities, to shirk public duties, and to find the whole meaning of life in the most elemental social group, the family, or even in the still more isolated and self-centered individual. What was properly a beginning was treated as an end.

★   ★   ★

Railroad Line, Greenbelt, Motor Sprawl
★   ★   ★

What has happened to the suburb is now a matter of historic record. As soon as the motor car became common, the pedestrian scale of the suburb disappeared, and with it most of its individuality and charm. The suburb ceased to be a neighborhood unit: it became a diffused low-density mass, enveloped by the conurbation and then further enveloping it. The suburb needed its very smallness, as it needed its rural background, to achieve its own kind of semi-rural perfection. Once that

---

* A general name used by Mumford for the coal-burning factory towns spawned by the Industrial Revolution.

limit was overpassed, the suburb ceased to be a refuge from the city and became part of the inescapable metropolis, "la ville tentaculaire," whose distant outlying open spaces and public parks were themselves further manifestations of the crowded city. This fact that will not cease to be true even if jet transportation brings an area twelve hundred miles away as near as one sixty miles distant today. For when one conquers space one also increases the populations to whom that distant space is accessible. The prospective net gain is considerably less than zero.

As long as the railroad stop and walking distances controlled suburban growth, the suburb had a form. The very concentration of shops and parking facilities around the railroad station in the better suburbs even promoted a new kind of market area, more concentrated than the linear market along an avenue. This was a spontaneous prototype of the suburban shopping center, whose easy facilities for parking gave it advantages over more central urban establishments, once the private motor car became the chief mode of transportation. But the motor car had done something more than remove the early limits and destroy the pedestrian scale. It either doubled the number of cars needed per family, or it turned the suburban housewife into a full time chauffeur.

These duties became even more imperative because the advent of the motor car was accompanied by the deliberate dismantling of the electric (rail) transportation system. In the more urbanized parts of America, electric transportation, often on its own private right of way, like the steam railroad, achieved far higher rates of speed than the present motor bus. Far from supplementing public rail transportation, the private motor car became largely a clumsy substitute for it. Instead of maintaining a complex transportation system, offering alternative choices of route and speed to fit the occasion, the new suburban sprawl has become abjectly dependent upon a single form, the private motor car, whose extension has devoured the one commodity the suburb could rightly boast: space. Instead of buildings set in a park, we now have buildings set in a parking lot.

Whilst the suburb served only a favored minority it neither spoiled the countryside nor threatened the city. But now that the drift to the outer ring has become a mass movement, it tends to destroy the value of both environments without producing anything but a dreary substitute, devoid of form and even more devoid of the original suburban values. We are faced by a curious paradox: the new suburban form has now produced an anti-urban pattern. With the destruction of walking distances has gone the destruction of walking as a normal means of human circulation: the motor car has made it unsafe and the extension of the suburb has made it impossible. . . .

What an effective network requires is the largest number of alternative modes of transportation, at varying speeds and volumes, for different functions and purposes. The fastest way to move a hundred thousand people within a limited urban area, say a half mile radius, is on foot: the slowest way of moving them would be to put them all into motor cars. The entire daytime population of historic Boston could assemble by foot on Boston Common, probably in less than an hour if the streets were clear of motor traffic. If they were transported by motor car, they would take many hours, and unless they abandoned their unparkable vehicles would never reach their destination.

Our highway engineers and our municipal authorities, hypnotized by the popularity of the private motor car, feeling an obligation to help General Motors to flourish, even if General Chaos results, have been in an open conspiracy to dismantle all the varied forms of transportation necessary to a good system, and have reduced our facilities to the private motor car (for pleasure, convenience, or trucking) and the airplane. They have even duplicated railroad routes and repeated all the errors of the early railroad engineers, while piling up in the terminal cities a population the private motor car cannot handle unless the city itself is wrecked to permit movement and storage of automobiles.

If technical experts and administrators had known their business, they would have taken special measures to safeguard more efficient methods of mass transportation, in order to maintain both the city's existence and the least time-wasting use of other forms of transportation. To have a complete urban structure capable of functioning fully, it is necessary to find appropriate channels for every form of transportation: it is the deliberate articulation of the pedestrian, the mass transit system, the street, the avenue, the expressway, and the airfield that alone can care for the needs of a modern community. Nothing less will do.

By favoring the truck over the railroad for long-distance traffic, we have replaced a safe and efficient service by a more dangerous and inefficient one. If we want to improve our highway system, we should be zealous to keep as large a part of goods haulage as possible on the rails. Not the least reason for saving the passenger and freight railroad service and mass transportation is to ensure free movement by private vehicles on highways. Similarly, if the expressways that we have built around our cities are to function as such, mass transit must be improved and widened, not permitted to go out of existence.

The only effective cure for urban congestion is to so relate industrial and business zones to residential areas that a large part of their personnel can either walk or cycle to work, or use a public bus, or take a railroad train. By pushing all forms of traffic onto high speed motor ways, we burden them with a load guaranteed to slow down peak traffic to a crawl; and if we try to correct this by multiplying motor ways, we only add to the total urban wreckage by flinging the parts of the city ever farther away in a formless mass of thinly spread semi-urban tissue. The spatial dissociation of functions in suburbia results in an extreme specialization of the individual parts: segregated residence areas without local shops: segregated shopping centers without industries: segregated industrial plants without eating facilities unless provided by the management. In escaping the complex co-operations of the city Suburbia recovers the original vices of over-specialization and rigid control.

Good urban planning must provide a place for the motor car: that goes without saying. But this does not in the least mean that the motor car must be permitted to penetrate every part of the city and stay there, even though it disrupts all other activities. Neither does it mean that the auto shall dictate the whole scheme of living; nor yet does it mean that its manufacturers should be permitted to flout the requirements of the city by designing ever broader and longer vehicles. Quite the contrary, the time has come to discriminate between two functions of the motor car—urban movement and countrywide movement. For the latter, a big car with plenty of room to house a family and hold their baggage is admirable. In the city, however, such cars should be encouraged to stay on the outskirts, and be heavily taxed for the privilege of parking within it; while special favors should be given to the design and distribution of small cars, electric powered, for ordinary intra-urban movement, to supplement rather than replace mass transportation. Moderate speed, quiet, ease and compactness of parking—these are the characteristics of a town car.

It is an absurdly impoverished technology that has only one answer to the problem of transportation; and it is a poor form of city planning that permits that answer to dominate its entire scheme of existence.

Mass Suburbia as Anti-city

Under the present dispensation we have sold our urban birthright for a sorry mess of motor cars. As poor a bargain as Esau's pottage.*Future generations will perhaps wonder at our willingness, indeed our eagerness, to sacrifice the education of our children, the care of the ill and the aged, the development of the arts, to say nothing of ready access to nature, for the lopsided system of mono-transportation, going through low density areas at sixty miles an hour, but reduced in high density areas to a bare six. But our descendants will perhaps understand our curious willingness to expend billions of dollars to shoot a sacrificial victim into planetary orbit, if they realize that our cities are being destroyed for the same superstitious religious ritual: the worship of speed and empty space. Lacking sufficient municipal budgets to deal adequately with all of life's requirements that can be concentrated in the city, we have settled for a single function, transportation, or rather for a single part of an adequate transportation system, locomotion by private motor car.

By allowing mass transportation to deteriorate and by building expressways out of the city and parking garages within, in order to encourage the maximum use of the private car, our highway engineers and city planners have helped to destroy the living tissue of the city and to limit the possibilities of creating a larger urban organism on a regional scale. Mass transportation for short distances, under a mile, should rely mainly upon the pedestrian. By discouraging and eliminating the pedestrian, by failing to extend and to perfect mass transportation, our municipal officials and highway engineers have created a situation that

---

* A reference to an Old Testament story. Esau, being very hungry, exchanged his paternal inheritance for a bowl of his brother Jacob's soup (Genesis 25:27-34).

calls for extremely low residential densities. Here again the monopoly of private space not merely reduces the social facilities of the city but sacrifices public open space to private.

The absurd belief that space and rapid locomotion are the chief ingredients of a good life has been fostered by the agents of mass suburbia. That habit of low density building is the residual bequest of the original romantic movement, and by now it is one of the chief obstacles to reassembling the parts of the city and uniting them in a new pattern that shall offer much richer resources for living than either the congested and disordered central metropolis or the outlying areas reached by its expressways. The *reductio ad absurdum* of this myth is, notoriously, Los Angeles. Here the suburban standards of open space, with free standing houses, often as few as five houses to the acre, has been maintained: likewise the private motor car, as the major means of transportation has supplanted what was only a generation or so ago an extremely efficient system of public transportation.

Los Angeles has now become an undifferentiated mass of houses, walled off into sectors by many-laned expressways, with ramps and viaducts that create special bottlenecks of their own. These expressways move but a small fraction of the traffic per hour once carried by public transportation, at a much lower rate of speed, in an environment befouled by smog, itself produced by the lethal exhausts of the technologically backward motor cars. More than a third of the Los Angeles area is consumed by these grotesque transportation facilities; *two-thirds* of central Los Angeles are occupied by streets, freeways, parking facilities, garages. This is space-eating with a vengeance. The last stage of the process already beckons truly progressive minds—to evict the remaining inhabitants and turn the entire area over to automatically propelled vehicles, completely emancipated from any rational human purpose.

Even in cities as spacious as Washington, it is only the original central area that has a residential density of ten or more families per acre: on the spreading outskirts, under ten is the rule, and a fast moving tide is putting an ever larger tract under a density of settlement less than five per acre. This is ruinous both to urban living and to leisured recreation; for the attempt to service the distant areas with expressways will not merely sterilize more and more of the land, but will scatter social facilities that should be concentrated in new cities, organized so as to diffuse and amplify the central facilities.

The conclusion should be plain. Any attempt to create an adequate transportation system without creating in advance sufficient reserves of public land, without laying down a desirable density for balanced urban occupation *higher than the present suburban level,* without providing for a regional network largely independent of the bigger trunk line highways, will degrade the landscape without bringing any permanent benefits to its new inhabitants.

To keep the advantages first incorporated in the romantic suburb, we must acclimate them to the building of cities. To keep the advantages first discovered in the closed city, we must create a more porous pattern, richer in both social and esthetic variety. Residential densities of about one hundred people per net acre, exclusive of streets and sidewalks, will provide usable private gardens and encourage small public inner parks for meeting and relaxing. This can be achieved without erecting the sterile, space-mangling high-rise slabs that now grimly parade, in both Europe and America, as the ultimate contribution of "modern" architecture. If we are concerned with human values, we can no longer afford either sprawling Suburbia or the congested Metropolis: still less can we afford a congested Suburbia, whose visual openness depends upon the cellular isolation and regimentation of its component families in mass structures.

Families in Space
As it has worked out under the impact of the present religion and myth of the machine, mass Suburbia has done away with most of the freedoms and delights that the original disciples of Rousseau* sought to find through their exodus from the city. Instead of centering attention on the child in the garden, we now have the image of "Families in Space." For the wider the scattering of the population, the greater the isolation of the individual household, and the more effort it takes to do privately, even with the aid of many machines and automatic devices,

---

* Jean Jacques Rousseau (1712-78), a French (Swiss-born) philosopher and writer. One of the forerunners of the romantic movement, he rejected civilization and asserted the moral superiority of the "return to nature."

what used to be done in company often with conversation, song, and the enjoyment of the physical presence of others.

The town housewife, who half a century ago knew her butcher, her grocer, her dairyman, her various other local tradesmen, as individual persons, with histories and biographies that impinged on her own, in a daily interchange, now has the benefit of a single weekly expedition to an impersonal supermarket, where only by accident is she likely to encounter a neighbor. If she is well-to-do, she is surrounded with electric or electronic devices that take the place of flesh and blood companions: her real companions, her friends, her mentors, her lovers, her fillers-up of unlived life, are shadows on the television screen, or even less embodied voices. She may answer them, but she cannot make herself heard: as it has worked out, this is a one-way system. The greater the area of expansion, the greater the dependence upon a distant supply center and remote control.

On the fringe of mass Suburbia, even the advantages of the primary neighborhood group disappear. The cost of this detachment in space from other men is out of all proportion to its supposed benefits. The end product is an encapsulated life, spent more and more either in a motor car or within the cabin of darkness before a television set: soon, with a little more automation of traffic, mostly in a motor car, travelling even greater distances, under remote control, so that the one-time driver may occupy himself with a television set, having lost even the freedom of the steering wheel. Every part of this life, indeed, will come through official channels and be under supervision. Untouched by human hand at one end: untouched by human spirit at the other. Those who accept this existence might as well be encased in a rocket hurtling through space, so narrow are their choices, so limited and deficient their permitted responses. Here indeed we find "The Lonely Crowd."*

The organizers of the ancient city had something to learn from the new rulers of our society. The former massed their subjects within a walled enclosure, under the surveillance of armed guardians within the smaller citadel, the better to keep them under control. That method is now

---

* *The Lonely Crowd: A Study of the Changing American Character* (1950) is a critical view of contemporary mass society written by David Riesman (1909-2002), an American sociologist.

obsolete. With the present means of long-distance mass communication, sprawling isolation has proved an even more effective method of keeping a population under control. With direct contact and face-to-face association inhibited as far as possible, all knowledge and direction can be monopolized by central agents and conveyed through guarded channels, too costly to be utilized by small groups or private individuals. To exercise free speech in such a scattered, dissociated community one must "buy time" on the air or "buy space" in the newspaper. Each member of Suburbia becomes imprisoned by the very separation that he has prized: he is fed through a narrow opening: a telephone line, a radio band, a television circuit. This is not, it goes without saying, the result of a conscious conspiracy by a cunning minority: it is an organic by-product of an economy that sacrifices human development to mechanical processing.

In a well-organized community, all these technological improvements might admirably widen the scope of social life: in the disorganized communities of today, they narrow the effective range of the person. Under such conditions, nothing can happen spontaneously or autonomously—not without a great deal of mechanical assistance. Does this not explain in some degree the passiveness and docility that has crept into our existence? In the recent Caracas revolution that deposed a brutal dictatorship in Venezuela, the starting signal, I have been told by an eye-witness, was the honking of motor car horns. That honking, growing louder, coming nearer, converging from every quarter of the city upon the palace, struck terror into the hearts of the rulers. That, too, was an urban phenomenon. Suburbia offers poor facilities for meeting, conversation, collective debate, and common action—it favors silent conformity, not rebellion or counter-attack. So Suburbia has become the favored home of a new kind of absolutism: invisible but all-powerful.

I might be uneasy about the validity of this analysis had not the prescient de Tocqueville* anticipated it long ago, in "Democracy in America." He sought to "trace the novel features under which despotism

* Alexis de Tocqueville (1805-59), an enlightened French aristocrat. His *Democracy in America* (1835, 1840) is a thorough survey of American society during the Age of Jackson.

may appear in the world." "The first thing that strikes observation," he says, "is an uncountable number of men, all equal and alike, incessantly endeavoring to produce the petty and paltry pleasures with which they glut their lives. Each of them living apart, is a stranger to the fate of all the rest—his children and his private friends constitute to him the whole of mankind; as for the rest of his fellow-citizens, he is close to them, but he sees them not; he touches them, but he feels them not; he exists but in himself and for himself alone; and if his kindred still remain to him, he may be said at any rate to have lost his country."

De Tocqueville was describing in anticipation the temper and habit of life in Suburbia, a habit that has worked back into the city and made even democratic nations submit, with hardly a murmur, to every manner of totalitarian compulsion and corruption. What this great political philosopher foresaw with his inner eye, less gifted observers can now see with their outer eye. This is the last stage in the breakup of the city. The expansion of our technology only quickens the pace of this change. What is left, if no counter-movement takes place, will not be worth saving. For when the container changes as rapidly as its contents nothing can in fact be saved.

★ ★ ★

The Myth of Megalopolis

★ ★ ★

The Removal of Limits

Let us now view the situation of the metropolis in more general terms: what some have called the urban explosion is in fact a symptom of a more general state—the removal of quantitative limits. This marks the change from an organic system to a mechanical system, from purposeful growth to purposeless expansion.

Until the nineteenth century the limitations of both local and regional transportation placed a natural restriction upon the growth of cities. Even the biggest centers, Rome, Babylon, Alexandria, Antioch, were forced to respect that limit. But by the middle of the nineteenth century the tendency toward metropolitan monopoly was supplemented with a new factor brought in by the effective utilization of coal and iron and the extension of the railroad: in terms of purely physical requirements the area of settlement coincided with the coal beds, the ore beds, the railroad network. Patrick Geddes, early in the present century, pointed out the significance of the new population maps, which graphically disclosed a general thickening and spreading of the urban mass: he showed that entire provinces and counties were becoming urbanized, and he proposed to differentiate such diffused formations by a name that would distinguish them from the historic city: the "conurbation."

Meanwhile the original forces that created the conurbation were supplemented by the electric power grid, the electric railway, and still later by the motor car and the motor road: so that a movement that was at first confined largely to the area accessible to the railroad now is taking place everywhere. Whereas the first extension of the factory system produced a multitude of new cities and greatly augmented the population of existing centers, the present diffusion of the area of settlement has largely halted this growth and has enormously increased the production of relatively undifferentiated urban tissue, without any relation either to an internally coherent nucleus or an external boundary of any sort.

The result threatens to be a universal conurbation. Those who ignored Geddes's original definition half a century ago have recently re-discovered the phenomenon itself, and treated it as if it were an entirely new development. Some have even misapplied to the conurbation the inappropriate term Megalopolis, though it represents, in fact, the precise opposite of the tendency that brought the original city of this name into existence. The overgrown historic city was still, residually, an entity: the conurbation is a nonentity, and becomes more patently so as it spreads.

What this removal of limits means can perhaps best be grasped by referring to the extension of historic centers. When Rome was surrounded by the Aurelian Wall in a.d. 274, it covered a little more than five square miles. The present area of London is 130 times as great as this; while it is roughly 650 times as big as the area of medieval London, which was 677 acres. The conurbation of New York is even more widespread: it covers something like 2,514 square miles. If no human purposes supervene to halt the blotting out of the countryside and to establish limits for the growth and colonization of cities, the whole coastal strip from Maine to Florida might coalesce into an almost undifferentiated conurbation. But to call this mass a "regional city" or to hold that it represents the new scale of settlement to which modern man must adapt his institutions and his personal needs is to mask the realities of the human situation and allow seemingly automatic forces to become a substitute for human purposes.

These vast urban masses are comparable to a routed and disorganized army, which has lost its leaders, scattered its battalions and companies, torn off its insignia, and is fleeing in every direction. "Sauve qui peut." *The first step toward handling this situation, besides establishment of an over-all command, is to re-group in units that can be effectively handled. Until we understand the function of the smaller units and can bring them under discipline we cannot command and deploy the army as a whole over a larger area. The scale of distances has changed, and the "regional city" is a potential reality, indeed a vital necessity. But the condition for success in these endeavors lies in our abilities to recognize and to impose organic limitations. This means the replacement of the machine-oriented metropolitan economy by one directed toward the goods and goals of life.

Though the removal of limits is one of the chief feats of the metropolitan economy, this does not imply any abdication of power on the part of the chiefs in charge: for there is one countervailing condition to this removal, and that is the processing of all operations through the metropolis and its increasingly complicated mechanisms. The metropolis is in fact a processing center, in which a vast variety of goods, material and spiritual, is mechanically sorted and reduced to a limited number of standardized articles, uniformly packaged, and distributed through controlled channels to their destination, bearing the approved metropolitan label.

"Processing" has now become the chief form of metropolitan control; and the need for its constant application has brought into existence a whole range of inventions, mechanical and electronic, from cash registers to electronic computers, which handle every operation

---

* French: save (himself) who can; that is, every man for himself.

from book-keeping to university examinations. Interests and aptitudes that do not lend themselves to processing are automatically rejected. So complicated, so elaborate, so costly are the processing mechanisms that they cannot be employed except on a mass scale: hence they eliminate all activities of a fitful, inconsecutive, or humanly subtle nature—just as "yes" or "no" answers eliminate those more delicate and accurate discriminations that often lie at one point or another in between the spuriously "correct" answer. That which is local, small, personal, autonomous, must be suppressed. Increasingly, he who controls the processing mechanism controls the lives and destinies of those who must consume its products, and who on metropolitan terms cannot seek any others. For processing and packaging do not end on the production line: they finally make over the human personality.

In short the monopoly of power and knowledge that was first established in the citadel has come back, in a highly magnified form, in the final stages of metropolitan culture. In the end every aspect of life must be brought under control: controlled weather, controlled movement, controlled association, controlled production, controlled prices, controlled fantasy, controlled ideas. But the only purpose of control, apart from the profit, power, and prestige of the controllers, is to accelerate the process of mechanical control itself.

The priests of this regime are easy to identify: the whole system, in its final stages, rests on the proliferation of secret, and thus controllable, knowledge; and the very division of labor that makes specialized scientific research possible also restricts the number of people capable of putting the fragments together. But where are the new gods? The nuclear reactor is the seat of their power: radio transmission and rocket flight their angelic means of communication and transportation: but beyond these minor agents of divinity the Control Room itself, with its Cybernetic Deity,* giving His lightning-like decisions and His infallible answers: omniscience and omnipotence, triumphantly mated by science. Faced with this electronic monopoly of man's highest powers, the human can come back only at the most primitive level. Sigmund

---

* Cybernetics is the comparative study of the controlling systems in the human body and of mechanical and electrical systems that incorporate similar controls; hence, Mumford's "Cybernetic Deity" would be essentially the computer viewed as God.

Freud* detected the beginnings of creative art in the infant's pride over his bowel movements. We can now detect its ultimate manifestation in paintings and sculpture whose contents betray a similar pride and a similar degree of autonomy—and a similar product.

One of the ancient prerogatives of the gods was to create man out of their flesh, like Atum,† or in their own image, like Yahweh.‡ When the accredited scientific priesthood go a little farther with their present activities, the new life-size homunculus [artificial man] will be processed, too: one can already see anticipatory models in our art galleries. He will look remarkably like a man accoutered in a "space-suit": outwardly a huge scaly insect. But the face inside will be incapable of expression, as incapable as that of a corpse. And who will know the difference?

Sprawling Giantism

* * *

The image of modern industrialism that Charlie Chaplin§ carried over from the past into "Modern Times" is just the opposite of megalopolitan reality. He pictured the worker as an old-fashioned drudge, chained to the machine, mechanically fed while he continued to operate it. That image belongs to Coketown. The new worker, in the metropolis, has been progressively released from the productive process: the grinding, impoverished toil that made the nineteenth-century factory so hideous has been lifted by social services and security, by mechanical aids and by complete automation. Work is no longer so brutal in the light industries: but automation has made it even more boring. The energy and application that once went into the productive process must now be addressed to consumption.

By a thousand cunning attachments and controls, visible and subliminal, the workers in an expanding economy are tied to a consumption mechanism: they are assured of a livelihood provided they devour without undue selectivity all that is offered by the machine— and demand nothing that is not produced by the machine. The whole organization

---

* An Austrian physician who became the founder of psychoanalysis (1856-1939).
† A primeval Egyptian god (often spelled "Atmu").
‡ Ancient form of the Hebrew name for God.
§ Great comic actor of the early cinema (1889-1977): his film *Modern Times* is a classic satire of the demands placed upon workers by the organization and machinery of the factory system.

of the metropolitan community is designed to kill spontaneity and self-direction. You stop on the red light and go on the green. You see what you are supposed to see, think what you are supposed to think: your personal contributions, like your income and security taxes, are deductible at source. To choose, to select, to discriminate, to exercise prudence or continence or forethought, to carry self-control to the point of abstinence, to have standards other than those of the market, and to set limits other than those of immediate consumption—these are impious heresies that would challenge the whole megalopolitan myth and deflate its economy. In such a "free" society Henry Thoreau* must rank as a greater public enemy than Karl Marx.†

The metropolis, in its final stage of development, becomes a collective contrivance for making this irrational system work, and for giving those who are in reality its victims the illusion of power, wealth, and felicity, of standing at the very pinnacle of human achievement. But in actual fact their lives are constantly in peril, their wealth is tasteless and ephemeral, their leisure is sensationally monotonous, and their pathetic felicity is tainted by constant, well-justified anticipations of violence and sudden death. Increasingly they find themselves "strangers and afraid," in a world they never made:‡ a world ever less responsive to direct human command, ever more empty of human meaning.

The Shadows of Success

To believe, therefore, that human culture has reached a marvellous final culmination in the modern metropolis one must avert one's eyes from the grim details of the daily routine. And that is precisely what the metropolitan denizen schools himself to do: he lives, not in the real world, but in a shadow world projected around him at every moment by means of paper and celluloid and adroitly manipulated lights: a world in which he is insulated by glass, cellophane, pliofilm from the

---

* An American essayist, poet, and naturalist (1817-62) who developed in his life and writings a doctrine of self-sufficiency and simplicity.

† A major originator of communist theory (1818-83).

‡ From "The Laws of God, The Laws of Man" (1922) by the English poet and classical scholar A. E. Housman (1859-1936):

   I, a stranger and afraid
   In a world I never made.

mortifications of living. In short, a world of professional illusionists and their credulous victims.

The swish and crackle of paper is the underlying sound of the metropolis. What is visible and real in this world is only what has been transferred to paper or has been even further etherialized on a microfilm or a tape recorder. The essential daily gossip of the metropolis is no longer that of people meeting face to face at a cross-roads, at the dinner table, in the marketplace: a few dozen people writing in the newspapers, a dozen or so more broadcasting over radio and television, provide the daily interpretation of movements and happenings with slick professional adroitness. Thus even the most spontaneous human activities come under professional surveillance and centralized control. The spread of manifolding devices of every sort gives to the most ephemeral and mediocre products of the mind a temporary durability they do not deserve: whole books are printed to justify the loose evacuations of the tape recorder. . . .

This metropolitan world, then, is a world where flesh and blood are less real than paper and ink and celluloid. It is a world where the great masses of people, unable to achieve a more full-bodied and satisfying means of living, take life vicariously, as readers, spectators, listeners, passive observers. Living thus, year in and year out, at second hand, remote from the nature that is outside them, and no less remote from the nature that is within, it is no wonder that they turn more and more of the functions of life, even thought itself, to the machines that their inventors have created. In this disordered environment only machines retain some of the attributes of life, while human beings are progressively reduced to a bundle of reflexes, without self-starting impulses or autonomous goals: "behaviorist man."*

Destiny of Megalopolis

In following the growth of megalopolitan culture to its conclusion we reach a whole series of terminal processes, and it would be simple-minded to believe that they have any prospect of continuing in existence indefinitely. A life that lacks any meaning, value, or purpose, except

---

* For a contrasting opinion of the value of "behaviorist man," see selection 9, from B. F. Skinner's *Beyond Freedom and Dignity*.

that of keeping the mechanism of breathing and ingestion going, is little better than life in an iron lung, which is only supportable because the patient still has hope of recovery and escape. The metropolitan regime now threatens to reach its climax in a meaningless war, one of total extermination, whose only purpose would be to relieve the anxieties and fears produced by the citadels' wholesale commitment to weapons of annihilation and extermination. Thus absolute power has become in fact absolute nihilism. Scientific and technological over-elaboration, unmodified by human values and aims, has committed countries like the United States and Russia to collective mechanisms of destruction so rigid that they cannot be modified or brought under control without being completely dismantled. Even instinctual animal intelligence remains inoperative in this system: the commitment to the machine overthrows all the safeguards to life, including the ancient law of self-preservation. For the sake of rapid locomotion, we in the United States kill some 40,000 people outright every year and fatally maim hundreds of thousands of others. For the sake of wielding absolute nuclear power our leaders are brazenly prepared to sacrifice from fifty to seventy-five million of their own citizens on the first day of an all-out nuclear war, and mutilate, or even possibly in the end eliminate the human race. The illusionist phrase to cover these psychotic plans is "national security," or even, more absurdly, "national survival."

Now, in every organism, the anabolic and the catabolic processes, the creative and the destructive, are constantly at work. Life and growth depend, not on the absence of negative conditions, but on a sufficient degree of equilibrium, and a sufficient surplus of constructive energy to permit continued repair, to absorb novelties, to regulate quantities, and to establish give-and-take relations with all the other organisms and communities needed to maintain balance. The negative factors in metropolitan existence might have provided the conditions for a higher development if the very terms of expansion had not given them the upper hand and tended to make their domination permanent, in ever more destructive processes. . . .

Remarkably, the wholesale rehabilitation of the cities of Europe [after World War II] at a higher level than they had achieved in the past, took place in less than a dozen years. That almost superhuman mobilization of energies demonstrated that urban reconstruction and renewal on a far greater scale might be accomplished, within a single generation, provided the economy was directly oriented to human needs, and that the major part of the national income was not diverted to the studious consumptive dissipations and planned destructions demanded by the expanding metropolitan economy: above all, by ceaseless preparations for collective genocide and suicide.

Unfortunately, as soon as the economy recovered and returned to the pursuit of its original ends, all its irrational features likewise came back: to keep going, an ever larger part of its energies must be dissipated in pyramid-building. Nowhere have the irrationalities of the current metropolitan myth been more fully exposed than in the development of so-called "absolute" weapons for limitless nuclear, bacterial, and chemical genocide. The building up of these weapons among the "Nuclear Powers" has given the "death-wish" the status of a fixed national policy, and made a universal extermination camp the ideal terminus of this whole civilization.

Even if the nations take timely measures to eliminate the stock of such weapons, it will be long before the vicious moral effects of this policy are dissipated: adult delinquency, on the scale not merely contemplated but actually prepared for in detail, requires therapeutic counter-measures that may take a full century to show any positive effect. This is the last and worst bequest of the citadel (read "Pentagon" and "Kremlin") to the culture of cities.

In a few short years our civilization has reached the point that Henry Adams,* with uncanny prescience, foresaw more than half a century ago. "At the present rate of progression, since 1600," he wrote, "it will not need another century or half a century to tip thought upside down. Law, in that case would disappear as theory or a priori principle and give place to force. Morality would become police. Explosives would reach cosmic violence. Disintegration would overcome integration." Every part of this prophecy has already been fulfilled; and it is useless to speculate about the future of cities until we have reckoned with the

---

* Henry Brooks Adams (1838-1918), an American historian, developed as the central thesis of his later writings the contrast between the integrating unity of the Middle Ages and the disintegrating multiplicity of the twentieth century.

forces of annihilation and extermination that now, almost automatically, and at an ever-accelerating rate, are working to bring about a more general breakdown.

Metropolitan civilization thus embodies and carries to its conclusion the radical contradiction we found already embedded in the life course of the city from the moment of its foundation: a contradiction that comes out of the dual origin of the city, and the perpetual ambivalence of its goals. From the village, the city derives its nature as a mothering and life-promoting environment, stable and secure, rooted in man's reciprocal relations with other organisms and communities. From the village, too, it derives the ways and values of an ungraded democracy in which each member plays his appropriate role at each stage in the life cycle.

On the other hand, the city owed its existence, and even more its enlargement, to concentrated attempts at mastering other men and dominating, with collective force, the whole environment. Thus the city became a power-trapping utility, designed by royal agents gathering the dispersed energies of little communities into a mighty reservoir, collectively regulating their accumulation and flow, and directing them into new channels—now favoring the smaller units by beneficently re-molding the landscape, but eventually hurling its energies outward in destructive assaults against other cities. Release and enslavement, freedom and compulsion, have been present from the beginning in urban culture.

Out of this inner tension some of the creative expressions of urban life have come forth: yet only in scattered and occasional instances do we discover political power well distributed in small communities, as in seventeenth-century Holland or Switzerland, or the ideals of life constantly regulating the eccentric manifestations of power. Our present civilization is a gigantic motor car moving along a one-way road at an ever-accelerating speed. Unfortunately as now constructed the car lacks both steering wheel and brakes, and the only form of control the driver exercises consists in making the car go faster, though in his fascination with the machine itself and his commitment to achieving the highest speed possible, he has quite forgotten the purpose of the journey. This state of helpless submission to the economic and technological mechanisms modern man has created is curiously disguised as progress, freedom, and the mastery of man over nature. As a result, every permission has become a morbid compulsion. Modern man has mastered every creature above the level of the viruses and bacteria—except himself.

Never before has the "citadel" exercised such atrocious power over the rest of the human race. Over the greater part of history, the village and the countryside remained a constant reservoir of fresh life, constrained indeed by the ancestral patterns of behavior that had helped make man human, but with a sense of both human limitations and human possibilities. No matter what the errors and aberrations of the rulers of the city, they were still correctible. Even if whole urban populations were destroyed, more than nine-tenths of the human race still remained outside the circle of destruction. Today this factor of safety has gone: the metropolitan explosion has carried both the ideological and the chemical poisons of the metropolis to every part of the earth; and the final damage may be irretrievable.

These terminal possibilities did not, I repeat, first become visible with the use of nuclear weapons: they were plain to alert and able minds, like Burckhardt in the eighteen-sixties, and like Henry Adams at the beginning of the present century.

Adams' contemporary, Henry James,* put the human situation in an image that curiously holds today: that of the Happy Family and the Infernal Machine. "The machine so rooted as to defy removal, and the family still so indifferent, while it carries on the family business of buying and selling, of chattering and dancing, to the danger of being blown up." The machine James referred to was the political machine of Philadelphia, then the classic embodiment of corruption and criminality; but only a too-guileless observer can fail to see that it applies to other demoralized mechanisms in our expanding metropolitan civilization. Once-local manifestations of criminality and irrationality now threaten our whole planet, smugly disguised as sound business enterprise, technological progress, communist efficiency, or democratic statesmanship. No wonder the popular existentialists, mirroring our time, equate "reality" with the "absurd." A large portion of the painting and sculpture of the past

* An American novelist (1843-1916).

generation symbolically anticipates the catastrophic end products of this death-oriented culture: total dismemberment and dehumanization in a lifeless, featureless void. Some of the best of this art, like Henry Moore's archaic pinheaded figures,* foretells a new beginning at a level so primitive that the mind has hardly yet begun to operate.

Now, if the total picture were as grim as that I have painted in the present chapter, there would be no excuse for writing this book; or rather, it would be just as irrational a contribution as the many other irrationalities and futilities I have touched on. If I have duly emphasized the disintegrations of the metropolitan stage, it has been for but one reason: only those who are aware of them will be capable of directing our collective energies into more constructive processes. It was not the diehard Romans of the fifth century a.d., still boasting of Rome's achievements and looking forward to another thousand years of them, who understood what the situation required: on the contrary, it was those who rejected the Roman premises and set their lives on a new foundation who built up a new civilization that in the end surpassed Rome's best achievements, even in engineering and government.

And so today: those who work within the metropolitan myth, treating its cancerous tumors as normal manifestations of growth, will continue to apply poultices, salves, advertising incantations, public relations magic, and quack mechanical remedies until the patient dies before their own failing eyes. No small part of the urban reform and correction that has gone on these last hundred years, and not least this last generation—slum demolition, model housing, civic architectural embellishment, suburban extension, "urban renewal" — has only continued in superficially new forms the same purposeless concentration and organic de-building that prompted the remedy.

Yet in the midst of all this disintegration fresh nodules of growth have appeared and, even more significantly, a new pattern of life has begun to emerge. This pattern necessarily is based on radically different premises from those of the ancient citadel builders or those of their modern counterparts, the rocket-constructors and nuclear exterminators.

---

* Moore (1898-), leading British sculptor. See selection 39 for some of Moore's comments on primitive art.

If we can distinguish the main outlines of this multidimensional, life-oriented economy we should also be able to describe the nature and the functions of the emerging city and the future pattern of human settlement. Above all, we should anticipate the next act in the human drama, provided mankind escapes the death-trap our blind commitment to a lopsided, power-oriented, anti-organic technology has set for it.

★ ★ ★

23

Hannah Arendt

Eichmann in Jerusalem: A Report on the Banality of Evil

Hannah Arendt (1906-1975), born and raised in Germany, was one of those creative European intellectuals who managed to flee their native lands in time to escape the Nazi grip. In the 1920s Arendt attended the University of Heidelberg, where, majoring in philosophy, she studied with such existentialists as Martin Heidegger and Karl Jaspers and, at age twenty-two, earned a doctorate with a dissertation on St. Augustine.

In 1933, with Hitler's rise to power, Arendt moved to Paris, where she worked for a relief organization that found homes in Palestine for orphaned Jewish children. Never ceasing to study and write, she immigrated to the United States in 1940 just before the fall of France; in 1950, she became a naturalized American citizen. Unable for several years to secure an academic position in her new country, Arendt worked as an editor and in various social agencies until the publication of her first major work, The Origins of Totalitarianism *(1951); this book analyzes Nazi and Communist forms of totalitarianism in terms of their roots in nineteenth-century imperialism and anti-Semitism. Other important volumes followed. Among them were* The Human Condition *(1958) and* Between Past and Future *(1961), both dealing with the general breakdown of the civilizing traditions of Western society;* On Revolution *(1963), which compares and contrasts the American and French revolutions; and* On Violence

From *Eichmann In Jerusalem: A Report on the Banality of Evil* by Hannah Arendt. Copyright © 1963 by Hannah Arendt. All rights reserved. Reprinted by permission of The Viking Press. [Pp. 25-34, 113-14, 126, 135-37, 148-50, 276.]

(1970), which argues that destructive acts appear in the modern bureaucratic state as people are denied creative power. At the time of her death Arendt had completed two volumes of a three-volume philosophical work called The Life of the Mind; it was published posthumously in 1978.

After the publication of The Origins of Totalitarianism, Arendt was much in demand at American universities. She became the first woman to be appointed a full professor at Princeton University and also taught, for various periods, at California, Chicago, Columbia, Northwestern, and Cornell universities. Her last academic post was as University Professor of Political Philosophy at the New School for Social Research, in New York City.

Arendt's Eichmann in Jerusalem: A Report on the Banality of Evil (1963), the source of the following selection, is a book based upon the author's personal observation of the trial of Adolf Eichmann, the notorious Nazi war criminal executed in 1962 for his role in Hitler's "final solution" for the Jewish people. Upon its publication, Eichmann in Jerusalem genera ted widespread critical antagonism, much of it focusing on two of the book's unusual theses: (1) Eichmann was not a demoniacal anti-Semitic monster but rather a normal "banal" mediocrity, content to function as a cog in a totalitarian system and (2) the victims—especially the leaders of the Jewish communities in Nazi-occupied Europe—willingly cooperated in the destruction of their own communities and themselves. In a sense, Arendt expands upon Bettelheim's view (expressed in the preceding selection) regarding the behavior-conditioning nature of totalitarian societies and their elimination of personal autonomy. But while Bettelheim's The Informed Heart deals mainly with concentration camp inmates, the following excerpt —based on the Eichmann trial record—analyzes the psyche of a "typical" administrator in the society outside the camps.

Throughout the trial, Eichmann tried to clarify, mostly without success, this second point in his plea of "not guilty in the sense of the indictment." The indictment implied not only that he had acted on purpose, which he did not deny, but out of base motives and in full knowledge of the criminal nature of his deeds. As for the base motives, he was perfectly sure that he was not what he called an *innerer Schweinehund*, a dirty bastard in the depths of his heart; and as for his conscience, he remembered perfectly well that he would have had a bad conscience only if he had not done what he had been ordered to do—to ship millions of men, women, and children to their death with great zeal and the most meticulous care. This, admittedly, was hard to take. Half a dozen psychiatrists had certified him as "normal"— "More normal, at any rate, than I am after having examined him," one of them was said to have exclaimed, while another had found that his whole psychological outlook, his attitude toward his wife and children, mother and father, brothers, sisters, and friends, was "not only normal but most desirable"—and finally the minister who had paid regular visits to him in prison after the Supreme Court had finished hearing his appeal reassured everybody by declaring Eichmann to be "a man with very positive ideas." Behind the comedy of the soul experts lay the hard fact that his was obviously no case of moral let alone legal insanity. . . . Worse, his was obviously also no case of insane hatred of Jews, of fanatical anti-Semitism or indoctrination of any kind. He "personally" never had anything whatever against Jews; on the contrary, he had plenty of "private reasons" for not being a Jew hater. . . .

Alas, nobody believed him. The prosecutor did not believe him, because that was not his job. Counsel for the defense paid no attention because he, unlike Eichmann, was, to all appearances, not interested in questions of conscience. And the judges did not believe him, because they were too good, and perhaps also too conscious of the very foundations of their profession, to admit that an average, "normal" person, neither feeble-minded nor indoctrinated nor cynical, could be perfectly incapable of telling right from wrong. They preferred to conclude from occasional lies that he was a liar—and missed the greatest moral and even legal challenge of the whole case. Their case rested on the assumption that the defendant, like all "normal persons," must have been aware of the criminal nature of his acts, and Eichmann was indeed normal insofar as he was "no exception within the Nazi regime." However, under the conditions of the Third Reich only "exceptions" could be expected to react "normally." This simple truth of the matter created a dilemma for the judges which they could neither resolve nor escape.

He was born on March 19, 1906, in Solingen, a German town in the Rhineland famous for its knives, scissors, and surgical instruments. Fifty-four years later, indulging in his favorite pastime of writing his memoirs, he described this memorable event as follows: "Today, fifteen years and a day after May 8, 1945, I begin to lead my thoughts back to that nineteenth of March of the year 1906, when at five o'clock in the morning I entered life on earth in the aspect of a human being." . . . According to his religious beliefs, which had not changed since the Nazi period (in Jerusalem Eichmann declared himself to be a *Gottgldubiger*, the Nazi term for those who had broken with Christianity, and he refused to take his oath on the Bible), this event was to be ascribed to "a higher Bearer of Meaning," an entity somehow identical with the "movement of the universe," to which human life, in itself devoid of "higher meaning," is subject. (The terminology is quite suggestive. To call God a *Hoheren Sinnes-trdger* meant linguistically to give him some place in the military hierarchy, since the Nazis had changed the military "recipient of orders," the *Befehlsempfanger,* into a "bearer of orders," a Befehl-*strdger,* indicating, as in the ancient "bearer of ill tidings," the burden of responsibility and of importance that weighed supposedly upon those who had to execute orders. Moreover, Eichmann, like everyone connected with the Final Solution, was officially a "bearer of secrets," a *Geheimnistrdger,* as well, which as far as self-importance went certainly was nothing to sneeze at.) But Eichmann, not very much interested in metaphysics, remained singularly silent on any more intimate relationship between the Bearer of Meaning and the bearer of orders, and proceeded to a consideration of the other possible cause of his existence, his parents: "They would hardly have been so overjoyed at the arrival of their first-born had they been able to watch how in the hour of my birth the Norn of misfortune, to spite the Norn of good fortune, was already spinning threads of grief and sorrow into my life. But a kind, impenetrable veil kept my parents from seeing into the future."

The misfortune started soon enough; it started in school. Eich-mann's father, first an accountant for the Tramways and Electricity Company in Solingen and after 1913 an official of the same corporation in Austria, in Linz, had five children, four sons and a daughter, of whom only Adolf, the eldest, it seems, was unable to finish high school, or even to graduate from the vocational school for engineering into which he was then put. Throughout his life, Eichmann deceived people about his early "misfortunes" by hiding behind the more honorable financial misfortunes of his father. In Israel, however, during his first sessions with Captain Avner Less, the police examiner who was to spend approximately 35 days with him and who produced 3,564 typewritten pages from 76 recorder tapes, he was in an ebullient mood, full of enthusiasm about this unique opportunity "to pour forth everything ... I know" and, by the same token, to advance to the rank of the most cooperative defendant ever. (His enthusiasm was soon dampened, though never quite extinguished, when he was confronted with concrete questions based on irrefutable documents.) The best proof of his initial boundless confidence, obviously wasted on Captain Less (who said to Harry Mulisch: "I was Mr. Eichmann's father confessor"), was that for the first time in his life he admitted his early disasters, although he must have been aware of the fact that he thus contradicted himself on several important entries in all his official Nazi records.

Well, the disasters were ordinary: since he "had not exactly been the most hard-working" pupil—or, one may add, the most gifted— his father had taken him first from high school and then from vocational school, long before graduation. Hence, the profession that appears on all his official documents: construction engineer, had about as much connection with reality as the statement that his birthplace was Palestine and that he was fluent in Hebrew and Yiddish—another outright lie Eichmann had loved to tell both to his S.S. comrades and to his Jewish victims. It was in the same vein that he had always pretended he had been dismissed from his job as salesman for the Vacuum Oil Company in Austria because of membership in the National Socialist Party. The version he confided to Captain Less was less dramatic, though probably not the truth either: he had been fired because it was a time of unemployment, when unmarried employees were the first to lose their jobs. (This explanation, which at first seems plausible, is not very satisfactory, because he lost his job in the spring of 1933, when he had been engaged for two full years to Veronika, or Vera, Liebl, who later became his wife. Why had he not married her before, when he still had a good job? He finally married in March, 1935, probably because bachelors in the S.S., as in the Vacuum Oil Company, were never sure of their jobs and could not be promoted.) Clearly, bragging had always been one of his cardinal vices.

While young Eichmann was doing poorly in school, his father left the Tramway and Electricity Company and went into business for himself. He bought a small mining enterprise and put his unpromising youngster to work in it as an ordinary mining laborer, but only until he found him a job in the sales department of the Oberòster-reichischen Elektrobau Company, where Eichmann remained for over two years. He was now about twenty-two years old and without any prospects for a career; the only thing he had learned, perhaps, was how to sell. What then happened was what he himself called his first break, of which, again, we have two rather different versions. In a handwritten biographical record he submitted in 1939 to win a promotion in the S.S., he described it as follows: "I worked during the years of 1925 to 1927 as a salesman for the Austrian Elek-trobau Company. I left this position of my own free will, as the Vacuum Oil Company of Vienna offered me the representation for Upper Austria." The key word here is "offered," since, according to the story he told Captain Less in Israel, nobody had offered him anything. His own mother had died when he was ten years old, and his father had married again. A cousin of his stepmother—a man he called "uncle"—who was president of the Austrian Automobile Club and was married to the daughter of a Jewish businessman in Czechoslovakia, had used his connection with the general director of the Austrian Vacuum Oil Company, a Jewish Mr. Weiss, to obtain for his unfortunate relation a job as traveling salesman. Eichmann was properly grateful; the Jews in his family were among his "private reasons" for not hating Jews. Even in 1943 or 1944, when the Final Solution was in full swing, he had not forgotten: "The daughter of this marriage, half-Jewish according to the Nuremberg Laws, . . . came to see me in order to obtain my permission for her emigration into Switzerland. Of course, I granted this request, and the same uncle came also to see me to ask me to intervene for some Viennese Jewish couple. I mention this only to show that I myself had no hatred for Jews, for my whole education through my mother and my father had been strictly Christian; my mother, because of her Jewish relatives, held different opinions from those current in S.S. circles."

He went to considerable lengths to prove his point: he had never harbored any ill feelings against his victims, and, what is more, he had never made a secret of that fact. "I explained this to Dr. Lòwen-herz [head of the Jewish Community in Vienna] as I explained it to Dr. Kastner [vice-president of the Zionist Organization in Budapest]; I think I told it to everybody, each of my men knew it, they all heard it from me sometime. Even in elementary school, I had a classmate with whom I spent my free time, and he came to our house; a family in Linz by the name of Sebba. The last time we met we walked together through the streets of Linz, I already with the Party emblem of the N.S.D.A.P. [the Nazi Party] in my buttonhole, and he did not think anything of it." Had Eichmann been a bit less prim or the police examination (which refrained from cross-examination, presumably to remain assured of his cooperation) less discreet, his "lack of prejudice" might have shown itself in still another aspect. It seems that in Vienna, where he was so extraordinarily successful in arranging the "forced emigration" of Jews, he had a Jewish mistress, an "old flame" from Linz. *Rassenschande,* sexual intercourse with Jews, was probably the greatest crime a member of the S.S. could commit, and though during the war the raping of Jewish girls became a favorite pastime at the front, it was by no means common for a Higher S.S. officer to have an affair with a Jewish woman. Thus, Eichmann's repeated violent denunciations of Julius Streicher, the insane and obscene editor *of Der Stürmer,* and of his pornographic anti-Semitism, were perhaps personally motivated, and the expression of more than the routine contempt an "enlightened" S.S. man was supposed to show toward the vulgar passions of lesser Party luminaries.

The five and a half years with the Vacuum Oil Company must have been among the happier ones in Eichmann's life. He made a good living during a time of severe unemployment, and he was still living with his parents, except when he was out on the road. The date when this idyll came to an end—Pentecost, 1933—was among the few he always remembered. Actually, things had taken a turn for the worse somewhat earlier. At the end of 1932, he was unexpectedly transferred from Linz to Salzburg, very much against his inclinations: "I lost all joy in my work, I no longer liked to sell, to make calls." From such sudden losses of *Arbeitsfreude* Eichmann was to suffer throughout his life. The worst of them occurred when he was told of the Fuhrer's order for the "physical extermination of the Jews," in which he was to play such an important role. This, too, came unexpectedly; he himself had "never thought of . . . such a solution through violence," and he described his reaction in the same words: "I now lost everything, all joy in my work, all initiative, all interest; I was, so to speak, blown out." A similar blowing out must have happened in 1932 in Salzburg, and from his own account it is clear that he cannot have been very surprised when he was fired, though one need not believe his saying that he had been "very happy" about his dismissal.

For whatever reasons, the year 1932 marked a turning point of his life. It was in April of this year that he joined the National Socialist Party and entered the S.S., upon an invitation of Ernst Kaltenbrunner, a young lawyer in Linz who later became chief of the Head Office for Reich Security (the *Reichssicherheitshauptamt* or R.S.H.A., as I shall call it henceforth), in one of whose six main departments— Bureau IV, under the command of Heinrich Müller—Eichmann was eventually employed as head of section B-4. In court, Eichmann gave the impression of a typical member of the lower middle classes, and this impression was more than borne out by every sentence he spoke or wrote while in prison. But this was misleading; he was rather the *déclassé* son of a solid middle-class family, and it was indicative of his comedown in social status that while his father was a good friend of Kaltenbrunner's father, who was also a Linz lawyer, the relationship of the two sons was rather cool: Eichmann was unmistakably treated by Kaltenbrunner as his social inferior. Before Eichmann entered the Party and the S.S., he had proved that he was a joiner, and May 8, 1945, the official date of Germany's defeat, was significant for him mainly because it then dawned upon him that thenceforward he would have to live without being a member of something or other. "I sensed I would have to live a leaderless and difficult individual life, I would receive no directives from anybody, no orders and commands would any longer be issued to me, no pertinent ordinances would be there to consult—in brief, a life never known before lay before me." When he was a child, his parents, uninterested in politics, had enrolled him in the Young Men's Christian Association, from which he later went into the German youth movement, the *Wandervogel*. During his four unsuccessful years in high school, he had joined the *Jungfrontkampfeverband*, the youth section of the German-Austrian organization of war veterans, which, though violently pro-German and anti-republican, was tolerated by the Austrian government. When Kaltenbrunner suggested that he enter the S.S., he was just on the point of becoming a member of an altogether different outfit, the Freemasons' Lodge Schlaraffia, "an association of businessmen, physicians, actors, civil servants, etc., who came together to cultivate merriment and gaiety. . . . Each member had to give a lecture from time to time whose tenor was to be humor, refined humor." Kaltenbrunner explained to Eichmann that he would have to give up this merry society because as a Nazi he could not be a Freemason—a word that at the time was unknown to him. The choice between the S.S. and Schlaraffia (the name derives from *Schlaraffenland*, the gluttons' Cloud-Cuckoo Land of German fairy tales) might have been hard to make, but he was "kicked out" of Schiaratila anyhow; he had committed a sin that even now, as he told the story in the Israeli prison, made him blush with shame: "Contrary to my upbringing, I had tried, though I was the youngest, to invite my companions to a glass of wine."

A leaf in the whirlwind of time, he was blown from Schlaraffia, the Never-Never Land of tables set by magic and roast chickens that flew into your mouth—or, more accurately, from the company of respectable philistines with degrees and assured careers and "refined humor," whose worst vice was probably an irrepressible desire for practical jokes—into the marching columns of the Thousand-Year Reich, which lasted exactly twelve years and three months. At any rate, he did not enter the Party out of conviction, nor was he ever convinced by it—whenever he was asked to give his reasons, he repeated the same embarrassed clichés about the Treaty of Versailles and unemployment; rather, as he pointed out in court, "it was like being swallowed up by the Party against all expectations and without previous decision. It happened so quickly and suddenly." He had no time and less desire to be properly informed, he did not even know the Party program, he never read *Mein Kampf*. Kaltenbrunner had said to him: Why not join the S.S.? And he had replied, Why not? That was how it had happened, and that was about all there was to it.

Of course, that was not all there was to it. What Eichmann failed to tell the presiding judge in cross-examination was that he had been an ambitious young man who was fed up with his job as traveling salesman even before the Vacuum Oil Company was fed up with him. From a humdrum life without significance and consequence the wind had blown him into History, as he understood it, namely, into a Movement that always kept moving and in which somebody like him—already a failure in the eyes of his social class, of his family, and hence in his own eyes as well—could start from scratch and still make a career. And if he did not always like what he had to do (for example, dispatching people to their death by the trainload instead of forcing them to emigrate), if he guessed, rather early, that the whole business would come to a bad end, with Germany losing the war, if all his most cherished plans came to nothing (the evacuation of European Jewry to Madagascar, the establishment of a Jewish territory in the Nisko region of Poland, the experiment with carefully built defense installations around his Berlin office to repel Russian tanks), and if, to his greatest "grief and sorrow," he never advanced beyond the grade of S.S. *Obersturmbannführer* (a rank equivalent to lieutenant colonel)—in short, if, with the exception of the year in Vienna, his life was beset with frustrations, he never forgot what the alternative would have been. Not only in Argentina, leading the unhappy existence of a refugee, but also in the courtroom in Jerusalem, with his life as good as forfeited, he might still have preferred—if anybody had asked him—to be hanged as *Obersturmbannführer a.D.* [Lieutenant Colonel in retirement] rather than living out his life quietly and normally as a traveling salesman for the Vacuum Oil Company.

[In January 1942 Reinhardt Heydrich, Chief of Security and Intelligence for the Gestapo (secret police), called a conference of Undersecretaries of the German government ministries and the Civil Service. The purpose of the meeting was to coordinate all efforts toward the implementation of the Final Solution, the Nazi plan for the total destruction of the Jewish people. *Ed.*]

It was a very important occasion for Eichmann, who had never before mingled socially with so many "high personages"; he was by far the lowest in rank and social position of those present. He had sent out the invitations and had prepared some statistical material (full of incredible errors) for Heydrich's introductory speech—eleven million Jews had to be killed, an undertaking of some magnitude— and later he was to prepare the minutes. In short, he acted as secretary of the meeting. This was why he was permitted, after the dignitaries had left, to sit down near the fireplace with his chief Muller and Heydrich, "and that was the first time I saw Heydrich smoke and drink." They did not "talk shop, but enjoyed some rest after long hours of work," being greatly satisfied and, especially Heydrich, in very high spirits.

There was another reason that made the day of this conference unforgettable for Eichmann. Although he had been doing his best right along to help with the Final Solution, he had still harbored some doubts about "such a bloody solution through violence," and these doubts had now been dispelled. "Here now, during this conference, the most prominent people had spoken, the Popes of the Third Reich." Now he could see with his own eyes and hear with his own ears that not only Hitler, not only Heydrich or the "sphinx" Müller, not just the S.S. or the Party, but the élite of the good old Civil

Service were vying and fighting with each other for the honor of taking the lead in these "bloody" matters. "At that moment, I sensed a kind of Pontius Pilate feeling, for I felt free of all guilt." *Who was he to judge?* Who was he "to have [his] own thoughts in this matter"? Well, he was neither the first nor the last to be ruined by modesty.

★ ★ ★

Eichmann, in contrast to other elements in the Nazi movement, had always been overawed by "good society," and the politeness he often showed to German-speaking Jewish functionaries was to a large extent the result of his recognition that he was dealing with people who were socially his superiors. He was not at all, as one witness called him, a *"Landsknechtnatur,"* a mercenary, who wanted to escape to regions where there aren't no Ten Commandments an' a man can raise a thirst. What he fervently believed in up to the end was success, the chief standard of "good society" as he knew it. Typical was his last word on the subject of Hitler—whom he and his comrade Sassen* had agreed to "shirr out" of their story; Hitler, he said, "may have been wrong all down the line, but one thing is beyond dispute: the man was able to work his way up from lance corporal in the German Army to Fuhrer of a people of almost eighty million. . . . His success alone proved to me that I should subordinate myself to this man." His conscience was indeed set at rest when he saw the zeal and eagerness with which "good society" everywhere reacted as he did. He did not need to "close his ears to the voice of conscience," as the judgment has it, not because he had none, but because his conscience spoke with a "respectable voice," with the voice of respectable society around him.

★ ★ ★

So Eichmann's opportunities for feeling like Pontius Pilate were many, and as the months and the years went by, he lost the need to feel anything at all. This was the way things were, this was the new law of the land, based on the Fuhrer's order; whatever he did he did, as far as he could see, as a law-abiding citizen. He did his *duty*, as he told the police and the court over and over again; he not only obeyed *orders*, he also obeyed the *law*. Eichmann had a muddled inkling that this could be an important distinction, but neither the defense nor the judges ever took him up on it. The well-worn coins of "superior orders" versus "acts of state" were handed back and forth; they had governed the whole discussion of these matters during the Nuremberg Trials,† for no other reason than that they gave the illusion that the altogether unprecedented could be judged according to precedents and the standards that went with them. Eichmann, with his rather modest mental gifts, was certainly the last man in the courtroom to be expected to challenge these notions and to strike out on his own. Since, in addition to performing what he conceived to be the duties of a law-abiding citizen, he had also acted upon orders— always so careful to be "covered"—he became completely muddled, and ended by stressing alternately the virtues and the vices

---

* Wilem Sassen, a journalist and former member of the S.S.—who, like Adolf Eichmann, was a fugitive from justice—interviewed Eichmann in 1955 in Argentina. After Eichmann was caught there in 1960 by Israeli agents, parts of the interview were published in American and German magazines.

† After the defeat of Germany in the Second World War, the victorious nations brought some of the major Nazi war criminals to trial at Nuremberg, Germany.

of blind obedience, or the "obedience of corpses," *Kadavergehorsam*, as he himself called it.

The first indication of Eichmann's vague notion that there was more involved in this whole business than the question of the soldier's carrying out orders that are clearly criminal in nature and intent appeared during the police examination, when he suddenly declared with great emphasis that he had lived his whole life according to Kant's moral precepts, and especially according to a Kantian definition of duty. This was outrageous, on the face of it, and also incomprehensible, since Kant's moral philosophy is so closely bound up with man's faculty of judgment, which rules out blind obedience. The examining officer did not press the point, but Judge Raveh, either out of curiosity or out of indignation at Eichmann's having dared to invoke Kant's name in connection with his crimes, decided to question the accused. And, to the surprise of everybody, Eichmann came up with an approximately correct definition of the categorical imperative: "I meant by my remark about Kant that the principle of my will must always be such that it can become the principle of general laws" (which is not the case with theft or murder, for instance, because the thief or the murderer cannot conceivably wish to live under a legal system that would give others the right to rob or murder him). Upon further questioning, he added that he had read Kant's *Critique of Practical Reason*. He then proceeded to explain that from the moment he was charged with carrying out the Final Solution he had ceased to live according to Kantian principles, that he had known it, and that he had consoled himself with the thought that he no longer "was master of his own deeds," that he was unable "to change anything." What he failed to point out in court was that in this "period of crimes legalized by the state," as he himself now called it, he had not simply dismissed the Kantian formula as no longer applicable, he had distorted it to read: Act as if the principle of your actions were the same as that of the legislator or of the law of the land—or, in Hans Frank's* formulation of "the categorical imperative in the Third Reich," which Eichmann might have known: "Act in such

---

* Hans Frank, tried and hanged at Nuremberg, had been Governor General of Poland during the German occupation.

a way that the Fuhrer, if he knew your action, would approve it" *(Die Technik des Staates,* 1942, pp. 15-16). Kant, to be sure, had never intended to say anything of the sort; on the contrary, to him every man was a legislator the moment he started to act: by using his "practical reason" man found the principles that could and should be the principles of law. But it is true that Eichmann's unconscious distortion agrees with what he himself called the version of Kant "for the household use of the little man." In this household use, all that is left of Kant's spirit is the demand that a man do more than obey the law, that he go beyond the mere call of obedience and identify his own will with the principle behind the law—the source from which the law sprang. In Kant's philosophy, that source was practical reason; in Eichmann's household use of him, it was the will of the Führer. Much of the horribly painstaking thoroughness in the execution of the Final Solution—a thoroughness that usually strikes the observer as typically German, or else as characteristic of the perfect bureaucrat—can be traced to the odd notion, indeed very common in Germany, that to be law-abiding means not merely to obey the laws but to act as though one were the legislator of the laws that one obeys. Hence the conviction that nothing less than going beyond the call of duty will do.

Whatever Kant's role in the formation of "the little man's" mentality in Germany may have been, there is not the slightest doubt that in one respect Eichmann did indeed follow Kant's precepts: a law was a law, there could be no exceptions. In Jerusalem, he admitted only two such exceptions during the time when "eighty million Germans" had each had "his decent Jew": he had helped a half-Jewish cousin, and a Jewish couple in Vienna for whom his uncle had intervened. This inconsistency still made him feel somewhat uncomfortable, and when he was questioned about it during cross-examination, he became openly apologetic: he had "confessed his sins" to his superiors. This uncompromising attitude toward the performance of his murderous duties damned him in the eyes of the judges more than anything else, which was comprehensible, but in his own eyes it was precisely what justified him, as it had once silenced whatever conscience he might have had left. No exceptions—this was the proof that he had always acted against his "inclinations," whether they were sentimental or inspired by interest, that he had always done his "duty." . . .

In Jerusalem, confronted with documentary proof of his extraordinary loyalty to Hitler and the Führer's order, Eichmann tried a number of times to explain that during the Third Reich "the Führer's words had the force of law" *(Führerworte haben Geset-zeskraft)*, which meant, among other things, that if the order came directly from Hitler it did not have to be in writing. He tried to explain that this was why he had never asked for a written order from Hitler (no such document relating to the Final Solution has ever been found; probably it never existed), but had demanded to see a written order from Himmler.* To be sure, this was a fantastic state of affairs, and whole libraries of very "learned" juridical comment have been written, all demonstrating that the Führer's *words,* his oral pronouncements, were the basic law of the land. Within this "legal" framework, every order contrary in letter or spirit to a word spoken by Hitler was, by definition, unlawful. Eichmann's position, therefore, showed a most unpleasant resemblance to that of the often-cited soldier who, acting in a normal legal framework, refuses to carry out orders that run counter to his ordinary experience of lawfulness and hence can be recognized by him as criminal. The extensive literature on the subject usually supports its case with the common equivocal meaning of the word "law," which in this context means sometimes the law of the land—that is, posited, positive law—and sometimes the law that supposedly speaks in all men's hearts with an identical voice. Practically speaking, however, orders to be disobeyed must be "manifestly unlawful" and unlawfulness must "fly like a black flag above [them] as a warning reading: 'Prohibited!' "—as the judgment pointed out. And in a criminal regime this "black flag" with its "warning sign" flies as "manifestly" above what normally is a lawful order—for instance, not to kill innocent people just because they happen to be Jews—as it flies above a criminal order under normal circumstances. To fall back on an unequivocal voice of conscience—or, in the even vaguer language of the jurists, on a "general sentiment of humanity" (Oppenheim-

---

* Heinrich Himmler was the director of all the German police forces during the Nazi regime; he was captured in 1945 but committed suicide before he could be brought to trial.

Lauter-pacht in *International Law,* 1952)—not only begs the question, it signifies a deliberate refusal to take notice of the central moral, legal, and political phenomena of our century.

To be sure, it was not merely Eichmann's conviction that Himmler was now giving "criminal" orders [to stop the murders and destroy the evidence as German defeat approached] that determined his actions. But the personal element undoubtedly involved was not fanaticism, it was his genuine, "boundless and immoderate admiration for Hitler" (as one of the defense witnesses called it)—for the man who had made it "from lance corporal to Chancellor of the Reich." It would be idle to try to figure out which was stronger in him, his admiration for Hitler or his determination to remain a law-abiding citizen of the Third Reich when Germany was already in ruins. Both motives came into play once more during the last days of the war, when he was in Berlin and saw with violent indignation how everybody around him was sensibly enough getting himself fixed up with forged papers before the arrival of the Russians or the Americans. A few weeks later, Eichmann, too, began to travel under an assumed name, but by then Hitler was dead, and the "law of the land" was no longer in existence, and he, as he pointed out, was no longer bound by his oath. For the oath taken by the members of the S.S. differed from the military oath sworn by the soldiers in that it bound them only to Hitler, not to Germany.

The case of the conscience of Adolf Eichmann, which is admittedly complicated but is by no means unique, is scarcely comparable to the case of the German generals, one of whom, when asked at Nuremberg, "How was it possible that all you honorable generals could continue to serve a murderer with such unquestioning loyalty?," replied that it was "not the task of a soldier to act as judge over his supreme commander. Let history do that or God in heaven." (Thus General Alfred Jodl, hanged at Nuremberg.) Eichmann, much less intelligent and without any education to speak of, at least dimly realized that it was not an order but a law which had turned them all into criminals. The distinction between an order and the Fuhrer's word was that the latter's validity was not limited in time and space, which is the outstanding characteristic of the former. This is also the true reason why the Fuhrer's order for the Final Solution was followed by a huge shower of regulations and directives, all drafted by expert lawyers and legal advisers, not by mere administrators; this order, in contrast to ordinary orders, was treated as a law. Needless to add, the resulting legal paraphernalia, far from being a mere symptom of German pedantry or thoroughness, served most effectively to give the whole business its outward appearance of legality.

And just as the law in civilized countries assumes that the voice of conscience tells everybody "Thou shalt not kill," even though man's natural desires and inclinations may at times be murderous, so the law of Hitler's land demanded that the voice of conscience tell everybody: "Thou shalt kill," although the organizers of the massacres knew full well that murder is against the normal desires and inclinations of most people. Evil in the Third Reich had lost the quality by which most people recognize it—the quality of temptation. Many Germans and many Nazis, probably an overwhelming majority of them, must have been tempted *not* to murder, *not* to rob, *not* to let their neighbors go off to their doom (for that the Jews were transported to their doom they knew, of course, even though many of them may not have known the gruesome details), and not to become accomplices in all these crimes by benefiting from them. But, God knows, they had learned how to resist temptation.

★ ★ ★

The trouble with Eichmann was precisely that so many were like him, and that the many were neither perverted nor sadistic, that they were, and still are, terribly and terrifyingly normal. From the viewpoint of our legal institutions and of our moral standards of judgment, this normality was much more terrifying than all the atrocities put together, for it implied—as had been said at Nuremberg over and over again by the defendants and their counsels—that this new type of criminal, who is in actual fact *hostis generis humani*,* commits his crimes under circumstances that make it well-nigh impossible for him to know or to feel that he is doing wrong. . . .

---

* Latin: an enemy of the human race.

24

Rev. Martin Luther King

Letter from a Birmingham Jail

16 April 1963
My Dear Fellow Clergymen:

While confined here in the Birmingham city jail, I came across your recent statement calling my present activities "unwise and untimely." Seldom do I pause to answer criticism of my work and ideas. If I sought to answer all the criticisms that cross my desk, my secretaries would have little time for anything other than such correspondence in the course of the day, and I would have no time for constructive work. But since I feel that you are men of genuine good will and that your criticisms are sincerely set forth, I want to try to answer your statement in what I hope will be patient and reasonable terms.

I think I should indicate why I am here in Birmingham, since you have been influenced by the view which argues against "outsiders coming in." I have the honor of serving as president of the Southern Christian Leadership Conference, an organization operating in every southern state, with headquarters in Atlanta, Georgia. We have some eighty five affiliated organizations across the South, and one of them is the Alabama Christian Movement for Human Rights. Frequently we share staff, educational and financial resources with our affiliates. Several months ago the affiliate here in Birmingham asked us to be on call to engage in a nonviolent direct action program if such were deemed necessary. We readily consented, and when the hour came we lived up to our promise. So I, along with several members of my staff, am here because I was invited here. I am here because I have organizational ties here.

But more basically, I am in Birmingham because injustice is here. Just as the prophets of the eighth century B.C. left their villages and carried their "thus saith the Lord" far beyond the boundaries of their home towns, and just as the Apostle Paul left his village of Tarsus and carried the gospel of Jesus Christ to the far corners of the Greco Roman world, so am I compelled to carry the gospel of freedom beyond my own home town. Like Paul, I must constantly respond to the Macedonian call for aid.

Moreover, I am cognizant of the interrelatedness of all communities and states. I cannot sit idly by in Atlanta and not be concerned about what happens in Birmingham. Injustice anywhere is a threat to justice everywhere. We are caught in an inescapable network of mutuality, tied in a single garment of destiny. Whatever affects one directly, affects all indirectly. Never again can we afford to live with the narrow, provincial "outside agitator" idea. Anyone who lives inside the United States can never be considered an outsider anywhere within its bounds.

You deplore the demonstrations taking place in Birmingham. But your statement, I am sorry to say, fails to express a similar concern for the conditions that brought about the demonstrations. I am sure that none of you would want to rest content with the superficial kind of social analysis that deals merely with effects and does not grapple with underlying causes. It is unfortunate that demonstrations are taking place in Birmingham, but it is even more unfortunate that the city's white power structure left the Negro community with no alternative.

In any nonviolent campaign there are four basic steps: collection of the facts to determine whether injustices exist; negotiation; self purification; and direct action. We have gone through all these steps in Birmingham. There can be no gainsaying the fact that racial injustice engulfs this community. Birmingham is probably the most thoroughly segregated city in the United States. Its ugly record of brutality is widely known. Negroes have experienced grossly unjust treatment in the courts. There have been more unsolved bombings of Negro homes and churches in Birmingham than in any other city in the nation. These are the hard, brutal facts of the case. On the basis of these conditions,

Negro leaders sought to negotiate with the city fathers. But the latter consistently refused to engage in good faith negotiation.

Then, last September, came the opportunity to talk with leaders of Birmingham's economic community. In the course of the negotiations, certain promises were made by the merchants—for example, to remove the stores' humiliating racial signs. On the basis of these promises, the Reverend Fred Shuttlesworth and the leaders of the Alabama Christian Movement for Human Rights agreed to a moratorium on all demonstrations. As the weeks and months went by, we realized that we were the victims of a broken promise. A few signs, briefly removed, returned; the others remained. As in so many past experiences, our hopes had been blasted, and the shadow of deep disappointment settled upon us. We had no alternative except to prepare for direct action, whereby we would present our very bodies as a means of laying our case before the conscience of the local and the national community. Mindful of the difficulties involved, we decided to undertake a process of self purification. We began a series of workshops on nonviolence, and we repeatedly asked ourselves: "Are you able to accept blows without retaliating?" "Are you able to endure the ordeal of jail?" We decided to schedule our direct action program for the Easter season, realizing that except for Christmas, this is the main shopping period of the year. Knowing that a strong economic-withdrawal program would be the by product of direct action, we felt that this would be the best time to bring pressure to bear on the merchants for the needed change.

Then it occurred to us that Birmingham's mayoral election was coming up in March, and we speedily decided to postpone action until after election day. When we discovered that the Commissioner of Public Safety, Eugene "Bull" Connor, had piled up enough votes to be in the run off, we decided again to postpone action until the day after the run off so that the demonstrations could not be used to cloud the issues. Like many others, we waited to see Mr. Connor defeated, and to this end we endured postponement after postponement. Having aided in this community need, we felt that our direct action program could be delayed no longer.

You may well ask: "Why direct action? Why sit ins, marches and so forth? Isn't negotiation a better path?" You are quite right in calling for negotiation. Indeed, this is the very purpose of direct action. Nonviolent direct action seeks to create such a crisis and foster such a tension that a community which has constantly refused to negotiate is forced to confront the issue. It seeks so to dramatize the issue that it can no longer be ignored. My citing the creation of tension as part of the work of the nonviolent resister may sound rather shocking. But I must confess that I am not afraid of the word "tension." I have earnestly opposed violent tension, but there is a type of constructive, nonviolent tension which is necessary for growth. Just as Socrates felt that it was necessary to create a tension in the mind so that individuals could rise from the bondage of myths and half truths to the unfettered realm of creative analysis and objective appraisal, so must we see the need for nonviolent gadflies to create the kind of tension in society that will help men rise from the dark depths of prejudice and racism to the majestic heights of understanding and brotherhood. The purpose of our direct action program is to create a situation so crisis packed that it will inevitably open the door to negotiation. I therefore concur with you in your call for negotiation. Too long has our beloved Southland been bogged down in a tragic effort to live in monologue rather than dialogue.

One of the basic points in your statement is that the action that I and my associates have taken in Birmingham is untimely. Some have asked: "Why didn't you give the new city administration time to act?" The only answer that I can give to this query is that the new Birmingham administration must be prodded about as much as the outgoing one, before it will act. We are sadly mistaken if we feel that the election of Albert Boutwell as mayor will bring the millennium to Birmingham. While Mr. Boutwell is a much more gentle person than Mr. Connor, they are both segregationists, dedicated to maintenance of the status quo. I have hope that Mr. Boutwell will be reasonable enough to see the futility of massive resistance to desegregation. But he will not see this without pressure from devotees of civil rights. My friends, I must say to you that we have not made a single gain in civil rights without determined legal and nonviolent pressure. Lamentably, it is an historical fact that privileged groups seldom give up their privileges voluntarily. Individuals may see the moral light and voluntarily give up their unjust posture; but, as Reinhold Niebuhr has reminded us, groups tend to be more immoral than individuals.

We know through painful experience that freedom is never voluntarily given by the oppressor; it must be demanded by the oppressed. Frankly, I have yet to engage in a direct action campaign that was "well timed" in the view of those who have not suffered unduly from the disease of segregation. For years now I have heard the word "Wait!" It rings in the ear of every Negro with piercing familiarity. This "Wait" has almost always meant "Never." We must come to see, with one of our distinguished jurists, that "justice too long delayed is justice denied."

We have waited for more than 340 years for our constitutional and God given rights. The nations of Asia and Africa are moving with jetlike speed toward gaining political independence, but we still creep at horse and buggy pace toward gaining a cup of coffee at a lunch counter. Perhaps it is easy for those who have never felt the stinging darts of segregation to say, "Wait." But when you have seen vicious mobs lynch your mothers and fathers at will and drown your sisters and brothers at whim; when you have seen hate filled policemen curse, kick and even kill your black brothers and sisters; when you see the vast majority of your twenty million Negro brothers smothering in an airtight cage of poverty in the midst of an affluent society; when you suddenly find your tongue twisted and your speech stammering as you seek to explain to your six year old daughter why she can't go to the public amusement park that has just been advertised on television, and see tears welling up in her eyes when she is told that Funtown is closed to colored children, and see ominous clouds of inferiority beginning to form in her little mental sky, and see her beginning to distort her personality by developing an unconscious bitterness toward white people; when you have to concoct an answer for a five year old son who is asking: "Daddy, why do white people treat colored people so mean?"; when you take a cross county drive and find it necessary to sleep night after night in the uncomfortable corners of your automobile because no motel will accept you; when you are humiliated day in and day out by nagging signs reading "white" and "colored"; when your first name becomes "nigger," your middle name becomes "boy" (however old you are) and your last name becomes "John," and your wife and mother are never given the respected title "Mrs."; when you are harried by day and haunted by night by the fact that you are a Negro, living constantly at tiptoe stance, never quite knowing what to expect next, and are plagued with inner fears and outer resentments; when you are forever fighting a degenerating sense of "nobodiness"—then you will understand why we find it difficult to wait. There comes a time when the cup of endurance runs over, and men are no longer willing to be plunged into the abyss of despair. I hope, sirs, you can understand our legitimate and unavoidable impatience. You express a great deal of anxiety over our willingness to break laws. This is certainly a legitimate concern. Since we so diligently urge people to obey the Supreme Court's decision of 1954 outlawing segregation in the public schools, at first glance it may seem rather paradoxical for us consciously to break laws. One may well ask: "How can you advocate breaking some laws and obeying others?" The answer lies in the fact that there are two types of laws: just and unjust. I would be the first to advocate obeying just laws. One has not only a legal but a moral responsibility to obey just laws. Conversely, one has a moral responsibility to disobey unjust laws. I would agree with St. Augustine that "an unjust law is no law at all."

Now, what is the difference between the two? How does one determine whether a law is just or unjust? A just law is a man made code that squares with the moral law or the law of God. An unjust law is a code that is out of harmony with the moral law. To put it in the terms of St. Thomas Aquinas: An unjust law is a human law that is not rooted in eternal law and natural law. Any law that uplifts human personality is just. Any law that degrades human personality is unjust. All segregation statutes are unjust because segregation distorts the soul and damages the personality. It gives the segregator a false sense of superiority and the segregated a false sense of inferiority. Segregation, to use the terminology of the Jewish philosopher Martin Buber, substitutes an "I it" relationship for an "I thou" relationship and ends up relegating persons to the status of things. Hence segregation is not only politically, economically and sociologically unsound, it is morally wrong and sinful. Paul Tillich has said that sin is separation. Is not segregation an existential expression of man's tragic separation, his awful estrangement, his terrible sinfulness? Thus it is that I can urge men to obey the 1954 decision of the Supreme Court, for it is morally right; and I can urge them to disobey segregation ordinances, for they are morally wrong.

Let us consider a more concrete example of just and unjust laws. An unjust law is a code that a numerical or power majority group compels a minority group to obey but does not make binding on itself. This is difference made legal. By the same token, a just law is a code that a majority compels a minority to follow and that it is willing to follow itself. This is sameness made legal. Let me give another explanation. A law is unjust if it is inflicted on a minority that, as a result of being denied the right to vote, had no part in enacting or devising the law. Who can say that the legislature of Alabama which set up that state's segregation laws was democratically elected? Throughout Alabama all sorts of devious methods are used to prevent Negroes from becoming registered voters, and there are some counties in which, even though Negroes constitute a majority of the population, not a single Negro is registered. Can any law enacted under such circumstances be considered democratically structured?

Sometimes a law is just on its face and unjust in its application. For instance, I have been arrested on a charge of parading without a permit. Now, there is nothing wrong in having an ordinance which requires a permit for a parade. But such an ordinance becomes unjust when it is used to maintain segregation and to deny citizens the First-Amendment privilege of peaceful assembly and protest.

I hope you are able to see the distinction I am trying to point out. In no sense do I advocate evading or defying the law, as would the rabid segregationist. That would lead to anarchy. One who breaks an unjust law must do so openly, lovingly, and with a willingness to accept the penalty. I submit that an individual who breaks a law that conscience tells him is unjust, and who willingly accepts the penalty of imprisonment in order to arouse the conscience of the community over its injustice, is in reality expressing the highest respect for law.

Of course, there is nothing new about this kind of civil disobedience. It was evidenced sublimely in the refusal of Shadrach, Meshach and Abednego to obey the laws of Nebuchadnezzar, on the ground that a higher moral law was at stake. It was practiced superbly by the early

332 Rev. Martin Luther King

Christians, who were willing to face hungry lions and the excruciating pain of chopping blocks rather than submit to certain unjust laws of the Roman Empire. To a degree, academic freedom is a reality today because Socrates practiced civil disobedience. In our own nation, the Boston Tea Party represented a massive act of civil disobedience.

We should never forget that everything Adolf Hitler did in Germany was "legal" and everything the Hungarian freedom fighters did in Hungary was "illegal." It was "illegal" to aid and comfort a Jew in Hitler's Germany. Even so, I am sure that, had I lived in Germany at the time, I would have aided and comforted my Jewish brothers. If today I lived in a Communist country where certain principles dear to the Christian faith are suppressed, I would openly advocate disobeying that country's antireligious laws.

I must make two honest confessions to you, my Christian and Jewish brothers. First, I must confess that over the past few years I have been gravely disappointed with the white moderate. I have almost reached the regrettable conclusion that the Negro's great stumbling block in his stride toward freedom is not the White Citizen's Counciler or the Ku Klux Klanner, but the white moderate, who is more devoted to "order" than to justice; who prefers a negative peace which is the absence of tension to a positive peace which is the presence of justice; who constantly says: "I agree with you in the goal you seek, but I cannot agree with your methods of direct action"; who paternalistically believes he can set the timetable for another man's freedom; who lives by a mythical concept of time and who constantly advises the Negro to wait for a "more convenient season." Shallow understanding from people of good will is more frustrating than absolute misunderstanding from people of ill will. Lukewarm acceptance is much more bewildering than outright rejection.

I had hoped that the white moderate would understand that law and order exist for the purpose of establishing justice and that when they fail in this purpose they become the dangerously structured dams that block the flow of social progress. I had hoped that the white moderate would understand that the present tension in the South is a necessary phase of the transition from an obnoxious negative peace, in which the Negro passively accepted his unjust plight, to a substantive and positive peace, in which all men will respect the dignity and worth of human personality. Actually, we who engage in nonviolent direct action are not the creators of tension. We merely bring to the surface the hidden tension that is already alive. We bring it out in the open, where it can be seen and dealt with. Like a boil that can never be cured so long as it is covered up but must be opened with all its ugliness to the natural medicines of air and light, injustice must be exposed, with all the tension its exposure creates, to the light of human conscience and the air of national opinion before it can be cured.

In your statement you assert that our actions, even though peaceful, must be condemned because they precipitate violence. But is this a logical assertion? Isn't this like condemning a robbed man because his possession of money precipitated the evil act of robbery? Isn't this like condemning Socrates because his unswerving commitment to truth and his philosophical inquiries precipitated the act by the misguided populace in which they made him drink hemlock? Isn't this like condemning Jesus because his unique God consciousness and never ceasing devotion to God's will precipitated the evil act of crucifixion? We must come to see that, as the federal courts have consistently affirmed, it is wrong to urge an individual to cease his efforts to gain his basic constitutional rights because the quest may precipitate violence. Society must protect the robbed and punish the robber. I had also hoped that the white moderate would reject the myth concerning time in relation to the struggle for freedom. I have just received a letter from a white brother in Texas. He writes: "All Christians know that the colored people will receive equal rights eventually, but it is possible that you are in too great a religious hurry. It has taken Christianity almost two thousand years to accomplish what it has. The teachings of Christ take time to come to earth." Such an attitude stems from a tragic misconception of time, from the strangely irrational notion that there is something in the very flow of time that will inevitably cure all ills. Actually, time itself is neutral; it can be used either destructively or constructively. More and more I feel that the people of ill will have used time much more effectively than have the people of good will. We will have to repent in this generation not merely for the hateful words and actions of the bad people but for the appalling silence of the good people. Human progress never rolls in on wheels of inevitability; it comes through the tireless efforts of men willing to be co workers with God, and without this hard work, time itself becomes an ally of the forces of social stagnation. We must use time creatively, in the knowledge that the time is always ripe to do right. Now is the time to make real the promise of democracy and transform our pending national elegy into a creative psalm of brotherhood. Now is the time to lift our national policy from the quicksand of racial injustice to the solid rock of human dignity.

You speak of our activity in Birmingham as extreme. At first I was rather disappointed that fellow clergymen would see my nonviolent efforts as those of an extremist. I began thinking about the fact that I stand in the middle of two opposing forces in the Negro community. One is a force of complacency, made up in part of Negroes who, as a result of long years of oppression, are so drained of self respect and a sense of "somebodiness" that they have adjusted to segregation; and in part of a few middle-class Negroes who, because of a degree of academic and economic security and because in some ways they profit by segregation, have become insensitive to the problems of the masses. The other force is one of bitterness and hatred, and it comes perilously close to advocating violence. It is expressed in the various black nationalist groups that are springing up across the nation, the largest and best known being Elijah Muhammad's Muslim movement. Nourished by the Negro's frustration over the continued existence of racial discrimination, this movement is made up of people who have lost faith in America, who have absolutely repudiated Christianity, and who have concluded that the white man is an incorrigible "devil."

I have tried to stand between these two forces, saying that we need emulate neither the "do nothingism" of the complacent nor the hatred and despair of the black nationalist. For there is the more excellent way of love and nonviolent protest. I am grateful to God that, through the influence of the Negro church, the way of nonviolence became an integral part of our struggle. If this philosophy had not emerged, by now many streets of the South would, I am convinced, be flowing with blood. And I am further convinced that if our white brothers dismiss as "rabble rousers" and "outside agitators" those of us who employ nonviolent direct action, and if they refuse to support our nonviolent efforts, millions of Negroes will, out of frustration and despair, seek solace and security in black nationalist ideologies—a development that would inevitably lead to a frightening racial nightmare.

Oppressed people cannot remain oppressed forever. The yearning for freedom eventually manifests itself, and that is what has happened to the American Negro. Something within has reminded him of his birthright of freedom, and something without has reminded him that it can be gained. Consciously or unconsciously, he has been caught up by the Zeitgeist, and with his black brothers of Africa and his brown and yellow brothers of Asia, South America and the Caribbean, the United States Negro is moving with a sense of great urgency toward the promised land of racial justice. If one recognizes this vital urge that has engulfed the Negro community, one should readily understand why public demonstrations are taking place. The Negro has many pent up resentments and latent frustrations, and he must release them. So let him march; let him make prayer pilgrimages to the city hall; let him go on freedom rides—and try to understand why he must do so. If his repressed emotions are not released in nonviolent ways, they will seek expression through violence; this is not a threat but a fact of history. So I have not said to my people: "Get rid of your discontent." Rather, I have tried to say that this normal and healthy discontent can be channeled into the creative outlet of nonviolent direct action. And now this approach is being termed extremist. But though I was initially disappointed at being categorized as an extremist, as I continued to think about the matter I gradually gained a measure of satisfaction from the label. Was not Jesus an extremist for love: "Love your enemies, bless them that curse you, do good to them that hate you, and pray for them which despitefully use you, and persecute you." Was not Amos an extremist for justice: "Let justice roll down like waters and righteousness like an ever flowing stream." Was not Paul an extremist for the Christian gospel: "I bear in my body the marks of the Lord Jesus." Was not Martin Luther an extremist: "Here I stand; I cannot do otherwise, so help me God." And John Bunyan: "I will stay in jail to the end of my days before I make a butchery of my conscience." And Abraham Lincoln: "This nation cannot survive half slave and half free." And Thomas Jefferson: "We hold these truths to be self evident, that all men are created equal . . ." So the question is not whether we will be extremists, but what kind of extremists we will be. Will we be extremists for hate or for love? Will we be extremists for the preservation of injustice or for the extension of justice? In that dramatic scene on Calvary's hill three men were crucified. We must never forget that all three were crucified for the same crime—the crime of extremism. Two were extremists for immorality, and thus fell below their environment. The other, Jesus Christ, was an extremist for love, truth and goodness, and thereby rose above his environment. Perhaps the South, the nation and the world are in dire need of creative extremists.

I had hoped that the white moderate would see this need. Perhaps I was too optimistic; perhaps I expected too much. I suppose I should have realized that few members of the oppressor race can understand the deep groans and passionate yearnings of the oppressed race, and still fewer have the vision to see that injustice must be rooted out by strong, persistent and determined action. I am thankful, however, that some of our white brothers in the South have grasped the meaning of this social revolution and committed themselves to it. They are still all too few in quantity, but they are big in quality. Some -such as Ralph McGill, Lillian Smith, Harry Golden, James McBride Dabbs, Ann Braden and Sarah Patton Boyle—have written about our struggle in eloquent and prophetic terms. Others have marched with us down nameless streets of the South. They have languished in filthy, roach infested jails, suffering the abuse and brutality of policemen who view them as "dirty nigger-lovers." Unlike so many of their moderate brothers and sisters, they have recognized the urgency of the moment and sensed the need for powerful "action" antidotes to combat the disease of segregation. Let me take note of my other major disappointment. I have been so greatly disappointed with the white church and its leadership. Of course, there are some notable exceptions. I am not unmindful of the fact that each of you has taken some significant stands on this issue. I commend you, Reverend Stallings, for your Christian stand on this past Sunday, in welcoming Negroes to your worship service on a nonsegregated basis. I commend the Catholic leaders of this state for integrating Spring Hill College several years ago.

But despite these notable exceptions, I must honestly reiterate that I have been disappointed with the church. I do not say this as one of those negative critics who can always find something wrong with the church. I say this as a minister of the gospel, who loves the church; who was nurtured in its bosom; who has been sustained by its spiritual blessings and who will remain true to it as long as the cord of life shall lengthen.

When I was suddenly catapulted into the leadership of the bus protest in Montgomery, Alabama, a few years ago, I felt we would be supported by the white church. I felt that the white ministers, priests and rabbis of the South would be among our strongest allies. Instead, some have been outright opponents, refusing to understand the freedom movement and misrepresenting its leaders; all too many others have been more cautious than courageous and have remained silent behind the anesthetizing security of stained glass windows.

In spite of my shattered dreams, I came to Birmingham with the hope that the white religious leadership of this community would see the justice of our cause and, with deep moral concern, would serve as the channel through which our just grievances could reach the power structure. I had hoped that each of you would understand. But again I have been disappointed.

I have heard numerous southern religious leaders admonish their worshipers to comply with a desegregation decision because it is the law, but I have longed to hear white ministers declare: "Follow this decree because integration is morally right and because the Negro is your brother." In the midst of blatant injustices inflicted upon the Negro, I have watched white churchmen stand on the sideline and mouth pious irrelevancies and sanctimonious trivialities. In the midst of a mighty struggle to rid our nation of racial and economic injustice, I have heard many ministers say: "Those are social issues, with which the gospel has no real concern." And I have watched many churches commit themselves to a completely other worldly religion which makes a strange, un-Biblical distinction between body and soul, between the sacred and the secular.

I have traveled the length and breadth of Alabama, Mississippi and all the other southern states. On sweltering summer days and crisp autumn mornings I have looked at the South's beautiful churches with their lofty spires pointing heavenward. I have beheld the impressive outlines of her massive religious education buildings. Over and over I have found myself asking: "What kind of people worship here? Who is their God? Where were their voices when the lips of Governor Barnett dripped with words of interposition and nullification? Where were they when Governor Wallace gave a clarion call for defiance and hatred? Where were their voices of support when bruised and weary Negro men and women decided to rise from the dark dungeons of complacency to the bright hills of creative protest?"

Yes, these questions are still in my mind. In deep disappointment I have wept over the laxity of the church. But be assured that my tears have been tears of love. There can be no deep disappointment where there is not deep love. Yes, I love the church. How could I do otherwise? I am in the rather unique position of being the son, the grandson and the great grandson of preachers. Yes, I see the church as the body of Christ. But, oh! How we have blemished and scarred that body through social neglect and through fear of being nonconformists.

There was a time when the church was very powerful—in the time when the early Christians rejoiced at being deemed worthy to suffer for what they believed. In those days the church was not merely a thermometer that recorded the ideas and principles of popular opinion; it was a thermostat that transformed the mores of society. Whenever the early Christians entered a town, the people in power became disturbed and immediately sought to convict the Christians for being "disturbers of the peace" and "outside agitators.'" But the Christians pressed on, in the conviction that they were "a colony of heaven," called to obey God rather than man. Small in number, they were big in commitment. They were too God-intoxicated to be "astronomically intimidated." By their effort and example they brought an end to such ancient evils as infanticide and gladiatorial contests. Things are different now. So often the contemporary church is a weak, ineffectual voice with an uncertain sound. So often it is an archdefender of the status quo. Far from being disturbed by the presence of the church, the power structure of the average community is consoled by the church's silent—and often even vocal—sanction of things as they are.

But the judgment of God is upon the church as never before. If today's church does not recapture the sacrificial spirit of the early church, it will lose its authenticity, forfeit the loyalty of millions, and be dismissed as an irrelevant social club with no meaning for the twentieth century. Every day I meet young people whose disappointment with the church has turned into outright disgust.

Perhaps I have once again been too optimistic. Is organized religion too inextricably bound to the status quo to save our nation and the world? Perhaps I must turn my faith to the inner spiritual church, the church within the church, as the true ekklesia and the hope of the world. But again I am thankful to God that some noble souls from the ranks of organized religion have broken loose from the paralyzing chains of conformity and joined us as active partners in the struggle for freedom. They have left their secure congregations and walked the streets of Albany, Georgia, with us. They have gone down the highways of the South on tortuous rides for freedom. Yes, they have gone to jail with us. Some have been dismissed from their churches, have lost the support of their bishops and fellow ministers. But they have acted in the faith that right defeated is stronger than evil triumphant. Their witness has been the spiritual salt that has preserved the true meaning of the gospel in these troubled times. They have carved a tunnel of hope through the dark mountain of disappointment. I hope the church as a whole will meet the challenge of this decisive hour. But even if the church does not come to the aid of justice, I have no despair about the future. I have no fear about the outcome of our struggle in Birmingham, even if our motives are at present misunderstood. We will reach the goal of freedom in Birmingham and all over the nation, because the goal of America is freedom. Abused and scorned though we may be, our destiny is tied up with America's destiny. Before the pilgrims landed at Plymouth, we were here. Before the pen of Jefferson etched the majestic words of the Declaration of Independence across the pages of history, we were here. For more than two centuries our forebears labored in this country without wages; they made cotton king; they built the homes of their masters while suffering gross injustice and shameful humiliation -and yet out of a bottomless vitality they continued to thrive and develop. If the inexpressible cruelties of slavery could not stop us, the opposition we now face will surely fail. We will win our freedom because the sacred heritage of our nation and the eternal will of God are embodied in our echoing demands. Before closing I feel impelled to mention one other point in your statement that has troubled me profoundly. You warmly commended the Birmingham police force for keeping "order" and "preventing violence." I doubt that you would have so warmly commended the police force if you had seen its dogs sinking their teeth into unarmed, nonviolent Negroes. I doubt that you would so quickly commend the policemen if you were to observe their ugly and inhumane treatment of Negroes here in the city jail; if you were to watch them push and curse old Negro women and young Negro girls; if you were to see them slap and kick old Negro men and young boys; if you were to observe them, as they did on two occasions, refuse to give us food because we wanted to sing our grace together. I cannot join you in your praise of the Birmingham police department.

It is true that the police have exercised a degree of discipline in handling the demonstrators. In this sense they have conducted themselves rather "nonviolently" in public. But for what purpose? To preserve the evil system of segregation. Over the past few years I have consistently preached that nonviolence demands that the means we use must be as pure as the ends we seek. I have tried to make clear that it is wrong to use immoral means to attain moral ends. But now I must affirm that it is just as wrong, or perhaps even more so, to use moral means to preserve immoral ends. Perhaps Mr. Connor and his policemen have been rather nonviolent in public, as was Chief Pritchett in Albany, Georgia, but they have used the moral means of nonviolence to maintain the immoral end of racial injustice. As T. S. Eliot has said: "The last temptation is the greatest treason: To do the right deed for the wrong reason."

I wish you had commended the Negro sit inners and demonstrators of Birmingham for their sublime courage, their willingness to suffer and their amazing discipline in the midst of great provocation. One day the South will recognize its real heroes. They will be the James Merediths, with the noble sense of purpose that enables them to face jeering and hostile mobs, and with the agonizing loneliness that characterizes the life of the pioneer. They will be old, oppressed, battered Negro women, symbolized in a seventy two year old woman in Montgomery, Alabama, who rose up with a sense of dignity and with her people decided not to ride segregated buses, and who responded with ungrammatical profundity to one who inquired about her weariness: "My feets is tired, but my soul is at rest." They will be the young high school and college students, the young ministers of the gospel and a host of their elders, courageously and nonviolently sitting in at lunch counters and willingly going to jail for conscience' sake. One day the South will know that when these disinherited children of God sat down at lunch counters, they were in reality standing up for what is best in the American dream and for the most sacred values in our Judaeo Christian heritage, thereby bringing our nation back to those great wells of democracy which were dug deep by the founding fathers in their formulation of the Constitution and the Declaration of Independence.

Never before have I written so long a letter. I'm afraid it is much too long to take your precious time. I can assure you that it would have been much shorter if I had been writing from a comfortable desk, but what else can one do when he is alone in a narrow jail cell, other than write long letters, think long thoughts and pray long prayers?

If I have said anything in this letter that overstates the truth and indicates an unreasonable impatience, I beg you to forgive me. If I have said anything that understates the truth and indicates my having a patience that allows me to settle for anything less than brotherhood, I beg God to forgive me.

I hope this letter finds you strong in the faith. I also hope that circumstances will soon make it possible for me to meet each of you, not as an integrationist or a civil-rights leader but as a fellow clergyman and a Christian brother. Let us all hope that the dark clouds of racial prejudice will soon pass away and the deep fog of misunderstanding will be lifted from our fear drenched communities, and in some not too distant tomorrow the radiant stars of love and brotherhood will shine over our great nation with all their scintillating beauty.

Yours for the cause of Peace and Brotherhood,
Martin Luther King, Jr.

25

Carl G. Jung

Approaching the Unconscious

For an ever larger number of followers, Carl G.Jung (1875-1961) is the leader who seems most capable of guiding humanity through a confusing and unintelligible world. Today, when the fruits of rationalism, that is, science and technology, threaten our world with disasters (including ecological and nuclear), Jung offers the vision of a healed world with humans integrated into a cosmic whole. To move toward such a world, Jung sees little need for additional discoveries of scientific facts or acquisition of technological know-how. Rather, he stresses the importance of rediscovering the images (archetypes) of man's past—which, in turn, point toward the divine (numinous).

Born in Switzerland to the family of a Swiss Reformed (Calvinist) pastor, Jung became aware of himself and the world around him while still very young. At an age when children ordinarily absorb their experiences in a matter-of-fact fashion, Jung pondered his observations and dreams, seeking an explanation for them. Even as a child he contemplated the existence of two worlds. One was the world of facts, the realm of the sciences, which in school demanded his attention. The other was the world of value, which gave meaning to what he had learned and experienced. Having a dual personality of complementary traits, rather than contradictory ones, Jung eventually had to choose between the sciences and the humanities. Though both were appealing, the sciences prevailed; and he decided to study medicine rather than archaeology or religion.

Approaching the Unconscious Carl G. Jung et al., *Man and His Symbols*, ed. Cari G. Jung (New York: Dell Publishing, 1964), 72-78, 80-88, 90-94. Copyright © 1964 Aldus Books, Ltd., London. Used by permission of publisher.

In 1900, while preparing for his final medical exam, Jung realized that psychiatry was the special field to which he wanted to devote his life. Psychiatry was then still in its infancy—groping for answers rather than offering them. Among those who were also captivated by psychiatry was the Viennese physician Sigmund Freud (see selection 30). When Freud's pioneering work came to his attention in the same year, Jung was fascinated by Freud's penetrating perceptions and daring speculations. In 1906 the two men met for the first time, and shortly thereafter Freud decided that this younger man should be the person to preserve and continue his work. Jung, however, had begun his research into mythology, and he soon came to the conclusion that Freud's dogmatic nature and their differing intellectual orientations would keep him from carrying on the Freudian psychological heritage.

Indeed, signs of disharmony between Jung and Freud appeared as early as 1912. The break came over a number of issues: for example, the role of sexuality in infant behavior, and Freud's insistence that sexuality is the prime psychological force in the life of a human being. Jung judged the latter an unwarranted conclusion, especially in view of the fact that inquiry into the human psyche was then of very recent date and, in his view, needed to be pursued without restrictions. Another reason for disagreement was the fact that Freud focused on certain key events in a person's life, rather than considering them in relation to the person's cultural heritage. Elements of this heritage, especially myth, folklore, and long-standing religious practices, were of primary importance to Jung; whereas Freud assigned them to the realm of the occult.

While pursuing his studies, Jung noted that people in the West engage in many visible acts whose meaning has been either lost or forgotten. He attributed this loss to the fact that Western culture has valued reasoning and experience over feeling and intuition, or result and process over meaning and vision. Jung made the rediscovery of meaning and vision the center of his life's work. He believed that as one progresses in unlocking myth, religion, and philosophy, one discovers the ancient images and impressions common to all humankind—which he termed archetypes. Jung came to the conclusion that dreams are often expressions of these repeated experiences of humankind. For Freud, on the other hand, dreams are responses, mainly, to sexual fantasies and certain disturbing experiences of particular individuals.

Some people have found Jung's work vague and mystical, a relapse into a spirit-world long believed to have been overcome by reason, science and "enlightenment."

Yet, for others, his message fills an inner emptiness—by restoring meaning and wholeness to their lives.

THE SOUL OF MAN

What we call civilized consciousness has steadily separated itself from the basic instincts. But these instincts have not disappeared. They have merely lost their contact with our consciousness and are thus forced to assert themselves in an indirect fashion. This may be by means of physical symptoms in the case of a neurosis,* or by means of incidents of various kinds, like unaccountable moods, unexpected forgetfulness, or mistakes in speech.

A man likes to believe that he is the master of his soul.† But as long as he is unable to control his moods and emotions, or to be conscious of the myriad secret ways in which unconscious factors insinuate themselves into his arrangements and decisions, he is certainly not his own master. These unconscious factors owe their existence to the autonomy of the archetypes.‡ Modern man protects himself against seeing his own split state by a system of compartments. Certain areas of outer life and of his own behavior are kept, as it were, in separate drawers and are never confronted with one another.

As an example of this so-called compartment psychology, I remember the case of an alcoholic who had come under the laudable influence of a certain religious movement, and, fascinated by its enthusiasm, had forgotten that he needed a drink. He was obviously and miraculously cured by Jesus, and he was correspondingly displayed as a witness to divine grace or to the efficiency of the said religious organization. But after a few weeks of public confessions, the novelty began to pale and

---

* An emotional or physical illness arising from unsolved conflicts between human drives and their environment.
† Mind, or essence of a human being.
‡ Subconscious images and impressions—tracing back to the earliest ages of the human species—which persons inherit, collectively, along with their physical traits.

some alcoholic refreshment seemed to be indicated, and so he drank again. But this time the helpful organization came to the conclusion that the case was "pathological"* and obviously not suitable for an intervention by Jesus, so they put him into a clinic to let the doctor do better than the divine Healer.

This is an aspect of the modern "cultural" mind that is worth looking into. It shows an alarming degree of dissociation and psychological confusion.

If, for a moment, we regard mankind as one individual, we see that the human race is like a person carried away by unconscious powers; and the human race also likes to keep certain problems tucked away in separate drawers. But this is why we should give a great deal of consideration to what we are doing, for mankind is now threatened by self-created and deadly dangers that are growing beyond our control. Our world is, so to speak, dissociated like a neurotic, with the Iron Curtain marking the symbolic line of division. Western man, becoming aware of the aggressive will to power of the East, sees himself forced to take extraordinary measures of defense, at the same time as he prides himself on his virtue and good intentions.

What he fails to see is that it is his own vices, which he has covered up by good international manners, that are thrown back in his face by the communist world, shamelessly and methodically. What the West has tolerated, but secretly and with a slight sense of shame (the diplomatic lie, systematic deception, veiled threats), comes back into the open and in full measure from the East and ties us up in neurotic knots. It is the face of his own evil shadow that grins at Western man from the other side of the Iron Curtain.

It is this state of affairs that explains the peculiar feeling of helplessness of so many people in Western societies. They have begun to realize that the difficulties confronting us are moral problems, and that the attempts to answer them by a policy of piling up nuclear arms or by economic "competition" is achieving little, for it cuts both ways. Many of us now understand that moral and mental means would be more

---

* Caused by disease.

efficient, since they could provide us with psychic* immunity against the ever-increasing infection.

But all such attempts have proved singularly ineffective, and will do so as long as we try to convince ourselves and the world that it is only *they* (that is, our opponents) who are wrong. It would be much more to the point for us to make a serious attempt to recognize our own shadow and its nefarious doings. If we could see our shadow (the dark side of our nature), we should be immune to any moral and mental infection and insinuation. As matters now stand, we lay ourselves open to every infection, because we are really doing practically the same thing as *they.*

Only we have the additional disadvantage that we neither see nor want to understand what we ourselves are doing, under the cover of good manners.

The communist world, it may be noted, has one big myth (which we call an illusion, in the vain hope that our superior judgment will make it disappear). It is the time-hallowed archetypal dream of a Golden Age (or Paradise), where everything is provided in abundance for everyone, and a great, just, and wise chief rules over a human kindergarten. This powerful archetype in its infantile form has gripped them, but it will never disappear from the world at the mere sight of our superior points of view. We even support it by our own childishness, for our Western civilization is in the grip of the same mythology. Unconsciously, we cherish the same prejudices, hopes, and expectations. We too believe in the welfare state, in universal peace, in the equality of man, in his eternal human rights, injustice, truth, and (do not say it too loudly) in the Kingdom of God on Earth.

The sad truth is that man's real life consists of a complex of inexorable opposites—day and night, birth and death, happiness and misery, good and evil. We are not even sure that one will prevail against the other, that good will overcome evil, or joy defeat pain. Life is a battleground. It always has been, and always will be; and if it were not so, existence would come to an end.

---

* Residing in the mind or soul.

It was precisely this conflict within man that led the early Christians to expect and hope for an early end to this world, or the Buddhists to reject all earthly desires and aspirations. These basic answers would be frankly suicidal if they were not linked up with peculiar mental and moral ideas and practices that constitute the bulk of both religions and that, to a certain extent, modify their radical denial of the world.

I stress this point because, in our time, there are millions of people who have lost faith in any kind of religion. Such people do not understand their religion any longer. While life runs smoothly without religion, the loss remains as good as unnoticed. But when suffering comes, it is another matter. That is when people begin to seek a way out and to reflect about the meaning of life and its bewildering and painful experiences.

It is significant that the psychological doctor (within my experience) is consulted more by Jews and Protestants than by Catholics. This might be expected, for the Catholic Church still feels responsible for the *cura animamm* (the care of the soul's welfare). But in this scientific age, the psychiatrist is apt to be asked the questions that once belonged in the domain of the theologian. People feel that it makes, or would make, a great difference if only they had a positive belief in a meaningful way of life or in God and immortality. The specter of approaching death often gives a powerful incentive to such thoughts. From time immemorial, men have had ideas about a Supreme Being (one or several) and about the Land of the Hereafter. Only today do they think they can do without such ideas.

Because we cannot discover God's throne in the sky with a radiotélescope or establish (for certain) that a beloved father or mother is still about in a more or less corporeal form, people assume that such ideas are "not true." I would rather say that they are not "true" *enough,* for these are conceptions of a kind that have accompanied human life from prehistoric times, and that still break through into consciousness at any provocation.

Modern man may assert that he can dispense with them, and he may bolster his opinion by insisting that there is no scientific evidence of their truth. Or he may even regret the loss of his convictions. But since we are dealing with invisible and unknowable things (for God is beyond human understanding, and there is no means of proving immortality), why should we bother about evidence? Even if we did not know by reason our need for salt in our food, we should nonetheless profit from its use. We might argue that the use of salt is a mere illusion of taste or a superstition; but it would still contribute to our well-being. Why, then, should we deprive ourselves of views that would prove helpful in crises and would give a meaning to our existence?

And how do we know that such ideas are not true? Many people would agree with me if I stated flatly that such ideas are probably illusions. What they fail to realize is that the denial is as impossible to "prove" as the assertion of religious belief. We are entirely free to choose which point of view we take; it will in any case be an arbitrary decision.

There is, however, a strong empirical* reason why we should cultivate thoughts that can never be proved. It is that they are known to be useful. Man positively needs general ideas and convictions that will give a meaning to his life and enable him to find a place for himself in the universe. He can stand the most incredible hardships when he is convinced that they make sense; he is crushed when, on top of all his misfortunes, he has to admit that he is taking part in a "tale told by an idiot."

It is the role of religious symbols to give a meaning to the life of man. The Pueblo Indians believe that they are the sons of Father Sun, and this belief endows their life with a perspective (and a goal) that goes far beyond their limited existence. It gives them ample space for the unfolding of personality and permits them a full life as complete persons. Their plight is infinitely more satisfactory than that of a man in our own civilization who knows that he is (and will remain) nothing more than an underdog with no inner meaning to his life.

A sense of a wider meaning to one's existence is what raises a man beyond mere getting and spending. If he lacks this sense, he is lost and miserable. Had St. Paul† been convinced that he was nothing more than a wandering weaver of carpets, he certainly would not have been the man he was. His real and meaningful life lay in the inner certainty that he

---

* Derived from experience and observation.
† Former Saul of Tarsus, martyred (probably 67 A.D.). "Apostle to the Gentiles" and a founder of Christian theology.

350   Carl G. Jung

was the messenger of the Lord. One may accuse him of suffering from megalomania,* but this opinion pales before the testimony of history and the judgment of subsequent generations. The myth that took possession of him made him something greater than a mere craftsman.

Such a myth, however, consists of symbols that have not been invented consciously. They have happened. It was not the man Jesus who created the myth of the god-man. It existed for many centuries before his birth. He himself was seized by this symbolic idea, which, as St. Mark[†] tells us, lifted him out of the narrow life of the Naza- rene[‡] carpenter.

Myths go back to the primitive storyteller and his dreams, to men moved by the stirring of their fantasies. These people were not very different from those whom later generations have called poets or philosophers. Primitive storytellers did not concern themselves with the origin of their fantasies; it was very much later that people began to wonder where a story originated. Yet, centuries ago, in what we now call "ancient" Greece, men's minds were advanced enough to surmise that the tales of the gods were nothing but archaic and exaggerated traditions of long-buried kings or chieftains. Men already took the view that the myth was too improbable to mean what it said. They therefore tried to reduce it to a generally understandable form. . . .

To the scientific mind, such phenomena as symbolic ideas are a nuisance because they cannot be formulated in a way that is satisfactory to intellect and logic. They are by no means the only case of this kind in psychology. The trouble begins with the phenomenon of "affect" or emotion, which evades all the attempts of the psychologist to pin it down with a final definition. The cause of the difficulty is the same in both cases—the intervention of the unconscious.

I know enough of the scientific point of view to understand that it is most annoying to have to deal with facts that cannot be completely or adequately grasped. The trouble with these phenomena is that the facts are undeniable and yet cannot be formulated in intellectual terms.

---

* Having grandiose self-delusions.
† Supposedly the writer of the second (New Testament) Gospel, which many consider the most reliable report concerning the life of Jesus.
‡ Refers to Nazareth in northern Palestine, where Jesus spent his childhood years.

For this one would have to be able to comprehend life itself, for it is life that produces emotions and symbolic ideas.

The academic psychologist is perfectly free to dismiss the phenomenon of emotion or the concept of the unconscious (or both) from his consideration. Yet they remain facts to which the medical psychologist at least has to pay due attention; for emotional conflicts and the intervention of the unconscious are the classical features of his science. If he treats a patient at all, he comes up against these irrationalities as hard facts, irrespective of his ability to formulate them in intellectual terms. It is, therefore, quite natural that people who have not had the medical psychologist's experience find it difficult to follow what happens when psychology ceases to be a tranquil pursuit for the scientist in his laboratory and becomes an active part of the adventure of real life. Target practice on a shooting range is far from the battlefield; the doctor has to deal with casualties in a genuine war. He must concern himself with psychic realities, even if he cannot embody them in scientific definitions. That is why no textbook can teach psychology; one learns only by actual experience.

We can see this point clearly when we examine certain well-known symbols:

The cross in the Christian religion, for instance, is a meaningful symbol that expresses a multitude of aspects, ideas, and emotions; but a cross after a name on a list simply indicates that the individual is dead.

The phallus* functions as an all-embracing symbol in the Hindu religion, but if a street urchin draws one on a wall, it just reflects an interest in his penis. Because infantile and adolescent fantasies often continue far into adult life, many dreams occur in which there are unmistakable sexual allusions. It would be absurd to understand them as anything else. But when a mason speaks of monks and nuns to be laid upon each other, or an electrician of male plugs and female sockets, it would be ludicrous to suppose that he is indulging in glowing adolescent fantasies. He is simply using colorful descriptive names for his materials. When an educated Hindu talks to you about the Lingam

---

* Latin: penis.

(the phallus that represents the god Siva in Hindu mythology), you will hear things we Westerns would never connect with the penis. The Lingam is certainly not an obscene allusion; nor is the cross merely a sign of death. Much depends upon the maturity of the dreamer who produces such an image.

The interpretation of dreams and symbols demands intelligence. It cannot be turned into a mechanical system and then crammed into unimaginative brains. It demands both an increasing knowledge of the dreamer's individuality and an increasing self-awareness on the part of the interpreter. No experienced worker in this field will deny that there are rules of thumb that can prove helpful, but they must be applied with prudence and intelligence. One may follow all the right rules and yet get bogged down in the most appalling nonsense, simply by overlooking a seemingly unimportant detail that a better intelligence would not have missed. Even a man of high intellect can go badly astray for lack of intuition or feeling.

When we attempt to understand symbols, we are not only confronted with the symbol itself, but we are brought up against the wholeness of the symbol-producing individual. This includes a study of his cultural background, and in the process one fills in many gaps in one's own education. I have made it a rule myself to consider every case as an entirely new proposition about which I do not even know the ABC. Routine responses may be practical and useful while one is dealing with the surface, but as soon as one gets in touch with the vital problems, life itself takes over and even the most brilliant theoretical premises become ineffectual words.

Imagination and intuition are vital to our understanding. And though the usual popular opinion is that they are chiefly valuable to poets and artists (that in "sensible" matters one should mistrust them), they are in fact equally vital in all the higher grades of science. Here they play an increasingly important role, which supplements that of the "rational" intellect and its application to a specific problem. Even physics, the strictest of all applied sciences, depends to an astonishing degree upon intuition, which works by way of the unconscious (although it is possible to demonstrate afterward the logical procedures that could have led one to the same result as intuition). . . .

THE ROLE OF SYMBOLS

When the medical psychologist takes an interest in symbols, he is primarily concerned with "natural" symbols, as distinct from "cultural" symbols. The former are derived from the unconscious contents of the psyche,[*] and they therefore represent an enormous number of variations on the essential archetypal images. In many cases they can still be traced back to their archaic roots—that is, to ideas and images that we meet in the most ancient records and in primitive societies. The cultural symbols on the other hand, are those that have been used to express "eternal truths," and that are still used in many religions. They have gone through many transformations and even a long process of more or less conscious development, and have thus become collective images accepted by civilized societies.

Such cultural symbols nevertheless retain much of their original numinosity[†] or "spell." One is aware that they can evoke a deep emotional response in some individuals, and this psychic charge makes them function in much the same way as prejudices. They are a factor with which the psychologist must reckon; it is folly to dismiss them because, in rational terms, they seem to be absurd or irrelevant. They are important constituents of our mental makeup and vital forces in the building up of human society; and they cannot be eradicated without serious loss. Where they are repressed or neglected, their specific energy disappears into the unconscious with unaccountable consequences. The psychic energy that appears to have been lost in this way in fact serves to revive and intensify whatever is uppermost in the unconscious—tendencies, perhaps, that have hitherto had no chance to express themselves or at least have not been allowed an uninhibited existence in our consciousness.

Such tendencies form an ever-present and potentially destructive "shadow" to our conscious mind. Even tendencies that might in some circumstances be able to exert a beneficial influence are transformed into demons when they are repressed. This is why many well-meaning

---

[*] Mind or soul, being.
[†] Awe-inspiring, incomprehensible divine power.

people are understandably afraid of the unconscious, and incidentally of psychology.

Our times have demonstrated what it means for the gates of the underworld to be opened. Things whose enormity nobody could have imagined in the idyllic harmlessness of the first decade of our century have happened and have turned our world upside down. Ever since, the world has remained in a state of schizophrenia.* Not only has civilized Germany disgorged its terrible primitivity, but Russia is also ruled by it, and Africa has been set on fire. No wonder that the Western world feels uneasy.

Modern man does not understand how much his "rationalism" (which has destroyed his capacity to respond to numinous symbols and ideas) has put him at the mercy of the psychic "underworld." He has freed himself from "superstition" (or so he believes), but in the process he has lost his spiritual values to a positively dangerous degree. His moral and spiritual tradition has disintegrated, and he is now paying the price for this break-up in worldwide disorientation and dissociation.

Anthropologists have often described what happens to a primitive society when its spiritual values are exposed to the impact of modern civilization. Its people lose the meaning of their lives, their social organization disintegrates, and they themselves morally decay. We are now in the same condition. But we have never really understood what we have lost, for our spiritual leaders unfortunately were more interested in protecting their institutions than in understanding the mystery that symbols present. In my opinion, faith does not exclude thought (which is man's strongest weapon), but unfortunately many believers seem to be so afraid of science (and incidentally of psychology) that they turn a blind eye to the numinous psychic powers that forever control man's fate. We have stripped all things of their mystery and numinosity; nothing is holy any longer.

In earlier ages, as instinctive concepts welled up in the mind of man, his conscious mind could no doubt integrate them into a coherent psychic pattern. But the "civilized" man is no longer able to do this. His "advanced" consciousness has deprived itself of the means by which

---

* Split consciousness; a type of illness of the psyche.

the auxiliary contributions of the instincts and the unconscious can be assimilated. These organs of assimilation and integration were numinous symbols, held holy by common consent.

Today, for instance, we talk of "matter." We describe its physical properties. We conduct laboratory experiments to demonstrate some of its aspects. But the word "matter" remains a dry, inhuman, and purely intellectual concept, without any psychic significance for us. How different was the former image of matter—the Great Mother— that could encompass and express the profound emotional meaning of Mother Earth. In the same way, what was the spirit is now identified with intellect and thus ceases to be the Father of All. It has degenerated to the limited ego-thoughts of man; the immense emotional energy expressed in the image of "our Father" vanishes into the sand of an intellectual desert. . . .

As scientific understanding has grown, so our world has become dehumanized. Man feels himself isolated in the cosmos, because he is no longer involved in nature and has lost his emotional "unconscious identity" with natural phenomena. These have slowly lost their symbolic implications. Thunder is no longer the voice of an angry god, nor is lightning his avenging missile. No river contains a spirit, no tree is the life principle of a man, no snake the embodiment of wisdom, no mountain cave the home of a great demon. No voices now speak to man from stones, plants, and animals, nor does he speak to them believing they can hear. His contact with nature has gone, and with it has gone the profound emotional energy that this symbolic connection supplied.

This enormous loss is compensated for by the symbols of our dreams. They bring up our original nature—its instincts and peculiar thinking. Unfortunately, however, they express their contents in the language of nature, which is strange and incomprehensible to us. It therefore confronts us with the task of translating it into the rational words and concepts of modern speech, which has liberated itself from its primitive encumbrances—notably from its mystical participation with the things it describes. Nowadays, when we talk of ghosts and other numinous figures, we are no longer conjuring them up. The power as well as the glory is drained out of such once-potent words. We have ceased to believe in magic formulas; not many taboos and similar restrictions are left; and our world seems to be disinfected of all such "superstitious" numina* as "witches, warlocks, and worricows," to say nothing of werewolves, vampires, bush souls, and all the other bizarre beings that populated the primeval forest.

To be more accurate, the surface of our world seems to be cleansed of all superstitious and irrational elements. Whether, however, the real inner human world (not our wish-fulfilling fiction about it) is also freed from primitivity is another question. Is the number of 13 not still taboo for many people? Are there not still many individuals possessed by irrational prejudices, projections, and childish illusions? A realistic picture of the human mind reveals many such primitive traits and survivals, which are still playing their roles just as if nothing had happened during the last 500 years.

It is essential to appreciate this point. Modern man is in fact a curious mixture of characteristics acquired over the long ages of his mental development. This mixed-up being is the man and his symbols that we have to deal with, and we must scrutinize his mental products very carefully indeed. Skepticism and scientific conviction exist in him side by side with old-fashioned prejudices, outdated habits of thought and feeling, obstinate misinterpretations, and blind ignorance.

Such are the contemporary human beings who produce the symbols we psychologists investigate. In order to explain these symbols and their meaning, it is vital to learn whether their representations are related to purely personal experience, or whether they have been chosen by a dream for its particular purpose from a store of general conscious knowledge.

Take, for instance, a dream in which the number 13 occurs. The question is whether the dreamer himself habitually believes in the unlucky quality of the number, or whether the dream merely alludes to people who still indulge in such superstitions. The answer makes a great difference to the interpretation. In the former case, you have to reckon

---

* Spirits.

with the fact that the individual is still under the spell of the unlucky 13, and therefore will feel most uncomfortable in Room 13 in a hotel or sitting at a table with 13 people. In the latter case, 13 may not mean any more than a discourteous or abusive remark. The "superstitious" dreamer still feels the "spell" of 13; the more "rational" dreamer has stripped 13 of its original emotional overtones.

This argument illustrates the way in which archetypes appear in practical experience: They are, at the same time, both images and emotions. One can speak of an archetype only when these two aspects are simultaneous. When there is merely the image, then there is simply a word-picture of little consequence. But by being charged with emotion, the image gains numinosity (or psychic energy); it becomes dynamic, and consequences of some kind must flow from it.

I am aware that it is difficult to grasp this concept, because I am trying to use words to describe something whose very nature makes it incapable of precise definition. But since so many people have chosen to treat archetypes as if they were part of a mechanical system that can be learned by rote, it is essential to insist that they are not mere names, or even philosophical concepts. They are pieces of life itself—images that are integrally connected to the living individual by the bridge of the emotions. That is why it is impossible to give an arbitrary (or universal) interpretation of any archetype. It must be explained in the manner indicated by the whole life-situation of the particular individual to whom it relates.

Thus, in the case of a devout Christian, the symbol of the cross can be interpreted only in its Christian context—unless the dream produces a very strong reason to look beyond it. Even then, the specific Christian meaning should be kept in mind. But one cannot say that, at all times and in all circumstances, the symbol of the cross has the same meaning. If that were so, it would be stripped of its numinosity, lose its vitality, and become a mere word.

Those who do not realize the special feeling tone of the archetype end with nothing more than a jumble of mythological concepts, which can be strung together to show that everything means anything—or nothing at all. All the corpses in the world are chemically identical, but living individuals are not. Archetypes come to life only when one patiently tries to discover why and in what fashion they are meaningful to a living individual. . . .

HEALING THE SPLIT

Our intellect has created a new world that dominates nature, and has populated it with monstrous machines. The latter are so indubitably useful that we cannot see even a possibility of getting rid of them or our subservience to them. Man is bound to follow the adventurous promptings of his scientific and inventive mind and to admire himself for his splendid achievements. At the same time, his genius shows the uncanny tendency to invent things that become more and more dangerous, because they represent better and better means for wholesale suicide.

In view of the rapidly increasing avalanche of world population, man has already begun to seek ways and means of keeping the rising flood at bay. But nature may anticipate all our attempts by turning against man his own creative mind. The H-bomb, for instance, would put an effective stop to overpopulation. In spite of our proud domination of nature, we are still her victims, for we have not even learned to control our own nature. Slowly but, it appears, inevitably, we are courting disaster.

There are no longer any gods whom we can invoke to help us. The great religions of the world suffer from increasing anemia,* because the helpful numina have fled from the woods, rivers, and mountains, and from animals, and the god-men have disappeared underground into the unconscious. There we fool ourselves that they lead an ignominious existence among the relics of our past. Our present lives are dominated by the goddess Reason, who is our greatest and most tragic illusion. By the aid of reason, so we assure ourselves, we have "conquered nature."

But this is a mere slogan, for the so-called conquest of nature overwhelms us with the natural fact of overpopulation and adds to our troubles by our psychological incapacity to make the necessary political arrangements. It remains quite natural for men to quarrel and

---

* Reduction in vitality.

to struggle for superiority over one another. How then have we "conquered nature"?

As any change must begin somewhere, it is the single individual who will experience it and carry it through. The change must indeed begin with an individual; it might be any one of us. Nobody can afford to look round and to wait for somebody else to do what he is loath to do himself. But since nobody seems to know what to do, it might be worth-while for each of us to ask himself whether by any chance his or her unconscious may know something that will help us. Certainly the conscious mind seems unable to do anything useful in this respect. Man today is painfully aware of the fact that neither his great religions nor his various philosophies seem to provide him with those powerful animating ideas that would give him the security he needs in face of the present condition of the world.

I know what the Buddhists would say: Things would go right if people would only follow the "noble eightfold path" of the *Dharma* (doctrine, law) and had true insight into the Self. The Christian tells us that if only people had faith in God, we should have a better world. The rationalist insists that if people were intelligent and reasonable, all our problems would be manageable. The trouble is that none of them manages to solve these problems himself.

Christians often ask why God does not speak to them, as he is believed to have done in former days. When I hear such questions, it always makes me think of the rabbi who was asked how it could be that God often showed himself to people in the olden days while nowadays nobody ever sees him. The rabbi replied: "Nowadays there is no longer anybody who can bow low enough."

This answer hits the nail on the head. We are so captivated by and entangled in our subjective consciousness that we have forgotten the age-old fact that God speaks chiefly through dreams and visions. The Buddhist discards the world of unconscious fantasies as useless illusions; the Christian puts his Church and his Bible between himself and his unconscious; and the rational intellectual does not yet know that his consciousness is not his total psyche. This ignorance persists today in spite of the fact that for more than 70 years the unconscious has been a basic scientific concept that is indispensable to any serious psychological investigation.

We can no longer afford to be so God-Almighty-like as to set ourselves up as judges of the merits or demerits of natural phenomena. We do not base our botany upon the old-fashioned division into useful and useless plants, or our zoology upon the naive distinction between harmless and dangerous animals. But we still complacently assume that consciousness is sense and the unconscious is nonsense. In science such an assumption would be laughed out of court. Do microbes, for instance, make sense or nonsense?

Whatever the unconscious may be, it is a natural phenomenon producing symbols that prove to be meaningful. We cannot expect someone who has never looked through a microscope to be an authority on microbes; in the same way, no one who has not made a serious study of natural symbols can be considered a competent judge in this matter. But the general undervaluation of the human soul is so great that neither the great religions nor the philosophies nor scientific rationalism have been willing to look at it twice.

In spite of the fact that the Catholic Church admits the occurrence of *somnia a Deo missa* (dreams sent by God), most of its thinkers make no serious attempt to understand dreams. I doubt whether there is a Protestant treatise or doctrine that would stoop so low as to admit the possibility that the *vox Dei** might be perceived in a dream. But if a theologian really believes in God, by what authority does he suggest that God is unable to speak through dreams?

I have spent more than half a century in investigating natural symbols, and I have come to the conclusion that dreams and their symbols are not stupid and meaningless. On the contrary, dreams provide the most interesting information for those who take the trouble to understand their symbols. The results, it is true, have little to do with such worldly concerns as buying and selling. But the meaning of life is not exhaustively explained by one's business life, nor is the deep desire of the human heart answered by a bank account.

---

* Latin: voice of God.

In a period of human history when all available energy is spent in the investigation of nature, very little attention is paid to the essence of man, which is his psyche, although many researches are made into its conscious functions. But the really complex and unfamiliar part of the mind, from which symbols are produced, is still virtually unexplored. It seems almost incredible that though we receive signals from it every night, deciphering these communications seems too tedious for any but a very few people to be bothered with it. Man's greatest instrument, his psyche, is little thought of, and it is often directly mistrusted and despised. "It's only psychological" too often means: It is nothing.

Where, exactly, does this immense prejudice come from? We have obviously been so busy with the question of what we think that we entirely forget to ask what the unconscious psyche thinks about us. . . .

This modern standpoint is surely one-sided and unjust. It does not even accord with the known facts. Our actual knowledge of the unconscious shows that it is a natural phenomenon and that, like Nature herself, it is at least *neutral*. It contains all aspects of human nature— light and dark, beautiful and ugly, good and evil, profound and silly. The study of individual, as well as of collective, symbolism is an enormous task, and one that has not yet been mastered. But a beginning has been made at last. The early results are encouraging, and they seem to indicate an answer to many so far unanswered questions of present- day mankind.

★　★　★

26

Philip Larkin

A Study of Reading Habits

Philip Larkin (1922–1985) was born in Coventry, England, and educated at St. John's College, Oxford. He worked in libraries most of his life and tried his hand at novels— such as Jill *(1946) and* A Girl in Winter *(1947)—but he made his reputation as a poet. Together with Donald Davie and Kinsley Amis, Larkin came to be associated with* The Movement, *a loose association of British writers who called for a return to more traditional literary techniques. His poems are collected in four volumes:* The North Ship *(1945),* The Less Deceived *(1955),* The Whitsun Wedding *(1965), and* High Windows *(1974).*

When getting my nose in a book
Cured most things short of school,
It was worth ruining my eyes
To know I could still keep cool,
And deal out the old right hook
To dirty dogs twice my size.

Later, with inch-thick specs,
Evil was just my lark:
Me and my cloak and fangs

"A Study of Reading Habits" by Philip Larkin from COLLECTED POEMS By Philip Larkin. Copyright © 1988, 2003 by the Estate of Philip Larkin. Reprinted by permission of Farrar, Straus and Giroux, LLC.

Had ripping times in the dark.
The women I clubbed with sex!
I broke them up like meringues.

Don't read much now: the dude
Who lets the girls down before
The hero arrives, the chap
Who's yellow and keeps the store,
Seem far too familiar. Get stewed:
Books are a load of crap.

UNDERSTANDING MEANING

1. What history of reading habits does the poem present?
2. How would you characterize the speaker in terms of level of emotional maturity and life experience?

EVALUATING ELEMENTS

1. What happens between the first and third stanzas that causes the speaker to give up on books?
2. How do the images in stanza two relate to reading habits?

APPRECIATING LANGUAGE

1. How do specific word choices and syntax contribute to tone in the poem?
2. What metaphors and allusions do you find in the poem?

WRITING SUGGESTIONS

1. Analyze slang in the poem. Then write a paper in which you argue that the poem is more about class than about reading habits.
2. Research theories of reading. Then apply what you learn to Larkin's "study."

27

Alvin Toffler

Future Shock

In addition to the cheerful optimists and gloomy doomsayers who survey the future, there are those who focus primarily on the process by which society will arrive at that uncertain circumstance. Prominent among them is Alvin Toffler (1928-), a writer who considers the now constantly accelerating rate of social change to be the critical new experience of the present age. Since people are not infinitely adaptable, Toffler maintains, they are not able to cope with the rapid and continuous changes forced upon them in modern life. Thus they suffer from what he calls 'future shock"—a psychic disorientation caused by premature arrival of the future.

Toffler was born in New York City to immigrants from Poland. Aspiring to be a writer, he majored in English literature at New York University and in 1949 received a bachelor's degree. He then spent about twelve years as — successively—laborer, Army private, editor of various industry and labor journals, free-lance magazine writer, and labor columnist for Fortune *magazine. An article Toffler wrote for Fortune on the rise of mass interest in the arts became the seed of his first book,* The Culture Consumers *(1964). In that book he documented the explosion of general interest and participation in the arts—and their financial plight. His recommendations for greater state and private support of artistic efforts had some measurable results.*

Toffler coined the term 'future shock" in a magazine article written in 1965. His book Future Shock, *a fuller study of severe stress due to the constant changes of contemporary culture, was published in 1970. The following selection is the first half of a condensation of the book that appeared in* Playboy *magazine in February and March 1970. In the book's introduction Toffler clearly states his principal aims: "to help us cope more effectively with both personal and social change by deepening our understanding of how men respond to it; . . . to show that the rate of change has implications . . . more important than the directions of change; . . . and . . . to increase the future-consciousness" of the reader.*

In The Eco-Spasm Report *(1975), Toffler continues his exploration of the inadequacy of traditional policies in dealing with the rapidly arriving future. He describes current economic upheavals as "the breakdown of industrial civilization . . . and the first fragmentary appearance of a wholly new and drastically different social order."*

In the three short decades between now and the turn of the next millennium, millions of psychologically normal people will experience an abrupt collision with the future. Affluent, educated citizens of the world's richest and most technically advanced nations, they will fall victim to tomorrow's most menacing malady: the disease of change. Unable to keep up with the supercharged pace of change brought to the edge of breakdown by incessant demands to adapt to novelty, many will plunge into future shock. For them, the future will have arrived too soon.

Future shock is more than an arresting phrase. It may prove to be the most obstinate and debilitating social problem of the future. Its symptoms range from confusion, anxiety and hostility to helpful authority, to physical illness, seemingly senseless violence and self-destructive apathy. Future-shock victims manifest erratic swings in interest and life style, followed by a panicky sense that events are slipping out of their control and, later, a desperate effort to "crawl into their shells" through social, intellectual and emotional withdrawal. They feel continuously harassed and attempt to reduce the number of changes with which they must cope, the number of decisions they must make. The ultimate casualties of future shock terminate by cutting off the outside world entirely—dropping out, spiraling deeper and deeper into disengagement.

In the decades immediately ahead, we face a torrent of change—in our jobs, our families, our sexual standards, our art, our politics, our values. This means that millions of us, ill prepared by either past experience or education, will be forced to make repeated, often painful adaptations. Some of us will be simply unable to function in this social flux and, unless we learn to treat—or prevent—future shock, we shall witness an intensification of the mass neurosis, irrationalism and violence already tearing at today's change-wracked society.

The quickest way to grasp the idea of future shock is to begin with a parallel term—culture shock—that has begun to creep from anthropology texts into the popular language. Culture shock is the queasy physical and mental state produced in an unprepared person who is suddenly immersed in an alien culture. Peace Corps volunteers suffer from it in Ethiopia or Ecuador. Marco Polo probably suffered from it in Cathay. Culture shock is what happens when a traveler suddenly finds himself surrounded by newness, cut off from meaning—when, because of a shift of culture, a yes may mean no, when to slap a man's back in friendly camaraderie may be to offer a mortal insult, when laughter may signify not joy but fury. Culture shock is the bewilderment and distress—sometimes culminating in blind fury or bone-deep apathy—triggered by the removal of the familiar psychological cues on which all of us must depend for survival.

The culture-shock phenomenon accounts for much of the frustration and disorientation that plague Americans in their dealings with other societies. It causes a breakdown in communication, a misreading of reality, an inability to cope. Yet culture shock is relatively mild in comparison with future shock. This malady will not be found in *Index Medicus* or in any listing of psychological abnormalities. Yet, unless intelligent steps are taken to combat it, millions of human beings will find themselves increasingly incompetent to deal rationally with their environments. A product of the greatly accelerated rate of change in society, future shock arises from the superimposition of a new culture on an old one. It is culture shock in one's own society. But its impact is far worse. For most Peace Corps men—in fact, most travelers—have the comforting knowledge that the culture they left behind will be there to return to. The victim of future shock does not.

Take an individual out of his own culture and set him down suddenly in an environment sharply different from his own, with a wholly novel set of cues to react to, different conceptions of time, space, work, love, religion, sex and everything else; then cut him off from any hope of retreat to a more familiar social landscape and the dislocation he suffers is doubly severe. Moreover, if this new culture is itself rife with change, and if, moreover, its values are incessantly changing, the sense of disorientation will be even further intensified. Given few clues as to what kind of behavior is rational under the radically new circumstances, the victim may well become a hazard to himself and others. Now, imagine not merely an individual but an entire society, an entire generation—including its weakest, least intelligent and most irrational members—suddenly transported into this new world. The result is mass disorientation, future shock on a grand scale.

This is the prospect man now faces. For a new society—superindustrial, fast-paced, fragmented, filled with bizarre styles, customs and choices—is erupting in our midst. An alien culture is swiftly displacing the one in which most of us have our roots. Change is avalanching upon our heads, and most people are unprepared to cope with it. Man is not infinitely adaptable, no matter what the romantics or mystics may say. We are biological organisms with only so much resilience, only a limited ability to absorb the physiological and mental punishment inherent in change. In the past, when the pace of change was leisurely, the substitution of one culture for another tended to stretch over centuries. Today, we experience a millennium of change in a few brief decades. Time is compressed. This means that the emergent superindustrial society will, itself, be swept away in the tidal wave of change—even before we have learned to cope adequately with it. In certain quarters, the rate of change is already blinding. Yet there are powerful reasons to believe that we are only at the beginning of the accelerative curve. History itself is speeding up.

This startling statement can be illustrated in a number of ways. It has been observed, for example, that if the past 50,000 years of man's existence were divided into lifetimes of approximately 62 years each, there have been about 800 such lifetimes. Of these 800, fully 650 were spent in caves. Only during the past 70 lifetimes has it been possible to communicate effectively from one lifetime to another— as writing made it possible to do. Only during the past six lifetimes have masses of men ever seen a printed word. Only during the past four has it been possible to measure time with any precision. Only in the past two has anyone anywhere used an electric motor. And the overwhelming majority of all the material goods we use in daily life today have been developed within the present, the 800th, lifetime.

Painting with the broadest of brush strokes, biologist Sir Julian Huxley informs us that "The tempo of human evolution during recorded history is at least 100,000 times as rapid as that of prehuman evolution." Inventions or improvements of a magnitude that took perhaps 50,000 years to accomplish during the early Paleolithic era were, he says, "run through in a mere millennium toward its close; and with the advent of settled civilization, the unit of change soon became reduced to the century." The rate of change, accelerating throughout the past 5000 years, has become, in his words, "particularly noticeable during the past 300 years." Indeed, says social psychologist Warren Bennis, the throttle has been pushed so far forward in recent years that "No exaggeration, no hyperbole, no outrage can realistically describe the extent and pace of change. ... In fact, only the exaggerations appear to be true."

What changes justify such supercharged language? Let us look at a few—changes in the process by which man forms cities, for example. We are now undergoing the most extensive and rapid urbanization the world has ever seen. In 1850, only four cities on the face of the earth had a population of 1,000,000 or more. By 1900, the number had increased to 19. But by 1960, there were 141; and today, world urban population is rocketing upward at a rate of 6.5 percent per year, according to Egbert de Vries and J. T. Thijsse of the Institute of Social Studies in The Hague. This single stark statistic means a doubling of the earth's urban population within 11 years.

One way to grasp the meaning of change on so phenomenal a scale is to imagine what would happen if all existing cities, instead of expanding, retained their present size. If this were so, in order to accommodate the new urban millions, we would have to build a duplicate city for each of the hundreds that already dot the globe. A new Tokyo, a new Hamburg, a new Rome and Rangoon—and all within 11 years.

This explains why Buckminster Fuller has proposed building whole cities in shipyards and towing them to coastal moorings adjacent to big cities. It explains why builders talk more and more about "instant" architecture—an "instant factory" to spring up here, an "instant campus" to be constructed there. It is why French urban planners are sketching subterranean cities—stores, museums, warehouses and factories to be built under the earth—and why a Japanese architect has blueprinted a city to be built on stilts out over the ocean.

The same accelerative tendency is instantly apparent in man's consumption of energy. Dr. Homi Bhabha, the late Indian atomic scientist, once analyzed this trend. "To illustrate," he said, "let us use the letter Q to stand for the energy derived from burning some 33 billion tons of coal. In the 18 V2 centuries after Christ, the total energy consumed averaged less than V2 Q per century. But by 1850, the rate had risen to one Q per century. Today, the rate is about 10 Q per century." This means, roughly speaking, that half of all the energy consumed by man in the past 2000 years has been consumed in the past 100.

Also dramatically evident is the acceleration of economic growth in the nations now racing toward superindustrialism. Despite the fact that they start from a large industrial base, the annual percentage increases in production in these countries are formidable. And the rate of increase is itself increasing. In France, for example, in the 29 years between 1910 and the outbreak of World War Two, industrial production rose only five percent. Yet between 1948 and 1965, in only 17 years, it increased by more than 220 percent. Today, growth rates of from 5 to 10 percent per year are not uncommon among the most industrialized nations. Thus, for the 21 countries belonging to the Organization for Economic Cooperation and Development—by and large, the "have" nations—the average annual rate of increase in gross national product in the years 1960-1968 ran between 4.5 and 5 percent. The U.S., despite a series of ups and downs, grew at a rate of 4.5 percent, and Japan led the rest with annual increases averaging 9.8 percent.

What such numbers imply is nothing less revolutionary than a doubling of the total output of goods and services in the advanced societies about every 15 years—and the doubling times are shrinking. This means that the child reaching his teens in any of these societies is literally surrounded by twice as much of everything newly man-made as his parents were at the time he was an infant. It means that by the time today's teenager reaches the age of 30, perhaps earlier, a second doubling will have occurred. Within a 70-year lifetime, perhaps five such doublings will take place—meaning, since the increases are compounded, that by the time the individual reaches old age, the society around him will be producing 32 times as much as when he was born. Such changes in the ratio between old and new have, as we shall show, an electric impact on the habits, beliefs and self-images of millions. Never in history has this ratio been transformed so radically in so brief a flick of time.

Behind such prodigious economic facts lies that great, growling engine of change—technology. This is not to say that technology is the only source of change in society. Social upheavals can be touched off by a change in the chemical composition of the atmosphere, by alterations in climate, by changes in fertility and many other factors. Yet technology is indisputably a major force behind the accelerative thrust. To most people, the term technology conjures up images of smoky steel mills and clanking machines. Perhaps the classic symbol of technology is still the assembly line created by Henry Ford half a century ago and transformed into a potent social icon by Charlie Chaplin in *Modern Times.** This symbol, however, has always been inadequate—indeed, misleading—for technology has always been more than factories and machines. The invention of the horse collar in the Middle Ages led to major changes in agricultural methods and was as much a technological advance as the invention of the Bessemer furnace centuries later. Moreover, technology includes techniques as well as the machines that may or may not be necessary to apply them. It includes ways to make chemical reactions occur, ways to breed fish, plant forests, light theaters, count votes or teach history.

The old symbols of technology are even more misleading today, when the most advanced technological processes are carried out far from assembly lines or open hearths. Indeed, in electronics, in space

---

* A classic cinematic satire of the demands placed upon workers by the organization and machinery of the factory system. Chaplin (1889-1977) was the director and comic star of the film.

technology, in most of the new industries, relative silence and clean surroundings are characteristic—sometimes even essential. And the assembly line—the organization of armies of men to carry out simple repetitive functions—is an anachronism. It is time for our symbols of technology to change—to catch up with the fantastic changes in technology itself.

This acceleration is graphically dramatized by a thumbnail account of the progress in transportation. It has been pointed out, for example, that in 6000 b.c. the fastest transportation over long distances available to man was the camel caravan, averaging eight miles per hour. It was not until about 3000 b.c., when the chariot was invented, that the maximum speed was raised to roughly 20 mph. So impressive was this invention, so difficult was it to exceed this speed limit that nearly 5000 years later, when the first mail coach began operating in England in 1784, it averaged a mere ten mph. The first steam locomotive, introduced in 1825, could muster a top speed of only 13 mph, and the great sailing ships of the time labored along at less than half that speed. It was probably not until the 1880s that man, with the help of a more advanced steam locomotive, managed to reach a speed of 100 mph. It took the human race millions of years to attain that record. It took only 50 years, however, to quadruple the limit; so that by 1931, airborne man was cracking the 400-mph line. It took a mere 20 years to double the limit again. And by the 1960s, rocket planes approached speeds of 4000 mph and men in space capsules were circling the earth at 18,000 mph. Plotted on a graph, the line representing progress in the past generation would leap vertically off the page.

Whether we examine distances traveled, altitudes reached, minerals mined or explosive power harnessed, the same accelerative trend is obvious. The pattern, here and in a thousand other statistical series, is absolutely clear and unmistakable. Millenniums or centuries go by, and then, in our own times, a sudden bursting of the limits, a fantastic spurt forward. The reason for this is that technology feeds on itself. Technology makes more technology possible, as we can see if we look for a moment at the process of innovation. Technological innovation consists of three stages, linked together into a self-reinforcing cycle. First, there is the creative, feasible idea. Second, its practical application.

Third, its diffusion through society. The process is completed, the loop closed, when the diffusion of technology embodying the new idea, in turn, helps generate new creative ideas. There is evidence now that the time between each of the steps in this cycle has been shortened.

It is not merely true, as frequently noted, that 90 percent of all the scientists who ever lived are now alive and that new scientific discoveries are being made every day. These new ideas are put to work much more quickly than ever before. The time between original concept and practical use has been radically reduced. This is a striking difference between ourselves and our ancestors. Apollonius of Perga discovered conic sections, but it was 2000 years before they were applied to engineering problems. It was literally centuries between the time Paracelsus discovered that ether could be used as an anesthetic and the time it began to be used for that purpose. Even in more recent times, the same pattern of delay prevailed. In 1836, a machine was invented that mowed, threshed, tied straw into sheaves and poured grain into sacks. This machine was itself based on technology at least 20 years old at the time. Yet it was not until a century later, in the 1930s, that such a combine was actually marketed. The first English patent for a typewriter was issued in 1714. But a century and a half elapsed before typewriters became commercially available. A full century passed between the time Nicolas Appert discovered how to can food and the time when canning became important in the food industry.

Such delays between idea and application are almost unthinkable today. It isn't that we are more eager or less lazy than our ancestors, but that, with the passage of time, we have invented all sorts of social devices to hasten the process. We find that the time between the first and second stages of the innovative cycle—between idea and application—has been radically shortened. Frank Lynn, for example, in studying 20 major innovations, such as frozen food, antibiotics, integrated circuits and synthetic leather, found that since the beginning of this century, more than 60 percent has been slashed from the average time needed for a major scientific discovery to be translated into a useful technological form. William O. Baker, vice-president of Bell Laboratories, itself the hatchery of such innovations as sound movies, computers, transistors and Telstar, underscores the narrowing gap between invention and application by noting that while it took 65 years for the electric motor to be applied, 33 years for the vacuum tube and 18 years for the X-ray tube, it took only 10 for the nuclear reactor, 5 for radar and only 3 for the transistor and the solar battery. A vast and growing research-and-development industry is working now to reduce the lag still further.

If it takes less time to bring a new idea to the market place, it also takes less time for it to sweep through society. The interval between the second and third stages of the cycle—between application and diffusion—has likewise been cut, and the pace of diffusion is rising with astonishing speed. This is borne out by the history of several familiar household appliances. Robert A. Young, at the Stanford Research Institute, has studied the span of time between the first commercial appearance of a new electrical appliance and the time the industry manufacturing it reaches peak production of the item. He found that for a group of appliances introduced in the United States before 1920—including the vacuum cleaner, the electric range and the refrigerator—the average span between introduction and peak production was 34 years. But for a group that appeared in the 1939-1959 period—including the electric frying pan, television and the washer-dryer combination—the span was only eight years. The lag had shrunk by more than 76 percent.

The stepped-up pace of invention, exploitation and diffusion, in turn, accelerates the whole cycle even further. For new machines or techniques are not merely a product, but a source, of fresh creative ideas. Each new machine or technique, in a sense, changes all existing machines and techniques, by permitting us to put them together into new combinations. The number of possible combinations rises exponentially as the number of new machines or techniques rises arithmetically. Indeed, each new combination may, itself, be regarded as a new supermachine. The computer, for example, made possible a sophisticated space effort. Linked with sensing devices, communications equipment and power sources, the computer became part of a configuration that, in aggregate, forms a single new supermachine—a machine for reaching into and probing outer space. But for machines or techniques to be combined in new ways, they have to be altered, adapted, refined or otherwise changed. So that the very effort to integrate machines into supermachines compels us to make still further technological innovations.

It is vital to understand, moreover, that technological innovation does not merely combine and recombine machines and techniques. Important new machines do more than suggest or compel changes in other machines—they suggest novel solutions to social, philosophical, even personal problems. They alter man's total intellectual environment, the way he thinks and looks at the world. We all learn from our environment, scanning it constantly—though perhaps unconsciously—for models to emulate. These models are not only other people. They are, increasingly, machines. By their presence, we are subtly conditioned to think along certain lines. It has been observed, for example, that the clock came along before the Newtonian image of the world as a great clocklike mechanism, a philosophical notion that has had the utmost impact on man's intellectual development. Implied in this image of the cosmos as a great clock were ideas about cause and effect and about the importance of external, as against internal, stimuli that shape the everyday behavior of all of us today. The clock also affected our conception of time, so that the idea that a day is divided into 24 equal segments of 60 minutes each has become almost literally a part of us.

Recently the computer has touched off a storm of fresh ideas about man as an interacting part of larger systems, about his physiology, the way he learns, the way he remembers, the way he makes decisions. Virtually every intellectual discipline, from political science to family psychology, has been hit by a wave of imaginative hypotheses triggered by the invention and diffusion of the computer—and its full impact has not yet struck. And so the innovative cycle, feeding on itself, speeds up.

If technology, however, is to be regarded as a great engine, a mighty accelerator, then knowledge must be regarded as its fuel. And we thus come to the crux of the accelerative process in society. For the engine is being fed a richer and richer fuel every day.

The rate at which man has been storing up useful knowledge about himself and the universe has been spiraling upward for 10,000 years. That rate took a sharp leap with the invention of writing; but even so, it remained painfully slow over centuries of time. The next great leap in knowledge acquisition did not occur until the invention of movable type in the 15th Century by Gutenberg and others. Prior to 1500, by the most optimistic estimates, Europe was producing books at a rate of 1000 titles per year. This means that it would take a full century to produce a library of 100,000 titles. By 1950, four and a half centuries later, the rate had accelerated so sharply that Europe was producing 120,000 titles a year. What once took a century now took only ten months. By 1960, a single decade later, that awesome rate of publication had made another significant jump, so that a century's work could be completed in seven and a half months. And by the mid-Sixties, the output of books on a world scale approached the prodigious figure of 1000 titles per *day*.

One can hardly argue that every book is a net gain for the advancement of knowledge, but we find that the accelerative curve in book publication does, in fact, roughly parallel the rate at which man has discovered new knowledge. Prior to Gutenberg, for example, only 11 chemical elements were known. Antimony, the 12th, was discovered about the time he was working on the printing press. It had been fully 200 years since the 11th, arsenic, had been discovered. Had the same rate of discovery continued, we would by now have added only two or three additional elements to the periodic table since Gutenberg. Instead, in the 500 years after his time, 73 additional elements were discovered. And since 1900, we have been isolating the remaining elements at a rate not of one every two centuries but of one every three years.

Furthermore, there is reason to believe that the rate is still rising sharply. The number of scientific journals and articles and the number of known chemical compounds are both doubling about every 15 years, like industrial production in the advanced countries. The doubling time for the number of asteroids known, the literature on non-Euclidean geometry, on experimental psychology and on the theory of determinants is only ten years. According to biochemist Philip Siekevitz, "What has been learned in the last three decades about the nature of living beings dwarfs in extent of knowledge any comparable period of scientific discovery in the history of mankind." The U.S. Government alone generates over 300,000 reports each year, plus 450,000 articles, books and papers. On a world-wide basis, scientific and technical literature mounts at a rate of some 60,000,000 pages a year.

The computer burst upon the scene around 1950. With its unprecedented power for analysis and dissemination of extremely varied kinds of data in unbelievable quantities and at mind-staggering speeds, it has become a major force behind the latest acceleration in knowledge acquisition. Combined with other increasingly powerful analytical tools for observing the invisible universe around us, it has raised the rate of knowledge acquisition to dumfounding speeds.

Francis Bacon told us that knowledge is power. This can now be translated into contemporary terms. In our social setting, knowledge is change—and accelerating knowledge acquisition, fueling the great engine of technology, means accelerating change.

Discovery. Application. Impact. Discovery. We see here a chain reaction of change, a long, sharply rising curve of acceleration in human social development. This accelerative thrust has now reached a level at which it can no longer, by any stretch of the imagination, be regarded as "normal." The established institutions of industrial society can no longer contain it, and its impact is shaking up all our social institutions. Acceleration is one of the most important and least understood of all social forces.

This, however, is only half the story. For the speed-up of change is more than a social force. It is a *psychological* force as well. Although it has been almost totally ignored by psychologists and psychiatrists, the rising rate of change in the world around us disturbs our inner equilibrium, alters the very way in which we experience life. The pace of life is speeding up.

Most of us, without stopping to think too deeply about it, sense this quickening of the pace of events. For it is not just a matter of explosive headlines, world crises and distant technological triumphs. The new pace of change penetrates our personal lives as well. No matter where we are, even the *sounds* of change are there. Cranes and concrete mixers keep up an angry clatter on the Champs Elysées and on Connecticut Avenue. I happen to live in mid-Manhattan, where the noise level created by traffic and the incessant jackham-mering is virtually intolerable. Recently, to escape the frenetic pace of New York and do some writing, I flew to a remote beach in Venezuela. At the crack of dawn on the first morning after arrival, I was awakened by the familiar sound of a jackhammer: The hotel was building an addition.

Other symptoms of change abound. In a 17th Century convent in a suburb of Paris, I walked through a long, sun-dappled cloister, up several flights of rickety wooden stairs, in a mood of silent reverie— until I turned a corner and found the man I had come to see: a Berkeley-trained operations researcher with a desktop computer, busy studying long-range change in the French education system and economy. In Amsterdam and Rotterdam, streets built only five years ago are already ridiculously narrow; no one anticipated the rapidity with which automobiles would proliferate. As I can attest from unpleasant personal experience, change is also present in the form of bumper-to-boot traffic hang-ups on Stockholm's once-peaceful Strandvagen. And in Japan, the pace is so swift that an American economist says wryly: "Stepping off a plane in San Francisco after arriving from Tokyo gives one the feeling of having returned to the 'unchanging West.' "

In Aldous Huxley's *Point Counter-Point,* Lucy Tantamount declared that "Living modernly is living quickly." She should have been here now. Eating, once a leisurely semisocial affair, has become for millions a gulp-and-go proposition, and an enormous "fast-food" industry has arisen to purvey doughnuts, hamburgers, French fries, milk shakes, *tacos* and hot dogs, not to mention machine-vended hot soup, sandwiches, packaged pies and a variety of other quasi-edibles intended to be downed in a hurry. The critic Russell Lynes once attended a convention of fast-food executives. "I am not quite sure," he wrote, "whether the fast-food industry gets its name from the speed with which the food is prepared, served and eaten, or on the other hand, from the fact that it is consumed by feeders of all ages on the run and, quite literally, on the wing." It was significant, he observed, that the convention was jointly held with a group of motelkeepers, whose prime passion in life is to keep the rest of us moving around.

As the pace accelerates, we seem to be always en route, never at our destination. The search for a place to stop, at least temporarily, is unwittingly symbolized by our increasingly hectic pursuit of that vanishing commodity—a parking place. As the number of autos grows and the number of places diminishes, so, too, does the allowable parking time. In New York and other major cities, what used to be one-hour meters have been converted to half-hour or 15-minute meters. The world awaits that crowning innovation: the 30-second parking slot. On the other hand, we may be bypassing that stage altogether by simply multiplying those disquieting signs that say NO STANDING.

Unconsciously, through exposure to a thousand such situations, we are conditioned to move faster, to interact more rapidly with other people, to expect things to happen sooner. When they don't, we are upset. Thus, economist W. Allan Beckett of Toronto recently testified before the Canadian Transport Commission that the country needed faster telephone service. Sophisticated young people, he declared, would not be willing to wait six seconds for a dial tone if it were technically possible to provide it in three.

★ ★ ★

Much of this might sound like subjective grousing based on impressionistic evidence—except that such facts fall into a vigorously definable, scientifically verifiable and historically significant pattern. They add up to a powerful trend toward transience in the culture: and unless this is understood, we cannot make sense of the contemporary world. Indeed, trying to comprehend the politics, economics, art or psychology of the present—let alone of the future—without the concept of transience is as futile as trying to write the history of the Middle Ages without mentioning religion.

If acceleration has become a primal social force in our time, transience, its cultural concomitant, has become a primal psychological force. The speed-up of change introduces a shaky sense of impermanence into our lives, a quality of transience that will grow more and more intense in the years ahead. Change is now occurring so rapidly that things, places, people, organizations, ideas all pass through our lives at a faster clip than ever before. Each individual's relationships with the world outside himself become foreshortened, compressed. They become transient. The throwaway product, the nonreturnable bottle, the paper dress, the modular building, the temporary structure, the portable playground, the inflatable command post are all examples of *things* designed for short-term, transient purposes, and they require a whole new set of psychological responses from man. In slower-moving societies, man's relationships were more durable. The farmer bought a mule or a horse, worked it for years, then put it out to pasture. The relationship between man and beast spanned a great many years. Industrial-era man bought a car, instead, and kept it for several years. Superindustrial man, living at the new accelerated pace, generally keeps his car a shorter period before turning it in for a new one, and some never buy a car at all, preferring the even shorter-term relationships made possible by leases and rentals.

Our links with *place* are also growing more transient. It is not simply that more of us travel more than ever before, by car, by jet and by boat, but more of us actually change our place of residence as well. In the United States each year, some 36,000,000 people change homes. This migration dwarfs all historical precedent, including the surge of the Mongol hordes across the Asian steppes. It also detonates a host of "micro-changes" in the society, contributing to the sense of transience and uncertainty. Example: Of the 885,000 listings in the Washington, D.C., telephone book in 1969, over half were different from the year before. Under the impact of this highly accelerated nomadism, all sorts of once-durable ties are cut short. Nothing stays put—especially us.

Most of us today meet more people in the course of a few months than a feudal serf did in his lifetime. This implies a faster *turnover* of people in our lives and, correspondingly, shorter-term relationships. We make and break ties with people at a pace that would have astonished our ancestors. This raises all kinds of profound questions about personal commitment and involvement, the quality of friendship, the ability of humans to communicate with one another, the function of education, even of sex, in the future. Yet this extremely significant shift from longer to shorter interpersonal ties is only part of the larger, more encompassing movement toward high-transience society.

This movement can also be illustrated by changes in our great corporations and bureaucracies. Just as we have begun to make temporary products, we are also creating temporary *organizations*. This explains the incredible proliferation of *ad hoc* committees, task forces and project teams. Every large bureaucracy today is increasingly honeycombed with such transient organizational cells that require, among other things, that people migrate from department to department, and from task to task, at ever faster rates. We see, in most large organizations, a frenetic, restless shuffling of people. The rise of temporary organizations may spell the death of traditional bureaucracy. It points toward a new type of organization in the future—one I call Ad-Hocracy. At the same time, it intensifies, or hastens, the foreshortening of human ties.

Finally, the powerful push toward a society based on transience can be seen in the impermanence of knowledge—the accelerating pace at which scientific notions, political ideologies, values and life-organizing concepts are turning over. This is, in part, based on the heavier loads of information transmitted to us by the communications media. In the U.S. today, the median time spent by adults reading newspapers is 52 minutes per day. The same person who commits nearly an hour to the newspaper also spends some time reading other things as well—magazines, books, signs, billboards, recipes, instructions, etc. Surrounded by print, he "ingests" between 10,000 and 20,000 edited words per day of the several times that many to which he is exposed. The same person also probably spends an hour and a quarter per day listening to the radio—more if he owns an FM set. If he listens to news, commercials, commentary or other such programs, he will, during this period, hear about 11,000 preprocessed words. He also spends several hours watching television—add another 10,000 words or so, plus a sequence of carefully arranged, highly purposive visuals.

Nothing, indeed, is quite so purposive as advertising, and the average American adult today is assaulted by a minimum of 560 advertising messages each day. The verbal and visual bombardment of advertising is so great that of the 560 to which he is exposed, he notices only 76. In effect, he blocks out 484 advertising messages a day to preserve his attention for other matters. All this represents the press of engineered messages against his nervous system, and the pressure is rising, for there is evidence that we are today tampering with our communications machinery in an effort to transmit even richer image-producing messages at an even faster rate. Communications people, artists and others are consciously working to make each instant of exposure to the mass media carry a heavier informational and emotional freight.

In this maelstrom of information, the certainties of last night become the ludicrous nonsense of this morning and the individual is forced to learn and relearn, to organize and reorganize the images that help him comprehend reality and function in it. The trend toward telescoped ties with things, places, people and organizations is matched by an accelerated turnover of information.

What emerges, therefore, are two interlinked trends, two driving forces of history: first, the acceleration of change itself: and, second, its cultural and psychological concomitant, transience. Together, they create a new ephemeralized environment for man—a high-transience society. Fascinating, febrile but, above all, fast, this society is racing toward future shock.

One of the astonishing, as-yet-unpublicized findings of medical research, for example, bears directly on the link-up between change and illness. Research conducted at the University of Washington Medical School, at the U.S. Navy Neuropsychiatrie Unit at San Diego, as well as in Japan, Europe and elsewhere, documents the disturbing fact that individuals who experience a great deal of change in their lives are more prone to illness—and the more radical and swift the changes, the more serious the illness. These studies suggest strongly that we cannot increase the rate at which we make and break our relationships with the environment without producing marked physiological changes in the human animal.

This is, of course, no argument against change. "There are worse things than illness," Dr. Thomas Holmes, a leader in life-change research, reminds us, dryly. Yet the notion that change can be endlessly accelerated without harm to the individual is sharply challenged by the work of Holmes and many others. There are distinct limits to the speed with which man can respond to environmental change.

These limits, moreover, are psychological as well as physiological. The neural and hormonal responses touched off in the human body when it is forced to adapt to change may well be accompanied by a deterioration of mental functioning as well. Research findings in experimental psychology, in communications theory, in management science, in human-factors engineering and in space biology all point to the conclusion that man's ability to make sound decisions—to adapt— collapses when the rate at which he must make them is too fast. Whether driving a car, steering a space capsule or solving intellectual problems, we operate most efficiently within a certain range of response speeds. When we are insufficiently stimulated by change, we grow bored and our performance deteriorates. But, by the same token, when the rate of responses demanded of us becomes too high, we also break down.

Thus we see people who, living in the midst of the most turbulent change, blindly deny its existence. We meet the world-weary executive who smiles patronizingly at his son and mouths nonsense to the effect that nothing ever really changes. Such people derive comfort from the misleading notions that history repeats itself or that young people were always rebellious. Focusing attention exclusively on the continuities in experience, they desperately attempt to block out evidence of discontinuities, in the unconscious hope that they will therefore not have to deal with them. Yet change, roaring through the social order, inevitably overtakes even those who blind themselves to it. Censoring reality, blocking out important warning signals from the environment, the deniers set themselves up for massive maladaptation, virtually guaranteeing that when change catches up with them, it will come not in small and manageable steps but in the form of a single overwhelming crisis.

Others respond to future shock by burrowing into a specialty—a job, a hobby, a social role—and ignoring everything else. We find the electronics engineer who tries manfully to keep in touch with the latest work in his field. But the more world strife there is, the more outbreaks there are in the ghetto, the more campuses erupt into violence, the more compulsively he focuses on servomechanisms and integrated circuits. Suffering from tunnel vision, monitoring an extremely narrow slice of reality, he becomes masterful at coping with a tightly limited range of life situations—but hopeless at everything else. Any sudden shift of the external environment poses for him the threat of total disorientation.

Yet another response to future shock is reversion to previously successful behavioral programs that are now irrelevant. The reversionist clicks back into an old routine and clings to it with dogmatic desperation. The more change whirls around him, the more blindly he attempts to apply the old action patterns and ideologies. The Barry Goldwaters and George Wallaces of the world appeal to his quivering gut through the politics of nostalgia. Police maintained order in the past; hence, to maintain order, we need only supply more police. Authoritarian treatment of children worked in the past; hence, the troubles of the present spring from permissiveness. The middle-aged, right-wing reversionist yearns for the simple, ordered society of the small town—the slow-paced social environment in which his old routines were appropriate. Instead of adapting to the new, he continues automatically to apply the old solutions, growing more and more divorced from reality as he does so.

If the older reversionist dreams of reinstating a small-town past, the youthful, left-wing reversionist dreams of reviving an even older social system. This accounts for some of the fascination with rural communes, the bucolic romanticism that fills the posters and poetry of the hippie and post-hippie subcultures, the deification of Ché Guevara (identified with mountains and jungles, not with urban or post-urban environments), the exaggerated veneration of pre-technological societies and the exaggerated contempt for science and technology. The left reversionist hands out anachronistic Marxist and Freudian clichés as knee-jerk answers for the problems of tomorrow.

Finally, there is the future-shock victim who attempts to cope with the explosion of information, the pulsing waves of data, the novelty and change in the environment, by reducing everything to a single neat equation. Complexity terrifies him. The world slips from control when it is too complex. This helps explain the intellectual faddism that seizes on a McLuhan or a Marcuse or a Maharishi to explain all the problems of past, present and future. Upset by the untidiness of reality, the supersimplifier attempts to force it into an overneat set of dogmas. He then invests these with tremendous emotional force and clings to them with total conviction—until the next new world-explaining concept is merchandised by the media.

In the field of action and activism, the passionate pursuit of the super simple leads to supersimple solutions—such as violence. For the older generation and the political establishment, police truncheons and military bayonets loom as attractive remedies, a way to end dissent once and for all. The vigilantes of the right and the brick-throwing cults of the left, overwhelmed by the onrushing complexities of change, employ violence to narrow their options and clarify their lives. Terrorism substitutes for thought.

These all-too-familiar forms of behavior can be seen as modes of response to future shock. They are the ways used by the future-shock victim to get through the thickening tangle of personal and social problems that seem to hit him with ever-increasing force and velocity. To the information scientist, these four responses— blocking-out, overspecialization, reversion and supersimplification— are instantly recognizable, for they are classical ways of coping with overload. But classical or not, these tactics, pushed beyond a reasonable point, flower into full-blown pathology, endangering not merely the individual who employs them but the people around him as well.

Asked to adapt too rapidly, increasing numbers of us grow confused, bewildered, irritable and irrational. Sometimes we throw a tantrum, lashing out against friends or family or committing acts of senseless violence. Pressured too hard, we fall into profound lethargy— the same lethargy exhibited by battle-shocked soldiers or by change-hassled young people who, even without the dubious aid of drugs, all too often seem stoned and apathetic. This is the hidden meaning of the dropout syndrome, the stop-the-world-I-want-to-get-off attitude, the search for tranquillity or nirvana in a host of moldy mystical ideas. Such philosophies are dredged up to provide intellectual justification for an apathy that is essentially unhealthy and anti-adaptive, and that is often a symptom not of intellectual profundity but of future shock.

For future shock is what happens to men when they are pushed beyond their adaptive tolerances. It is the inevitable and crushing consequence of a society that is running too fast for its own good— without even having a clear picture of where it wants to go.

Change is good. Change is life itself. The justifications for radical changes in world society are more than ample. The ghetto, the campus, the deepening misery in the Third World all cry out for rapid change. But every time we accelerate a change, we need to take into account the effect it has on human copability. Just as we need to accelerate some changes, we need to decelerate others. We need to design "future-shock absorbers" into the very fabric of the emergent society. If we don't, if we simply assume that man's capacity for change is infinite, we are likely to suffer a rude awakening in the form of massive adaptive breakdown. We shall become the world's first future-shocked society.

28

Heron

The Revolution Will Not Be Televised

You will not be able to stay home, brother.
You will not be able to plug in, turn on and cop out.
You will not be able to lose yourself on skag and skip,
Skip out for beer during commercials,
Because the revolution will not be televised.

The revolution will not be televised.
The revolution will not be brought to you by Xerox
In 4 parts without commercial interruptions.
The revolution will not show you pictures of Nixon blowing a
    bugle and leading a charge by John
Mitchell, General Abrams and Spiro Agnew to eat hog maws
    confiscated from a Harlem sanctuary.
The revolution will not be televised.

The revolution will not be brought to you by the Schaefer Award
    Theatre and will not star Natalie Woods and Steve McQueen or
    Bullwinkle and Julia.
The revolution will not give your mouth sex appeal.
The revolution will not get rid of the nubs.
The revolution will not make you look five pounds thinner,
    because the revolution will not be televised, Brother.

There will be no pictures of you and Willie May pushing that
    shopping cart down the block on the dead run, or trying to slide
    that color television into a stolen ambulance.

NBC will not be able predict the winner at 8:32
or report from 29 districts.
The revolution will not be televised.

There will be no pictures of pigs shooting down brothers in the
   instant replay.
There will be no pictures of pigs shooting down brothers in the
   instant replay.
There will be no pictures of Whitney Young being run out of
   Harlem on a rail with a brand new process.
There will be no slow motion or still life of Roy
Wilkens strolling through Watts in a Red, Black and
Green liberation jumpsuit that he had been saving
For just the proper occasion.

Green Acres, The Beverly Hillbillies, and Hooterville
Junction will no longer be so damned relevant, and women will
   not care if Dick finally gets down with
Jane on Search for Tomorrow because Black people will be in the
   street looking for a brighter day.
The revolution will not be televised.

There will be no highlights on the eleven o'clock news and no
   pictures of hairy armed women liberationists and Jackie Onassis
   blowing her nose.
The theme song will not be written by Jim Webb,
Francis Scott Key, nor sung by Glen Campbell, Tom
Jones, Johnny Cash, Englebert Humperdink, or the Rare Earth.
The revolution will not be televised.

The revolution will not be right back after a message bbout a white
   tornado, white lightning, or white people.
You will not have to worry about a dove in your bedroom, a tiger
   in your tank, or the giant in your toilet bowl.
The revolution will not go better with Coke.
The revolution will not fight the germs that may cause bad
   breath.
The revolution will put you in the driver's seat.

The revolution will not be televised, will not be televised, will not
  be televised, will not be televised.
The revolution will be no re-run brothers;
The revolution will be live.

29

Orson Scott Card

Ender's Game

"Whatever your gravity is when you get to the door, remember—the enemy's gate is down. If you step through your own door like you're out for a stroll, you're a big target and you deserve to get hit. With more than a flasher." Ender Wiggins paused and looked over the group. Most were just watching him nervously. A few understanding. A few sullen and resisting.

First day with this army, all fresh from the teacher squads, and Ender had forgotten how young new kids could be. He'd been in it for three years, they'd had six months—nobody over nine years old in the whole bunch. But they were his. At eleven, he was half a year early to be a commander. He'd had a toon of his own and knew a few tricks, but there were forty in his new army. Green. All marksmen with a flasher, all in top shape, or they wouldn't be here—but they were all just as likely as not to get wiped out first time into battle.

"Remember," he went on, "they can't see you till you get through that door. But the second you're out, they'll be on you. So hit that door the way you want to be when they shoot at you. Legs up under you, going straight *down*." He pointed at a sullen kid who looked like he was only seven, the smallest of them all. "Which way is down, greenoh!"

"Toward the enemy door." The answer was quick. It was also surly, as if to say, Yeah, yeah, now get on with the important stuff.

"Name, kid?"

"Bean."

First appeared in the August 1977 issue of *Analog*.

"Get that for size or for brains?"

Bean didn't answer. The rest laughed a little. Ender had chosen right. This kid *was* younger than the rest, must have been advanced because he was sharp. The others didn't like him much, they were happy to see him taken down a little. Like Ender's first commander had taken him down.

"Well, Bean, you're right onto things. Now I tell you this, nobody's gonna get through that door without a good chance of getting hit. A lot of you are going to be turned into cement somewhere. Make sure it's your legs. Right? If only your legs get hit, then only your legs get frozen, and in nullo that's no sweat." Ender turned to one of the dazed ones. "What're legs for? Hmmm?"

Blank stare. Confusion. Stammer.

"Forget it. Guess I'll have to ask Bean here."

"Legs are for pushing off walls." Still bored.

"Thanks, Bean. Get that, everybody?" They all got it, and didn't like getting it from Bean. "Right. You can't see with legs, you can't *shoot* with legs, and most of the time they just get in the way. If they get frozen sticking straight out you've turned yourself into a blimp. No way to hide. So how do legs go?"

A few answered this time, to prove that Bean wasn't the only one who knew anything. "Under you. Tucked up under."

"Right. A shield. You're kneeling on a shield, and the shield is your own legs. And there's a trick to the suits. Even when your legs are flashed you can *still* kick off. I've never seen anybody do it but me—but you're all gonna learn it."

Ender Wiggins turned on his flasher. It glowed faintly green in his hand. Then he let himself rise in the weightless workout room, pulled his legs under him as though he were kneeling, and flashed both of them. Immediately his suit stiffened at the knees and ankles, so that he couldn't bend at all.

"Okay, I'm frozen, see?"

He was floating a meter above them. They all looked up at him, puzzled. He leaned back and caught one of the handholds on the wall behind him, and pulled himself flush against the wall.

"I'm stuck at a wall. If I had legs, I'd use legs, and string myself out like a string *bean*, right?"

They laughed.

"But I don't have legs, and that's *better*, got it? Because of this." Ender jackknifed at the waist, then straightened out violently, He was across the workout room in only a moment. From the other side he called to them. "Got that? I didn't use hands, so I still had use of my flasher. *And* I didn't have my legs floating five feet behind me. Now watch it again."

He repeated the jackknife, and caught a handhold on the wall near them. "Now, I don't just want you to do that when they've flashed your legs. I want you to do that when you've still got legs, because it's better. And because they'll never be expecting it. All right now, everybody up in the air and kneeling."

Most were up in a few seconds. Ender flashed the stragglers, and they dangled, helplessly frozen, while the others laughed. "When I give an order, you move. Got it? When we're at the door and they clear it, I'll be giving you orders in two seconds, as soon as I see the setup. And when I give the order you better be out there, because whoever's out there first is going to win, unless he's a fool. I'm not. And you better not be, or I'll have you back in the teacher squads." He saw more than a few of them gulp, and the frozen ones looked at him with fear. "You guys who are hanging there. You watch. You'll thaw out in about fifteen minutes, and let's see if you can catch up to the others."

For the next half hour Ender had them jackknifing off walls. He called a stop when he saw that they all had the basic idea. They were a good group, maybe. They'd get better.

"Now you're warmed up," he said to them, "we'll start working."

★ ★ ★

Ender was the last one out after practice, since he stayed to help some of the slower ones improve on technique. They'd had good teachers, but like all armies they were uneven, and some of them could be a real drawback in battle. Their first battle might be weeks away. It might be tomorrow. A schedule was never posted. The commander just woke up and found a note by his bunk, giving him the time of his battle and the name of his opponent. So for the first while he was going to drive his boys until they were in top shape—all of them. Ready for anything, at any time. Strategy was nice, but it was worth nothing if the soldiers couldn't hold up under the strain.

He turned the corner into the residence wing and found himself face to face with Bean, the seven-year-old he had picked on all through practice that day. Problems. Ender didn't want problems right now.

"Ho, Bean."

"Ho, Ender."

Pause

"Sir," Ender said softly.

"We're not on duty."

"In my army, Bean, we're always on duty." Ender brushed past him.

Bean's high voice piped up behind him. "I know what you're doing, Ender, sir, and I'm warning you."

Ender turned slowly and looked at him. "Warning me?"

"I'm the best man you've got. But I'd better be treated like it."

"Or what?" Ender smiled menacingly.

"Or I'll be the worst man you've got. One or the other."

"And what do you want? Love and kisses?" Ender was getting angry now.

Bean was unworried. "I want a toon."

Ender walked back to him and stood looking down into his eyes. "I'll give a toon," he said, "to the boys who prove they're worth something. They've got to be good soldiers, they've got to know how to take orders, they've got to be able to think for themselves in a pinch, and they've got to be able to keep respect. That's how I got to be a commander. That's how you'll get to be a toon leader. Got it?"

Bean smiled. "That's fair. If you actually work that way, I'll be a toon leader in a month."

Ender reached down and grabbed the front of his uniform and shoved him into the wall. "When I say I work a certain way, Bean, then that's the way I work."

Bean just smiled. Ender let go of him and walked away, and didn't look back. He was sure, without looking, that Bean was still watching, still smiling, still just a little contemptuous. He might make a good toon leader at that. Ender would keep an eye on him.

★ ★ ★

Captain Graff, six foot two and a little chubby, stroked his belly as he leaned back in his chair. Across his desk sat Lieutenant Anderson, who was earnestly pointing out high points on a chart.

"Here it is, Captain," Anderson said. "Ender's already got them doing a tactic that's going to throw off everyone who meets it. Doubled their speed."

Graff nodded.

"And you know his test scores. He thinks well, too."

Graff smiled. "All true, all true, Anderson, he's a fine student, shows real promise."

They waited.

Graff sighed. "So what do you want me to do?"

"Ender's the one. He's got to be."

"He'll never be ready in time, Lieutenant. He's eleven, for heaven's sake, man, what do you want, a miracle?"

"I want him into battles, every day starting tomorrow. I want him to have a year's worth of battles in a month."

Graff shook his head. "That would be his army in the hospital."

"No, sir. He's getting them into form. And we need Ender."

"Correction, Lieutenant. We need somebody. You think it's Ender."

"All right, I think it's Ender. Which of the commanders if it isn't him?"

"I don't know, Lieutenant." Graff ran his hands over his slightly fuzzy bald head. "These are children, Anderson. Do you realize that? Ender's army is nine years old. Are we going to put them against the older kids? Are we going to put them through hell for a month like that?"

Lieutenant Anderson leaned even farther over Graff's desk.

"Ender's test scores, Captain!"

"I've seen his bloody test scores! I've watched him in battle, I've listened to tapes of his training sessions, I've watched his sleep patterns, I've heard tapes of his conversations in the corridors and in the bathrooms,

I'm more aware of Ender Wiggins that you could possibly imagine! And against all the arguments, against his obvious qualities, I'm weighing one thing. I have this picture of Ender a year from now, if you have your way. I see him completely useless, worn down, a failure, because he was pushed farther than he or any living person could go. But it doesn't weigh enough, does it, Lieutenant, because there's a war on, and our best talent is gone, and the biggest battles are ahead. So give Ender a battle every day this week. And then bring me a report."

Anderson stood and saluted. "Thank you, sir."

He had almost reached the door when Graff called his name. He turned and faced the captain.

"Anderson," Captain Graff said. "Have you been outside, lately I mean?"

"Not since last leave, six months ago."

"I didn't think so. Not that it makes any difference. But have you ever been to Beaman Park, there in the city? Hmm? Beautiful park. Trees. Grass. No mallo, no battles, no worries. Do you know what else there is in Beaman Park?"

"What, sir?" Lieutenant Anderson asked.

"Children," Graff answered.

"Of course children," said Anderson.

"I mean children. I mean kids who get up in the morning when their mothers call them and they go to school and then in the afternoons they go to Beaman Park and play. They're happy, they smile a lot, they laugh, they have fun. Hmmm?"

"I'm sure they do, sir."

"Is that all you can say, Anderson?"

Anderson cleared his throat. "It's good for children to have fun, I think, sir. I know I did when I was a boy. But right now the world needs soldiers. And this is the way to get them."

Graff nodded and closed his eyes. "Oh, indeed, you're right, by statistical proof and by all the important theories, and dammit they work and the system is right but all the same Ender's older than I am. He's not a child. He's barely a person."

"If that's true, sir, then at least we all know that Ender is making it possible for the others of his age to be playing in the park."

"And Jesus died to save all men, of course." Graff sat up and looked at Anderson almost sadly. "But we're the ones," Graff said, "we're the ones who are driving in the nails."

       ★ ★ ★

Ender Wiggins lay on his bed staring at the ceiling. He never slept more than five hours a night—but the lights went off at 2200 and didn't come on again until 0600. So he stared at the ceiling and thought.

He'd had his army for three and a half weeks. Dragon Army. The name was assigned, and it wasn't a lucky one. Oh, the charts said that about nine years ago a Dragon Army had done fairly well. But for the next six years the name had been attached to inferior armies, and finally, because of the superstition that was beginning to play about the name, Dragon Army was retired. Until now. And now, Ender thought, smiling, Dragon Army was going to take them by surprise.

The door opened quietly. Ender did not turn his head. Someone stepped softly into his room, then left with the sound of the door shutting. When soft steps died away Ender rolled over and saw a white slip of paper lying on the floor. He reached down and picked it up.

"Dragon Army against Rabbit Army, Ender Wiggins and Carn Carby, 0700."

The first battle. Ender got out of bed and quickly dressed. He went rapidly to the rooms of each of the toon leaders and told them to rouse their boys. In five minutes they were all gathered in the corridor, sleepy and slow. Ender spoke softly.

"First battle, 0700 against Rabbit Army. I've fought them twice before but they've got a new commander. Never heard of him. They're an older group, though, and I knew a few of their olds tricks. Now wake up. Run, doublefast, warmup in workroom three."

For an hour and a half they worked out, with three mock battles and calisthenics in the corridor out of the nullo. Then for fifteen minutes they all lay up in the air, totally relaxing in the weightlessness. At 0650 Ender roused them and they hurried into the corridor. Ender led them down the corridor, running again, and occasionally leaping to touch a light panel on the ceiling. The boys all touched the same light panel. And at 0658 they reached their gate to the battleroom.

The members of toons C and D grabbed the first eight handholds in the ceiling of the corridor. Toons A, B, and E crouched on the floor. Ender hooked his feet into two handholds in the middle of the ceiling, so he was out of everyone's way.

"Which way is the enemy's door?" he hissed.

"Down!" they whispered back, and laughed.

"Flashers on." The boxes in their hands glowed green. They waited for a few seconds more, and then the gray wall in front of them disappeared and the battleroom was visible.

Ender sized it up immediately. The familiar open grid of most early games, like the monkey bars at the park, with seven or eight boxes scattered through the grid. They called the boxes *stars*. There were enough of them, and in forward enough positions, that they were worth going for. Ender decided this in a second, and he hissed, "Spread to near stars. E hold!"

The four groups in the corners plunged through the forcefield at the doorway and fell down into the battleroom. Before the enemy even appeared through the opposite gate Ender's army had spread from the door to the nearest stars.

Then the enemy soldiers came through the door. From their stance Ender knew they had been in a different gravity, and didn't know enough to disorient themselves from it. They came through standing up, their entire bodies spread and defenseless.

"Kill 'em, E!" Ender hissed, and threw himself out the door knees first, with his flasher between his legs and firing. While Ender's group flew across the room the rest of Dragon Army lay down a protecting fire, so that E group reached a forward position with only one boy frozen completely, though they had all lost the use of their legs—which didn't impair them in the least. There was a lull as Ender and his opponent, Carn Carby, assessed their positions. Aside from Rabbit Army's losses at the gate, there had been few casualties, and both armies were near full strength. But Carn had no originality—he was in the four-corner spread that any five-year-old in the teacher squads might have thought of. And Ender knew how to defeat it.

He called out, loudly, "E covers A, C down. B, D angle east wall." Under E toon's cover, B and D toons lunged away from their stars.

While they were still exposed, A and C toons left their stars and drifted toward the near wall. They reached it together, and together jackknifed off the wall. At double the normal speed they appeared behind the enemy's stars, and opened fire. In a few seconds the battle was over, with the enemy almost entirely frozen, including the commander, and the rest scattered to the corners. For the next five minutes, in squads of four, Dragon Army cleaned out the dark corners of the battleroom and shepherded the enemy into the center, where their bodies, frozen at impossible angles, jostled each other. Then Ender took three of his boys to the enemy gate and went through the formality of reversing the one-way field by simultaneously touching a Dragon Army helmet at each corner. Then Ender assembled his army in vertical files near the knot of frozen Rabbit Army soldiers.

Only three of Dragon Army's soldiers were immobile. Their victory margin—38 to 0—was ridiculously high, and Ender began to laugh. Dragon Army joined him, laughing long and loud. They were still laughing when Lieutenant Anderson and Lieutenant Morris came in from the teachergate at the south end of the battleroom.

Lieutenant Anderson kept his face stiff and unsmiling, but Ender saw him wink as he held out his hand and offered the stiff, formal congratulations that were ritually given to the victor in the game.

Morris found Carn Carby and unfroze him, and the thirteen-year-old came and presented himself to Ender, who laughed without malice and held out his hand. Carn graciously took Ender's hand and bowed his head over it. It was that or be flashed again.

Lieutenant Anderson dismissed Dragon Army, and they silently left the battleroom through the enemy's door—again part of the ritual. A light was blinking on the north side of the square door, indicating where the gravity was in that corridor. Ender, leading his soldiers, changed his orientation and went through the forcefield and into gravity on his feet. His army followed him at a brisk run back to the workroom. When they got there they formed up into squads, and Ender hung in the air, watching them.

"Good first battle," he said, which was excuse enough for a cheer, which he quieted. "Dragon Army did all right against Rabbits. But the enemy isn't always going to be that bad. And if that had been a good army we would have been smashed. We still would have won, but we would have been smashed. Now let me see B and D toons out here. Your takeoff from the stars was way too slow. If Rabbit Army knew how to aim a flasher, you all would have been frozen solid before A and C even got to the wall."

They worked out for the rest of the day.

That night Ender went for the first time to the commanders' mess hall. No one was allowed there until he had won at least one battle, and Ender was the youngest commander ever to make it. There was no great stir when he came in. But when some of the other boys saw the Dragon on his breast pocket, they stared at him openly, and by the time he got his tray and sat at an empty table, the entire room was silent, with the other commanders watching him. Intensely self-conscious, Ender wondered how they all knew, and why they all looked so hostile.

Then he looked above the door he had just come through. There was a huge scoreboard across the entire wall. It showed the win/loss record for the commander of every army; that day's battles were lit in red. Only four of them. The other three winners had barely made it—the best of them had only two men whole and eleven mobile at the end of the game. Dragon Army's score of thirty-eight mobile was embarrassingly better.

Other new commanders had been admitted to the commanders' mess hall with cheers and congratulations. Other new commanders hadn't won thirty-eight to zero.

Ender looked for Rabbit Army on the scoreboard. He was surprised to find that Carn Carby's score to date was eight wins and three losses. Was he that good? Or had he only fought against inferior armies? Whichever, there was still a zero in Carn's mobile and whole columns, and Ender looked down from the scoreboard grinning. No one smiled back, and Ender knew that they were afraid of him, which meant that they would hate him, which meant that anyone who went into battle against Dragon Army would be scared and angry and less competent. Ender looked for Carn Carby in the crowd, and found him not too far away. He stared at Carby until one of the other boys nudged the Rabbit commander and pointed to Ender. Ender smiled again and waved slightly. Carby turned red, and Ender, satisfied, leaned over his dinner and began to eat.

★ ★ ★

At the end of the week Dragon Army had fought seven battles in seven days. The score stood 7 wins and 0 losses. Ender had never had more than five boys frozen in any game. It was no longer possible for the other commanders to ignore Ender. A few of them sat with him and quietly conversed about game strategies that Ender's opponents had used. Other much larger groups were talking with the commanders that Ender had defeated, trying to find out what Ender had done to beat them.

In the middle of the meal the teacher door opened and the groups fell silent as Lieutenant Anderson stepped in and looked over the group. When he located Ender he strode quickly across the room and whispered in Ender's ear. Ender nodded, finished his glass of water, and left with the lieutenant. On the way out, Anderson handed a slip of paper to one of the older boys. The room became very noisy with conversation as Anderson and Ender left.

Ender was escorted down corridors he had never seen before. They didn't have the blue glow of the soldier corridors. Most were wood paneled, and the floors were carpeted. The doors were wood, with nameplates on them, and they stopped at one that said "Captain Graff, supervisor." Anderson knocked softly, and a low voice said, "Come in."

They went in. Captain Graff was seated behind a desk, his hands folded across his potbelly. He nodded, and Anderson sat. Ender also sat down. Graff cleared his throat and spoke.

"Seven days since your first battle, Ender."

Ender did not reply.

"Won seven battles, one every day."

Ender nodded.

"Scores unusually high, too."

Ender blinked.

"Why?" Graff asked him.

Ender glanced at Anderson, and then spoke to the captain behind the desk. "Two new tactics, sir. Legs doubled up as a shield, so that a flash doesn't immobilize. Jackknife takeoffs from the walls. Superior strategy, as Lieutenant Anderson taught, think places, not spaces. Five toons of eight instead of four of ten. Incompetent opponents. Excellent toon leaders, good soldiers."

Graff looked at Ender without expression. Waiting for what, Ender wondered. Lieutenant Anderson spoke up.

"Ender, what's the condition of your army?"

Do they want me to ask for relief? Not a chance, he decided. "A little tired, in peak condition, morale high, learning fast. Anxious for the next battle."

Anderson looked at Graff. Graff shrugged slightly and turned to Ender.

"Is there anything you want to know?"

Ender held his hands loosely in his lap. "When are you going to put us up against a good army?"

Graff's laughter rang in the room, and when it stopped, Graff handed a piece of paper to Ender. "Now," the captain said, and Ender read the paper. "Dragon Army against Leopard Army, Ender Wiggins and Pol Slattery, 2000."

Ender looked up at Captain Graff. "That's ten minutes from now, sir."

Graff smiled. "Better hurry, then, boy."

As Ender left he realized Pol Slattery was the boy who had been handed his orders as Ender left the mess hall.

He got to his army five minutes later. Three toon leaders were already undressed and lying naked on their beds. He sent them all flying down the corridors to rouse their toons, and gathered up their suits himself. When all his boys were assembled in the corridor, most of them still getting dressed, Ender spoke to them.

"This one's hot and there's no time. We'll be late to the door, and the enemy'll be deployed right outside our gate. Ambush, and I've never heard of it happening before. So we'll take our time at the door. A and B toons, keep your belts loose, and give your flashers to the leaders and seconds of the other toons."

Puzzled, his soldiers complied. By then all were dressed, and Ender led them at a trot to the gate. When they reached it the forcefield was already on one-way, and some of his soldiers were panting. They had had one battle that day and a full workout. They were tired.

Ender stopped at the entrance and looked at the placements of the enemy soldiers. Some of them were grouped not more than twenty feet out from the gate. There was no grid, there were no stars. A big empty space. Where were most of the enemy soldiers? There should have been thirty more.

"They're flat against this wall," Ender said, "where we can't see them."

He took A and B toons and made them kneel, their hands on their hips. Then he flashed them, so that their bodies were frozen rigid.

"You're shields," Ender said, and then had boys from C and D kneel on their legs and hook both arms under the frozen boys' belts. Each boy was holding two flashers. Then Ender and the members of E toon picked up the duos, three at a time, and threw them out the door.

Of course, the enemy opened fire immediately. But they mainly hit the boys who were already flashed, and in a few moments pandemonium broke out in the battleroom. All the soldiers of Leopard Army were easy targets as they lay pressed flat against the wall or floated, unprotected, in the middle of the battleroom; and Ender's soldiers, armed with two flashers each, carved them up easily. Pol Slattery reacted quickly, ordering his men away from the wall, but not quickly enough—only a few were able to move, and they were flashed before they could get a quarter of the way across the battleroom.

When the battle was over Dragon Army had only twelve boys whole, the lowest score they had ever had. But Ender was satisfied. And during the ritual of surrender Pol Slattery broke form by shaking hands and asking, "Why did you wait so long getting out of the gate?"

Ender glanced at Anderson, who was floating nearby. "I was informed late," he said. "It was an ambush."

Slattery grinned, and gripped Ender's hand again. "Good game."

Ender didn't smile at Anderson this time. He knew that now the games would be arranged against him, to even up the odds. He didn't like it.

★   ★   ★

404   Orson Scott Card

It was 2150, nearly time for lights out, when Ender knocked at the door of the room shared by Bean and three other soldiers. One of the others opened the door, then stepped back and held it wide. Ender stood for a moment, then asked if he could come in. They answered, of course, of course, come in, and he walked to the upper bunk, where Bean had set down his book and was leaning on one elbow to look at Ender.

"Bean, can you give me twenty minutes?"

"Near lights out," Bean answered.

"My room," Ender answered. "I'll cover for you."

Bean sat up and slid off his bed. Together he and Ender padded silently down the corridor to Ender's room. Ender entered first, and Bean closed the door behind them.

"Sit down," Ender said, and they both sat on the edge of the bed, looking at each other.

"Remember four weeks ago, Bean? When you told me to make you a toon leader?"

"Yeah."

"I've made five toon leaders since then, haven't I? And none of them was you."

Bean look at him calmly.

"Was I right?" Ender asked.

"Yes, sir," Bean answered.

Ender nodded. "How have you done in these battles?"

Bean cocked his head to one side. "I've never been immobilized, sir, and I've immobilized forty-three of the enemy. I've obeyed orders quickly, and I've commanded a squad in mop-up and never lost a soldier."

"Then you'll understand this." Ender paused, then decided to back up and say something else first.

"You know you're early, Bean, by a good half year. I was, too, and I've been made a commander six months early. Now they've put me into battles after only three weeks of training with my army. They've given me eight battles in seven days. I've already had more battles than boys who were made commander four months ago. I've won more battles than many who've been commanders for a year. And then tonight. You know what happened tonight."

Bean nodded. "They told you late."

"I don't know what the teachers are doing. But my army is getting tired, and I'm getting tired, and now they're changing the rules of the game. You see, Bean, I've looked in the old charts. No one has ever destroyed so many enemies and kept so many of his own soldiers whole in the history of the game. I'm unique—and I'm getting unique treatment.

Bean smiled. "You're the best, Ender."

Ender shook his head. "Maybe. But it was no accident that I got the soldiers I got. My worst soldier could be a toon leader in another army. I've got the best. They've loaded things my way—but now they're loading it all against me. I don't know why. But I know I have to be ready for it. I need your help."

"Why mine?"

"Because even though there are some better soldiers than you in Dragon Army—not many, but some—there's nobody who can think better and faster than you." Bean said nothing. They both knew it was true.

Ender continued. "I need to be ready, but I can't retrain the whole army. So I'm going to cut every toon down by one, including you. With four others you'll be a special squad under me. And you'll learn to do some new things. Most of the time you'll be in the regular toons just like you are now. But when I need you. See?"

Bean smiled and nodded. "That's right, that's good, can I pick them myself?"

"One from each toon except your own, and you can't take any toon leaders."

"What do you want us to do?"

"Bean, I don't know. I don't know what they'll throw at us. What would you do if suddenly our flashers didn't work, and the enemy's did? What would you do if we had to face two armies at once? The only thing I know is—there may be a game where we don't even try for score. Where we just go for the enemy's gate. I want you ready to do that any time I call for it. Got it? You take them for two hours a day during regular workout. Then you and I and your soldiers, we'll work at night after dinner."

"We'll get tired."

"I have a feeling we don't know what tired is." Ender reached out and took Bean's hand, and gripped it. "Even when it's rigged against us, Bean. We'll win."

Bean left in silence and padded down the corridor.

★   ★   ★

Dragon Army wasn't the only army working out after hours now. The other commanders had finally realized they had some catching up to do. From earlymorning to lights out soldiers all over Training and Command Center, none of them over fourteen years old, were learning to jackknife off walls and use each other as shields.

But while other commanders mastered the techniques that Ender had used to defeat them, Ender and Bean worked on solutions to problems that had never come up.

There were still battles every day, but for a while they were normal, with grids and stars and sudden plunges through the gate. And after the battles, Ender and Bean and four other soldiers would leave the main group and practice strange maneuvers. Attacks without flashers, using feet to physically disarm or disorient an enemy. Using four frozen soldiers to reverse the enemy's gate in less than two seconds. And one day Bean came in workout with a 30-meter cord.

"What's that for?"

"I don't know yet." Absently Bean spun one end of the cord. It wasn't more than an eighth of an inch thick, but it would have lifted ten adults without breaking.

"Where did you get it?"

"Commissary. They asked what for. I said to practice tying knots."

Bean tied a loop in the end of the rope and slid it over his shoulders.

"Here, you two, hang on to the wall here. Now don't let go of the rope. Give me about twenty meters of slack." They complied, and Bean moved about ten feet from them along the wall. As soon as he was sure they were ready, he jackknifed off the wall and flew straight out, fifty yards. Then the rope snapped taut. It was so fine that it was virtually invisible, but it was strong enough to force Bean to veer off at almost a right angle. It happened so suddenly that he had inscribed a perfect arc and hit the wall hard before most of the other soldiers knew what had happened. Bean did a perfect rebound and drifted quickly back to where Ender and the others waited for him.

Many of the soldiers in the five regular squads hadn't noticed the rope, and were demanding to know how it was done. It was impossible to change direction that abruptly in nullo. Bean just laughed.

"Wait till the next game without a grid! They'll never know what hit them."

They never did. The next game was only two hours later, but Bean and two others had become pretty good at aiming and shooting while they flew at ridiculous speeds at the end of the rope. The slip of paper was delivered, and Dragon Army trotted off to the gate, to battle with Griffin Army. Bean coiled the rope all the way.

When the gate opened, all they could see was a large brown star only fifteen feet away, completely blocking their view of the enemy's gate.

Ender didn't pause. "Bean, give yourself fifty feet of rope and go around the star." Bean and his four soldiers dropped through the gate and in a moment Bean was launched sideways away from the star. The rope snapped taut, and Bean flew forward. As the rope was stopped by each edge of the star in turn, his arc became tighter and his speed greater, until when he hit the wall only a few feet away from the gate he was barely able to control his rebound to end up behind the star. But he immediately moved all his arms and legs so that those waiting inside the gate would know that the enemy hadn't flashed him anywhere.

Ender dropped through the gate, and Bean quickly told him how Griffin Army was situated. "They've got two squares of stars, all the away around the gate. All their soldiers are under cover, and there's no way to hit any of them until we're clear to the bottom wall. Even with shields, we'd get there at half strength and we wouldn't have a chance."

"They moving?" Ender asked.

"Do they need to?"

"I would." Ender thought for a moment. "This one's tough. We'll go for the gate, Bean."

Griffin Army began to call out to them.

"Hey, is anybody there?"

"Wake up, there's a war on!"

"We wanna join the picnic!"

They were still calling when Ender's army came out from behind their star with a shield of fourteen frozen soldiers. William Bee, Griffin Army's commander, waited patiently as the screen approached, his men waiting at the fringes of their stars for the moment when whatever was behind the screen became visible. About ten yards away the screen suddenly exploded as the soldiers behind it shoved the screen north. The momentum carried them south twice as fast, and at the same moment the rest of Dragon Army burst from behind their star at the opposite end of the room, firing rapidly.

William Bee's boys joined battle immediately, of course, but William Bee was far more interested in what had been left behind when the shield disappeared. A formation of four frozen Dragon Army soldiers were moving headfirst toward the Griffin Army gate, held together by another frozen soldier whose feet and hands were hooked through their belts. A sixth soldier hung to the waist and trailed like the tail of a kite. Griffin Army was winning the battle easily, and William Bee concentrated on the formation as it approached the gate. Suddenly the soldier trailing in back moved—he wasn't frozen at all! And even though William Bee flashed him immediately, the damage was done. The format drifted in the Griffin Army gate, and their helmets touched all four corners simultaneously. A buzzer sounded, the gate reversed, and the frozen soldiers in the middle were carried by momentum right through the gate. All the flashers stopped working, and the game was over.

The teachergate opened and Lieutenant Anderson came in. Anderson stopped himself with a slight movement of his hands when he reached the center of the battleroom. "Ender," he called, breaking protocol. One of the frozen Dragon soldiers near the south wall tried to call through jaws that were clamped shut by the suit. Anderson drifted to him and unfroze him.

Ender was smiling.

"I beat you again, sir," Ender said.

Anderson didn't smile. "That's nonsense, Ender," Anderson said softly. "Your battle was with William Bee of Griffin Army."

Ender raised an eyebrow.

"After that maneuver," Anderson said, "the rules are being revised to require that all of the enemy's soldiers must be immobilized before the gate can be reversed."

"That's all right," Ender said. "It could only work once anyway."

Anderson nodded, and was turning away when Ender added, "Is there going to be a new rule that armies be given equal positions to fight from?"

Anderson turned back around. "If you're in one of the positions, Ender, you can hardly call them equal, whatever they are."

William Bee counted carefully and wondered how in the world he had lost when not one of his soldiers had been flashed and only four of Ender's soldiers were even mobile.

And that night as Ender came into the commanders' mess hall, he was greeted with applause and cheers, and his table was crowded with respectful commanders, many of them two or three years older than he was. He was friendly, but while he ate he wondered what the teachers would do to him in his next battle. He didn't need to worry. His next two battles were easy victories, and after that he never saw the battleroom again.

★ ★ ★

It was 2100 and Ender was a little irritated to hear someone knock at his door. His army was exhausted, and he had ordered them all to be in bed after 2030. The last two days had been regular battles, and Ender was expecting the worst in the morning.

It was Bean. He came in sheepishly, and saluted.

Ender returned his salute and snapped, "Bean, I wanted everybody in bed."

Bean nodded but didn't leave. Ender considered ordering him out. But as he looked at Bean, it occurred to him for the first time in weeks just how young Bean was. He had turned eight a week before, and he was still small and—no, Ender thought, he wasn't young. Nobody was young. Bean had been in battle, and with a whole army depending on him he had come through and won. And even though he was small, Ender could never think of him as young again.

Ender shrugged and Bean came over and sat on the edge of the bed. The younger boy looked at his hands for a while, and finally Ender grew impatient and asked, "Well, what is it?"

"I'm transferred. Got orders just a few minutes ago."

Ender closed his eyes for a moment. "I knew they'd pull something new. Now they're taking—where are you going?"

"Rabbit Army."

"How can they put you under an idiot like Carn Carby!"

"Carn was graduated. Support squad."

Ender looked up. "Well, who's commanding Rabbit then?"

Ben held his hands out helplessly.

"Me," he said.

Ender nodded, and the smiled. "Of course. After all, you're only four years younger than the regular age."

"It isn't funny," Bean said. "I don't know what's going on here. First all the changes in the game. And now this. I wasn't the only one transferred, either, Ender. Ren, Peder, Brian, Wins, Younger. All commanders now."

Ender stood up angrily and strode to the wall. "Every damn toon leader I've got!" he said, and whirled to face Bean. "If they're going to break up my army, Bean, why did they bother making me a commander at all?"

Bean shook his head. "I don't know. You're the best, Ender. Nobody's ever done what you've done. Nineteen battles in fifteen days, sir, and you won every one of them, no matter what they did to you."

"And now you and the other are commanders. You know every trick I've got, I trained you, and who am I supposed to replace you with? Are they going to stick me with six greenohs?"

"It stinks, Ender, but you know that if they gave you five crippled midgets and armed you with a roll of toilet paper you'd win."

They both laughed, and then they noticed that the door was open.

Lieutenant Anderson stepped in. He was followed by Captain Graff.

"Ender Wiggins," Graff said, holding his hands across his stomach.

"Yes, sir." Ender answered.

"Orders."

Anderson extended a slip of paper. Ender read it quickly, then crumpled it, still looking at the air where the paper had been. After a few minutes he asked, "Can I tell my army?"

"They'll find out," Graff answered. "It's better not to talk to them after orders. It makes it easier."

"For you or for me?" Ender asked. He didn't wait for an answer. He turned quickly to Bean, took his hand for a moment, and then headed for the door.

"Wait," Bean said. "Where are you going? Tactical or Support School?"

"Command School," Ender answered, and then he was gone and Anderson closed the door.

Command School, Bean thought. Nobody went to Command School until they had gone through three years of Tactical. But then, nobody went to Tactical until they had been through at least five years of Battle School. Ender had only had three.

The system was breaking up. No doubt about it, Bean thought. Either somebody at the top was going crazy, or something was going wrong with the war—the real war, the one they were training to fight in. Why else would they break down the training system, advance somebody—even somebody as good as Ender—straight to Command School? Why else would they ever have an eight-year-old greenoh like Bean command an army?

Bean wondered about it for a long time, and then he finally lay down on Ender's bed and realized that he'd never see Ender again, probably. For some reason that made him want to cry. But he didn't cry, of course. Training in the preschools had taught him how to force down emotions like that. He remembered how his first teacher, when he was three, would have been upset to see his lip quivering and his eyes full of tears.

Bean went through the relaxing routine until he didn't feel like crying anymore. Then he drifted off to sleep. His hand was near his mouth. It lay on his pillow hesitantly, as if Bean couldn't decide whether to bite his nails or suck on his fingertips. His forehead was creased and furrowed. His breathing was quick and light. He was a soldier, and if anyone had asked him what he wanted to be when he grew up, he wouldn't have known what they meant.

★ ★ ★

There's a war on, they said, and that was excuse enough for all the hurry in the world. They said it like a password and flashed a little card at every ticket counter and customs check and guard station. It got them to the head of every line.

Ender Wiggins was rushed from place to place so quickly he had no time to examine anything. But he did see trees for the first time. He saw men who were not in uniform. He saw women. He saw strange animals that didn't speak, but that followed docilely behind women and small children. He saw suitcases and conveyor belts and signs that said words he had never heard of. He would have asked someone what the words meant, except that purpose and authority surrounded him in the persons of four very high officers who never spoke to each other and never spoke to him.

Ender Wiggins was a stranger to the world he was being trained to save. He did not remember ever leaving Battle School before. His earliest memories were of childish war games under the direction of a teacher, of meals with other boys in the gray and green uniforms of the armed forces of his world. He did not know that the gray represented the sky and the green represented the great forests of his planet. All he knew of the world was from vague references to "outside."

And before he could make any sense of the strange world he was seeing for the first time, they enclosed him again within the shell of the military, where nobody had to say There's a war on anymore because no one within the shell of the military forgot it for a single instant of a single day.

They put him in a spaceship and launched him to a large artificial satellite that circled the world.

This space station was called Command School. It held the ansible.

On his first day Ender Wiggins was taught about the ansible and what it meant to warfare. It meant that even though the starships of today's battles were launched a hundred years ago, the commanders of the starships were men of today, who used the ansible to send messages to the computers and the few men on each ship. The ansible sent words as they were spoken, orders as they were made. Battleplans as they were fought. Light was a pedestrian.

For two months Ender Wiggins didn't meet a single person. They came to him namelessly, taught him what they knew, and left him to other teachers. He had no time to miss his friends at Battle School. He only had time to learn how to operate the simulator, which flashed battle patterns around him as if he were in a starship at the center of the battle. How to command mock ships in mock battles by manipulating the keys on the simulator and speaking words into the ansible. How to recognize instantly every enemy ship and the weapons it carried by the pattern that the simulator showed. How to transfer all that he learned in the nullo battles at Battle School to the starship battles at Command School.

He had thought the game was taken seriously before. Here they hurried him through every step, were angry and worried beyond reason every time he forgot something or made a mistake. But he worked as he had always worked, and learned as he had always learned. After a while he didn't make any more mistakes. He used the simulator as if it were a part of himself. Then they stopped being worried and gave him a teacher.

★ ★ ★

Maezr Rackham was sitting cross-legged on the floor when Ender awoke. He said nothing as Ender got up and showered and dressed, and Ender did not bother to ask him anything. He had long since learned that when something unusual was going on, he would often find out more information faster by waiting than by asking.

Maezr still hadn't spoken when Ender was ready and went to the door to leave the room. The door didn't open. Ender turned to face the man sitting on the floor. Maezr was at least forty, which made him the oldest man Ender had ever seen close up. He had a day's growth of black and white whiskers that grizzled his face only slightly less than his close-cut hair. His face sagged a little and his eyes were surrounded by creases and lines. He looked at Ender without interest.

Ender turned back to the door and tried again to open it.

"All right," he said, giving up. "Why's the door locked?"

Maezr continued to look at him blankly.

Ender became impatient. "I'm going to be late. If I'm not supposed to be there until later, then tell me so I can go back to bed." No answer. "Is it a guessing game?" Ender asked. No answer. Ender decided that maybe the man was trying to make him angry, so he went through a relaxing exercise as he leaned on the door, and soon he was calm again. Maezr didn't take his eyes off Ender.

For the next two hours the silence endured. Maezr watching Ender constantly, Ender trying to pretend he didn't notice the old man. The boy became more and more nervous, and finally ended up walking from one end of the room to the other in a sporadic pattern.

He walked by Maezr as he had several times before, and Maezr's hand shot out and pushed Ender's left leg into his right in the middle of a step. Ender fell flat on the floor.

He leaped to his feet immediately, furious. He found Maezr sitting calmly, cross-legged, as if he had never moved. Ender stood poised to fight. But the man's immobility made it impossible for Ender to attack, and he found himself wondering if he had only imagined the old man's hand tripping him up.

The pacing continued for another hour, with Ender Wiggins trying the door every now and then. At last he gave up and took off his uniform and walked to his bed.

As he leaned over to pull the covers back, he felt a hand jab roughly between his thighs and another hand grab his hair. In a moment he had been turned upside down. His face and shoulders were being pressed into the floor by the old man's knee, while his back was excruciatingly bent and his legs were pinioned by Maezr's arm. Ender was helpless to use his arms, and he couldn't bend his back to gain slack so he could use his legs. In less than two seconds the old man had completely defeated Ender Wiggins.

"All right," Ender gasped. "You win."

Maezr's knee thrust painfully downward.

"Since when," Maezr asked in a soft, rasping voice, "do you have to tell the enemy when he has won?"

Ender remained silent.

"I surprised you once, Ender Wiggins. Why didn't you destroy me immediately? Just because I looked peaceful? You turned your back on me. Stupid. You have learned nothing. You have never had a teacher."

Ender was angry now. "I've had too many damned teachers, how was I supposed to know you'd turn out to be a—" Ender hunted for the word. Maezr supplied one.

"An enemy, Ender Wiggins," Maezr whispered. "I am your enemy, the first one you've ever had who was smarter than you. There is no teacher but the enemy, Ender Wiggins. No one but the enemy will ever tell you what the enemy is going to do. No one but the enemy will ever teach you how to destroy and conquer. I am your enemy, from now on. From now on I am your teacher."

Then Maezr let Ender's legs fall to the floor. Because the old man still held Ender's head to the floor, the boy couldn't use his arms to compensate, and his legs hit the plastic surface with a loud crack and a sickening pain that made Ender wince. Then Maezr stood and let Ender rise.

Slowly the boy pulled his legs under him, with a faint groan of pain, and he knelt on all fours for a moment, recovering. Then his right arm flashed out. Maezr quickly danced back and Ender's hand closed on air as his teacher's foot shot forward to catch Ender on the chin.

Ender's chin wasn't there. He was lying flat on his back, spinning on the floor, and during the moment that Maezr was off balance from his kick Ender's feet smashed into Maezr's other leg. The old man fell on the ground in a heap.

What seemed to be a heap was really a hornet's nest. Ender couldn't find an arm or a leg that held still long enough to be grabbed, and in the meantime blows were landing on his back and arms. Ender was smaller—he couldn't reach past the old man's flailing limbs.

So he leaped back out of the way and stood poised near the door.

The old man stopped thrashing about and sat up, cross-legged again, laughing. "Better, this time, boy. But slow. You will have to be better with a fleet than you are with your body or no one will be safe with you in command. Lesson learned?"

Ender nodded slowly.

Maezr smiled. "Good. Then we'll never have such a battle again. All the rest with the simulator. I will program your battles, I will devise the strategy of your enemy, and you will learn to be quick and discover what tricks the enemy has for you. Remember, boy. From now on the enemy is more clever than you. From now on the enemy is stronger than you. From now on you are always about to lose."

Then Maezr's face became serious again. "You will be about to lose, Ender, but you will win. You will learn to defeat the enemy. He will teach you how."

Maezr got up and walked to the door. Ender stepped out of the way. As the old man touched the handle of the door, Ender leaped into the air and kicked Maezr in the small of the back with both feet. He hit hard enough that he rebounded onto his feet, as Maezr cried out and collapsed on the floor.

Maezr got up slowly, holding on to the door handle, his face contorted with pain. He seemed disabled, but Ender didn't trust him. He waited warily. And yet in spite of his suspicion he was caught off guard by Maezr's speed. In a moment he found himself on the floor near the opposite wall, his nose and lip bleeding where his face had hit the bed. He was able to turn enough to see Maezr open the door and leave. The old man was limping and walking slowly.

Ender smiled in spite of the pain, then rolled over onto his back and laughed until his mouth filled with blood and he started to gag. Then he got up and painfully made his way to his bed. He lay down and in a few minutes a medic came and took care of his injuries.

As the drug had its effect and Ender drifted off to sleep he remember the way Maezr limped out of his room and laughed again. He was still laughing softly as his mind went blank and the medic pulled the blanket over him and snapped off the light. He slept until pain woke him in the morning. He dreamed of defeating Maezr.

The next day Ender went to the simulator room with his nose bandaged and his lip still puffy. Maezr was not there. Instead, a captain who had worked with him before showed him an addition that had been made. The captain pointed to a tube with a loop at one end. "Radio. Primitive, I know, but it loops over your ear and we tuck the other end into your mouth like this."

"Watch it," Ender said as the captain pushed the end of the tube into his swollen lip.

"Sorry. Now you just talk."

"Good. Who to?"

The captain smiled. "Ask and see."

Ender shrugged and turned to the simulator. As he did a voice reverberated through his skull. It was too loud for him to understand, and he ripped the radio off his ear.

"What are you trying to do, make me deaf?"

The captain shook his head and turned a dial on a small box on a nearby table. Ender put the radio back on.

"Commander," the radio said in a familiar voice.

Ender answered, "Yes."

"Instructions, sir?"

The voice was definitely familiar. "Bean?" Ender asked.

"Yes, sir."

"Bean, this is Ender."

Silence. And then a burst of laughter from the other side. Then six or seven more voices laughing, and Ender waited for silence to return. When it did, he asked, "Who else?"

A few voices spoke at once, but Bean drowned them out. "Me, I'm Bean, and Peder, Wins, Younger, Lee, and Vlad."

Ender thought for a moment. Then he asked what the hell was going on. They laughed again.

"They can't break up the group," Bean said. "We were commanders for maybe two weeks, and here we are at Command School, training with the simulator, and all of a sudden they told us we were going to form a fleet with a new commander. And that's you."

Ender smiled. "Are you boys any good?"

"If we aren't, you'll let us know."

Ender chuckled a little. "Might work out. A fleet."

For the next ten days Ender trained his toon leaders until they could maneuver their ships like precision dancers. It was like being back in the battleroom again, except that now Ender could always see everything, and could speak to his toon leaders and change their orders at any time.

One day as Ender sat down at the control board and switched on the simulator, harsh green lights appeared in the space—the enemy.

"This is it," Ender said. "X, Y, bullet, C, D, reserve screen, E, south loop, Bean, angle north."

The enemy was grouped in a globe, and outnumbered Ender two to one. Half of Ender's force was grouped in a tight, bulletlike formation, with the rest in a flat circular screen—except for a tiny force under Bean that moved off the simulator, heading behind the enemy's formation. Ender quickly learned the enemy's strategy: whenever Ender's bullet formation came close, the enemy would give way, hoping to draw Ender inside the globe where he would be surrounded. So Ender obligingly fell into the trap, bringing his bullet to the center of the globe.

The enemy began to contract slowly, not wanting to come within range until all their weapons could be brought to bear at once. Then Ender began to work in earnest. His reserve screen approached the outside of the globe, and the enemy began to concentrate his forces there. Then Bean's force appeared on the opposite side, and the enemy again deployed ships on that side.

Which left most of the globe only thinly defended. Ender's bullet attacked, and since at the point of attack it outnumbered the enemy overwhelmingly, he tore a hole in the formation. The enemy reacted to try to plug the gap, but in the confusion the reserve force and Bean's small force attacked simultaneously, while the bullet moved to another part of the globe. In a few more minutes the formation was shattered, most of the enemy ships destroyed, and the few survivors rushing away as fast as they could go.

Ender switched the simulator off. All the lights faded. Maezr was standing beside Ender, his hands in his pockets, his body tense. Ender looked up at him.

"I thought you said the enemy would be smart," Ender said.

Maezr's face remained expressionless. "What did you learn?"

"I learned that a sphere only works if your enemy's a fool. He had his forces so spread out that I outnumbered him whenever I engaged him."

"And?"

"And," Ender said, "you can't stay committed to one pattern. It makes you too easy to predict."

"Is that all?" Maezr asked quietly.

Ender took off his radio. "The enemy could have defeated me by breaking the sphere earlier."

Maezr nodded. "You had an unfair advantage."

Ender looked up at him coldly. "I was outnumbered two to one."

Maezr shook his head. "You have the ansible. The enemy doesn't. We include that in the mock battles. Their messages travel at the speed of light."

Ender glanced toward the simulator. "Is there enough space to make a difference?"

"Don't you know?" Maezr asked. "None of the ships was ever closer than thirty thousand kilometers to any other."

Ender tried to figure the size of the enemy's sphere. Astronomy was beyond him. But now his curiously was stirred.

"What kind of weapons are on those ships? To be able to strike so fast?"

Maezr shook his head. "The science is too much for you. You'd have to study many more years than you've lived to understand even the basics. All you need to know is that the weapons work."

"Why do we have to come so close to be in range?"

"The ships are all protected by forcefields. A certain distance away the weapons are weaker and can't get through. Closer in the weapons are stronger than the shields. But the computers take care of all that. They're constantly firing in any direction that won't hurt one of our ships. The computers pick targets, aim; they do all the detail work. You just tell them when and get them in a position to win. All right?"

"No," Ender twisted the tube of the radio around his fingers. "I have to know how the weapons work."

"I told you, it would take—"

"I can't command a fleet—not even on the simulator—unless I know." Ender waited a moment, then added, "Just the rough idea."

Maezr stood up and walked a few steps away. "All right, Ender. It won't make any sense, but I'll try. As simply as I can." He shoved his hands into his pockets. "It's this way, Ender. Everything is made up of atoms, little particles so small you can't see them with your eyes. These atoms, there are only a few different types, and they're all made up of even smaller particles that are pretty much the same. These atoms can be broken, so that they stop being atoms. So that this metal doesn't hold together anymore. Or the plastic floor. Or your body. Or even the air. They just seem to disappear, if you break the atoms. All that's left is the pieces. And they fly around and break more atoms. The weapons on the ships set up an area where it's impossible for atoms of anything to stay together. They all break down. So things in that area—they disappear."

Ender nodded. "You're right, I don't understand it. Can it be blocked?"

"No. But it gets wider and weaker the farther it goes from the ship, so that after a while a forcefield will block it. OK? And to make it strong at all, it has to be focused so that a ship can only fire effectively in maybe three or four directions at once."

Ender nodded again, but he didn't really understand, not well enough. "If the pieces of the broken atoms go breaking more atoms, why doesn't it just make everything disappear?"

"Space. Those thousands of kilometers between the ships, they're empty. Almost no atoms. The pieces don't hit anything, and when they finally do hit something, they're so spread out they can't do any harm." Maezr cocked his head quizzically. "Anything else you need to know?"

"Do the weapons on the ships—do they work against anything besides ships?"

Maezr moved in close to Ender and said firmly, "We only use them against ships. Never anything else. If we used them against anything else, the enemy would use them against us. Got it?"

Maezr walked away, and was nearly out the door when Ender called to him.

"I don't know your name yet," Ender said blandly.

"Maezr Rackham."

"Maezr Rackham," Ender said, "I defeated you."

Maezr laughed.

"Ender, you weren't fighting me today," he said. "You were fighting the stupidest computer in the Command School, set on a ten-year-old program. You don't think I'd use a sphere, do you?" He shook his head. "Ender, my dear little fellow, when you fight me, you'll know it. Because you'll lose." And Maezr left the room.

★ ★ ★

Ender still practiced ten hours a day with his toon leaders. He never saw them, though, only heard their voices on the radio. Battles came every two or three days. The enemy had something new every time, something harder—but Ender coped with it. And won every time. And after every battle Maezr would point out mistakes and show Ender that he had really lost. Maezr only let Ender finish so that he would learn to handle the end of the game.

Until finally Maezr came in and solemnly shook Ender's hand and said, "That, boy, was a good battle."

Because the praise was so long in coming, it pleased Ender more than praise had ever pleased him before. And because it was so condescending, he resented it.

"So from now on." Maezr said, "we can give you hard ones."

From then on Ender's life was a slow nervous breakdown.

He began fighting two battles a day, with problems that steadily grew more difficult. He had been trained in nothing but the game all his life, but now the game began to consume him. He woke in the morning with new strategies for the simulator and went fitfully to sleep at night with the mistakes of the day preying on him. Sometimes he would wake up in the middle of the night crying for a reason he didn't remember. Sometimes he woke up with his knuckles bloody from biting them. But every day he went impassively to the simulator and drilled his toon leaders until the battles, and drilled his toon leaders after the battles, and endured and studied the harsh criticism that Rackham piled on him. He noted that Rackham perversely criticized him more after his hardest battles. He noted that every time he thought of a new strategy the enemy was using it within a few days. And he noted that while his fleet always stayed the same size, the enemy increased in numbers every day.

He asked his teacher.

"We are showing you what it will be like when you really command. The ratios of enemy to us."

"Why does the enemy always outnumber us?"

Maezr bowed his gray head for a moment, as if deciding whether to answer Finally he looked up and reached out his hand and touched Ender on the shoulder. "I will tell you, even though the information is secret. You see, the enemy attacked us first. He had good reason to attack us, but that is a matter for politicians, and whether the fault was ours or his, we could not let him win. So when the enemy came to our worlds, we fought back, hard, and spent the finest of our young men in the fleets. But we won, and the enemy retreated."

Maezr smiled ruefully. "But the enemy was not through, boy. The enemy would never be through. They came again, with more numbers, and it was harder to beat them. And another generation of young men was spent. Only a few survived. So we came up with a plan—the big men came up with the plan. We knew that we had to destroy the enemy once and for all, totally, eliminate his ability to make war against us. To do that we had to go to his home worlds—his home world, really, since the enemy's empire is all tied to his capital world."

"And so?" Ender asked.

"And so we made a fleet. We made more ships than the enemy ever had. We made a hundred ships for every ship he had sent against us. And we launched them against his twenty-eight worlds. They started leaving a hundred years ago. And they carried on them the ansible, and only a few men. So that someday a commander could sit on a planet somewhere far from the battle and command the fleet. So that our best minds would not be destroyed by the enemy."

Ender's questions had still not been answered. "Why do they outnumber us?"

Maezr laughed. "Because it took a hundred years for our ships to get there. They've had a hundred years to prepare for us. They'd be fools, don't you think, boy, if they waited in old tugboats to defend their harbors. They have new ships, great ships, hundreds of ships. All we have is the ansible, that and the fact that they have to put a commander with every fleet, and when they lose—and they will lose—they lose one of their best minds every time."

Ender started to ask another question.

"No more, Ender Wiggins. I've told you more than you ought to know as it is."

Ender stood angrily and turned away. "I have a right to know. Do you think this can go on forever, pushing me through one school and another and never telling me what my life is for? You use me and the others as a tool, someday we'll command your ships, someday maybe we'll save your lives, but I'm not a computer, and I have to *know*!"

"Ask me a question, then, boy," Maezr said, "and if I can answer, I will."

"If you use your best minds to command the fleets, and you never lose any, then what do you need me for? Who am I replacing, if they're all still there?"

Maezr shook his head. "I can't tell you the answer to that, Ender. Be content that we will need you, soon. It's late. Go to bed. You have a battle in the morning."

Ender walked out of the simulator room. But when Maezr left by the same door a few moments later, the boy was waiting in the hall.

"All right, boy," Maezr said impatiently, "what is it? I don't have all night and you need to sleep."

Ender wasn't sure what his question was, but Maezr waited. Finally Ender asked softly, "Do they live?"

"Do who live?"

"The other commanders. The ones now. And before me."

Maezr snorted. "Live. Of course they live. He wonders if they live." Still chuckling, the old man walked off down the hall. Ender stood in the corridor for a while, but at last he was tired and he went off to bed. They live, he thought. They live, but he can't tell me what happens to them.

That night Ender didn't wake up crying. But he did wake up with blood on his hands.

★ ★ ★

Months wore on with battles every day, until at last Ender settled into the routine of the destruction of himself. He slept less every night, dreamed more, and he began to have terrible pains in his stomach. They put him on a very bland diet, but soon he didn't even have an appetite for that. "Eat," Maezr said, and Ender would mechanically put food in his mouth. But if nobody told him to eat he didn't eat.

One day as he was drilling his toon leaders the room went black and he woke up on the floor with his face bloody where he had hit the controls.

They put him to bed then, and for three days he was very ill. He remembered seeing faces in his dreams, but they weren't real faces, and he knew it even while he thought he saw them. He thought he saw Bean sometimes, and sometimes he thought he saw Lieutenant Anderson and Captain Graff. And then he woke up and it was only his enemy, Maezr Rackham.

"I'm awake," he said to Maezr Rackham.

"So I see," Maezr answered. "Took you long enough. You have a battle today."

So Ender got up and fought the battle and he won it. But there was no second battle that day, and they let him go to bed earlier. His hands were shaking as he undressed.

During the night he thought he felt hands touching him gently, and he dreamed he heard voices saying, "How long can he go on?"

"Long enough."

"So soon?"

"In a few days, then he's through."

"How will he do?"

"Fine. Even today, he was better than ever."

Ender recognized the last voice as Maezr Rackham's. He resented Rackham's intruding even in his sleep.

He woke up and fought another battle and won.

Then he went to bed.

He woke up and won again.

And the next day was his last day in Command School, though he didn't know it. He got up and went to the simulator for the battle.

★ ★ ★

Maezr was waiting for him. Ender walked slowly into the simulator room. His step was slightly shuffling, and he seemed tired and dull. Maezr frowned.

"Are you awake, boy?" If Ender had been alert, he would have cared more about the concern in his teacher's voice. Instead, he simply went to the controls and sat down. Maezr spoke to him.

"Today's game needs a little explanation, Ender Wiggins. Please turn around and pay strict attention."

Ender turned around, and for the first time he noticed that there were people at the back of the room. He recognized Graff and Anderson from Battle School, and vaguely remembered a few of the men from Command School—teachers for a few hours at some time or another. But most of the people he didn't know at all.

"Who are they?"

Maezr shook his head and answered, "Observers. Every now and then we let observers come in to watch the battle. If you don't want them, we'll send them out."

Ender shrugged. Maezr began his explanation. "Today's game, boy, has a new element. We're staging this battle around a planet. This will complicate things in two ways. The planet isn't large, on the scale we're using, but the ansible can't detect anything on the other side of it—so there's a blind spot. Also, it's against the rules to use weapons against the planet itself. All right?"

"Why, don't the weapons work against planets?"

Maezr answered coldly, "There are rules of war, Ender, that apply even in training games."

Ender shook his head slowly. "Can the planet attack?"

Maezr looked nonplussed for a moment, then smiled. "I guess you'll have to find that one out, boy. And one more thing. Today, Ender, your opponent isn't the computer. I am your enemy today, and today I won't be letting you off so easily. Today is a battle to the end. And I'll use any means I can to defeat you."

Then Maezr was gone, and Ender expressionlessly led his toon leaders through maneuvers. Ender was doing well, of course, but several of the observers shook their heads, and Graff kept clasping and unclasping his hands, crossing and uncrossing his legs. Ender would be slow today, and today Ender couldn't afford to be slow.

A warning buzzer sounded, and Ender cleared the simulator board, waiting for today's game to appear. He felt muddled today, and wondered why people were there watching. Were they going to judge him today? Decide if he was good enough for something else? For another two years of grueling training, another two years of struggling to exceed his best? Ender was twelve. He felt very old. And as he waited for the game to appear, he wished he could simply lose it, lose the battle badly and completely so that they would remove him from the program, punish him however they wanted, he didn't care, just so he could sleep.

Then the enemy formation appeared, and Ender's weariness turned to desperation.

The enemy outnumbered them a thousand to one, the simulator glowed green with them, and Ender knew that he couldn't win.

And the enemy was not stupid. There was no formation that Ender could study and attack. Instead the vast swarms of ships were constantly moving, constantly shifting from one momentary formation to another, so that a space that for one moment was empty was immediately filled with a formidable enemy force. And even though Ender's fleet was the largest he had ever had, there was no place he could deploy it where he would outnumber the enemy long enough to accomplish anything.

And behind the enemy was the planet. The planet, which Maezr had warned him about. What difference did a planet make, when Ender couldn't hope to get near it? Ender waited, waited for the flash of insight that would tell him what to do, how to destroy the enemy. And as he waited, he heard the observers behind him begin to shift in their seats, wondering what Ender was doing, what plan he would follow. And finally it was obvious to everyone that Ender didn't know what to do, that there was nothing to do, and a few of the men at the back of the room made quiet little sounds in their throats.

Then Ender heard Bean's voice in his ear. Bean chuckled and said, "Remember, the enemy's gate is *down*." A few of the other toon leaders laughed, and Ender thought back to the simple games he had played and won in Battle School. They had put him against hopeless odds there, too. And he had beaten them. And he'd be damned if he'd let Maezr Rackham beat him with a cheap trick like outnumbering him a thousand to one. He had won a game in Battle School by going for something the enemy didn't expect, something against the rules—he had won by going against the enemy's gate.

And the enemy's gate was down.

Ender smiled, and realized that if he broke this rule they'd probably kick him out of school, and that way he'd win for sure. He would never have to play a game again.

He whispered into the microphone. His six commanders each took a part of the fleet and launched themselves against the enemy. They pursued erratic courses, darting off in one direction and then another. The enemy immediately stopped his aimless maneuvering and began to group around Ender's six fleets.

Ender took off his microphone, leaned back in his chair, and watched. The observers murmured out loud, now. Ender was doing nothing—he had thrown the game away.

But a pattern began to emerge from the quick confrontations with the enemy. Ender's six groups lost ships constantly as they brushed with each enemy force—but they never stopped for a fight, even when for a moment they could have won a small tactical victory. Instead they continued on their erratic course that led, eventually, down. Toward the enemy planet.

And because of their seemingly random course the enemy didn't realize it until the same time that the observers did. By then it was too late, just as it had been too late for William Bee to stop Ender's soldiers from activating the gate. More of Ender's ships could be hit and destroyed, so that of the six fleets only two were able to get to the planet, and those were decimated. But those tiny groups *did* get through, and they opened fire on the planet.

Ender leaned forward now, anxious to see if his guess would pay off. He half expected a buzzer to sound and the game to be stopped, because he had broken the rule. But he was betting on the accuracy of the simulator. If it could simulate a planet, it could simulate what would happen to a planet under attack.

It did.

The weapons that blew up little ships didn't blow up the entire planet at first. But they did cause terrible explosions. And on the planet there was no space to dissipate the chain reaction. On the planet the chain reaction found more and more fuel to feed it.

The planet's surface seemed to be moving back and forth, but soon the surface gave way to an immense explosion that sent light flashing in all directions. It swallowed up Ender's entire fleet. And then it reached the enemy ships.

The first simply vanished in the explosion. Then, as the explosion spread and became less bright, it was clear what happened to each ship. As the light reached them they flashed brightly for a moment and disappeared. They were all fuel for the fire of the planet.

It took more than three minutes for the explosion to reach the limits of the simulator, and by then it was much fainter. All the ships were gone, and if any had escaped before the explosion reached them, they were few and not worth worrying about. Where the planet had been there was nothing. The simulator was empty.

Ender had destroyed the enemy by sacrificing his entire fleet and breaking the rule against destroying the enemy planet. He wasn't sure whether to feel triumphant at his victory or defiant at the rebuke he was certain would come. So instead he felt nothing. He was tired. He wanted to go to bed and sleep.

He switched off the simulator, and finally heard the noise behind him.

There were no longer two rows of dignified military observers. Instead there was chaos. Some of them were slapping each other on the back, some of them were bowed, head in hands, others were openly weeping. Captain Graff detached himself from the group and came to Ender. Tears streamed down his face, but he was smiling. He reached out his arms, and to Ender's surprise he embraced the boy, held him tightly, and whispered, "Thank you, thank you, thank you, Ender."

Soon all the observers were gathered around the bewildered child, thanking him and cheering him and patting him on the shoulder and shaking his hand. Ender tried to make sense of what they were saying. Had he passed the test after all? Why did it matter so much to them?

Then the crowd parted and Maezr Rackham walked through. He came straight up to Ender Wiggins and held out his hand.

"You made the hard choice, boy. But heaven knows there was no other way you could have done it. Congratulations. You beat them, and it's all over."

All over. Beat them. "I beat *you*, Maezr Rackham."

Maezr laughed, a loud laugh that filled the room. "Ender Wiggins, you never played me. You never played a *game* since I was your teacher."

Ender didn't get the joke. He had played a great many games, at a terrible cost to himself. He began to get angry.

Maezr reached out and touched his shoulder. Ender shrugged him off. Maezr then grew serious and said, "Ender Wiggins, for the last months you have been the commander of our fleets. There were no games. The battles were real. Your only enemy was *the* enemy. You won every battle. And finally today you fought them at their home world, and you destroyed their world, their fleet, you destroyed them completely, and they'll never come against us again. You did it. You."

Real. Not a game. Ender's mind was too tired to cope with it all. He walked away from Maezr, walked silently through the crowd that still whispered thanks and congratulations by the boy, walked out of the simulator room and finally arrived in his bedroom and closed the door.

★   ★   ★

He was asleep when Graff and Maezr Rackham found him. They came in quietly and roused him. He awoke slowly, and when he recognized them he turned away to go back to sleep.

"Ender," Graff said. "We need to talk to you."

Ender rolled back to face them. He said nothing.

Graff smiled. "It was a shock to you yesterday, I know. But it must make you feel good to know you won the war."

Ender nodded slowly.

"Maezr Rackham here, he never played against you. He only analyzed your battles to find out your weak spots, to help you improve. It worked, didn't it?"

Ender closed his eyes tightly. They waited. He said, "Why didn't you tell me?"

Maezr smiled. "A hundred years ago, Ender, we found out some things. That when a commander's life is in danger he becomes afraid, and fear slows down his thinking. When a commander knows that he's killing people, he becomes cautious or insane, and neither of those help him do well. And when he's mature, when he has responsibilities and an understanding of the world, he becomes cautious and sluggish and can't do his job. So we trained children, who didn't know anything but the game, and never knew when it would become real. That was the theory, and you proved that the theory worked."

Graff reached out and touched Ender's shoulder. "We launched the ships so that they would all arrive at their destination during these few months. We knew that we'd probably have only one good commander, if we were lucky. In history it's been very rare to have more than one genius in a war. So we planned on having a genius. We were gambling. And you came along and we won."

Ender opened his eyes again and they realized that he was angry. "Yes, you won."

Graff and Maezr Rackham looked at each other. "He doesn't understand," Graff whispered.

"I understand," Ender said. "You needed a weapon, and you got it, and it was me."

"That's right," Maezr answered.

"So tell me," Ender went on, "how many people lived on that planet that I destroyed."

They didn't answer him. They waited awhile in silence, and then Graff spoke. "Weapons don't need to understand what they're pointed at, Ender. We did the pointing, and so we're responsible. You just did your job."

Maezr smiled. "Of course, Ender, you'll be taken care of. The government will never forget you. You served us all very well."

Ender rolled over and faced the wall, and even though they tried to talk to him, he didn't answer them. Finally they left.

Ender lay in his bed for a long time before anyone disturbed him again. The door opened softly. Ender didn't turn to see who it was. Then a hand touched him softly.

"Ender, it's me, Bean."

Ender turned over and looked at the little boy who was standing by his bed.

"Sit down," Ender said.

Bean sat. "That last battle, Ender. I didn't know how you'd get us out of it."

Ender smiled. "I didn't. I cheated. I thought they'd kick me out."

"Can you believe it! We won the war. The whole war's over, and we thought we'd have to wait till we grew up to fight in it, and it was us fighting it all the time. I mean, Ender, we're little kids. I'm a little kid, anyway." Bean laughed and Ender smiled. Then they were silent for a little while, Bean sitting on the edge of the bed, Ender watching him out of half-closed eyes.

Finally Bean thought of something else to say.

"What will we do now that the war's over?" he said.

Ender closed his eyes and said, "I need some sleep, Bean."

Bean got up and left and Ender slept.

★　★　★

Graff and Anderson walked through the gates into the park. There was a breeze, but the sun was hot on their shoulders.

"Abba Technics? In the capital?" Graff asked.

"No, in Biggock County. Training division," Anderson replied. "They think my work with children is good preparation. And you?"

Graff smiled and shook his head. "No plans. I'll be here for a few more months. Reports, winding down. I've had offers. Personnel development for DCIA, executive vice-president for U and P, but I said no. Publisher wants me to do memoirs of the war. I don't know."

They sat on a bench and watched leaves shivering in the breeze. Children on the monkey bars were laughing and yelling, but the wind and the distance swallowed their words. "Look," Graff said, pointing.

A little boy jumped from the bars and ran near the bench where the two men sat. Another boy followed him, and holding his hands like a gun he made an explosive sound. The child he was shooting at didn't stop. He fired again.

"I got you! Come back here!"

The other little boy ran on out of sight.

"Don't you know when you're dead?" The boy shoved his hands in his pockets and kicked a rock back to the monkey bars. Anderson smiled and shook his head. "Kids," he said. Then he and Graff stood up and walked on out of the park.

30

B. F. Skinner

Beyond Freedom and Dignity

Behaviorism, a leading school of modern psychology, explains human behavior as physical responses to environmentally based stimuli and holds that the scientific method of studying behavior is the only way to understand human nature. B(urrhus) F(rederic) Skinner (1904-1990) is the most notable American exponent of the behavioral doctrine.

Born in Pennsylvania, Skinner received a bachelor's degree in English literature in 1926 from Hamilton College in Clinton, New York. After an unsuccessful period as a writer of fiction, he became interested in the behavioral theories of the Russian physiologist Ivan Pavlov and the American psychologist John Watson. He then undertook graduate work in experimental psychology at Harvard University, earning a doctorate in 1931. After teaching at Minnesota and Indiana universities, Skinner returned to Harvard in 1947 and remained on the faculty there until his retirement in 1975.

During the Second World War his interests in behavior led Skinner to the directorship of a secret government project aimed at training pigeons to pilot explosive missiles, such as bombs and torpedoes, by pecking at the center of target images. Such pecking by a pigeon placed in the nose of a missile would generate electrical impulses that would, in turn, control the missile's guidance system. Although the training was successful, the pecking pilots were never used in combat.

After the war, Skinner turned his inventiveness to more pacific pursuits. Seeking an optimum crib for his own infant, he devised the Air-Crib, a glass-sided, atmospherically controlled baby-tender. Later he developed the Skinner

From *Beyond Freedom and Dignity* by B. F. Skinner. Copyright © 1971 by B. F. Skinner. Condensed by permission of Alfred A. Knopf, Inc. [Pp. 19-22, 24-25, 185-89, 198-214.]

box, a mechanism for observing and measuring changes in animal behavior; it is now used primarily by pharmaceutical researchers studying the effects of drugs on laboratory animals.

In the late 1950s, Skinner developed the concept of programmed instruction. As proposed by Skinner, this instructional method includes the devising of a series of minute steps through which the learner is led to acquire complex forms of behavior or knowledge; such steps are presented to the learner by means of a "teaching machine." The deviser of the machine's "program" is seeking to control behavior. The learner—whether beast or human—is led through the program by the techniques of reinforcement, or reward. For humans using a teaching machine, the reinforcement at each step is the achievement of a correct answer. Food is often used in the training of other species. When Skinner trained pigeons to play ping-pong, for example, their reward was a grain of corn for every correct move.

The major works written by Skinner—including a Utopian novel, Walden Two *(1948)—all tend to advance his behavioral thesis.* Beyond Freedom and Dignity *(1971), from which the following selection is taken, provoked especially bitter criticism among those who saw its views as destructive of traditional human values. In it, Skinner approves, as necessary for human survival, those same manipulative techniques that Ellul and Galbraith warn against. To adopt Skinner's "science of behavior" is to abandon the old notions of individual autonomy and free will. These concepts—like freedom and dignity—are "pre-scientific" ideas that Skinner believes are no longer appropriate to the human condition.*

Two features of autonomous man are particularly troublesome. In the traditional view, a person is free. He is autonomous in the sense that his behavior is uncaused. He can therefore be held responsible for w⁷hat he does and justly punished if he offends. That view, together with its associated practices, must be re-examined when a scientific analysis reveals unsuspected controlling relations between behavior and environment. A certain amount of external control can be tolerated. Theologians have accepted the fact that man must be predestined to do what an omniscient God knows he will do, and the Greek dramatist took inexorable fate as his favorite theme. Soothsayers and astrologers often claim to predict what men will do, and they have always been in demand. Biographers and historians have searched for "influences" in the lives of individuals and peoples. Folk wisdom and the insights of essayists like Montaigne and Bacon imply some kind of predictability in human conduct, and the statistical and actuarial evidences of the social sciences point in the same direction.

Autonomous man survives in the face of all this because he is the happy exception. Theologians have reconciled predestination with free will, and the Greek audience, moved by the portrayal of an inescapable destiny, walked out of the theater free men. The course of history has been turned by the death of a leader or a storm at sea, as a life has been changed by, a teacher or a love affair, but these things do not happen to everyone, and they do not affect everyone in the same way. Some historians have made a virtue of the unpredictability of history. Actuarial evidence is easily ignored; we read that hundreds of people will be killed in traffic accidents on a holiday weekend and take to the road as if personally exempt. Very little behavioral science raises "the specter of predictable man." On the contrary, many anthropologists, sociologists, and psychologists have used their expert knowledge to prove that man is free, purposeful, and responsible. Freud* was a determinisi—on faith, if not on the evidence— but many Freudians have no hesitation in assuring their patients that they are free to choose among different courses of action and are in the long run the architects of their own destinies.

This escape route is slowly closed as new evidences of the predictability of human behavior are discovered. Personal exemption from a complete determinism is revoked as a scientific analysis progresses, particularly in accounting for the behavior of the individual. Joseph Wood Krutch has acknowledged the actuarial facts while insisting on personal freedom: "We can predict with a considerable degree of accuracy how many people will go to the seashore on a day when the temperature reaches a certain point, even how many will jump off a bridge . . . although I am not, nor are you, compelled to do either." But he can scarcely mean that those who go to the seashore do not go for good reason, or that circumstances in the life of a suicide do not have some bearing on the fact that he jumps off a bridge. The distinction is tenable only so long as a word like "compel" suggests a particularly conspicuous and

---

* Sigmund Freud (1856-1939), an Austrian physician, was the founder of the therapeutic technique of psychoanalysis, which reveals the instinctual drives that dominate human behavior.

forcible mode of control. A scientific analysis naturally moves in the direction of clarifying all kinds of controlling relations.

By questioning the control exercised by autonomous man and demonstrating the control exercised by the environment, a science of behavior also seems to question dignity or worth. A person is responsible for his behavior, not only in the sense that he may be justly blamed or punished when he behaves badly, but also in the sense that he is to be given credit and admired for his achievements. A scientific analysis shifts the credit as well as the blame to the environment, and traditional practices can then no longer be justified. These are sweeping changes, and those who are committed to traditional theories and practices naturally resist them.

There is a third source of trouble. As the emphasis shifts to the environment, the individual seems to be exposed to a new kind of danger. Who is to construct the controlling environment and to what end? Autonomous man presumably controls himself in accordance with a built-in set of values: he works for what he finds good. But what will the putative controller find good, and will it be good for those he controls? Answers to questions of this sort are said, of course, to call for value judgments.

Freedom, dignity, and value are major issues, and unfortunately they become more crucial as the power of a technology of behavior becomes more nearly commensurate with the problems to be solved. The very change which has brought some hope of a solution is responsible for a growing opposition to the kind of solution proposed. This conflict is itself a problem in human behavior and may be approached as such. A science of behavior is by no means as far advanced as physics or biology, but it has an advantage in that it may throw some light on its own difficulties. Science *is* human behavior, and so is the opposition to science. What has happened in man's struggle for freedom and dignity, and what problems arise when scientific knowledge begins to be relevant in that struggle? Answers to these questions may help to clear the way for the technology we so badly need. . . .

Almost all our major problems involve human behavior, and they cannot be solved by physical and biological technology alone. What is needed is a technology of behavior, but we have been slow to develop the science from which such a technology might be drawn. One difficulty is that almost all of what is called behavioral science continues to trace behavior to states of mind, feelings, traits of character, human nature, and so on. Physics and biology once followed similar practices and advanced only when they discarded them. The behavioral sciences have been slow to change partly because the explanatory entities often seem to be directly observed and partly because other kinds of explanations have been hard to find. The environment is obviously important, but its role has remained obscure. It does not push or pull, it *selects,* and this function is difficult to discover and analyze. The role of natural selection in evolution was formulated only a little more than a hundred years ago, and the selective role of the environment in shaping and maintaining the behavior of the individual is only beginning to be recognized and studied. As the interaction between organism and environment has come to be understood, however, effects once assigned to states of mind, feelings, and traits are beginning to be traced to accessible conditions, and a technology of behavior may therefore become available. It will not solve our problems, however, until it replaces traditional prescientifie views, and these are strongly entrenched. Freedom and dignity illustrate the difficulty. They are the possessions of the autonomous man of traditional theory, and they are essential to practices in which a person is held responsible for his conduct and given credit for his achievements. A scientific analysis shifts both the responsibility and the achievement to the environment. It also raises questions concerning "values." Who will use a technology and to what ends? Until these issues are resolved, a technology of behavior will continue to be rejected, and with it possibly the only way to solve our problems.

★ ★ ★

The evidence for a crude environmentalism is clear enough. People are extraordinarily different in different places, and possibly just because of the places. The nomad on horseback in Outer Mongolia and the astronaut in outer space are different people, but, as far as we know, if they had been exchanged at birth, they would have taken each other's place. (The expression "change places" shows how closely we identify a person's behavior with the environment in which it occurs.) But we need to know a great deal more before that fact becomes useful. What is it about the environment that produces a Hottentot?* And what would need to be changed to produce an English conservative instead?

Both the enthusiasm of the environmentalist and his usually ignominious failure are illustrated by Owen's Utopian experiment at New Harmony.† A long history of environmental reform—in education, penology, industry, and family life, not to mention government and religion—has shown the same pattern. Environments are constructed on the model of environments in which good behavior has been observed, but the behavior fails to appear. Two hundred years of this kind of environmentalism has very little to show for itself, and for a simple reason. We must know how the environment works before we can change it to change behavior. A mere shift in emphasis from man to environment means very little.

Let us consider some examples in which the environment takes over the function and role of autonomous man. The first, often said to involve human nature, is *aggression*. Men often act in such a way that they harm others, and they often seem to be reinforced by signs of damage to others. The ethologists have emphasized contingencies of survival which would contribute these features to the genetic endowment of the species, but the contingencies of reinforcement in the lifetime of the individual are also significant, since anyone who acts aggressively to harm others is likely to be reinforced in other ways— for example, by taking possession of goods. The contingencies explain the behavior quite apart from any state or feeling of aggression or any initiating act by autonomous man.

Another example involving a so-called "trait of character" is *industry*. Some people are industrious in the sense that they work energetically for long periods of time, while others are lazy and idle in the sense that they do not. "Industry" and "laziness" are among thousands of so-called "traits." The behavior they refer to can be explained in other ways. Some of it may be attributed to genetic idiosyncrasies (and subject to change only through genetic measures), and the rest to environmental

---

* A people native to southern Africa.

† Robert Owen (1771-1858) was a British industrialist, socialist, and philanthropist. Utilizing his environmentalist ideas, he established a "co-operative" community at New Harmony, Indiana, in 1825.

contingencies, which are much more important than is usually realized. Regardless of any normal genetic endowment, an organism will range between vigorous activity and complete quiescence depending upon the schedules on which it has been reinforced. The explanation shifts from a trait of character to an environmental history of reinforcement.

A third example, a "cognitive" activity, is *attention*. A person responds only to a small part of the stimuli impinging upon him. The traditional view is that he himself determines which stimuli are to be effective by "paying attention" to them. Some kind of inner gatekeeper is said to allow some stimuli to enter and to keep all others out. A sudden or strong stimulus may break through and "attract" attention, but the person himself seems otherwise to be in control. An analysis of the environmental circumstances reverses the relation. The kinds of stimuli which break through by "attracting attention" do so because they have been associated in the evolutionary history of the species or the personal history of the individual with important—e.g., dangerous—things. Less forceful stimuli attract attention only to the extent that they have figured in contingencies of reinforcement. We can arrange contingencies which ensure that an organism—even such a "simple" organism as a pigeon—will attend to one object and not to another, or to one property of an object, such as its color, and not to another, such as its shape. The inner gatekeeper is replaced by the contingencies to which the organism has been exposed and which select the stimuli to which it reacts.

In the traditional view a person perceives the world around him and acts upon it to make it known to him. In a sense he reaches out and grasps it. He "takes it in" and possesses it. He "knows" it in the Biblical sense in which a man knows a woman. It has even been argued that the world would not exist if no one perceived it. The action is exactly reversed in an environmental analysis. There would, of course, be no perception if there were no world to be perceived, but an existing world would not be perceived if there were no appropriate contingencies. We say that a baby perceives his mother's face and knows it. Our evidence is that the baby responds in one way to his mother's face and in other ways to other faces or other things. He makes this distinction not through some mental act of perception but because of prior contingencies. Some of these may be contingencies of survival. Physical features of a species are particularly stable parts of the environment in which a species evolves. (That is why courtship and sex and relations between parent and offspring are given such a prominent place by ethologists.) The face and facial exprèssions of the human mother have been associated with security, warmth, food, and other important things, during both the evolution of the species and the life of the child.

We learn to perceive in the sense that we learn to respond to things in particular ways because of the contingencies of which they are a part. We may perceive the sun, for example, simply because it is an extremely powerful stimulus, but it has been a permanent part of the environment of the species throughout its evolution and more specific behavior with respect to it could have been selected by contingencies of survival (as it has been in many other species). The sun also figures in many current contingencies of reinforcement: we move into or out of sunlight depending on the temperature; we wait for the sun to rise or set to take practical action; we talk about the sun and its effects; and we eventually study the sun with the instruments and methods of science. Our perception of the sun depends on what we do with respect to it. Whatever we do, and hence however we perceive it, the fact remains that it is the environment which acts upon the perceiving person, not the perceiving person who acts upon the environment.

The perceiving and knowing which arise from verbal contingencies are even more obviously products of the environment. We react to an object in many practical ways because of its color; thus, we pick and eat red apples of a particular variety but not green. It is clear that we can "tell the difference" between red and green, but something more is involved when we say that we *know* that one apple is red and the other green. It is tempting to say that knowing is a cognitive process altogether divorced from action, but the contingencies provide a more useful distinction. When someone asks about the color of an object which he cannot see, and we tell him that it is red, *we* do nothing about the object in any other way. It is the person who has questioned us and heard our answer who makes a practical response which depends on color. Only under verbal contingencies can a speaker respond to an isolated property to which a nonverbal response cannot be made. A response made to the property of an object without responding to the object in any other way is called *abstract*. Abstract thinking is the product of a particular kind of environment, not of a cognitive faculty.

As listeners we acquire a kind of knowledge from the verbal behavior of others which may be extremely valuable in permitting us to avoid direct exposure to contingencies. We learn from the experienee of others by responding to what they say about contingencies. When we are warned against doing something or are advised to do something, there may be no point in speaking of knowledge, but when we learn more durable kinds of warnings and advice in the form of maxims or rules, we may be said to have a special kind of knowledge about the contingencies to which they apply. The laws of science are descriptions of contingencies of reinforcement, and one who knows a scientific law may behave effectively without being exposed to the contingencies it describes. (He will, of course, have very different feelings about the contingencies, depending on whether he is following a rule or has been directly exposed to them. Scientific knowledge is "cold," but the behavior to which it gives rise is as effective as the "warm" knowledge which comes from personal experience.) . . .

It is in the nature of an experimental analysis of human behavior that it should strip away the functions previously assigned to autonomous man and transfer them one by one to the controlling environment. The analysis leaves less and less for autonomous man to do. But what about man himself? Is there not something about a person which is more than a living body? Unless something called a self survives, how can we speak of self-knowledge or self-control? To whom is the injunction "Know thyself addressed?

It is an important part of the contingencies to which a young child is exposed that his own body is the only part of his environment which remains the same *(idem)* from moment to moment and day to day. We say that he discovers his *identity* as he learns to distinguish between his body and the rest of the world. He does this long before the community teaches him to call things by name and to distinguish "me" from "it" or "you."

A self is a repertoire of behavior appropriate to a given set of contingencies. A substantial part of the conditions to which a person is exposed may play a dominant role, and under other conditions a person may report, "I'm not myself today," or, "I couldn't have done what you said I did, because that's not like me." The identity conferred upon a self arises from the contingencies responsible for the behavior. Two or more repertoires generated by different sets of contingencies compose two or more selves. A person possesses one repertoire appropriate to his life with his friends and another appropriate to his life with his family, and a friend may find him a very different person if he sees him with his family or his family if they see him with his friends. The problem of identity arises when situations are intermingled, as when a person finds himself with both his family and his friends at the same time.

Self-knowledge and self-control imply two selves in this sense. The self-knower is almost always a product of social contingencies, but the self that is known may come from other sources. The controlling self (the conscience or superego) is of social origin, but the controlled self is more likely to be the product of genetic susceptibilities to reinforcement (the id,* or the Old Adam). The controlling self generally represents the interests of others, the controlled self the interests of the individual.

The picture which emerges from a scientific analysis is not of a body with a person inside, but of a body which 15 a person in the sense that it displays a complex repertoire of behavior. The picture is, of course, unfamiliar. The man thus portrayed is a stranger, and from the traditional point of view he may not seem to be a man at all. "For at least one hundred years," said Joseph Wood Krutch, "we have been prejudiced in every theory, including economic determinism, mechanistic behaviorism, and relativism, that reduces the stature of man until he ceases to be man at all in any sense that the humanists of an earlier generation would recognize." Matson has argued that "the empirical behavioral scientist . . . denies, if only by implication, that a unique being, called Man, exists." "What is now under attack," said Maslow, "is the 'being' of man." C. S. Lewis put it quite bluntly: Man is being abolished.

---

* In Freudian psychoanalysis, the unconscious part of the psyche that is the source of instinctual energies.

There is clearly some difficulty in identifying the man to whom these expressions refer. Lewis cannot have meant the human species, for not only is it not being abolished, it is filling the earth. (As a result it may eventually abolish itself through disease, famine, pollution, or a nuclear holocaust, but that is not what Lewis meant.) Nor are individual men growing less effective or productive. We are told that what is threatened is "man *qua* man," or "man in his humanity," or "man as Thou not It," or "man as a person not a thing." These are not very helpful expressions, but they supply a clue. What is being abolished is autonomous man—the inner man, the homuncuius, the possessing demon, the man defended by the literatures of freedom and dignity.

His abolition has long been overdue. Autonomous man is a device used to explain what we cannot explain in any other way. He has been constructed from our ignorance, and as our understanding increases, the very stuff of which he is composed vanishes. Science does not dehumanize man, it de-homunculizes him, and it must do so if it is to prevent the abolition of the human species. To man *qua* man we readily say good riddance. Only by dispossessing him can we turn to the real causes of human behavior. Only then can we turn from the inferred to the observed, from the miraculous to the natural, from the inaccessible to the manipulable.

It is often said that in doing so we must treat the man who survives as a mere animal. "Animal" is a pejorative term, but only because "man" has been made spuriously honorific. Krutch has argued that whereas the traditional view supports Hamlet's exclamation, "How like a god!," Pavlov, the behavioral scientist, emphasized "How like a dog!" But that was a step forward. A god is the archetypal pattern of an explanatory fiction, of a miracle-working mind, of the metaphysical. Man is much more than a dog, but like a dog he is within range of a scientific analysis.

It is true that much of the experimental analysis of behavior has been concerned with lower organisms. Genetic differences are minimized by using special strains; environmental histories can be controlled, perhaps from birth; strict regimens can be maintained during long experiments; and very little of this is possible with human subjects. Moreover, in working with lower animals the scientist is less likely to put his own responses to the experimental conditions among his data, or to design contingencies with an eye to their effect on him rather than on the experimental organism he is studying. No one is disturbed when physiologists study respiration, reproduction, nutrition, or endocrine systems in animals; they do so to take advantage of very great similarities. Comparable similarities in behavior are being discovered. There is, of course, always the danger that methods designed for the study of lower animals will emphasize only those characteristics which they have in common with men, but we cannot discover what is "essentially" human until we have investigated nonhuman subjects. Traditional theories of autonomous man have exaggerated species differences. Some of the complex contingencies of reinforcement now under investigation generate behavior in lower organisms which, if the subjects were human, would traditionally be said to involve higher mental processes.

Man is not made into a machine by analyzing his behavior in mechanical terms. Early theories of behavior, as we have seen, represented man as a push-pull automaton, close to the nineteenth-century notion of a machine, but progress has been made. Man is a machine in the sense that he is a complex system behaving in lawful ways, but the complexity is extraordinary. His capacity to adjust to contingencies of reinforcement will perhaps be eventually simulated by machines, but this has not yet been done, and the living system thus simulated will remain unique in other ways.

Nor is man made into a machine by inducing him to use machines. Some machines call for behavior which is repetitious and monotonous, and we escape from them when we can, but others enormously extend our effectiveness in dealing with the world around us. A person may respond to very small things with the help of an electron microscope and to very large things with radiotélescopes, and in doing so he may seem quite inhuman to those who use only their unaided senses. A person may act upon the environment with the delicate precision of a micromanipulator or with the range and power of a space rocket, and his behavior may seem inhuman to those who rely only on muscular contractions. (It has been argued that the apparatus used in the operant laboratory misrepresents natural behavior because it introduces an external source of power, but men use external sources when they fly kites, sail boats, or shoot bows and arrows. They would have to abandon all but a small fraction of their achievements if they used only the power of their muscles.) People record their behavior in books and other media, and the use they make of the records may seem quite inhuman to those who can use only what they remember. People describe complex contingencies in the form of rules, and rules for manipulating rules, and they introduce them into electronic systems which "think" with a speed that seems quite inhuman to the unaided thinker. Human beings do all this with machines, and they would be less than human if they did not. What we now regard as machine-like behavior was, in fact, much commoner before the invention of these devices. The slave in the cotton field, the bookkeeper on his high stool, the student being drilled by a teacher—these were the machine-like men.

Machines replace people when they do what people have done, and the social consequences may be serious. As technology advances, machines will take over more and more of the functions of men, but only up to a point. We build machines which reduce some of the aversive features of our environment (grueling labor, for example) and which produce more positive reinforcers. We build them precisely because they do so. We have no reason to build machines to be reinforced by these consequences, and to do so would be to deprive ourselves of reinforcement. If the machines man makes eventually make him wholly expendable, it will be by accident, not design.

An important role of autonomous man has been to give human behavior direction, and it is often said that in dispossessing an inner agent we leave man himself without a purpose. As one writer has put it, "Since a scientific psychology must regard human behavior objectively, as determined by necessary laws, it must represent human behavior as unintentional." But "necessary laws" would have this effect only if they referred exclusively to antecedent conditions. Intention and purpose refer to selective consequences, the effects of which can be formulated in "necessary laws." Has life, in all the forms in which it exists on the surface of the earth, a purpose, and is this evidence of intentional design? The primate hand evolved *in order that* things might be more successfully manipulated, but its purpose is to be found not in a prior design but rather in the process of selection. Similarly, in operant conditioning the purpose of a skilled movement of the hand is to be found in the consequences which follow it. A pianist neither acquires nor executes the behavior of playing a scale smoothly because of a prior intention of doing so. Smoothly played scales are reinforcing for many reasons, and they select skilled movements. In neither the evolution of the human hand nor in the acquired use of the hand is any prior intention or purpose at issue.

The argument for purpose seems to be strengthened by moving back into the darker recesses of mutation. Jacques Barzun has argued that Darwin* and Marx† both neglected not only human purpose but the creative purpose responsible for the variations upon which natural selection plays. It may prove to be the case, as some geneticists have argued, that mutations are not entirely random, but nonran-domness is not necessarily the proof of a creative mind. Mutations will not be random when geneticists explicitly design them in order that an organism will meet specific conditions of selection more successfully, and geneticists will then seem to be playing the role of the creative Mind in pre-evolutionary theory, but the purpose they display will have to be sought in their culture, in the social environment which has induced them to make genetic changes appropriate to contingencies of survival.

There is a difference between biological and individual purpose in that the latter can be felt. No one could have felt the purpose in the development of the human hand, whereas a person can in a sense feel the purpose with which he plays a smooth scale. But he does not play a smooth scale *because* he feels the purpose of doing so; what he feels is a by-product of his behavior in relation to its consequences. The relation of the human hand to the contingencies of survival under which it evolved is, of course, out of reach of personal observation; the relation of the behavior to contingencies of reinforcement which have generated it is not.

---

* Charles Darwin (1809-82), an English naturalist who developed a theory of biological evolution based on natural selection.
† Karl Marx (1818-83), a German-born political philosopher, was the major originator of the modern socialist theory that human history is determined by the conflict of impersonal economic forces.

A scientific analysis of behavior dispossesses autonomous man and turns the control he has been said to exert over to the environment. The individual may then seem particularly vulnerable. He is henceforth to be controlled by the world around him, and in large part by other men. Is he not then simply a victim? Certainly men have been victims, as they have been victimizers, but the word is too strong. It implies despoliation, which is by no means an essential consequence of interpersonal control. But even under benevolent control is the individual not at best a spectator who may watch what happens but is helpless to do anything about it? Is he not "at a dead end in his long struggle to control his own destiny"?

It is only autonomous man who has reached a dead end. Man himself may be controlled by his environment, but it is an environment which is almost wholly of his own making. The physical environment of most people is largely man-made. The surfaces a person walks on, the walls which shelter him, the clothing he wears, many of the foods he eats, the tools he uses, the vehicles he moves about in, most of the things he listens to and looks at are human products. The social environment is obviously man-made—it generates the language a person speaks, the customs he follows, and the behavior he exhibits with respect to the ethical, religious, governmental, economic, educational, and psychotherapeutic institutions which control him. The evolution of a culture is in fact a kind of gigantic exercise in self-control. As the individual controls himself by manipulating the world in which he lives, so the human species has constructed an environment in which its members behave in a highly effective way. Mistakes have been made, and we have no assurance that the environment man has constructed will continue to provide gains which outstrip the losses, but man as we know him, for better or for worse, is what man has made of man.

This will not satisfy those who cry "Victim!" C. S. Lewis protested: ". . . the power of man to make himself what he pleases . . . means . . . the power of some men to make other men what they please." This is inevitable in the nature of cultural evolution. The controlling *self* must be distinguished from the controlled self, even when they are both inside the same skin, and when control is exercised through the design of an external environment, the selves are, with minor exceptions, distinct. The person who unintentionally or intentionally introduces a new cultural practice is only one among possibly billions who will be affected by it. If this does not seem like an act of self-control, it is only because we have misunderstood the nature of self-control in the individual.

When a person changes his physical or social environment "intentionally"— that is, in order to change human behavior, possibly including his own—he plays two roles: one as a controller, as the designer of a controlling culture, and another as the controlled, as the product of a culture. There is nothing inconsistent about this; it follows from the nature of the evolution of a culture, with or without intentional design.

The human species has probably not undergone much genetic change in recorded time. We have only to go back a thousand generations to reach the artists of the caves of Lascaux.* Features which bear directly on survival (such as resistance to disease) change substantially in a thousand generations, but the child of one of the Lascaux artists transplanted to the world of today might be almost indistinguishable from a modern child. It is possible that he would learn more slowly than his modern counterpart, that he could maintain only a smaller repertoire without confusion, or that he would forget more quickly; we cannot be sure. But we can be sure that a twentieth-century child transplanted to the civilization of Lascaux would not be very different from the children he met there, for we have seen what happens when a modern child is raised in an impoverished environment.

Man has greatly changed himself as a person in the same period of time by changing the world in which he lives. Something of the order of a hundred generations will cover the development of modern religious practices, and something of the same order of magnitude modern government and law. Perhaps no more than twenty generations will account for modern industrial practices, and possibly no more than four or five for education and psychotherapy. The physical and biological technologies which have increased man's sensitivity to the

---

* The ceilings and walls of these caves in central France bear paintings (mainly of animals) that were done by hunter-artists of nearly fifteen thousand years ago.

world around him and his power to change that world have taken no more than four or five generations.

Man has "controlled his own destiny," if that expression means anything at all. The man that man has made is the product of the culture man has devised. He has emerged from two quite different processes of evolution: the biological evolution responsible for the human species and the cultural evolution carried out by that species. Both of these processes of evolution may now accelerate because they are both subject to intentional design. Men have already changed their genetic endowment by breeding selectively and by changing contingencies of survival, and they may now begin to introduce mutations directly related to survival. For a long time men have introduced new practices which serve as cultural mutations, and they have changed the conditions under which practices are selected. They may now begin to do both with a clearer eye to the consequences.

Man will presumably continue to change, but we cannot say in what direction. No one could have predicted the evolution of the human species at any point in its early history, and the direction of intentional genetic design will depend upon the evolution of a culture which is itself unpredictable for similar reasons. "The limits of perfection of the human species," said Etienne Cabet in *Voyage en Icarie,* "are as yet unknown." But, of course, there are no limits. The human species will never reach a final state of perfection before it is exterminated—"some say in fire, some in ice," and some in radiation.

The individual occupies a place in a culture not unlike his place in the species, and in early evolutionary theory that place was hotly debated. Was the species simply a type of individual, and if so, in what sense could it evolve? Darwin himself declared species "to be purely subjective inventions of the taxonomist." A species has no existence except as a collection of individuals, nor has a family, tribe, race, nation, or class. A culture has no existence apart from the behavior of the individuals who maintain its practices. It is always an individual who behaves, who acts upon the environment and is changed by the consequences of his action, and who maintains the social contingencies which *are* a culture. The individual is the carrier of both his species and his culture. Cultural practices, like genetic traits, are transmitted from individual to individual. A new practice, like a new genetic trait, appears first in an individual and tends to be transmitted if it contributes to his survival as an individual.

Yet, the individual is at best a locus in which many lines of development come together in a unique set. His individuality is unquestioned. Every cell in his body is a unique genetic product, as unique as that classic mark of individuality, the fingerprint. And even within the most regimented culture every personal history is unique. No intentional culture can destroy that uniqueness, and, as we have seen, any effort to do so would be bad design. But the individual nevertheless remains merely a stage in a process which began long before he came into existence and will long outlast him. He has no ultimate responsibility for a species trait or a cultural practice, even though it was he who underwent the mutation or introduced the practice which became part of the species or culture. Even if Lamarck had been right in supposing that the individual could change his genetic structure through personal effort, we should have to point to the environmental circumstances responsible for the effort, as we shall have to do when geneticists begin to change the human endowment. And when an individual engages in the intentional design of a cultural practice, we must turn to the culture which induces him to do so and supplies the art or science he uses.

One of the great problems of individualism, seldom recognized as such, is death—the inescapable fate of the individual, the final assault on freedom and dignity. Death is one of those remote events which are brought to bear on behavior only with the aid of cultural practices. What we see is the death of others, as in Pascal's famous metaphor: "Imagine a number of men in chains, all under sentence of death, some of whom are each day butchered in the sight of the others; those remaining see their own condition in that of their fellows, and looking at each other with grief and despair await their turn. This is an image of the human condition." Some religions have made death more important by picturing a future existence in heaven or hell, but the individualist has a special reason to fear death, engineered not by a religion but by the literatures of freedom and dignity. It is the prospect of personal annihilation. The individualist can find no solace in reflecting upon any contribution which will survive him. He has refused to act for the good of others and is therefore not reinforced by the fact that others whom he has helped will outlive him. He has refused to be concerned for the survival of his culture and is not reinforced by the fact that the culture will long survive him. In the defense of his own freedom and dignity he has denied the contributions of the past and must therefore relinquish all claim upon the future.

Science has probably never demanded a more sweeping change in a traditional way of thinking about a subject, nor has there ever been a more important subject. In the traditional picture a person perceives the world around him, selects features to be perceived, discriminates among them, judges them good or bad, changes them to make them better (or, if he is careless, worse), and may be held responsible for his action and justly rewarded or punished for its consequences. In the scientific picture a person is a member of a species shaped by evolutionary contingencies of survival, displaying behavioral processes which bring him under the control of the environment in which he lives, and largely under the control of a social environment which he and millions of others like him have constructed and maintained during the evolution of a culture. The direction of the controlling relation is reversed: a person does not act upon the world, the world acts upon him.

It is difficult to accept such a change simply on intellectual grounds and nearly impossible to accept its implications. The reaction of the traditionalist is usually described in terms of feelings. One of these, to which the Freudians have appealed in explaining the resistance to psychoanalysis, is wounded vanity. Freud himself expounded, as Ernest Jones has said, "the three heavy blows which narcissism or self-love of mankind had suffered at the hands of science. The first was cosmological and was dealt by Copernicus;* the second was biological and was dealt by Darwin; the third was psychological and was dealt by Freud." (The blow was suffered by the belief that something at the center of man knows all that goes on within him and that an instrument called will power exercises command and control over the rest of one's personality.) But what are the signs or symptoms of wounded vanity, and how shall

---

* Nicolaus Copernicus (1473-1543), a Polish astronomer, was the first modern scientist to state that the sun—not the earth—is the center of the solar system.

we explain them? What people *do* about such a scientific picture of man is call it wrong, demeaning, and dangerous, argue against it, and attack those who propose or defend it. They do so not out of wounded vanity but because the scientific formulation has destroyed accustomed reinforcers. If a person can no longer take credit or be admired for what he does, then he seems to suffer a loss of dignity or worth, and behavior previously reinforced by credit or admiration will undergo extinction. Extinction often leads to aggressive attack.

Another effect of the scientific picture has been described as a loss of faith or "nerve," as a sense of doubt or powerlessness, or as discouragement, depression, or despondency. A person is said to feel that he can do nothing about his own destiny. But what he feels is a weakening of old responses which are no longer reinforced. People are indeed "powerless" when long-established verbal repertoires prove useless. For example, one historian has complained that if the deeds of men are "to be dismissed as simply the product of material and psychological conditioning," there is nothing to write about; "change must be at least partially the result of conscious mental activity."

Another effect is a kind of nostalgia. Old repertoires break through, as similarities between present and past are seized upon and exaggerated. Old days are called the good old days, when the inherent dignity of man and the importance of spiritual values were recognized. Such fragments of outmoded behavior tend to be "wistful"—that is, they have the character of increasingly unsuccessful behavior.

These reactions to a scientific conception of man are certainly unfortunate. They immobilize men of good will, and anyone concerned with the future of his culture will do what he can to correct them. No theory changes what it is a theory about. Nothing is changed because we look at it, talk about it, or analyze it in a new way. Keats drank confusion to Newton for analyzing the rainbow, but the rainbow remained as beautiful as ever and became for many even more beautiful. Man has not changed because we look at him, talk about him, and analyze him scientifically. His achievements in science, government, religion, art, and literature remain as they have always been, to be admired as one admires a storm at sea or autumn foliage or a mountain peak, quite apart from their origins and untouched by a scientific analysis. What does change is our chance of doing something about the subject of a theory. Newton's analysis of the light in a rainbow was a step in the direction of the laser.

The traditional conception of man is flattering; it confers reinforcing privileges. It is therefore easily defended and can be changed only with difficulty. It was designed to build up the individual as an instrument of countercontrol, and it did so effectively but in such a way as to limit progress. We have seen how the literatures of freedom and dignity, with their concern for autonomous man, have perpetuated the use of punishment and condoned the use of only weak nonpunitive techniques, and it is not difficult to demonstrate a connection between the unlimited right of the individual to pursue happiness and the catastrophes threatened by unchecked breeding, the unrestrained affluence which exhausts resources and pollutes the environment, and the imminence of nuclear war.

Physical and biological technologies have alleviated pestilence and famine and many painful, dangerous, and exhausting features of daily life, and behavioral technology can begin to alleviate other kinds of ills. In the analysis of human behavior it is just possible that we are slightly beyond Newton's position in the analysis of light, for we are beginning to make technological applications. There are wonderful possibilities—and all the more wonderful because traditional approaches have been so ineffective. It is hard to imagine a world in which people live together without quarreling, maintain themselves by producing the food, shelter, and clothing they need, enjoy themselves and contribute to the enjoyment of others in art, music, literature, and games, consume only a reasonable part of the resources of the world and add as little as possible to its pollution, bear no more children than can be raised decently, continue to explore the world around them and discover better ways of dealing with it, and come to know themselves accurately and, therefore, manage themselves effectively. Yet all this is possible, and even the slightest sign of progress should bring a kind of change which in traditional terms would be said to assuage wounded vanity, offset a sense of hopelessness or nostalgia, correct the impression that "we neither can nor need to do anything for ourselves," and promote a "sense of freedom and dignity" by building "a sense of confidence and worth." In other words, it should abundantly reinforce those who have been induced by their culture to work for its survival. . . .

31

Elie Wiesel

The Death of God

In the years since the Second World War, "the death of God" has been a significant theological expression. For some, the "atheist" mood it suggests grew out of the inability of traditional religions to explain "God's silence" in the face of the Nazis' deliberate abuse and slaughter of millions of civilians. Among the most memorable eyewitness accounts of the Nazi death camps is the one by Elie Wiesel (1928-).

Born and raised in the town of Sighet in the Transylvanian highlands-an area that had been controlled alternately by Hungary and Romania-Wiesel, at age fifteen, was sent with his family to the concentration camp in Auschwitz, Poland. It was the spring of 1944, and all the Jews of Transylvania were being shipped out of that area as part of the German racial policy. His mother and youngest sister were selected for extermination on the night they arrived at Auschwitz. His father was killed, before Elie's eyes, in early 1945, soon after the father and son were marched to the concentration camp at Buchenwald, Germany.

Liberated by the advancing American army two months after his father's death, Wiesel refused repatriation to eastern Europe at the end of the war. Now stateless, he was denied immigration to Palestine, his first choice, which was still under the authority of the British government. Eventually he moved to Paris where, from 1948 to 1951, he studied philosophy, while earning his living as a choir director and teacher of the Bible.

From *Night* by Elie Wiesel. Copyright © Les Editions de Minuit, 1958. Translated by Stella Rodway. English translation copyright © MacGibbon & Kee, 1960. Reprinted by permission of Farrar, Straus and Giroux. Inc. [Pp. 69-75.]

During his sojourn in Paris, Wiesel took a brief assignment from a French newspaper to report on Israel's war of independence; later, he became chief foreign correspondent for a Tel Aviv daily. In 1956, while in New York on a reporting mission for his newspaper, he was struck by a taxicab. During his ensuing period of confinement in a New York hospital, he decided to apply for American citizenship, which was granted to him in 1963. While continuing his journalistic and literary careers, Wiesel has also been a professor, from 1973 to 1916, at the City University of New York and since then at Boston University.

The ambition to become a "serious" writer has been with Wiesel since his agony in the concentration camps. As a survivor he feels profoundly the need "to bear witness, to testify" to their horrors. The selection that follows is from his first book, Night *(1960), which recounts his experiences in the camps — the death of his father, and the death of his own faith in God. Having witnessed dehumanizing suffering and death, Wiesel accuses and rejects God for His "silence."*

Wiesel's many other writings also deal largely with the themes of Jewish remembrance, survival, and identity in a world that permitted Auschwitz. Among these works are Dawn *(1961), a novel in which a death-camp survivor, now a member of a Jewish terrorist group in British-controlled Palestine, is given the ironically grim task of executing a British officer; and* The Gates of the Forest *(1966), a complex novel of a Transylvanian Jew, sole survivor of his village, who portrays Judas in a passion play, joins a partisan group to fight the Germans, and eventually settles in the United States where—like the author—he comes to a passionate reaffirmation of his own identity, his relationship to other people and to God.*

Wiesel, apart from his novels, has often concerned himself with the ongoing plight of his co-religionists in other lands. In The Jews of Silence *(1966), for example, he recounts his 1965 journey to the Soviet Union and speaks out against the silence of Western Jews regarding the oppression of Soviet Jews. In recent years Wiesel has also written about happier aspects of his tradition, as in* Souls on Fire *(1972), which retells tales of the mystical Hasidic Jews.*

One day, the electric power station at Buna was blown up. The Gestapo,* summoned to the spot, suspected sabotage. They found a trail. It eventually led to the Dutch Oberkapo.† And there, after a search, they found an important stock of arms.

The Oberkapo was arrested immediately. He was tortured for a period of weeks, but in vain. He would not give a single name. He was transferred to Auschwitz. We never heard of him again.

But his little servant had been left behind in the camp in prison. Also put to torture, he too would not speak. Then the SS‡ sentenced him to death, with two other prisoners who had been discovered with arms.

One day when we came back from work, we saw three gallows rearing up in the assembly place, three black crows. Roll call. SS all round us, machine guns trained: the traditional ceremony. Three victims in chains—and one of them, the little servant, the sad-eyed angel.

The SS seemed more preoccupied, more disturbed than usual. To hang a young boy in front of thousands of spectators was no light matter. The head of the camp read the verdict. All eyes were on the child. He was lividly pale, almost calm, biting his lips. The gallows threw its shadow over him.

This time the Lagerkapo§ refused to act as executioner. Three SS replaced him.

The three victims mounted together onto the chairs.

The three necks were placed at the same moment within the nooses.

"Long live liberty!" cried the two adults.

But the child was silent.

"Where is God? Where is He?" someone behind me asked.

At a sign from the head of the camp, the three chairs tipped over.

Total silence throughout the camp. On the horizon, the sun was setting.

---

* The secret police of the Nazi regime.
†Head prisoner foreman (selected by the Nazis from among the prisoners).
‡ A special police force; one of its functions was to operate the camps.
§ Prisoner foreman of the warehouse.

"Bare your heads!" yelled the head of the camp. His voice was raucous. We were weeping.

"Cover your heads!"

Then the march past began. The two adults were no longer alive. Their tongues hung swollen, blue-tinged. But the third rope was still moving; being so light, the child was still alive. . . .

For more than half an hour he stayed there, struggling between life and death, dying in slow agony under our eyes. And we had to look him full in the face. He was still alive when I passed in front of him. His tongue was still red, his eyes were not yet glazed.

Behind me, I heard the same man asking:

"Where is God now?"

And I heard a voice within me answer him:

"Where is He? Here He is—He is hanging here on this gallows. . . ."

That night the soup tasted of corpses.

The summer was coming to an end. The Jewish year was nearly over.

On the eve of Rosh Hashanah, the last day of that accursed year, the whole camp was electric with the tension which was in all our hearts. In spite of everything, this day was different from any other. The last day of the year. The word "last" rang very strangely. What if it were indeed the last day?

They gave us our evening meal, a very thick soup, but no one touched it. We wanted to wait until after prayers. At the place of assembly, surrounded by the electrified barbed wire, thousands of silent Jews gathered, their faces stricken.

Night was falling. Other prisoners continued to crowd in, from every block, able suddenly to conquer time and space and submit both to their will.

"What are You, my God," I thought angrily, "compared to this afflicted crowd, proclaiming to You their faith, their anger, their revolt? What does Your greatness mean, Lord of the Universe, in the face of all this weakness, this decomposition, and this decay? Why do You still trouble their sick minds, their crippled bodies?"

Ten thousand men had come to attend the solemn service, heads of the blocks, Kapos, functionaries of death.

"Bless the Eternal. . . ."

The voice of the officiant had just made itself heard. I thought at first it was the wind.

"Blessed be the Name of the Eternal!"

Thousands of voices repeated the benediction; thousands of men prostrated themselves like trees before a tempest.

"Blessed be the Name of the Eternal!"

Why, but why should I bless Him? In every fiber I rebelled. Because He had had thousands of children burned in His pits? Because He kept six crematories working night and day, on Sundays and feast days? Because in His great might He had created Auschwitz, Birkenau, Buna, and so many factories of death? How could I say to Him: "Blessed art Thou, Eternal, Master of the Universe, Who chose us from among the races to be tortured day and night, to see our fathers, our mothers, our brothers, end in the crematory? Praised be Thy Holy Name, Thou Who hast chosen us to be butchered on Thine altar?"

I heard the voice of the officiant rising up, powerful yet at the same time broken, amid the tears, the sobs, the sighs of the whole congregation:

"All the earth and the Universe are God's!"

He kept stopping every moment, as though he did not have the strength to find the meaning beneath the words. The melody choked in his throat.

And I, mystic that I had been, I thought:

"Yes, man is very strong, greater than God. When You were deceived by Adam and Eve, You drove them out of Paradise. When Noah's generation displeased You, You brought down the Flood. When Sodom no longer found favor in Your eyes, You made the sky rain down fire and sulphur. But these men here, whom You have betrayed, whom You have allowed to be tortured, butchered, gassed, burned, what do they do? They pray before You! They praise Your name!"

"All creation bears witness to the Greatness of God!"

Once, New Year's Day had dominated my life. I knew that my sins grieved the Eternal; I implored his forgiveness. Once, I had believed profoundly that upon one solitary deed of mine, one solitary prayer, depended the salvation of the world.

This day I had ceased to plead. I was no longer capable of lamentation. On the contrary, I felt very strong. I was the accuser, God the accused. My eyes were open and I was alone—terribly alone in a world without God and without man. Without love or mercy. I had ceased to be anything but ashes, yet I felt myself to be stronger than the Almighty, to whom my life had been tied for so long. I stood amid that praying congregation, observing it like a stranger.

The service ended with the Kaddish.* Everyone recited the Kaddish over his parents, over his children, over his brothers, and over himself.

We stayed for a long time at the assembly place. No one dared to drag himself away from this mirage. Then it was time to go to bed and slowly the prisoners made their way over to their blocks. I heard people wishing one another a Happy New Year!

I ran off to look for my father. And at the same time I was afraid of having to wish him a Happy New Year when I no longer believed in it.

He was standing near the wall, bowed down, his shoulders sagging as though beneath a heavy burden. I went up to him, took his hand and kissed it. A tear fell upon it. Whose was that tear? Mine? His? I said nothing. Nor did he. We had never understood one another so clearly.

The sound of the bell jolted us back to reality. We must go to bed. We came back from far away. I raised my eyes to look at my father's face leaning over mine, to try to discover a smile or something resembling one upon the aged, dried-up countenance. Nothing. Not the shadow of an expression. Beaten.

Yom Kippur. The Day of Atonement.

Should we fast? The question was hotly debated. To fast would mean a surer, swifter death. We fasted here the whole year round. The whole year was Yom Kippur. But others said that we should fast simply

---

* A prayer of the Jewish liturgy that is recited at the end of a religious service and is also used as a mourner's prayer for those who have died.

because it was dangerous to do so. We should show God that even here, in this enclosed hell, we were capable of singing His praises.

I did not fast, mainly to please my father, who had forbidden me to do so. But further, there was no longer any reason why I should fast. I no longer accepted God's silence. As I swallowed my bowl of soup, I saw in the gesture an act of rebellion and protest against Him.

And I nibbled my crust of bread.

In the depths of my heart, I felt a great void. . . .

32

Gary Zukav

Nonsense

BEGINNER'S MIND

The importance of nonsense hardly can be overstated. The more clearly we experience something as "nonsense," the more clearly we are experiencing the boundaries of our own self-imposed cognitive structures. "Nonsense" is that which does not fit into the prearranged patterns which we have superimposed on reality. There is no such thing as "nonsense" apart from a judgmental intellect which calls it that.

True artists and true physicists know that nonsense is only that which, viewed from our present point of view, is unintelligible. Nonsense is nonsense only when we have not yet found that point of view from which it makes sense.

In general, physicists do not deal in nonsense. Most of them spend their professional lives thinking along well-established lines of thought. Those scientists who establish the established lines of thought, however, are those who do not fear to venture boldly into nonsense, into that which any fool could have told them is clearly not so. This is the mark of the creative mind; in fact, this *is* the creative process. It is characterized by a steadfast confidence that there exists a point of view from which the "nonsense" is not nonsense at all—in fact, from which it is obvious.

In physics, as elsewhere, those who most have felt the exhilaration of the creative process are those who best have slipped the bonds of the known to venture far into the unexplored territory which lies beyond the barrier of the obvious. This type of person has two characteristics. The first is a childlike ability to see the world as it is, and not as it appears according to what we know about it. This is the moral of the (child's?) tale, "The Emperor's New Clothes." When the emperor rode naked through the streets, only a child proclaimed him to be without clothes, while the rest of his subjects forced themselves to believe, because they had been told so, that he wore his finest new clothing.

The child in us is always naive, innocent in the simplistic sense. A Zen story tells of Nan-in, a Japanese master during the Meiji era who received a university professor. The professor came to inquire about Zen. Nan-in served tea. He poured his visitor's cup full, and then kept on pouring. The professor watched the overflow until he no longer could restrain himself.

"It is overfull. No more will go in!"

"Like this cup," Nan-in said, "you are full of your own opinions and speculations. How can I show you Zen unless you first empty your cup?"

Our cup usually is filled to the brim with "the obvious," "common sense," and "the self-evident."

Suzuki Roshi, who established the first Zen center in the United States (without trying, of course, which is very Zen), told his students that it is not difficult to attain enlightenment, but it is difficult to keep a beginner's mind. "In the beginner's mind," he told them, "there are any possibilities, but in the expert's there are few." When his students published Suzuki's talks after his death, they called the book, appropriately, *Zen Mind, Beginner's Mind*. In the introduction, Baker Roshi, the American Zen Master, wrote:

> *The mind of the beginner is empty, free of the habits of the expert, ready to accept, to doubt, and open to all the possibilities. . . }*

The beginner's mind in science is wonderfully illustrated by the story of Albert Einstein and his theory of relativity. That is the subject of this chapter.

The second characteristic of true artists and true scientists is the firm confidence which both of them have in themselves. This confidence is an expression of an inner strength which allows them to speak out, secure in the knowledge that, appearances to the contrary, it is the world that is confused and not they. The first man to see an illusion by which men have flourished for centuries surely stands in a lonely place. In that moment of insight he, and he alone, sees the obvious which to the uninitiated (the rest of the world) yet appears as nonsense or, worse, as madness or heresy. This confidence is not the obstinacy of the fool, but the surety of him who knows what he knows, and knows also that he can convey it to others in a meaningful way.

The writer, Henry Miller, wrote:

> *I obey only my own instincts and intuition. I know nothing in advance. Often I put down things which I do not understand myself, secure in the knowledge that later they will become clear and meaningful to me. I have faith in the man who is writing, who is myself, the writer.*[2]

The songwriter Bob Dylan told a press conference:

> *I just write a song and I know it's going to be all right. I don't even know what it's going to say.*[3]

An example of this kind of faith in the realm of physics was the theory of light quanta. In 1905, the accepted and proven theory of light was that light was a wave phenomenon. In spite of this, Einstein published his famous paper proposing that light was a particle phenomenon (page 58). Heisenberg described this fascinating situation this way:

> *[In 1905] light could either be interpreted as consisting of electromagnetic waves, according to Maxwell's theory, or as consisting of light quanta, energy packets traveling through space with high velocity [according to Einstein]. But could it be both? Einstein knew, of course, that the well-known phenomena of diffraction and interference can be explained only on the basis of the wave picture. He was not able to dispute the complete contradiction between this wave picture and the idea of the light quanta; nor did he even attempt to remove the inconsistency of this interpretation. He simply took the contradiction as something which would probably be understood much later.*[4]

That is exactly what happened. Einstein's thesis led to the wave-particle duality from which quantum mechanics emerged, and with it, as we know, a way of looking at reality and ourselves that is vastly different from that to which we were accustomed. Although Einstein is known popularly for his theories of relativity, it was his paper on the quantum nature of light that won him the Nobel Prize. It is also a fine example of confidence in nonsense.

What is nonsense and what is not, then, may be merely a matter of perspective.

"Wait a minute," interrupts Jim de Wit. "My uncle, Weird George, believes that he is a football. Of course, we know that this is nonsense, but Uncle George thinks that *we* are mad. He is quite certain that he is a football. He talks about it constantly. In other words, he has abundant confidence in his nonsense. Does this make him a great scientist?

No. In fact, Weird George has a problem. Not only is he the only person who has this particular perspective, but also this particular perspective is in no way relative to that of any other observer, which brings us to the heart of Einstein's special theory of relativity. (Einstein created two theories of relativity. The first theory is called the special theory of relativity. The second theory, which came later and is more general, is called the general theory of relativity. This chapter and the next are about the first theory, the special theory of relativity).

The special theory of relativity is not so much about what is relative as about what is not. It describes in what way the relative aspects of physical reality appear to vary, depending upon the point of view of different observers (actually depending upon their state of motion relative to each other), but, in the process, it defines the nonchanging, absolute aspect of physical reality as well.

The special theory of relativity is not a theory that everything is relative. It is a theory that *appearances* are relative. What may appear to us as a ruler (physicists say "rod") one foot long, may appear to an observer traveling past us (very fast) as being only ten inches long. What may appear to us as one hour, may appear to an observer traveling past us (very fast) as two hours. However, the moving observer can use the special theory of relativity to de termine how our ruler and our clock appear to us (if he knows his motion relative to us) and, likewise, we can use the special theory of relativity to determine how our stick and our clock appear to the moving observer (if we know our motion relative to him).

If we were to perform an experiment at the same moment that the moving observer came past us, both we and the moving observer would see the same experiment, but each of us would record different times and distances, we with our rod and clock and he with his rod and clock. Using the special theory of relativity, however, each of us could transpose our data to the other's frame of reference. The final numbers would come out the same for both of us. In essence, the special theory of relativity is not about what is relative, it is about what is absolute.

However, the special theory of relativity does show that appearances are dependent upon the state of motion of the observers. For example, the special theory of relativity tells us that (1) a moving object measures shorter in its direction of motion as its velocity increases until, at the speed of light, it disappears; (2) the mass of a moving object measures more as its velocity increases until, at the speed of light, it becomes infinite; and (3) moving clocks run more slowly as their velocity increases until, at the speed of light, they stop running altogether.

All of this is from the point of view of an observer to whom the object is moving. To an observer traveling along with the moving object, the clock keeps perfect time, ticking off sixty seconds each minute, and nothing appears to get any shorter or more massive. The special theory of relativity also tells us that space and time are not two separate things, but that together they form space-time, and that energy and mass are actually different forms of the same thing, mass- energy.

"This is not possible!" we cry. "It is nonsense to think that increasing the velocity of an object increases its mass, decreases its length, and slows its time."

Our cup runneth over.

These phenomena are not observable in everyday life because the velocities required to make them noticeable are those approaching the speed of light (186,000 miles per *second*). At the slow speeds that we encounter in the macroscopic world, these effects are virtually unde-tectable. If they were, we would discover that a car traveling down the freeway is shorter than it is at rest, weighs more than it does at rest, and that its clock runs slower than it does at rest. In fact, we even would find that a hot iron weighs more than a cold one (because energy has mass and heat is energy).

How Einstein discovered all of this is another version of "The Emperor's New Clothes."

Only Albert Einstein looked at two of the major puzzles of his day and saw them with a beginner's mind. The result was the special theory of relativity. The first puzzle of Einstein's time was the constancy of the speed of light. The second puzzle of Einstein's time was the uncertainty, both physical and philosophical, about what it means to be moving or not moving. *

"Wait a minute," we say. "What is uncertain about that? If I am sitting in a chair and another person walks past me, then the person walking past me is in motion, and I, sitting in my chair, am not in motion."

"Quite right," says Jim de Wit, appearing on cue, "but still, it is not that simple. Suppose that the chair in which you are sitting is on an airplane and that the person walking past you is a stewardess. Suppose also that I am on the ground watching both of you go by. From your point of view, you are at rest and the stewardess is in motion, but from my point of view, I am at rest and *both* of you are in motion. It all depends upon your frame of reference. Your frame of reference is the airplane, but my frame of reference is the earth."

De Wit, as usual, has discovered the problem exactly. Unfortunately, he has not solved it. The earth itself hardly is standing still. Not only is it spinning on its axis like a top, it and the moon are revolving around a common center of gravity while both of them circle the sun at eighteen miles per second.

"That's not fair," we say. "Of course, it is true, but the earth does not seem to be moving to us who live on it. It is only in motion if we change our frame of reference from it to the sun. If we start playing that game, it is impossible to find anything in the entire universe that is

*Einstein's point of departure for the special theory of relativity came from the conflict of classical relativity and Maxwell's prediction of a light speed, "c." An often-told story tells how Einstein tried to imagine what it would be like to travel as fast as a light wave. He saw, for example, that the hands on a clock would appear to stand still, since no other light waves from the clock would be able to catch up with him until he slowed down.

'standing still.' From the point of view of the galaxy, the sun is moving; from the point of view of another galaxy, our galaxy is moving; from the point of view of a third galaxy, the first two galaxies are moving. In fact, from the point of view of each of them, the others are moving."

"Nicely said," laughs Jim de Wit, "and that is exactly the point. There is no such thing as something being absolutely at rest, unequivocally not moving. Motion, and the lack of it, is always relative to something else. Whether we are moving or not depends upon what frame of reference we use."

The discussion above is *not* the special theory of relativity. In fact, the discussion above is a part of the Galilean relativity principle which is over three hundred years old. Any physical theory is a theory of relativity if, like Jim de Wit, it acknowledges the difficulty of detecting absolute motion or absolute nonmotion. A theory of relativity assumes that the only kind of motion that we ever can determine is motion, or lack of it, relative to something else. Galileo's principle of relativity says, in addition, that the laws of mechanics are equally valid in all frames of reference (physicists say "co-ordinate systems") that move uniformly in relation to each other.

The Galilean relativity principle assumes that somewhere in the universe there exists a frame of reference in which the laws of mechanics are completely valid—that is, a frame of reference in which experiment and theory agree perfectly. This frame of reference is called an "inertial" frame of reference. An inertial frame of reference simply means a frame of reference in which the laws of mechanics are completely valid. All other frames of reference moving uniformly, relative to an inertial frame of reference, are also inertial frames of reference. Since the laws of mechanics are equally valid in all inertial frames of reference, this means that there is no way that we can distinguish between one inertial frame of reference and another by performing mechanical experiments in them.

Frames of reference moving uniformly, relative to each other, are co-ordinate systems that move with a constant speed and direction. In other words, they are frames of reference that move with a constant velocity. For example, if, by accident, we drop a book while standing in line at the library, the book falls directly downward in accordance with Newton's law of gravity, and strikes the ground directly beneath the place from which it was dropped. Our frame of reference is the earth. The earth is moving at a fantastic speed on its trip around the sun, but this speed is constant.*

If we drop the same book while we are traveling on an ideally smooth train which is moving at a constant speed, the same thing happens. The book falls directly downward in accordance with Newton's laws of gravitation, and strikes the floor of the train directly beneath the place from which it was dropped. This time, our frame of reference is the train. Because the train is moving uniformly, with no increases or decreases of speed, in relation to the earth, and because the earth is moving in a similar manner in relation to the train, the two frames of reference are moving uniformly relative to each other, and the laws of mechanics are valid in both of them. It does not matter in the least which of the frames of reference is "moving." A person in either frame of reference can consider himself moving and the other frame of reference at rest (the earth is at rest and the train is moving) or the other way round (the train is at rest and the earth is moving). From the point of view of physics, there is no difference.

What happens if the engineer suddenly accelerates while we are doing our experiment? Then, of course, everything is upset. The falling book still will strike the floor of the train, but at a spot farther back since the floor of the train has moved forward beneath the book while it was falling. In this case, the train is not moving uniformly in relation to the earth, and the Galilean relativity principle does not apply.

Provided that all of the motion involved is uniformly relative, we can translate motion as perceived in one frame of reference into another frame of reference. For example, suppose that we are standing on the shore watching a ship move past us at thirty miles per hour. The ship is a frame of reference moving uniformly relative to us. There is a passenger, a man, standing on the deck of the ship, leaning against the railing. Since he is standing still, his velocity is the same as that of the ship, thirty miles per hour. (From his point of view, we are moving past *him* at thirty miles per hour).

* Although we do not experience it directly, the orbital motion of the earth is accelerating.

Suppose now that the man begins to walk toward the front of the ship at three miles per hour. His velocity now, relative to us, is thirty-three miles per hour. The ship carries him forward at thirty miles per hour, and his walking adds three miles per hour to that. (You get to the top of an escalator faster if you walk.)

Suppose that the man turns around and walks back toward the rear of the ship. His velocity relative to the ship is, again, three miles per hour, but his velocity relative to the shore is now twenty-seven miles per hour.

In other words, to calculate how fast this passenger moves relative to us, we add his velocity to the velocity of his co-ordinate system (the ship) if he is walking in the same direction that it is moving, and we subtract his velocity from the velocity of his co-ordinate system if he is walking in the opposite direction. This calculation is called a classical (Galilean) transformation. Knowing the uniform relative motion of our two frames of reference, we can transform the passenger's velocity in reference to his own co-ordinate system (three miles per hour) into his velocity in reference to our co-ordinate system (thirty-three miles per hour).

The freeway provides abundant examples of classical transformations from one frame of reference to another. Suppose that we are driving at 75 miles per hour. We see a truck coming toward us. Its speedometer also reads 75 miles per hour. Making a classical transformation, we can say that, relative to us, the truck is approaching at 150 miles per hour, which explains why head-on collisions so often are fatal.

Suppose now that a car going in the same direction that we are going passes us. His speedometer reads 110 miles per hour (it's a Ferrari). Again, making a classical transformation, we can say that, relative to us, the Ferrari is departing our location at 35 miles per hour.

The transformation laws of classical mechanics are common sense. They say that, even though we cannot determine whether a frame of reference is absolutely at rest or not, we can translate velocities (and positions) from one frame of reference into velocities (and positions) in other frames of reference, provided that the frames of reference are moving uniformly, relative to each other. Furthermore, the Galilean relativity principle, from which Galilean transformations come, says that if the laws of mechanics are valid in any one frame of reference, they also are valid in any other frame of reference moving uniformly relative to it.

Unfortunately, there is one catch in all this. No one yet has found a co-ordinate system in which the laws of mechanics are valid!*

"What! Impossible! Can't be!" we cry, aghast. "What about the earth?"

Well, it is true that Galileo, who first probed the laws of classical mechanics, used the earth as a frame of reference, although not consciously. (The idea of co-ordinate systems did not come along until Descartes). However, our present measuring devices are more accurate than Galileo's, who occasionally even used his pulse (which means that the more excited he got, the more inaccurate his measurements became!). Whenever we reconstruct Galileo's falling body experiments, we always find discrepancies between the theoretical results that we should get and the experimental results that we actually do get. These discrepancies are due to the rotation of the earth. The bitter truth is that the laws of mechanics are not valid for a co-ordinate system rigidly attached to the earth. The earth is *not* an inertial frame of reference. Since their very inception, the poor laws of classical mechanics have been left, so to speak, without a home. No one has discovered a co-ordinate system in which they manifest themselves perfectly.

This leaves us, from a physicist's point of view, in a pretty mess. On the one hand, we have the laws of classical mechanics, which are indispensable to physics, and, on the other hand, these same laws are predicated upon a co-ordinate system which may not even exist.

This problem is related to relativity, which is the problem of determining absolute nonmotion, in an intimate way. If such a thing as absolute nonmotion were detected, then a co-ordinate system attached to it would be the long-lost inertial frame of reference, the co-ordinate system in which the classical laws of mechanics are perfectly valid. Then everything would make sense again because, given a frame of reference in which the classical laws of mechanics are valid, *any* frame of

---

* The fixed stars provide such a reference frame as far as defining non-rotation.

reference, the classical laws of mechanics at last would have a permanent mailing address.

Physicists do not enjoy theories with loose ends. Before Einstein, the problem of detecting absolute motion (or absolute non- motion—if we find one, we find the other), and the problem of finding an inertial co-ordinate system were, to say the least, loose ends. The entire structure of classical mechanics was based on the fact that somewhere, somehow, there must be a frame of reference in which the laws of classical mechanics are valid. The inability of physicists to find it made classical mechanics appear exactly like a huge castle built on sand.

Although no one, including Einstein, discovered absolute non-motion, the inability to detect it was a major concern of Einstein's day. The second major controversy of Einstein's day (not counting Planck's discovery of the quantum) was an incomprehensible, logic- defying characteristic of light.

In the course of their experiments with the speed of light, physicists discovered something very strange. The speed of light disregards the transformation laws of classical mechanics. Of course, that's impossible, but nevertheless, experiment after experiment proved just the opposite. The speed of light just happens to be the most nonsensical thing ever discovered. That is because it never changes.

"So light always travels at the same speed," we ask, "what's so strange about that?"

"Oh my, oh my," says a distraught physicist, circa 1887, "you simply don't understand the problem. The problem is that no matter what the circumstances of the measurement, no matter what the motion of the observer, the speed of light *always* measures 186,000 miles per second."*

"Is this bad?" we say, beginning to sense that something *is* strange here.

"Worse," says the physicist. "It's impossible. Look," he tells us, trying to calm himself, "suppose that we are standing still and that somewhere in front of us is a light bulb that also is standing still. The

---

* In a vacuum. The speed of light changes in matter depending upon the index of refraction of the matter: $c_{matter} = c \div$ index of refraction.

light bulb flashes on and off and we measure the velocity of the light that comes from it. What do you suppose that velocity will be?"

"186,000 miles per second," we answer, "the speed of light."

"Correct!" says the physicist, with a knowing look that makes us uncomfortable. "Now, suppose the light bulb still is standing still, but we are moving toward it at 100,000 miles per second. Now what will we measure the speed of the light to be?"

"286,000 miles per second," we answer, "the speed of light »(186,000 miles per second) plus our speed (100,000 miles per second)." (This is a typical example of a classical transformation.)

"Wrong!" shouts the physicist. "That's just the point. *The speed of the light is still 186,000 miles per second.*"

"Wait a minute," we say. "That can't be. You say that if the light bulb is at rest and we are at rest, the speed of photons emitted from it will measure the same to us as the speed of photons emitted from it when we are rushing toward the light bulb? That doesn't make sense. When the photons are emitted, they are traveling at 186,000 miles per second. If we also are moving, and moving toward them, their velocity should measure that much faster. In fact, they should appear to be traveling with the speed at which they were emitted *plus* our speed. Their velocity should measure 186,000 miles per second plus 100,000 miles per second."

"True," says our friend, "but it doesn't. It measures 186,000 miles per second, just as if we still were standing still."

Pausing for that to sink in, he continues, "Now consider the opposite situation. Suppose that the light bulb still is standing still, and this time we are moving *away* from it at 100,000 miles per second. What will the velocity of the photons measure now?"

"86,000 miles per second?" we say, hopefully, "the speed of light minus our speed as we move away from the approaching photons?"

"Wrong, again!" exclaims our friend again. "It should, but it doesn't. The speed of the photons still measures 186,000 miles per second."

"This is very hard to believe. Do you mean that if a light bulb is at rest and we measure the speed of the photons emitted from it while we also are at rest, and if we then measure the speed of the photons from it while we are moving toward it, and lastly, if we measure the speed of the photons emitted from it while we are moving away from it, we get *the same result in* all three cases?"

"Exactly!" says the physicist. "186,000 miles per second."*

"Do you have any evidence?" we ask him.

"Unfortunately," he says, "I do. Two American physicists, Albert Michelson and Edward Morley, have just completed an experiment which seems to show that the speed of light is constant, regardless of the state of motion of the observer.

"This can't happen," he sighs, "but it *is* happening. It just doesn't make sense."

The problem of absolute nonmotion and the problem of the constancy of the speed of light converged in the Michelson-Morley experiment. The Michelson-Morley experiment (1887) was a crucial experiment. A crucial experiment is an experiment which determines the life or death of a scientific theory. The theory that was tested by the Michelson-Morley experiment was the theory of the ether.

The theory of the ether was that the entire universe lies in and is permeated by an invisible, tasteless, odorless substance that has no properties at all, and exists simply because it has to exist so that light waves can have something to propagate in. For light to travel as waves, according to the theory, something has to be waving. That something was the ether. The theory of the ether was the last attempt to explain the universe by explaining *something*. Interpreting the universe in terms of things (like the Great Machine idea) was the distinguishing characteristic of the mechanical view, which means all of physics from Newton until the middle 1800s.

The ether, according to the theory, is everywhere and in everything. We live and perform our experiments in a sea of ether. To the ether, the hardest substance is as porous as a sponge to water. There are no

---

* The reverse situation (the source moves and the observer remains stationary) is explainable in terms of prerelativistic physics. In fact, if light is assumed to be a wave phenomenon governed by a wave equation, it is expected that its measured velocity will be independent of the velocity of its source. The velocity of the sound waves reaching us from a jet plane, for example, does not depend upon the velocity of the aircraft. They propagate through a medium (the atmosphere) at a given velocity, from their point of origin, regardless of the motion of the plane (the frequency of the sound shifts as the source moves, e.g., the Doppler effect). Prerelativity theory assumes a medium (like the atmosphere, for sound waves, or the ether, for light waves) through which the waves propagate. The paradox is that the measured velocity of light has been found (the Michelson-Morley experiment) to be independent of the motion of the observer. In other words, assuming a light wave propagating through a medium, how can we move through the same medium toward the approaching wave without increasing its measured velocity?

doors to the ether. Although we move in the ether sea, the ether sea does not move. It is absolutely, unequivocally not moving.

Therefore, although the primary reason for the existence of the ether was to give light something to propagate through, its existence also solved the old problem of locating the original inertial coordinate system, that frame of reference in which the laws of mechanics are completely valid. If the ether existed (and it *had* to exist), the co-ordinate system attached to it was *the* co-ordinate system against which all others could be compared to see if they were moving or not.

The findings of Michelson and Morley gave a verdict of death to the theory of the ether.* Equally important, they led to the mathematical foundations of Einstein's revolutionary new theory.

The idea of the Michelson-Morley experiment was to determine the motion of the earth through the ether sea. The problem was how to do this. Two ships at sea can determine their motion relative to one another, but if only one ship moves through a smooth sea, it has no reference point against which to measure its progress. In the old days, seamen would throw a log overboard and measure their progress relative to it. Michelson and Morley did the same thing, except that the log that they threw overboard was a beam of light.

Their experiment was conceptually simple and ingenious. If the earth is moving, they reasoned, and the ether sea is at rest, then the movement of the earth through the ether sea must cause an ether breeze. Therefore, a beam of light traveling against the ether breeze should have a slower velocity than a beam of light sent across the ether breeze. This is the essence of the Michelson-Morley experiment.

Every pilot knows that it takes longer to fly a given distance if one leg of the trip is against a head wind (even though the return leg is with a tail wind) than it takes to fly the same distance across the same wind. Similarly, thought Michelson and Morley, if the theory of the ether sea is correct, a light beam sent upstream against the ether breeze and then downstream with it will take longer to return to its starting point than a light beam sent back and forth across the either breeze.

To establish and detect this difference in velocity, Michelson and Morley created a device called an interferometer (from the word

---

* Quantum field theory resurrects a new kind of ether, e.g., particles are excited states of the featureless ground state of the field (the vacuum state). The vacuum state is so featureless and has such high symmetry that we cannot assign a velocity to it experimentally.

"interference"). It was designed to detect the interference pattern created by the two beams of light as they returned to a common point. (A diagram is on the next page.)

A light source emits a beam of light toward a half-silvered mirror (similar to the lenses in sunglasses that look like a mirror on one side, but are transparent from the other side). The original beam of light ($\Longrightarrow$) is split by the half-silvered mirror into two segments ($\longrightarrow$) ($- - - \rightarrow$), each of which travels an equal distance, but at right angles to each other, and back again. The two beams then reunite via the same half-silvered mirror and travel ($\Longrightarrow$) into a measuring device. By observing the interference created by these converging beams in the measuring device, any difference in velocity between them can be determined accurately.

When the experiment was performed, not the slightest difference in velocity could be detected between the two beams of light. The interferometer was turned 90 degrees so that the beam going against

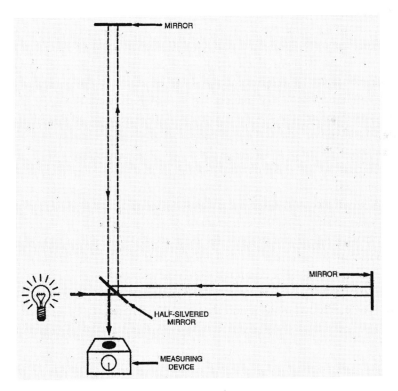

the ether wind now was directed across it, and the beam going across the ether wind now was sent directly into it. Again not the slightest difference in velocity between the two beams could be detected.

In other words, the Michelson-Morley experiment had failed to prove the existence of the ether. Unless an explanation could be found, physicists would be faced with choosing between two unsetding alternatives: either (1) the earth is not moving (and Copernicus was wrong), or (2) the ether does not exist. Neither of these was very acceptable.

Michelson and Morley thought that perhaps the earth carried a layer of ether with it as it moved through the ether set, just as it carries its atmosphere with it as it travels through space and, therefore, close to the surface of the earth, the ether breeze cannot be detected. No one had a better hypothesis until an Irishman named George Francis FitzGerald proposed (in 1892) an outrageous explanation.

FitzGerald reasoned that perhaps the pressure of the ether wind compresses matter just as an elastic object moving through water becomes shortened in the direction that it is traveling. If this were true, then the arm of the interferometer pointing into the ether wind would be somewhat shorter than the arm that is not pointing into it. Therefore, a reduction in the velocity of the light traveling into the ether wind and back might not be detected because the distance that the light travels also is reduced. In fact, if the amount by which the interferometer arm pointing into the ether wind is shortened just corresponds to the amount by which the velocity of the light traveling up that arm and back is reduced, then both beams of light in the experiment will reach the measuring device at exactly the same time (the beam with the higher velocity traversing a greater distance in the same time that the beam with the slower velocity traverses a lesser distance).

FitzGerald's hypothesis had a major advantage over all the others. It was impossible to disprove. It said simply that there is a one-dimensional contraction (in the direction of motion) that increases as velocity increases. The catch is that *everything* contracts. If we want to measure the length of an object that is moving very fast compared to the speed of light, we have to catch up with it first, and when we do, according to the theory, the measuring stick that we are carrying with us also contracts. If the object measured seventeen inches at rest, it still would measure seventeen inches. Nor would anything look contracted because the lenses in our eyes also would contract, distorting them just enough to make everything look normal.

One year later a Dutch physicist, Hendrik Antoon Lorentz, while working on another problem, independently arrived at FitzGerald's hypothesis. Lorentz, however, expressed his discovery in rigorous mathematical terms. This, of course, upgraded FitzGerald's hypothesis to a position of respectability and it began to gain a surprising degree of acceptance, considering its fantasy-like quality. Lorentz's mathematical formulations of the FitzGerald-Lorentz contraction became known as the Lorentz transformations.

The stage was now set. All of the scenery was in place. The failure to detect the ether. The Michelson-Morley experiment.* The constancy of the speed of light. The FitzGerald-Lorentz contractions. The Lorentz transformations. These are the facts that continued to confuse physicists at the beginning of the century. All of them but Albert Einstein. When he looked at these pieces of scenery, what his beginner's mind saw was the special theory of relativity.

SPECIAL NONSENSE

Einstein's first professional act, upon reviewing the facts, was the equivalent of saying, "But the Emperor's not wearing any clothes!" except what he said was, "The ether does not exist."[1] The first message of the special theory of relativity is that since the ether is undetectable and, in effect, useless, there is no reason to continue to search for it. It is undetectable because every attempt to measure it or determine its quality, culminating with the Michelson-Morley experiment, failed utterly even to indicate its presence. It is useless because light propagation can be envisioned as the propagation of energy through *empty space (in vacuo)* according to Maxwell's field equations as well as it can be

---

* It is said that the reasoning process by which Einstein discovered the special theory of relativity did not include the results of the Michelson-Morley experiment. However, the results of this well-publicized experiment were "in the air" for eighteen years prior to Einstein's paper on special relativity (1905) and they led to the Lorentz transformations which became central to the mathematical formalism of special relativity.

envisioned as a disturbance of the ether medium. Einstein stated clearly what already was implicit in Maxwell's equations. (Maxwell was the discoverer of the electromagnetic field.) "The electromagnetic fields," he wrote, "are not states of a medium [the ether] and are not bound down to any bearer, but they are independent realities which are not reducible to anything else . . ."[2] This assertion was supported by the inability of physicists to detect the ether.

With this statement, Einstein brought to a close the illustrious history of mechanics, the idea that physical events are explicable in terms of things. Classical mechanics is the story of objects and forces between them. It was a remarkable break from a three-century-old tradition to assert blatantly, in the early 1900s, that electromagnetic fields involve no object whatever, that they are not states of the ether medium, but "ultimate, irreducible realities"[3] in themselves. Henceforth, as in quantum mechanics, there would be no concrete imagery associated with physical theory.

Both relativity and quantum theory heralded the unprecedented remoteness from experience which has characterized physical theory ever since. In fact, the trend is continuing. As though governed by an inexorable law, physics is becoming more and more abstract as it covers wider and wider tracts of experience. Only the future will tell if this trend is reversible.

The second victim of Einstein's inability to see clothes that weren't there was absolute nonmotion. Why should we make one particular frame of reference "privileged"[4] in respect to all others by saying that it alone absolutely is not moving? It may be desirable theoretically, but since such a frame of reference does not constitute a part of our experience, it should be disregarded. It is "intolerable"[5] to place in a theoretical structure a characteristic which has no corresponding characteristic in our system of experience.

In one stroke, Einstein eliminated the two major physical and philosophical blocks to a radically new way of perceiving reality. With no ether and no concept of absolute motion to confuse the situation, the situation became much simpler.

Einstein's next step was to confront the puzzle which had come to light (no pun) in the Michelson-Morley experiment, namely, the constancy of the speed of light. How could the speed of light *always* be 186,000 miles per second regardless of the state of motion of the observer?

In an ingenious mental turnaround, Einstein turned this puzzle into a postulate! Instead of worrying, for the moment, about how it can happen, he simply accepted the experimentally irrefutable fact that it *does* happen. This evident (to us) recognition of the obvious was the first step in a logical process, which, once set in motion, was to explain not only the puzzle of the constant speed of light, but a great deal more.

The puzzle of the constancy of the velocity of light became the principle of the constancy of the velocity of light. The principle of the constancy of the velocity of light is the first foundation stone of the special theory of relativity.

The principle of the constancy of the velocity of light is that whenever we make a measurement of the velocity of light, regardless of whether we are in motion or at rest relative to the light source, we always get the same result. The speed of light is invariably 186,000 miles per second.* This is what Michelson and Morley discovered in their famous experiment.

From the point of view of classical mechanics, the principle of the constancy of the velocity of light makes no sense at all. In fact, it conflicts violently with common sense. Before Einstein, the totalitarian grasp of "common sense" held the constancy of the speed of light to the status of a paradox. (Whenever we bump into the limits of our self-imposed cognitive reality, the result is always paradox.) It took a pure beginner's mind, such as Albert Einstein's, to accept that if what is, is (the constancy of the velocity of light), then *common sense must be wrong.*

The most important victim of Einstein's beginner's mind was the whole structure of classical (Galilean) transformations, that sweet but illusory fruit of a common sense anchored in macroscopic dimensions and velocities. To give up common sense is not an easy task. Einstein was the first person to do it in such a wholesale manner that his perception of the very nature of space and time changed radically. More-

---

* In a vacuum. The speed of light changes in matter depending upon the index of refraction of the matter.

over, when all was said and done, Einstein's vision of space and time turned out to be more useful than that of common sense.

The second foundation stone of the special theory of relativity is the principle of relativity. When Einstein dismissed the idea of absolute nonmotion, his theory became, *ipso facto,* a theory of relativity. Since there was no better principle of relativity to be had than Galileo's, Einstein simply borrowed it, but first, of course, he brought it up to date.

Galileo's principle of relativity says that the laws of mechanics (such as the laws governing falling bodies) that are valid in one frame of reference are valid in all frames of reference that move uniformly (without jerkiness) in relation to it. Another way of saying the same thing is that it is impossible to determine, by doing experiments involving the laws of mechanics, whether or not our frame of reference is moving or at rest in relation to another frame of reference in which the laws of mechanics also are valid.

Einstein expanded the Galilean relativity principle to include *all* the laws of physics, and not just the laws of classical mechanics. In particular he included the laws governing electromagnetic radiation, which were unknown in Galileo's time.

Einstein's updated principle of relativity, then, is that all the laws of nature are exactly identical in all frames of references that move uniformly relative to each other and that, therefore, there is no way of distinguishing absolute uniform motion (or nonmotion).

In short, the two foundation stones of the special theory of relativity are the principle of the constancy of the velocity of light (the Michelson-Morley experiment) and the principle of relativity (Galileo). Said more specifically, the special theory of relativity rests upon these two postulates:

(1) The velocity of light in a vacuum is the same in all frames of reference (for all observers) moving uniformly, relative to each other, and

(2) All laws of nature are the same in all frames of reference moving uniformly, relative to each other.

Of these two postulates, the first one, the principle of the constancy of the velocity of light, is the troublemaker. There is no way that it and the classical transformation laws both can be true. According to the classical transformation laws (and common sense) the speed of light must be its velocity as it is emitted from a source plus or minus the velocity of the observer, if the observer is moving toward the source or away from the source. According to experiment, the speed of light remains constant regardless of the state of motion of the observer. Common sense and experimental findings are in violent disagreement.

Einstein's beginner's mind told him that, since we cannot argue with what is (the experimental evidence), then our common sense must be wrong. With this decision to disregard common sense and to base his new theory on the only clothes he could see that the emperor *was* wearing (the constant speed of light and the principle of relativity) Einstein stepped boldly into the unknown, in fact, into the unimaginable. Already on new territory, he proceeded to explore where no person had gone before.

How could it be that to every observer the speed of light is the same regardless of their state of motion? To measure speed, it is necessary to use a clock and ruler (a rigid rod). If the speed of light as measured by an observer at rest relative to a light source is the same as the speed of light as measured by an observer in motion relative to the source, then it must be that, somehow, *the measuring instruments* change from one frame of reference to the other in just such a way that the speed of light always appears to be the same.

The speed of light appears constant because the rods and clocks used to measure it vary from one frame of reference to another depending upon their *motion*. In short, to an observer at rest, a moving rod changes its length and a moving clock changes its rhythm. At the same time, to an observer traveling along with a moving rod and clock, there is no apparent change at all in length or rhythm. Therefore, both observers measure the speed of light to be the same, and neither can detect anything unusual in the measurement or in the measuring apparatus.

This is very similar to the case of the Michelson-Morley experiment. According to FitzGerald and Lorentz, the arm of the interferometer that faces into the ether wind (now dismissed from our theory) is shortened by the pressure of the ether wind. Therefore, the light that travels the interferometer arm facing into the "ether wind" has less distance to travel and more time to do it in than does the light traveling the other arm. As a result, the speed of light traveling both arms appears to be the same. This is what the Lorentz transformations describe. Come to think of it, *the Lorentz transformations can be used to describe contractions due to motion* as well as contractions due to a fictitious ether wind.

FitzGerald and Lorentz imagined that rigid rods were compressed under the pressure of the ether wind, but according to Einstein, it is *motion itself* that causes contraction, and, in addition, time dilation.

Here is another way of looking at it. A "constant velocity of light" is exactly what would result if moving measuring rods became shorter and moving clocks ran more slowly because a moving observer would measure the speed of light with a shorter measuring rod (less distance for the light to travel) and a slower clock (more time to do it in) than an observer at rest. Each observer, however, would consider his own rod and clock to be quite normal and unimpaired. Therefore, both observers would find the speed of light to be 186,000 miles per second and both of them would be puzzled by this fact if they were still bound by the classical transformation laws.

These were the initial fruits of Einstein's basic assumptions (the principle of the constancy of the velocity of light and the principle of relativity): First, a moving object appears to contract in its direction of motion and become shorter as its velocity increases until, at the speed of light, it disappears altogether. Second, a moving clock runs more slowly than a clock at rest and continues to slow its rhythm as its velocity increases until, at the speed of light, it stops running altogether.

These effects only appear to a "stationary" observer; one who is at rest relative to the moving clock and rod. They do not appear to an observer who is traveling along with the clock and rod. To make this clear, Einstein introduced the labels "proper" and "relative." What we see when we observe our stationary rod and our stationary clock, if we ourselves are stationary, is their *proper* length and *proper* time. ("Proper" means "one's own.") Proper lengths and proper times always appear normal. What we see if we are stationary and observe a rod and a clock traveling very fast relative to us is the *relative* length of the moving rod and the *relative* time of the moving clock. The relative length is always shorter than the proper length, and the relative time is always slower than the proper time.

The time that you see on your own watch is your proper time, and the time that you see on the watch of the person moving past you is the relative time (which appears to you—not to the person moving past you—to run more slowly). The length of the measuring rod in your own hand is its proper length, and the length of the measuring rod in the hand of the person moving past you is its relative length (which appears to you—but not to the other person—to be shorter). From the point of view of the person moving past you, he is at rest, you are moving, and the situation is reversed.

Suppose that we are aboard a spacecraft outward bound on an exploration. We have made arrangements to press a button every fifteen minutes to send a signal back to earth. As our speed steadily increases our earthbound colleagues notice that instead of every fifteen minutes, our signals begin to arrive seventeen minutes apart, and then twenty-five minutes apart. After several days, our colleagues, to their distress, find that our signals arrive every two days. As our velocity continues to increase our signals become years apart. Eventually, generations of earthlings come and go between our signals.

Meanwhile, on the spacecraft, we are entirely unaware of the predicament back on earth. As far as we are concerned, everything is proceeding according to plan, although we are becoming bored with the routine of pressing a button every fifteen minutes. When we return to earth, a few years older (our proper time) we may find that we have been gone, according to earth time, for centuries (their relative time). Exactly how long depends upon how fast we have been going.

This scene is not science fiction. It is based upon a well-known (to physicists) phenomenon called the Twin Paradox of the special theory of relativity. Part of the paradox is that one twin remains on earth while the other goes on a space voyage and returns younger than his brother.

There are many examples of proper time and relative time. Suppose that we are in a space station observing an astronaut who is traveling at a speed of 161,000 miles per second relative to us. As we watch him, we notice a certain sluggishness in his movements, as though he were moving in slow motion. We also notice that everything in his spaceship also seems to function in slow motion. His rolled cigarette, for example, lasts twice as long as one of ours.

Of course, part of his sluggishness is due to the fact that he is fast increasing the distance between us, and with each passing moment, it takes the light from his spaceship longer to reach us. Nonetheless, after making allowances for the travel time of the light involved, we find that the astronaut still is moving more slowly than usual.

However, to the astronaut, it is we who are zipping past him at 161,000 miles per second, and after he makes all the necessary allowances, he finds that it is we who are sluggish. Our cigarette lasts twice as long as his.

This situation could be the ultimate illustration of how the grass is always greener on the other side. Each man's cigarette lasts twice as long as the other's. (Unfortunately, so does each man's trip to the dentist.)

The time that we ourselves experience and measure is our proper time. Our cigarette lasts the normal length of time. The time that we measure for the astronaut is the relative time. His cigarette appears to last twice as long as ours because his time passes twice as slowly. The situation is similar regarding proper lengths and relative lengths. From our point of view, the astronaut's cigarette, provided that it is pointing in the direction that his spaceship is moving, is shorter than our own cigarette.

The other side of the coin is that the astronaut sees himself as stationary and his cigarettes as normal. He also sees us as traveling at 161,000 miles per second relative to him, and our cigarettes as shorter than his and slower burning.

Einstein's theory has been substantiated in many ways. All of them verify it with awesome accuracy.

The most common verifications of time dilation come from high-energy particle physics. A very light elementary particle, called a muon (pronounced moo'on), is created at the top of the earth's atmosphere by the collision of protons (one form of "cosmic radiation") and air molecules. We know from experiments in which muons are created in accelerators that they live a very short time. By no means do they live long enough to reach the earth from the upper atmosphere. Long before the time it takes to traverse this distance, they should decay spontaneously into other types of particles. Yet this does not happen because we detect them in abundance here at the earth's surface.

Why do the muons created by cosmic radiation live longer, in fact, *seven times longer* than those muons created in the laboratory? The answer is that the muons produced by collisions of cosmic radiation and air molecules travel much faster than any muons that we can create experimentally. Their velocity is approximately 99 percent of the speed of light. At that speed, time dilation is quite noticeable. They do not live longer than usual from *their* point of view, but from our point of view they live seven times longer than they would at slower velocities.

This is true not only of muons, but of almost all subatomic particles, and there are many of them. For example, pions (pie'ons), another type of subatomic particle, which move at 80 percent of the speed of light, live, on the average, 1.67 times as long as slow pions. The special theory of relativity tells us that the intrinsic lifetime of these high-speed particles does not increase, but that their relative rate of time flow slows down. The special theory of relativity also made the calculation of these phenomena possible long before we had the technical capability to create them.

In 1972, four of the most accurate atomic clocks available were put aboard an aircraft: and flown around the world. At the end of the trip, they were found to be slightly behind their stationary, earth- bound counterparts with which they were synchronized before the flight.* The next time that you fly, remember that, even if minutely, your watch is running slower, your body had more mass, and, if you stand facing the cockpit, you are thinner.

According to the special theory of relativity, a moving object appears to contract in the direction of motion as its velocity increases. James Terrell, a physicist, has demonstrated mathematically that this phenomenon is something like a visual illusion, and, in fact, is analogous to a projection of the real world onto the wall of Plato's cave.[6]

Plato's famous parable of the cave describes a group of people who are chained inside a cave in such a way that they can see only the shadows on the wall of the cave. These shadows are the only world that these people know. One day one of these people escapes into the

---

* The clocks were flown around the world each way (east and west). Both general relativistic and special relativistic effects were noted. (J. C. Hafele and R. E. Keating, Science, vol. 177, 1972, pp. 168ff.)

world outside the cave. At first he is blinded by the sunlight, but when he recovers, he realizes that *this* is the real world, and what he previously considered to be the real world was, in fact, only the projection of the real world onto the wall of the cave. (Unfortunately, when he returned to the people who still were chained inside the cave, they thought he was mad.)

Figure A, on the next page, depicts a view looking down on the top of our head and the top of a sphere. The lines connect our eyes with points on either side of the sphere. If we are far enough away from the sphere, the distance between these points is almost equal to the diameter of the sphere. Figure A is drawn as if the artist were looking down on the top of our head, our eyes, and the sphere.

The first step in Terrell's explanation is to draw lines downward (back into the page) from each of the two points on the sphere to a screen directly below the sphere. Figure B is a side view showing the two points, the lines that we have drawn downward, and the screen. (If you hold this book directly in front of you, your eyes are in the same position relative to the dotted lines as the eyes drawn in Figure A.)

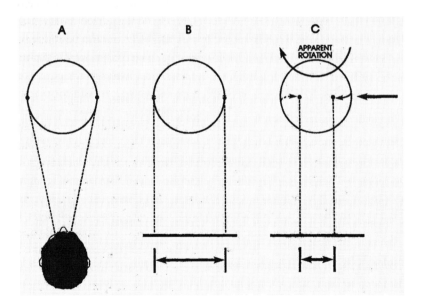

To understand Terrell's explanation, suppose that the sphere is moving *very fast* relative to the speed of light from right to left. If the sphere moves fast enough, some very interesting things happen. For example, before the light from the point on the far left edge of the sphere can reach us, the ball moves in front of it, blocking it from our vision! The reverse happens on the far right. The ball moves out from between us and the light signals originating from points that used to be on the "back" side of the ball. These signals now are visible to us, while the signals coming from the point that used to be on the leading edge of the ball now are blocked by the ball itself as it moves to the left. The effect of this is an illusion of sorts. What we see is the same thing that we would see if someone had *rotated* the ball around its axis!

Look what happened to the distance between the two points as projected on the screen. It is considerably less than when we started. The equations in the special theory of relativity (the Lorentz transformations) which show a contraction due to motion describe these *projections*. (Is this beginning to sound like Plato's cave?)

The fact that the ball, by moving fast enough, gets in the way of some of its own light signals and out of the way of others causes the ball to appear to rotate. This causes the *projected* distance between any two points on it which are aligned with the direction of motion to decrease, just as if someone really had rotated the ball. The faster the ball moves, the more it appears to "rotate," and the closer together come the points projected on the screen. It is the projection that contracts. Instead of "screen" substitute "view of the ball from our frame of reference" and we have the Terrell explanation of relativistic contraction.

As yet, no analogous explanations have been found for the time dilation that accompanies moving clocks or the increase of mass that accompanies moving objects, but the effort, relatively speaking, is young.

The special theory of relativity shows that the mass of a moving object increases as the velocity of the object increases. Newton would not have hesitated to call this nonsense, but then Newton's experience was limited to velocities that are quite slow compared to the speed of light.

Classic physics tells us that a specific amount of force is required to increase the velocity of a moving object by a given amount, for example, one foot per second. Once we know what that amount of force is, whenever we want to increase the velocity of that particular object by one foot per second, all we need do is apply that amount of force to it. If the object has a velocity of 100 feet per second, that specific amount of force will increase its velocity to 101 feet per second. According to Newton's physics, the same amount of force that increases the velocity of an object from 100 feet per second to 101 feet per second also will increase the velocity of the same object from 8,000 feet per second to 8,001 feet per second.

The problem is that Newtonian physics is wrong. It takes much more force to increase by one foot per second the velocity of an object moving at 8,000 feet per second than it takes to increase by one foot per second the velocity of the same object moving at 100 feet per second.

That is because a faster-moving object has more kinetic energy (energy of motion). This additional energy makes it behave exactly as if it had more mass. A given amount of force applied for a given amount of time will accelerate a force applied for the same amount of time to an entire train. Of course, this is because an entire train has more mass than a single car.

When particles travel at velocities that are fast relative to the speed of light, their high kinetic energy makes them behave as though they have more mass than they have at lower velocities. In fact, the special theory of relativity shows that the effective mass of a moving object *does* increase with velocity.

Since most subatomic particles travel at different velocities, each one of them can have many different relative masses. Therefore, physicists have calculated the "rest mass" of each particle. The rest mass of a subatomic particle is its mass when it is not moving. Subatomic particles are never really at rest, but these calculations provide a uniform method of comparing their masses. This is necessary since, as the velocity of a particle approaches the speed of light, its relative mass depends upon how fast it is moving.

Einstein's discovery that moving clocks change their rhythm led to some spectacular revisions in the way that we see the world. It showed that there is no "universal" time that permeates the universe. There are only proper times associated with various observers. The proper time of each observer is different, unless two of them happen to be at rest relative to each other. If the universe has a heart beat, its rate depends upon the hearer.

The special theory of relativity shows that two events which happen at the same time in one frame of reference may occur at different times when seen from another frame of reference. To illustrate this point, Einstein used one of his famous thought experiments.

A thought experiment is a mental exercise. It has the advantage of requiring no apparatus other than the mind, which frees it from the practical limitations of laboratory experiments. Most physicists accept the use of thought experiments as a valid theoretical tool, provided they are satisfied that if the experiment could be performed, the results of the actual experiment would be the same as those of the thought experiment.

Suppose that we are in a moving room. The room is moving with a uniform velocity. Exactly in the center of the room is a light bulb which flashes periodically. The room is made of glass so that an outside observer can see what happens inside.

At the precise moment that we pass an outside observer, the light flashes. The question is, is there any difference between what we see inside the moving room and what the outsider observer sees? According to the special theory of relativity, the answer is an extraordinary, concept-shattering *Yes*. There is a big difference.

Inside the room, we see the bulb flash and we see the light spread out in all directions at the same speed. Since the walls of the room are equidistant from the bulb, we see the light strike the forward wall and rearward wall of the room simultaneously.

The outside observer also sees the flash, and he also sees the light propagate in all directions at the same speed. However, in addition, he sees that the room is moving. From his point of view the forward wall tries to escape the approaching light while the rearward wall rushes to meet it. Therefore, to the outside observer, the light reaches the rearward wall before it reaches the forward wall. If the speed of the room is small compared to the speed of light, the light reaches the rearward wall only slightly ahead of the forward wall. Nonetheless, the light reaches the rearward and forward walls in a one-two order, and not at the same time.

Although both of us observed the same two events, the light striking the forward wall and the light striking the rearward wall, we each have different stories to tell. To us, inside the room, the two events were simultaneous. To the outside observer, one event came first and the other event came later.

Einstein's revolutionary insight was that events which are simultaneous for one observer may occur at different times for another observer depending upon their relative motion. Put another way, two events, one of which occurs before the other as seen from the frame of reference of one observer, may occur at the same time when seen from the frame of reference of another observer. One observer uses the words "sooner" and "later." The other observer uses the word "simultaneous," even though both of them are describing the same two events.

In other words, "sooner," "later," and "simultaneous" are local terms. They have no meaning in the universe at large unless they are tied down to a specific frame of reference. What is "sooner" in one frame of reference may be "later" in another frame of reference and "simultaneous" in a third.*

The mathematics which translate what an observer in one frame of reference sees into what an observer in another frame of reference sees are the Lorentz transformations. Einstein adopted the Lorentz transformations—which are a set of equations—virtually intact.

No one before Einstein got these startling results from this simple type of thought experiment because no one before Einstein had the audacity to postulate something as outrageous as the principle of the constancy of the velocity of light. No one had the audacity to postulate something as outrageous as the principle of the constancy of the velocity

---

* This is only true for events that are space-like separated. For time-like separated events the relation earlier-later is preserved for all observers. Time-like separated events can never appear simultaneous in any frame of reference moving with a velocity less than c. (Space-like separation is explained later.)

of light because the principle of the constancy of the velocity of light completely and unequivocally contradicts common sense; specifically, common sense as represented by the classical transformation laws. The classical transformation laws are so embedded in our everyday experience that it simply never occurred to anybody to question them.

Even when the Michelson–Morley experiment produced results that were incompatible with the classical transformation laws, no beginner's mind but Einstein's conceived that the classical transformation laws might be wrong. Only Einstein suspected that at very high velocities, velocities far faster than those that we encounter through our senses, the classical transformation laws do not apply. This is not to say that they are incorrect. At low velocities (compared to 186,000 miles per second) contraction and time dilation are not detectable sensorily. In this limited situation, the classical transformations are a good guide for practical experience. After all, we do reach the top of an escalator faster if we walk.

If we do the moving-room experiment with sound instead of light, we do not get the special theory of relativity. We get a confirmation of the classical transformation laws. There is no principle of the constancy of the velocity of sound because the velocity of sound is not constant. It varies depending upon the motion of the observer (hearer) as dictated by common sense. The important word here is "dictated."

We live out our lives in a limited situation of low velocities where the speed of sound (about 700 miles per hour) seems "fast." Therefore, our common sense is based upon our experiences in this limited environment. If we want to expand our understanding beyond the limitations of this environment, it is necessary to drastically rearrange our conceptual constructs. This is what Einstein did. He was the first person to see that this is what had to be done in order to make sense of such impossible experimental findings as the constancy of the velocity of light for each and every person who measures it, regardless of their states of motion.

This led him to turn the puzzle of the constancy of the velocity of light into the principle of the constancy of the velocity of light. In turn, that led him to the conclusion that, if the velocity of light really is constant for all observers, then the measuring instruments used by different observers in different states of motion somehow must vary so that all of them give the same result. By a stroke of luck, Einstein discovered that these same variances were expressed in the equations of the Dutch physicist Hendrik Lorentz, and so he borrowed them. Lastly, the fact that moving clocks change their rhythm led Einstein to the inescapable conclusion that "now," "sooner," "later," and "simultaneous" are *relative* terms. They all depend upon the state of motion of the observer.

This conclusion is precisely the opposite of the assumption upon which Newtonian physics is based. Newton assumed, as did we all, that there is one clock ticking off the seconds by which the entire universe grows older. For every second of time that passes in this corner of the universe, one second of time passes also in every other corner of the universe.

According to Einstein, this is incorrect. How can anyone say when it is "now" throughout the universe? If we try to designate "now" by the occurrence of two simultaneous events (like my arrival at the doctor's office and my watch indicating 3 o'clock), we find that an observer in another frame of reference sees one of our events happening before the other. Absolute time, wrote Newton, "flows equably . . . ,"[7] but he was wrong. There is no single time which flows equally for all observers. There is no absolute time.

The existence of one ultimate flow of time throughout the physical universe, which we all tacitly acknowledged, turned out to be another piece of clothing that the Emperor wasn't wearing.

Newton made one more mistake in this regard. He said that time and space were separate. According to Einstein, time and space are not separate. Something cannot exist at some place without existing at some time, and neither can it exist at some time without existing at some place.

Most of us think of space and time as separate because that is the way that we think that we experience them. For example, we seem to have some control over our position in space, but none at all over our position in time. There is nothing that we can do about the flow of time. We can choose to stand perfectly still, in which case our position in space does not change, but there is no way that we can stand still in time.

This notwithstanding, there is something very elusive about "space" and especially about "time"; something that prevents us from "resting our accounts with them prematurely." Subjectively, time has a fluid quality which much resembles a running brook; sometimes bubbling past in a furious rush, sometimes slipping by quietly unnoticed, and sometimes lying languid, almost stationary, in deep pools. Space, too, has an ubiquitous quality about it which belies the common notion that it serves only to separate things.

William Blake's famous poem reaches out toward these intangible qualities:

> To see a World in a Grain of Sand
> And a Heaven in a Wild Flower,
> Hold Infinity in the palm of your hand
> And Eternity in an hour.

(Its title, by no coincidence is "Auguries of Innocence.")

The special theory of relativity is a physical theory. Its concern is with the mathematically calculable nature of reality. It is *not* a theory of subjectivity. Although it shows that the appearances of physical reality may vary from one frame of reference to another, it is a theory about the unchanging (physicists say "invariant") aspect of physical reality. Nonetheless, the special theory of relativity was the first mathematically rigorous physical theory to explore areas whose expression previously had been the domain of poets. Like any concise and poignant *re-presentation* of reality, the theories of relativity *are* poetry to mathematicians and physicists. However, Albert Einstein's enormous public renown perhaps was due in part to a shared intuition that he had something profoundly relevant to say about space and time.

What Einstein had to say about space and time is that there is no such thing as space *and* time; there is only space-time. Space-time is a continuum. A continuum is something whose parts are so close together, so "arbitrarily small," that the continuum really cannot be broken down into them. There are no breaks in a continuum. It is called a continuum because it flows continuously.

For example, a one-dimensional continuum is a line drawn on a wall. Theoretically we might say that the line is comprised of a series of points, but the points are each infinitely close to one another. The result is that the line flows continuously from one end of it to the other.

An example of a two-dimensional continuum is the wall. It has two dimensions, length and width. Similarly, all of the points on the wall are in contact with other points on the wall, and the wall itself is a continuous surface.

A three-dimensional continuum is what we commonly call "space." A pilot flying his airplane navigates in a three-dimensional continuum. To give his location he must state, for example, not only how far north and how far east of a given point he is, but he also must report his altitude. The airplane itself, like all things physical, is three- dimensional. It has a width, a height, and a depth. This is why mathematicians call our reality (their reality, too) three-dimensional.

According to Newtonian physics, our three-dimensional reality is separate from, and moves forward in, a one-dimensional time. Not so, says the special theory of relativity. Our reality is *four-dimensional,* and the fourth dimension is time. We live, breathe, and exist in a four-dimensional space-time continuum.

The Newtonian view of space and time is a *dynamic* picture. Events *develop* with the passage of time. Time is one-dimensional and *moves* (forward). The past, present, and future happen in that order. The special theory of relativity, however, says that it is preferable, and more useful, to think in terms of a *static,* nonmoving picture of space and time. This is the space-time continuum. In this static picture, the space-time continuum, events do not develop, they just are. If we could view our reality in a four-dimensional way, we would see that everything that now seems to unfold before us with the passing of time, already exists *in toto* painted, as it were, on the fabric of space-time. We would see all, the past, the present, and the future with one glance. Of course, this is only a mathematical proposition (isn't it?).

Don't worry about visualizing a four-dimensional world. Physicists can't do it, either. For the moment, just assume that Einstein might be right since the evidence so far suggests that he is. His message is that space and time are related in an intimate manner. For lack of a better way of saying it, he expressed this relationship by calling time a fourth dimension.

"Fourth dimension" is a translation from one language to another. The original language is mathematics and the second language is English. The problem is that there is simply no way of precisely expressing what the first language says in terms of the second language. Therefore, "time as a fourth dimension" is merely a label that we give to a *relationship*. The relationship in question is the relationship between space and time as it is expressed mathematically in the theories of relativity.

The relationship between space and time that Einstein discovered is similar to the relationship between the sides of a right triangle which Pythagoras the Greek (a contemporary of Confucius) discovered about 550 B.C.

A right triangle is a triangle that contains a right angle. A right angle is formed whenever two perpendicular lines intersect. Below is a right triangle. The side of a right triangle that is opposite the right angle is called the hypotenuse (hi pot′ n ōōs′). The hypotenuse is always the longest side of a right triangle.

Pythagoras discovered that as long as we know the length of the two shorter sides of a right triangle, we can calculate the length of the longest side. This relationship, expressed mathematically, is the Pythagorean theorem: The first leg squared plus the second leg squared equals the hypotenuse squared.

A hypotenuse of a given length can be calculated from many different combinations of shorter legs. In other words, there are many combinations of different-size legs that all calculate to have the same hypotenuse.

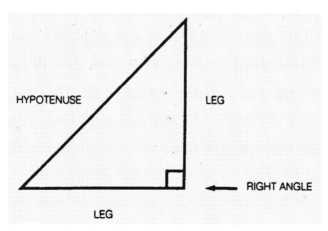

HYPOTENUSE   LEG

RIGHT ANGLE

LEG

For example, the first leg might be very short and the second leg very long.

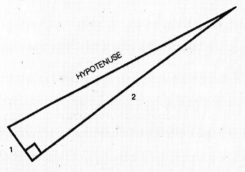

or the other way round,

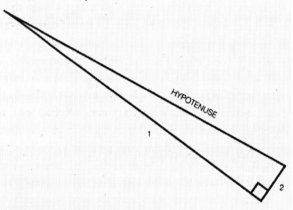

or anything in between.

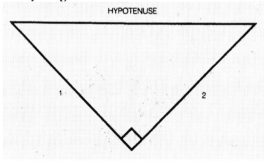

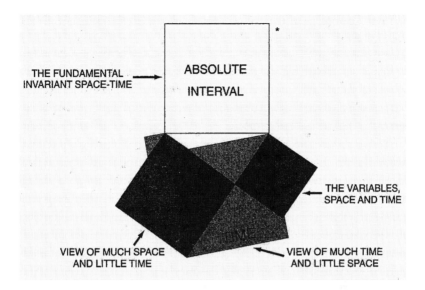

THE FUNDAMENTAL → ABSOLUTE
INVARIANT SPACE-TIME   INTERVAL

THE VARIABLES, ←
SPACE AND TIME

VIEW OF MUCH SPACE   VIEW OF MUCH TIME →
AND LITTLE TIME   AND LITTLE SPACE

If we substitute "space" for one of the legs of a right triangle, "time" for the other leg, and "space-time interval" for the hypotenuse, we have a relationship which is conceptually analogous to the relationship between space, time, and the space-time interval described in the special theory of relativity.* The space-time interval between two events is an absolute. It never varies. It can appear differently to observers in different states of motion, but it is, itself, invariant. The special theory of relativity shows how observers in different frames of reference can observe the same two events and calculate the space-time interval between them. The answer that all of the observers get will be the same.[†]

One observer may be in a state of motion such that for him there is a time and a distance involved between the two events, and another

---

* The Pythagorean theorem is c2 = a2 + b2. The equation for the space - time interval in the special theory of relativity is s2 = t2 − x2. The Pythagorean theorem describes properties in Euclidean space. The equation for the space-time interval describes properties in Minkowski's flat space-time (Euclidean and non- Euclidean space are discussed in the next chapter). There are other differences as well, but the fundamental relationship between space, time, and the space-time interval is very similar to the relationship expressed in the Pythagorean theorem between the three sides of a right triangle.

† Thanks to Guy Murchie who drew the original version of this drawing in his fine book, *Music of the Spheres,* New York, Dover, 1961.

observer may be in a state of motion such that his measuring devices indicate a different distance and a different time between the events, but the space-time interval between the two events does not vary. For example, the space-time interval, the absolute separation, between two exploding stars is the same whether it is viewed from a slow- moving frame of reference, like a planet, or from a fast-moving frame of reference, like a speeding rocket.

Let us return to our experiment with the moving glass room. Although we inside the room saw the light strike the rearward and forward walls simultaneously, the outside observer saw the light strike the rearward wall before it reached the forward wall. Nevertheless, by using a Pythagorean-like equation, into which we and the outside observer feed our time and distance measurements, we both get the same space-time interval between the events.

Actually, this Pythagorean-like relationship was the discovery of Einstein's mathematics teacher, Hermann Minkowski, who was inspired by his most famous student's special theory of relativity. In 1908 Minkowski announced his vision this way:

Henceforth space by itself, and time by itself, are doomed to fade away into mere shadows, and only a kind of union of the two will preserve an independent reality.[8]

Minkowski's mathematical explorations of space and time were both revolutionary and fascinating. Out of them came a simple diagram of space-time showing the mathematical relationship of the past, present, and the future. Of the wealth of information contained in this diagram, the most striking is that all of the past and all of the future, for each individual, meet and forever meet, at one single point, *now*. Furthermore, the *now* of each individual is specifically located and will never be found in any other place than *here* (wherever the observer is at).

Sixty-three years before Ram Dass's great book, *Be Here Now*, established the watchwords of the awareness movement, Hermann Minkowski proved that, in physical reality, no choice exists in the matter (pun?). Unfortunately for physicists, the realization is not always the experience. Nonetheless, after two thousand years of use in the East, being here now, the beginning step in meditation, received the validation of western science via Minkowski's rigorous mathematical confirmation of it, inspired by the special theory of relativity.

The last and the most famous aspect of the special theory of relativity is the revelation that mass is a form of energy, and that energy has mass. In Einstein's words, "Energy has mass and mass represents energy."[9]

Although this sounds shocking in one sense, in the sense that we have believed ever so long that matter, stuff, is different from energy just as the body is different from the mind (another form of the same theory), in another sense, it sounds surprisingly natural. The matter-energy dichotomy goes back at least as far as the Old Testament. Genesis portrays man as a sort of ceramic creation. God scoops up a handful of clay (matter) and breathes life (energy) into it. The Old Testament is a product of the western world (or the other way round). Physics also is a product of the western world.

In the East, however, there never has been much philosophical or religious (only in the West are these two separate) confusion about matter and energy. The world of matter is a relative world, and an illusory one: illusory not in the sense that it does not exist, but illusory in the sense that we do not see it as it really is. The way it really is cannot be communicated verbally, but in the attempt to talk around it, eastern literature speaks repeatedly of dancing energy and transient, impermanent forms. This is strikingly similar to the picture of physical reality emerging from high-energy particle physics. Buddhist literature does not speak of learning new things about reality, but about removing veils of ignorance that stand between us and what we already *are*. Perhaps this accounts for the fact that the preposterous claim that mass is only a form of energy is unexpectedly palatable.

The formula which expresses the relationship of mass to energy is the most famous formula in the world: $E = mc^2$. The energy contained in a piece of matter is equal to the mass of the matter multiplied by an extraordinarily large number, the speed of light squared. This means that even the tiniest, the very tiniest particle of matter has within it a tremendous amount of concentrated energy.

Although Einstein didn't know it at the time, he discovered the secret of stellar energy. Stars continuously convert matter into energy. It is because of the very large ratio of energy released to matter consumed that stars can continue to burn through countless millennia.

At the center of a star, hydrogen atoms, the primordial "stuff" of the physical world, are squeezed together so tightly by the enormous gravitational force of the star's dense mass that they fuse together, making a new element, helium. Every four hydrogen atoms become one helium atom. However, the mass of one helium atom is not the same as the mass of four hydrogen atoms. It is slightly less. This small difference in mass is released as radiant energy—heat and light. The process of fusing lighter elements into heavier elements is called, of course, fusion. The fusion of hydrogen into helium causes a hydrogen explosion. In other words, a (young) burning star literally is one huge, continuously exploding hydrogen bomb.*

The formula $E = mc^2$ also resulted in the atomic bomb. Atomic bombs and atomic reactors obtain energy from mass by the process of fission, which is the opposite of fusion. Instead of fusing smaller atoms into larger ones, the process of fission splits atoms of uranium, which are quite large, into atoms which are smaller.

This is done by firing a subatomic particle, a neutron, at an atom of uranium. When the neutron hits the uranium atom, it splits it into lighter atoms, but the mass of these smaller atoms together is less than the mass of the parent atom of uranium. The difference in mass explodes into energy. This process also produces additional neutrons which fly off to strike other uranium atoms, creating more fissions, more light atoms, more energy, and more neutrons. The whole phenomenon is called a chain reaction. An atomic bomb is an uncontrolled chain reaction.

A hydrogen (fusion) bomb is produced by detonating an atomic (fission) bomb in the midst of hydrogen. The heat from the atomic explosion (in place of the heat of friction caused by gravity) fuses hydrogen atoms into helium atoms and releases heat in the process which fuses together more hydrogen atoms, releasing more heat, and so on. There is no limit to the size of a potential hydrogen bomb, and it is constructed from the most plentiful element in the universe.

---

* As its hydrogen becomes exhausted, a star begins to fuse the helium at its core. Helium fusion is hotter than hydrogen fusion and produces heavier elements, such as neon, oxygen, and carbon, which, in turn, becomes the solar fuel as its helium becomes exhausted.

For better or worse, a major revelation of the special theory of relativity is that mass and energy are different forms of the same thing. Like space and time, they are not separate entities. There is no qualitative difference between mass and energy; there is only mass-energy. Mathematically, this discovery meant that the two conservation laws of mass and energy could be replaced by a single conservation law of mass-energy.

A conservation law is a simple statement that a quantity of something, whatever it may be, never changes no matter what happens. For example, suppose that there were a conservation law governing the number of guests at a party. If such a thing were true, we would notice that every time a new guest arrived at the party, some other guest would leave. Similarly, every time a guest at the party left, another one would arrive. The rate of guest turnover at the party might be great or small, and the guests might arrive and depart singly or in groups, but in all circumstances the number of guests at the party would remain the same.

The conservation law concerning energy says that the total amount of energy in the universe always has been and always will be the same. We can convert energy from one form to another (like mechanical energy to thermal energy via friction), but the total amount of energy in the universe does not change. Similarly, the law of the conservation of matter says that the total amount of matter in the universe always has been and always will be the same. We can convert matter from one form to another (like ice to water or water to steam), but the total amount of matter in the universe does not change.

When the special theory of relativity combined mass and energy into mass-energy, it also combined the law of the conservation of mass and the law of the conservation of energy into the law of the conservation of mass-energy. The law of the conservation of mass-energy says that the total amount of mass-energy in the universe always has been and always will be the same. Mass may be converted into energy and energy may be converted into mass, but the total amount of mass- energy in the universe does not change.

The sun, the stars, even wood burning in the fireplace, are examples of mass being converted into energy. Physicists who study subatomic particles are so familiar with the concept of exchanging mass for energy and energy for mass that they routinely designate the mass size of particles in terms of their energy content.

In all, there are roughly twelve conservation laws. These simple laws are becoming more and more important, especially in high-energy particle physics, because they are derived from what physicists now believe to be the ultimate principles (latest dance) governing the physical world. These are the laws of symmetry.

The laws of symmetry are pretty much what they sound like. Something is symmetrical if certain aspects of it remain the same under varying conditions. For example, one half of a circle mirrors the other half, no matter how we cut it. Regardless of how we turn a circle, the right half always mirrors the left half. The position of the circle changes, but its symmetry remains.

The Chinese have a similar concept (perhaps the same?). One side of a circle is called "yin" and other side is called "yang." Where there is yin, there is yang. Where there is high, there also is low. Where there is day, there also is night. Where there is death, there also is birth. The concept of yin-yang, which is really a very old law of symmetry, is yet another way of saying that the physical universe is a whole which seeks balance within itself.

The irony of the special theory of relativity, as apparent by now, is that it is not about those aspects of reality that are relative, but about those aspects that are not relative. Like quantum mechanics, its impact on the assumptions of Newtonian physics was shattering. Not because it proved them wrong, but because it proved them to be quite limited. The special theory of relativity and quantum mechanics have propelled us into unimaginably expansive areas of reality, areas about which we literally had not one previous idea.

The assumptions of Newtonian physics correspond to the clothes we always thought that the Emperor was wearing: a universal time whose uniform passage equally affects every part of the universe; a separate space, independent though empty; and the belief that there exists somewhere in the universe a place which stands absolutely still, quiet and unmoving.

Every one of these assumptions has been proven untrue (not useful) by the special theory of relativity. The Emperor wasn't wearing them at all. The only motion in the physical universe is motion relative to something else. There is no separate space and time. Mass and energy are different names for the same thing.

In place of these assumptions, the special theory of relativity provides a new and unified physics. Measurements of distance and duration may vary from one frame of reference to another, but the space- time interval between events never changes.

For all this, however, the special theory of relativity has one shortcoming. It is based on a rather uncommon situation. The special theory of relativity applies only to frames of reference that move uniformly, relative to each other. Most movement, unfortunately, is neither constant nor ideally smooth. In other words, the special theory of relativity is built upon an idealization. It is limited to and premised upon the special situation of uniform motion. That is why Einstein called it the "special," or restricted, theory.

Einstein's vision was to construct a physics that is valid for *all* frames of reference, such as those moving with non-uniform motion (acceleration and deceleration) relative to each other, as well as those moving uniformly relative to each other. His idea was to create a physics which could describe events in terms of *any* frame of reference, no matter how it moves relative to any other frame of reference.

In 1915, Einstein succeeded in achieving the complete generalization of his special theory. He called this achievement the general theory of relativity.

GENERAL NONSENSE

The general theory of relativity shows us that our minds follow different rules than the real world does. A rational mind, based on the impressions that it receives from its limited perspective, forms structures which thereafter determine what it further will and will not accept freely. From that point on, regardless of how the real world actually operates, this rational mind, following its self-imposed rules, tries to superimpose on the real world its own version of what must be.

This continues until at long last a beginner's mind cries out, "This is not right. What 'must be' is not happening. I have tried and tried to discover why this is so. I have stretched my imagination to the limit to preserve my belief in what 'must be.' The breaking point has come. Now I have no choice but to admit that the 'must' I have believed in does not come from the real world, but from my own head."

This narrative is not poetic hyperbole. It is a concise description of the major conclusion of the general theory of relativity and the means by which it was reached. The limited perspective is the perspective of our three-dimensional rationality and its view of one small part of the universe (the part into which we were born). The things that "must be" are the ideas of geometry (the rules governing straight lines, circles, triangles, etc.). The beginner's mind was Albert Einstein's. The long-held belief was that these rules govern, without exception, the entirety of the universe. What Einstein's beginner's mind realized was that this is so only in our minds.*

Einstein discovered that certain laws of geometry are valid only in limited regions of space. This makes them useful since our experience physically is limited to very small regions of space, like our solar system. However, as our experience expands, we encounter more and more difficulty in trying to superimpose these rules upon the entire expanse of the universe.

Einstein was the first person to see that the geometrical rules which apply to one small part of the universe as seen from a limited perspective (like ours) are not universal. This freed him to behold the universe in a way that no person had seen it before.

What he saw is the content of the general theory of relativity.

---

* The view presented here is not that geometry comes from the mind. There are many possible geometries (as Riemann and Lobachevsky showed before Einstein), but the actual geometry that we have is determined by the physics. For example, Euclid considered geometry to be closely related to experience (he defined congruence by moving triangles about in space) and he considered his parallel axiom to be not self-evident, i.e., not a product purely of the mind.

The view presented here is that idealizations abstracted from experience (like Euclidean geometry) form a rigid structure of such durability that, when subsequent sensory experience contradicts it, we question the validity of the sensory data rather than the validity of the idealized abstractions. Once such a set of idealized abstractions is erected (verified) in the mind, we thereafter superimpose it upon all subsequent actual and projected sense data (i.e., upon the entire universe as we picture it according to this set of abstractions), whether it fits or not.

Einstein did not set out to prove anything about the nature of our minds. His interest was in physics. "Our new idea," he wrote, "is simple: to build a physics valid for all co-ordinate systems."[1] The fact that he *did* illustrate something of importance about the way that we structure our perceptions is indicative of an inevitable trend toward the merger of physics and psychology.

How did Einstein get from a theory of physics to a revolutionary statement of geometry? How did that lead to a significant insight into our mental processes? The answer to these questions is one of the least known, but one of the most important and intriguing intellectual adventures recorded.

Einstein started with his special theory of relativity. As successful as it was, Einstein was not satisfied with it because it applied only to co-ordinate systems moving uniformly relative to each other. Is it possible, thought Einstein, to explain the same phenomenon as seen from two different frames of reference, one of them moving uniformly and the other of them moving non-uniformly, in such a way that there is a consistent explanation for the phenomenon in terms of both the uniformly moving frame of reference and the non-uniformly moving frame of reference. In other words, can we describe events which happen in a co-ordinate system which is moving non-uniformly in terms which are meaningful to an observer in a co-ordinate system which is moving uniformly, and the other way round? Can we create *one* physics that is valid for observers in both frames of reference?

Yes, discovered Einstein, it is possible for observers in the two different frames of reference to relate in a manner which is both meaningful in terms of their own state of motion and in terms of the other's state of motion. To illustrate this, he used another famous thought experiment.

Imagine an elevator in an extraordinarily tall building. The cable which supports the elevator has snapped, and the elevator is plummeting downward. Inside the elevator are several physicists. They are not aware that the cable has broken, and, since there are no windows, they cannot look outside.

The question is, what is the appraisal of this situation by the observers on the outside of the elevator (us) and by the observers on the inside of the elevator (the physicists)? Since this is an idealized experiment, we can disregard the effects of friction and the resistance of the air.

To us, the situation is apparent. The elevator is falling and soon it will strike the earth and all of its inhabitants will be dead. As the elevator falls, it accelerates according to Newton's law of gravity. The motion of the elevator is not uniform, but accelerated, because of the gravitational field of the earth.

We can predict many things that might happen inside the elevator. For example, if someone inside the elevator dropped a handkerchief, nothing would happen. It would appear to the inside observers to float where it was released because it would be accelerating toward the earth at the same rate as the elevator and the people inside of it. Nothing really would be floating, everything would be falling, but, since everything would be falling at the same rate, there would be no change in their relative positions.

To a generation of physicists born and brought up inside the elevator, however, things would appear quite differently. To them, dropped objects do not fall, they simply hang in midair. If someone gives a floating object a shove, off it goes in a straight line until it hits the side of the elevator. To the observers inside the elevator, there are no forces acting on any objects inside the elevator. In short, the observers inside the elevator would conclude that they are in an iner- tial co-ordinate system! The laws of mechanics are perfectly valid. Their experiments always produce results which agree exactly with theoretical predictions. An object at rest remains at rest. An object in motion remains in motion. Moving objects are deflected from their paths only by forces which are proportional to the amount of deflection. For every reaction there is an equal and opposite reaction. If we give a shove to a floating chair, it goes off in one direction, and we go off in the opposite direction with an equal momentum (although with a slower speed because of our greater mass).

The inside observers have a consistent explanation for the phenomena inside the elevator: They are in an inertial co-ordinate system, and they can prove it by the laws of mechanics.

The outside observers also have a consistent explanation for the phenomena inside the elevator: The elevator is falling in a gravitational field. Its passengers are unaware of this because, without being able to see outside the elevator, there is no way for them to detect it while they are falling. Their co-ordinate system is in accelerated motion, even though they believe that it is not moving at all.

The bridge between these two explanations is gravity.

The falling elevator is a pocket edition of an inertial co-ordinate system. A real inertial co-ordinate system is not limited in space or time. The elevator edition is limited in both. It is limited in space because a moving object inside the elevator will not move in a straight line forever, but only until it reaches one of the walls of the elevator. It is limited in time because sooner or later the elevator and its passengers are going to collide with the earth, ending their existence abruptly.

According to the special theory of relativity, moreover, it is significant that the elevator is limited in size because otherwise it would not appear to its inhabitants as an inertial co-ordinate system. For example, if the physicists inside the elevator simultaneously drop two baseballs, the baseballs float in the air exactly where they are released, and remain there. This, to the outside observer, is because they are falling parallel to each other. However, if the elevator were the size of Texas and the baseballs were as far apart when they were dropped as Texas is wide, the baseballs would not fall parallel to each other. They would *converge,* since each of them would be drawn by gravity to the center of the earth. The observers inside the elevator would notice that the baseballs, and any other floating objects in the elevator, move toward each other with the passage of time, as though there were a mutual attraction between them. This mutual attraction would appear as a "force" affecting the objects in the elevator, and the physicists inside hardly would conclude, under those circumstances, that they were in an inertial co-ordinate system.

In short, if it is small enough, *a co-ordinate system falling in a gravitational field is the equivalent of an inertial co-ordinate system.* This is Einstein's principle of equivalence. It is a telling piece of mental dexterity. Anything like an "inertial co-ordinate system" that can be "wiped out"[2] (Einstein's words) by the assumption of a gravitational field hardly deserves to be called absolute (as in "absolute motion," and "absolute nonmotion"). While the observers inside the elevator experience a lack of motion and the absence of gravity, the observers outside the elevator see a co-ordinate system (the elevator) accelerating through a gravitational field.

Now let us imagine a variation of this situation.

Assume that *we,* the outside observers, are in an inertial coordinate system. We already know what happens in inertial coordinate systems; the same things that happened in the falling elevator. There are no forces, including gravity, to affect us. Therefore, let us assume that we are comfortably floating. Objects at rest remain at rest, objects in motion continue in a straight line forever, and every action produces an equal and opposite reaction.

In our inertial co-ordinate system is an elevator. Someone has attached a rope to the elevator and is pulling it in the direction indicated.

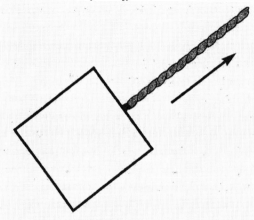

Since this is a thought experiment, it does not matter how this is done. The elevator is being pulled with a constant force, which means that it is in a state of constant acceleration in the direction of the arrow. How will observers outside the elevator and observers inside the elevator appraise this situation:[1]

As we float outside the elevator, we experience that our frame of reference is absolutely at rest and that there is no gravity affecting it.

We see the elevator being pulled with a constant acceleration by the rope, and so we can predict certain things about it. Everything inside the elevator that is not attached quickly collides with the floor of the elevator. If someone in the elevator drops a handkerchief, the elevator floor rushes up to meet it. If someone in the elevator tries to jump off the floor, the floor, rushing upward, is instantly under his feet again. The floor of the elevator continually crashes into anything in its path as it accelerates upward.

Inside the elevator, however, the appraisal of the situation is quite different. To a generation of physicists born and brought up inside the elevator, talk of acceleration upward is fantasy (remember, the elevator has no windows). To them, their co-ordinate system is quite at rest. Objects fall downward to the floor because of a gravitational field, just as objects on the earth fall downward to the floor because of a gravitational field.

Both the observers inside the elevator and the observers outside the elevator have consistent explanations for the phenomena inside the elevator. We observers outside the elevator explain them by the accelerated motion of the elevator. The observers inside the elevator explain them by the presence of a gravitational field. *There is absolutely no way to determine which of us is right.*

"Wait a minute," we say, "suppose that we cut a small hole in one wall of the elevator and shine a light beam through it. If the elevator really were motionless, the light beam would strike the opposite wall of the elevator at a spot exactly opposite the hole. Since we can see that the elevator is accelerating upward, we know that the elevator wall will move upward slightly in the time it takes the light beam to cross the elevator. Therefore, the light beam will strike the far wall slightly below the spot just opposite the hole it entered through. In effect, it will seem to curve downward from the point of view of the people inside the elevator instead of traveling in a straight line. This should prove to them that their elevator is in motion."

"It does not prove anything of the sort," says Jim de Wit, who, of course, is inside the elevator. "The light beams in this elevator do not travel in straight lines. How could they? We are in a gravitational field. Light is energy, and energy has mass. Gravity attracts mass, and a light beam traveling through our elevator will be drawn downward by our gravitational field exactly like a baseball thrown horizontally at the speed of light."

There is no way that we can convince de Wit that his co-ordinate system is in a state of accelerated motion. Everything that we can say to prove this to him he dismisses (accounts for) as a result of his "gravitational field." *There is absolutely no way of distinguishing between uniform accelerated motion and a constant gravitational field.*

This is another expression of Einstein's principle of equivalence. In limited areas, *gravity is equivalent to acceleration.* We already saw that acceleration (falling) through a "gravitational field" is the equivalent of an inertial co-ordinate system. Now we see that a "gravitational field" is equivalent to accelerated motion. At last we are approaching a *general* theory of relativity, a theory valid for all frames of reference regardless of their states of motion.

The bridge which links the explanations of the observers inside of the elevator and the explanations of the observers outside of the elevator is gravity. The clue which indicated to Einstein that gravity was the key to his general theory was as old as physics itself.

There are two kinds of mass, which means that there are two ways of talking about it. The first is gravitational mass. The gravitational mass of an object, roughly speaking, is the weight of the object as measured on a balance scale. Something that weighs three times more than another object has three times more mass. Gravitational mass is the measure of how much force the gravity of the earth exerts on an object. Newton's laws describe the effects of this force, which vary with the distance of the mass from the earth. Although Newton's laws describe the effects of this force, they do not define it. This is the mystery of action-at-a-distance (page 24). How does the earth invisibly reach up and pull objects downward?

The second type of mass is inertial mass. Inertial mass is the measure of the resistance of an object to acceleration (or deceleration, which is negative acceleration). For example, it takes three times more force to move three railroad cars from a standstill to twenty miles per hour (positive acceleration) than it takes to move one railroad car from a standstill to twenty miles per hour (page 161). Similarly, once they are moving, it takes three times more force to stop three cars than it takes to stop the single car. This is because the inertial mass of the three railroad cars is three times more than the inertial mass of the single railroad car.

Inertial mass and gravitational mass are equal. This explains why a feather and a cannonball fall with equal velocity in a vacuum. The cannonball has hundreds of times more gravitational mass than the feather (it weighs more) but it also has hundreds of times more resistance to motion than the feather (its inertial mass). Its attraction to the earth is hundreds of times stronger than that of the feather, but then so is its inclination not to move. The result is that it accelerates downward at the same rate as the feather, although it seems that it should fall much faster.

The fact that inertial mass and gravitational mass are equal was known three hundred years ago, but physicists considered it a coincidence. No significance was attached to it until Einstein published his general theory of relativity.

The "coincidence" of the equivalence of gravitational mass and inertial mass was the "clew,"[3] to use Einstein's word, that led him to the principle of equivalence, which refers via the equivalence of gravitational mass and inertial mass to the equivalence of gravity and acceleration themselves. These are the things that he illustrated with his famous elevator examples.

The special theory of relativity deals with unaccelerated (uniform) motion.* If acceleration is neglected, the special theory of relativity applies. However, since gravity and acceleration are equivalent, this is the same as saying that the special theory of relativity is applicable whenever gravity is neglected. If the effects of gravity are to be considered, then we must use the general theory of relativity. In the physical world the effects of gravity can be neglected in (1) remote regions of space which are far from any centers of gravity (matter), and (2) in very small regions of space.

Why gravity can be ignored in very small regions of space leads to the most psychedelic aspect of all Einstein's theories. Gravity can be ignored in very small regions of space because, if the region is small enough, the mountainous terrain of space-time is not noticeable.†

---

* The special theory deals with the unaccelerated (uniform) motion of coordinate systems. The special theory can be used to describe the accelerated (nonuniform) motion of objects as long as the co-ordinate system from which the object is being observed is itself in uniform motion.
† Some physicists think that general relativity will be useful on the microscale of high-energy physics (where the effects of gravity usually are ignored), e.g., strong fluctuations of the gravitational field have been detected at very short distances (10~14 cm).

The nature of the space-time continuum is like that of a hilly country-side. The hills are caused by pieces of matter (objects). The larger the piece of matter, the more it curves the space-time continuum. In remote regions of space far from any matter of significant size, the space-time continuum resembles a flat plain. A piece of matter the size of the earth causes quite a bump in the space-time continuum, and a piece of matter the size of a star causes a relative mountain.

As an object travels through the space-time continuum, it takes the easiest path between two points. The easiest path between two points in the space-time continuum is called a geodesic (geo dee' sic). A geodesic is not always a straight line owing to the nature of the terrain in which the object finds itself.

Suppose that we are in a balloon looking down on a mountain that has a bright beacon on the top of it. The mountain rises gradually out of the plain, and becomes more and more steep as its elevation increases, until, close to the top, it rises almost straight up. There are many villages surrounding the mountain, and there are footpaths connecting all of the villages with each other. As the paths approach the mountain, all of them begin to curve in one way or another, to avoid going unnecessarily far up the mountain.

Suppose that it is nighttime and that, looking down, we can see neither the mountain nor the footpaths. All that we can see is the beacon and the torches of the travelers below. As we watch, we notice that the torches deflect from a straight path when they approach the vicinity of the beacon. Some of them curve gently around the beacon in a graceful arc some distance away from it. Others approach the beacon more directly, but the closer they get to it, the more sharply they turn away from it.

From this, we probably would deduce that some force emanating from the beacon was repelling all attempts to approach it. For example, we might speculate that the beacon is extremely hot and painful to approach.

With the coming of daylight, however, we can see that the beacon is situated on the top of a large mountain and that it has nothing whatever to do with the movement of the torch-bearers. They simply followed the easiest paths available to them over the terrain between their points of origin and destination.

This masterful analogy was created by Bertrand Russell. In this case, the mountain is the sun, the travelers are the planets, asteroids, comets (and debris from the space program), the footpaths are their orbits, and the coming of daylight is the coming of Einstein's general theory of relativity.

The point is that the objects in the solar system move as they do not because of some mysterious force (gravity) exerted upon them at a distance by the sun, but because of the nature of the neighborhood through which they are traveling.

Arthur Eddington illustrated this same situation in another way. Suppose, he suggested, that we are in a boat looking down into clear water. We can see the sand on the bottom and the fishes swimming beneath us. As we watch, we notice that the fish seem to be repelled from a certain point. As they approach it, they swim either to the right or to the left of it, but never over it. From this we probably would deduce that there is a repellant force at that point which keeps the fish away.

However, if we should go into the water to get a closer look, we would see that an enormous sunfish has buried himself in the sand at that point, creating a sizable mound. As fish swimming along the bottom approach the mound, they follow the easiest path available to them, which is around it rather than over it. There is no "force" causing the fish to avoid that particular spot. If all had been known from the first, that spot was merely the top of a large mound which the fish found easier to swim around than to swim over.

The movement of the fish was determined not by a force emanating from the mysterious spot, but by the nature of the neighborhood through which they were passing. (Eddington's sunfish was called "Albert") (really). If we could see the geography (the geometry) of the space-time continuum, we would see that, similarly, it, and not "forces between objects," is the reason that planets move in the ways that they do.

It is not possible for us actually to see the geometry of the space-time continuum because it is four-dimensional and our sensory experience is limited to three dimensions. For that reason, it is not even possible to picture it.

For example, suppose that there existed a world of two- dimensional people. Such a world would look like a picture on a television or a movie screen. The people and the objects in a two- dimensional world would have height and width, but not depth. If these two-dimensional figures had a life and an intelligence of their own, their world would appear quite different to them than our world appears to us, for they could not experience the third dimension.

A straight line drawn between two of these people would appear to them as a wall. They would be able to walk around either end of it, but they would not be able to "step over" it, because their physical existence is limited to two dimensions. They cannot step off the screen into the third dimension. They would know what a circle rs, but there is no way that they could know what a sphere is. In fact, a sphere would appear to them as a circle.

If they like to explore, they soon would discover that their world is flat and infinite. If two of them went off in opposite directions, they would never meet.

They also could create a simple geometry. Sooner or later they would generalize their experiences into abstractions to help them do and build the things that they want to do and build in their physical world. For example, they would discover that whenever three straight metal bars form a triangle, the angles of the triangle always total 180 degrees. Sooner or later, the more perceptive among them would substitute mental idealizations (straight lines) for the metal bars. That would allow them to arrive at the abstract conclusion that a triangle, which by definition is formed by three straight lines, always contains 180 degrees. To learn more about triangles, they no longer would need actually to construct them.

The geometry that such a two-dimensional people would create is the same geometry that we studied in school. It is called Euclidean geometry, in honor of the Greek, Euclid, whose thoughts on the subject were so thorough that no one expanded on them for nearly two thousand years. (The content of most high-school geometry books is about two millennia old.)

Now let us suppose that someone, unbeknownst to them, transported these two-dimensional people from their flat world onto the surface of an enormously large sphere. This means that instead of being perfectly flat, their physical world now would be somewhat curved. At first, no one would notice the difference. However, if their technology improved enough to allow them to begin to travel and to communicate over great distances, these people eventually would make a remarkable discovery. They would discover that their geometry could not be verified in their physical world.

For example, they would discover that if they surveyed a large enough triangle and measured the angles that form it, it would have more than 180 degrees! This is a simple phenomenon for *us* to picture. Imagine a triangle drawn on a globe. The apex (top) of the triangle is at the north pole. The two lines intersecting there form a right angle. The equator is the base of the triangle. Look what happens. Both sides of the triangle, upon intersecting the equator, also form right angles. According to Euclidean geometry, a triangle contains only two right angles (180 degrees), yet this triangle contains *three* right angles (270 degrees).

Remember that in our example, the two-dimensional people actually have surveyed a triangle on what they presumed was their flat world, measured the angles, and come up with 270 degrees. What a confusion. When the dust setdes they would realize that there are only two possible explanations.

The first possible explanation is that the straight lines used to construct the triangle (like light beams) were not actually straight, although they seemed to be straight. This could account for the excessive number of degrees in the triangle. However, if this is the explanation that they choose to adopt, then they must create a "force" responsible for somehow distorting the straight lines (like "gravity"). The second possible explanation is that their abstract geometry does not apply to their real world. This is another way of saying that, impossible as it sounds, their universe is not Euclidean.

The idea that their physical reality is not Euclidean probably would sound so fantastic to them (especially if they had had no reason to question the reality of Euclidean geometry for two thousand years) that they probably would choose to look for forces responsible for distorting their straight lines.[*]

---

[*] *Eddington expressed this concept most concisely:* "A field of force represents the discrepancy between the natural geometry of a co-ordinate system and the abstract geometry arbitrarily ascribed to

The problem is that, having chosen this course, they would be obligated to create a responsible force every time that their physical world failed to validate Euclidean geometry. Eventually the structure of these necessary forces would become so complex that it would be much simpler to forget them altogether and admit that their physical world does not follow the logically irrefutable rules of Euclidean geometry.

Our situation is parallel to that of the two-dimensional people who cannot perceive, but who can deduce that they are living in a three-dimensional world. We are a three-dimensional people who cannot perceive, but who can deduce that we are living in a four-dimen- sional universe.

For two thousand years we have assumed that the entire physical universe, like the geometry that the ancient Greeks created from their experience with this part of it, was Euclidean. That the geometry of Euclid is universally valid means that it can be verified anywhere in the physical world. That assumption was wrong. Einstein was the first person to see that the universe is not bound by the rules of Euclidean geometry, even though our minds tenaciously cling to the idea that it is.

Although we cannot perceive the four-dimensional space-time contin-uum directly, we can deduce from what we already know of the special theory of relativity that our universe is not Euclidean. Here is another of Einstein's thought experiments.

Imagine two concentric circles, one with a small radius and one with a very large radius. Both of them revolve around a common cen-ter as shown.

Imagine also that we, the observers, are watching these revolving circles from an inertial co-ordinate system. Being in an inertial co-ordinate system simply means that our frame of reference is at rest relative to everything, including the revolving circles. Drawn over the revolving circles are two identical concentric circles which are in our co-ordinate system. They are not revolving. They are the same size as the revolving circles and have the same common center, but they remain motionless. While we and our nonrevolving circles are motionless, we

it." (Arthur Eddington, *The Mathematical Theory of Relativity,* Cambridge, England, Cambridge University Press, 1923, pp. 37-38. Italics in the original.)

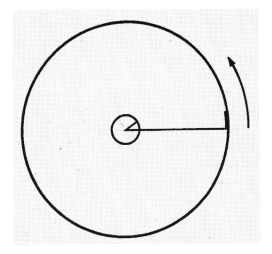

are in communication with an observer who is on the revolving circles. He actually is going around with them.

According to Euclidean geometry, the ratio of the radius to the circumference of all circles is the same. If we measure the radius and the circumference of the small circle, for example, the ratio of these two measurements will be the same as the ratio of the radius to the circumference of the large circle. The object of this thought experiment is to determine whether this is true or not for both the observers on the stationary circles (us) and the observer on the revolving circles. If the geometry of Euclid is valid throughout the physical universe, as it should be, we should discover that the ratio between the radius and the circumference of *all* the circles involved is identical.

Both we and the observer on the revolving circles will use the same ruler to do our measuring. "The same ruler" means that either we actually hand him the same ruler that we have used, or that we use rulers that have the same length when at rest in the same co-ordinate system.

We go first. Using our ruler, we measure the radius of our small circle, and then we measure the circumference of our small circle. Then we note the ratio between them. The next step is to measure the radius of our large circle and then the circumference of our large circle. Then we note the ratio between them. Yes, it is the same ratio that we found between the radius and the circumference of our small circle. We have proved that Euclidean geometry *is* valid in our coordinate system, which is an inertial co-ordinate system.

Now we hand the ruler to the observer on the revolving circles as he passes by us. Using this ruler he first measures the radius of his small circle and finds that it is the same as ours, since our circles are drawn directly over his circles. Next he measures the circumference of his small circle. Remember that motion causes rulers to contract in the direction that they are moving. However, since the radius of the small circle is so short, the velocity of the ruler when it is placed on the circumference of the small circle is not fast enough to make the effect of relativistic contraction noticeable. Therefore, the observer on the revolving circles measures the circumference of his small circle and finds it to be the same as the circumference of our small circle. Naturally, the ratio between them also is the same. So far so good. The ratios between the radius and the circumference of three circles have been determined (our small circle, our large circle, and his small circle) and they are all identical. This is exactly what should happen according to high-school geometry books across the country. Only one more circle to go.

The observer on the revolving circles measures the radius of his large circle and finds it to be the same length as the radius of our large circle. Now he comes to the last measurement, the circumference of his large circle. However, as soon as he puts his ruler into position to make a measurement on the circumference of the large revolving circle, his ruler contracts! Because the radius of his large circle is much larger than the radius of his small circle, the velocity of the circumference of the large revolving circle is considerably faster than the velocity of the circumference of the small revolving circle.

Since the ruler must be aligned in the direction that the circumference is moving, it becomes shorter. When the revolving observer uses this ruler to measure the circumference of the large revolving circle, he finds that it is larger than the circumference of our large circle. This is because his ruler is shorter. (Contraction also affected his ruler when he measured the radius of his large circle, but since it then was placed perpendicular to the direction of motion, it became skinnier, nor shorter).

This means that the ratio of the radius to the circumference of the small revolving circle is not the same as the ratio of the radius to the circumference of the large revolving circle. According to Euclidean geometry, this is not possible, but there it is.

If we want to be old-fashioned about it (before-Einstein) we can say that this situation is nothing unusual. By definition, the laws of mechanics and the geometry of Euclid are valid only in inertial systems (that is what makes them inertial systems). We simply don't consider co-ordinate systems which are not inertial. (This was really the position of physicists before Albert Einstein.) This is exactly what seemed wrong to Einstein. His idea was to create a physics valid for *all* co-ordinate systems, since the universe abounds with the non-inertial as well as the inertial kind.

If we are to create such a universally valid physics, a general physics, then we must treat both the observers in the stationary (inertial) system and the observer on the revolving circles (a non-inertial system) with equal seriousness. The person on the revolving circles has as much right to relate the physical world to his frame of reference as we have to relate it to ours. True, the laws of mechanics as well as the geometry of Euclid are not valid in his frame of reference, but every deviation from them can be explained in terms of a gravitational field which affects his frame of reference.

This is what Einstein's theory allows us to do. It allows us to express the laws of physics in such a way that they are independent of specific space-time co-ordinates. Space and time co-ordinates (measurements) vary from one frame of reference to another, depending upon the state of motion of the frame of reference. The general theory of relativity allows us to universalize the laws of physics and to apply them to all frames of reference.

"Wait a minute," we say, "how can anyone measure distance or navigate in a co-ordinate system like the one on the revolving circles? The length of a ruler varies from place to place in such a system. The farther we go from the center, the faster the velocity of the ruler, and the more it contracts. This doesn't happen in an inertial co-ordinate system, which, in effect, is a system that is at rest. Because there is no change of velocity throughout an inertial co-ordinate system, rulers do not change length.

"This allows us to organize inertial systems like a city, block by block. Since rulers do not change length in inertial systems, all the blocks that are laid out with the same ruler will be the same length. No matter where we travel, we know that ten blocks is twice the distance of five blocks.

"In a non-inertial system the velocity of the system varies from place to place. This means that the length of a ruler varies from place to place. If we used the same ruler to lay out all the city blocks in a non-inertial co-ordinate system, some of them would be larger than others depending upon where they were located."

"What is wrong with that," asks Jim de Wit, "as long as we still can determine our position in the co-ordinate system? Imagine a sheet of india rubber on which we have drawn a grid so that it looks like a piece of graph paper (first drawing, next page). This is a co-ordinate system. Assuming that we are at the lower left corner (we can start anywhere) let us say that a party Saturday night is being held at the intersection marked 'Party.' To get there we have to go two squares to the right and two squares up.

"Now suppose that we stretch the sheet of rubber so that it looks like the second drawing.

"The same directions (two squares right and two squares up) still bring us to the party. The only difference is that unless we are familiar with this part of the co-ordinate system, we cannot calculate the distance that we have to travel as easily as we could if all of the squares were the same size."

According to the general theory of relativity, gravity, which is the equivalent of acceleration, is what distorts the space-time continuum in a manner analogous to our stretching the sheet of rubber. Where the effects of gravity can be neglected, the space-time continuum is like the sheet of rubber before we stretched it. All of the lines are straight lines and all of the clocks are synchronized. In other words, the undistorted sheet of rubber is analogous to the space-time continuum of an inertial co-ordinate system and the special theory of relativity applies.

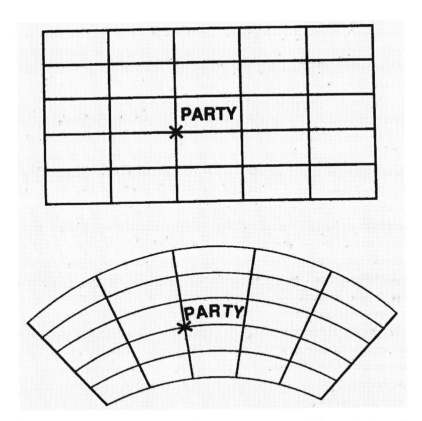

However, in the universe at large gravity cannot be neglected. Wherever there is a piece of matter, it warps the space-time continuum. The larger the piece of matter, the more pronounced the warp.

In the example of the revolving circles, the variation of velocity in different parts of the co-ordinate system caused the ruler to change size. With that in mind, remember that *acceleration (change in velocity) is the equivalent of gravity.* Therefore, changes in the strength of a gravitational field will produce the same contractions of the ruler as changes in velocity. "Acceleration" and "gravity" are two ways of saying the same thing. That means that if a ruler is subjected to gravitational fields of different strength, it changes length.

Of course, it is impossible to travel through our solar system, much less our galaxy, without encountering gravitational fields of varying intensity, which would cause any maps that we somehow could produce to look distorted like the stretched piece of india rubber. The terrain of the space-time continuum in which our earth moves is like a hilly countryside with a mountain (the sun) dominating the geography.

According to Newton, the earth wants to continue forever in a straight line, but forever is deflected from its inclination by the gravitational force of the sun. A balance of the two keeps the earth in orbit around the sun. According to Einstein, the earth's orbit is simply the easiest path for the earth to take as it moves through the space-time continuum, warped as it is in this neighborhood by the sun.

Imagine how complex is the geography of the space-time continuum which is our universe with its solar systems, star systems, galaxies, and galaxy clusters, each of them causing major and minor bumps, curves, hills, valleys, and mountains in the four-dimensional space-time continuum.

Would it be possible to navigate under such circumstances?

Yes. Although it is a crude example, sailors navigate under somewhat analogous circumstances. We cover the earth with squares which are formed by lines of latitude and longitude. The size of these squares varies depending upon where they are located. The closer they are to the equator, the larger they are. (If this is unclear, look at a globe). Nonetheless, we still can locate physical points on the surface of the earth by designating the intersection of a line of latitude and a line of longitude. Knowing the number of squares between us and where we want to sail does not give us the distance to our destination because the squares may vary in size. However, if we know the nature of our terrain (a globe) we can calculate distances on it (using spherical trigonometry).

Similarly, once we know the properties of an area of the space- time continuum (by exploring it) we can determine not only the position of, but also the distance (interval) between two events in the space-time continuum.* The mathematical structure of the general theory of

---

* This distance, of course, is "invariant," i.e., the same for all co-ordinate systems (page 171). The invariance is the absolute objective aspect of Einstein's theory that complements the subjective arbitrary choice of co-ordinate system.

relativity, which Einstein created over a period of ten years, permits us to do just that.

The equations of the general theory of relativity are structural formulas. They describe the structure of changing gravitational fields. (Newton's formula describes a situation between two objects at a given time. Einstein's formulas relate a situation here and now to a situation in the immediate vicinity a litde later.) By feeding the results of actual observations into these equations, they give us a picture of the space-time continuum in the neighborhood of our observations. In other words, they reveal the geometry of space-time in that area. Once we know that, our situation is roughly analogous to that of a sailor who knows that the earth is round and also knows spherical trigonometry.*

We have said, up to now, that matter distorts, or causes a curvature of, the space-time continuum in its vicinity. According to Einstein's ultimate vision, which he never "proved" (demonstrated mathematically), a piece of matter *is* a curvature of the space-time continuum! In other words, according to Einstein's ultimate vision, there are no such things as "gravitational fields" and "masses." They are only mental creations. No such things exist in the real world. There is no such thing as "gravity"—gravity is the equivalent of acceleration, which is motion. There is no such thing as "matter"—matter is a curvature of the space-time continuum. There is not even such a thing as "energy"—energy equals mass and mass is space-time curvature.

What we considered to be a planet with its own gravitational field moving around the sun in an orbit created by the gravitational attraction (force) of the sun is actually a pronounced curvature of the space-time continuum finding its easiest path through the space-time continuum in the vicinity of a very pronounced curvature of the space-time continuum.

There is nothing but space-time and motion and they, in effect, are the same thing. Here is an exquisite presentation, in completely western terms, of the most fundamental aspect of Taoist and Buddhist philosophies.

---

* The space-time continuum is not only curved, it also has topological properties, i.e., it can be connected in crazy ways, e.g., like a donut (O)· It also can twist (i.e., torsion).

Physics is the study of physical reality. If a theory does not relate to the physical world, it may be pure mathematics, poetry, or blank verse, but it is not physics. The question is, does Einstein's fantastic theory really work?

The answer is a slightly tentative, but generally accepted "Yes." Most physicists agree that the general theory of relativity is a valid way of viewing large-scale phenomena, and at the same time, most physicists still are eager to see more evidence to confirm (or challenge) this position.

Since the general theory of relativity deals with vast expanses of the universe, its proof (or usefulness, not of "truth"—the watch is still unopenable) cannot come from observations of phenomena limited to the earth. For this reason, its verifications come from astronomy.

Thus far, the general theory of relativity has been verified in four ways. The first three ways are straightforward and convincing. The last way, if early observations are correct, may be more fantastic than the theory itself.

The first verification of the general theory of relativity came as an unexpected benefit to astronomers. Newton's law of gravity purported to describe the orbits of the planets around the sun, and it did—all of them except Mercury. Mercury orbits the sun in such a way that some parts of its orbit bring it closer to the sun than others. The part of Mercury's orbit closest to the sun is called its perihelion. The first verification of Einstein's general theory of relativity turned out to be the long-sought explanation of the problem of Mercury's perihelion.

The problem with Mercury's perihelion—in fact, with Mercury's entire orbit—is that it moves. Instead of continuously retracing its path around the sun relative to a co-ordinate system attached to the sun, Mercury's orbit itself revolves around the sun. The rate of revolution is extremely slow (it completes one revolution around the sun every three million years). This still was enough to puzzle astronomers. Prior to Einstein, this precession in Mercury's orbit had been attributed to an undiscovered planet in our solar system. By the time Einstein published his general theory of relativity, the search for this mysterious planet was well underway.

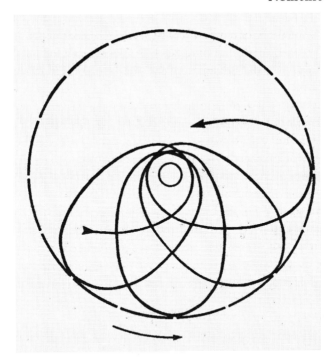

Einstein created his general theory of relativity without special attention to the perihelion of Mercury. However, when the general theory of relativity was applied to this problem, it showed that Mercury moves precisely as Mercury has to move through the space-time continuum in that vicinity of the sun! The other planets do not move significantly in this way because they are farther away from the sun's gravity. Score one for the general theory.

The second verification of the general theory of relativity was the fulfillment of a prediction specifically made by Einstein. Einstein predicted that light beams are bent by gravitational fields. He also predicted exacdy how much they are bent, and he suggested an experiment to test this prediction. Einstein suggested that astronomers measure the deflection of starlight by the gravitational field of the sun.

According to Einstein, the presence of the sun between a group of visible stars and the earth will cause an apparent change in the position of the stars because light coming from them will be bent by the gravitational field of the sun. In order to perform this experiment, it is necessary to photograph a group of stars at night, noting their positions relative to each other and other stars in their periphery, and then to photograph the same group during the day when the sun is between them and us. Of course, stars only can be photographed in the daytime during a total eclipse of the sun by the moon.

Astronomers consulted their star charts and discovered that May 29 is the ideal day for such an undertaking. This is because the sun, in its apparent journey across a varied stellar background, is in front of an exceptionally rich grouping of bright stars on that date. By incredible coincidence, a total eclipse of the sun occurred on May 29, 1919, only four years after the general theory was published. Preparations were made to use this event to test Einstein's new theory.

Light signals from a star are bent in the neighborhood of the sun. Because we assume that starlight travels in a straight line, we assume that the star is in a position other than it actually is.

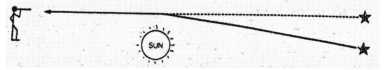

Although light was supposed to travel in a straight line in a vacuum, a certain amount of bending already was theorized before Einstein's general theory of relativity. Newton's law of gravity was used to calculate this bending, even though it could not explain it. Einstein's theory predicted roughly *twice* the deflection that Newton's law predicted, and, in addition, it supplied an explanation for it. Physicists and astronomers alike eagerly awaited the outcome of this confrontation between the new theory and the old.

The 1919 eclipse was photographed by two different expeditions sent to two different parts of the world. These expeditions also took photographs of the same stellar background at times when the sun was not in the area. The results of both expeditions vindicated Einstein's calculations, not Newton's. Since 1919, the same verdict has been reached again and again during other eclipses. All of them confirm Einstein's predictions. Score two for the general theory.

The third verification of the general theory of relativity is called gravitational redshift. Remember that gravity (because it is the equivalent of acceleration) not only causes rulers to contract, but it also causes clocks to run more slowly.

A clock is anything that repeats itself periodically. An atom is a type of clock. It vibrates at a certain frequency. When a substance, like sodium, is made to glow, the wavelength of the light that it emits can be measured accurately. This wavelength tells us exactly the frequency of the vibrations of the atoms that comprise the substance. If the frequency should vary, the wavelength also will vary.

If we want to compare the rhythm of a clock here on the earth with the rhythm of a clock that is influenced by an intense gravitational field, like that of the sun, we do not need to send a clock to the surface of the sun. The clocks already are in place.

Einstein predicted that any periodic process that takes place in an atom on the sun, where the gravity is very intense, must take place at a slightly slower rate than it does here on the earth. To test this prediction, all we need do is compare the wavelength of the radiation of a given element as it is found in sunlight and as it is found here on earth in the laboratory. This has been done many times. In each case, the wavelength measured from the sunlight was found to be longer than its laboratory counterpart. A longer wavelength means a lower (slower) frequency. Sodium atoms, for example, vibrate more slowly under the influence of the sun's strong gravitational field than they do on the earth. So do all the atoms.

This phenomenon is called gravitational redshift because the wavelengths involved appear to be shifted slightly toward the red end of the visible light spectrum where the wavelengths are the longest. Score three for the general theory.

Mercury's moving perihelion, starlight deflection, and gravitational redshift are all observable phenomena. Now we come to an area where theory is still predominant and observation is minimal. Nonetheless, it is an area that is by far the most exciting and perhaps the most stimulating in the entire history of science. The fourth verification of the general theory of relativity appears to be the phenomenon of the black hole.

In 1958, David Finkelstein published a paper in which he theorized, on the basis of Einstein's general theory of relativity, a phenomenon that he called a "one-way membrane."[4] Finkelstein showed that under certain conditions involving an extremely dense gravitational field, an invisible threshold can occur into which light and physical objects can enter, but from which they never again can escape.*

The following year, a young graduate student at the University of London heard Finkelstein, who was speaking there as a guest lecturer, explain his one-way membrane. The idea caught his attention and then his imagination. The young student was Roger Penrose. Expanding on Finkelstein's discovery, he developed it into the modern theory of the "Black Hole."

A black hole is an area of space which appears absolutely black because the gravitation there is so intense that not even light can escape into the surrounding areas.† Gravitation is negligible on the laboratory level, but quite important when bodies of large mass are concerned. Therefore, the exploration of black holes naturally became a joint venture of physicists and astronomers.

Astronomers speculated that a black hole may be one of several possible products of stellar evolution. Stars do not burn indefinitely. They evolve through a life cycle which begins with hydrogen gas and sometimes ends with a very dense, burned-out, rotating mass. The exact end product of this process depends upon the size of the star undergoing it. According to one theory, stars which are about three times the size of our sun or larger end up as black holes. The remains of such stars are unimaginably dense. They may be only a few miles in diameter and yet contain the entire mass of a star three times larger than the sun. Such a dense mass produces a gravitational field strong enough to pull everything in its vicinity into it, while at the same time allowing nothing, not even light, to escape from it.

Surrounding this remainder of a star is an "event horizon." An event horizon is created by the enormous gravitational field of the burned-

---

* This phenomenon was theorized by Pierre-Simon La Place in 1795 using Newtonian physics. Finkelstein was the first physicist to formulate it from the modern point of view, i.e., relativity theory. This modern formulation triggered the current theories on the black hole.

The very first modern paper on black holes was done by J. R. Oppenheimer and S. Snyder in 1939. The current theories of the black hole, i.e., black hole singularities which are beyond space-time, were developed independently by R. Penrose and S. W. Hawking.

† To a first approximation. Physicists currently theorize that black holes actually shine due to photons and other particles quantum-tunneling out of the oneway membranes.

out star. It functions precisely like Finkelstein's one-way membrane. Anything within the gravitational field of this mass quickly is pulled toward it, and once past the event horizon, never can return. It is the event horizon which constitutes the essential feature of the black hole. What happens to an object that passes through an event horizon is even more fantastic than the wildest (currently) science fiction.

If the black hole is not rotating, the object will be pulled directly to the center of the black hole to a point called the singularity. There it literally will be squeezed out of existence, or as physicists say, to zero volume. At the black hole singularity all of the laws of physics break down completely, and even space and time disappear. It is speculated that everything which is sucked into a black hole is spilled out again on "the other side"—the "other side" being another universe!

If the black hole is rotating, an object that is sucked into the event horizon could miss the black hole singularity (which is shaped like a "ring" in a rotating black hole) and emerge into another time and another place in this universe (through "wormholes"), or into another universe (through "Einstein-Rosen bridges"). In this way, rotating black holes may be the ultimate time machines.

Although black holes are almost invisible, we can search for observable phenomena that may be characteristic of them. The first of these is a large amount of electromagnetic radiation. A black hole continuously attracts hydrogen atoms, cosmic particles, and everything else to it. As these particles and objects are drawn to the black hole, they steadily accelerate through its gravitational field until they approach the velocity of light itself. This causes tremendous amounts of electromagnetic radiation. (Any accelerating charged particle creates electromagnetic radiation.)

The second observable characteristic of an invisible black hole is its effect on a nearby visible star. If a visible star can be found which moves as though it were revolving around an invisible star (i.e., as though it were half of a binary star system), we might speculate that it actually *is* revolving around an invisible star, and that its invisible partner is a black hole.

The search for black holes consequently became the search for these two phenomena. In 1970, the satellite Uhuru located both of them in one area. It pinpointed a high-energy x-ray source in the constellation Cygnus which emits a million times more energy than the sun. This high-energy source of electromagnetic radiation, which came to be known as Cygnus X-1, is very close to a visible blue-hot supergiant star. Scientists now believe that this blue supergiant forms a binary system with the black hole, Cygnus X-1.

As the visible star and the invisible black hole orbit each other, the blue supergiant literally is being sucked into the black hole. As material is torn away from its surface, it plunges into the black hole at tremendous speed, emitting x-rays. Incredible as Cygnus X-1 is, more than one hundred similar objects have been detected within our own Milky Way galaxy since its discovery. Although black holes stretch our imagination to the limit, the evidence is mounting that they actually do exist.

For example, if black holes are as we have speculated them to be, whatever disappears in them reappears somewhere. Is it possible, therefore, that there are black holes in other universes which are sucking matter from those universes into our universe? This is a seriously considered possibility. There are objects in our universe that appear to be the reverse of black holes. They are called white holes (of course). These objects are quasi-stellar radio sources, or quasars for short.

Quasars are extraordinarily intense energy sources. Most of them are only several times the diameter of our solar system, yet they emit more energy than an entire galaxy of over 150 billion stars! Some astronomers believe that quasars are the most distant objects ever detected, yet their incredible brightness allows us to see them clearly.

The relationship between black holes and quasars is purely speculation, but the speculation is mind-boggling. For example, some physicists speculate that black holes swallow up matter from one universe and pump it either into another universe or into another part and time of the same universe. The "output" side of a black hole, according to this hypothesis, is a quasar. If this speculation is correct, then our universe is being sucked into its many black holes, only to reappear in other universes, while other universes are being pumped into our own universe, which is being sucked through black holes and into other universes again. The process goes on and on, feeding on itself, another beginningless, endless, endless, beginningless dance.

One of the most profound by-products of the general theory of relativity is the discovery that gravitational "force," which we had so long taken to be a real and independentiy existing thing, is actually our mental creation. There is no such thing in the real world. The planets do not orbit the sun because the sun exerts an invisible gravitational force on them, they follow the paths that they do because those paths are the easiest ways for them to traverse the terrain of the space-time continuum in which they find themselves.

The same is true for "nonsense." It is a mental creation. There is no such thing in the real world. From one frame of reference black holes and event horizons make sense. From another frame of reference absolute nonmotion makes sense. Neither is "nonsense" except as seen from another point of view.

We call something nonsense if it does not agree with the rational edifices that we carefully have constructed. However, there is nothing intrinsically valuable about these edifices. In fact, they themselves often are replaced by more useful ones. When that happens, what was nonsensical from an old frame of reference can make sense from a new frame of reference, and the other way round. Like measurements of space and time, the concept of nonsense (itself a type of measurement) is relative, and we always can be sure when we use it that from some frame of reference it applies to us.

Endnotes

Beginner's Mind

1. Shunryu Suzuki, Zen Mind, Beginner's Mind, New York, Weatherhill, 1970,pp. 13-14.
2. Henry Miller, "Reflections on Writing," in Wisdom of the Heart, Norfolk, Connecticut, New Directions Press, 1941 (reprinted in The Creative Process, by B. Ghiselin (ed.), Berkeley, University of California Press, 1954, p. 186).
3. KQED Television press conference, San Francisco, California, December 3,1965.
4. Werner Heisenberg, Physics and Philosophy, Harper Torchbooks, New York, Harper & Row, 1958, p. 33.

Special Nonsense

1. Albeit Einstein, "Aether und Relativitätstheorie," 1920, trans. W. Perret and G. B. Jeffery, Side Lights on Relativity, London, Methuen, 1922 (reprinted in Physical Thought from the

Preso cratics to the Quantum Physicists by Shmuel Sambursky, New York, Pica Press, 1975, p. 497).

2. Ibid.

3. Ibid.

4. Albert Einstein, "Die Grundlage der Allgemeinen Relativitätstheorie," 1916, trans. W. Perret and G. B. Jeffery, *Side Lights on Relativity*, London, Methuen, 1922 (reprinted in *Physical Thought from the Presocratics to the Quantum Physicists* by Shmuel Sambursky, New York, Pica Press, 1975, p. 491).

5. Einstein, „Aether und Relativitätstheorie," *op. cit.*, p. 496.

6. J. Terrell, *Physical Review*, 116,1959,1041.

7. Isaac Newton, Philosophiae Naturalis Principia Mathematica (trans. Andrew Motte), reprinted in Sir Isaac Newton's Mathematical Principles of Natural Philosophy and His System of the World (revised trans. Florian Cajori), Berkeley, University of California Press, 1946, p. 6.

8. From "Space and Time," an address to the 80th Assembly of German Natural Scientists and Physicians, Cologne, Germany, September 21,1908 (reprinted in *The Principles of Relativity*, by A. Lorentz, A. Einstein, H. Minkowski, and H. Weyle, New York, Dover, 1952, p. 75).

9. Albert Einstein and Leopold Infeld, *The Evolution of Physics*, New York, Simon and Schuster, 1961, p. 197.

General Nonsense

1. Albert Einstein and Leopold Infeld, *The Evolution of Physics*, New York, Simon and Schuster, 1961, p. 197.

2. *Ibid.*, p. 219.

3. *Ibid.*, pp. 33-34.

4. David Finkelstein, "Past-Future Asymmetry of the Gravitational Field of a Point Particle," *Physical Review*, 110, 1958, 965.

33

John Hick

The Problem of Evil

To many, the most powerful positive objection to belief in god is the fact of evil. Probably for most agnostics it is the appalling depth and extent of human suffering, more than anything else, that makes the idea of a loving Creator seem so implausible and disposes them toward one or another of the various naturalistic theories of religion.

As a challenge to theism, the problem of evil has traditionally been posed in the form of a dilemma: if God is perfectly loving, he must wish to abolish evil; and if he is all-powerful, he must be able to abolish evil. But evil exists; therefore God cannot be both omnipotent and perfectly loving.

Certain solutions, which at once suggest themselves, have to be ruled out so far as the Judaic-Christian faith is concerned.

To say, for example (with contemporary Christian Science), that evil is an illusion of the human mind, is impossible within a religion based upon the stark realism of the Bible. Its pages faithfully reflect the characteristic mixture of good and evil in human experience. They record every kind of sorrow and suffering, every mode of man's inhumanity to man and of his painfully insecure existence in the world. There is no attempt to regard evil as anything but dark, menacingly ugly, heart-rending, and crushing. In the Christian scriptures, the climax of this history of evil is the crucifixion of Jesus, which is presented

From *Philosophy of Religion,* 1st ed. by John Hick, © 1965. Reprinted by permission of Prentice-Hall Inc., Upper Saddle River, NJ. Burt/Goldinger: Philosophy and Contemporary Issues. 8th edition (Prentice Hall)

not only as a case of utterly unjust suffering, but as the violent and murderous rejection of God's Messiah. There can be no doubt, then, that for biblical faith, evil is unambiguously evil, and stands in direct opposition to God's will.

Again, to solve the problem of evil by means of the theory (sponsored for example, by the Boston "Personalist" School) of a finite deity who does the best he can with a material, intractable and coeternal with himself, is to have abandoned the basic premise of Hebrew-Christian monotheism; for the theory amounts to rejecting belief in the infinity and sovereignty of God.

Indeed, any theory which would avoid the problem of the origin of evil by depicting it as an ultimate constituent of the universe, coordinate with good, has been repudiated in advance by the classic Christian teaching, first developed by Augustine, that evil represents the going wrong of something which in itself is good. Augustine holds firmly to the Hebrew-Christian conviction that the universe is *good*—that is to say, it is the creation of a good God for a good purpose. He completely rejects the ancient prejudice, widespread in his day, that matter is evil. There are, according to Augustine, higher and lower, greater and lesser goods in immense abundance and variety; but everything which has being is good in its own way and degree, except in so far as it may have become spoiled or corrupted. Evil—whether it be an evil will, an instance of pain, or some disorder or decay in nature has not been set there by God, but represents the distortion of something that is inherently valuable. Whatever exists is, as such, and in its proper place, good; evil is essentially parasitic upon good, being disorder and perversion in a fundamentally good creation. This understanding of evil as something negative means that it is not willed and created by God; but it does not mean (as some have supposed) that evil is unreal and can be disregarded. On the contrary, the first effect of this doctrine is to accentuate even more the question of the origin of evil.

Theodicy,* as many modern Christian thinkers see it, is a modest enterprise, negative rather than positive in its conclusions. It does not claim to explain, nor to explain away, every instance of evil in human

---

*The word "theodicy," from the Greek theos (God) and dike (righteous), means the justification of God's goodness in the face of the fact of evil.

experience, but only to point to certain considerations which prevent the fact of evil (largely incomprehensible though it remains) from constituting a final and insuperable bar to rational belief in God.

In indicating these considerations it will be useful to follow the traditional division of the subject. There is the problem of *moral evil* or wickedness: why does an all-good and all-powerful God permit this? And there is the problem of the *non-moral evil* of suffering or pain, both physical and mental: why has an all-good and all-powerful God created a world in which this occurs?

Christian thought has always considered moral evil in its relation to human freedom and responsibility. To be a person is to be a finite center of freedom, a (relatively) free and self-directing agent responsible for one's own decisions. This involves being free to act wrongly as well as to act rightly. The idea of a person who can be infallibly guaranteed always to act rightly is self-contradictory. There can be no guarantee in advance that a genuinely free moral agent will never choose amiss. Consequently, the possibility of wrongdoing or sin is logically inseparable from the creation of finite persons, and to say that God should not have created beings who might sin amounts to saying that he should not have created people.

This thesis has been challenged in some recent philosophical discussions of the problem of evil, in which it is claimed that no contradiction is involved in saying that God might have made people who would be genuinely free and who could yet be guaranteed always to act rightly. A quote from one of these discussions follows:

If there is no logical impossibility in a man's freely choosing the good on one, or on several occasions, there cannot be a logical impossibility in his freely choosing the good on every occasion. God was not, then, faced with a choice between making innocent automata and making beings who, in acting freely, would sometimes go wrong: there was open to him the obviously better possibility of making beings who would act freely but always go right. Clearly, his failure to avail himself of this possibility is inconsistent with his being both omnipotent and wholly good.*

---

* J. L. Mackie, "Evil and Omnipotence." *Mind* (April 1955), 209.

A reply to this argument is suggested in another recent contribution to the discussion.* If by a free action we mean an action which is not externally compelled but which flows from the nature of the agent as he reacts to the circumstances in which he finds himself, there is, indeed, no contradiction between our being free and our actions being "caused" (by our own nature) and therefore being in principle predictable. There is a contradiction, however, in saying that God is the cause of our acting as we do but that we are free beings in relation to God. There is, in other words, a contradiction in saying that God has made us so that we shall of necessity act in a certain way, and that we are genuinely independent persons in relation to him. If all our thoughts and actions are divinely predestined, however free and morally responsible we may seem to be to ourselves, we cannot be free and morally responsible in the sight of God, but must instead be his helpless puppets. Such "freedom" is like that of a patient acting out a series of post-hypnotic suggestions: he appears, even to himself, to be free, but his volitions have actually been predetermined by another will, that of the hypnotist, in relation to whom the patient is not a free agent.

A different objector might raise the question of whether or not we deny God's omnipotence if we admit that he is unable to create persons who are free from risks inherent in personal freedom. The answer that has always been given is that to create such beings is logically impossible. It is no limitation upon God's power that he cannot accomplish the logically impossible, since there is nothing here to accomplish, but only a meaningless conjunction of words—in this case "person who is not a person." God is able to create beings of any and every conceivable kind; but creatures who lack moral freedom, however superior they might be to human beings in other respects, would not be what we mean by persons. They would constitute a different form of life which God might have brought into existence instead of persons. When we ask why God did not create such beings in place of persons, the traditional answer is that only persons could, in any meaningful sense, become "children of God," capable of entering into a personal relationship with their Creator by a free and uncompelled response to his love.

---

* Flew, in *New Essays on Philosophical Theology.*

When we turn from the possibility of moral evil as a correlate of man's personal freedom to its actuality, we face something which must remain inexplicable even when it can be seen to be possible. For we can never provide a complete causal explanation of a free act; if we could, it would not be a free act. The origin of moral evil lies forever concealed within the mystery of human freedom.

The necessary connection between moral freedom and the possibility, now actualized, of sin throws light upon a great deal of the suffering which afflicts mankind. For an enormous amount of human pain arises either from the inhumanity or the culpable incompetence of mankind. This includes such major scourges as poverty, oppression and persecution, war, and all the injustice, indignity, and inequity which occur even in the most advanced societies. These evils are manifestations of human sin. Even disease is fostered to an extent, the limits of which have not yet been determined by psychosomatic medicine, by moral and emotional factors seated both in the individual and in his social environment. To the extent that all of these evils stem from human failures and wrong decisions, their possibility is inherent in the creation of free persons inhabiting a world which presents them with real choices which are followed by real consequences.

We may now turn more directly to the problem of suffering. Even though the major bulk of actual human pain is traceable to man's misused freedom as a sole or part cause, there remain other sources of path which are entirely independent of the human will, for example, earthquake, hurricane, storm, flood, drought, and blight. In practice it is often impossible to trace a boundary between the suffering which results from human wickedness and folly and that which falls upon mankind from without. Both kinds of suffering are inextricably mingled together in human experience. For our present purpose, however, it is important to note that the latter category does exist and that it seems to be built into the very structure of our world. In response to it, theodicy, if it is wisely conducted, follows a negative path. It is not possible to show positively that each item of human path serves the divine purpose of good; but, on the other hand, it does seem possible to show that the divine purpose as it is understood in Judaism and Christianity could not be forwarded in a world which was designed as a permanent hedonistic paradise.

An essential premise of this argument concerns the divine purpose in creating the world. The skeptic's assumption is that man is to be viewed as a completed creation and that God's purpose in making the world was to provide a suitable dwelling-place for this fully-formed creature. Since God is good and loving, the environment which he has created for human life to inhabit is naturally as pleasant and comfortable as possible. The problem is essentially similar to that of a man who builds a cage for some pet animal. Since our world, in fact, contains sources of hardship, inconvenience, and danger of innumerable kinds, the conclusion follows that this world cannot have been created by a perfectly benevolent and all-powerful deity.

Christianity, however, has never supposed that God's purpose in the creation of the world was to construct a paradise whose inhabitants would experience a maximum of pleasure and a minimum of pain. The world is seen, instead, as a place of "soul-making" in which free beings, grappling with the tasks and challenges of their existence in a common environment, may become "children of God" and "heirs of eternal life." A way of thinking theologically of God's continuing creative purpose for man was suggested by some of the early Hellenistic Fathers of the Christian Church, especially Irenaeus. Following hints from St. Paul, Irenaeus taught that man has been made as a person in the image of God but has not yet been brought as a free and responsible agent into the finite likeness of God, which is revealed in Christ. Our world, with all its rough edges, is the sphere in which this second and harder stage of the creative process is taking place.

This conception of the world (whether or not set in Irenaeus' theological framework) can be supported by the method of negative theodicy. Suppose, contrary to fact, that this world were a paradise from which all possibility of pain and suffering were excluded. The consequences would be very far-reaching. For example, no one could ever injure anyone else: the murderer's knife would turn to paper or his bullets to thin air; the bank safe, robbed of a million dollars, would miraculously become filled with another million dollars (without this device, on however large a scale, proving inflationary); fraud, deceit, conspiracy, and treason would somehow always leave the fabric of society undamaged. Again, no one would ever be injured by accident the mountain-climber, steeplejack, or playing child falling from a height would float unharmed to the ground; the reckless driver would never meet with disaster. There would be no need to work, since no harm could result from avoiding work; there would be no call to be concerned for others in time of need or danger, for in such a world there could be no real needs or dangers.

To make possible this continual series of individual adjustments, nature would have to work by "special providence" instead of running according to general laws which men must learn to respect on penalty of pain or death. The laws of nature would have to be extremely flexible: sometimes gravity would operate, sometimes not, sometimes an object would be hard and solid, sometimes soft. There could be no sciences, for there would be no enduring world structure to investigate. In eliminating the problems and hardships of an objective environment, with its own laws, life would become like a dream in which, delightfully but aimlessly, we would float and drift at ease.

One can at least begin to imagine such a world. It is evident that our present ethical concepts would have no meaning in it. If, for example, the notion of harming someone is an essential element in the concept of a wrong action, in our hedonistic paradise there could be no wrong actions—nor any right actions in distinction from wrong. Courage and fortitude would have no point in an environment in which there is, by definition, no danger or difficulty. Generosity, kindness, the *agape* aspect of love, prudence, unselfishness, and all other ethical notions which presuppose life in a stable environment, could not even be formed. Consequently, such a world, however well it might promote pleasure, would be very ill adapted for the development of the moral qualities of human personality. In relation to this purpose it would be the worst of all possible worlds.

It would seem, then, that an environment intended to make possible the growth in free beings of the finest characteristics of personal life, must have a good deal in common with our present world. It must operate according to general and dependable laws: and it must involve real dangers, difficulties, problems, obstacles, and possibilities of pain, failure, sorrow, frustration, and defeat. If it did not contain the particular trials and perils which—subtracting man's own very considerable contribution—our world contains, it would have to contain others instead.

To realize this is not, by any means, to be in possession of a detailed theodicy It is to understand that this world, with all its "heartaches and the thousand natural shocks that flesh is heir to," and environment so manifestly not designed for the maximization of human pleasure and the minimization of human pain, may be rather well adapted to the quite different purpose of "soul-making."

34

Sharon Olds

Sex without Love

How do they do it, the ones who make love
without love? Beautiful as dancers,
gliding over each other like ice skaters
over the ice, fingers hooked
inside each other's bodies, faces
red as steak, wine, wet as the
children at birth whose mothers are going to
give them away. How do they
come to the   come to the   come to the   God   come to the
still waters, and not love
the one who came there with them, light
rising slowly as steam off their joined
skin? These are the true religious,
the purists, the pros, the ones who will not
accept a false Messiah, love the
priest instead of the God. They do not
mistake the lover for their own pleasure,
they are like great runners: they know they are alone
with the road surface, the cold, the wind,
the fit of their shoes, their over-all cardio-
vascular health—just factors, like the partner
in the bed, and not the truth, which is the
single body alone in the universe
against its own best time.

"Sex without Love" from THE DEAD AND THE LIVING by Sharon Olds, copyright © 1987
by Sharon Olds. Used by permission of Alfred A. Knopf, a division of Random House, Inc.

35

Richard Kamber

Sartre: Life and Works

A. SARTRE'S CHILDHOOD AND EDUCATION: 1905-1929

Jean-Paul Charles Aymard Sartre was born in Paris on June 21, 1905. His father, Jean-Baptiste Sartre, was an officer in the French navy. His mother, Anne-Marie (née Schweitzer) was the youngest child of a family from Alsace who had moved to France after the Franco-Prussian War to avoid living under German rule. Her first cousin was Albert Schweitzer, who later become famous as a missionary in Africa. When Sartre was fifteen months old his father died of an intestinal disease he contracted in the French colony of Cochin China (now part of Vietnam). As a result, Sartre never knew his father. Lacking any opportunity to support herself, Anne-Marie returned to her parents' home, where she and her son shared "the children's room." Although Sartre and his mother were very close, their relationship in the Schweitzer household was rather like that of an older sister and little brother. Anne-Marie's mother, Louise, ran the house and her father, Charles, ran the family.

According to Sartre, the ten years he spent in the Schweitzer household, first at Meudon and then in Paris, shaped the ambitions that would drive him for the rest of his life. Both of his grandparents were readers, and their rooms were full of books. Charles Schweitzer was a teacher of languages, still handsome, energetic, and sexually profligate at age sixty-five with a long white beard that made him look like traditional pictures of God the Father. Having quarreled with his own sons, Charles was delighted to have a grandson to himself, a child whose character he could mold. He took charge of Sartre's education and encouraged the boy to develop a love for good literature. He warned him not to become a writer—an unreliable profession, but to make a career as a teacher and scholar.

In the meantime, Sartre's mother bought him picture books and adventure stories in order to ensure that her son could enjoy his childhood. But, children, as Sartre would later emphasize, are never merely passive recipients of adult influence. Searching for his own identity, young Sartre was torn between allegiance to his grandfather's high literary values and dreams of being a man of action, a knight errant who would rescue damsels in distress and battle the forces of evil. Between the ages of eight and twelve, Sartre decided to become a writer, or, more precisely, he convinced himself that he was destined to become a writer. Here was a destiny that would allow him to justify his existence by becoming indispensable to the world of letters. He would be a hero, but the weapon of his heroism would be a pen not a sword. (Significantly, perhaps, Sartre always preferred a pen to a typewriter.)

In 1917, Sartre's mother remarried. Her new husband was Joseph Mancy, a former admirer, who was now a prosperous engineer, managing shipbuilding yards in La Rochelle. The next three years were among the unhappiest in Sartre's life. He disliked being in La Rochelle and resented his stepfather. Although Mancy was generous with Sartre, the boy despised his authoritarian manner and middle-class values. Neither did Sartre appreciate his stepfather's efforts to tutor him in science and mathematics. Perhaps, most of all, Sartre resented having to share the affections of his mother with an intruder. In school, he had difficulty making friends. He fought with his classmates, and then tried to buy their friendship with pastries he purchased by selling books from his home and stealing money from his mother's handbag. He was caught and knew the shame of being treated as a thief. When his grandfather dropped a coin in a store he stooped in pain to pick it up rather than let his dishonest grandson retrieve it.

Although Sartre had been raised as a Catholic, religion had never gripped his soul with any notable force. At about this time, he suddenly discovered that he no longer believed in God.

In 1920, his grandfather arranged for him to attend school in Paris at the distinguished *Lycée Henri IV.* (In the French system of education, a *lycée* provided preparation for university studies. A student entered at age twelve and graduated at nineteen.) There, Sartre came under the influence of a talented and iconoclastic philosopher who called himself Alain (Emile Auguste Chartier). There too, he formed his first close friendship, with a student named Paul Nizan. Despite truancy and rebelliousness, Sartre did well in school.

Sartre's greatest gift was what he would later call his "golden brain." The rest of his body was another matter. Like his father, Sartre was short. As a young man, his height was just five foot two. But unlike either of his parents, he was ugly. At the age of four, he caught a cold at the beach, which led to near-blindness in his right eye and loss of muscular control. Later, his face was disfigured by acne that left pockmarks and bloated features. Short and stocky, walleyed, and pockmarked, Sartre described himself as a "toad." To compensate for his appearance, he developed his muscles, took boxing lessons, and cultivated a remarkably engaging personality. He had an impressive voice, a good sense of humor, and an astonishing capacity for conversation. Despite his ugliness, he managed to have long-term sexual relationships with many attractive women.

In 1924, he was admitted to the exclusive L'Ecole Normale Supérieure (ENS) to prepare for a university degree. The ENS provided complementary instruction to the regular course of studies at the Sorbonne, but Sartre seldom went to the Sorbonne. Most of what Sartre learned during his five years of university studies he learned from books and conversations with other students. Luckily, there were brilliant students taking a degree in Paris at that time. Among them were Simone Weil, Raymond Aron, Maurice Merleau-Ponty, Jean Hyppolite, and Simone de Beauvoir. Sartre's closest friends were Paul Nizan and René Maheu. It was Maheu, who may have been Beauvoir's first lover, who gave her her nickname. He called her "the Beaver" (*le Castor*) because she enjoyed company and worked so constructively. As mentioned above, Sartre failed the written examination for the *agégation* in 1928, but ranked in first place in 1929.

B. SOLDIER, TEACHER, PHILOSOPHER, AND WRITER: 1930-1938

Although Sartre left the university eager to fulfill his destiny as a writer, nearly seven years would pass before his first book was published. In spite of partial blindness, he was required by French law to complete eighteen months of military training. Stationed at Fort Saint Cyr in November 1924, he was trained as an army meteorologist, and for the first time in his adult life, experienced the boredom of days that repeated themselves without change. In April, 1931 he began a teaching appointment at a *lycée* in Le Havre, a commercial seaport in northeastern France. He soon became popular with students, who enjoyed his casual manners and style of teaching. While other teachers took care to maintain "the proper distance" between themselves and students, he made a practice of socializing with students. He ate with them, drank with them, played Ping-Pong with them, and joined their picnics. At the end of one term, he went drinking with a group of students, and they ended up in whorehouse. This episode gave him an enduring reputation at the lycée. On the other hand, he found Le Havre to be a dull, dreary, and provincial town. He particularly disliked the smug self-righteousness of its civic leaders and prominent businessmen.

The first two books Sartre wrote as an adult were inspired by his reading of Nietzsche and a biography of Nietzsche. The first was a novel entitled *A Defeat* (*Une défaite*) written about 1927-28 and based on the story of Nietzsche's unrequited love for Richard Wagner's wife Cosima. The second, *The Legend of Truth* (*La Légende de la vérité*), was written between 1929 and 1931. It consisted of essays in the form of myths on three different kinds of truth: the certainty of science, the probability of philosophy, and the living truth of the solitary man. Both books were rejected for publication, and Sartre moved on to other interests.

He began to concentrate in earnest on his belief in the irreducibility and contingency of the physical world. He believed that ordinary objects like tables and trees had a reality that is independent of (i.e. not reducible to) our perceptions and ideas of them. He also believed that this reality, the existence of physical objects, is unexplainable. The world exists, but there is no reason for it to exist. It is not, for example, the necessary result of divine creation or, as Hegel thought, the unfolding of spirit through space and time. Furthermore, he believed that the irreducibility and contingency of the physical world could be known through direct experience. What Sartre lacked was a method and language for developing these beliefs.

The break for Sartre came in an unexpected way. During a visit to Paris in 1933, Sartre and Beauvoir spent an evening with their friend Raymond Aron, who was studying phenomenology at the French Institute in Berlin. Beauvoir describes what happened:

> We spent an evening together at the Bec de Gaz on the Rue Montparnasse. We ordered the specialty of the house, Apricot Cocktails; Aron said, pointing to his glass: 'You see my dear fellow, if you are a phenomenologist, you can talk about this cocktail and make philosophy out of it!' Sartre turned pale with emotion at this. Here was just the thing that he had been longing to achieve for years—to describe objects just as he saw and touched them, and extract philosophy from the process. . . Sartre decided to make a serious study of [Husserl], and took the necessary steps to succeed Aron at the French Institute in Berlin for the coming year" (Beauvoir 1966, 112).

In September of 1933, Sartre began his studies in Berlin. Adolph Hitler had been appointed Chancellor in January, and the grip of Nazism had begun to tighten on all aspects of life in Germany, as it would a few years later on Europe as a whole. But in 1933 Sartre was less concerned with the future of Europe than with his own development as a philosopher and writer. He spent his mornings reading Husserl and his evenings working on a new novel. He learned that Husserl had been educated as a mathematician, not as a philosopher, and had turned to philosophy in order to gain a better understanding of the foundations of mathematics. Although Husserl's philosophical interests soon expanded beyond mathematical phenomena, he sought to bring to philosophy the methodological rigor of science and mathematics. The result was an ambitious program for a science of appearances. (The word phenomenology means the science of that which appears or shows itself.) By 1911, Husserl thought of phenomenology as a rigorous descriptive science for examining whatever appears, insofar as it appears and only insofar as it appears.

In the fall of 1934, Sartre returned to his teaching duties at Le Havre braced with new optimism about his future. Inspired by Husserl, he adopted key insights and methods from phenomenology and began using them in original ways. His first book to be published, *The Imagination* (*L'Imagination*, *1936*), used phenomenological methods to address the longstanding philosophical and psychological problem of how to explain the difference between a perception and an image. Everyone recognizes that seeing a wolf is different from imagining a wolf, but what exactly is that difference? Sartre rejects the view that both are ideas in the mind: the perception being a vivid idea and the image less vivid. For Sartre, nothing is *in* the mind. Imagining and perceiving are both ways of being conscious of the world at large.

When I perceive a wolf I am conscious of the wolf as present, when I imagine a wolf I am conscious of the wolf as absent or non-existent.

The Imagination was followed in 1937 by a book-length essay entitled "The Transcendence of the Ego" ("*La Transcendance de l'ego*" 1937). Here again, Sartre affirms the view that consciousness has nothing inside of itself: it is pure awareness. But if this is so, how can we explain the continuity of consciousness? What is that connects my thoughts now with the thoughts I had ten minutes ago? Why do I recognize those past thoughts as *mine*? To do deal with this problem, Husserl had posited a "transcendental ego": an "I" behind consciousness that connects and constitutes the stream of conscious experiences. Sartre rejects Husserl's solution and argues that the connections between my consciousness now and my consciousness at other times are the connections my consciousness now creates for itself. There is an ego, says Sartre, but that ego is an ideal object, a fiction, that consciousness invents to reinforce its sense of identity. Consciousness itself is:

> [an] impersonal spontaneity. It determines its existence at each instant, without being able to conceive of anything before it. Thus each instance of our conscious life reveals to us creation ex nihilo [from nothing]. Not a new arrangement but a new existence. (Sartre, TE 1957, 98-99)

This bold thesis would become part of the foundation for his most important philosophical work.

Sartre's other major project at this time was his novel on the theme of contingency. It had begun as a poem on the irreducible contingency of a chestnut tree, but Sartre had no gift for poetry and the result was embarrassing. He gave up the poem and began writing a pamphlet which combined phenomenological description with a fictional speaker. He showed it to Beauvoir who found it promising but suggested that he use his talents as a writer and his fondness for mystery novels to work the theme of contingency into a novel with a real story line. He took her advice and began working on a novel entitled *Melancholia* (taking the name from a famous engraving by Albrecht Dürer). The setting for the novel is a fictional seaport city called Bouville [literally Mudville], modeled closely on Le Havre. The main character, Antoine Roquentin, is a thirty-year old intellectual who has come to Bouville to conduct research in the city's archives for a historical biography he is attempting to complete. The novel is written in the form of diary, which Roquentin keeps in an effort to makes sense out of his increasingly oppressive struggles with contingency. He is afflicted, on the one hand, with recurrent bouts of nausea that make him acutely aware of the independent reality of physical objects. He is troubled, on the other hand, by the contingency and meaninglessness of his own life. Roquentin's gradual discoveries about himself and the world constitute a remarkably interesting tale: a kind metaphysical mystery novel. In 1936, Sartre submitted his novel to the distinguished publisher Gallimard. Confident of the magnitude of his achievement, he was shocked when his book was rejected. "I had put the whole of myself into the book . . ." he said, "To reject it was to reject me" (Hayman 1992, 123-124). When he met Beauvoir at Christmastime, he could not hold back his tears. Fortunately, two of his friends arranged for the book to be reconsidered. After reading book himself, Gaston Gallimard met with Sartre. His only objection was the title of the book. He suggested that the book be called *Nausea* (*La Nausée*). Sartre agreed, and Gallimard scheduled *Nausea* for release in 1938. There is little doubt that *Nausea* is one of Sartre's most enduring accomplishments. It may well be the most densely philosophical novel ever written.

By 1939, Sartre had achieved his ambition of becoming a writer. Although far from famous and still teaching at a *lycée* (in Neuilly), his essays, short stories, literary criticism, and new novel were being printed and read. In Paris especially, he was gaining recognition as a new voice in

French literature. Five of his short stories were published as a collection under the title *The Wall* (*Le Mur*). The lead story of the collection, also called "The Wall," dealt with the civil war that was going on Spain and the psychology of men of waiting to be executed. This story may also reflect Sartre's growing interest in Heidegger's revolutionary book *Being and Time*—especially Heidegger's views on authenticity as "freedom towards death." Another story in the collection, "The Childhood of a Leader" ("*L'Enfance d'un chef*") contains elements of Sartre's theory of bad faith (self-deception) and the formation of personal identity in childhood. In addition, Sartre completed the second half of his study of imagination, *The Psychology of Imagination* (*L' Imaginaire*) and most of a novel, *The Age of Reason* (*L'Age de raison*).

During the same period, Sartre also wrote (in three months!) 400 pages of a treatise on phenomenological psychology which he planned to call "The Psyche" ("*Le Psyché*"). Although only one fragment of this treatise was published, that fragment *The Emotions: Outline of a Theory* (*Esquisse d'une théorie des émotions*) is a significant work in its own right and part of the foundation for Sartre's later philosophy.

This book registers Sartre's growing debt to Heidegger's *Being and Time*. He borrows from Heidegger the general thesis that emotions are not internal states which sweep over us but ways that we choose to be in the world. He then argues that strong emotions such as fear, joy, anger, and sadness are also ways in which we choose to deceive ourselves about the world. According to Sartre, strong emotions typically involve physiological change to one's body (changes in blood pressure, muscle tension, breathing, etc.), but they always involve attempts to transform the world (beyond one's body) by means of magic. Thus, by permitting myself to slip into the grip of a strong emotion such as anger, I transform the object of my resentment into something inherently hateful, something that stains the world and needs to be eliminated—if not physically at least symbolically. Furthermore, for the object of my emotion the realities that guide practical behavior are "magically" suspended or adjusted. I may, for example, see the object of my anger as far more evil and powerful than any rational assessment could possibly justify.

Given Sartre's remarkable productivity as a philosopher and writer and his obligations as a teacher, one might imagine that he had little time left for anything else. Yet he worked with astonishing speed and somehow found time for vacations with Beauvoir, the pleasures of café life, correspondence with friends, and a number of extended love affairs. Although Beauvoir would have preferred a more monogamous relationship, she yielded to Sartre's preference for complete sexual freedom and, over the years, had affairs with both men and women, including an intense affair with American novelist Nelson Algren. Sartre's relationship with women, other than Beauvoir, tended to follow a curious pattern. Although he enjoyed being intimate with women, sexual intercourse was not his primary source of pleasure:

I was more a masturbator of women than a copulator. . . . For me what mattered most in a sexual relationship was embracing, caressing, moving my lips over a body . . . I came erect quickly, easily: I made love often, but without very much pleasure. Just a little pleasure at the end, but fairly second-rate (Hayman, 1992, 144).

Sartre liked having affairs with women who, in addition to being young and pretty, were exotic, childish, or mysterious—women whose intuitive personalities contrasted with his own relentlessly analytic frame of mind. Among Sartre's earliest conquests were two sisters, Olga and Wanda Kosakiewicz, the daughters of a Russian nobleman.

Sometimes, Sartre's relationships with women began with seduction and ended with adoption. By the 1960s, Sartre was providing financial support and acting roles for a number of current or former mistresses. In March 1965, he legally adopted his last and youngest mistress, Arlette Elkaïm, a Jewish woman from Algeria.

C. THE WAR YEARS: 1939-1944

On September 1, 1939, Germany invaded Poland and World War II began. Sartre was called up for duty and sent to a small village thirteen miles from the front to take wind measurements for the French artillery. After smashing Poland, Germany waited for six months before taking action again. But the following spring, the German army swept through Holland and Belgium and into northeastern France with astonishing and overwhelming force. The French military lacked the leadership, technology, and will to deal with the German *Blitzkrieg*, and the army of France collapsed in defeat. One of the soldiers killed during the invasion was Sartre's old friend, Paul Nizan. Sartre was taken prisoner on the morning of his 35th birthday, June 21, 1940. The soldiers who captured him were the first German soldiers he had seen since the war began.

Under the terms of the 1940 armistice, all French prisoners-of war were required to remain in captivity until the end of the war. Sartre was sent to Stalag XII-D in Trier near the Luxembourg border. Despite the usual hardships of life in a prisoner-of-war camp, he learned to enjoy the rough company of his fellow prisoners. "What I liked at the camp was the feeling of belonging to a crowd." (Hayman 1992, 176) He also became friends with several of the priests in the camp. One priest, Fr. Marius Perrin, was interested in phenomenology and Sartre tutored him by translating Heidegger's *Being and Time* into French. At Christmas, Sartre wrote and staged a "resistance" play, *Bariona*, about a rebel leader who plans to strangle the infant Jesus in order to keep up the spirit of rebellion against the Romans in ancient Judea. In the end, the wise man Balthazar, played by Sartre, convinces Bariona to spares the infant by offering an existentialist gospel: "Christ is here to teach you that you are responsible for yourself and your suffering." (Sartre, *B* 1974, 2:130). Bariona accepts Christ as an ally and leads his men against the Romans in the name of freedom. One member of the audience who misunderstood the point of the play was so touched by Balthazar's speech that he subsequently converted to Christianity. For

Sartre, life in Stalag XII-D had proven rather gratifying, but he had other goals to fulfill. After nine months of captivity, he used a fake medical certificate to obtain his release.

Back in Paris, Sartre found himself in an occupied city. Although living under Nazi occupation was humiliating, it was not too difficult at first for French citizens who were neither Jews, Communists, nor recognized political opponents. The Nazis were eager to win support from the French, whom they viewed as a kindred people, and therefore treated them far better than they did the conquered peoples of Eastern Europe. They permitted the southern half of France (the Vichy régime) to govern itself as a closely-watched ally under the leadership of a retired French general, the eighty-five year old Marshal Henri Pétain. They also hoped to lure French intellectuals into collaborating with Nazi leadership.

Sartre had returned to Paris full of plans. After reestablishing contact with his friends and lovers, he put the finishing touches on *The Age of Reason* and produced a new system of philosophy, inspired in part by his reading of Heidegger. (The fact that Sartre was borrowing from Heidegger, a Nazi Party member, may have helped him to avoid harassment by the occupation officials in Paris.) Having laid the foundations of a system through his phenomenological studies of imagination, the ego, and emotions, and his exploration of contingency in *Nausea*, he was ready to complete the final synthesis. He had begun the writing while still a prisoner-of war. Now at liberty, he finished his single most important work: *Being and Nothingness: An Essay in Phenomenological Ontology* (*L'Être et le Néant: Essai d'ontologie phénoménologique*). It was published by Gallimard in June 1943. Given the magnitude of this book and its centrality to Sartre's career, there is no responsible way to summarize its conclusions in the space of a few paragraphs. I will spend most of the next three chapters on *Being and Nothingness*. For the purposes of this chapter, it will suffice to consider just three theses that are particularly important for understanding Sartre's later work. The theses are: limitless freedom, limitless responsibility, and the futility of bad faith. For readers unfamiliar with the free will debate and Sartre's unusual take on this debate, these theses may sound quite strange at first. The following paragraphs are intended as a starting place, a first exposure. What is said here will be amplified and clarified in Chapter 4.

Limitless Freedom

In *Being and Nothingness*, Sartre defends the remarkable thesis that the being of human beings is freedom. Part of what he means by that is that human beings do not merely *have* free will, they are freedom incarnate. To exist as a human being is to be an embodied agent-consciousness. Through our bodies we are able to be in the world, to be conscious of the world, and to act on the world. But consciousness remains causally independent of the world. It is also causally independent of its past. What has happened in the past, be it physical or mental, cannot causally determine my present choice because I am separated from that past by a gap across which causality cannot travel: I am separated from that past by nothingness (*néant*). Thus, I can truly say of any conscious action I have ever done "I could have done otherwise, even if everything else had been precisely the same." According to Sartre, only freedom itself can limit freedom. This means two things. First, we are not free not to choose. We are, says Sartre, "condemned to be free" (Sartre *BN* 1956, 439). Second, we cannot control the free will of others.

Although my freedom is limitless, it is never abstract. Freedom for Sartre is always freedom *in* a particular situation, and in every situation there are givens (facticity) to which freedom must respond. My body, my past, and my relations with others are among the factors that define my facticity. I may want to fly like a bird, or like Superman, but my body is not capable of flight. In order to fly, I will need to choose and use appropriate technology. I may regret having said angry words to my friend, but I cannot change the past. At most, I can change the *meaning* the past will have in the future. I can do that by apologizing, making amends, promising not to get angry again, etc. I may wish that my boss had a higher opinion of my abilities, but I cannot change his opinion by wishful thinking. If he doubts my abilities for objective reasons, I may be able to change his future opinion by demonstrating abilities that he has not yet recognized. If he doubts my abilities for prejudicial reasons (e.g. because I am woman, a black, a Jew, etc.), then my efforts to demonstrate unrecognized abilities may be futile. He too is free, and he may choose to remain in bad faith.

Limitless Responsibility

Sartre also tries to show that since human beings are free they are responsible, not only for the lives they lead, but also, for the world in which they live. If, for example, I am born into poverty, then my opportunities for achieving a life free of want and grueling labor may be very limited, but it is up to me to decide how to deal with my condition. I may endure it as my "natural" state or I may find it intolerable and strive to escape from it. (Although to choose the latter, I must first conceive a better condition, and, by contrast, recognize the deficiencies of my present condition.) Yet this is only half of the story, for I must also share responsibility for a world, my world, in which people are born into poverty, go to war, etc. The soldier who is called up to fight in a war assumes responsibility, not only for his own condition, but for the war itself. If I fight in the war, rather than desert or commit suicide, I make the war mine. I cannot excuse myself by saying "I did not declare the war" or "I don't agree with its aims." Sartre quotes with favor Jules Romains' remark: "In war there are no innocent victims," and adds for good measure: "We have the war we deserve" (Sartre *BN* 1956, 554-555).

The Futility of Living in Bad Faith

Limitless freedom and limitless responsibility might not be overwhelming burdens if we were not conscious of them. But according to Sartre, we are conscious of them. In fact, we are directly and continuously conscious of them through the emotion of anguish. What prevents us from feeling anguished most of the time are our persistent efforts to hide from freedom and responsibility through self-deception or, what Sartre prefers to call, bad faith (*mauvaise foi*). Through bad faith, we strive to achieve the kind of being that non-conscious things have. We strive to be a writer, or a parent, or a boss in the way that a rock is a rock or a table is a table. (Rocks never have to choose or excuse what they are.)

Furthermore, Sartre links this theory of bad faith to a psychoanalytic theory of human development. He argues that between the ages of eight and twelve, every child makes a fundamental choice of being. The child fastens on to a vaguely formulated project of self-realization (e.g. to be a writer, a leader, a solitary, a failure, a thief) and begins building a life in pursuit of that project. What makes this project more than just an early step in the process of growing up is that it is undertaken in bad faith. It is undertaken as a personal destiny, something one *has to be* rather than something one has freely chosen *to do*. According to Sartre, most people spend their lives in bad faith passionately seeking to complete their projects of being and thereby escape freedom. But this is a futile endeavor. "Man," Sartre declares, "is a useless passion" (Sartre, *BN* 1956, 615).

Although Sartre had always favored liberal socialism over capitalism, fascism, and Soviet-style communism, he had never engaged in any kind of political of action. (He thought it pointless to vote.) When his friend Nizan joined the French Communist Party (PCF) in 1929, he was impressed by his friend's commitment but unwilling to make a political commitment of his own. By 1941 that had changed. His experiences as soldier and prisoner-of-war, especially his production of the Christmas play *Bariona*, had shown him the possibility of acting in solidarity with large numbers of people and the potential of theatre as a vehicle for political communication. Within a month of his return to Paris, Sartre founded a resistance group called "Socialism and Freedom." It was made up of his "family" (Beauvoir, Olga and Wanda and Kosakiewicz, J.-L. Bost, Jean Pouillon,) and friends (like Maurice Merleau-Ponty) and committed to encouraging French men and women to maintain their pride and avoid collaboration with the Germans. During the summer of 1941, Sartre and Beauvoir slipped across the border into the Free Zone (Vichy France) for a bicycle trip and a chance to recruit converts for Socialism and Liberty. They approached two of the most famous writers in France, André Gide and André Malraux, but neither was interested in joining Sartre's group. Britain was fighting for its own life and the Soviet Union was reeling under the invasion that Germany had launched in June of 1941. What, they asked, could French civilians do? Sartre and Beauvoir returned to Paris disappointed with their efforts and a few months later dissolved Socialism and Freedom. But the French Resistance was really just beginning. By December 1942, the Soviet Union had stopped the German advance at Stalingrad, Britain was no longer under threat of invasion, and British and American troops were rapidly gaining control of North Africa. In France, followers of Charles de Gaulle, the French colonel who had fled to England into 1940 rather than surrender, and French Communists began to build resistance organizations that carried out espionage, sabotage and relayed valuable information to Allied agents. Although Sartre was willing to do what he could for the Resistance, his actual contributions were minor. As a politically independent philosopher, he tended to be seen as unreliable and/or ineffectual. In 1944, his friend Albert Camus provided Sartre with writing assignments for *Combat,* the underground newspaper that Camus was helping to edit.. However, Sartre's most memorable contribution to the cause of resistance was his play *The Flies* (*Les Mouches*).

Like *Bariona*, *The Flies* used an ancient story to carry a message of empowerment and resistance to French men and women without provoking German authorities into closing the play. The story in this case is the Greek legend of the House of Atreus, a tale of family bloodguilt and revenge set around the time of the Trojan War. The elements of the story are these: Agamemnon, King of Argos, sacrifices one of his daughters in order to appease the gods and sail to Troy; when he returns home his wife, Clytemnestra, and her lover, Aegistheus, take revenge by killing Agamemnon; seven years later Agamemnon's son, Orestes, returns from abroad, kills his mother and her lover, and frees his sister, Electra.

A distinctive feature of Sartre's play is the way that guilt has been dispersed among all the citizens of Argos. Instead of assuming full responsibility for their own crime, the new King and Queen have convinced the people of Argos that everyone shares in the guilt and needs to suffer for that guilt. The furies of guilt have turned into flies, and they are everywhere. The guilt of Argos' rulers has become collective guilt, and everybody must suffer for it. Since this was essentially the message that Marshal Pétain had conveyed to the French people, there is a clear parallel between ancient Argos and France during World War II. After Orestes kills his mother and Aegistheus he is approached by the god Jupiter, who is willing to support Orestes as king as long as he agrees to maintain Argos' cult of collective guilt. Orestes refuses, insisting that he alone is responsible and that Jupiter has no power over him. Of course, Jupiter does have some power over him. He has the power to punish him and even to kill him. What Orestes means is that that Jupiter does not control his freedom.

Although *The Flies* was not particularly successful in 1943, either financially or critically, it inspired Sartre to write additional plays. In 1944, Sartre wrote and staged a one act play entitled *No Exit*. It was a philosophical play based on ideas that Sartre had developed in *Being and Nothingness*. It had little to do with the war or the political scene in France, but it was brilliant. *No Exit* has proved to be Sartre's most popular play and is often cited as a model for the Theater of Ideas.

D. HUMANISTIC EXISTENTIALIST: 1945–1951

In August of 1944, Paris was liberated from German occupation. Allied troops, led by De Gaulle's Free French Forces, entered the city amidst sporadic sniper fire and wildly cheering crowds. Although Hitler had ordered that Paris be destroyed rather than surrendered to the allies, his orders were disobeyed. In October, the Allies recognized De Gaulle as head of the French provisional government. On April 30, 1945, Hitler committed suicide in his bunker in Berlin. Eight days later, Germany surrendered unconditionally, and the war in Europe was over.

It was not until after World War II that Sartre became well known outside of France. The liberation of France meant that his books and plays could be published, circulated, translated, and performed abroad. As Sartre's fame spread, new readers often assumed that the gloomy vision of human existence presented in works like *Nausea, Being and Nothingness* and *No Exit* was a reaction to Hitler's domination of Europe and the horrors of World War II. What, they asked themselves, could explain the bleakness of Sartre's worldview—his emphasis on the bankruptcy of humanism, the meaninglessness of the universe, the absence of God, endless conflict with other people, and the bad faith of our deepest aspirations? The answer seemed obvious: his experiences in a nightmare world in which the veneer of civilization had been stripped away and human beings had been exposed at their weakest and ugliest. Ironically, the opposite was true! Sartre's experiences during World War II made him more optimistic not more pessimistic. His experiences as a soldier, a prisoner-of-war, and a minor player in the French Resistance opened his eyes to the possibility of collective action, personal heroism, and political commitment.

A few days after the liberation of Paris, Sartre wrote:

We were never more free than under the Nazi Occupation. We had lost all our rights, beginning with our right to speak. We were insulted daily and had to bear those insults in silence. On one pretext or another—as workers, Jews, political prisoners—Frenchmen were deported. . . . Every instant we lived to the full meaning of that banal little phrase "All men are mortal." Everyone of us who knew the truth about the Resistance asked himself anxiously "If they torture me, shall I be able to keep silent?" Thus the basic question of freedom was set before us; and we were brought to the point of the deepest knowledge a man can have of himself. The secret of man is not his Oedipus complex or his inferiority complex; it is the limit of his own freedom; his capacity for standing up to torture and death (Cranston 1966, 10).

The year 1944 was a year of profound transition for Sartre. It was a year in which ideas that had been simmering through the war years replaced some of the older ideas that he had woven into the fabric of his philosophy. Although he did not give up the terminology that he had adopted in *Being and Nothingness*, he began to take his philosophy and life in a new direction. He began to emphasize the possibilities of authenticity and commitment.

This change in direction is reflected in his trilogy "The Roads to Liberty." The first two volumes, *The Age of Reason* and *The Reprieve (Le Sursis)* were published in 1945 but written before that; the third volume *Troubled Sleep (La Mort dans l'âme)* was written mainly in 1948 and published in 1949. In this volume, the trilogy's anti-hero, Mathieu, finds freedom and purpose in the heroism of self-sacrifice during the German offensive of 1940. Without hope of success or even survival, he chooses to fight to the death from his perch in a church steeple rather than surrender. His goal is to last for fifteen minutes.

This focus on commitment is also reflected in Sartre's willingness to embrace the label of existentialist and to defend existentialism as a humanistic philosophy of commitment. Without a doubt, Sartre's best known essay is the printed version of a lecture that he gave at the Club Maintenant on October 28, 1945, entitled "Existentialism is a Humanism" (*"L'Existentialisme est un humanisme"*). One purpose of this essay was to define existentialism and to distinguish atheistic from religious existentialism. A second purpose was to show that existentialism was not a philosophy of despair, solitude, and hopelessness, but a kind of humanism. A third purpose was to demonstrate that existentialism offered a viable alternative to Christianity and Marxism, not only as a way of understanding the human condition but also as a basis for choice and action. To make good on this claim, Sartre had to show that his brand of existentialism had ethical implications about what people ought or ought not to do. Near the end of the essay, he outlines some strategies for deriving ethical conclusions from his existentialist premises. Still, the question remained: could this outline become a coherent theory?

Actually, Sartre had already promised to develop the ethical implications of his philosophy. In *Being and Nothingness*, he had promised a "future work" that would examine the possibility of choosing freedom as a value rather being, authenticity rather than bad faith. (Sartre *BN* 1956, 70n., 627-628). But his critics doubted that he could fulfill this promise. Any systematic account of the human condition is bound to offer insights into why people do what they do, and such insights may be useful for understanding areas of human conduct that are ethically important. Thus, a philosophy like Sartre's is bound to offer insights for *descriptive ethics*. If, however, one is looking for guidance on what people *ought* to do, on *norms* (i.e. standards) of good or bad, right or wrong, then something more is required. In order demonstrate that a particular account of the human condition can support *normative ethics*, it is necessary to find a normative anchor within that account. (Remember that 'normative' does not mean 'normal.') In Judaism, Christianity, and Islam that anchor is a single, perfect divinity. In some versions of Marxism that anchor is the inescapable progression of history. For some philosophers that anchor is a theory of human nature, for example: that man is a rational animal (Aristotle); that man is a pleasure-seeker (Bentham and Mill), that man is a power-seeker (Nietzsche). The trouble with Sartre's account of the human condition is that it seemed to offer no place to anchor a normative ethics. He denied the existence of God, he denied that there was an inescapable progression in history, and he denied that human beings had a fixed nature. What he attributed to humans were nasty dispositions to deceive themselves, deny their contingency, and engage in conflict with one another.

From 1945 until 1951, Sartre and Beauvoir devoted considerable time and talent to the quest for a normative theory of existentialist ethics. But the results of their efforts were ultimately disappointing. On the one hand, they had impressive success in applying Sartre's theory of bad faith and Beauvoir's theory of the socially constructed Other to the analysis of anti-Semitism, gender discrimination, and color-based prejudice. Sartre's *Anti-Semite and Jew* (*Réflexions sur la question juivre* 1946) and Beauvoir's *The Second Sex* (*Le Deuxieme Sexe* 1949) are brilliant examples of philosophical psychology and sociology in areas of ethical importance. Both books are excellent on the prejudices they treat, although Beauvoir's account of what it means to be a woman is far superior to Sartre's narrow account of what it means to be a Jew. Sartre also framed some promising insights on the issues of "blackness" and color-prejudice in a preface to an anthology of African poetry entitled *Black Orpheus* (*Orphée Noir* 1948.) Impressive, too, are Sartre's discussions of "committed literature": his efforts to demonstrate that writers of prose ought to consider writing a form of action and write on behalf of social and political causes. *What is Literature* (*Qu'est-ce que la littérature?* 1947) remains an insightful exploration of the intersection between ethics and aesthetics.

On the other hand, neither Sartre nor Beauvoir had much success in creating a coherent ethical theory. Beauvoir's *The Ethics of Ambiguity* (*Pour une morale de l'ambiguïté* 1947) amplified the outline Sartre had drawn in "Existentialism is a Humanism" by providing a richer array of examples and by responding to critics of existentialist ethics, but it did not supply the missing theoretical framework. In 1947-48, Sartre began compiling extensive notes for a book on ethics. He called these notes "Notebooks for an Ethics, Volume I and Volume II," but he did not weave them into a completed text or attempt to publish them. Indeed, he insisted that they not be published until after his death (Sartre, *NFE* 1992, xxiii). He did, however, incorporate some of his reflections on ethics into his play *The Devil and the Good God* (*Le Diable et le bon dieu* 1951) and his long psycho-biography of Jean Genet, *Saint Genet: Actor and Martyr* (*Saint Genet; comédian et martyr* 1952).

Although Sartre and Beauvoir had reached an impasse in the development of a normative theory of existentialist ethics, they had no hesitation about committing themselves and their work to political and social causes. As writers with rapidly growing international reputations and the chief exponents of existentialism, they now had the capacity to reach large audiences. They also had sufficient income to resign from their teaching posts and use that time for other purposes. Too famous to work comfortably in cafes, they found new living quarters and wrote at home. (After the death Joseph Mancy in 1946, Sartre's mother bought an apartment on the Rue Bonaparte in Paris and Sartre moved in with her. He remained there for sixteen years.)

Fame also brought them invitations to visit and lecture abroad. In 1945, Sartre spent four months in the United States. During his stay in New York, he fell in love with Dolores Vanetti, who had once been an actress in Paris. For a brief time this relationship was so intense that Sartre seriously considered taking a two-year teaching position at Columbia University. But Sartre did not like or understand the United States. Unable to speak English, antagonistic to capitalism, and rightfully indignant at American traditions of racial discrimination, he felt little kinship with the United States.

The fame that Sartre and Beauvoir had achieved guaranteed that their opinions would be noticed, but political effectiveness required a way of responding quickly to current events. To provide themselves with a fast and dependable outlet for their writing, they had joined in September of 1944 with a group of friends (including Maurice Merleau-Ponty and Raymond Aron) to produce a new monthly journal. The name of this journal, *Les Temps Modernes* (Modern Times), was chosen in part because of Sartre's fondness for a 1936 Charlie Chaplin movie by that title and in part because the journal was committed to dealing with contemporary issues. Although *Les Temps Modernes* was pitched to a highly literate audience rather than to the working class, whose interests they hoped to serve, it enabled Sartre and Beauvoir to carry on a monthly dialogue with other intellectual and ideological leaders.

Yet political commitment turned out to be nastier and more complicated than they had expected. In America, the start of the Cold War led to anti-Communist crusades and made it difficult to defend any political program that was left of center, even the mildest forms of socialism. In France, the start of the Cold War led to bitter divisions across a much broader spectrum of political ideologies. For example, the elections of 1951 left the French Assembly with most of its seats split fairly evenly among six political parties, the largest being the Gaullists (RPF), the Socialists (SFIO), and the Communists (PCF).

Until 1952, Sartre and Beauvoir attempted to steer an independent course. They rejected both American-style capitalism and Soviet-style Communism. Fearing American domination of Europe, they opposed NATO. (Although they agreed with the U.S. on the creation of Israel.) They condemned the Gaullists and other centrists for their attachment to American capitalism and support for French colonialism. (The French had been fighting in Vietnam since 1946). They praised the Soviet Union for striving to perfect socialism, but they criticized its repression of civil liberties, brutal labor camps, and imperialistic stance toward other communist nations. They attacked the French Communist Party (PCF) for slavish obedience to the Soviet party line and unwillingness to tolerate independent thinking in its own ranks. They admired Marxist ideology for its staunch commitment to the interests of the working class, but disagreed with its insistence that human action and history were causally determined. These views were advanced by Sartre not only in essays but also in his novel, *Troubled Sleep*, his play, *Dirty Hands (Les Mains Sales*, 1948), and his film script, *In the Mesh (L'Engrenage*, 1948). For a period of eighteen months, Sartre served on the management committee of a new political party, The Revolutionary Peoples Assembly (RDP), but he broke with the leaders of the party when they favored France's involvement in NATO.

E. COMMUNIST FELLOW TRAVELER: 1952-1956

In 1952, Sartre changed his political stance and began a four-year period as a supporter of the French Communist Party, the *Parti Communist Français*, or PCF. Although he never became a member of the PCF, he was a fellow traveler and sought to defend the party against its critics. The reasons for this change were both philosophical and practical. One philosophical reason was his failure to develop a normative theory for existentialist ethics. This failure had made him reconsider the advantages of anchoring ethical commitment in a Marxist interpretation of history. Another philosophical reason was his growing suspicion that *Being and Nothingness* had exaggerated the real independence of individual human beings. On a political plane, Sartre had become convinced that the only party capable of uniting the workers of France and bringing about revolutionary change in the social order was the PCF, therefore anti-Communism in all its forms hurt the long-term interest of the working class. He had begun to accept the Communist argument that one should avoid public criticism of the PCF or the Soviet Union, even when such criticism was valid, because it harmed the working class and helped the enemies of the working class.

Yet Sartre's conversion in 1952 also owed a good deal to the events of the moment. One events was the arrest of Jacques Duclos, leader of the Communists in the National Assembly. In retaliation for a public demonstration that had ended in violence, several leading Communists, including Duclos, were arrested in May 1952. Two pigeons were found in Duclos' car, and he was charged with espionage on the assumption that they were carrier pigeons. In fact, he was planning to eat the pigeons. (Pigeons are considered a delicacy in France.) The Communists tried to organize a protest strike for June 2, but the strike failed and the right-wing press celebrated this failure as a sign that the Communists were losing credibility with workers.

In June 1952 Sartre exploded in anger. He had finally come to see for himself "how much shit can be crammed into a middle-class heart" (Sartre, *SBH*, 1978, 72). Writing about this moment years later, he said:

> *My vision was transformed: an anti-Communist is a swine, I can see no way out of that, and I never will. . . . After ten years of brooding about it, I had reached a breaking point and I needed only a gentle push. In the language of the Church, this was a conversion (Hayman 1987, 301-302).*

Sartre's conversion to active support for PCF at home and the Communist cause abroad led to profound changes in his life. His defense of Communism and his condemnation of anti-Communism in *The Communists and Peace* (*Les Communistes et la Paix*, 1952, 1954) provoked public quarrels with Albert Camus and Maurice Merleau-Ponty. After a bitter exchange of letters in the *Les Temps Modernes*, Sartre never saw Camus again. Merleau-Ponty, who had initially been responsible for pushing Sartre toward a more sympathetic view of the Communists, resigned as Editor-in-Chief of *Les Temps Modernes*. Sartre had broken with Raymond Aron in 1947, but their differences now became wider and angrier. Aron, for example, characterized as "hyper-Stalinism" Sartre's 1953 essay accusing the United States of fascism for executing Julius and Ethel Rosenberg as atomic spies.

In May 1954, Sartre visited the Soviet Union. Stalin had died the year before and Nikita Khrushchev was now first secretary of the Central Committee. A year and a half later, Khurshchev would startle both Communists and anti-Communists around the world by denouncing Stalin's "bloody crimes" proclaiming "de-Stalinization," and conceding that "different roads to Socialism" were possible. Yet Sartre's reports on the USSR in 1954, before de-Stalinization, were overwhelmingly positive. In December, Sartre accepted the post of Vice President of the French-Soviet Association. He also attempted to suppress production of his own play *Dirty Hands* to avoid giving comfort to anti-Communists. The following year, Sartre and Beauvoir spent two months in China as guests of the new Communist regime. But Sartre's stint as a fellow traveler was about to end.

F. INDEPENDENT MARXIST: 1956–1960

In October 1956, the Soviet Union sent an army bristling with tanks and artillery into Hungary to crush an uprising of students, workers, and soldiers who were demanding better standards of living, greater democracy, and more national independence. Khrushchev might have avoided bloodshed by restoring to power Hungary's former liberal premier, Imre Nagy, just he had restored Wladyslaw Gomulka in Poland. Instead, he chose to meet the Hungarians with the might of the Red Army. In the end, between 25,000 and 50,000 Hungarians were killed and thousands more imprisoned. The new premier János Kádár repealed reforms and even abolished his country's "Workers Councils."

Sartre's response was swift and furious. He condemned the Soviet invasion as a crime committed by hypocrites who were trying to outdo Stalinism at the same time they were denouncing it. He blamed the crisis on the Soviet Union's stupid and oppressive policy of trying to impose the same economic structure on all Communist nations. He denounced their use of force as a cruel blunder which presented the Red Army as the enemy of the Hungarian people. In a series of essays under the title "The Ghost of Stalin" ("*Le Fantôme de Stalin*"), he argued that the Soviet Union's crime against Hungary was not an accident, but a logical expression of its misguided efforts to interpret and apply the lessons of Marxism. He was equally scathing in his denunciation of the leaders of the French Communist Party (PCF) for their support of the Soviet Union's crime. "All their comments, all their actions," Sartre said, "are the result of thirty years of lying and sclerosis." (Hayman 1987, 326). He declared that he would never again tie himself to the leaders of the PCF. He resigned from the French-Soviet Association.

Once more, Sartre had readjusted his deepest political convictions in response to current events. This time, however, his new convictions would set him on a course that would continue until almost the end of his life. Although disillusioned with Soviet-style Communism and the PCF, he was more enthusiastic than ever about Marxism. The problem, as he now saw it, was that Communism had twisted and falsified Marxism. His new goal would be to stimulate the reform of Communism by helping to reinterpret Marxism. His new role would be that of an independent Marxist.

For nearly five years, Sartre had not written much except political essays. (He wrote one mediocre play, *Nekrassov*, and began his book on Flaubert.) Now, he was eager to return to technical philosophy and begin a dialogue with Marx and his followers. He was also intent on continuing his longstanding interest in psychobiography, but with a new twist: he would write Marxist biographies.

For most writers, philosophy and biography would be an odd pair of interests, yet for Sartre this pair made sense. Sartre had always aimed his philosophy at trying to explain why people have certain values and do certain things. At the end of *Being and Nothingness*, he sketched an outline of existential psychoanalysis which would allow him to use this framework as a practical tool for analyzing in minute detail the values and actions of individual lives. It resembled Sigmund Freud's theory of psychoanalysis in its emphasis on the influence of childhood experiences on adult behavior, but unlike Freud's theory, it did not appeal to an "unconscious." (In 1959, Sartre wrote a long screenplay about Freud's early career for director John Huston; part of that screenplay was used in Huston's 1962 film, *Freud*.)

With mixed success, Sartre attempted to use his psychoanalytic theory to explain the development of several French writers. He used it in his 1946 biography of the 19th century poet Charles Baudelaire, his unpublished 1948 book on the 19th century poet Stéphane Mallarmé, and his 1952 biography of his friend, the playwright and former thief Jean Genet. Now, as an independent Marxist, Sartre wanted to reconstruct his explanatory framework and psychoanalytic applications based on a Marxist understanding of history. In fact, it was precisely this focus on using Marxist principles to explain the particulars of human history, individual *and* collective, that he intended to be his distinctive contribution to Marxist thought. Phenomenology had enabled him to philosophize about apricot cocktails; Marxism, he believed, would enable him to discover the historical meaning in particular human actions.

For three years, Sartre worked furiously on his new philosophical treatise, *The Critique of Dialectical Reason*. The first fruit of this effort was a remarkable essay on Marxism and existentialism entitled *Search for a Method* (*Questions de méthode*). In this essay Sartre declares that existentialism is not a philosophy on a par with Marxism, but an ideology that needs to be integrated into Marxism. Marxism, he says, is not one philosophy among many, but the *only* legitimate "system of coordinates" for contemporary thought. He claims that attempts to go beyond Marxism today must result in outmoded, pre-Marxist thought. A philosophy of freedom may be possible in the future, but it will not be possible to formulate until there is freedom from need and class oppression for everyone. On the other hand, existentialism must retain its independence as an ideology of human existence until Marxism learns how to incorporate "the human dimension" into its knowledge of history and society (Sartre, *SM* 1963, 181). The perspective of existentialism is necessary because Marxist thinkers have oversimplified Marxism and imposed a mechanistic view on the workings of history.

When *The Critique of Dialectical Reason*, (*La Critique de raison dialectique*, 1960) was published three years later, it included this essay as an introduction. The book as a whole had 755 pages of very fine print. It was longer than *Being and Nothingness* and more difficult to read. Even professional philosophers found it difficult to wade through the thick terminology and multi-page paragraphs that filled this volume. Some pages were clear and powerful, others were obscure and rambling. To help quicken the pace of his writing, Sartre had taken heavy doses of a stimulant called Corydrane. Much that he wrote was not properly edited. He started to write a second volume, but never completed it. Yet, despite its shortcomings, *The Critique of Dialectical Reason* is a work of depth and importance. It does not claim to present a new system of philosophy, but rather to show how the principles established in the 19th century by Karl Marx *ought* to be used to understand the workings of history

What remains unchanged in Sartre's *Critique* is his view of human beings as conscious and purposive agents. On this point, he makes no concessions to Marxists who want to view humans as objects rather than subjects. However, he is willing to concede that the scope of free will and responsibility is a good deal narrower than he previously claimed. He acknowledges that social, economic, and historical factors play a much larger role in influencing and limiting individual choices than he had previously recognized. As he expressed it some years later:

> For I believe that man can always make something out of what is made of him. This is the limit I would accord to freedom: the small movement which makes of a totally conditioned social being someone who does not render back completely what his conditioning has given him. (Sartre, BEM 1974, 35).

Some of the ideas in *The Critique of Dialectical Reason* are also presented in a play that Sartre wrote at about the same time, *The Condemned of Altona* (*Les Séquestrés d'Altona*, 1959). This play tells the story of a wealthy German family, who despite their efforts to act decisively and according to their own lights, are thwarted by their own bad faith and by their thorough entanglement in the net of history— family history, German history, and economic class history. In the last act of the play, we learn that during World War II, the play's main character, Franz von Gerlach, tortured to death several Russian peasants. His excuse for this atrocity was the need to extract information about Russian partisans in order to help his men survive during their desperate retreat through Russia, but his primary motive was to preserve his own authority. Although Franz had resisted the efforts of his father to make him a leader and the efforts of Hitler's regime to make him a Nazi, he ended up committing a heartless atrocity in order not to compromise his status as a leader. Sartre also intended Franz's story to suggest a perspective on the atrocities of French officials in Algeria. Indeed, the name Franz (Frantz in the French text) suggests France itself. Over the next eleven years, the course of events, first in the French colony of Algeria, and then in the former French colony of Vietnam would deeply affect Sartre's life.

G. ANTI-IMPERIALIST: 1960-1967

At the end of World War II, France had regained its overseas empire, but the age of European imperialism was rapidly coming to an end. In Asia, Africa, and the Middle East, people began demanding independence with demonstrations, strikes, and, sometimes, open warfare. Very quickly, colonies became financial burdens rather than financial assets. The capacity and willingness of the French to hold on to their colonies varied from place to place. In spite of American arms and money, the French military was not able to defeat the Communist-led Viet Minh. After a decisive Viet Minh victory at the battle of Dien Bien Phu in 1954, peace accords were signed in Geneva and the countries of Indochina became independent. The largest of these countries, Vietnam, was temporarily partitioned, with a Communist government in the North and non-Communist government in the South.

The loss of Indochina was a blow to the dignity of France and its hopes of remaining an empire, but that loss was more easily digested than the threat of losing Algeria. Technically, Algeria was part of France, and for many French "settlers," it was home. In 1956, over a million Europeans (mainly of French descent) lived in Algeria. Many belonged to families that had lived there for generations. (Albert Camus, for example, was born and raised in Algeria.) On the other hand, the native population numbered about 8.5 million, mostly poor, illiterate, and subject to constant discrimination. In October 1954, a revolutionary organization, the National Liberation Front (*Front de Libération Nationale*) or FLN, began attacks on French Algerians. In 1955, the French retaliated against FLN massacres with indiscriminate bloodshed based on a policy of "collective responsibility." During the battle of Algiers, the French used torture to intimidate prisoners and extract information.

In 1958, French settlers seized control of Algeria and brought about the fall of the Fourth Republic. Charles de Gaulle returned to power in France and a new constitution for France was approved by referendum, but even de Gaulle's prestige could not bring peace to Algeria. The FLN would not agree to anything less than full independence and the French settlers were determined to resist. In April 1960, four generals in the French army attempted to lead a military coup. When the coup failed, they set up an underground organization, the Secret Army Organization (*Organisation de l'Armée Secrète*) or OAS to commit acts of terror in Algeria and France in hope of preventing a cease-fire in Algeria.

In August 1960, Sartre and Beauvoir were among the first of 121 dissidents who signed a manifesto pledging civil disobedience on behalf of Algerian independence. A month later, Sartre allowed a letter to be written in his name for the trial of his friend Francis Jeanson. The letter, which Sartre had not seen, endorsed Jeanson's aid to Algerian militants, declared that Sartre would have assisted him if asked to do so, and challenged the authority of the government to judge Jeanson.

On October 3, over 6,000 war veterans marched through Paris shouting "French Algeria" and "Shoot Sartre." When Sartre and Beauvoir returned from visits to Cuba and Brazil, they expected to be arrested, like others signers of the manifesto. To their surprise, the police refused to arrest them. De Gaulle had given orders that Sartre and his "family" were to be left alone, saying that one does not arrest Voltaire. The greater danger, however, was from the OAS and other right-wing militants who threatened Sartre with death. In January 1962, a bomb destroyed the apartment where Sartre and his mother had lived for nearly sixteen years. Luckily, Sartre had already moved his mother into a hotel and was sharing a new apartment with Beauvoir.

Although the threats to Sartre's life ended in July 1962, when Algeria became an independent nation, Sartre's involvement with the Algerian crisis helped him to look beyond Europe, the Soviet Union and the United States. Distrustful of Soviet-style Communism and antagonistic to American-style capitalism, he began to invest his hopes in the development of third-world socialism. Both he and Beauvoir had been deeply impressed by their first visit to Castro's Cuba in 1960. Here, perhaps, was a model for a Marxist society in which a visionary leadership worked directly with the masses, avoiding the pitfalls of elitism, oppression, and leaden bureaucracy. Sartre and Beauvoir were also deeply impressed by their meetings with Frantz Fanon, a black physician from Martinique who had been influenced by Sartre's writings, and was now a forceful spokesman for third world liberation. In 1961, Sartre wrote the preface for Fanon's last and most important work, *The Wretched of the Earth* (1961). In that preface, he celebrates the emergence of an independent voice and vision for people of the third world and warns Europeans that the violence they have used to maintain colonial power is about to be repaid in kind. This book was translated in seventeen languages and sold over a million copies.

In 1963, Sartre completed *The Words* (*Les Mots*, 1964), his autobiography to age ten. It was a beautifully written and very personal book, not always accurate on details, but consistently witty and engaging. The principal purpose of *The Words* is to give a psychoanalytic account of how Sartre chose to become a writer and transformed that choice through bad faith into the illusion of a destiny and personal justification. What is odd about the book is that it does so in terms of his earlier existential theory of psychoanalysis and with no explicit attention to Marxist principles of history. *The Words'* most interesting revelation is Sartre's confession that long after he had formulated his views on the futility of living in bad faith, he himself continued to live the lie that he condemned in others.

> *Fake to the marrow of my bones and hoodwinked, I joyfully wrote about our unhappy state. Dogmatic though I was, I doubted everything except that I was the elect of doubt. I built with one hand what I destroyed with the other, and I regarded anxiety as the guarantee of my security; I was happy. . . . For a long time, I took my pen for a sword ; I now know we're powerless. . . . Culture doesn't save anything or anyone, it doesn't justify (Sartre Words 1964, 254-255).*

Partially on the strength of this book and its popularity, Sartre was selected to receive the 1964 Nobel Prize for Literature. When he learned that he was likely to be the recipient, he warned the Swedish Academy that he did not want the prize. When they chose him anyway, he refused to accept it and the 26 million francs that went with it. He refused the prize because he did not want to be bought off or even appear to be bought off by the middle-class establishment. He also noted that the Swedish Academy had never before offered this prize to a Marxist writer and the only Soviet writer to receive the prize was the dissident Boris Pasternak.

In the Fall of 1966, Sartre and Beauvoir agreed to serve on the International War Crimes Tribunal that had been initiated by the distinguished British philosopher Lord Bertrand Russell to protest America's escalation of the war in Vietnam and the lethal consequences of that escalation for the civilian population. Although Russell's tribunal had no legal status, it was intended to serve as a public relations platform for shaping world opinion. It was modeled on the Nuremberg trials that the Allies had used after World War II to prosecute Nazi war criminals. The tribunal met in Stockholm and Copenhagen during 1967, and, after months of debate, found the United States guilty of genocidal intent. Sartre, who had been elected Executive President, wrote the final verdict.

In retrospect, Sartre's verdict seems at once perceptive and naïve, cogent and exaggerated. He recognizes that the North Vietnamese, the Viet Cong, and their numerous supporters are committed to total war and will not be stopped by anything short of total defeat. Thus, he reasons that the United States is faced with a choice of making peace [on North Vietnamese terms] or physically eliminating its enemy. Since America is not willing to make peace, it is "guilty of continuing and intensifying the war despite the fact that everyday its leaders realize more accurately . . . that the only way to win is "to free Vietnam of all the Vietnamese" (Sartre, OG 1968, 42). He also draws the clearly erroneous conclusion that the Vietnam War meets all of Hitler's specifications. "Hitler killed Jews because they were Jews. The armed forces of the United States torture and kill men, women, and children in Vietnam *merely because they are Vietnamese*" (Sartre, OG 1968, 42).

As enemies of colonialism and champions of people who had suffered under the heel of European powers, Sartre and Beauvoir were unequivocal in their enthusiasm for emerging nations and their sympathy with victims of oppression, like blacks in South Africa. But conflicts *between* victims of oppression posed a different kind of problem. Shortly, before the 1967 Arab-Israeli War, Sartre and Beauvoir visited Egypt and Israel. In both countries they told their hosts that they supported the right of Israel to exist as an independent state and the right of Palestinians living outside of Israel to return home. In both countries they were told these rights were incompatible. As President Nasser of Egypt explained "if Israel took in 1.2 million Palestinians it would no longer be Israel; 'it would burst apart'" (Thompson 1984, 157).

H. LEFTIST GUARDIAN AND FLAUBERT BIOGRAPHER: 1968-1972

By 1965 Sartre had given up writing fiction and systematic philosophy, although he continued to write literary criticism and philosophically informed essays. His last major work was a three-volume biography of the 19th century novelist Gustave Flaubert, entitled *The Family Idiot* (*L'Idiot de la famille*, 1971). Many of his working hours from 1968 until his health began to fail in 1972 were spent as a leftist activist (*gauchiste*) on behalf of radical student groups and their newspapers, making public statements on political issues, and giving interviews. As Sartre grew older he sought out the company of young people. In 1965, he adopted his twenty-six year old mistress, Arlette Elkaïm and made her executor of his literary estate. (Although Beauvoir was deeply wounded by Sartre's action at the time, she would eventually follow his example and adopt a young woman, Sylvie le Bon, as her daughter and literary executor.) But Sartre's attraction to young people was philosophical as well as personal and sexual. In *Search for a Method* he had complained about the inability of Marxists of his own generation to think "dialectically" because of their pre-Marxist education. But he held out hope for the future. "Far from being exhausted, Marxism is still very young, almost in its infancy, it has scarcely begun to develop" (Sartre, *SM* 1967, 30).

Two events in 1968 pushed Sartre even further in pinning his hopes on the next generation. One was the invasion of Czechoslovakia by Soviet and other Warsaw Pact troops in August of 1968 in order to crush the liberal Communist government that had come to power earlier in the year. Sartre not only denounced the Soviet Union but also finally severed all ties with its government. He also rebuked Fidel Castro for his support of the invasion. The other event was the outbreak of violent demonstrations by French university students which began in March 1968 and continued for months. The immediate causes of the student uprising were rather concrete: dissatisfaction with overcrowding, too few professors, antiquated educational requirements, and lack of job opportunities after graduation. But these concrete complaints were merged with idealistic concerns about American and Soviet imperialism and the lack of social justice in France.

After violent clashes between police and students in May, Sartre told Radio Luxembourg:

> These youngsters don't want the future of their fathers—our future—a future which proved we were cowardly, weary, worn out, stupefied by total obedience. . . . The only relationship they can have with this university is to smash it (Hayman 1987, 424).

He also arranged an interview with the student's radical young spokesman, Daniel Cohn-Bendit. According to Cohn-Bendit, some of the students in the rebellion had read Marx, "perhaps Bakunin and of the moderns, Althusser, Mao, Guevera, Lefebvre. Nearly, all the militants have read Sartre" (Hayman 1987, 423). The bond was irresistible. Sartre became the grown-up the students could trust, and he, in turn, repaid their trust by employing his fame as a shield to help protect them from violent police and angry officials.

In 1970, Sartre and Beauvoir permitted their names to be listed as "editors" of a Maoist, student newspaper dedicated to the promotion of subversive activities, La Cause du Peuple. (Maoism was a version of Communism based on the teaching of China's leader, Mao Zedong. What Sartre did not know was that Mao's atrocities would rival Stalin's.) Among the real editors of this newspaper was a mysterious young man who called himself "Pierre Victor," but whose real name was Benny Lévy. Lévy would play an important role in the last seven years of Sartre's life. For the present, however, he was just one of the student leaders with whom Sartre had joined hands to bring about revolution. For the first time since the Nazi Occupation, Sartre could enjoy being a man of action while experiencing the empowerment that came from being a member of a group united by a common purpose. He appeared at protest rallies, distributed newspapers on the street, and made speeches at factories.

As the French authorities cracked down on the revolutionary left and their publications, Sartre began to experience some embarrassment at his inability to get arrested. In September 1970, he announced that he was making himself available to any revolutionary newspaper in order to force the bourgeoisie (middle-class establishment) to put him on trial or, by failing to put him on trial, to reveal the illegality of its repression. Soon he was listed as "editor" on a dozen extremist newspapers and his name was added to articles he had never seen. One right-wing newspaper, Minute, called him "the nation's red cancer" and said he should be in prison (Hayman 187, 445). Finally, in June 1971, he was formally charged with libel of the police and the police system. The charge was based on two unsigned articles in La Cause du Peuple and a third unsigned article in a similar publication. On September 24, he appeared in court before two judges, who released him immediately.

Sartre's last major work was his three-volume biography of Flaubert. The first two volumes, *The Family Idiot: Gustave Flaubert from 1821 to 1857* (*L'Idiot de la famille: Gustave Flaubert de 1821 à 1857*) were published in 1971. Although each volume was over a thousand pages long, the two volumes together covered little more than half of Flaubert's life! The third volume, a mere 667 pages, dealt with Flaubert's life and work in relationship to his times.

Why did Sartre choose to write about this mid-19th century novelist whose obsession with the craft of writing prose was so different from Sartre's free-flowing style of composition. Why did he devote so many words to the development of an author whose "art for art's sake" ethic contrasted so sharply with his own dedication to politically committed literature? In the Preface to *The Family Idiot*, he mentions four reasons. The first was personal. Sartre disliked Flaubert and what he stood for. He felt he "had a score to settle" with him. But as he studied Flaubert's letters his dislike changed to empathy and understanding. Second, since Flaubert's life was "objectified" in his work, he offered an exceptional opportunity to examine the relationship between man and work. Third, Flaubert's early fiction and extensive correspondence provided a wealth of personal information: "We might imagine we were hearing a neurotic 'free associating' on the psychoanalyst's couch" (Sartre, *FI* 1981, x). Fourth, "Flaubert, creator, of the 'modern' novel, stands at the crossroads of all our literary problems today" (Sartre, *FI* 1981, x). A fifth reason, which Sartre does not mention in the Preface, but is clearly important, is that Flaubert's life (1821-1880) coincided almost exactly with Karl Marx's life (1818-1883). The historical period that shaped Marx as a philosopher also shaped Flaubert as a writer.

In the first two volumes of *The Family Idiot*, Sartre attempts to explain how Gustave Flaubert became a writer of a very particular kind as a result of the family and social circumstances in which he was raised and the choices he made in response to those circumstances. He speculates about his mother's disappointment with young Gustave for not being the daughter she wanted and his father's disappointment with him for Gustave's slowness in learning to read. He imagines, Flaubert's father, who was a successful doctor with high ambitions for his family, telling his seven-year old son that he will be "the idiot of the family." Thus, at an early age the boy was deprived of a sense of self-worth. Wounded by the judgments of both parents, he saw himself in bleakly negative terms—as a nothingness. What choice did he make in response to these circumstances? According to Sartre, he chose to take revenge on society by reducing everyone to his own negative condition. Of course, he could not do this in reality, but he could do it through the creation of an imaginary world, a world of fiction. Thus, Flaubert gradually formed the project of using the beauty of language to seduce readers into seeing the world as "horrible, cruel, and naked" (Collins 1980, 122).

The third volume of *The Family Idiot* deals with the correspondences between Flaubert's literary works and the history of the bourgeoisie (middle-class establishment) during his most productive years. Although the old aristocracy had been stripped of its hereditary power by the French Revolution (1789-1799), it was not until the industrialization of the 1830s and 1840s that the bourgeoisie came into its own as an immensely wealthy, powerful, and self-conscious class. The distinctive values of this class included: ambition, self-enrichment, hard work, and competition. But the bourgeoisie soon discovered their success was built in part on the misery of the working class. In order to drive up profits, they drove down wages and sacrificed humane working conditions to productivity. Food was scare, infant mortality was rampant, and children were often sent to work before the age of eight. (The bitter poverty of that time is described vividly by Victor Hugo in *Les Miserable*.)

According to Sartre, Flaubert found an enthusiastic audience in the bourgeoisie of his age precisely because this self-conscious class was *comforted* by his grim picture of the world. What Flaubert's novels and stories implied to them was that they were not to blame for the harshness, inequalities, and selfishness in the world. Thus, Flaubert's revenge on his own class became the source of his popularity, and he, in turn, reveled in the heartlessness with which the bourgeoisie confirmed his nasty depiction of them. He was pleased when the failed revolution of 1848 led to the crowning of Napoleon's scheming nephew, Louis Bonaparte, as Emperor Napoleon III. It was a triumph of baseness over idealism.

I. PROPHET OF HOPE AND FRATERNITY: 1973-1980

Following a stroke in 1973, Sartre's health began to deteriorate rapidly. For many years he had treated his body as one might treat an old car, driving it recklessly with little care for its basic needs. He smoked two packs of cigarettes a day, drank a good deal of alcohol, and used sedatives and stimulants to regulate his sleep and work habits. Now, his circulation was so poor that his brains and legs were seriously affected. He had lost control of his bladder. He had diabetes and was going blind. Although he had earned a good deal of money from his writings, he had given nearly all of it way. Fortunately for Sartre, Beauvoir and her sister Hélène, Arlette Elkaïm-Sartre, and his long-time mistresses Wanda Kosakiewicz and Michelle Vian provided him with company and physical care. Nevertheless, by the fall of 1973 Sartre's vision was so bad that he could no longer read or write.

A friend suggested that he hire his former "co-editor" from *La Cause du Peuple*, Benny Lévy to read to him and help him with his writing. Lévy was a Egyptian Jew who had immigrated to France with his family during the Suez crisis of 1956. Although he could not return to Egypt, he had neither French citizenship nor permanent resident status. Employment as Sartre's secretary would help protect him from deportation. (Later, at Sartre's request, the President of France, Valéry Giscard d'Estaing, granted Lévy full citizenship.)

Over the next seven years Sartre and Lévy developed a relationship that astonished and upset most of Sartre's friends. Lévy was a philosophy student with a prodigious memory, a brash personality, and a very good knowledge of Sartre's works. Instead of merely reading to him, Lévy insisted on challenging Sartre by asking him tough questions and engaging him in vigorous debate. Eager for intellectual stimulation, Sartre welcomed Lévy's persistent questioning and presumptuous familiarity. Gradually, Sartre and Lévy formed plans for writing a book together under the title *Power and Freedom*. Although most of Sartre's friends found this idea ridiculous and believed that Lévy was taking advantage of a sick, old man, some also recognized that Lévy efforts were helping to keep Sartre alive by promising him a future, however illusory, to which he could look forward.

In March 1980, a month before Sartre's death, Lévy published a slim volume entitled *Hope Now: The 1980 Interviews* (*L'espoir de maintenant: les entretiens de 1980*, 1980). This book contains Sartre's last words on philosophical matters and two brief commentaries by Lévy. What makes *Hope Now* surprising and controversial are statements by Sartre that seem inconsistent with his earlier views or express interest in things that are decidedly new. Sartre confesses that he used the concepts of despair and anguish in his philosophy during the 1940s because they were in vogue, even though he had never experienced despair or anguish. He also admits that his account of Jewish identity in *Anti-Semite and Jew* was seriously inadequate because it overlooked the historical, metaphysical, and messianic aspects of Jewish identity. Despite his twenty-year association with Marxism, Sartre dismisses Marxism in *Hope Now* and affirms the ideals of hope, democracy, and an ethical future based on universal brotherhood. He says, for example:

> *What does it mean to be human, and to be capable—along with one's neighbor, who is also a human being—of producing laws, institutions, of making oneself a citizen by means of the vote? All Marx's distinctions among superstructures are a fine bit of work, but it's utterly false because the primary relationship of individual to individual is something else, and that's what we're here to discover (Sartre and Lévy, HN 1996, 86).*

The publication of *Hope Now* provoked intense debate, first among Sartre's friends and then among scholars. There is no reason to doubt that the words attributed to Sartre in the text of the interview are Sartre's actual words. Arlette reread the interview to Sartre before its publication "repeating word after word, as well as the whole text several times. . . . Sartre added and corrected as he wished" (Sartre and Lévy, *HN* 1996, 8). On the other hand, there is reason to wonder whether Lévy, who had changed his own views from Maoism to messianic Judaism, had pressured Sartre into saying things he did not really believe. Raymond Aron, who had for decades disagreed with Sartre on most political issues, said that the ideas expressed in the interview were far too reasonable to be Sartre's work. François Truffaut, the famous French film director, described the interview as "pure shit." Beauvoir attempted to discredit *Hope Now* by publishing *Adieux* (*La Cérémonie des adieux* 1981), in which she gave her own account of Sartre's last ten years accompanied by an edited transcript of conversations she had with Sartre in 1974.

My view is that the *Hope Now* interview is a genuine reflection of ideas that Sartre was "trying out" in response to new circumstances. Sartre was a philosopher who was always willing to "think against himself" in order to make sense out of the concrete realities that the world presented to him. I believe that at the end of his life, he did what he had so often done before: he readjusted the language and emphasis of his worldview to accommodate the world in which he found himself. This time, however, the world had shrunk rather than expanded. Blind and helpless, yet eager as always to move on to new projects, he concentrated his attention on Benny Lévy, and attempted to make sense out of the abandonment of revolutionary Marxism by Lévy and other student radicals.

Sartre died in a coma on April 15, 1980. His circulation had become so poor that his bedsores were infected with gangrene. Shortly before lapsing into consciousness, he told Beauvoir "I love you very much, my dear Castor [Beaver]" (Beauvoir 1984, 123). The hearse that carried Sartre's body from the hospital to the cemetery was followed by a crowd of about 50,000 people. The mass of people following the hearse was met by another mass of people waiting at the cemetery. Many people were standing on top of tombstones. The crowd had to be pushed back in order to get the coffin out of the hearse. There was no speech or ceremony. Beauvoir asked for a chair and sat at the open grave for about ten minutes. A few days later, Sartre's body was removed from the grave and cremated.

Since Sartre left no will, his adopted daughter Arlette received legal rights over everything he had written, including his letters to Beauvoir. When Arlette refused to give Beauvoir permission to publish Sartre's letters, Beauvoir published them without her permission. Beauvoir died six years after Sartre on April 14, 1986.

36

Arthur Jones

America's Invisible Poor

Arthur Jones is editor-at-large for the National Catholic Reporter and a contributor to the Tablet, England's leading Catholic weekly. His book New Catholics for a New Century was published in 2000.

CONTEXT: In the following article, which appeared in the April 30, 1999, issue of the National Catholic Reporter, Jones challenges the notion that a strong economy is all that is needed to combat poverty. In the midst of a bullish stock market and a brief period of surpluses in the federal budget, the gap between America's rich and poor grew ever larger.

In 1964 the United States government, at the urging of President Lyndon B. Johnson, declared an "unconditional war on poverty."

Thirty-two years later, in 1996, the Clinton administration and the U.S. Congress—in the eyes of many antipoverty activists—declared war on the poor.

Johnson's decision to combat poverty and his ability to persuade Congress to go along with him was in major part based on a personal concern for the poor and in minor measure a continuation of the legacy of President John F. Kennedy.

Kennedy's attitude toward the poor in America had been greatly influenced by social critic Michael Harrington's 1962 book, *The Other*

America: Poverty in the United States, a landmark work that drew the nation's attention to the extent of poverty throughout the country.

By contrast, Clinton's decision to accede to a conservative Congress' anti-welfare, antipoor initiative was electoral politics, a move to appeal to centrist and right-of-center voters.

If, as the critics put it, a war is being waged against poor people, the weapon Clinton and Congress employ is The Personal Responsibility and Work Opportunity Reconciliation Act of 1996, billed as the means "to end welfare as we know it."

The description is proving to be correct: Welfare rolls are down, and the number of poor disconnected from any filament of the now-tattered social safety net is beginning to climb. Overall, how fares America?

"America's Invisible Poor" by Arthur Jones from NATIONAL CATHOLIC REPORTER, April 30, 1999. Reprinted with permission from National Catholic Reporter (www.NCRonline.org).

Spring 1999 figures show the U.S. economy is bounding along as merrily as in 1998. Inflation is low; unemployment is at the lowest level in 29 years; mortgage rates are down, and house sales are up. Some ordinary Americans, who 10 or 15 years ago took a chance and started sticking their money into the right stocks and mutual funds, now are worrying about capital gains and tax offsets. The Dow index has risen past the 10,000 mark and continues to set records almost daily.

The top 1 percent of America is becoming wealthier, and to protect their corporate asset wealth, they pay their retainers highly. The Children's Defense Fund, in its 1998 "State of America's Children" report, found that in 1960 the average CEO—corporate executive officer—made 41 times the average worker's wage. In 1998, top CEOs averaged $7.8 million annually, 185 times as much as the average worker. In the past decade, states the Children's Defense Fund, while the nation's poorest fifth of families have lost $587 each in purchasing power, the richest 5 percent added $29,533.

Adds the defense fund, "Six years of economic expansion with low inflation and a soaring stock market has not filtered down to the 36.5 million poor people."

In addition, the number of extremely poor people, those whose incomes are less than 50 percent of the poverty level, has increased.

Federal Reserve Board chairman Alan Greenspan explains the reality behind the appearances.

WEALTH AT TOP

The typical view, said Greenspan in a speech given at Jackson Hole, Wyo., last September, is that the booming market has benefited individuals "further down in the wealth distribution. Certainly, while in the 1990s those households are more likely to own stocks and mutual funds than a decade or two ago, the stock market rise did not lead to a rise in the share of stocks and mutual fund assets owned by the bottom 90 percent but suggests a further increase in the concentration of net worth [at the top]."

How does the rising stock market concentrate assets? Both through wealthy investors rising with the tide and through corporate managers and owner-entrepreneurs cashing in on their stock options.

Financial writer Allan Sloan notes that spring is also proxy statement time when multibillionaires like Michael Dell of Dell Computer (who owns $16.4 billion in Dell stock) and Ted Turner ($7.6 billion in Time War ner stock), can exercise their options. That means they can buy more of their stock very cheaply as a perk for being successful or canny. If they sell some of that cheaply acquired stock while the market is high, they can buy other assets, thus converting paper holdings in their own corporations into concentrated wealth. And those new options, now turned into stock, are bought up by other wealthy investors, mutual funds and the like.

In the Other America—to borrow Harrington's title—almost 37 million Americans, 15 percent of the population, live below the poverty line. According to a just-released two-year study by Network, the Catholic social justice lobby, many of the poor, directed toward the welfare-to-work conveyer belt, are not finding jobs and are losing benefits. Consequently, states Network, at least 1 million children "lack basic necessities."

And while some welfare recipients have received adequate training and found decent jobs, the number of them still employed 6 and 12 months later is not encouraging. Even welfare recipients who get jobs may not be better off than before. In Michigan, one of the organizations cooperating in the Network study, Groundwork for a Just World, finds severe hardship among those welfare recipients who have "graduated" to work.

"Our findings," said Groundwork's Beverly McDonald, "is that people are cycling on and off work, are making less than $7 an hour, with only 25 percent having health coverage on the job and 60 percent with no benefits whatsoever, not even sick time."

Fo r those who made it to jobs, many, she said, "are working nonstandard hours. They're leaving their children with friends and relatives and relocating their children in the middle of the night.

"Even where the state provides child care support, it is very hard to get when you work nonstandard, fluctuating hours," McDonald said, "and there's a huge lag between when you had to pay for the care and when you got reimbursed for it weeks later."

STATES PROCLAIM REDUCED CASE LOADS

All that state governments care about, said Groundwork's Beverly McDonald, is proclaiming reduced welfare case loads. Few state governments track what happens to those who slip off welfare or the welfare-to-work conveyer belt, she said.

How does Greenspan see the jobs situation? In the speech last September, he said a rising demand for skilled workers who can "effectively harness new technologies" has been outpacing supply and driving up their wages.

He mentioned that "earnings inequality occurs within groups of workers with similar skills," but made no mention of the gross inequalities between men's and women's pay for similar jobs (NCR, March 5).

Greenspan also looked at wealth distribution and consumption distribution. Inequality in household wealth, he said, was higher in 1989 than in 1963 but hasn't changed much in a decade—"though that masks the apparent rise in the share of wealth held by the wealthiest families. The distribution of wealth," he said, "more fundamentally than earnings or income, measures the ability of households to consume."

Writing on Americans in poverty 37 years ago, Harrington referred to those "maimed in body and spirit, existing at levels beneath those necessary for human decency," and said that they were becoming "invisible."

The Personal Responsibility and Work Opportunity Reconciliation Act of 1996, by pretending that lower welfare rolls equate with fewer people in poverty, has provided Americans with an additional curtain to shield from them the sight and condition of the poor.

UNDERSTANDING MEANING

1. What does Jones believe is the difference between President Johnson's attitude toward the poor and President Clinton's? (What's the difference between declaring war on poverty and declaring war on the poor?)
2. How has the economy changed for Americans between 1996 and 1999? Who is in better shape financially? Who is doing worse financially?
3. According to Jones, how are the jobs working out for those who got them through welfare-to-work? What does Jones suggest is the government attitude toward the problems that these citizens new to the work force are experiencing?
4. *CRITICAL THINKING.* Jones suggests wealthier Americans are happy just as long as they don't have to see the suffering of the poor. Do you feel that is an accurate perception?

EVALUATING STRATEGY

1. In the opening paragraphs, Jones is making use of comparison and contrast. Whom is he contrasting?
2. Are Jones's statistics clear and convincing? Do they persuade you that the successes reported for welfare-to-work are deceptive?
3. Jones is appealing in part to his readers' sense of reason and in part to their emotion. Do you feel it is a successful blend?

APPRECIATING LANGUAGE

1. What does Jones mean in paragraph 7 when he says that the poor have been "disconnected from any filament of the now-tattered social safety net"? Explain this metaphor.

2. In the metaphors about the fight against poverty being a war, what is President Clinton's weapon?
3. What does Jones mean when he refers to welfare-to-work as a "conveyor belt" in paragraph 16?

WRITING SUGGESTIONS

1. *PREWRITING.* Do some quick informal writing about your earliest memories of seeing real poverty. Was it, for example, the first time a beggar approached you on the street or when you saw a homeless person? If you have not had any direct contact with the poor, what are some images that stick in your mind from television or movies?
2. Agencies that help the poor often point out that there is an outpouring of generosity around Christmas and Hanukkah but not enough help the rest of the year. Is it true that those who live in relative wealth would rather forget about the poor except at those times of year when it is traditional to donate to them? Write a brief essay about people's attitudes toward the poor.
3. Do you feel that Americans have lost their desire to help those in need? Defend your answer with specific examples.
4. *COLLABORATIVE WRITING.* Discuss this essay with a group of students and draft a statement agreeing or disagreeing with Jones's view of welfare-to-work. If members disagree, consider drafting opposing statements.

37

Amiri Baraka

Ka'Ba

"A closed window looks down
on a dirty courtyard, and Black people
call across or scream across or walk
across defying physics in the stream of their will.

Our world is full of sound
Our world is more lovely than anyone's
tho we suffer, and kill each other
and sometimes fail to walk the air.

We are beautiful people
With African imaginations
full of masks and dances and swelling chants
with African eyes, and noses, and arms
tho we sprawl in gray chains in a place
full of winters, when what we want is sun.

We have been captured,
and we labor to make our getaway, into
the ancient image; into a new

Correspondence with ourselves
and our Black family. We need magic
now we need the spells, to raise up
return, destroy, and create. What will be

the sacred word?